WORLD
THE DEFINITIVE VISUAL GUIDE
WAR I

WORLD
THE DEFINITIVE VISUAL GUIDE
WAR I

FROM SARAJEVO TO VERSAILLES

R.G. GRANT

DK Penguin Random House

Senior Editor Janet Mohun	**Senior Art Editor** Ina Stradins
Editors Laura Wheadon, Claire Gell	**Project Art Editors** Anna Hall, Steve Woosnam-Savage
Pre-Production Producers Rebekah Parsons-King, Rachel Ng, Jacqueline Street-Elkayam	**Producer** Alice Sykes
Senior Producer Alex Bell	**Jacket Designers** Mark Cavanagh, Paul Drislane
Jacket Editor Manisha Majithia	**Jacket Design Development Manager** Sophia MTT
Managing Editor Angeles Gavira Guerrero	**Managing Art Editors** Michelle Baxter, Michael Duffy
Cartographers Simon Mumford Encompass Graphics Ltd, Brighton, UK	**Art Directors** Philip Ormerod, Karen Self
	Publisher Sarah Larter
Associate Publishing Director Liz Wheeler	**Publishing Director** Jonathan Metcalf

DK INDIA

Editorial Manager Rohan Sinha	**Deputy Design Manager** Sudakshina Basu
Senior Editor Vineetha Mokkil	**Senior Art Editor** Mahua Mandal
Editors Sudeshna Dasgupta, Dharini Ganesh	**Art Editors** Sanjay Chauhan, Suhita Dharamjit, Arijit Ganguly, Amit Malhotra, Kanika Mittal, Shreya Anand Virmani
Production Manager Pankaj Sharma	
DTP Manager Balwant Singh	**DTP Designers** Neeraj Bhatia, Syed Md Farhan, Shanker Prasad, Sachin Singh, Tanveer Abbas Zaidi

TOUCAN BOOKS LTD

Managing Editor Ellen Dupont	**Senior Art Editor** Thomas Keenes
Senior Editor Dorothy Stannard	**Picture Research** Roland Smithies (Luped)
Assistant Editor David Hatt	**Indexer** Marie Lorimer
Proofreader Caroline Hunt	

Editorial Consultants

Barton C. Hacker, Senior Curator of Armed Forces History, National Museum of American History, Kenneth E. Behring Center, Smithsonian Institution; Richard Overy, Professor of History, University of Exeter

This edition published in 2018
First published in Great Britain in 2014 by
Dorling Kindersley Limited
80 Strand, London, WC2R 0RL

Copyright © 2014, 2018 Dorling Kindersley Limited
A Penguin Random House Company
10 9 8 7 6 5 4 3
004 – 308091 – April/2018

ISBN: 978-0-2413-1765-5

Printed and bound in Dubai

A WORLD OF IDEAS:
SEE ALL THERE IS TO KNOW

www.dk.com

CONTENTS

1

THE TROUBLED CONTINENT 1870–1914

THE TROUBLED CONTINENT 1870–1914 ... 10

Introduction ... 12

Timeline ... 14

Europe's High Noon ... 16
The power and prosperity of Europe, its political systems and empires. The web of alliances between the great powers.

Crises and Conflicts ... 18
Tensions between rival European powers. The first and second Moroccan crises. The Austro-Hungarian annexation of Bosnia-Herzegovina. Slav nationalism and the Balkan Wars.

■ KAISER WILHELM II ... 20

Planning for War ... 22
The armies of the major European powers prepare for war. The German Schlieffen Plan. British hesitancy. French belief in the offensive.

■ EVOLVING MILITARY TECHNOLOGY ... 24

■ RIFLES ... 26

Assassination at Sarajevo ... 28
The shooting dead of the heir to the Austro-Hungarian throne, Archduke Franz Ferdinand, by a Bosnian Serb in Sarajevo. The reactions of Austria-Hungary and Germany.

The Slide to War ... 30
Austria-Hungary declares war on Serbia. Germany declares war on Russia and France. Britain enters the war in defence of Belgian neutrality.

Pulling Together ... 32
Political and social interest groups in combatant countries voice their support for the war. Opposing voices are quickly silenced.

■ THE DECLARATION OF WAR ... 34

2

NOT OVER BY CHRISTMAS 1914

NOT OVER BY CHRISTMAS 1914 ... 36

Introduction ... 38

Timeline ... 40

The Invasion of Belgium ... 42
Belgian troops fight the German army to defend the country's independence. Germany carries out massacres and brutal acts of destruction.

The French Offensive ... 44
French forces attack in Alsace, Lorraine, and the Ardennes. Germany launches successful counter-offensives. French eventually halt Germans in front of Nancy.

The British Go into Action ... 46
Arrival of the British Expeditionary Force (BEF) in France. The battles of Mons and Le Cateau. The BEF retreats from Belgium.

■ BATTLE OF MONS   48

■ ARTILLERY   50

The Great Retreat   52
French and British troops are pursued by
German armies. Paris comes under threat.
France plans to strike back.

The Battle of the Marne   54
France and Britain end their retreat
and launch a counterattack. Germany
is forced on to the defensive. German hopes
of a quick victory come to an end.

■ JOSEPH JOFFRE   56

The Race to the Sea   58
Allied advance from the Marne is halted on
the Aisne river. A war of movement continues
further north. Belgium is halted by the
Germans at the Battle of the Yser.

Fighting to a Standstill   60
The First Battle of Ypres in Flanders. The end
of the mobile phase of the war. Trenches are
dug along the entire Western Front.

■ THE CHRISTMAS TRUCE   62

The Battle of Tannenberg   64
Russia invades East Prussia. German forces
soundly defeat the Russians at Tannenberg.
German commanders Hindenburg and
Ludendorff become national heroes.

■ PAUL VON HINDENBURG   66

Austro-Hungarian Failures   68
Russia makes successful attacks in Galicia.
The Austro-Hungarian invasion of Serbia is
repulsed by Serbian forces.

The Battle for Poland   70
Germany launches offensive operations
against Russia in Poland in support of
Austria-Hungary. After the indecisive Battle
of Lodz, both sides prepare for winter.

■ CAVALRY   72

Turkey Enters the War   74
The Ottoman Empire sides with Germany
and Austria-Hungary. The British take
Basra and successfully defend the Suez
Canal. Turkey attacks Russia in the Caucasus.

African Diversions   76
The Allies strike at German colonies, seizing
Togoland, Kamerun, and Southwest Africa.
The British lose the Battle of Tanga. Fighting
continues in East Africa.

Confrontation at Sea   78
British naval blockade of Germany. Threats
to Allied shipping posed by mines and
submarines. British victory at the Battle
of Heligoland Bight.

■ WARSHIPS AT SEA   80

Coronel and the Falklands   82
Allied trade threatened by German cruisers.
The battles of Coronel and the Falklands
in the South Atlantic. German East Asiatic
Squadron is destroyed by Britain's Royal Navy.

War in the East   84
Japan declares war on Germany and captures
Tsingtao. New Zealand seizes Samoa, and
Australia occupies Kaiser Wilhelmsland. The
contribution of China to the Allied war effort.

Mobilizing Resources   92
Combatants attempt to harness resources
efficiently and maximize production of military
supplies. Increased employment of women in
many countries. War profiteering.

■ TRENCH WARFARE   94

■ LIFE IN THE TRENCHES   96

Failure on the Western Front   98
The Allies launch costly offensives at
Champagne and Neuve Chapelle. German
defences hold.

■ TRENCH FIGHTING   100
EQUIPMENT

Second Ypres   102
The Germans attack at Ypres. Chlorine gas
spreads panic in the Allied lines. Germany
makes limited gains before the front stabilizes.

■ CHEMICAL WARFARE   104

Italy Enters the War   106
In a bid to gain territory, Italy joins the Allies
and declares war on Austria-Hungary. Italy
launches first Isonzo offensive but captures
only a small area.

■ ANZAC TROOPS   108

The Gallipoli Campaign   110
Allied attempt to seize the Dardanelles
Straits. British and Commonwealth troops
land on the Gallipoli peninsula. Turkey
repulses the Allied attack.

■ BATTLE OF LONE PINE   114

The Armenian Massacre   116
Deportation and slaughter of Armenians
living in Turkey's Ottoman Empire. War
between Russian and Turkish forces on the
Caucasus front.

■ IN SERVICE OF THE EMPIRE   118

■ COLONIAL TROOPS   120

Disaster in Mesopotamia   122
British Indian forces advance from Basra
to Baghdad. They surrender to the Turks
at Kut al-Amara.

The Battle at Dogger Bank   124
British and German naval confrontation
in the North Sea. German battlecruisers
narrowly avoid a major defeat.

The Sinking of the *Lusitania* 126
German submarines begin attacking merchant
shipping off the British coastline. The sinking
of the transatlantic liner RMS *Lusitania*.
Subsequent outrage in the USA.

■ WARTIME POSTERS   128

America and the European War   130
President Woodrow Wilson declares the
USA neutral. American anger at perceived
German aggression. US economic support.
The Preparedness Movement.

The Zeppelin Raids   132
Germany bombs Paris, London, and
other cities. Fighter aircraft deployed
to counteract attacks.

Campaigns on the Eastern Front 134
Austro-German Gorlice-Tarnow offensive.
German forces advance across Poland.
Russian army embarks on its Great Retreat.

■ ANIMALS AT WAR   136

■ MACHINE-GUNS   138

Serbia Crushed   140
Austro-Hungarian, Bulgarian, and German
forces occupy Serbia. Corfu becomes the
seat of the Serbian government in exile.

The Artois-Loos Offensive   142
Allied autumn offensives in Champagne and
Artois. German defence tactics. Heavy losses
on both sides.

■ RECONNAISSANCE AND   144
COMMUNICATION

3

STALEMATE
1915   86

Introduction   88

Timeline   90

4

YEAR OF BATTLES
1916

146

Introduction 148

Timeline 150

Facing Deadlock 152
The combatant powers search for strategies
to end the war. US President Woodrow Wilson's
"peace note". The resumption of offensives.

The German Offensive at Verdun 154
One of the bloodiest battles of the war.
General Philippe Pétain takes over French
defence. Initial German success turns
to stalemate.

■ VERDUN 156

■ PHILIPPE PÉTAIN 158

The French Fight Back at Verdun 160
German and French armies remain locked
in battle. Combat between fighter aircraft.
Defensive victory for the French.

■ FORT DOUAUMONT 162

The Easter Rising 164
Armed rebellion against British rule in Ireland
is crushed. Execution of perpetrators.

■ INTELLIGENCE AND 166
ESPIONAGE

Slav Nationalism 168
Subject Slavic peoples of Austria-Hungary,
Germany, and Russia seek independence.

The Battle of Jutland 170
Indecisive clash between British and German
fleets in the North Sea.

■ ON BOARD THE 172
SMS DERFFLINGER

The Brusilov Offensive 174
Russia's most successful operation of the war.
Austro-Hungarian forces driven back across a
wide front.

Kitchener's Armies 176
Britain creates a New Army through appealing
for volunteers. The creation of pals battalions.
Social pressure to join the army.

■ DOUGLAS HAIG 178

The Somme Offensive 180
Britain and France launch a joint attack at
the Somme. It results in the heaviest loss
of life in a single day's fighting in British
military history.

■ THE FIRST DAY OF 182
THE SOMME

Attrition on the Somme 184
Lack of a decisive British breakthrough leads
to costly fighting.

■ MEDICAL TREATMENT 186

Dogfights and Aces 188
Development of single-seat fighter aircraft
and aerial combat tactics. The glorification
of fighter "aces".

■ DOGFIGHT 190

■ WARPLANES 192

The Romanian Campaign 194
Romania's decision to join the Allies. The
German-led invasion of Romania.

The Arab Revolt 196
Guerrilla war waged by Arab rebels
against Ottoman Turkey. The role of
British intelligence officer T.E. Lawrence.

The Strains of War 198
Mounting economic hardship for European
civilians. "Turnip winter" in Germany.
Breakdown of social cohesion. The threat
of revolution in Russia.

■ DAVID LLOYD GEORGE 200

Germany's New Order 202
Ludendorff and Hindenburg control the
German war effort. The formulation of plans
to populate Eastern Europe with Germans.

5

REVOLUTION AND
DISILLUSION
1917

204

Introduction 206

Timeline 208

The Tsar Overthrown 210
Russia's February Revolution and abdication
of the Tsar. The Provisional Government's
decision to continue the war. Lenin's return
to Russia from exile.

America Enters the War 212
New U-boat attacks and the uncovering
of a plot to invade USA from Mexico.
US President Woodrow Wilson declares
war on Germany.

■ WOODROW WILSON 214

Organizing America for War 216
The USA creates a mass army. Conscription
is introduced. Unprecedented federal
intervention in the economy.

Peace Initiatives and War Aims 218
Rise of anti-war forces in combatant
countries. Wilson's Fourteen Points and
statement of Allied war aims. German plans
to dominate Europe.

The U-boat Onslaught 220
Germany's unrestricted submarine warfare
against Allied merchant shipping. The use of
convoys, nets, and mines.

■ ERIC LUDENDORFF 222

The Nivelle Offensive 224
A French attack fails to break the German
defensive line. Morale of the French soldiers
breaks down. Widespread mutinies sweep
the French army.

The Battle of Arras 226
British launch dawn attack at Arras to
support the Nivelle Offensive. Canadians
capture Vimy Ridge.

■ SHELL CASINGS 228

■ CANADIANS IN THE WAR 230

The German Bomber Offensive 232
Large heavy bombers launch raids against
British cities. Effect on civilians.

The Kerensky Offensive 234
Last Russian offensive of the war.
The disintegration of the Russian army.

■ THE REVOLUTIONARY ARMY 236

Messines Ridge 238
British detonate mines under the German
lines and seize Messines Ridge.

Third Ypres 240
Major British offensive bogs down in the
Flanders mud.

■ PASSCHENDAELE 244

Italian Disaster at Caporetto 246
Attack by Austro-German forces the Italian
army into retreat. Events on the Italian
home front.

False Dawn at Cambrai 248
British offensive against the German
Hindenburg Line. Led by tanks, the operation
achieves a short-lived breakthrough.

■ TANK WARFARE 250

The Bolshevik Revolution 252
Seizure of power by revolutionary Bolshevik
Party in Russia. The new Bolshevik
government seeks an armistice with the
Central Powers.

Guerilla War in East Africa 254
Campaign mounted against the British by
German colonial troops. Impact on the local
African population.

Naval War in the Mediterranean 256
Allied intervention in Greece. Japanese help
counter the U-boat threat to Allied merchant
shipping. Italian attacks on the Austro-
Hungarian navy.

From Gaza to Jerusalem 258
British and Commonwealth forces, aided by
their Arab allies, mount a successful campaign
against the Turks in Palestine.

■ RECORDING THE WAR 260

6
VICTORY AND DEFEAT
1918 262

Introduction 264

Timeline 266

Home Fronts 268
Government attempts to raise civilian
morale in combatant countries. Rationing,
strikes, and falling standards of living.

■ THE GERMAN HOME FRONT 270

Trench Warfare Transformed 272
New innovations end deadlock of the
trenches. Infiltration tactics developed by
Germany. Use of ground attack aircraft.
Greater coordination between infantry
and artillery.

■ STORMTROOPER 274
EQUIPMENT

German Victory in the East 276
Bolsheviks and Germans sign the Treaty of
Brest-Litovsk, ending hostilities. Germany
receives vast areas of Russia.

The Michael Offensive 278
Germany launches the first of its Spring
Offensives. Ludendorff's gamble to win the
war before US troops arrive.

■ THE OPENING OF THE 280
MICHAEL OFFENSIVE

The German Search for Victory 282
German offensive continues with Operation
Georgette. British and Portuguese troops
come under pressure. Ferdinand Foch becomes
Supreme Commander of the Allied Armies.

The Battle of Belleau Wood 284
US marines engage advancing German
troops near the Marne river.

The Second Battle of the Marne 286
German offensive at Reims halted. German
troops are transferred from Flanders.
Successful French-led counter-offensive
ends hope of a German victory.

■ GAS ATTACK 288

■ FERDINAND FOCH 290

The Zeebrugge Raid 292
British attempt to block the movements of
U-boats from the port of Zeebrugge ends in
failure, but boosts civilian morale.

Climax of the Air War 294
Allies win fight for air supremacy over the
Western Front. Strategic bombing campaign
begins against German industrial targets.

■ AERIAL COMBAT 296

■ MANFRED VON RICHTHOFEN 298

Allied Intervention in Russia 300
Attempts to revive Russia's war effort against
Germany causes Allied troops to become
embroiled in the Russian Civil War.

■ WRITERS AT WAR 302

Turning Point at Amiens 304
A British and Commonwealth offensive at
Amiens inflicts a sharp defeat on the German
army. Loss of morale among German troops.

Taking the St Mihiel Salient 306
US army enters battle for the first time.
It defeats the exposed German troops in
the St Mihiel salient.

The Meuse-Argonne Offensive 308
The largest battle in the history of the US
army. American and French troops push the
Germans back across the Meuse river.

■ JOHN PERSHING 310

Attacking the Hindenburg Line 312
A series of Allied offensives break through
the fortifications of the Hindenburg Line.

■ ST QUENTIN CANAL 314

Turkey and Bulgaria Defeated 316
Military defeats force Germany's allies to
seek armistices with the Allies. Germany
is unable to intervene.

Italy Victorious 318
The Italians repulse an Austro-Hungarian
offensive at the Piave river, then launch a
successful attack at Vittorio Veneto.
Austria-Hungary collapses.

Mutiny and Revolution 320
Germany seeks an armistice. German naval
revolt at Kiel. The abdication of the Kaiser.
Germany becomes a republic.

The Armistice 322
More than four years of fighting come to
an end. The last shots of the war. Public
reactions to the news.

■ CELEBRATIONS 324

The Versailles Treaty 338
The Allies impose a peace treaty upon the
Germans. They regard it as unjust.

■ SIGNING THE VERSAILLES 340
TREATY

Postwar Conflicts 342
Red Army victory in the Russian Civil War.
Violence in Ireland. The rise of fascism.
The Greco-Turkish War.

Never Again 344
Mourning the dead. Isolationism and
pacifism in the postwar world.

■ MONUMENT TO THE FALLEN 346

In Memoriam 348
Country by country register of key World
War I battle sites, cemeteries, memorials,
and museums.

Centenary events 358
One hundred years after World War I, people
around the globe commemorate the conflict
and honour those who died.

Index 364

Acknowledgments 370

7
AFTERMATH
1919–1923 326

Introduction 328

Timeline 330

Devastated World 332
The horrific death toll. Malnutrition, Spanish
flu epidemic, and poverty. The rise of extreme
nationalism and new conflicts.

The Paris Peace Conference 334
Attempts to create a lasting peace. Conflicting
demands of the national delegations. Creation
of the League of Nations.

Foreword

When Winston Churchill reflected on World War I in the 1920s he claimed that "all the horrors of all the ages" were brought together in a terrible conflict that sucked in not only armies, but whole populations". The war of 1914–1918, or the "Great War" as it came to be known, was indeed a war of exceptional intensity, scale, and ruthlessness. It destroyed the fabric of European political life and set in motion movements worldwide that did not come to rest until much later in the 20th century. The effects of the war were deadly and devastating for every country dragged into its orbit.

A war that was supposed to be over in weeks soon became a long, drawn-out war of attrition. Military and naval belief in the decisive battle between rival navies and armies shifted inexorably towards a new concept of "total war" in which whole populations found themselves unexpected participants. This book describes and illustrates the war in all its many guises, from the brief colonial skirmishes in the Far East, when Japan seized Germany's Pacific colonies, to the slaughterhouses of the Western Front, which consumed millions of young men in four years of unabated combat.

Almost a century later, historians still debate why the Allies won and why the Central Powers – Germany, Austria-Hungary, and Turkey – were forced late in 1918 to sue for an armistice. The answer has a lot to do with resources: the Allies controlled the seas and denied trade to the enemy; the British and French empires, and the United States, could supply food and raw materials to keep populations fed and factories supplied. Germany was forced to improvise and invent in order to keep the war effort going, and shortages slowly undermined the domestic war effort of all the Central Powers.

The war changed the map of the world. In 1919, four of the great pre-war empires – German, Russian, Austro-Hungarian, and Ottoman – disappeared, while Britain and France faced an uncertain future in their surviving empires, where nationalist sentiment had been woken by the world crisis. Peace was welcomed, but its survival was uncertain. On 11 November 1918, Armistice Day, Churchill, then Minister of Munitions, looked out of his office in Whitehall as people streamed out on to the street in scenes of "triumphant pandemonium". But in his history of the war, Churchill concluded on a more sombre note: "Is this the end? Is it merely to be a chapter in a cruel and senseless story?" Sadly for humanity, it proved to be the prologue to the devastations to come a generation later.

Richard Overy,
University of Exeter

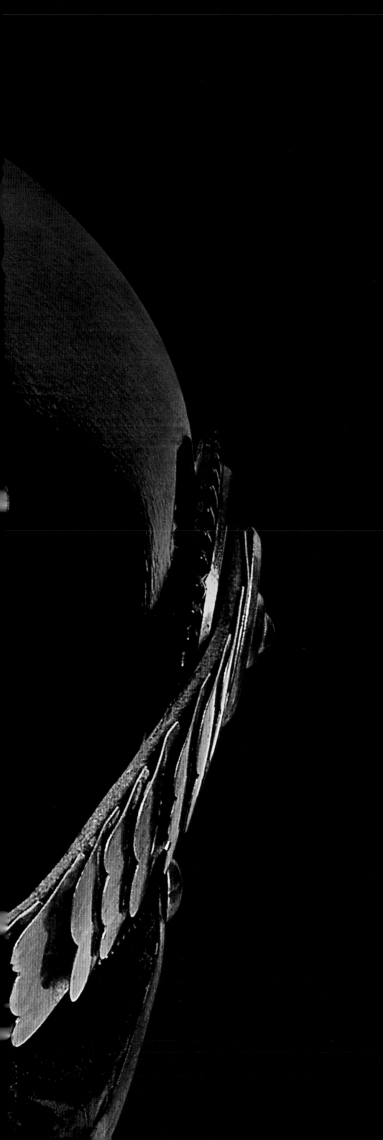

1
THE TROUBLED CONTINENT
1870 – 1914

In the early 20th century, Europe was dominated by ambitious imperial states. This produced an unstable international system and fuelled an arms race. War broke out in Europe with the assassination of Austrian Archduke Franz Ferdinand in the summer of 1914.

THE TROUBLED CONTINENT

German Chancellor
Otto von Bismarck masterminded the creation of a united Germany in the 1860s and 1870s. He created the Dual Alliance with Austria-Hungary and kept friendly relations with Russia.

The assination of Archduke Franz Ferdinand, heir to the Austrian throne, and his wife by Bosnian Serb Gavrilo Princip, in Sarajevo on 28 June 1914, led Austria-Hungary to declare war on Serbia.

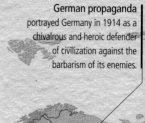

German propaganda portrayed Germany in 1914 as a chivalrous and heroic defender of civilization against the barbarism of its enemies.

EUROPE

[Map of Europe showing: FAEROE ISLANDS (Denmark), NORWAY, SWEDEN, North Sea, Baltic Sea, DENMARK, BRITAIN, NETH., GERMANY, RUSSIAN EMPIRE, BEL., LUX., FRANCE, SWITZ., AUSTRIA-HUNGARY, ITALY, ROMANIA, MONT., SERBIA, BULGARIA, Black Sea, ALB., PORTUGAL, SPAIN, Mediterranean Sea, GREECE, OTTOMAN EMPIRE, DODECANESE (Italy), ALGERIA (France), TUNISIA (France), CYPRUS (Britain), MOROCCO (France), LIBYA (Italy), EGYPT (Britain)]

[World map showing: ICELAND, NORWAY, SWEDEN, BRITAIN, GERMANY, FRANCE, AUSTRIA-HUNGARY, RUSSIAN EMPIRE, ATLANTIC OCEAN, ITALY, Black Sea, Caspian Sea, PORTUGAL, SPAIN, OTTOMAN EMPIRE, PERSIA, AFGHANISTAN, TIBET (autonomous), NEPAL, SPANISH MOROCCO, TUNISIA, CYPRUS, KUWAIT, BAHRAIN, QATAR, MOROCCO, ALGERIA, LIBYA, EGYPT, NEJD (Saudi), TRUCIAL OMAN, OMAN, INDIA, RIO DE ORO, ANGLO-EGYPTIAN SUDAN (British mandate), HIJAZ, HADHRAMAUT, ADEN PROTECTORATE, GAMBIA, FRENCH WEST AFRICA, TOGO, FRENCH EQUATORIAL AFRICA, ERITREA, FRENCH SOMALILAND, PORTUGUESE GUINEA, SIERRA LEONE, NIGERIA, ABYSSINIA, BRITISH SOMALILAND, LIBERIA, GOLD COAST, CAMEROON, ITALIAN SOMALILAND, CEY..., RIO MUNI (Spain), FRENCH CONGO, BELGIAN CONGO, BRITISH EAST AFRICA, INDIAN OCEAN, GERMAN EAST AFRICA, NORTHERN RHODESIA, ANGOLA, MADAGASCAR, GERMAN SOUTHWEST AFRICA, SOUTHERN RHODESIA, BECHUANALAND, PORTUGUESE EAST AFRICA, UNION OF SOUTH AFRICA]

Austro-Hungarian Emperor
Franz Joseph, here holding court in Schönbrunn Palace in Vienna, was head of a vast but restless empire with a large Slav population. Its annexation of Bosnia-Herzegovina in 1908 angered Serbia.

In the Balkan Wars of 1912–13, Serbia, Greece, Romania, and Bulgaria fought against Ottoman Turkey and one another. Serbia gained military strength and confidence in these conflicts.

The arrival of the German gunboat *Panther* off Agadir in July 1911 was a challenge to French imperial ambitions in Morocco. The episode brought Europe to the brink of war.

Unterhaltungs-Beilage

A series of wars in the 1860s and 1870s established Germany as Europe's dominant military power. In the 1890s, France and Russia formed an alliance to counter the might of Germany and its close ally, Austria-Hungary. In the first decade of the 20th century, Britain, feeling threatened by the growth of the German navy, abandoned its traditional isolationism and a formed an entente – a loose unofficial alliance – with France and Russia. In the years leading up to World War I, peace was maintained by a balance of power between the two hostile alliance systems. The European states expanded their armed forces and equipped them with the latest technology. They developed plans for the rapid mobilization of mass conscript armies that threatened to turn any confrontation into full-scale war. Every country felt that the side that struck first would have a decisive advantage.

New technology transformed the nature of warfare. This Russian Ilya Mourometz was the world's largest aircraft on the eve of World War I. Capable of carrying bombs, it was widely imitated.

Woodrow Wilson, US president from 1913, here addressing an American audience, was a high-principled political leader who, in August 1914, declared the USA strictly neutral.

CANADA

UNITED STATES OF AMERICA

CHINA

JAPANESE EMPIRE

FRENCH INDOCHINA

PHILIPPINE ISLANDS

BRITISH NORTH BORNEO

BRUNEI

SARAWAK

MALAYA

DUTCH EAST INDIES

PORTUGUESE TIMOR

AUSTRALIA

Mariana Islands

GUAM

Marshall Islands

GERMAN PACIFIC TERRITORIES

Caroline Islands

KAISER WILHELMSLAND

Bismarck Archipelago

Nauru

PAPUA

Solomon Islands

Gilbert Islands

Ellice Islands

German Samoa (Western)

New Hebrides

Fiji

Tonga

Cook Islands

New Caledonia

Hawaiian Islands

PACIFIC OCEAN

Christmas Island

French Polynesia

MEXICO

BRITISH HONDURAS

CUBA

HAITI

DOMINICAN REPUBLIC

VIRGIN ISLANDS

LEEWARD ISLANDS

WINDWARD ISLANDS

BARBADOS

TRINIDAD AND TOBAGO

GUATEMALA

HONDURAS

EL SALVADOR

NICARAGUA

COSTA RICA

CANAL ZONE

PANAMA

VENEZUELA

COLOMBIA

ECUADOR

BRITISH GUIANA

DUTCH GUIANA

FRENCH GUIANA

ATLANTIC OCEAN

PERU

BRAZIL

BOLIVIA

PARAGUAY

CHILE

URUGUAY

ARGENTINA

FALKLAND ISLANDS

An industrial giant by the beginning of the 20th century, the USA was manufacturing munitions to supply the European arms race well before 1914. The USA's own army was small, and it relied upon its navy for defence.

THE WORLD IN JULY 1914

— Frontiers

TIMELINE 1870 – 1914

Franco-Prussian War ▪ Rival military alliances ▪ **Wilhelm II is Kaiser** ▪
Boer War ▪ **Anglo-German naval race** ▪ Moroccan crises ▪ **Wars in the**
Balkans ▪ Assassination in Sarajevo ▪ **Declarations of war**

1870 – 1880	1881 – 1890	1891 – 1900	1901 – 1902	1903 – 1904	1905 – 1906
JULY 1870 Outbreak of the Franco-Prussian War. **JANUARY 1871** France is defeated. The King of Prussia is declared Emperor of Germany.	**1881** Russia joins Germany and Austria-Hungary in the League of the Three Emperors. **1882** The Triple Alliance is formed between Germany, Austria-Hungary, and Italy.	**1891** Architect of Germany's pre-war planning Alfred von Schlieffen becomes German Chief of the General Staff. **JANUARY 1894** Franco-Russian Alliance is concluded. ⌄ Alfred von Schlieffen	**1901** Discussions about a possible alliance between Britain and Germany come to nothing. **JANUARY 1901** Death of Queen Victoria.		
	1884 The Maxim gun, the first true machine-gun, is invented. The Berlin Conference formalizes the division of Africa between European colonial powers.		**MARCH 1901** In the Boer War, the British adopt the policy of moving Boer civilians into concentration camps. **SEPTEMBER 1901** China signs a humiliating treaty with foreign powers after suppression of the Boxer Rebellion.	**MARCH 1903** Germans make plans with Ottoman Turkey to build a railway between Berlin and Baghdad. **DECEMBER 1903** The Wright brothers make the first powered heavier-than-air flight.	⌃ King Edward VII visits Paris for the Entente Cordiale **1905** German army adopts the Schlieffen Plan for fighting a war on two fronts.
	JUNE 1888 Wilhelm II becomes Emperor (Kaiser) of Germany. **1889** Russia begins a rapprochement with France.	**1898** Germany begins naval expansion, starting an Anglo-German naval race. **OCTOBER 1899** The Boer War in South Africa reveals deficiencies in the British Army.	**JANUARY 1902** Britain agrees a military alliance with Japan.	**FEBRUARY 1904** Russo-Japanese War begins. **APRIL 1904** Britain forms the Entente Cordiale with France.	**MARCH 1905** Japanese army defeats the Russians at the Battle of Mukden. Germany provokes the First Moroccan Crisis to test the Anglo-French Entente, which holds firm.
⌃ French Legion of Honour medal **MARCH 1878** Defeated in war with Russia, Ottoman Turkey is forced to recognize the independence of Serbia and Romania. **1879** Germany and Austria-Hungary form the Dual Alliance.	**1890** European armies begin to adopt bolt-action repeater rifles, increasing infantry rate of fire.	**1900** First effective submarines come into service. First flight of Zeppelin airship.	**MAY 1902** Boer War ends in British victory. **JUNE 1902** Triple Alliance between Germany, Austria-Hungary, and Italy is renewed.		**MAY 1905** The Imperial Japanese Navy destroys a Russian fleet at the Battle of Tsushima. **SEPTEMBER 1905** Russo-Japanese War ends in humiliating defeat for Russia. **FEBRUARY 1906** HMS *Dreadnought* is launched, rendering all earlier battleships obsolete.

» Belgian machine-gun

« Kaiser Wilhelm II

"The accelerating arms race is... a crushing burden that weighs on all nations and, if prolonged, will lead to the very cataclysm it seeks to avert."

TSAR NICHOLAS II, ADDRESSING THE HAGUE CONFERENCE, 1899

1907 – 1908	1909 – 1910	1911	1912	1913	1914

MARCH 1909
Germany backs Austria-Hungary over the annexation of Bosnia-Herzegovina, forcing Russia to withdraw its opposition by threatening war.

« Political postcard of European balancing act

JULY
General Joseph Joffre is appointed commander-in-chief of the French army.

1 JULY
Arrival of German gunboat in Tangier provokes the Second Moroccan Crisis, taking Europe to the brink of war.

12 FEBRUARY
China becomes a republic as the last emperor abdicates.

23 MARCH–30 MAY
Bulgarians capture Adrianople, Turkey, in First Balkan War. Treaty of London redraws boundaries.

29 JUNE
Second Balkan War begins. Bulgaria fights Serbia, Greece, and Romania.

AUGUST 1907
Russia and Britain sign a convention settling outstanding disputes in Central Asia.

1908
German army adopts the MG 08 machine-gun.

APRIL 1909
Young Turks depose Ottoman Sultan Abdul Hamid II and replace him with Mehmed V.

≽ German Uhlan helmet

☆ German holidaymakers, summer 1914

28 JUNE
Archduke Franz Ferdinand is assassinated by a Bosnian Serb in Sarajevo.

6 JULY
Germany agrees to support Austro-Hungarian action against Serbia.

NOVEMBER 1909
Britain creates an Imperial General Staff to coordinate military planning in Britain and its dominions.

☆ The German High Seas Fleet in the North Sea

29 SEPTEMBER
Italy declares war on Turkey in pursuit of territorial claims in Libya.

28 MARCH
British House of Commons rejects votes for women, provoking suffragettes into adoption of militant tactics.

7 AUGUST
France enacts the Three-Year Law, extending conscription.

10 AUGUST
Second Balkan War ends with defeat of Bulgaria.

23 JULY
Austria-Hungary issues the Serbians with an ultimatum.

28 JULY
Austria-Hungary declares war on Serbia.

1910
Armies and navies of the major powers begin to acquire planes and train military pilots.

JULY 1908
Young Turk revolution begins drive to modernize Ottoman Turkey.

UNITED SUFFRAGISTS

USQUE AD FINEM

≫ Suffragette banner

8 OCTOBER
First Balkan War begins, pitting Turkey against the Balkan League: Serbia, Montenegro, Greece, and Bulgaria.

18 OCTOBER
Italo-Turkish War ends. Italy takes possession of Libya.

OCTOBER 1908
Austria-Hungary announces the annexation of Bosnia-Herzegovina.

MAY 1910
In Britain, George V becomes king on the death of Edward VII.

1 NOVEMBER
First combat use of aircraft by Italians in North Africa.

4 NOVEMBER
Treaty of Fez resolves the Moroccan crisis.

NOVEMBER
Britain and France agree to share naval responsibilities, the French concentrating on the Mediterranean.

5 NOVEMBER
Woodrow Wilson is elected president of the USA.

☆ Announcement of war in Berlin

30 JULY
Russia begins general mobilization.

« BEFORE

A series of localized wars in the 1860s and 1870s redrew the borders of major European states.

GERMAN UNIFICATION
In 1860, Germany was a collection of separate states. **Prussia** was acknowledged as its **leading power** and, in 1870–71, defeated France in the **Franco-Prussian War**. This victory led directly to the founding of the German Empire under the king of Prussia, who later became the German Kaiser.

AUSTRIA-HUNGARY
The Austrian Habsburgs survived in power by forming **Austria-Hungary**, the Dual Monarchy, held together by allegiance to the emperor of Austria, who was also the king of Hungary.

GERMAN ARMY HELMET

Europe's High Noon

Convinced of the superiority of their civilization, Europeans had achieved a dominant position in the world, rooted in the spectacular growth of their industries and populations, and in the strength of their military forces.

At the dawn of the 20th century, Europe was at the height of its military and economic power. States such as Britain and France controlled huge empires, encompassing nearly all of Africa and large parts of Asia. European capital and commerce created enormous influence and wealth. Worldwide transport and communication networks tied the global economy to its European hub. The US was the only major non-European economic power, although Japan had emerged as an industrializing military force in the 1890s. The leading European powers were Britain, France, Germany, Russia, and Austria-Hungary. Italy and Ottoman Turkey aspired to join them. Of these states, Germany was the most dynamic force.

Since the unification of Germany in 1871 the country had undergone rapid industrialization. The population had grown a massive 43 per cent between 1880 and 1910. France, in contrast, had an almost static population growth and less developed industries, despite ruling an extensive empire. Russia lagged even further behind industrially, but was by far the most populous European state. Britain had lost its industrial lead but still exercised unchallenged dominance over international finance, maritime trade, and its vast overseas empire.

1.63 BILLION The estimated global population in 1900. Around one-quarter of this number resided in Europe.

Precarious balance
A 1910 postcard shows various heads of state embarked upon an uncertain journey, precariously mounted aboard a motor vehicle. In the early 20th century, the political balance was always threatening to tip over into war.

AFTER

Tensions between the European powers mounted over disputes outside Europe and in the Balkans.

THE MOROCCAN CRISES
Germany challenged French **imperial ambitions in Morocco**, leading to diplomatic crises in 1905 and 1911 **18–19 ≫**.

CENTRAL POWERS Name given to Germany, Austria-Hungary, and their allies in World War I.

ENTENTE POWERS Name given to Britain, France, and Russia, which are also referred to as the Allies.

OTTOMAN DECLINE
The long-term decline of the **Turkish Ottoman Empire** was a serious source of instability, triggering an **Italian invasion of Libya**, an Ottoman-ruled area of North Africa, in 1911, and two **Balkan Wars in 1912–13 18–19 ≫**. Ottoman weakness and Balkan conflicts were a temptation for both Russia and Austria-Hungary to intervene in an area on their southern borders where they had competing interests. This was where World War I would start, after the assassination of **Austrian Archduke Franz Ferdinand** in June 1914 **28–29 ≫**.

Oppressed nationalities' demands for self-rule were a threat to the multinational Austro-Hungarian Empire. Governments feared a breakdown of order and responded by asserting the military and diplomatic prestige of the state. They hoped this would serve as an antidote to internal forces of disintegration and subversion.

All the major powers spent large amounts on their armed forces. Mass education and a popular press united in spreading a message of patriotism that easily slipped into jingoism. As no formal institution existed for regulating international affairs, states sought security in alliances. Germany allied itself with Austria-Hungary and Italy, and France with Russia. Britain was

Imperial splendour
Emperor Franz Joseph of Austria receives guests at Schönbrunn Palace in Vienna. A member of the Habsburg dynasty, he was Europe's longest-ruling monarch in 1914, having come to the throne in 1848.

traditionally isolationist, but its fear of Germany led to agreements with France, and later Russia. These divisive alliance systems existed among nations bound by cultural similarities, economic interdependence, and the ties that linked the various royal families. The inability of the countries to stop the slide to war was to be a catastrophe for Europe, from which it would never recover its global power.

Political systems
Most European states were ruled by hereditary monarchs. In Germany, Austria-Hungary, and Russia, these monarchs retained a large measure of political power, despite the existence of elected parliaments. Britain had retained its monarchy, but kings and queens scrupulously respected the authority of the Houses of Parliament. France, conversely, was a republic. Both Britain and France had restricted electoral franchises – women could not vote, and in Britain the poor were also excluded.

Threats and alliances
Although often seen in retrospect as a golden age of tranquil prosperity, the years before World War I were racked by political conflict. Mass Socialist movements preached the overthrow of the capitalist system. Anarchists practised "propaganda of the deed", assassinating monarchs, such as the Italian King Umberto I in July 1900, and bombing symbols of power. Suffragettes turned to violence in their quest for women's voting rights.

European alliances, 1878–1918
By 1900, shifting military alliances had resolved into a fixed confrontation between Russia and France on one side and Germany and Austria-Hungary on the other.

KEY
◆ Austro–German alliance 1878–1918
◆ Three Emperors' alliance 1881–87
◆ Austro–Serbian alliance 1881–95
◇ Triple alliance 1882–1915
◆ Austro–German–Romanian alliance 1883–1916
◆ Franco–Russian alliance 1894–1917
◆ Russo–Bulgarian military convention 1902–13
◇ Anglo–French Entente 1904–1918
◆ Anglo–Russian Entente 1907–1917

ALLIANCES DURING FIRST WORLD WAR 1914–18
▦ The Allies (and allied states)
▦ Central Powers (and allied states)
▦ Neutral states

Crises and Conflicts

In the years before the outbreak of World War I, the European powers engaged in brinkmanship and an accelerating arms race. A series of diplomatic crises and conflicts in the Balkans accustomed Europeans to the possibility of a major war.

Germany was indisputably a major military and economic power by the end of the 19th century. However, it lacked two of the attributes then regarded as indicative of great power status: a substantial overseas empire and an ocean-going navy.

Under the unstable Kaiser Wilhelm II, Germany set out to flex its muscles on the world stage. A plan to build a world-class fleet, proposed by Admiral Alfred von Tirpitz, was adopted in 1897. To Britain, this appeared a hostile act. The German naval programme presented a direct challenge to the Royal Navy's dominance of its home waters, the cornerstone of Britain's national security. The British responded with a massive warship-building programme of their own, setting a new standard for battleships with HMS *Dreadnought* in 1906. As the naval race gathered pace, the British buried old rivalries to form an entente with France in 1904 and with France's ally, Russia, in 1907.

Moroccan crises

While making an enemy of Britain, Germany also manufactured a confrontation with France. In 1905, Kaiser Wilhelm made a provocative visit to Morocco, a nominally independent country that France was absorbing into its sphere of influence. He called for all the powers to be given equal access to Morocco, a claim rejected by a subsequent international conference. The Germans took up the issue again in 1911, sending the gunboat SMS *Panther* to the Moroccan port of Agadir. This move provoked a diplomatic crisis, briefly raising fears of a general European war. By the end of 1911, a settlement had been negotiated, involving a small concession of territory to Germany from French Equatorial Africa. This sabre-rattling, along with some anti-British remarks dropped by the Kaiser, drove Britain to strengthen its links with France.

When the crisis of 1911 blew over, the prospect of a general war appeared to recede. Yet at a private meeting in December 1912, the Kaiser and his senior military commanders discussed launching a preventive war against France and Russia. They argued that with the strength of the Russian army increasing, it was in Germany's best interest to make the conflict happen sooner rather than later.

Crisis in Morocco
The dispatch of the German gunboat *Panther* to Agadir, caricatured in this contemporary German illustration, took Europe to the brink of war in 1911. Diplomacy solved the crisis but strengthened Anglo-French resolve.

Slav nationalism

In southeastern Europe, tensions were rising. The Balkans was a traditional area of rivalry between Austria-Hungary and Russia. The Russians had adopted the role of protectors and leaders of the area's Slav states,

« **BEFORE**

The accession of German Kaiser Wilhelm II in 1888 was followed by a fatal shift in great power relations.

LEAGUE OF THE THREE EMPERORS
In 1873, German Chancellor Otto von Bismarck tried to stabilize Europe through an **alliance of three empires**: Germany, Russia, and Austria-Hungary. In the 1880s, **rivalry between Russia and Austria-Hungary** undermined this system. Germany formed the **Dual Alliance** with Austria-Hungary, but maintained friendly relations with Russia. This policy was abandoned by Wilhelm II. By 1894, **Russia had allied itself with France** against Germany.

OTTO VON BISMARCK

German fleet, pre-1914
Dreadnought battleships of the German High Seas Fleet steam into the North Sea before World War I. The navy was a source of pride to the German people, its expansion supported by a patriotic Navy League with more than a million members.

including Serbia and Bulgaria. Russia also had long-term ambitions to expand at the expense of the declining Ottoman Turkish Empire. For Austria-Hungary, Slavs were a domestic problem, a restive part of the empire's ethnic mix. By asserting itself against the Balkan Slavs, especially Serbia, which was not in the Habsburg Empire, Austria-Hungary hoped to reinforce its authority over its own Slav minorities.

In 1908, the Austro-Hungarian annexation of Bosnia Herzegovina, an area it already administered, provoked a hostile response from Russia, but its allies, Britain and France, refused to back military action. The annexation left the Russians humiliated and angered Serbia, which covertly backed a campaign of attacks on Austro-Hungarian officials by Bosnian Serbs.

The Ottoman Empire
The weakness of Ottoman Turkey was another source of instability. In 1908, Turkish nationalists, known as the Young Turks, rebelled against the sultan, Abdul Hamid II, opening a

Balkan soldiers
The two Balkan Wars of 1912–13 were fought with great ferocity, resulting in more than half a million casualties. The instability of the region drew Russia and Austria-Hungary into a dangerous confrontation.

period of political upheaval. In 1912, the Balkan League – an alliance of Serbia, Bulgaria, Greece, and Montenegro – attacked and defeated Turkey in the First Balkan War. The victors then fell out over the spoils. Bulgaria attacked Serbia and Greece to start the Second Balkan War. When Romania also joined the

hostilities, Bulgaria was heavily defeated. The major winner of both wars was Serbia, which almost doubled its territory.

After the war, Bulgaria was left a discontented state, eager for revenge on the Serbs, while the strengthening of a hostile Serbia was a disaster for Austria-Hungary. The split between

Serbia and Bulgaria was a major setback for Russia's Balkan policy. Unable to back both countries, Russia was left with Serbia as its sole ally in the Balkans.

Germany, meanwhile, sought to extend its influence southwards, and planned to build a Berlin-to-Baghdad railway. This was interpreted by Britain as a threat to its interests in the Middle East. Enver Pasha, a Young Turk army officer who became Turkish leader in 1913, was pro-German. He invited a German military mission, headed by General Otto Liman von Sanders, to modernize the Turkish army.

None of these crises, fears, and conflicting ambitions made a general European war inevitable, but it had become distinctly imaginable and even tempting for some as a possible solution to intractable problems.

> **"If the German fleet becomes superior to ours, the German army can conquer this country."**
> SIR EDWARD GREY, BRITISH FOREIGN SECRETARY, 1906

AFTER ≫

In the years leading up to World War I, a growing arms race was a clear sign of insecurity and potential conflict.

THE ARMS RACE
In its **naval race with Britain**, Germany had built 17 dreadnoughts and five battlecruisers by August 1914. Due to Britain's massive financial investment, however, it retained its superiority over Germany, boasting 24 dreadnoughts and 10 battlecruisers.

DREADNOUGHT The name of a British battleship that entered service in 1906. It became a general term for all modern battleships of comparable armament and performance.

France extended conscription by the Three Year Law of 1913, attempting to match the size of the German army from a much smaller population base. **Russia increased military spending**.

BALKAN TROUBLES
World War I was in part a third Balkan War, following on from the two wars of 1912–13. Triggered by the assassination of **Austrian Archduke Franz Ferdinand** by Bosnian Serbs at Sarajevo in June 1914 **28–29 ≫**, World War I began when **Austria-Hungary declared war on Serbia 30–31 ≫**.

EMPEROR OF GERMANY Born 1859 Died 1941

Kaiser Wilhelm II

"England, France, and Russia have conspired ... to wage a war of annihilation against us."

KAISER WILHELM II, MEMORANDUM WRITTEN 30 JULY 1914

To his enemies, Wilhelm II, King of Prussia and Kaiser (Emperor) of Germany was the embodiment of aggressive Prussian militarism. Yet in many ways, Wilhelm had struggled to adapt to the requirements of his social status and official role. A difficult birth had left him with a withered and paralysed left arm. To this disability, about which he was self-conscious, was added a neurotic nature. He hero-worshipped his stern and warlike paternal ancestors, and moulded himself in the image of the Prussian military tradition – strict, hard, pitiless,

Young leader
In the early part of his reign, Wilhelm was a fresh force in German life, promising to lead the country on a new course to global power and prosperity.

and patriarchal. He was, however, neither physically nor emotionally fit for the role. A weak man trying to prove he was strong, he developed a habit of erratic posturing, alternately bullying and ingratiating. The other European powers viewed Germany as unreliable and dangerous.

On the global stage
Coming to the throne at the age of 29, Wilhelm was determined to assert his personal rule. He quickly disposed of the experienced Chancellor Otto von Bismarck. *Weltpolitik*, the theory that Germany should take its place as a global superpower, was adopted as official German policy in 1897. This expansionist outlook was not his own invention. It reflected the ideas and aspirations of a host of German nationalists, who demanded that their country should have a colonial empire, an ocean-going navy, and possibly *Lebensraum* (living space) in eastern Europe.

For Wilhelm, diplomacy was partly a family affair. He was a grandson of Britain's Queen Victoria, on his mother's side, and cousin to Tsar Nicholas II of Russia. These blood connections were important to him, but did not necessarily imply friendship. His attitude towards Britain in particular was contradictory. He

Churchill meets the Kaiser
The Kaiser hosted Winston Churchill during military manoeuvres in 1909. Churchill described him as a man who wanted to be like Napoleon "without having to fight his battles".

The Kaiser at war
Wilhelm was sidelined by military leaders, but could not be ignored completely. Here, he stands between generals Paul von Hindenburg and Erich Ludendorff at German General Headquarters in 1917.

In the years leading up to World War I, the German high command under General Helmuth von Moltke and the chancellor, Theobald von Bethmann-Hollweg, dictated policy. In the crisis of summer 1914, Wilhelm wavered between violent assertions of the need for war and feeble attempts to preserve peace.

The war years
Although the spirit of national unity that gripped Germany in August 1914 carried the Kaiser to an unprecedented level of popularity, his marginalization continued. He intervened in the direction of the German war effort, but did not control it. He took a special interest in naval affairs, limiting the operations of the High Seas Fleet in order to avoid loss of his precious battleships. His attitudes showed his habitual instability, one moment advocating genocidal policies on the Eastern Front, the next considering a peace initiative based on an appeal to his royal relatives. From 1916, he lost control of senior appointments and

veered from clear admiration to a conviction that the British were intent on seeking his destruction. Such instability was typical of the Kaiser, as was his impulsiveness.

Waning authority
Wilhelm liked dramatic diplomatic initiatives, such as his unexpected appearance in Tangier in 1905, provoking the First Moroccan Crisis. Yet the language of his speeches could be blustering in a way that damaged Germany's international image.

November 1908, General Dietrich, Count von Hülsen-Haeseler, the Chief of the German Imperial Military Cabinet, died while dancing in front of the Kaiser dressed in a ballerina's tutu. More damagingly, from 1907 the Kaiser's closest confidant, Prince Philip of Eulenburg, had to defend himself against press allegations of homosexual behaviour.

Germany's military and bureaucratic establishment was beginning to tire of Wilhelm's ill-considered public statements and erratic attempts to

Epaulettes
These shoulder boards formed part of the Kaiser's Hussar Life Guard uniform. Wilhelm loved military regalia and was deeply captivated by the grandeur of parades and ceremonies.

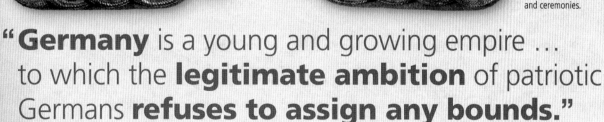

"**Germany** is a young and growing empire ... to which the **legitimate ambition** of patriotic Germans **refuses to assign any bounds.**"

KAISER WILHELM II, INTERVIEW IN BRITAIN'S "DAILY TELEGRAPH", 28 OCTOBER 1908

In 1900, he told German troops sent to suppress the Boxer Rebellion in China that they should behave like "Huns", a reference to the devastating attacks on European areas of the Roman Empire by the hordes of Attila the Hun in the fifth century.

Beginning in 1908, Wilhelm's personal position weakened and his influence on policy-making waned. His reputation was damaged by association with scandal. At a private party in

exercise personal diplomacy. The last straw was an interview the Kaiser accorded to a British journalist for the *Daily Telegraph* in October 1908, in which he described the British as "mad as March hares", suggested German naval expansion was aimed at Japan, and claimed to have personally shown the British how to win the Boer War in South Africa. This outburst alienated public opinion inside Germany as well as abroad.

was forced to accept the ascendancy of General Erich Ludendorff, whom he loathed. Almost powerless, he was dubbed the "Shadow Kaiser". His last exercise of authority was to sack Ludendorff as the war effort fell apart in October 1918. In November, facing defeat and revolution, the army insisted that he abdicate. Wilhelm was spirited away into exile in the Netherlands, an irrelevant figure as Germany entered a new era.

TIMELINE

- **January 1859** Born in Berlin, the son of Prince Friedrich Wilhelm of Prussia and Princess Victoria of Great Britain.
- **February 1881** Marries Augusta Victoria, Princess of Schleswig-Holstein.
- **June 1888** Becomes Kaiser after the death of his father, Friedrich III.
- **March 1890** Forces the resignation of veteran Chancellor Otto von Bismarck.
- **January 1896** Sends a personal telegram to South Africa to congratulate Boer leader Paul Kruger for defeating the British-backed Jameson Raid. This causes offence to Britain.
- **1897** Backs Admiral von Tirpitz's plan to build a modern navy capable of challenging the British in the North Sea.
- **March 1905** Visits Tangier to assert German interests in Morocco, antagonizing France and causing a diplomatic crisis.
- **April 1907** Prince Philip of Eulenburg, Wilhelm's closest friend and personal adviser, is accused in the press of homosexual activities, initiating a major scandal.
- **October 1908** Gives an ill-considered interview to the British *Daily Telegraph* that includes wild statements on foreign affairs.
- **July 1914** Assures Austria-Hungary of German support for military action against Serbia following the assassination of Archduke Franz Ferdinand.
- **August 1914** Delivers an eloquent address to the deputies of the German Reichstag welcoming national unity.
- **August 1916** Sidelined as generals Hindenburg and Ludendorff take control of the German war effort.
- **January 1917** Approves the decision to resort to unrestricted U-boat warfare, which will bring the US into the war.
- **November 1918** Having lost the support of his army commanders and the German people, Wilhelm abdicates and flees to exile in the neutral Netherlands.
- **June 1919** The Treaty of Versailles attempts to prosecute Wilhelm for "supreme offence against international morality". The Dutch government refuses to extradite him.
- **November 1922** After the death of Victoria Augusta, Wilhelm marries his second wife, Princess Hermine Reuss of Greiz.
- **June 1941** Dies in his country house at Doorn in the Netherlands.

WILHELM AND HERMINE IN EXILE

Part-time soldiers
A British soldier, British lion, and the figure of Britannia advertise a military exhibition held at the Earl's Court Exhibition Centre in London in 1901.

‹‹ BEFORE

Prussian victories in wars against Austria in 1866 and France in 1870–71 convinced all European powers of the need for meticulous war planning by a properly trained general staff.

PROFESSIONAL PLANNERS
Staff officers trained at the **Prussian War Academy** had excelled in the organizational task of moving masses of men swiftly to the borders by rail and of supplying them once they arrived. After 1870, other European countries imitated the Prussian system – France, for example, creating its **École de Guerre** in 1880. New **railways** were built to **facilitate mobilization**, and the drawing up of railway timetables was recognized as a vital staff function.

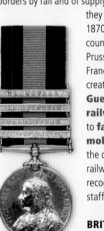

BRITISH BOER
WAR MEDAL

BRITISH REFORMS
The British Army lagged behind Continental Europe, but serious failings revealed during Britain's war against the Boers in South Africa in 1899–1902 led to **major military reforms**. Pushed through by War Minister Richard Haldane from 1905, these reforms created the post of Chief of the Imperial General Staff and instituted **detailed planning for mobilization** in case of war.

Planning for War

The armies of the major European powers had long prepared for the conflict that erupted in 1914. Their military plans were a crucial factor in fuelling the build-up to war, although its actual course confounded all their expectations.

The war plans of all the Continental powers were built on the rapid mobilization of mass armies. European states maximized their manpower by conscripting a large proportion of their male population into short-term peacetime service. These trained men formed a reserve that could be easily deployed in the event of war.

This created armies of unprecedented size in Germany, France, Austria-Hungary, and Russia. Britain, which did not have conscription, had a relatively small number of regular troops and reserves, backed up by a part-time Territorial Army intended for home service only.

Plans for a war on two fronts
The assumption behind Germany's war planning was that it would have to fight France and Russia simultaneously, a Franco-Russian military alliance having been in place since the 1890s. The German army's Chief of the General Staff from 1891 to 1906, Alfred von Schlieffen, believed that a two-front war could be won only through bold aggression. He devised a plan to hurl most of the German army into an initial offensive against France. Approaching via Belgium, his troops would encircle the French, attacking from the rear and crushing them within six weeks of mobilization. The German troops would then move by train to the Eastern Front and defeat the Russians.

The Schlieffen Plan
Germany's plan for defeating France involved an advance through neutral Belgium, the Netherlands, and Luxembourg to sweep behind the French armies, which were to be enveloped and swiftly destroyed.

KEY
⇒ Planned routes of German armies
⊠ German fortified town
⊠ Belgian fortified town
⊠ French fortified town

> **42** **The number of days it would take for France to fall to Germany, according to the Schlieffen Plan.**

This risky plan, based on optimistic assumptions about everything from the marching speed of German troops to the slowness of Russian mobilization, was adopted in 1905.

Schlieffen's successor as Chief of the General Staff, Helmuth von Moltke (known as Moltke the Younger), tinkered with details of the plan, such as avoiding the violation of Dutch neutrality and shifting some troops from the enveloping manoeuvre to reinforce the border with France. The consequences of violating Belgian neutrality were not addressed.

At the time the Schlieffen Plan was adopted, French war planning was essentially defensive. Fearing German military strength, France had built a line of fortresses on its eastern border. In 1911, however, General Joseph Joffre took over as French commander-in-chief, and French tactics changed.

Offence versus defence
Influenced by military theorists such as General Ferdinand Foch, who argued that in modern warfare the offence would always triumph over the defence, Joffre adopted Plan XVII, prescribing an immediate invasion of German-annexed Alsace and Lorraine should war break out. By 1913, the French had also managed to extract from their Russian allies, whose rearmament they were financing, a promise to launch an offensive against Germany within 15 days of mobilization. The Russians continued to have separate plans for a possible war with Austria-Hungary alone.

> " Let the **last man** on the right **brush the Channel** with his sleeve. "
>
> REMARK ATTRIBUTED TO COUNT ALFRED VON SCHLIEFFEN, 1905

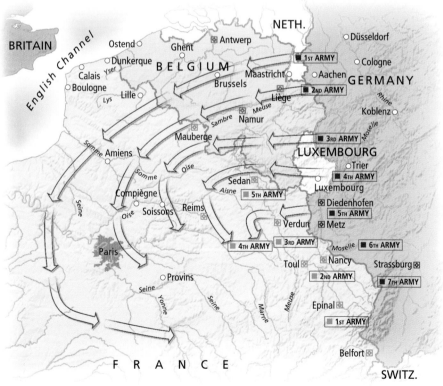

German troops on manoeuvres
A crowd watches soldiers cross a pontoon bridge during Germany's 1912 military manoeuvres. These annual occasions were a testing ground for new tactics and technology and a display of military strength.

Austria-Hungary faced a problem of split objectives. The Austro-Hungarian chief of staff, Conrad von Hötzendorf, favoured an offensive war against Serbia, and was inclined to stand on the defensive against Russia. But Austria-Hungary's German allies needed Austro-Hungarian forces to attack the Russians in Poland, to relieve pressure on Germany's Eastern Front. Despite Austro-Hungarian plans for a "swing force" to be mobilized against Serbia or Russia as required, the issue was still unresolved in 1914.

British commitments

Britain's front line of defence was its Royal Navy, which had long enabled British governments to adopt a detached pose in relation to European affairs. But its entente with France in 1904, designed to deter German aggression, led to the development of war plans that would commit the British to a European war.

From 1911, informal talks between British and French army commanders resulted in an understanding that, were France attacked by Germany, Britain would send an expeditionary force across the English Channel to take up position on the left of the French line, facing the border with Belgium. However, the British were careful to avoid making any formal promise to carry out this commitment to their French allies.

The pre-1914 war plans were worked out in great detail by staff officers, with timetables that had to be adhered to if the military machine was to function smoothly. Collectively they created a situation in which the mobilization of armies could only with great difficulty be prevented from leading to large-scale battles. The planners had written the script for a Europe-wide war that could be precipitated at any moment by a single incident.

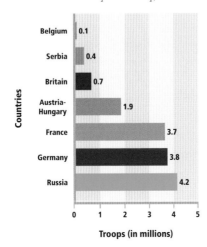

Army sizes at the outbreak of war
Russia's army was substantially larger than those of other European nations, but it was poorly equipped and badly organized. Britain had a relatively small army, and depended on the Royal Navy for defence.

Bar chart — Troops (in millions) by country:

Country	Troops (in millions)
Belgium	0.1
Serbia	0.4
Britain	0.7
Austria-Hungary	1.9
France	3.7
Germany	3.8
Russia	4.2

Axis: Countries (y) / Troops (in millions) 0 1 2 3 4 5 (x)

AFTER »

The mobilization of European armies in 1914 mostly proceeded with an efficiency that was a credit to the professionalism of army staff officers. Once the fighting had started, however, little went as planned.

THWARTED EXPECTATIONS
None of the plans of the initial protagonists worked out as they had expected. Attacking on their eastern frontier, the French army quickly discovered their troops' **vulnerability to defensive firepower**. At the same time, instead of achieving the rapid defeat of France they had envisaged, German forces were driven back at the **Battle of the Marne** in September 1914 **54–55** ». On Germany's eastern front, **advancing Russian armies** suffered heavy defeats. There was to be no quick victory for anyone.

Evolving Military Technology

"Everybody will be **entrenched...** The **spade** will be **indispensable.**"

JAN BLOCH, POLISH FINANCIER AND INDUSTRIALIST, IN "THE FUTURE OF WAR", 1897

The European armies and navies of 1914 were the beneficiaries of a century of progress in industry, science, and technology. Change was often not specifically driven by military requirements. Railways transformed the speed at which armies could be deployed to frontiers. New means of communication, from the electric telegraph to the telephone and radio, were adapted to military uses. Progress in precision engineering made it much easier to mass-produce weapons with complex mechanisms. Chemists experimented with new explosives that would provide a more powerful replacement for gunpowder.

Arming the infantry

In 1815, at the end of the Napoleonic Wars, armies fought with smoothbore flintlock muskets, loaded by ramming a ball and powder down the barrel, and cannon firing solid shot. Navies went to sea in wooden sailing ships. The pace of change was slow at first, but by the 1870s a firepower revolution was under way.

In the Franco-Prussian War of 1870–71, both sides armed their infantry (foot soldiers) with breech-loading single-shot rifles. By the 1880s, these already effective infantry weapons were being replaced by bolt-action rifles with ammunition fed from a magazine. A well-trained soldier using the Lee-Enfield, the British Army's standard rifle from 1895, could fire more than 20 rounds a minute. This rate of fire was far exceeded by machine-guns. The Maxim gun, the first true machine-gun, brought into active service in the 1890s, fired 600 rounds a minute. The German army took to machine-guns enthusiastically, while other countries struggled to find a good tactical use for the weapon.

Rapid-fire artillery

Artillery guns (long-range weaponry used for bombardment) also adopted rifled barrels and breech-loading. The range of guns greatly increased, and gunners began practising the bombardment of targets beyond their field of view.

The invention in the 1870s of a hydraulic mechanism that returned the gun's barrel to its original position after recoil cleared the way for rapid-fire artillery. Most important of all, scientifically designed shells packed with nitrate-based high-explosives ensured that artillery fire

Potential bomber
Just before the outbreak of World War I, Russian aviation pioneer Igor Sikorski (right) built the first multi-engine aircraft. These flying machines could carry a substantial load and were turned into bombers during the war.

High-explosive shells
Mass-produced in factories and fired from breech-loading rifled guns, these shells marked a revolutionary advance in destructive power over the gunpowder and smoothbore cannon of the mid-19th century.

The rapid developments in military technology from the 1870s occurred during a long period of peace between the great powers. The Russo-Japanese War of 1904–05, the first conflict to use modern armaments, provided a preview of what was to come in World War I. At sea, torpedoes and mines proved capable of sinking the largest warships. On land, troops were entrenched behind barbed wire. Invented to control cattle in the American West, barbed wire inflicted massive casualties on infantry attempting frontal assaults.

The old ways die hard
In Europe, naval commanders continued to focus on bigger and better battleships, while army commanders preached the triumph of offensive spirit over defensive firepower. Openness to technological innovation coexisted with an attachment to venerated traditions, such as the cavalry charge with sabre and lance, and the infantry assault with fixed bayonets. World War I would be characterized by the contrast between the efficient exploitation of weaponry supplied by science and industry and the persistence of many attitudes to war belonging to an earlier era.

> "Aviation is fine as a **sport. But as an instrument of war,** it is **worthless.**"

FERDINAND FOCH, FRENCH GENERAL, 1911

was more destructive. Rifled guns and high-explosive shells were also used at sea, mounted in rotating turrets aboard steam-driven steel warships.

New technology
By the early 20th century, armies and navies were keen to explore other new inventions that might give them an advantage over the enemy. Wireless telegraphy (radio), first demonstrated experimentally in the 1890s, was in use by navies by 1904. However, early radio equipment proved cumbersome on land, and armies preferred to use field telephones.

Inventors Wilbur and Orville Wright developed a heavier-than-air flying machine between 1903 and 1905. European armies showed interest but adoption of the invention was delayed by the brothers' refusal to demonstrate their aircraft in public.

Meanwhile, airships were developed by, among others, German Count Ferdinand von Zeppelin. From 1909, the year in which French pilot Louis Blériot flew a monoplane across the Channel, an air craze gripped Europe. Air enthusiasts and fantasy fiction writers envisaged future aerial wars with mass bombing of cities. More

> **12,000** The number of machine-guns in service with the German army in August 1914. In contrast, the British and French armies had only a few hundred machine-guns each.

soberly, armies and navies explored the potential of aeroplanes and airships for reconnaissance, integrating both into manoeuvres from 1911.

By that date, motor transport was having a major impact on civilian life, but armies remained overwhelmingly reliant upon horse-drawn vehicles. Armoured cars began to come into service, and were used by Italy in its war with Turkey in 1911.

Clément-Bayard II airship
Built in 1910 for the French army, this airship never entered service. It was the first airship to fly over the English Channel, and its wireless transmitter achieved the first air-ground radio communication.

1840s Prussia is the first European state to equip its infantry with a breech-loading rifle, the Dreyse needle gun.

1859 In France, the army makes the first mass movement of troops by railway, transporting an army to fight the Austrians in northern Italy.

BELGIAN MACHINE-GUN, 1869

1860s The first hand-cranked rapid-fire weapons are introduced, including the Belgian Montigny Mitrailleuse and the American Gatling gun.

1866 British engineer Robert Whitehead invents the first self-propelled naval torpedo.

1870–71 In the Franco-Prussian War, Krupp's rifled artillery guns prove their effectiveness.

1880s High explosives such as picric acid (Lyddite) and TNT come into widespread use as fillings for artillery and naval shells, greatly increasing their destructive effect.

1884 The first recoil-operated machine-gun is invented by Sir Hiram Maxim. The Maxim gun, as it is known, is used by the British Army in colonial wars in the 1890s. Its derivatives include the German MG 08 (1908) and the British Vickers gun (1912) used in World War I.

1886 Replacing gunpowder with a smokeless propellent makes rifle fire more effective.

1890s European armies are equipped with the bolt-action repeater rifles they will use in World War I, such as the German Mauser Gewehr 98, French Lebel, and Russian Mosin-Nagant.

1897 The US Navy adopts the first successful powered submarine.

1898 France introduces the 75 mm field gun that can fire up to 30 rounds a minute to a range of 8.5 km (5 miles).

1904–05 In the Russo-Japanese War, the combination of trenches and barbed wire, artillery firing high-explosive shells beyond line of sight, and the use of field telephones and radio anticipate the warfare of World War I.

1906 The British battleship HMS *Dreadnought* enters service, making all previous leading warships obsolescent.

1911 The military use of aircraft begins as Italy drops grenades on Ottoman Turks in Libya.

1 MAUSER GEWEHR 98 (GERMAN)

2 7.92MM X57 MAUSER CARTRIDGE (GERMAN)

5 PATTERN 1907 SWORD BAYONET (BRITISH)

7 KNIFE BAYONET (GERMAN)

8 .303 MKVII CARTRIDGE (BRITISH)

9 SHORT MAGAZINE LEE-ENFIELD (BRITISH)

Rifles

The infantry was armed with bolt-action rapid-fire rifles, with ammunition fed from a box magazine. These were reliable, efficient weapons, and armies saw no need for substantial innovations during the war.

11 HALES NO. 3 RIFLE GRENADE (BRITISH)

1 **Mauser Gewehr 98 (German)** entered service in 1898. This model has been fitted with a telescopic sight for use by a sniper. 2 **7.92mm X57 Mauser cartridge (German)** was adopted in 1905. Its use with the Gewehr 98 rifle led to the name "Mauser" being added. 3 **Ross .303IN MK III (Canadian)** Produced until 1916, the Ross was favoured by many snipers due to its long-range accuracy. However, it often jammed in the muddy conditions of the trenches. 4 **M91 Moschetto de Cavalleria (Italian)** This was a shorter variant of the Carcano M91 rifle, the standard Italian infantry weapon. 5 **Pattern 1907 sword bayonet (British)** Designed for the Lee-Enfield rifle, this was based on the Japanese Arisaka bayonet, but its long blade was unwieldy in the trenches. 6 **Steyr-Mannlicher M1895 (Austro-Hungarian)** was used by Austro-Hungarian troops, who called it the "Ruck-Zuck" (very quick) due to its high firing rate. 7 **Knife bayonet (German)** Short and double-edged, this fitted to the Gewehr 98 rifle and doubled as a trench knife. 8 **.303 MKVII cartridge (British)** This version of the Lee-Enfield cartridge had a heavy lead base, which caused

the cartridge to twist and deform, inflicting more severe wounds on the enemy. 9 **Short Magazine Lee-Enfield (British)** was the standard British infantry weapon. The rifle shown is the Mark III Star, introduced in late 1915. 10 **Berthier MLE 1916 (French)** A modified version of the earlier MLE 1907/15, this increased the magazine size from three rounds to five. 11 **Hales No. 3 rifle grenade (British)** Rifle grenades, which clipped to the muzzle, provided greater range for explosives. 12 **Cartridge belt (American)** Standard issue for infantrymen, these belts enabled them to carry extra ammunition. 13 **Mosin Nagant M1891 (Russian)** was the main weapon of the Russian infantry. Due to shortages, Russia issued contracts to American firms for over three million of these rifles. 14 **M1903 Springfield (American)** After encountering Mauser rifles in the Spanish-American War of 1898, the US negotiated a licence to manufacture a Mauser-style rifle of its own. 15 **Cartridge belt (Turkish)** This belt with its cartridge pouches was made in Germany, as was most of the equipment used by the Turkish troops.

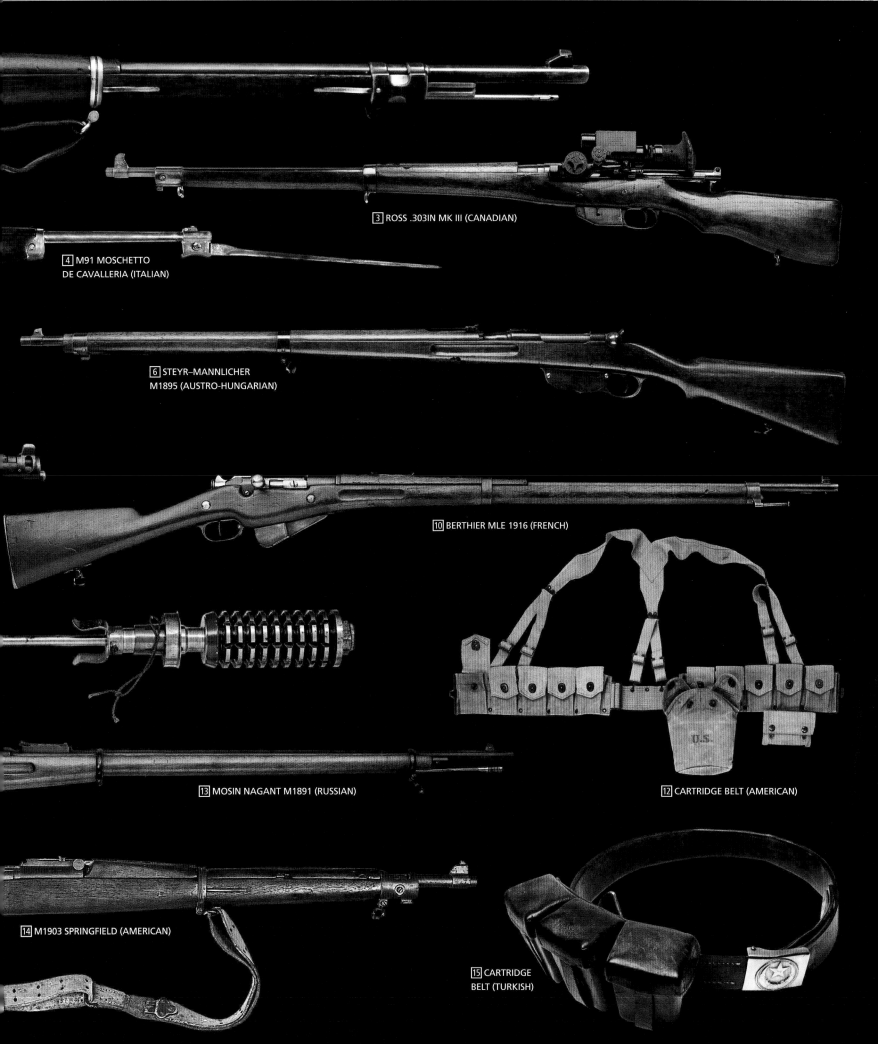

3 ROSS .303IN MK III (CANADIAN)

4 M91 MOSCHETTO
DE CAVALLERIA (ITALIAN)

6 STEYR–MANNLICHER
M1895 (AUSTRO-HUNGARIAN)

10 BERTHIER MLE 1916 (FRENCH)

13 MOSIN NAGANT M1891 (RUSSIAN)

12 CARTRIDGE BELT (AMERICAN)

14 M1903 SPRINGFIELD (AMERICAN)

15 CARTRIDGE
BELT (TURKISH)

‹‹ BEFORE

Austria-Hungary was a multi-ethnic state in crisis. Its stability was under threat from growing discontent among its Slav subject peoples.

AUSTRO-HUNGARIAN WEAKNESS
The country's ruler, **Emperor Franz Joseph**, had come to the throne in 1849. His regime was splendid in its public ceremonies but shaky in its political foundations. In 1908, Austria-Hungary **annexed Bosnia-Herzegovina ‹‹ 18–19**, a province with a mixed Serb, Croat, and Bosnian Muslim population. This annexation **angered Serbia**, an aggressive Balkan state with ambitions to unite the region's Slav population under its rule. The Austro-Hungarian government felt the **rising power of Serbia** was a threat to its authority over its restive Slav subjects in the Balkans.

EMPEROR FRANZ JOSEPH

Assassination at Sarajevo

On 28 June 1914, the heir to the Austro-Hungarian throne, Archduke Franz Ferdinand, and his wife, Sophie, were shot dead by a Bosnian Serb in Sarajevo. This act triggered a chain of events that would lead to the outbreak of war.

Archduke Franz Ferdinand's visit to Sarajevo, the capital of Bosnia-Herzegovina, was a blunt assertion of imperial authority in a recently annexed province. Even its timing was provocative – 28 June was a day sacred to Serb nationalists as the anniversary of the 1389 Battle of Kosovo, in which a defeat by the Turks had cost Serbia its independence.

Bosnian Serb separatists, who were armed, trained, and organized by shadowy nationalist groups and military intelligence officers in Serbia, had been carrying out attacks against the Austro-Hungarian authorities in Bosnia-Herzegovina. The Austrian government had received specific warning of a planned assassination attempt against the Archduke, but the

> The Habsburgs of Austria-Hungary were one of Europe's oldest royal families. They took their name from a castle in Switzerland.

visit went ahead regardless. To cancel it, or even to mount a heavy-handed security operation, would have been an admission that the Habsburgs did not fully control one of the provinces in their empire. The archduke's planned route and schedule were publicized in advance of the visit.

Imperial visitor
Franz Ferdinand arrived in Sarajevo by train at 9:50am. He was delighted to be accompanied by his wife, who was usually excluded from all public ceremonies under the terms of their marriage. The archduke first inspected troops drawn up on the Filipovic parade ground and then set off for the town hall in a procession of cars.

Assassin apprehended
Gavrilo Princip is arrested after shooting Archduke Franz Ferdinand and his wife on 28 June 1914. Princip declared himself inspired by a mission to free Slavs from Austrian rule "by means of terror".

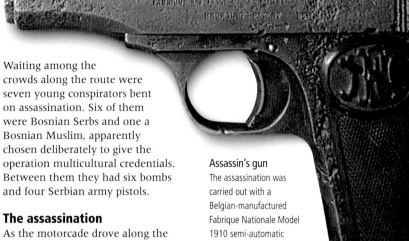

Waiting among the crowds along the route were seven young conspirators bent on assassination. Six of them were Bosnian Serbs and one a Bosnian Muslim, apparently chosen deliberately to give the operation multicultural credentials. Between them they had six bombs and four Serbian army pistols.

Assassin's gun
The assassination was carried out with a Belgian-manufactured Fabrique Nationale Model 1910 semi-automatic pistol, supplied by the Serbian army.

The assassination

As the motorcade drove along the quay by the Miljacka river, one of the conspirators, Nedjelko Cabrinovic, threw a bomb that bounced off the back of the archduke's car and exploded. This injured a number of bystanders, including a police officer. The would-be assassin then swallowed a cyanide pill and jumped into the shallow river, where he was arrested, the cyanide dose proving non-lethal. Angry and shocked by the incident, Franz Ferdinand continued making his way to the town hall. The conspirators dispersed into the crowds, their assassination bid having seemingly ended in failure.

Nineteen-year-old Gavrilo Princip went into a delicatessen to buy a sandwich. Coming out of the shop, he found the archduke's car stopped directly in front of him. Franz Ferdinand had decided to visit the injured police officer in hospital, but his driver had taken a wrong turn and was trying to reverse. Seizing his opportunity, Princip pulled out his pistol and fired twice, hitting the archduke in the neck and his wife in the abdomen. The couple died within minutes, while still in the car. Princip tried to kill himself but was overpowered by onlookers and arrested.

Austria-Hungary reacts

The news of the couple's death was a shock to the Habsburg court. There was no state funeral. Franz Ferdinand and Sophie were interred side by side in a private crypt at Artstetten Castle in the Danube valley. Emperor Franz Joseph was privately relieved that he would never be succeeded by a nephew he neither liked nor trusted. "A higher power," the emperor said, "has restored that order which I could unfortunately not maintain." But the public affront to the Austro-Hungarian state was gross. Although there was no clear evidence that the Serbian government had been directly involved, the operation had definitely been planned and organized in Serbia. This was enough.

A band of assassins, with Serbian backing, had killed the heir to the throne. Austria-Hungary's honour, prestige, and credibility required that Serbia be made to pay.

The road to war

Austro-Hungarian ruling circles were split between hawks and doves. Chief of the General Staff Count Franz Conrad von Hötzendorf had long sought a war with Serbia. He saw the assassinations as an ideal pretext for military action. Other important figures, including Count István Tisza, prime minister of Hungary, were more cautious, preferring a diplomatic solution. In the first week of July,

47 PER CENT of the population of Austria-Hungary were Slavs. They included Poles, Czechs, Croats, Slovaks, Slovenes, and Serbs. Only 24 per cent of the population were ethnic Germans.

Austria-Hungary sought the opinion of its ally Germany. Kaiser Wilhelm II had been outraged by the assassinations. His advisers, including Chancellor Theobald von Bethmann-Hollweg, agreed that Austria-Hungary should be encouraged to take decisive, but unspecified, action against Serbia. Whatever the Austro-Hungarian government chose to do, it could be assured of Germany's support.

This loose guarantee of German backing – often referred to as the "blank cheque" – put the hawks firmly in control in Vienna. Austria-Hungary then drew up a series of demands deliberately designed to prove unacceptable. Their rejection by Serbia would provide a pretext for an attack by the Austro-Hungarian army.

No one was planning for a full-scale war. The idea was for a swift punitive invasion followed by a harsh peace settlement to humiliate and permanently weaken Serbia. However, nothing could happen quickly. Much of the army was on leave, helping to bring in the harvest. After some hesitation, the date for delivery of an ultimatum was set for 23 July.

Private burial
Franz Ferdinand knew his Czech wife would be denied burial in the Habsburg imperial crypt below the Capuchin Church in Vienna. He therefore specified in his will that they be buried at Artstetten Castle, Austria.

Franz Ferdinand was the nephew of Emperor Franz Joseph. He became heir apparent to the Habsburg throne in 1889. His relations with Franz Joseph were soured by his insistence on marrying an impoverished Czech aristocrat, Sophie Chotek, in 1900. He was forced to agree to humiliating terms in order to marry her. She was denied royal status, and any offspring would be barred from inheriting the throne. Franz Ferdinand's political position varied over time, but he was viewed by the Austro-Hungarian establishment as dangerously liberal on the key issue of Slav nationalism.

AFTER »

The interrogation and trial of the conspirators failed to dispel the mystery surrounding the event.

TRIALS AND EXECUTIONS
Twenty-five **Bosnian conspirators** implicated in the archduke's assassination were **tried in Austria-Hungary** in October 1914. Sixteen were found guilty and three hanged. Gavrilo Princip was spared execution because he had been under 20 years old when the crime was committed. He died of tuberculosis in prison in April 1918.

The **planning of the operation** was traced to the head of **Serbian military intelligence**, Colonel Dragutin Dimitrijevic. Using the code name Apis, he also led a Serbian secret society known as the **Black Hand**. In 1917, the Serbian government had Dimitrijevic and three other Black Hand members executed after a rigged trial.

THE OUTBREAK OF WAR
Austria-Hungary **declared war on Serbia** on 28 July 1914 **30–31** ». Within a week, a wider European war had broken out. World War I led directly to the collapse of Austria-Hungary and the fall of the Habsburg dynasty.

The Slide to War

In late July 1914, an Austro-Hungarian confrontation with Serbia plunged Europe into crisis. Such situations had been resolved before by diplomacy, but this time the major powers slid with startling rapidity from peace to a long-anticipated war.

On 23 July, at 6pm, the Austro-Hungarian ambassador delivered an ultimatum to the Serbian government, starting the world on the road to war. The ultimatum demanded that the Serbs suppress anti-Austrian terrorist organizations, stop anti-Austrian propaganda, and allow Austro-Hungarian officials to take part in the investigation of those who were responsible for the Sarajevo assassinations. The Serbians were given 48 hours to accept the demands of the ultimatum or face war. Serbia accepted most of them but, assured of support from Russia, rejected outright the idea of Austrian officials operating on its territory.

A diplomatic solution was still possible. On 26 July, British Foreign Secretary Sir Edward Grey proposed a conference of the major powers. Kaiser Wilhelm, returning from his holiday cruise in the North Sea, enthused over the humiliation of Serbia and suggested that war was no longer necessary.

The Russian reaction

The dominant elements within the Austro-Hungarian military and political establishment did not want a diplomatic triumph. They wanted a military victory to dismember Serbia and bolster Habsburg authority. Thus on 28 July, Austria-Hungary formally declared war on Serbia.

To stand by while Serbia was defeated by Austria-Hungary would have been a severe humiliation for Russia. It would have signalled the end of its long-nourished ambition to expand its influence in the Balkans and towards Constantinople (modern Istanbul). So, on 28 July, Russia declared the mobilization of its armed forces in those regions facing Austria-Hungary, but not along its border with Germany. Suddenly the great European powers faced the prospect of war spreading to engulf them all. The insecurity and crises of the last decade had strengthened rival alliances and hardened mutual suspicions. France and Russia felt that they must stand or fall together. Neither had the military or industrial capability to stand up to Germany alone. By making no effort to restrain their ally, the French in effect abandoned all influence over the evolving situation.

German mobilization

At this point in the crisis, a general war was still far from inevitable. Yet leading figures in the German political and military ruling circle, including the Chief of the General Staff, Helmuth von Moltke, and Prussian War Minister Erich von Falkenhayn, decided the moment for the long-predicted war with France and Russia had come. Moltke had argued on previous occasions that, for Germany, it was better the war should come sooner rather than later. On 29 July, he urged mobilization to support Austria-Hungary. German war plans dictated that this had to be directed against both Russia and France and involve the invasion of neutral Belgium.

Meanwhile, in St Petersburg, debate raged about the practicality of partial mobilization. The Russian foreign minister Sergei Sazonov, fearful of German intentions, forced through a shift to general mobilization on the evening of 30 July. This played into the hands of the German hawks, who could now present themselves as responding to Russian aggression.

BEFORE

The assassination of Archduke Franz Ferdinand and his wife by a Bosnian Serb in Sarajevo on 28 June 1914 ≪ 28–29 was followed by an interlude in which, in public at least, little happened.

PLANNING FOR WAR
Dominant figures in Austria-Hungary, notably Chief of Staff Franz Conrad von Hötzendorf, were determined to use the assassination as a pretext for **war against Serbia**. They had received clearance from Germany to take whatever action they wanted. It took time for Austria-Hungary to organize its blow against Serbia, so through the first three weeks of July the crisis appeared to subside.

BUSINESS AS USUAL
Maintaining a facade of normality, Kaiser Wilhelm left for a summer cruise. Meanwhile, French President Raymond Poincaré made a prearranged visit to Russia to confirm the long-established **Franco-Russian alliance**. The issue of Serbia was mentioned, but without the urgency of a matter that might **threaten war**.

TSARIST STATE EMBLEM

Life as usual
The gravity of the diplomatic crisis in July 1914 was masked by summer holidays. Relaxation in the sun distracted ordinary German citizens and cloaked the machinations of military and political leaders.

> **"The lights are going out all over Europe; we shall not see them lit again in our lifetime."**
>
> ATTRIBUTED TO SIR EDWARD GREY, BRITISH FOREIGN SECRETARY, 3 AUGUST 1914

Naval review
In July 1914, Britain's Royal Navy conducted a test mobilization, followed by a review at Spithead. Submarines were among the ships on show.

Through 1914, there were more declarations of war as the conflict took on a global scale. Other countries asserted neutrality.

THE WIDENING WAR

Britain and France also **brought their empires into the war 118–19 »**. In Britain's case, this included the British dominions of Australia, New Zealand, Canada, and South Africa – although in South Africa entry into the war was contested by anti-British Boers. **Japan**, an ally of Britain since 1902, **declared war on Germany** on 23 August 1914 **84–85 »**. The **Ottoman Empire** entered the war as an **ally of Germany** at the end of October **74–75 »**.

NEUTRALITY

Italy opted to **stay neutral**. It had been a member of the **Triple Alliance** with Germany and Austria-Hungary since 1882 but, with the Italian people in equal measure **hostile to Austria-Hungary** and hostile to going to war, in August 1914 neutrality seemed the best policy. The **USA** also **declared neutrality 130–31 »**.

PUBLIC UNITY

Combatant countries experienced a wave of **social solidarity** and **patriotic fervour** at the outbreak of war **32–33 »**.

FRENCH MEDAL OF HONOUR

Rallying the nation
Germania, the personification of the German nation, stands ready for war in Friedrich August von Kaulbach's 1914 painting of the same name. The German government presented itself as the armed defender of civilization against tsarist Russia in the East.

On 31 July, German Chancellor Bethmann-Hollweg asked Moltke: "Is the fatherland in danger?". Moltke answered in the affirmative. On 1 August, Germany declared war on Russia. The Kaiser made a last-ditch bid for peace by sending a telegram to his cousin, Tsar Nicholas II, but the two heads of state were not in control. When the Kaiser ordered Moltke to limit the war to Russia, he was told that mobilization for a war on two fronts could not be changed. A German declaration of war on France followed on 3 August.

Enter the British

For the Germans, a crucial but unknown factor in the crisis was the reaction of Britain. The British Liberal government was horrified by the prospect of war. An inner circle of ministers had gone much further than was publicly known in committing British military support to France in case of war. As fighting broke out on the continent, they could not carry the rest of the government with them. More clear-cut than Britain's ententes with France and Russia, however, was its commitment to Belgium. Britain was a guarantor of Belgian neutrality under the terms of the 1839 Treaty of London. In order to implement the Schlieffen Plan, the German army had to cross Belgium. On 2 August, Germany demanded right of passage for its troops.

The Belgians opted to fight. When German troops entered Belgium on 3 August, Britain responded with an ultimatum demanding their withdrawal. A British declaration of war on Germany followed on 4 August. Chancellor Bethmann-Hollweg, appalled at this turn of events, told the departing British ambassador, Edward Goschen, that Britain had gone to war "just for a scrap of paper".

Pulling Together

The outbreak of war in August 1914 produced a remarkable show of solidarity in deeply divided societies. As the mobilization of mass citizen armies proceeded smoothly, revolutionary aspirations and anti-war sentiments drowned in a flood of patriotism.

Before 1914, war was a divisive issue in Europe. Nationalists and imperialists praised war as a healthy struggle for survival. Liberals and socialists denounced it as an offence against civilized values or an evil product of capitalism and autocracy. Although newspapers were often aggressively jingoistic, most ordinary people were not, as their voting patterns showed.

A general election in France in spring 1914 brought a landslide victory for radicals and socialists opposed to the country's virulently anti-German president, Raymond Poincaré.

In Germany, the Social Democrats, outspoken critics of Prussian militarism, were the largest party in the Reichstag. European socialists took the slogan "Workers of the world, unite!" seriously. The Second International, to which the socialist

Called to war

German reservists, some in uniform and others still in civilian dress, are mobilized at the start of World War I. Part-time, non-professional troops, reservists were soon to be thrown into battle.

parties of all the major European countries belonged, believed it could make war impossible through coordinated working-class resistance.

On 31 July 1914, France's most prominent antiwar socialist, Jean Jaurès, was killed by a nationalist extremist in a Parisian café. This act of violence might have been expected on a wider scale – a struggle between those in favour of the war and those against it. Instead, the outbreak of war was followed by an extraordinary social and political solidarity.

Growing patriotism

In every country, the vast majority of people were convinced that their nation's cause was just, a necessary act of defence or the fulfilment of an obligation. Accepting the need to defend their country against tsarist Russia, the most reactionary regime in Europe, the German Social Democrats voted in support of the war. Surprised and elated, Kaiser Wilhelm stated that he "no longer saw parties, but only Germans". In Austria-Hungary, to general astonishment, even the empire's Slav minorities showed initial enthusiasm for the war.

In France, squabbling politicians buried their differences in response

‹‹ BEFORE

If the slide to war took Europe by surprise in summer 1914, it was partly because other crises and scandals were holding governments' attention.

INTERNAL UNREST

Russia faced widespread strikes that threatened to develop into revolutionary upheaval. In France, the public was preoccupied with the sensational trial of Henriette Caillaux, wife of a former prime minister. She had shot a French newspaper editor for publishing her love letters. The British were wrestling with a grave crisis over **Irish Home Rule 106–07 ››**, which threatened civil war between Irish Protestants and Catholics, and an arson campaign by **suffragettes** seeking voting rights for women.

SUFFRAGETTE BANNER

Unity in support of the war was never complete and did not last. Social conflicts soon resurfaced and opposition mounted.

DISSENTING VOICES

Socialists who opposed the war from the start included Kier Hardie in Britain, Karl Liebknecht in Germany, and Russian Bolshevik leader **Vladimir Ilyich Lenin**. In 1915, Liebknecht and Rosa Luxemburg formed the revolutionary **Spartacus League** to oppose the war.

HONOURING THE SPARTICUS LEAGUE, BERLIN

to President Poincaré's appeal for a *Union sacrée* (Sacred Union) in defence of the Fatherland. French socialists redirected their hostility against German militarism. In Russia, widely believed to be on the brink of a revolution in the summer of 1914, a vast crowd assembled with banners and icons in St Petersburg to pledge their support to Tsar Nicholas II.

Britain was similarly swept by a wave of patriotism. This was stimulated by fear of an increasingly powerful Germany and widespread sympathy for the plight of Belgium. Suffragettes negotiated a halt to their violent campaign for women's voting rights, with the government freeing suffragette prisoners in return for the movement's support in the war.

Reviewing the Ulstermen

The Ulster Volunteers are reviewed by their founder, Edward Carson. On the outbreak of war, this Protestant militia, set up to fight Irish Home Rule, formed the basis of the British 36th (Ulster) Division.

Rule when it ended. Somewhat reluctantly accepted by the British Army, Redmond's Irish Volunteers formed the basis of the 16th (Irish) Division. Some Volunteers refused to follow Redmond and continued their campaign against British rule.

Conscript armies

Mobilization of Europe's conscript armies – a complex operation on a vast scale – mostly proceeded smoothly. Millions of men and horses were assembled, equipped, and sent by train to the front. Before the war, French military authorities had estimated that up to 13 per cent of those called up might not appear; in fact, only 1.5 per cent failed to present themselves as instructed. There were anti-draft riots in some Russian towns and country districts, but they were the exception. Nonetheless, the popular image of smiling soldiers leaving for the front cheered by crowds is deceptive. There were tears, anxiety, and resigned acceptance, as well as enthusiasm.

> " A **fateful hour** has fallen upon **Germany...** The sword is being forced into our hands. "

KAISER WILHELM II, IN A SPEECH IN BERLIN, 31 JULY 1914

British trade unions also rallied behind the call for war, cancelling a planned series of strikes.

Irish support

Most remarkably, a perilous situation in Ireland was transformed. The war broke out as Britain was about to grant the Irish a measure of self-government, known as Home Rule. This was opposed by the Protestants in Ulster, who had formed an armed militia, the Ulster Volunteer Force (UVF), to resist such moves. Pro-Home Rule Catholics had responded by arming a militia of their own, the Irish Volunteers.

The outbreak of the European war prevented a civil war in Ireland. UVF leaders offered the services of their militia to the British Army, which readily accepted them. Irish nationalist leader John Redmond also supported Britain in the war, calculating this would ensure implementation of Home

715,000 The number of horses mobilized by Germany in 1914.

The large number of those not liable for military service who volunteered to fight in August 1914 is evidence of the war fever gripping European nations. Britain was the only combatant country that did not conscript. Responding to an appeal for volunteers launched by the newly appointed Minister for War, Lord Kitchener, over 750,000 men had enlisted by the end of September. World War I was, at least initially, a people's war.

SUFFRAGETTE (1858–1928)

EMMELINE PANKHURST

Born in Manchester, Emmeline Pankhurst was the founder of the Women's Social and Political Union (WSPU) suffragist movement. From 1903, she adopted militant tactics, including attacks on property and hunger strikes, in pursuit of women's right to vote. On the outbreak of war in 1914, she dedicated her organization to support of the war effort. She called on women to "fight for their country as they fought for the vote". Pankhurst felt her stance was vindicated by the British parliament's partial extension of voting rights to women in 1918.

The **Declaration** of **War**

The outbreak of war in the summer of 1914 was greeted with a range of emotions from the people of Europe. Most imagined it would be a brief conflict, with short, murderous battles and a clear result. Thousands of young men immediately rushed to take part in the glory, while mobilization papers soon took others – fathers, brothers, and sons – away from their worried families.

❝Up and down the wide road… crowds paced incessantly by day and night, singing the German war songs: 'Was blasen die Trompeten?', which is the finest, 'Deutschland, Deutschland über Alles', which comes next, and 'Die Wacht am Rhein', which was most popular. As I walked to and fro among the patriot crowds, I came to know many of the circling and returning faces by sight… Sometimes a company of infantry, sometimes a squadron of horses went down the road westward, wearing the new grey uniforms in place of the familiar Prussian blue… Sometimes the Kaiser in full uniform swept along in his fine motor, cheered he was certainly… [But] the most mighty storm of cheering was reserved for the crown prince, known to be at variance with his father in longing to test his imagined genius in the field.❞

MR H.W. NEVINSON, A CORRESPONDENT FOR THE "LONDON DAILY NEWS", IN BERLIN DURING THE FIRST DAYS OF AUGUST 1914

❝'The tocsin!' cried someone in the field. 'There's a fire in the fields!' Then we saw men running… Soon the field was swept with a wave of agitation. My husband and I stared without understanding before we heard, right in our faces, the news that a neighbour, in his turn, was yelling, 'War! It's war!'

Then, we dropped our tools… and joined the crowd, running as fast as our legs could carry us, to the farmhouse. The men usually so calm… were seized with frenzy. Horses entered at quick trot, whipped by their drivers, while the oxen, goaded until they bled, hurried in reluctantly. In this coming and going of wagons and animals, I could hear disjointed phrases: 'General mobilization…', 'What a misfortune, what an awful misfortune!', 'I'll have to leave right away!', 'It was all bound to come to this.'❞

MÉMÉ SANTERRE, A WEAVER FROM A FRENCH VILLAGE NEAR THE BELGIAN BORDER

War is declared
News of the much-anticipated announcement of war in August 1914 drew huge crowds on to the streets of Berlin. It was greeted with a mixture of solemnity and excitement, for a swift victory was expected.

2
NOT OVER BY CHRISTMAS
DECEMBER 1914

When Europe went to war in summer 1914, most people expected a decisive victory for one side or the other by the year's end. In fact, although battles were fought on a vast scale, costing hundreds of thousands of lives, the outcome of the war remained undecided.

NOT OVER BY CHRISTMAS

Britain's naval supremacy allows it to impose a blockade on Germany from the start of the war. Its warship HMS *Queen Elizabeth*, launched in 1913, was a super-dreadnought, at the time the world's most advanced battleship.

King Albert I of Belgium leads his nation's defiance of German military might. Belgium is overrun by the German army and subjected to brutal reprisals for alleged acts of resistance.

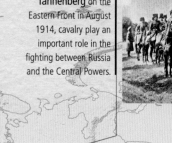

At the **Battle of Tannenberg** on the Eastern Front in August 1914, cavalry play an important role in the fighting between Russia and the Central Powers.

EUROPE

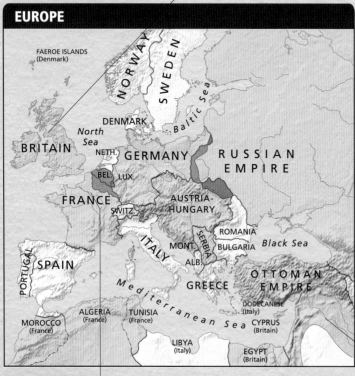

FAEROE ISLANDS
(Denmark)

NORWAY

SWEDEN

Baltic Sea

DENMARK

North Sea

BRITAIN

NETH.

GERMANY

RUSSIAN EMPIRE

BEL. LUX.

FRANCE

SWITZ.

AUSTRIA-HUNGARY

ITALY

SERBIA

MONT.

ROMANIA

BULGARIA

Black Sea

ALB.

SPAIN

GREECE

OTTOMAN EMPIRE

DODECANESE (Italy)

Mediterranean Sea

CYPRUS (Britain)

PORTUGAL

ALGERIA (France)

TUNISIA (France)

MOROCCO (France)

LIBYA (Italy)

EGYPT (Britain)

ICELAND

NORWAY

SWEDEN

BRITAIN

GERMANY

ATLANTIC OCEAN

FRANCE

AUSTRIA-HUNGARY

RUSSIAN EMPIRE

ITALY

Black Sea

Caspian Sea

PORTUGAL

SPAIN

OTTOMAN EMPIRE

SPANISH MOROCCO

TUNISIA

CYPRUS

PERSIA

AFGHANISTAN

MOROCCO

ALGERIA

LIBYA

EGYPT

KUWAIT

BAHRAIN

QATAR

TIBET (autonomous)

NEPAL

RIO DE ORO

NEJD (Saudi)

TRUCIAL OMAN

OMAN

INDIA

HEJAZ

FRENCH WEST AFRICA

ANGLO-EGYPTIAN SUDAN

FRENCH (British mandate)

HADHRAMAUT

ADEN PROTECTORATE

GAMBIA

PORTUGUESE GUINEA

TOGO

EQUATORIAL AFRICA

ERITREA

FRENCH SOMALILAND

SIERRA LEONE

NIGERIA

ABYSSINIA

BRITISH SOMALILAND

CEYLON

LIBERIA

GOLD COAST

CAMEROON

ITALIAN SOMALILAND

INDIAN OCEAN

RIO MUNI (Spain)

FRENCH CONGO

BELGIAN CONGO

BRITISH EAST AFRICA

ANGOLA

GERMAN EAST AFRICA

NORTHERN RHODESIA

SOUTHERN RHODESIA

MADAGASCAR

GERMAN SOUTHWEST AFRICA

BECHUANA-LAND

PORTUGUESE EAST AFRICA

UNION OF SOUTH AFRICA

General Joseph Gallieni is entrusted with the defence of Paris in 1914. He leads the counterattack against the flank of invading German forces in September, using taxis to move troops from Paris to the front.

Ottoman Turkey joins the war on the side of the Central Powers in late October 1914. Russia declares war on Turkey after it bombs Russian Black Sea ports.

The King's African Rifles, a British colonial force, fight the Germans in East Africa. German colonial troops sustain a guerrilla campaign throughout the war, led by Colonel Lettow-Vorbeck.

I n August 1914, Germany implemented the Schlieffen Plan. German leaders intended to defeat France in six weeks before turning to fight the Russians on the Eastern Front. Courageous resistance from the Belgians, although soon swept aside, slowed the advance of the main German armies into northern France. The French suffered tremendous losses attacking Germany's western border but, aided by the British Expeditionary Force (BEF), turned the tide with a counter-offensive at the Battle of the Marne. Germany was denied its swift victory and a series of battles progressing northwards to Ypres and the Yser river left both sides dug into trenches by December 1914. Meanwhile, on the Eastern Front, a Russian invasion of Germany was halted at Tannenberg. In warfare involving large-scale manoeuvres, the Russians generally had the better of Austria-Hungary but lost when fighting German forces.

1914

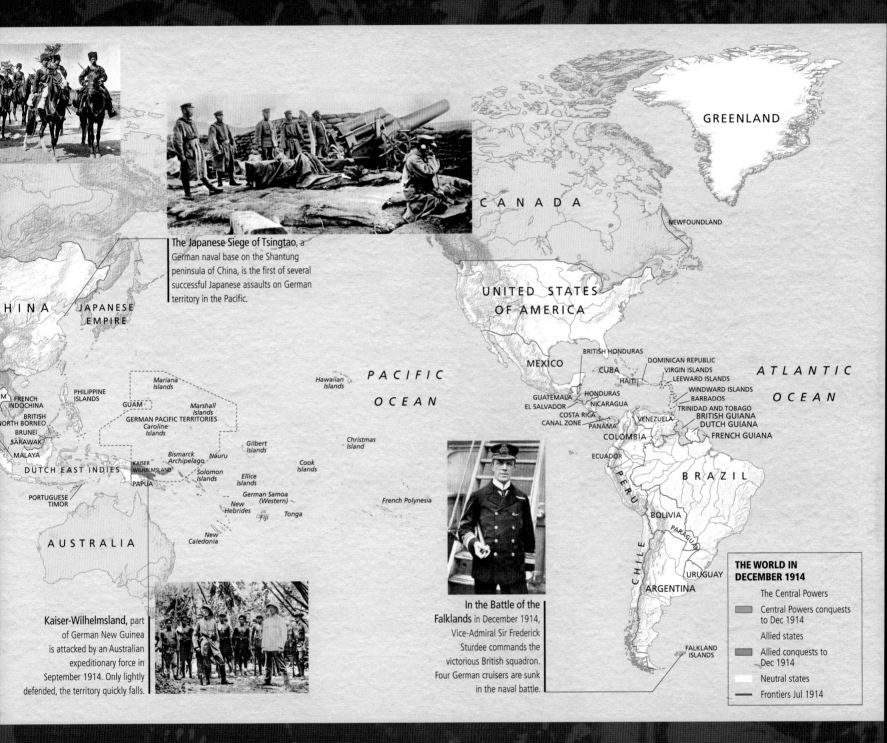

The Japanese Siege of Tsingtao, a German naval base on the Shantung peninsula of China, is the first of several successful Japanese assaults on German territory in the Pacific.

GREENLAND

CANADA

NEWFOUNDLAND

UNITED STATES
OF AMERICA

MEXICO

BRITISH HONDURAS
CUBA
DOMINICAN REPUBLIC
VIRGIN ISLANDS
HAITI
LEEWARD ISLANDS
GUATEMALA
HONDURAS
WINDWARD ISLANDS
EL SALVADOR
NICARAGUA
BARBADOS
COSTA RICA
TRINIDAD AND TOBAGO
CANAL ZONE
PANAMA
VENEZUELA
BRITISH GUIANA
DUTCH GUIANA
COLOMBIA
FRENCH GUIANA

ATLANTIC
OCEAN

ECUADOR

BRAZIL

PERU

PACIFIC
OCEAN

Hawaiian
Islands

Christmas
Island

Mariana
Islands

GUAM

Marshall
Islands

GERMAN PACIFIC TERRITORIES
Caroline
Islands

Gilbert
Islands

Náuru

Cook
Islands

Bismarck
Archipelago

KAISER
WILHELMSLAND

Solomon
Islands

PAPUA

Ellice
Islands

German Samoa
(Western)

French Polynesia

New
Hebrides

Fiji

Tonga

New
Caledonia

AUSTRALIA

CHINA

JAPANESE
EMPIRE

FRENCH
INDOCHINA

PHILIPPINE
ISLANDS

BRITISH
NORTH BORNEO

BRUNEI

SARAWAK

MALAYA

DUTCH EAST INDIES

PORTUGUESE
TIMOR

BOLIVIA

PARAGUAY

CHILE

URUGUAY

ARGENTINA

FALKLAND
ISLANDS

Kaiser-Wilhelmsland, part of German New Guinea is attacked by an Australian expeditionary force in September 1914. Only lightly defended, the territory quickly falls.

In the Battle of the Falklands in December 1914, Vice-Admiral Sir Frederick Sturdee commands the victorious British squadron. Four German cruisers are sunk in the naval battle.

THE WORLD IN DECEMBER 1914

The Central Powers

Central Powers conquests to Dec 1914

Allied states

Allied conquests to Dec 1914

Neutral states

Frontiers Jul 1914

At sea, the superiority of the British Royal Navy mostly kept the German High Seas Fleet pinned in port. German cruisers stationed outside Europe when the war began threatened Allied merchant shipping but were tracked down and destroyed. A German squadron commanded by Vice-Admiral Maximilian von Spee was at large in the Pacific, but after a victory at Coronel, off Chile, was sunk off the Falkland Islands.

Germany's colonies in Africa, China, and the Pacific were mostly taken with ease by the Allies, including Japan, which entered the war at Britain's request. Only in East Africa would prolonged German resistance require a large-scale campaign. The entry of Ottoman Turkey into the war as one of the Central Powers extended the conflict into the Middle East. The Ottoman sultan called for a Muslim holy war against the European empires.

TIMELINE 1914

Declarations of war ▪ **Germany invades Belgium** ▪ Battle of Tannenberg ▪
First Battle of the Marne ▪ Turkey enters the war ▪ **First Battle of Ypres**
▪ Start of trench warfare ▪ **Christmas Truce**

AUGUST

1 AUGUST
Germany declares war on Russia.

3 AUGUST
Germany declares war on France.

≫ French infantry uniform

4 AUGUST
Germany invades Belgium. Britain declares war on Germany.

5 AUGUST
Austria-Hungary declares war on Russia.

6 AUGUST
Belgian city of Liège surrenders to the Germans but its forts continue resistance.

7 AUGUST
First troops of British Expeditionary Force (BEF) land in France.

12 AUGUST
Austro-Hungarian forces invade Serbia.

14 AUGUST
French offensive in Lorraine begins, opening the Battle of the Frontiers.

16 AUGUST
Germans capture Belgium's Liège forts, using siege artillery.

20 AUGUST
Brussels falls to the Germans. Belgian army withdraws to Antwerp. Germans retreat in East Prussia after Battle of Gumbinnen.

21 AUGUST
Serbs drive back Austro-Hungarians at the Jadar river.

≫ German knife

23 AUGUST
British encounter German troops for the first time at Mons, Belgium. More than 600 Belgian civilians are massacred by Germans at Dinant. Japan declares war on Germany.

≪ The Battle of Mons

15 AUGUST
Russian troops advance into East Prussia.

24 AUGUST
French and British forces begin a retreat from Belgium.

25 AUGUST
Belgian city of Louvain is sacked by German troops. Fortress of Namur falls to the Germans.

26 AUGUST
First day of the Battle of Tannenberg between Russian and German forces. British fight rearguard action at Le Cateau in France.

28 AUGUST
Clash of British and German warships at Heligoland Bight results in British victory.

29 AUGUST
Russians suffer defeat at Tannenberg. German advance from Belgium delayed by French counterattack at Guise and St Quentin.

SEPTEMBER

⌃ Indian cavalry in northern France

2 SEPTEMBER
French government evacuated from Paris to Bordeaux.

3 SEPTEMBER
Russians take Lvov (Lemberg) from Austria-Hungary in Galicia.

⌃ British recruitment poster

5 SEPTEMBER
French Sixth Army counterattacks German troops marching east of Paris.

6 SEPTEMBER
French General Joffre launches a counter-offensive, the First Battle of the Marne.

7 SEPTEMBER
French fortress of Maubeuge surrenders after 13-day siege.

11 SEPTEMBER
Australian troops land in German New Guinea.

13 SEPTEMBER
German troops retreating from the Marne dig into trenches at the Aisne.

14 SEPTEMBER
Defeated at the Masurian Lakes, Russians are driven out of East Prussia. Falkenhayn becomes German Chief of Staff.

22 SEPTEMBER
Three British cruisers are sunk by a German submarine in the North Sea.

26 SEPTEMBER
First British Indian troops arrive in France.

≪ French refugees

BRITONS
"WANTS"
YOU
JOIN YOUR COUNTRY'S ARMY!
GOD SAVE THE KING
Reproduced by permission of LONDON OPINION

"In a battle on which the **country's fate depends,** every effort must be made to attack… A **soldier must be killed** where he stands **rather than retreat.**"

FRENCH GENERAL JOSEPH JOFFRE, ORDER NO 6, ISSUED 5 SEPTEMBER 1914

OCTOBER   ## NOVEMBER   ## DECEMBER   »

1 OCTOBER
French offensive at Arras is halted by the Germans during the "Race to the Sea".

8 OCTOBER
Belgian army abandons Antwerp under bombardment from German siege guns.

17 OCTOBER
Arrival of Russian reinforcements obliges the Germans to begin withdrawal from Poland.

19 OCTOBER
First Battle of Ypres begins as Germans fight to reach the Channel ports.

12 OCTOBER
Germans occupy the French city of Lille. British Expeditionary Force is moved to positions in Flanders.

15 OCTOBER
First Canadian troops arrive in Britain. Germans and Russians fight in front of Warsaw.

22 OCTOBER
Germans suffer heavy losses at the Battle of Langemarck, known as the *Kindermord*.

27 OCTOBER
Britain's Royal Navy dreadnought HMS *Audacious* is sunk by a mine.

« German pilot's badge

9 NOVEMBER
Australian cruiser *Sydney* sinks the German commerce raider SMS *Emden* in the Indian Ocean.

11 NOVEMBER
German offensive in Poland launches the month-long Battle of Lodz.

12 NOVEMBER
At the First Battle of Ypres, fierce German attacks are repulsed at Gheluvelt.

16 DECEMBER
German battlecruisers shell Scarborough and other towns on the English east coast.

8 DECEMBER
At the Battle of the Falkland Islands, the British Royal Navy destroys a German squadron commanded by Admiral von Spee.

» Field Marshal Paul von Hindenburg

1 NOVEMBER
Royal Navy squadron is defeated by Admiral von Spee at the Battle of Coronel in the Pacific.

≫ The Battle of the Yser

16 OCTOBER
Belgians resist the Germans at the Battle of the Yser. Japanese attack the German base at Tsingtao in China.

29 OCTOBER
Turkey enters the war on the side of the Central Powers, bombarding Russian Black Sea ports. Renewed German offensive at Ypres drives back Allied forces.

4 NOVEMBER
In German East Africa, a British Indian invasion force is defeated by German colonial troops at Tanga.

7 NOVEMBER
Japanese take the German base of Tsingtao in China.

16 NOVEMBER
Sultan of Turkey calls for a jihad (holy war) against the British Empire.

21 NOVEMBER
British Indian forces take Basra in southern Mesopotamia.

10 DECEMBER
With opposing armies in France and Belgium dug into trench lines, the French launch an offensive in Champagne. It is a costly failure.

17 DECEMBER
The British depose the pro-Turkish Khedive of Egypt. Egypt becomes a British protectorate.

22 DECEMBER
On the Caucasus front, the Russians launch a counter-offensive at Sarikamish that crushes Turkish forces.

8 NOVEMBER
Austria-Hungary relaunches its invasion of Serbia.

29 NOVEMBER
Germans launch a final offensive at the First Battle of Ypres.

30 OCTOBER
Belgians flood land at the Yser Canal, halting the German advance.

« Barbed wire

15 DECEMBER
Austro-Hungarian forces are driven out of Belgrade by the Serbs after occupying the city for a fortnight.

≫ British and German soldiers during the Christmas Truce

25 DECEMBER
Soldiers of the opposing armies fraternize at many points along the Western Front in the "Christmas truce". British naval aircraft raid German airship sheds at Cuxhaven.

BEFORE «

Neutral Belgium was a small country, but densely populated and heavily industrialized. In 1914, it stood in the path of the German attack on France.

GERMAN THREATS

The German **Schlieffen Plan** « 22–23, adopted in 1905, required the bulk of the German army to **advance through Belgium**. On 2 August, the German ambassador delivered a note to the Belgian government, stating that the **German army was going to enter Belgium** to forestall a violation of Belgian neutrality by France. The note gave the Belgians 12 hours to decide on whether to allow this or go to war. The next day, Belgium informed Germany that it **would resist** "by all means at its power".

BELGIUM PREPARES

Belgium's **army was weak**, and military service had only been introduced in 1913. In their favour, the Belgians had built state-of-the-art **fortresses at Liège and Namur**. In addition, Britain was a **guarantor of Belgian neutrality** under the 1839 Treaty of London « 30–31. At the outset of war, the Belgian government told civilians **not to carry out acts** that might give the Germans a pretext for "bloodshed or pillage or massacre of the innocent population".

The **Invasion** of **Belgium**

In August 1914, the Belgians fought the German army to defend their independence. Outraged by Belgium's determined stand, which they had not expected, the Germans carried out massacres and acts of destruction that shocked the world.

German forces invaded Belgium on 4 August. Immediately in their path lay the industrial city of Liège, surrounded by fortresses. Expecting only token resistance, the Germans instructed a force of 39,000 men, under General Otto von Emmich, to seize the city in 48 hours.

Belgium's King Albert I entrusted the defence of Liège to the reliable General Gérard Leman, with firm instructions to hold out to the end. The Belgians blew up the bridges over the River Meuse to slow the German advance. When Emmich's infantry and cavalry reached Liège, their frontal assaults on prepared Belgian defensive positions were repulsed by artillery and machine-gun fire, with heavy losses.

The great German offensive was immobilized until, on 7 August, staff officer Erich Ludendorff and his forces

Belgian refugees
Carrying a few belongings, Belgians fleeing the German invasion cross into the Netherlands in August 1914. About 300,000 Belgians sought refuge in the Netherlands, Britain, or France for the duration of the war.

penetrated the city and received the surrender of its citadel. Most of the other fortresses held out, their concrete and armour plate invulnerable to German artillery. But, on 12 August, Krupp 420 mm and Skoda 305 mm howitzers – monstrous siege guns – reached Liège. Within three days the Germans had bombarded the fortresses into submission, and the way was open for them to flood across Belgium.

German troops were under orders to respond to any Belgian civilian resistance with summary executions and collective reprisals. From the first day of the invasion, soldiers shot Belgian civilians and burned down houses as a punishment for alleged acts of resistance.

Civilians pay the price

Many German officers seem to have regarded the fact that Belgium fought at all as a form of treachery and a cause for outrage. Rumours of attacks on soldiers by Belgian civilians and of the mutilation of corpses were rife in the German ranks and repeated by the German press. In the confusion of war fought amid towns and villages, it was easy for troops to convince themselves that they had been shot at by civilians, when in fact they were victims of friendly fire or Belgian troops firing from houses.

There is no evidence that civilians resisted the Germans at all, but non-resistance did them no good. In many places prominent individuals – typically the parish priest and the mayor – were shot. Occasionally, massacres occurred. In the town of Dinant on 23 August, 674 civilians, including women and children, were executed by German firing squads. At Tamines, the death toll was 384.

German advance

News of German attacks on civilians and the burning of towns and villages was inflated by rumour, such as the false allegation that German soldiers were cutting off the right hands of male children. A flood of Belgian refugees was soon fleeing from the advancing German forces.

Determined to continue the struggle but incapable of facing the Germans in the field, King Albert withdrew the bulk of his army to Antwerp, which had a fortified perimeter. Brussels was abandoned to occupation by the German First Army. Further south, the fortress complex of Namur, in the path of the German Second Army, held out for only three days after the German siege guns arrived on 21 August.

"**Our advance** in Belgium is certainly **brutal,** but we are **fighting for** our **lives...**"

HELMUT VON MOLTKE, GERMAN CHIEF OF STAFF, 5 AUGUST 1914

Effects of German bombardment
Pre-World War I fortresses were armour-plated structures buried deep in the earth, with their guns mounted on rotating turrets. Only the largest German siege guns could bombard them to rubble.

By the third week in August, British and French troops were beginning to engage with the Germans on Belgian soil. As the next phase of the war opened, however, there was a final paroxysm of German rage against the Belgian nation. On 25 August, German troops occupying the historic city of Louvain, 30 km (19 miles) east of Brussels, fired on one another in a confused night-time incident. Convinced they had

> **5,521** The number of Belgian civilians who were massacred by advancing German forces during their invasion of Belgium. According to official figures, at least 14,000 buildings were deliberately destroyed.

been attacked by civilians rather than by friendly fire, German soldiers reacted ruthlessly, looting and burning the town's buildings (including its famous medieval library), executing more than 200 people, and emptying the town of its population.

The destruction of Louvain proved to be a propaganda disaster for Germany, confirming an image of the brutal "Huns" that would sustain its enemies in war for four years.

KING OF BELGIUM (1875–1934)

ALBERT I

Albert I had come to the Belgian throne in 1909 and was a popular king. As a constitutional monarch, he had no control over military matters until the outbreak of war, when the constitution made him commander-in-chief. His resistance to Germany was motivated by a determination to preserve Belgium as an independent nation. He kept his army intact in 1914, first in Antwerp and then through withdrawing westwards along the Flanders coast. He headed a government-in-exile in Le Havre, France. In October 1918, he commanded Allied forces in the Courtrai Offensive, in Belgium, re-entering Brussels in triumph in November 1918.

Pickelhaube

M1898 bayonet

Cartridge pouch

Scabbard

Model 1866 boots

German infantry uniform
The uniform of a German noncommissioned officer at the start of World War I included a Pickelhaube (spiked helmet), made of boiled leather (no army used steel helmets in 1914). The cloth cover prevented the helmet from glistening in the sun.

AFTER

The Germans occupied almost the whole of Belgium. Antwerp fell in early October, but Belgian forces held on to a strip of the Flanders coast in the Battle of the Yser later that month.

PLUNDERED NATION
The Germans placed **Belgium under military government**. In 1916–17, Belgians were deported to work in German factories. **Belgian resistance workers** who spied on German troop movements or aided escaping Allied prisoners of war were **executed**. Many Belgians also suffered from malnutrition, despite food aid from the USA. Flemish separatism was encouraged by the Germans, and the **annexation of Belgium** became a **German war aim 202–03 »**.

The **French Offensive**

France's attacking strategy at the start of the war, flawed in conception and naively executed, led to heavy losses in Alsace, Lorraine, and the Ardennes. Despite the scale of the casualties, this military disaster did not break French resolve.

Celebrating victory
French propaganda shows Alsace-Lorraine as a woman carried off by a Prussian in 1870 but returned to her true French lover in 1914. Optimism about the recovery of the lost provinces proved to be premature.

« BEFORE

In the first week of August 1914, five French armies mobilized on the country's eastern borders, ready to implement General Joffre's Plan XVII.

FAST FORWARDS
French mobilization was efficiently conducted. The French First and Second armies faced **Alsace and Lorraine**, the provinces lost by France to Germany in 1871. The other three armies took up positions from **Verdun** northwards. The **British Expeditionary Force (BEF)** was stationed to their left at **Maubeuge**.

FRENCH CONFIDENCE
The French anticipated a **German move through southern Belgium**, but not the large-scale sweeping movement planned by Alfred von Schlieffen **« 22**. By 14 August, **German troops were pouring into Belgium « 42–43**, but General Joffre remained confident of success, dismissing fears expressed by **General Charles Lanrezac**, who was commanding troops on the left of the French line.

VON SCHLIEFFEN

On 8 August, French commander-in-chief General Joseph Joffre issued General Instruction No. 1, ordering a general offensive to open on 14 August. Two armies were to advance into Lorraine and three into the Ardennes forest and southern Belgium. By the time the order was issued, one French force had already crossed the German border. An army corps and a cavalry division under General Louis Bonneau was sent into Alsace on 7 August to take the city

> **84** **PER CENT** of eligible French men were called up for military service. From 1913, the service period was three years.

of Mulhouse. The Alsatians, supposedly groaning under German rule since 1871, were expected to rise up against their oppressors. Overcoming light German resistance, Bonneau entered Mulhouse, triggering a fanfare from French propagandists euphorically celebrating the liberation of Alsace.

The Germans quickly counterattacked and Bonneau embarrassingly scampered back across the French border, where he became the first of many French generals in the war to be sacked by Joffre. A hastily organized Army of Alsace retook Mulhouse, but the French effort in Alsace was overtaken by events further north and soon abandoned.

Attempt on Lorraine
The main French offensive opened in Lorraine on 14 August. The French First and Second armies crossed the border, advancing with banners and bands playing. The German Sixth and Seventh armies withdrew, fighting stiff delaying actions in which their machine-guns took a heavy toll of the brightly clad French

Royal commander
Crown Prince Rupprecht of Bavaria, depicted on this medal, commanded German forces in Lorraine in August 1914. Bavaria was part of the German Empire but had its own monarchy.

infantry. The Schlieffen Plan dictated that the Germans should hold prepared defensive positions at Morhange and Sarrebourg, but Crown Prince Rupprecht of Bavaria, commanding in Lorraine, obtained permission from German General Staff to launch a counteroffensive.

Forced back
On 20 August, German infantry moved forward after a concentrated artillery bombardment. Stunned by the power of the German heavy guns, the French Second Army reeled back from Morhange, forcing the First Army to fall back as well. By 23 August, the French troops, much depleted in numbers, had been thrown back to their starting points on the Meurthe river.

By then, the French Third and Fourth armies were engaged further north, with similarly disastrous results. They marched into the heavily wooded Ardennes expecting to achieve surprise and find it lightly held. For the Germans, this sector formed the innermost part of their great wheeling movement through Belgium. Their Fourth and Fifth armies, respectively commanded by Albrecht, Duke of Württemberg, and German Crown Prince Wilhelm, were advancing in the opposite direction to the French. German reconnaissance aircraft reported the presence of French troops, alerting the Germans to the imminence of battle. Depending on cavalry for reconnaissance, the French plunged forward, believing that, as Joffre's headquarters informed them, "no serious opposition need be anticipated". On 22 August, the opposing armies collided in morning fog. Both sides suffered heavy casualties. The rapid fire of the French 75 mm

Uncovered kepi

Tunic

Bayonet

Hobnailed boots

Regimental markings

Cartridge pouch

Haversack

Scabbard

Trousers

> "In an instant it had become clear that **all** the **courage** in the world **could not withstand** this **fire.**"

CHARLES DE GAULLE, A PLATOON COMMANDER IN THE FRENCH FIFTH ARMY, AUGUST 1914

field guns slaughtered German troops caught on open ground, but the French came off worst. They were too often thrown forward in futile bayonet charges and reluctant to dig trenches, the only effective protection against artillery and machine-gun fire.

140,000 The estimated number of French casualties in the Battle of the Frontiers, 14–24 August, out of some 1.25 million troops deployed.

The French Third Colonial Division lost 11,000 of its 15,000 men in a day. Despite receiving orders from Joffre to resume their advance in the Ardennes, the French armies fell back in disarray behind the Meuse river.

End of the offensive

By 24 August, the French offensive laid down in Plan XVII had clearly failed. On the attack, French forces had proved naive, launching infantry assaults without artillery support and without adequate reconnaissance. Lack of heavy guns and entrenching equipment had proved fatal defects.

At the same time that French offensives failed in Lorraine and the Ardennes, French and British forces encountered the main German armies advancing through Belgium.

SAMBRE AND MONS

The **French Fifth Army**, under General Charles Lanrezac, fought the **German Second Army** at the Battle of the Sambre. On Lanrezac's left, the British Expeditionary Force confronted the German First Army at **Mons 46–47 »**. **Overwhelmed by the German forces**, the French and British began a **retreat** from Belgium that took them south of Paris **52–53 »**.

FRENCH RECOVERY

Departing from the **Schlieffen Plan**, Chief of the General Staff Helmuth von Moltke provided **reinforcements** to continue the German offensive in Lorraine. In **desperate fighting** in early September, France's eastern line held in front of Nancy and Verdun. Meanwhile, Joffre set about **rearranging his armies**. On 5 September, he launched a **major counteroffensive** at the **Battle of the Marne 54–55 »**.

Forced on the defensive, however, the French troops fought like tigers. The Germans, in their turn, discovered how difficult it was to assault determinedly held defensive positions. By 26 August, the French had halted their enemy in front of the town of Nancy.

African soldiers

Arab and Berber troops of the French Army of Africa were brought to France from Algeria, Morocco, and Tunisia on the outbreak of war. These colonial soldiers soon moved into frontline positions.

French infantry uniform

The French army entered the war with uniforms that made little concession to the need for camouflage. Dark blue overcoats and bright red trousers offered a clear target for enemy fire, although the red kepi was hidden by a cloth cover.

BEFORE

Britain declared war on Germany on 4 August 1914. By the time the British Expeditionary Force (BEF) had deployed to France, the fighting was already well under way.

BRITAIN JOINS FRANCE

First organized in 1907, the BEF consisted of **six infantry divisions** and a **cavalry division**. Under plans discussed with the French army from 1911, the BEF was to take up position on the left of the French line. Home defence was to be entrusted to the Territorial Army and reserves. At the outbreak of war,

BRITISH FORCES ARRIVE AT BOULOGNE

however, the nervous British government insisted on two infantry divisions remaining at home. **Mobilization was punctual and efficient**, with large numbers of horses also sent to the front. The BEF was in position around Maubeuge in France by 20 August. By then, the **Lorraine offensive was in trouble ≪ 44–45**, and **Belgium** was being **put to the sword ≪ 42–43**.

BRITISH GENERAL (1852–1925)

JOHN FRENCH

The first commander of the British Expeditionary Force, Field Marshal Sir John French made his reputation as a dashing cavalry officer fighting the Boers in South Africa.

Appointed Chief of the Imperial General Staff in 1912, he resigned in April 1914 over government policy on Ireland. His seniority made him a natural choice to lead the BEF, but he soon proved to be out of his depth. He was reluctant to liaise with the French and, after initial setbacks in August, was persuaded only with great difficulty to return to the fight at the Battle of the Marne. Considered ill-equipped to cope with the challenges of trench warfare, he was replaced by Sir Douglas Haig in December 1915.

The British Go into Action

The regular professional soldiers of the British Expeditionary Force arrived in France in August 1914 to find themselves directly in the path of the main German offensive through Belgium. They received their first taste of war at the Battle of Mons.

Placed in command of the British Expeditionary Force (BEF), Field Marshal Sir John French was given written instructions by the newly appointed Secretary of State for War, Lord Kitchener. These told him to "support and cooperate with the French army", while at the same time stressing that he would "in no case come under the orders of any Allied general". The field marshal was also instructed to take the greatest care to minimize "losses and wastage".

How the BEF was to remain independent and intact while wholeheartedly supporting the French was not explained. Kitchener also sent a personal message to the troops in which they were advised, among other things, to behave courteously in foreign lands and resist "temptations both in wine and women".

The BEF's position on the Belgian frontier at the extreme left of the French line was considered a quiet sector. By 16 August, when Field Marshall French went for his first meeting with General Charles Lanrezac, commander of the French Fifth Army, it was becoming apparent this would not be the case.

Mutual incomprehension

Ordered by a complacent General Joffre to advance into southern Belgium, Lanrezac was convinced he was about to be overwhelmed by German forces. He did not trust the British to protect his left flank, especially as they had arrived with only four divisions instead of the promised six. The meeting between French and Lanrezac ended in mutual incomprehension.

The British advanced into Belgium, reaching the Condé-Mons canal on 22 August, a day ahead of General Alexander von Kluck's German First Army, which was advancing from the east. Under orders to maintain the pace of the advance through Belgium, Kluck mounted a frontal assault on the British, who were in defensive positions along the far bank of the canal. The Battle of Mons, as it became known, was a fierce skirmish.

Gunned down

The British were short of machine-guns but the rapid rifle fire of the regular soldiers mowed down the massed columns of German infantry. British field artillery was pushed dangerously forward, because the gunners were unpractised in firing beyond line of sight, but its shrapnel was brutally effective against soldiers advancing in the open. By the end of the day, the BEF had suffered 1,600 casualties, and the Germans 5,000. Outnumbered two to one in soldiers and guns, the British had been forced to pull back, but they were ready to resume the next day.

> **100,000** The number of British soldiers deployed by the BEF in August 1914. By the end of the year, 90 per cent were killed, wounded, or missing.

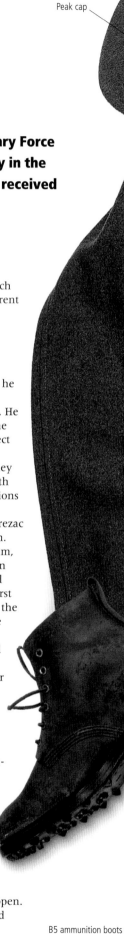

Peak cap

B5 ammunition boots

Knapsack

Tunic

Cartridge pouch

British uniform
The British army adopted khaki as its campaign uniform in 1897, replacing the traditional red coats. This camouflage increased soldiers' chances of survival, but the cloth and leather headgear gave no protection against shrapnel.

Pattern 1907 bayonet

Scabbard

The Battle of Mons was a minor engagement, but because it was the first entry of British troops in the war it was portrayed as an epic battle to the British public.

THE MONS MYTH
Mons was soon being compared to historic examples of British forces defying much larger enemy armies, such as the **Battle of Agincourt**. A popular myth developed in 1915 that **angels** had intervened to protect British soldiers. The "angel of Mons" became a standard theme of British **propaganda**.

THE GREAT RETREAT
Mons was the starting point for the **Great Retreat 52–53 》**, in which **French and British troops** marched **from Belgium to south of the Marne river**, with German armies advancing behind them. Joffre struggled to **reorganize French forces**. With some difficulty he revived cooperation with the British, convincing their commander to **resume the fight**.

MUSIC SCORE MARKING BRITISH SUCCESS AT MONS

To the right of the British position, however, Lanrezac's army was in serious trouble. The French faced a large-scale attack by General Karl von Bülow's German Second Army, which had established bridgeheads across the Sambre and Meuse rivers.

Retreat and pursuit
Lanrezac needed to extricate his army from potential encirclement and destruction. On the night of 23 August, he sent Joffre the unwelcome news that he was going to withdraw the following day. The BEF had no choice but to follow Lanrezac's example. Beginning on 24 August, there was

38 The number of British field guns that were lost to the Germans at the Battle of Le Cateau during the British retreat.

a series of hard-fought actions as the British sought to disengage from an enemy in close pursuit. Getting the field guns away before they were seized was often a hazardous operation, as batteries kept firing until the very last moment, covering the infantry as it fell back from the German advance.

The largest engagement was at Le Cateau, northern France, where the Germans caught up with the BEF's II Corps, commanded by General Sir Horace Smith-Dorrien, on the night of 25 August. Disobeying an order

from French to continue the withdrawal, which he considered impossible, Smith-Dorrien turned to fight. On the morning of 26 August, the British delivered a sufficient check to the Germans to allow an orderly withdrawal later in the day, but this was achieved at the cost of some 8,000 men, including a battalion of Gordon Highlanders who, failing to receive the order to retreat, fought on until all were dead or captured.

The war had hardly begun and the BEF had already lost about 10 per cent of its original strength.

Retreating troops
A British officer with a head wound is aided to walk in the retreat from Mons. Combat against the odds, followed by a long retreat, placed immense strain upon British morale and physical endurance.

"You'd have to load your rifle and fire, tip the case out, fire, fire, fire, fire."

CORPORAL BILL HOLBROOK, ROYAL FUSILIERS, AT THE BATTLE OF MONS

Retreat from Mons
Richard Caton Woodville's painting *Charge of the Ninth Lancers* shows British troops fighting to save a battery of field guns on 24 August 1914, the first day of the retreat from Mons. Captain Francis Grenfell of the Ninth Lancers won a Victoria Cross for his part in the incident.

Artillery

At the start of the war, field artillery was relatively mobile and often loaded with shrapnel to scythe down advancing infantry. Trench systems demanded heavier guns that could saturate enemy defences with shellfire.

[1] **18-Pounder field gun (British)** The standard British field gun lacked the power or angle of fire to be effective against trenches. [2] **149 mm Obice Krupp M14 Howitzer (Italian)** This German design was built in Italy under licence. Howitzers were used to fire heavy shells on a high trajectory, enabling them to reach concealed targets. [3] **2.75 in mountain gun (British)** This weapon saw service in Mesopotamia (Iraq) and on the Macedonian front. [4] **75 mm field gun (French)** The hydraulic recoil mechanism of this gun enabled accurate and rapid fire, without the need to reposition the gun after each shot. [5] **Gas shell (German)** The first use of artillery fired chemical shells was at Neuve-Chapelle in October 1914. [6] **77 mm shrapnel shell (German)** Packed with a large number of bullets, shrapnel shells were effective against massed troops in open terrain. [7] **Munitions carriage with 38 cm shell (German)** Some shells were so large that they had to be transported by carriage. [8] **75 mm shells (French)** Shells for the 75 mm field gun contained either shrapnel or high-explosives. [9] **Schneider mortar (French)** Designed to fire at a steep angle, mortars were useful in trench warfare. [10] **Fahrpanzer (German)** This gun was mounted on narrow gauge railway tracks and operated by a two-man crew. [11] **149 mm Howitzer M14/16 (Austro-Hungarian)** This howitzer was built by Skoda, the largest industrial enterprise in the Austro-Hungarian Empire. [12] **21 cm Mörser 16 (German)** This howitzer, here packed for transportation, was used by the German army until 1940.

[1] 18-POUNDER FIELD GUN (BRITISH)

[4] 75 MM FIELD GUN (FRENCH)

[5] GAS SHELL (GERMAN)

[6] 77 MM SHRAPNEL SHELL (GERMAN)

[7] MUNITIONS CARRIAGE WITH 38 CM SHELL (GERMAN)

[11] 149 MM HOWITZER M14/16 (AUSTRO–HUNGARIAN)

2 149 MM OBICE KRUPP
M14 HOWITZER (ITALIAN)

3 2.75 IN MOUNTAIN GUN (BRITISH)

9 SCHNEIDER MORTAR (FRENCH)

8 75 MM SHELLS (FRENCH)

10 FAHRPANZER (GERMAN)

12 21 CM MÖRSER 16 (GERMAN)

The Great Retreat

In the last days of August 1914, French and British troops were retreating as fast as they could march, pursued by German armies. The Germans were occupying French territory and threatening Paris. Faced with this debacle, General Joffre calmly set about organizing a counter-offensive.

« BEFORE

In August 1914, the German Schlieffen Plan, intended to defeat France in six weeks, appeared to be working. But in reality, the German offensive was going awry.

FATALLY WEAKENED
The basis of the **Schlieffen Plan « 22–23** was the concentration of German forces on their right wing to sweep through Belgium and northern France. These forces became **fatally weakened**. Troops had to be detached to besiege the Belgians at **Antwerp** and the French fortress at **Maubeuge**. The **German offensive from Lorraine « 44–45** was reinforced at the expense of the armies on the right. On 26 August, two German corps were sent to the Eastern Front to face the **Russian threat to East Prussia 64–65 »**.

ALLIED RESPONSE
In spite of their **massive losses**, the French maintained their coherence and fighting spirit. The **British confirmed their commitment to the war** by sending another infantry division to France on 19 August.

On 25 August, Joffre issued his General Instruction No. 2. This envisaged a withdrawal of the French and British armies to a defensible line – initially set at the Somme, but later revised to the Marne – where the German advance would be halted. A new French Sixth Army would be created and moved by rail north of Paris to help repel the German armies flooding into France from Belgium. This strategic vision seemed

220 The number of kilometres (137 miles) marched by the British Expeditionary Force from Mons during the Great Retreat.

mere fantasy when set against the reality faced by French and British troops on the ground.

The battered British Expeditionary Force (BEF) and French Fifth Army were marching up to 20 km (12 miles) a day in burning summer heat with the German First and Second armies at their heels. Occasionally, British and French troops fought rearguard actions, including a successful French counterattack at St Quentin. Mostly they marched, often short of food and drink, their feet blistered, and snatching sleep by the roadside.

General Gallieni
French General Joseph Gallieni was recalled from retirement to take command of the defence of Paris in August 1914. In September, he turned the capital into the base for a counterattack against the German flank.

In Paris, there was panic as the Germans approached. The French government fled to Bordeaux while General Gallieni defended the capital. Meanwhile, the BEF commander, Field Marshal Sir John French, had lost all confidence in his allies. Determined to save his army from destruction, he

planned to withdraw his army. The British war minister, Lord Kitchener, made a lightning visit to Paris and told him to stay in line.

The line holds
By early September, Joffre's plans were taking shape. The French continued to hold against German attacks in front of Nancy and Verdun. The French Third and Fourth armies lost more ground, including the city of Reims on 5 September, but a defensive line was emerging, with a new Ninth Army under the command of General Ferdinand Foch inserted between the Fourth and Fifth armies.

Meanwhile, the strains imposed on Allied troops by the Great Retreat were mirrored on the German side. Soldiers on the German right wing had been marching for a month since crossing the Belgian border. Dependent on horse-drawn transport, their supplies failed to keep up, leaving troops hungry and thirsty. The German First and Second armies, advancing in

Invasion of France

The course of the German invasion departed from the Schlieffen Plan, turning east of Paris instead of west. Joffre refused to allow his armies to be enveloped and prepared a counter-offensive for 5 September.

KEY

- ➤ German advance (2 Aug–5 Sept)
- ■ German army
- ■ Belgian army
- ■ British army
- ■ French army
- ⌣ German position 5 Sept
- ⌣ Belgian position 5 Sept
- ⌣ British position 5 Sept
- ⌣ French position 5 Sept
- ⊙ German GHQ
- ⊙ French GHQ
- ⊠ German fortified towns
- ⊠ Belgian fortified towns
- ⊠ French fortified towns
- ✺ Major battle or siege

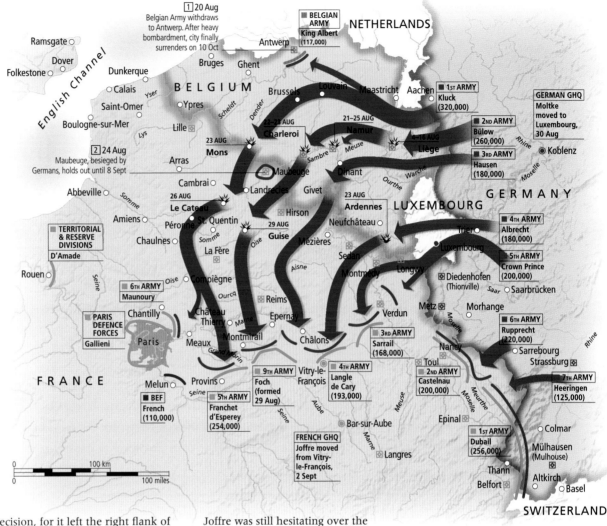

parallel, had difficulty keeping in touch with one another and with Moltke's staff headquarters in Luxembourg. Although Moltke had planned for the

170

The distance in kilometres (106 miles) between the German Second Army's front and its supporting railways on 4 September – too far for the supply system to work properly.

First Army to march west of Paris, its commander, General von Kluck, chose to turn east of the capital, heading for the Marne river. This was a disastrous

Refugees on the road

As the German armies advanced, thousands of Belgian and French citizens fled their homes. In northern France, the Germans burned down villages and killed civilians as they had in Belgium.

decision, for it left the right flank of Kluck's army exposed to potential attack by both the Paris garrison and Joffre's newly formed Sixth Army.

Time to attack

In the first days of September, the Great Retreat was still under way. The BEF and French Fifth Army withdrew across the Marne river on 2 September with Kluck a day behind them, his rapid advance opening up a gap between his army and General von Bülow's Second Army.

Joffre was still hesitating over the optimum moment to launch his counter-blow, but Gallieni, with not only the Paris troops but also the Sixth Army under his overall command, forced Joffre's hand. Informed from various sources, including aerial reconnaissance, of Kluck's exposed flank, on 4 September Gallieni sent out orders to prepare to attack. Accepting Gallieni's initiative, on the following day Joffre informed his armies "the time for retreat has ended".

AFTER »

As the Great Retreat came to a halt, Joffre launched the Battle of the Marne. This counter-offensive was a turning point of the war.

THE BATTLE OF THE MARNE
Pressure for a **swift counterattack** came from General Gallieni in Paris and General Louis Franchet d'Espèrey, the new commander of the French Fifth Army. They obtained Joffre's agreement for the offensive on the **Marne 54–55 »** to start on 6 September. Field Marshal Sir John French agreed to stop retreating only after Joffre appealed to "the honour of England" on 5 September.

FIGHTING WITHDRAWAL
On the German side, Kluck's First Army advanced across the Marne on 5 September, despite orders from Moltke to go on the defensive. Kluck did not pull back until the following day. The **Germans** managed the transition from **headlong attack** to a **fighting withdrawal** skilfully. They eventually stabilized a defensive position at the **Aisne river 58–59 »**.

GERMAN GENERAL (1848–1916)

HELMUTH VON MOLTKE

Helmuth von Moltke was known as "the Younger" to distinguish him from his uncle, whose victories had created the German Empire. A neurotic personality, the younger Moltke preferred playing the cello to riding a horse, but also liked to strike poses of brutal ruthlessness. Appointed Chief of the General Staff in 1906, he argued the case for preventive war against Russia and France. In the crisis of July 1914, he was pessimistic about Germany's chances but insistent that war must be launched. In the early weeks of the war, he took poor decisions that undermined the Schlieffen Plan and failed to control his generals. In poor health, he was relieved of command on 14 September.

German offensive
Initially overcoming the French Sixth Army, a German machine-gun detachment advances at full gallop into the battle zone, September 1914.

The Battle of the Marne

The French and British counter-offensive launched on 5–6 September 1914 was one of the decisive battles in world history. By forcing the German armies in France on to the defensive, it ended Germany's hopes of a quick victory and set the course for a drawn-out global conflict.

◀◀ BEFORE

Up to the first week in September, when the Battle of the Marne began, the war had brought a remarkable series of German victories on both the Eastern and Western fronts.

RAPID GERMAN ADVANCE
French offensives were **thrown back in Lorraine and the Ardennes ‹‹ 44–45**. Driven out of Belgium, the French Fifth Army and the BEF were **pursued by German armies**

400 The number of kilometres (250 miles) German's First Army had advanced before the order was given to retreat.

and forced to **retreat** beyond the **Marne river ‹‹ 52–53**. This rapid **German advance**, however, left the flank of the German First Army exposed to a **counterattack** by General Joseph Gallieni's forces around Paris.

Transport to the front
Parisian buses and taxis were requisitioned by the French army to rush reinforcements to the front on 7 September. The "taxis of the Marne" became a French national legend, although their contribution to victory was limited.

The Battle of the Marne opened prematurely. General Joseph Joffre ordered the Allied counter-offensive to begin on 6 September. In preparation, on 5 September the eager General Gallieni, commanding in Paris, moved General Michel-Joseph Maunoury's Sixth Army forward towards the exposed flank of the German First Army.

Strengths and weaknesses
The Germans' main strength had advanced to the south, leaving only a reserve corps under General Hans von Gronau defending the flank. Spotting the French advance, Gronau boldly opted to attack, exploiting the advantage of high ground. Soon an already familiar spectacle was being repeated: French troops in their bright uniforms, poorly supported by artillery, cut down in swathes by superior German firepower. The German First Army commander, General Alexander von Kluck, responded to the outbreak of fighting by skilfully shifting troops back to confront the threat.

The French Sixth Army was a hastily assembled formation, chiefly comprising reserves and Moroccan troops. Facing the increasing weight of

Kluck's forces, it was soon in severe difficulties. Despite Gallieni's commandeering of Parisian taxis and buses to rush troops to the front – the French army had almost no motor transport – by 8 September, Kluck was threatening Paris.

Nonetheless, the strategic situation was shifting in favour of the Allies. While the French Ninth Army under Ferdinand Foch fought a desperate holding action in the Gond marshes, General Louis Franchet d'Espèrey led his Fifth Army forward against General Karl von Bülow's German Second Army. The Allies were short of supplies and exhausted by weeks of marching, but after tough fighting it was the Germans who fell back.

Lost opportunity
Meanwhile, Franchet d'Espèrey fumed at the tardiness of the British on his left. Field Marshal Sir John French, who had been persuaded with some difficulty to promise Joffre his cooperation, was asked to advance into a gap that had opened between the German First and Second armies. He did so, but with excessive caution and a distinct lack of urgency. To the French commanders, it seemed that a chance to impose a decisive defeat on the Germans was being lost.

The German Chief of the General Staff Helmuth von Moltke, at his headquarters in Luxembourg, was a worried man. Unclear about the state of the fighting, he sent a staff intelligence officer, Lieutenant Colonel Richard Hentsch, to visit each of the army headquarters in turn.

The counter-offensive, 5–6 September

Rapid advance of German 1st and 2nd armies had left them exposed to counterattack. The French 6th Army struck from the flank while the BEF and other French armies attacked from the south.

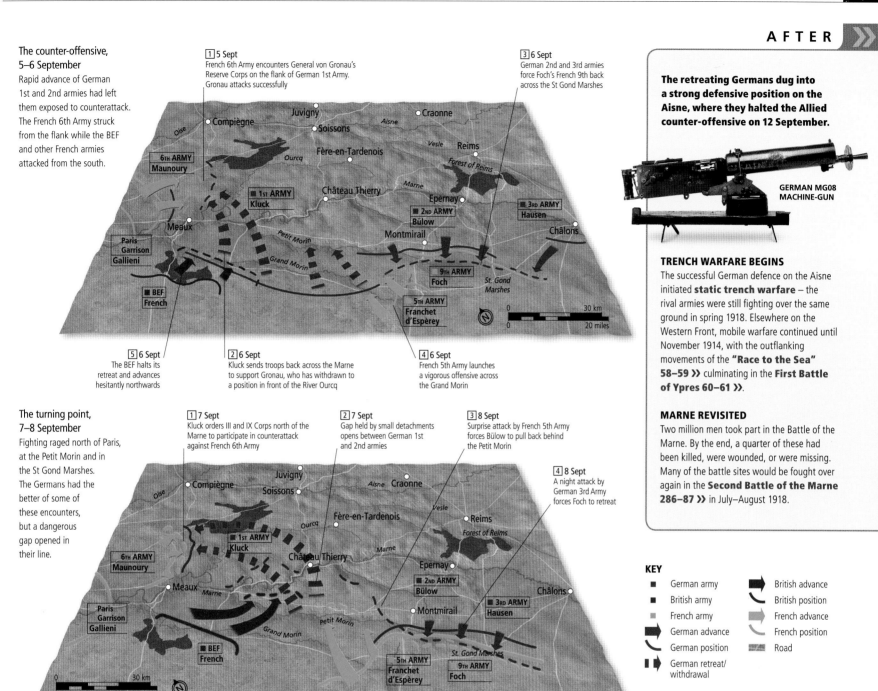

1 5 Sept
French 6th Army encounters General von Gronau's Reserve Corps on the flank of German 1st Army. Gronau attacks successfully

3 6 Sept
German 2nd and 3rd armies force Foch's French 9th back across the St Gond Marshes

5 6 Sept
The BEF halts its retreat and advances hesitantly northwards

2 6 Sept
Kluck sends troops back across the Marne to support Gronau, who has withdrawn to a position in front of the River Ourcq

4 6 Sept
French 5th Army launches a vigorous offensive across the Grand Morin

The turning point, 7–8 September

Fighting raged north of Paris, at the Petit Morin and in the St Gond Marshes. The Germans had the better of some of these encounters, but a dangerous gap opened in their line.

1 7 Sept
Kluck orders III and IX Corps north of the Marne to participate in counterattack against French 6th Army

2 7 Sept
Gap held by small detachments opens between German 1st and 2nd armies

3 8 Sept
Surprise attack by French 5th Army forces Bülow to pull back behind the Petit Morin

4 8 Sept
A night attack by German 3rd Army forces Foch to retreat

After discussing the situation with Bülow, Hensch judged a German withdrawal was urgently needed. On 9 September, Bülow began to disengage his forces, while Hensch passed on the news to Kluck. Although the German First Army was winning its part of the battle, Kluck had no choice but to pull back his troops along with Bülow.

Last act

Belatedly intervening in a situation that had slipped beyond his control, Moltke set the Aisne river as the line to which the armies would withdraw. It was his last act as Chief of Staff. Having failed to implement the Schlieffen Plan, he was dismissed. Joffre, the architect of the "miracle of the Marne", was hailed as the saviour of France.

The German retreat, 9–12 September

British and French troops advanced into the gap between the German 1st and 2nd armies. With the situation perilous, the Germans mounted a general withdrawal to the River Aisne.

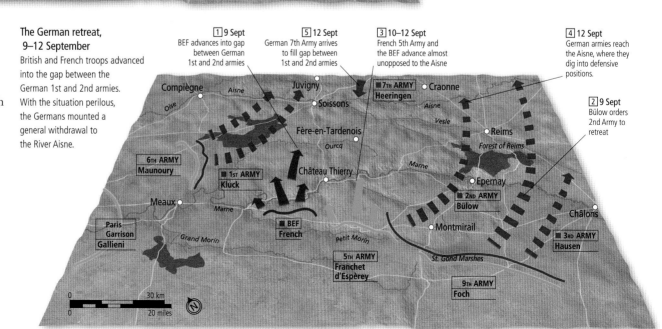

1 9 Sept
BEF advances into gap between German 1st and 2nd armies

5 12 Sept
German 7th Army arrives to fill gap between 1st and 2nd armies

3 10–12 Sept
French 5th Army and the BEF advance almost unopposed to the Aisne

4 12 Sept
German armies reach the Aisne, where they dig into defensive positions.

2 9 Sept
Bülow orders 2nd Army to retreat

AFTER

The retreating Germans dug into a strong defensive position on the Aisne, where they halted the Allied counter-offensive on 12 September.

GERMAN MG08 MACHINE-GUN

TRENCH WARFARE BEGINS

The successful German defence on the Aisne initiated **static trench warfare** – the rival armies were still fighting over the same ground in spring 1918. Elsewhere on the Western Front, mobile warfare continued until November 1914, with the outflanking movements of the **"Race to the Sea" 58–59 ≫** culminating in the **First Battle of Ypres 60–61 ≫**.

MARNE REVISITED

Two million men took part in the Battle of the Marne. By the end, a quarter of these had been killed, were wounded, or were missing. Many of the battle sites would be fought over again in the **Second Battle of the Marne 286–87 ≫** in July–August 1918.

KEY

- ■ German army
- ■ British army
- ■ French army
- ➤ German advance
- ▶ German retreat/withdrawal
- ◥ British advance
- ⌐ British position
- ◤ French advance
- ⌐ French position
- ▦ Road

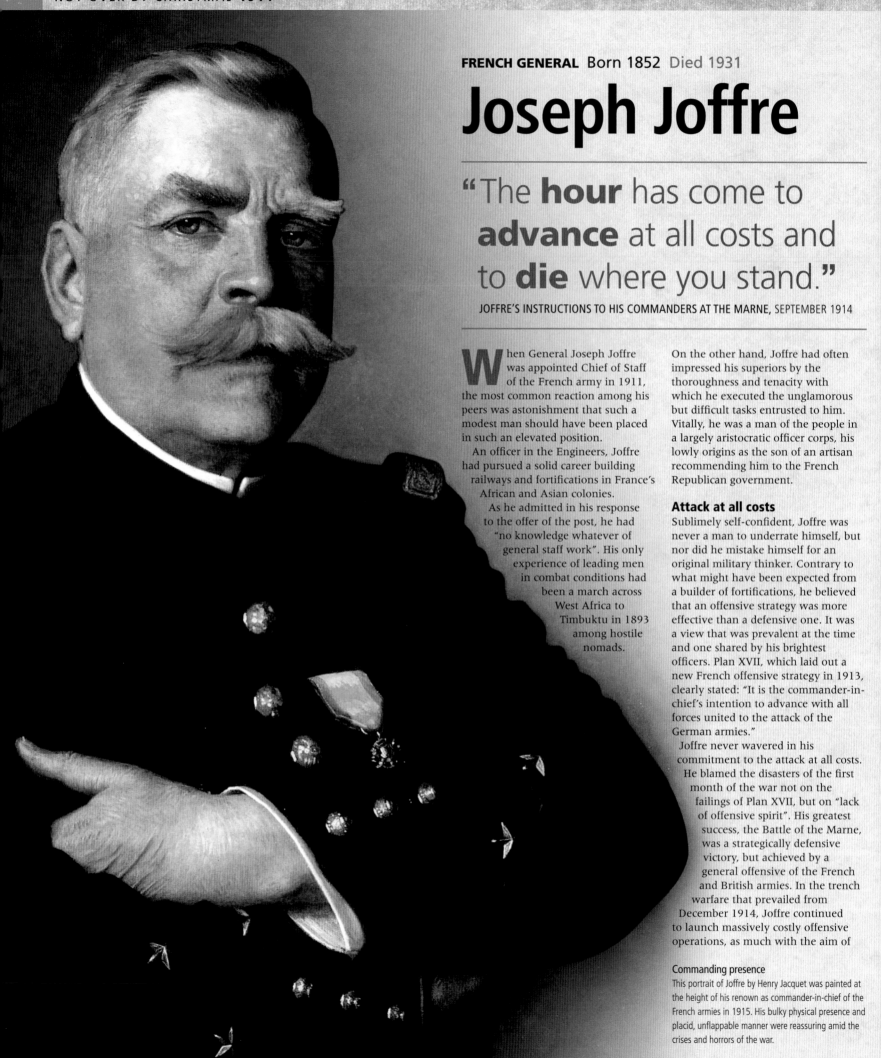

FRENCH GENERAL Born 1852 Died 1931

Joseph Joffre

> "The **hour** has come to **advance** at all costs and to **die** where you stand."

JOFFRE'S INSTRUCTIONS TO HIS COMMANDERS AT THE MARNE, SEPTEMBER 1914

When General Joseph Joffre was appointed Chief of Staff of the French army in 1911, the most common reaction among his peers was astonishment that such a modest man should have been placed in such an elevated position.

An officer in the Engineers, Joffre had pursued a solid career building railways and fortifications in France's African and Asian colonies.

As he admitted in his response to the offer of the post, he had "no knowledge whatever of general staff work". His only experience of leading men in combat conditions had been a march across West Africa to Timbuktu in 1893 among hostile nomads.

On the other hand, Joffre had often impressed his superiors by the thoroughness and tenacity with which he executed the unglamorous but difficult tasks entrusted to him. Vitally, he was a man of the people in a largely aristocratic officer corps, his lowly origins as the son of an artisan recommending him to the French Republican government.

Attack at all costs

Sublimely self-confident, Joffre was never a man to underrate himself, but nor did he mistake himself for an original military thinker. Contrary to what might have been expected from a builder of fortifications, he believed that an offensive strategy was more effective than a defensive one. It was a view that was prevalent at the time and one shared by his brightest officers. Plan XVII, which laid out a new French offensive strategy in 1913, clearly stated: "It is the commander-in-chief's intention to advance with all forces united to the attack of the German armies."

Joffre never wavered in his commitment to the attack at all costs. He blamed the disasters of the first month of the war not on the failings of Plan XVII, but on "lack of offensive spirit". His greatest success, the Battle of the Marne, was a strategically defensive victory, but achieved by a general offensive of the French and British armies. In the trench warfare that prevailed from December 1914, Joffre continued to launch massively costly offensive operations, as much with the aim of

Commanding presence
This portrait of Joffre by Henry Jacquet was painted at the height of his renown as commander-in-chief of the French armies in 1915. His bulky physical presence and placid, unflappable manner were reassuring amid the crises and horrors of the war.

Meeting of Allies
Joffre meets, from left to right, President Poincaré, King George V, General Foch, and General Haig in August 1916, during the Battle of the Somme. He cultivated a good relationship with his British allies.

maintaining the aggression and spirit of his troops as with any real hope of achieving a breakthrough.

If his commitment to attack showed Joffre as stubborn and unimaginative, his strengths as a commander grew out of the same powerful, unshakeable root of his character.

"Papa" Joffre

While his opponent at the start of the war, German Chief of the General Staff Helmuth von Moltke, came close to a nervous breakdown through the strains of an apparently victorious campaign, Joffre remained calm and resolute in the face of the failure of his offensives and the invasion of France. He lost neither appetite nor sleep. Visitors to his headquarters in the early weeks of the war, first at Vitry-le-François and then at Bas-sur-Aube, marvelled at the long, copious lunches, always followed by an hour's siesta, which no one would dare interrupt.

His absolute self-confidence communicated itself to his staff and to his subordinate commanders. Even while they were being killed in their tens of thousands in the offensives ordered by their commander-in-chief, French soldiers responded to his firm but benevolent paternal appearance by dubbing him "Papa" Joffre.

Joffre was implacably authoritarian. He ruled the battle zones in eastern France like a military dictator. Despising politicians, he rejected all political interference in military decisions and barely kept his government informed of his intentions.

Sound judgement

Joffre was famous for sacking generals whom he believed incompetent or lacking in offensive spirit – more than 70 corps or divisional commanders were dismissed in the first two months of the war. His judgement was usually shrewd, if not always fair. The replacement of Lanrezac by the energetic Franchet d'Espèrey as commander of the Fifth Army before the Battle of the Marne was essential to victory, although unjust to Lanrezac

whom Joffre wrongly blamed for ordering the necessary retreat from Belgium. The choice of Foch to lead the Ninth Army at the Marne and of Pétain to oversee the defence of Verdun in February 1916 were other inspired appointments.

Winning over the British

In dealing with France's allies, whom he could neither order nor sack, Joffre proved effective at eliciting cooperation. Like everyone else, he found the first BEF commander, Sir John French, intractable, but in a dramatic visit to French's headquarters on the eve of the Marne counter-offensive, he won British cooperation through an emotional appeal that came across despite the lack of a common language. With French's successor, Douglas Haig, Joffre built a relationship of trust and mutual aid, helped by Haig's own wholehearted commitment to the alliance.

The Battle of the Marne was the high point of Joffre's career. In a rapidly changing situation, with armies in retreat, he pursued the goal of establishing a line facing the invader from which a counter-offensive could be launched. His means of

achieving this goal were flexible. He repositioned armies and created new ones, keeping a tight hold on his commanders through clear and concise orders. Nothing went according to a plan, yet Joffre controlled the battle, taking decisions in his measured manner.

Victory at the Marne made Joffre a French hero. For a while, his prestige saved him from criticism, but the stalemate of trench war eroded his reputation. By late 1915, after a series of failed offensives in Artois and Champagne, Joffre's magic began to fail. In February 1916, he was blamed for the poor state of the defences at Verdun.

Sidelined

Politicians who were offended by Joffre's arrogance plotted his downfall. With losses unbearable, and Joffre unable to propose a quick route to winning the war, in December 1916 he was replaced by Robert Nivelle, whom Joffre had promoted. Still popular, Joffre was made a Marshal of France – the first to be accorded the title since 1870 – but was sidelined from then on. After the war, Joffre retired from military and public life. He died in Paris in 1931.

Sword of honour
Joffre won adulation both in France and abroad, and was presented with numerous swords of honour and other symbolic gifts. Although known for his modest demeanour, he was not averse to a little hero worship.

> ## "My faith in the **soldiers of France** had been justified... How gloriously they **fought!**"
>
> JOSEPH JOFFRE DESCRIBING THE BATTLE OF THE MARNE

TIMELINE

- **January 1852** Joseph Jacques Césaire Joffre is born at Rivesaltes in Rousillon, southern France, one of 11 children of a barrel-maker.

- **1870** Enters the École Polytechnique, France's elite school of military engineering, afterwards becoming an officer in the Corps of Engineers, serving mostly in France's colonies.

- **1893** Promoted to lieutenant-colonel after leading a column of troops to Timbuktu, Mali, through territory dominated by Tuareg.

- **1899** Serves under General Joseph Gallieni in Madagascar, impressing Gallieni with his diligent work on fortifications.

- **1908** Promoted to general and given command of the French Second Army Corps.

- **July 1911** Appointed French Chief of Staff on the recommendation of Gallieni.

- **1913** As Chief of Staff, endorses a new war strategy, Plan XVII, which envisages a general offensive by French armies on the outbreak of war.

- **8 August 1914** Issues General Instruction No. 1, which orders French armies to take the offensive; these offensives are repulsed with exceptionally heavy losses.

- **5–6 September 1914** Launches a counter-offensive at the Battle of the Marne, forcing the German armies in France to retreat.

- **1915** Launches the Champagne and Artois offensives, in which French troops suffer heavy casualties for little or no gain.

- **February 1916** Widely blamed for the poor state of Verdun's defences when the Germans launch an offensive at Verdun.

- **13 December 1916** Replaced as commander-in-chief by Robert Nivelle, but accorded the title of Marshal of France.

- **1917** Heads French military missions to Romania and the USA.

- **3 January 1931** Dies in Paris and is buried at his estate in Louveciennes.

WORLD WAR I POSTCARD

The **Race** to the **Sea**

The Allied advance from the Marne was brought to an abrupt halt in front of the German trenches on the Aisne in mid-September 1914, but a war of movement continued further north in the "Race to the Sea".

Destroying a bridge over the Aisne
As the Germans withdrew across the Aisne river, they blew up bridges to stop the French and British pursuing them. Allied troops had great difficulty crossing the river under enemy fire.

« BEFORE

On the Western Front, the first six weeks of the war had been dramatic but indecisive, leaving both sides options for offensive operations.

STRATEGIC DECISIONS
Despite the **Allied victory at the Marne « 54–55**, German troops controlled a large area of northeastern France and Belgium. The **Belgian army had withdrawn** inside a defensive perimeter around **Antwerp**. Fighting along France's eastern borders subsided, but battle raged at the **city of Reims**, retaken by the French after a brief German occupation on 12 September. The French fortress of **Maubeuge** fell after a two-week siege on 8 September. **German armies** retreating from the Marne had **orders to stand at the Aisne river**, but this left open space to be exploited between the Aisne and the coast.

Pursuing a supposedly defeated enemy northwards in the second week in September, French and British commanders were in an optimistic mood. They estimated that it would take their advancing forces from three weeks to a month to reach Belgium's border with Germany. But they did not know that the outgoing German Chief of General Staff, General Moltke, had ordered his withdrawing armies to fortify and defend a line along the Aisne river.

Battle of the Aisne

When Allied troops reached the Aisne on 12 September, they found the Germans entrenched on the Chemin des Dames ridge, easily defensible heights on the far side of the river. Determined to maintain the rhythm of their advance, the British and French attacked immediately. Under heavy shelling from the German guns, they found a precarious way across bridges partially destroyed by German engineers or built their own pontoon bridges over the broad river, which was swollen by heavy rain. Once they were on the other side, Allied infantry mounted uphill assaults against the German lines and were repeatedly driven back by German firepower.

The Germans followed up with their own counterattacks, but these proved equally unsuccessful as Allied troops dug in. Soon two lines of trenches faced one another immovably – the start of the

trench system that would eventually extend from Switzerland to the coast. At Reims, the armies were equally stuck, with the French holding the city but suffering under a heavy German bombardment, which devastated the city's cathedral.

Neither French commander-in-chief Joffre, nor Moltke's replacement as German Chief of the General Staff, Erich von Falkenhayn, was interested in accepting a stalemate. The country was almost empty of troops north from the Aisne to the coast, and both commanders hastened to assemble forces for an outflanking move into this inviting space. They transferred troops from other sectors – chiefly the now largely dormant front line

48 **The number of fortresses surrounding Antwerp to defend it from attack.**

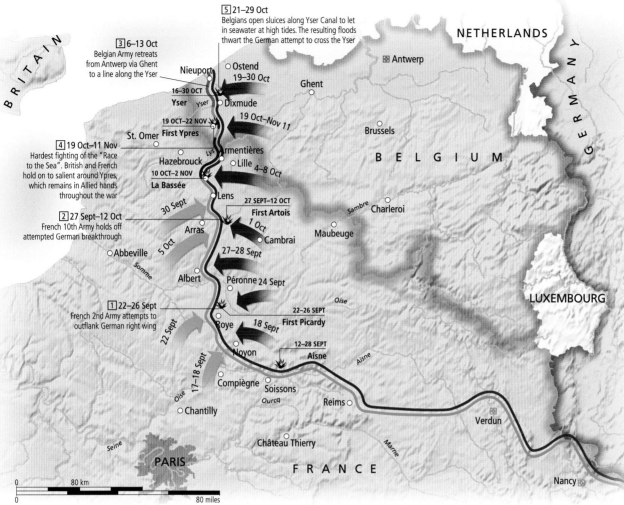

5 21–29 Oct
Belgians open sluices along Yser Canal to let in seawater at high tides. The resulting floods thwart the German attempt to cross the Yser

3 6–13 Oct
Belgian Army retreats from Antwerp via Ghent to a line along the Yser

4 19 Oct–11 Nov
Hardest fighting of the "Race to the Sea". British and French hold on to salient around Ypres, which remains in Allied hands throughout the war

2 27 Sept–12 Oct
French 10th Army holds off attempted German breakthrough

1 22–26 Sept
French 2nd Army attempts to outflank German right wing

Troop movements
A series of attempted outflanking moves by armies on both sides carried the fighting from the Aisne north to the coast, where Belgian troops retreating from Antwerp held the line at the Yser.

KEY
- Major French attack (with date)
- Major German attack (with date)
- Major battle (with date)
- Allied front line November
- Belgian sector
- British sector
- French sector
- German front line November 1914
- Belgian fortified town/city
- French fortified town/city

AFTER

The Race to the Sea culminated in the First Battle of Ypres, fought from mid-October to late November.

APPROACHING STALEMATE
Beginning while fighting raged to the north at the Battle of the Yser and to the south at La Bassé, **intensive combat at Ypres 60–61 »** continued until the third week in November. With neither side able to make a breakthrough, **this ended the first mobile phase of the war** on the Western Front. Joffre launched another **offensive in Champagne** in December, but **no further substantial movement** could be achieved by either side. The trenches that were dug by troops at various points in these battles were gradually joined together to **create a continuous trench line**.

along France's eastern border – and flung them forward in a series of offensives, each of which met the enemy head on.

Clashes in northern France
Once troops entrenched, no progress could be made and a new flanking manoeuvre had to be attempted further north. The French came close to a major defeat at Arras, but held firm after General Foch, put in overall command in the northern sector, issued the order: "No retirement; every man to the battle."
Making aggressive use of massed cavalry divisions, the Germans captured Lille in early October. Meanwhile, the British Expeditionary Force (BEF) was moved by train to the far left of the Allied line. Advancing towards Lille, it ran into German cavalry at La Bassée.

Driving to battle
In 1914, the Belgian army fitted a number of Minerva automobiles with steel plate and mounted guns on top, creating the first armoured cars. They were used as rescue vehicles and for reconnaissance.

"**We established a rough firing line** and there **we stayed... We bogged down**."

DRUMMER E.L. SLAYTOR, COLDSTREAM GUARDS, AT THE AISNE, 16 SEPTEMBER 1914

While infantry and cavalry clashed in northern France, the Belgians, led in person by King Albert I, were engaged in a desperate defence of Antwerp. From 28 September, the Germans mounted a major attack on the fortified city. Their array of heavy siege guns had the same effect as at Liège, Namur, and Maubeuge, and battered Antwerp's fortresses to destruction.
As the defence wavered, Britain sent the Naval Division to Antwerp to bolster Belgian morale, and a British infantry division landed at the Belgian port of Zeebrugge. The First Lord of the Admiralty, Winston Churchill, travelled to Antwerp to persuade the Belgians to continue resistance. It was in vain. The city's defences were penetrated and on 9 October the king and his government left for the coastal town of Ostende. Antwerp surrendered to the Germans the following day. Most of the Belgian army escaped to continue the fight at the Yser river.

KEY MOMENT
THE BATTLE OF THE YSER

Abandoning the defence of Antwerp on 9 October, Belgian troops withdrew along the coast to the Yser Canal between Nieuport and Dixmude, where they took up position on high embankments dominating low-lying land. The German Fourth Army attacked, hoping to break through to the vital Channel ports of

Boulogne and Calais. With battle raging, on 25 October King Albert ordered engineers to open the locks. As water flooded a wide area, German troops were forced to retreat or drown. The Belgians were left in possession of a coastal strip of their national territory that they held throughout the war.

Fighting to a Standstill

The collision of Allied and German forces in Flanders at the First Battle of Ypres was a bloody climax to the opening mobile phase of the war on the Western Front. After the battle proved indecisive, the armies settled into trench warfare.

French commander-in-chief, General Joffre, regarded the area around the Belgian city of Ypres as the gateway through which Allied forces would advance to liberate northern France and Belgium from German occupation. To German Chief of the General Staff Erich von Falkenhayn, it was the route by which his forces could seize the Channel ports of Dunkirk, Calais, and Boulogne – Britain's links to the battlefields.

« BEFORE

Between August and September 1914, it became clear that plans drawn up before the war had failed to work. Fresh offensives were improvised by generals still seeking a quick victory.

INSPECTION OF INDIAN TROOPS, 1914

BATTLE MOVES NORTH
A series of attempted outflanking movements known as the **Race to the Sea** « 58–59, carried the fighting northwards from the Aisne to **Flanders**. The BEF was moved by train to Flanders, where it fought the Germans at **La Bassée** from 10 October. The Belgian army, retreating from Antwerp, defended a coastal strip at the **Yser**. The British rushed troops to Flanders, including elements of the Indian army.

The Indian troops who took part in the "Race to the Sea" had only been in Europe for six weeks. Their first engagement was at the Battle of La Bassée in October 1914.

Falkenhayn succeeded in assembling superior forces to the Allies, partly through calling on corps of enthusiastic young volunteers, many of them still students, who had joined up in the early days of the war. These reservists – whose numbers included the young Adolf Hitler, an Austrian enrolled in the Bavarian forces – had received only two months of military training.

By this stage in the war, the British were able to field seven infantry divisions plus three cavalry divisions, which fought dismounted, alongside the foot soldiers. After some initial fighting, the first major German offensive was launched on 20 October. Because of Allied inferiority, the battle turned into a desperate Anglo-French defence of a salient around Ypres, with British troops holding positions in front of the town and the French defending the flanks.

360,000 The number of French, British, and Belgian troops killed in action by the end of 1914. The majority (300,000) were French.

240,000 The number of German troops who were killed during this period.

Heavy losses on both sides
The British and French improvised defensive positions, digging shallow trenches and exploiting the protection of stone walls, ditches, and village houses. The British were chronically short of heavy artillery and machine-guns, but their rapid rifle fire, which the Germans persistently mistook for the fire of machine-guns, imposed heavy losses on the massed German infantry.

The slaughter of German troops marching into gunfire while singing patriotic songs at Langemarck, near Ypres, on 22 October became one the best-known German stories of the war. In fact, this was a half-truth, since the troops were singing only to identify themselves in the morning mist.

By late October, the Allies had ceded ground, but the initial German offensive had stalled.

German commemorative bayonet
The Iron Cross on this bayonet is a reference to Germany's most common military decoration. Four million Iron Crosses were awarded in the war, including one to Adolf Hitler at First Ypres.

Falkenhayn then launched a fresh attack towards Ypres along the Menin Road. His expectations of success were high, for the British forces had been severely depleted. When Kaiser Wilhelm came to forward headquarters on 31 October, it was in the hope of celebrating a major victory. In fact, the Germans did achieve a potentially important breakthrough at the village of Gheluvelt on the outskirts of Ypres. Their heavy guns hit a British divisional headquarters at Hooge Château, just east of the village, unusually adding staff officers to the lengthening list of casualties.

The Allies lost the vital high ground dominating Ypres, but remnants of half-broken British battalions were assembled to mount a counterattack and, with the help of just a handful of French reinforcements, a line was held. The British were desperately short of soldiers and ammunition. The arrival of forces from India helped alleviate the problem, and a number of Territorial battalions were sent across the Channel for the first time.

Nonetheless, the German renewal of the offensive in the second week of November came perilously close to overwhelming the British line.

British counterattack
At the climax of the battle, on 11 November, elite Prussian Foot Guards were at one point resisted only by hastily armed British cooks and officers' servants. By the end of that day, however, a

TECHNOLOGY

BARBED WIRE

Invented in the US in the 1860s, barbed wire was originally designed to control cattle. It had seen extensive military use in the Russo-Japanese War of 1904–05. By the end of 1914, barbed wire was being planted in front of trenches to block infantry assaults or raiding parties. When attacking infantry found their path barred by uncut wire, they were stranded under the fire of enemy guns and massacred. Soldiers devoted perilous night hours to repairing their own wire and sabotaging the enemy's with wire-cutters.

Simple but effective

Barbed wire increased the dominance of defence over offence by entrapping the attacking troops. Later in the war, barbed wire entanglements in front of trenches could be up to 30 m (100 ft) deep.

Troops dig in

The original trenches on the Western Front were hastily dug temporary field fortifications. These hard-pressed British soldiers will have been grateful even for this primitive protection against enemy fire.

> " We must... **strike** the decisive **blow against our** most **detested enemy.** "

GERMAN ORDER OF THE DAY, YPRES, 30 OCTOBER 1914

counterattack by British light infantry at Nonnebosschen succeeded in driving the Guards back, and Falkenhayn knew the Ypres offensive had ended in failure. Although some fighting continued around Ypres until 22 November, the official date of the end of the battle, the German armies no longer threatened a breakthrough.

For the British, First Ypres was the graveyard of the pre-war regular army – the "Old Contemptibles", so named because of an alleged derisory reference by the Kaiser to their puny fighting strength. The original BEF troops that landed in France in August 1914 had suffered around 90 per cent casualties, with a large proportion of the losses at Ypres.

German setback

Strategically, the failed offensive at Ypres was a serious setback for Germany. Falkenhayn informed the Kaiser that there was no further chance of achieving an early victory on the Western Front. The German high command eventually concluded that it was best to create a strong defensive trench system on the Western Front while taking the offensive against the Russians in the east. Irrepressible in his pursuit of the offensive, General Joffre continued to order his troops to attack in Champagne and Artois in December, but elsewhere on the Western Front the fighting subsided. Soldiers had dug themselves into trenches as best they could wherever the fighting had come to a halt. As time passed, these trench lines were gradually reinforced, joined together, and extended. Troops on both sides settled in.

As the final weeks of 1914 approached, it was apparent that there would not be a swift victory for the Allies or the Germans. War would certainly not be over by Christmas.

AFTER »

The First Battle of Ypres resulted in many casualties. But it was inconclusive, and fighting at Ypres continued for the next four years.

REMEMBERING THE DEAD
Germans remember First Ypres as the *Kindermord* ("massacre of children"), because of the heavy losses among young volunteers. One victim was the youngest son of sculptress Käthe Kollwitz, who made **grieving statues** for the war cemetery at Vladslo, Belgium.

HARD TO DEFEND
The battle left the Allies occupying an exposed salient. Over the next four years the fighting continued, including **Second Ypres 102–103** » in 1915 and **Third Ypres 240–241** » in 1917.

KOLLWITZ SCULPTURE

The **Christmas Truce**

The Christmas Truce was actually a series of ceasefires that took place along the Western Front in 1914. Although it was not an official truce, and in some areas the fighting continued, it is thought that up to 100,000 British and German troops took part. Troops sang carols across the trenches and met in No Man's Land to exchange gifts and souvenirs.

"On Christmas Eve the Germans entrenched opposite us began calling out to us... 'Pudding', 'A Happy Christmas' and 'English-means good'... so two of our fellows climbed over the parapet... and went towards the German trenches. Halfway they were met by four Germans, who said they would not shoot on Christmas Day if we did not. They gave our fellows cigars and a bottle of wine and were given cake and cigarettes.

When they came back I went out with some more of our fellows and we were met by about 30 Germans, who seemed to be very nice fellows. I got one of them to write his name and address on a postcard as a souvenir. All through the night we sang carols to them and they sang to us and one played 'God Save the King' on a mouth organ.

On Christmas Day we all got out of the trenches and walked about with the Germans, who, when asked if they were fed up with the war, said 'Yes, rather'... Between the trenches there were a lot of dead Germans whom we helped to bury. In one place where the trenches are only 25 yards apart we could see dead Germans half buried. Their legs and gloved hands sticking out of the ground. The trenches in this position are called 'The Death Trap' as hundreds have been killed there.

A hundred yards or so in the rear... there were old houses that had been shelled. These were explored... and we found old bicycles, top hats, straw hats, umbrellas, etc. We dressed ourselves up in these and went over to the Germans. It seemed so comical to see our fellows walking about in top hats and with umbrellas up... We made the Germans laugh.

No firing took place on Christmas night and at four the next morning we were relieved by regulars."

RIFLEMAN C.H. BRAZIER, QUEEN'S WESTMINSTERS, EXTRACT FROM A LETTER WRITTEN HOME, PUBLISHED IN THE *HERTFORDSHIRE MERCURY* ON 9 JANUARY 1915

A temporary peace
Among the many soldiers who participated in the truce were these British soldiers from the 11th Brigade, Fourth Division, and their German counterparts, gathered at Ploegsteert, Belgium, on Christmas Day 1914.

The Battle of Tannenberg

The war on Germany's Eastern Front opened in August 1914 with a Russian invasion of East Prussia. The defeat of a Russian army at Tannenberg was greeted by the German people as a miracle of deliverance, making national heroes of generals Hindenburg and Ludendorff.

Eye in the sky

This German pilot's badge shows a Taube monoplane, the main aircraft used by Germany for reconnaissance in August 1914. These frail machines had a decisive effect at the Battle of Tannenberg.

BEFORE

At the start of the war, Germany intended to stand on the defensive against Russia until France had been defeated in the west.

PLANS FOR THE EAST

Germany assumed **Russian mobilization** would take at least 40 days to complete. The Russians, however, had promised the French that Russian forces would **launch an attack against Germany within 15 days** of the outbreak of war. Russia planned to begin its role in the war by taking the offensive against **Austria-Hungary**.

Russian prisoners

The Germans took over 90,000 Russian soldiers prisoner at Tannenberg. Remaining captives until 1918, they provided valuable labour for Germany's war effort, including building trench systems on the Western Front.

Following the dictates of the Schlieffen Plan, the Germans had sent seven of their eight armies to Belgium and France. The Eighth Army, commanded by General Maximilian Prittwitz, was to act as a holding force until troops could be transferred from the west. The Russians, their forces divided between the German and Austro-Hungarian fronts, had two armies available for an invasion of East Prussia, giving them considerable local superiority in manpower. Honouring their agreement with France, the Russians attacked on day 15 of the war, even though their mobilization was far from complete.

The advance of Russian troops on to German soil, preceded by marauding Cossack cavalry, sent a wave of panic through Germany. Roads were clogged with East Prussian refugees fleeing westwards. Abandoning prepared defensive positions, the German Eighth Army advanced towards the Russian First Army. Commanded by General Paul von Rennenkampf, the Russians repelled German attacks at Gumbinnen.

Role of intelligence

When reconnaissance aircraft reported the advance of the Russian Second Army to the south of the Masurian Lakes, Prittwitz panicked and ordered a general withdrawal to the Vistula, angering the German high command. Prittwitz was sacked and replaced by veteran General Paul von Hindenburg, with General Ludendorff – the hero of the recent siege of Liège – as his Chief of Staff.

Hindenburg and Ludendorff arrived in East Prussia to find a perfectly viable plan for a counter-offensive already in place, devised by Prittwitz's staff. Gambling that the fighting at Gumbinnen would have temporarily halted Rennenkampf, the Germans decided to concentrate their forces against the Russian Second Army, commanded by General Alexander Samsonov, which was blithely pushing forward almost unopposed through the forests to the south.

The German plan took advantage of aerial reconnaissance, by both primitive Taube aeroplanes and

> **EAST PRUSSIA** The easternmost area of Germany, on the Baltic coast, which is now divided between Poland, Russia, and Lithuania.

airships. An intercepted Russian radio message, transmitted uncoded, confirmed that Rennenkampf was not intending to resume his advance.

Setting the trap

Leaving a thin screen of cavalry and reserves in front of the Russian First Army, an entire German corps under General Hermann von François was moved by train to the south of the Russian Second Army. Other German troops marched from Gumbinnen towards Samsonov's northern flank.

Samsonov was ignorant of the position of German forces and had no contact with the Russian First Army. Nonetheless, a spirit of optimism reigned. When German flank attacks began on 26–27 August, Samsonov pressed forward. By 29 August, the German pincers had closed behind him and most of the Second Army was trapped. Having lost control of his forces, Samsonov walked into the forest and shot himself. Claiming a great victory, the Germans named it Tannenberg after a 15th-century battle famed in Prussian history.

Fighting switches to the south, 24–26 August

Hindenburg and Ludendorff took command and ordered German 8th Army south to attack the Russian 2nd Army. While Rennenkampf's 1st Army dithered and Samsonov's 2nd Army advanced, by 26 August the Germans were ready to spring the trap and destroy Samsonov's army.

The Russian advance, 17–23 August

The Russian 1st and 2nd armies advanced with a wide gap between them. When the Germans moved against the Russian 1st Army, they were defeated at Gumbinnen. The Russian 2nd Army threatened to advance behind the German forces from south of the Masurian Lakes.

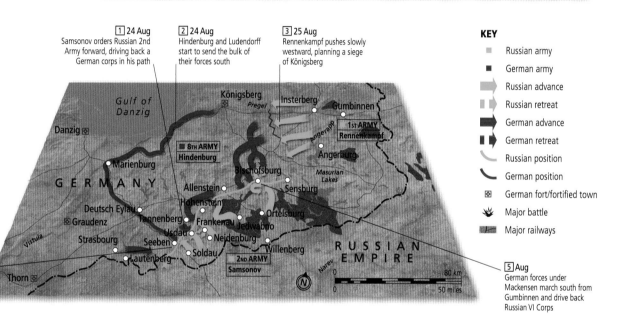

4 20–23 Aug
Two German corps move by train to reinforce the line in front of Russian 2nd Army

2 20 Aug
German forces attack at Gumbinnen, despite some success they are forced to withdraw westwards

1 15–20 Aug
Russian 1st Army crosses the East Prussian border. Part of German 8th Army moves to block them

3 20 Aug
Russian 2nd Army crosses the East Prussian border

1 24 Aug
Samsonov orders Russian 2nd Army forward, driving back a German corps in his path

2 24 Aug
Hindenburg and Ludendorff start to send the bulk of their forces south

3 25 Aug
Rennenkampf pushes slowly westward, planning a siege of Königsberg

KEY

▪	Russian army
▪	German army
⇨	Russian advance
⇥	Russian retreat
⬛	German advance
▮▯	German retreat
⟍	Russian position
⟍	German position
⊗	German fort/fortified town
💥	Major battle
▬	Major railways

4 Night of 25 Aug
German I Corps under François reaches Seeben by train and prepares to attack Samsonov's southern flank

5 Aug
German forces under Mackensen march south from Gumbinnen and drive back Russian VI Corps

A German victory, 27–31 August

The Russian forces were defeated in every major engagement. Outgunned and outmanoeuvred, they tried to retreat, but their route was barred by German I Corps.

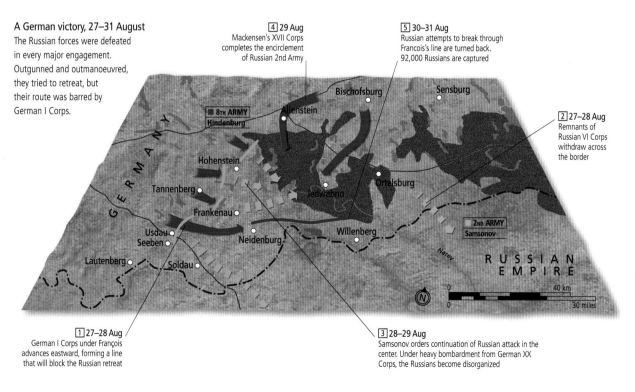

4 29 Aug
Mackensen's XVII Corps completes the encirclement of Russian 2nd Army

5 30–31 Aug
Russian attempts to break through Francois's line are turned back. 92,000 Russians are captured

2 27–28 Aug
Remnants of Russian VI Corps withdraw across the border

1 27–28 Aug
German I Corps under François advances eastward, forming a line that will block the Russian retreat

3 28–29 Aug
Samsonov orders continuation of Russian attack in the center. Under heavy bombardment from German XX Corps, the Russians become disorganized

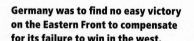

AFTER

Germany was to find no easy victory on the Eastern Front to compensate for its failure to win in the west.

RUSSIA RALLIES

The Russians recovered from Tannenberg. When the Germans turned their forces against the Russian First Army in September, Rennenkampf managed **a fighting withdrawal** at the **Battle of the Masurian Lakes 134 »**, and then mounted a successful counter-offensive. Russia was also scoring successes against the **Austro-Hungarians in Galicia 68–69 »**, and fighting on the **Eastern Front continued in Poland 70–71 »**. Hindenburg and Ludendorff took the credit for saving Germany from the Russian hordes, and were endowed the two generals with almost magical prestige. Their rise to power had begun.

GERMAN GENERAL Born 1847 Died 1934

Paul von Hindenburg

"With clean hearts we **marched** out to defend the **Fatherland.**"

PAUL VON HINDENBURG, SPEECH AT THE OPENING OF THE TANNENBERG MEMORIAL, SEPTEMBER 1927

If Paul von von Hindenburg had died at the age of 65, no one in the world would have heard of him. Born a Junker – a member of the landed aristocracy who formed the social, political, and military elite of the Prussian state – he adopted the conservative values of his class and pursued a military career. Joining the elite Prussian Foot Guards as a junior officer in 1865, he swore the standard oath to behave as "an upright, fearless, dutiful, and honourable soldier".

Prussian wars

That is no doubt how Hindenburg saw himself throughout his life. He experienced at first hand the dramatic events that created the German Empire, serving in Prussia's victorious wars against Austria and France, and witnessing the proclamation of the king of Prussia as emperor (Kaiser) of Germany in Versailles in 1871, at the end of the Franco-Prussian War. Recognized as solid, able, and reliable, he made a successful career through four decades in the peacetime army,

but always fell short of the highest appointments. In 1911, he retired – not, he later claimed, because of "professional or personal friction", but in fulfilment of "the duty to make way for younger officers".

Call of duty

After the outbreak of war in August 1914, all recently retired officers expected the call to return to arms. For Hindenburg, it came three weeks into the war. The German General Staff had decided that Erich Ludendorff, who had distinguished himself at the siege of Liège, was the man to handle a threatening situation on the Eastern Front. Ludendorff was ordered to East Prussia, where he would take over as Chief of Staff. He needed an army commander to serve under.

Hindenburg was living in Hanover, on the rail route Ludendorff would take from Belgium. On the evening of 22 August, he was informed that he was to take command of the Eighth Army. At 4am the next morning, he joined Ludendorff's train at Hanover

Hero of Tannenberg

Painted after the victory at Tannenberg, this portrait shows Hindenburg as the stern, paternal embodiment of the Prussian military tradition. Germans were reassured by his air of calm strength and simplicity.

Austro-Prussian War
As a young officer, Hindenburg was commended for his bravery against the Austrians at the Battle of Königgrätz. He was one of a few German commanders old enough to have fought against European powers.

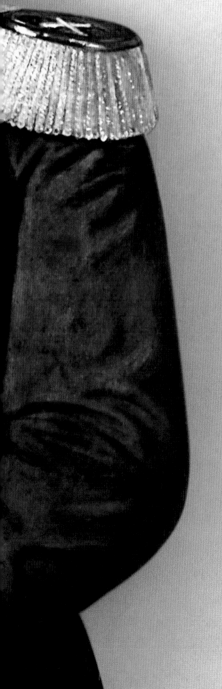

station, dressed in an old Prussian uniform, the only military outfit that he possessed. Within a week, the Eighth Army had won the Battle of Tannenberg.

Hindenberg and Ludendorff were to be an inseparable pair in military command and political power through the following four years. Together, they mounted large-scale campaigns against the Russians, and fought a long and vicious power struggle against Chief of the General Staff Erich von Falkenhayn. Together they led the Third Supreme Command that ran the German war effort from Falkenhayn's downfall in August 1916 to the final collapse in 1918. Although contrasting in social background and personality, they were perfectly matched in attitudes and opinions. Coming from a lower social stratum, Ludendorff had made himself both respected and disliked for his aggressive ambition and ruthless intelligence. Hindenburg's Prussian dignity and implacable calm were the perfect foil to Ludendorff's nervous energy and abrasiveness.

Fervent nationalist

The two men shared the typical views of German nationalists. Hindenburg was anti-semitic and regarded socialists – a substantial part of the German population – as a potential threat to the war effort. He advocated the clearance of the Slav population from territories around the Baltic and their replacement by German settlers. He rejected the pursuit of peace except on terms that would include permanent German control of northeastern France and Belgium and German domination of Central and Eastern Europe.

In these matters Hindenburg and Ludendorff were as one. In terms of public image, it was Hindenburg who replaced the sidelined Kaiser as the focus of wartime patriotism. He became the object of a personality cult, which was fostered by German propagandists. From August 1916, his name was appended to major initiatives such as the Hindenburg Programme to mobilize German society for total war and the Hindenburg Line for fortifications along the Western Front.

Taking responsibility

Ludendorff is generally credited with the real exercise of power in the partnership, whether in planning and executing military campaigns or in determining strategic policy, but Hindenburg was much more than

Wooden titan
In September 1915, a colossal wooden statue of Hindenburg was erected in Berlin, a gesture imitated in other German cities. Members of the public paid for a chance to hammer a nail into the statue, a scheme devised to raise funds for war widows.

that was never healed. In theory a monarchist, but with no great personal regard for Kaiser Wilhelm, he presided over the Kaiser's abdication and the transition to a German republic.

Postwar president

Hindenburg never lost his hold over the German people. His image as an honourable soldier survived, while he helped shift the blame for the country's defeat on to the subversive socialists and Jews who had allegedly stabbed the army in the back. After the war,

> ## "**Hindenburg** is extraordinarily well versed in **military history** and has a **clear mind.**"
>
> GENERAL WILHELM GROENER, MEMBER OF THE GENERAL STAFF, OCTOBER 1916

a passive front man. He took responsibility for all the decisions that eventually led Germany to disaster, from the adoption of unrestricted submarine warfare in 1917 to the large-scale Spring Offensives on the Western Front in 1918.

Whereas Ludendorff came close to nervous collapse as the German position disintegrated in October 1918, Hindenburg remained calm, advocating acceptance of an armistice because of the lack of any alternative. When Ludendorff was forced to resign, Hindenburg stayed in place, causing a breach between the two men

he was persuaded to return from retirement a second time in 1925 to stand as the right-wing candidate for the presidency of the Weimar Republic, and was elected.

Hindenburg's enduring popularity ensured he remained president until his death in 1934, overseeing the collapse of democratic government. He disliked Adolf Hitler as a social upstart and a dangerously socialist politician, but was persuaded to appoint the Nazi leader on the promise he could be controlled by the old elite. By default he became the bridge between the old Prussia and the Third Reich.

HINDENBURG WITH ADOLF HITLER

Austro-Hungarian Failures

In the first months of the war, Austro-Hungarian forces suffered serious setbacks against both Russians and Serbs. The scale of their early casualties, which included many of their finest troops and officers, was a severe shock to this fragile and divided state.

« BEFORE

In August 1914, Austria-Hungary found itself at war with Serbia and Russia, a two-front conflict for which it was ill-prepared.

WAR ON SERBIA
Austria-Hungary triggered World War I with its declaration of **war on Serbia << 30–31** on 28 July 1914, provoking Russian mobilization in support of the Serbs. Austro-Hungarian Chief of Staff Franz Conrad von Hötzendorf's priority was to defeat Serbia, but he was under pressure from Germany to **mount an offensive against Russia**.

RUSSIAN STRATEGY
Also committed to **splitting their forces between two fronts**, the Russians intended to invade Germany through **East Prussia << 64–65**, while also attacking Austria-Hungary's eastern province of Galicia.

The mobilization of the Austro-Hungarian armies was plagued by indecision about whether their initial target should be Russia or Serbia. Pre-war planning had given Austro-Hungarian Chief of Staff Franz Conrad von Hötzendorf the Second Army, to send against either the Serbs or Russians. At the outbreak of war, he ordered it to Serbia, but then realized he needed to use it against the mobilizing Russians. The Second Army went to the Serbian front, stayed for three weeks, and then went by train to Austria-Hungary's eastern province of Galicia. It played no part in the opening battles on either front.

Misplaced confidence
Austria-Hungary expected an easy victory against Serbia, but its divided forces left inadequate strength to overcome a country that had mobilized most of its male population. The Serbs were commanded by Field Marshal Radomir Putnik, who had been allowed to return to Serbia from an

Elite Austrian troops
A regiment of the Tyrolean Kaiserjäger, elite riflemen, is led forward by Colonel Brosch von Aarenau. The colonel and many of his men died fighting in Galicia in early September 1914.

Austrian spa when war broke out. The Austro-Hungarian invasion was entrusted to Oskar Potiorek, governor of Bosnia, who had ridden in Franz Ferdinand's car on the day of the Sarajevo assassination. He was fiercely committed to punishing the Serbs, giving his troops licence to kill civilians and destroy property.

Falling apart
Potiorek's plans proceeded woefully, however. Crossing the Drina and Sava rivers, his forces advanced only as far as Putnik's defensive line. After heavy fighting, they were thrown back, and by 24 August the attack against Serbia had fallen apart.

In early September, Serbian forces advanced into Bosnia. By then, the Serbian front was a sideshow, dwarfed by the clash of the Russian and Austro-Hungarian armies in Poland and Galicia. This was warfare conducted across wide plains where armies could manoeuvre freely, inhibited only by the obstacle of major rivers. Both sides used large bodies of cavalry to spearhead their movements.

Operations proceeded in a fog of confusion, with commanders ill-informed of the scale and position

A partial Austro-Hungarian revival in the last three months of 1914 could not disguise its military weakness.

AUSTRIA-HUNGARY REELS

The spirit of unity achieved between Austria-Hungary's diverse ethnic groups at the outbreak of war began to fray, and the country could not sustain the losses it was facing. In response to the near collapse of their allies, the Germans created a **new army in Silesia** to mount an offensive against Warsaw, thus threatening the rear of the **Russian armies in Galicia 70–71 »**. On the Serbian front,

400,000 The number of Austro-Hungarian casualties on the Eastern Front by the end of September. Some 300,000 of these were taken prisoner.

the **Serb invasion of Bosnia** was repulsed and Austro-Hungarian forces briefly **occupied Belgrade** before being forced to withdraw.

Serbian determination
The Serbian army was a highly motivated force, with recent experience of battle in the Balkan Wars of 1912–13. It was also supplied with state-of-the-art military equipment.

" The war is **taking us into a country** [Serbia]… with a **fanatical hatred** toward us."

COMMANDER OSKAR POTIOREK, AUSTRO-HUNGARIAN GENERAL, AUGUST 1914

128mm-long barrel

Butt houses eight-round fixed magazine

Steyr pistol
The Steyr M1912 semi-automatic 9mm pistol was used by the Austrian and German armies. It was manufactured by Steyr-Mannlicher, part of Austria-Hungary's advanced weapons industry.

of enemy forces. Conrad opened with an advance northwards from Galicia into Russian Poland, as demanded by his German allies. Barely across the border, Austro-Hungarian forces unexpectedly met Russian armies heading southwards. Put into the field before mobilization was complete, the Russians had arrived more quickly than Conrad had anticipated.

In the last week of August, the Austro-Hungarian forces – which included formations of ethnic Poles eager to liberate their people from Russian oppression – won encounters at Krasnik and Komarov in Poland. Hypnotized by the prospect of crushing the Russian armies in Poland, Conrad paid little attention to the advance of other Russian forces over Galicia's

eastern border near the fortress of Lemberg (now Lviv). The Austro-Hungarian army in front of Lemberg, which had been depleted to provide troops for the Polish operation, advanced to meet the Russians, who were far stronger than expected.

Suffering heavy losses at Zlotchow, the Austro-Hungarians fell back in disarray. Neither side understood the situation, the Russians not realizing the weakness of enemy forces, and the Austro-Hungarians underestimating Russian strength. The Austrian Second Army was thrown into an offensive in eastern Galicia on 29 August, only to be repulsed with many casualties.

Conrad's strategy was to pull back behind Lemberg, drawing the Russians forward, while his Fourth Army, in Poland, turned to attack the Russian flank. Disaster ensued. Lemberg fell to the Russians on 3 September. Three days later the Fourth Army was cut to pieces attacking the Russians at Rava Russka, north of Lemberg.

Withdrawal to the Carpathians

Conrad suddenly awoke to the possibility that his forces in Poland could be surrounded by Russians advancing westwards across Galicia.

AUSTRO-HUNGARIAN GENERAL (1852–1925)

FRANZ CONRAD VON HÖTZENDORF

Austro-Hungarian Chief of Staff from 1906, Conrad was a determined advocate of war against Serbia. As such, he probably did more than any other individual to start World War I. His military operations were over-optimistic but sporadically successful. He claimed much of the credit for victory over the Russians in the Gorlice-Tarnow offensive in 1915, but his use of Austro-Hungarian forces to settle scores with Serbia and Italy often left insufficient strength for the war with Russia. After the accession of Emperor Charles, Conrad was dismissed as chief of staff in March 1917, serving as a field commander until the end of the war.

On 11 September, he ordered a general withdrawal to the natural barrier of the Carpathians. Pursued by Russian Cossack cavalry, the Austro-Hungarian armies fled westwards, some retreating over 160 km (100 miles) in two days. Przemysl, with a garrison of 150,000 soldiers, was left surrounded by Russians. By the time the Austro-Hungarians stabilized a defensive position at the end of September, they were reduced to a quarter of their original strength. Only German intervention could avoid defeat.

BEFORE

Divided between Russia, Germany, and Austria since the 18th century, the Polish lands became a major battlefield in World War I.

POLAND DIVIDED BY RUSSIA, GERMANY, AND AUSTRIA, 1766

SPLIT LOYALTIES

Most of Poland was a **province of the Russian Empire**, but many Poles also lived in **Galicia in Austria-Hungary** and a smaller number in **East Prussia**. Poles served as conscripts in all three armies.

Polish nationalists seeking independence were split at the start of the war. The **Polish Legions** under Jozef Pilsudski fought with the **Austro-Hungarian army**, while other nationalists sided with **Russia and its allies**. Austria-Hungary was **defeated by the Russians in Galicia** in August–September 1914 and forced to abandon **an invasion of Russian Poland ≪ 68–69**.

FORMIDABLE FORCE

The successful partnership of German generals Erich Ludendorff and Paul von Hindenburg had already been proved at the **Battle of Tannenberg ≪ 64–65** on the Eastern Front in August 1914.

The **Battle** for **Poland**

The weakness of Austria-Hungary drew Germany into offensive operations against Russia in Poland. In a war of movement on a monumental scale, battles were fought at the cost of previously unimaginable levels of casualties.

In the opinion of the German general staff, the main function of Austro-Hungarian forces at the start of the war was to invade Russian Poland, therefore preventing the Russians from mounting an offensive against Germany from that direction. But by mid-September 1914, instead of aiding German plans, Austria-Hungary was becoming a liability. After heavy defeats in Galicia, Austro-Hungarian Chief of Staff Conrad von Hötzendorf pleaded for German troops to rescue his threatened armies.

Germany to the rescue

The German commanders had little sympathy for Austria-Hungary's plight, but they could not ignore the fact that their ally's military failures left Germany exposed to a possible Russian thrust through Silesia towards Berlin. The Russian central command, Stavka, under Grand Duke Nikolai, was indeed assembling its forces at Warsaw for just such an offensive.

The German General Staff decided to create a new Ninth Army in Silesia, under the command of generals Hindenburg and Ludendorff, the victors of Tannenberg. Most of the troops for the Ninth Army came

from East Prussia, transferred south by the German railway system. On 29 September, Ludendorff launched an offensive towards Warsaw, coordinated with an Austro-Hungarian advance in Galicia. The Russians had begun their advance towards Silesia.

Great bodies of troops marched along Poland's muddy roads, with only fragmentary information about the movement of the enemy gleaned from radio intercepts and reconnaissance by cavalry or aircraft.

In the second week of October, approaching Warsaw, Ludendorff became aware that Russians were preparing to cross the Vistula behind him, threatening to encircle his forces. The German advance was reversed, turning into a fighting retreat, accompanied by the destruction of

Grand Duke Nikolai
The uncle of Tsar Nicholas II, Grand Duke Nikolai Nikolaievich was appointed commander-in-chief of Russian forces at the outbreak of the war. His personal authority was reinforced by his imposing physical presence.

railways, bridges, villages, and cattle. The Ninth Army got back to its start lines relatively intact. Further south, the Austro-Hungarians, attempting to support the Germans, were defeated at Ivangorod.

Reinforcements

Both sides intended to return to the offensive with the shortest possible delay. The Russians were steadily receiving reinforcements, as conscripts mobilized in Siberia and Central Asia arrived at the front. At the start of November, the Germans transferred forces to the Ninth Army from the Western Front.

The Russians had superiority of numbers but were short of rifles, bullets, and artillery shells, as well as food and clothing. Their forces were overstretched, since they were attempting to sustain offensive operations over a vast area, from the Vistula in the north to the Carpathians in the south. Nonetheless, through early November Russian forces pressed the Austro-Hungarians back towards Cracow and to the Carpathian mountain passes, through which General Aleksei Brusilov's Eighth Army hoped to capture Budapest.

Warfare on a vast scale

As the Russians attempted their offensive on the Vistula, Ludendorff sent the Ninth Army around their northern flank by rail to Posen and Thorn. Under the command of General August von Mackensen, the Germans attacked on 11 November, initiating the Battle of Lodz. This was warfare on a vast scale, with more than 600,000

> **"We run around in thin topcoats.** There is **not much** to **eat...** Perhaps we'd be **better off dead."**
>
> LETTER FROM A RUSSIAN SOLDIER, 1914

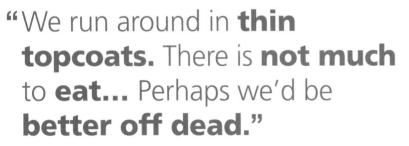

German epaulettes
These epaulettes were worn by a German conscript in a transport battalion during World War I. The efficient transport of troops by rail was essential to German military operations.

troops engaged in combat. The weather was freezing, daytime temperatures dropping to -13°C (9°F). Ludendorff was in effect attempting to repeat the encirclement of Tannenberg, but Russian commanders had learned their lesson. They cancelled the advance on Silesia and pulled back at high speed through forced marches – some units covered as much as 100 km (60 miles) in two days.

Mackensen smashed through the Russian flank but then found his army caught by a flanking attack from the Russian Fifth Army. By the time the Germans extricated themselves, the Russians had entrenched in front of Lodz. Ludendorff demanded and received reinforcements from the Western Front, while launching frontal assaults in an attempt to take the city.

By 6 December, the men were near exhaustion. The Russians decided upon a strategic withdrawal towards Warsaw and left Lodz to the Germans. Within a week the fighting ran down, as both sides dug in for the rest of the winter in trench lines.

The fighting of 1914 had an unexpected conclusion in Galicia. In the first week of December, Austria-Hungary achieved a successful offensive at Limonova, south of Cracow. The Russians were forced into a withdrawal that ended the threat to the Carpathian passes, although the fortress at Przemysl remained under Russian siege. This was not enough to restore German faith in Austro-Hungarian Chief of Staff Conrad, but it enabled him to fight off a German bid to place all the forces of the Central Powers on the Eastern Front under unified command.

1.5 MILLION The number of Russian casualties.

1 MILLION The number of Austro-Hungarian losses on all fronts by the end of 1914.

The human impact of the fighting had been immense, with more than two million troops killed, wounded, or taken prisoner. The fate of civilians in the territory was dismal. Cholera and typhus, the traditional companions of war, had made their appearance. No end to the war between the three empires was in sight.

Entrenched and ready for action
German troops with MG 08 machine-guns and Mauser rifles wait for the enemy in a hastily dug trench on the Eastern Front. Their combined firepower could repel almost any infantry assault.

The situation in late 1914 provoked a bitter debate between German commanders over priorities while fighting continued through winter.

THE BATTLE RESUMES
Generals Hindenburg and Ludendorff were **convinced that they could defeat Russia**. German Chief of the General Staff Erich von Falkenhayn was not prepared to focus exclusively on the Eastern Front, but did support major German operations there in 1915. Meanwhile, Austria-Hungary faced **successful resistance by Serbia**. In March 1915, the besieged Austrian fortress at Przemysl **fell to the Russians**, entailing the surrender of 120,000 men.

AUSTRIAN ARMY TAG

Cavalry

"The rifle... cannot replace the effect produced by the **speed of the horse** ... and the **terror of cold steel**."

BRITISH ARMY CAVALRY TRAINING MANUAL, 1907

Italian carbine
Cavalry were mostly issued with carbines such as this Carcano, a shorter-barrelled but less accurate version of the Italian infantry rifle.

Before 1914, cavalry formed a social elite in all European armies, their colourful uniforms and dashing appearance a striking feature of military parades and state ceremonies. They were also an essential element in fighting wars. In the absence of motor vehicles, still in their infancy, cavalry offered speed of movement. Their roles included reconnaissance, direct frontal charges to overrun enemy infantry (foot soldiers) and capture guns, the pursuit of retreating troops, and rapid advance through undefended territory.

Army commanders were well aware of the problems that cavalry faced when confronted with modern firepower – a man on a horse was a large target and could not easily exploit cover – but cavalry had adapted to the firepower revolution of the period, equipping their formations with machine-guns and field artillery.

There were undeniably archaic aspects to European cavalry. Most uniforms were designed for show rather than camouflage – German and Austrian Uhlans, for example, wore unusually tall headgear, while French cuirassiers donned shiny breastplates and plumed helmets. Many regiments carried lances decorated with brightly coloured pennons. In contrast, the British, with recent experience of fighting in the Boer War, wore khaki.

Armies differed in the extent to which their cavalry were trained to fight dismounted with their carbines or rifles. The need for this was widely acknowledged, but the tradition of the charge, with drawn sword, still held its grip on the military imagination.

World War I was in many ways a disappointment for cavalry. Even in the mobile campaigns of 1914, aircraft proved superior at reconnaissance. On the Eastern Front, the Russians,

Cossack cavalry
A column of Russian Cossack horsemen rides towards battle in their traditional fur hats. Feared for their raiding tactics, they also knew how to form a dismounted firing line when defence was needed.

> "In order to **shorten the war...** we must **make use** of the mobility of the **cavalry.**"

GENERAL DOUGLAS HAIG, JUNE 1916

deploying some 30 cavalry divisions, sent masses of horsemen charging across Galicia. On the Western Front, German cavalry swept across northern France during the "Race to the Sea". But problems quickly grew. Cavalry strained supply systems, because of the horses' need for fodder. Losses were heavy from the start. Mostly obliged to dismount to fight, cavalrymen often proved second-rate infantry, their carbines less accurate than rifles and their shooting inferior.

Cavalry and the trenches

In the trench warfare of the Western Front from 1915, there were no spaces in which cavalry could operate. The British, in particular, continued to believe that by charging through a gap

in the German trench lines opened up by infantry and artillery, their cavalry could turn a defeat into a rout, but it did not work. Advancing on horseback under machine-gun and artillery fire, across terrain made treacherous by mud, shell holes, trenches, and barbed wire, was simply too difficult.

In all European armies, the ratio of cavalry to infantry declined sharply in the course of the war, and many cavalrymen ended up serving their turn in the trenches as infantry.

However, cavalry did have something to offer in World War I. Even on the Western Front, cavalry occasionally carried out successful charges against entrenched infantry and machine-gun posts. Away from the main European theatres, especially in Russian operations in the Caucasus and British campaigns in Palestine, well-handled cavalry forces were frequently decisive.

General Edmund Allenby, commanding on the Palestine front from 1917, had an army with more than 20 per cent cavalry. The Desert Mounted Corps, including Light Horse regiments from India, Australia, and New Zealand, and the Territorials of the British Yeomanry, carried out sweeping manoeuvres and successful cavalry charges against entrenched Turkish infantry and artillery.

Last charge

By 1918, in the crucial European theatres of operations, cavalry was no longer a potentially decisive arm. The Russian Civil War, from 1918–21, was the last major conflict in which cavalry played a prominent role. The growth of motorized forces in the 1920s and '30s finally spelled the end of the long tradition of the mounted warrior in Europe.

Horse gas mask

Gas masks were designed for horses as well as for their riders. The mask protected the animals against poison gasses such as chlorine and phosgene.

TIMELINE

- **August 1914** All European armies start the war with large bodies of cavalry, constituting between 10 and 30 per cent of their total forces. The advance of Russian Cossacks into East Prussia and Galicia provokes panic among the populations of Germany and Austria.

- **August–September 1914** French and British cavalry fight fierce rearguard actions against the Germans during the Great Retreat.

GERMAN UHLAN HAT

- **September 1914** Six German cavalry divisions take the offensive around Lille in northern France, probably the largest body of horsemen ever to fight in Western Europe.

- **October 1914** Dismounted to form a firing line, the British Cavalry Corps fights a famous action to defend Messines Ridge during the First Battle of Ypres.

- **1915** Large numbers of cavalrymen, especially on the Western Front, are made to serve as infantry in trench warfare.

- **March–May 1915** South African cavalry carry out a successful campaign to occupy German Southwest Africa (now Namibia).

- **January–April 1916** On the Caucasus front, Russian General Nikolai Yudenich captures Erzurum and Trebizond (now Trabzon) from Turkey, making bold use of massed cavalry.

- **July 1916** Ordered to attack German positions at High Wood during the Battle of the Somme, an Indian cavalry division fails to exploit a brief opportunity for a breakthrough.

- **April 1917** At Monchy-le-Preux, during the Battle of Arras on the Western Front, British cavalry suffer heavy losses attempting to exploit a gap in the German line created by the advance of tanks and infantry.

- **October 1917** At Beersheba in Palestine, Australian cavalry execute a successful charge against Turkish defensive lines that contributes decisively to a British victory.

- **November 1917** At the Battle of Cambrai on the Western Front, a Canadian cavalry brigade advances 13 km (8 miles) and captures 100 German machine-guns in one of the most ambitious of failed breakthrough attempts.

- **October 1918** Australian Light Horse Regiment, serving with the British Desert Mounted Corps, occupies Damascus in Syria towards the end of the campaign against Ottoman Turkey.

- **1918–21** All armies engaged in the Russian Civil War and the Russo-Polish War make extensive use of cavalry. The Battle of Komarow, fought between Polish and Soviet horsemen, in August 1920, is often considered the last significant cavalry battle.

BEFORE

For over a century before World War I, the Turkish-ruled Ottoman Empire was in decline. Attempts at reform failed to restore its military strength.

DIMINISHING EMPIRE
Ottoman military weakness was revealed by the **Italo-Turkish War of 1911–12**, which enabled Italy to seize Libya, and the Balkan Wars of 1912–13, which deprived Turkey of almost all its remaining territory in Europe. The Ottoman Empire **lost a third of its area ‹‹ 18–19** in the years leading up to World War I.

THE YOUNG TURKS
A revolt by **"Young Turk" military officers** deposed Ottoman Sultan Abdulhamid II in 1909 and **replaced him with Mehmed V**. Attempts at constitutional government were undermined by the strains of defeat in war. By 1914, the government was dominated by Interior Minister **Talaat Pasha** and War Minister **Enver Pasha**.

Turkey Enters the War

The decision of Ottoman Turkey to go to war as an ally of the Central Powers was a crucial moment in modern history. It not only shaped the course of World War I but also profoundly influenced the future of the entire region, including Iraq, Syria, Palestine, and Egypt.

Desperate to restore Turkey's status as a military power, Turkish governments before World War I sought foreign expertise and investment, without tying themselves to the European alliance system. The Turkish army established close links with Germany, which sent a military mission under General Liman von Sanders to modernize Turkish land forces. The Turkish navy, on the other hand, traditionally looked to Britain for ships and advisers.

As the war crisis erupted in Europe in July–August 1914, pro-German figures in the Turkish government signed a secret treaty with Germany aimed specifically against Russia, the historic enemy of the Ottoman Empire. Meanwhile, the Turkish people were eagerly awaiting delivery of two dreadnoughts, *Reshadieh* and *Sultan Osman I*, paid for by public subscription and being built at shipyards in Britain. Possession of such warships was the mark of great power status.

At the start of August, the British Admiralty, facing war with Germany, seized the dreadnoughts for the Royal Navy. In response, a wave of anti-British feeling swept through Turkey.

On 10 August, the German warships *Goeben* and *Breslau* sailed through the Dardanelles and were handed to the Turks. With this action, Turkish commitment to Germany was sealed.

Enver Pasha
Turkey's war minister, Enver Pasha, played a leading role in bringing Turkey into World War I on the side of Germany. Also commander of the Ottoman forces, Enver was virtually a military dictator during the war.

British naval advisers were asked to leave, and German Rear Admiral Wilhelm Souchon took command of Turkish naval operations.

Shelling Russian ports
On 29 October, sailing aboard *Goeben*, renamed *Yavuz Sultan Selim*, Souchon took his fleet and bombarded Russian Black Sea ports, including Odessa and Sebastopol. Russia responded by declaring war on Turkey, followed in the first week of November by France and Britain.

The Ottoman Sultan, Mehmed V, was also the caliph – the head of the worldwide

Turkish troops on the march
Although Turkish forces fought with determination, they were often let down by the misjudgements of their senior commanders. At the Battle of Sarikamish, only 18,000 out of an intial force of 95,000 survived.

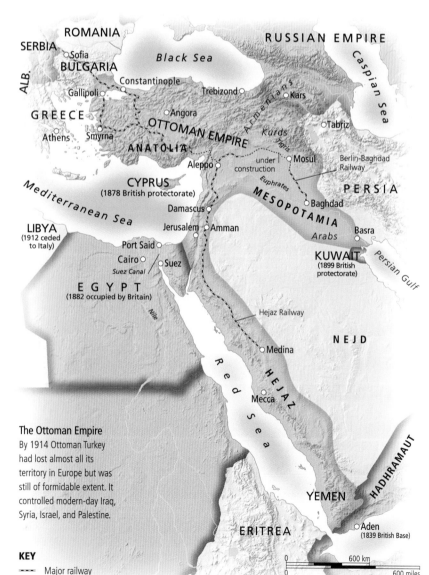

The Ottoman Empire
By 1914 Ottoman Turkey had lost almost all its territory in Europe but was still of formidable extent. It controlled modern-day Iraq, Syria, Israel, and Palestine.

KEY
- - - Major railway

community of Islam. On 11 November, he declared a jihad (holy war), calling on Muslims in the British, French, and Russian empires to rise in revolt. This raised German hopes of the collapse of British India, but its effect was muted.

Arab unrest

In Arab lands under Turkish rule, the appeal to Islamic solidarity was overtaken by Arab nationalism. Britain moved swiftly to protect its imperial interests. Khedive Abbas Hilmi II was nominally the ruler of Egypt, itself still part of the Ottoman Empire. From the safety of his residence in Turkey, he called on Egyptians to join the jihad against British occupation of their country. Britain responded by declaring Egypt a British protectorate and deposed Abbas Hilmi in favour of his uncle, Hussein Kamil.

Britain also formally annexed Cyprus, a protectorate since 1878. In the Gulf, Britain's priority was to defend oilfields in southern Persia (Iran), bordering on Ottoman Mesopotamia (Iraq).

MESOPOTAMIA An area between the Tigris and Euphrates rivers, mainly comprising modern-day Iraq.

To pre-empt a Turkish attack, British Indian troops occupied the port of Basra in late November.

For Russia, war with Turkey opened up the possibility of controlling Constantinople (Istanbul) and gaining access to the Mediterranean from the Black Sea. For Young Turks such as War Minister Enver Pasha, war was a chance to liberate the Muslims of the Caucasus, conquered by Russia in the 19th century.

PURSUIT OF THE *GOEBEN* AND *BRESLAU*

At the start of August 1914, Germany had two warships in the Mediterranean, the battlecruiser *Goeben* and the light cruiser *Breslau*, commanded by Rear Admiral Wilhelm Souchon. Outclassed by Allied naval forces, Souchon decided to steam to neutral Constantinople. The German force was briefly engaged by the British cruiser *Gloucester*, but then, through misunderstandings, was allowed to sail unmolested to the Dardenelles. The Royal Navy's blunder caused a scandal in Britain.

Enver went in person to the Caucasian front in December, planning a bold offensive. Poorly supplied Turkish forces advanced through mountain terrain in bitterly cold weather, some dying of frostbite. When the Russians counterattacked at Sarikamish, near Kars, the Turks were routed.

Attack on Egypt

This inauspicious start for Turkish forces was mirrored far to the south, where they mounted an attack on Egypt that had been planned in Berlin. Supplied by the Germans with pontoon bridges, an Ottoman army crossed the Sinai desert to the Suez Canal in February 1915. The army's approach was detected by French aircraft and repulsed by British resistance at the canal. The expectation of an Egyptian uprising against British rule failed to materialize. Instead, the Ottoman Empire faced the beginnings of an Arab revolt against Turkish rule in Syria and the Hejaz (Saudi Arabia).

> " Of those who go to **jihad...** the rank of those who depart to the next world is **martyr.** "
>
> SHEIKH AL-ISLAM, RELIGIOUS LEADER OF TURKEY, 14 NOVEMBER 1914

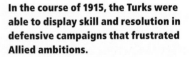

In the course of 1915, the Turks were able to display skill and resolution in defensive campaigns that frustrated Allied ambitions.

TRIUMPHS AND REPRISALS

In early 1915, Turkish plans for offensive action were in tatters. However, the Allied attempt to break through the Dardanelles and the subsequent landings at **Gallipoli were defeated 110–13 ≫**. Later that year, the British extended their **invasion of Mesopotamia** (Iraq) and were **defeated by Turkish forces at Kut 122–23 ≫**. Meanwhile, the Turks, believing Armenian nationalists to be supporting Russia, embarked upon the deportation and massacre of Turkey's **Armenians 116–17 ≫**.

BEFORE ❮❮

In 1914, all of Africa except Ethiopia and Liberia was directly or indirectly ruled by Europeans. The colonial powers were Britain, Spain, France, Italy, Portugal, Belgium, and Germany.

THE SCRAMBLE FOR AFRICA

Germany acquired its African colonies in the 1880s. These were **German East Africa** (now Tanzania, Burundi, and Rwanda), **German South West Africa** (now Namibia), and Kamerun and Togoland in West Africa (parts of modern-day Cameroon and Togo). In the Union of South Africa, the **Afrikaners**, descended from Dutch and German settlers, were defeated by Britain in the **Second Boer War of 1899–1902**.

BOER MAUSER PISTOL

African Diversions

Military campaigns in Africa were particularly arduous because of disease and difficult terrain with few roads or railways. Cut off from Europe by British naval power, German colonial forces were forced on to the defensive.

Given the scale of the war in Europe, the fate of the combatant powers' overseas colonies was a low priority. It was, however, of major importance for the British. By taking control of the coasts of Germany's African colonies, Britain would deny coaling and radio stations to German warships, thus countering threats posed by the German navy to maritime trade.

In August 1914, an invasion of German Togoland from the British Gold Coast (now Ghana) seized a vital radio station. In September, British and South African naval forces attacked the coast of German South West Africa, occupying the port of Lüderitz and destroying the radio

transmitter at Swakopmund. In the same month, Douala, the principal port and radio station in Kamerun, fell.

British setbacks

An attack on German East Africa did not run so smoothly. A German light cruiser, the SMS *Königsberg*, had been operating off the East African coast since the start of the war. Seeing this as a threat, Britain decided to mount an invasion of East Africa by troops from India. On 2 November, an 8,000-strong Anglo-Indian expeditionary force landed near the East African port of Tanga.

> **ASKARI** The standard term used for black African troops serving in colonial armies in East and Central Africa.

The defence of the German colony was in the hands of Lieutenant Colonel Paul von Lettow-Vorbeck, with about 1,000 Schutztruppe (colonial soldiers) under his command. The Indian expeditionary force was low on morale and short of training and leadership. Its slow approach gave Lettow-Vorbeck sufficient warning to move his troops to Tanga by train.

A confused battle ensued on 4 November, and the shaken Anglo-Indian troops fled back to their ships, leaving most of their equipment behind.

Lettow-Vorbeck pursued a prolonged defensive campaign designed to absorb maximum British resources.

East African soldiers
Locally recruited troops in British-ruled East Africa, named the King's African Rifles, fought in the protracted campaigns against German colonial forces led by Lettow-Vorbeck.

German slouch hat
A grey felt slouch hat with blue trim was the regulation headwear of officers in the Schutztruppe, the German colonial armed forces. The officers of German colonial armies were always white.

While the British were organizing their response to this humiliation on land, the *Königsberg* was pursued by Royal Navy warships into the mangrove swamps of the Rufiji delta.

Although it could not escape the Royal Navy's blockade, the *Königsberg* held out until July 1915. Even after the cruiser was bombarded by British river monitors (flat-bottomed gunboats) and had to be abandoned, its sailors continued to fight, joining Lettow-Vorbeck's army and bringing their ship's heavy naval guns with them.

The Maritz Rebellion
Britain had a potentially valuable source of troops in South Africa. Although the dominion's prime minister, Louis Botha, was an Afrikaner who had fought the British in the Second Boer War, he wholeheartedly supported the war against Germany. But not all Afrikaners were of the same mind. Making contact from neighbouring German South West Africa, the Germans encouraged discontent among the Afrikaners to flare into open revolt. In early October, Solomon Maritz, a colonel in the South African Defence Force, and Boer War hero Christiaan de Wet declared a rebellion. They sought to make South Africa an independent republic.

But Botha and his defence minister, Jan Smuts, handled the situation with skill. Using loyal troops, they mounted

a series of operations that defeated the rebel forces by January 1915. The rebels were on the whole treated leniently, with widespread amnesties. Opponents of the government returned to political channels of dissent, and South African troops became available for British operations.

The fall of Windhoek
The South Africans' first task was the conquest of German South West Africa. After the initial British attacks on the colony's ports, the Germans had withdrawn to the interior. From February to July 1915, Botha and Smuts, commanding South African mounted troops, penetrated South West Africa from the coast, the Namib Desert or from South Africa. In the

process, they uncovered evidence of German massacres of the Herero and Hottentot populations carried out in the decade before the war. They took the capital, Windhoek, in May and the Germans surrendered the colony seven weeks later.

South African forces were then transferred to East Africa, where they spearheaded the campaign to hunt down Lettow-Vorbeck, who was still at large. The South African mounted columns proved far less effective in East Africa, however. The tsetse fly took an enormous toll on their horses, while malaria debilitated the troops.

> ## "Swamps and jungles… what a dismal prospect there is in front of me."
> JAN SMUTS, SOUTH AFRICAN GENERAL, COMMANDING IN EAST AFRICA, 1916

War in Africa 1914–1916
The German colonies in Africa were scattered and of less strategic and economic value than British, French, and Belgian colonies. Defending them depended more on exploiting difficult terrain than on military force.

KEY
- British Empire
- French possessions
- German possessions
- Belgian possessions
- Italian possessions
- Portuguese possessions
- Ottoman Empire
- ✸ Area of conflict

1 6–8 Aug 1914
French and British forces invade. Germans capitulate on 26 Aug

3 Sept 1914
Allies capture Douala, the capital. A lenghty campaign follows. Allies' converging offensives lead to eventual German surrender, 18 Feb 1916

2 Sept 1914
German forces withdraw to capital, Windhoek. South African forces capture Windhoek 20 May 1915, and Germans surrender 9 July

4 1914–18
A protracted campaign. German forces extend campaign to Portuguese East Africa

Confrontation at Sea

In 1914, there had been no major naval conflict between European powers for a century. When war began, the public in Germany and Britain expected a great battle between the rival fleets, but naval commanders took a more cautious approach.

At the start of the war, the British and French navies successfully fulfilled their first essential task – to protect the transport of troops to the European battlefield across the English Channel from Britain and across the Mediterranean from North Africa. The Allies also set about clearing the oceans of German and Austro-Hungarian merchant shipping and roaming warships. Meanwhile, the British Grand Fleet and the German High Seas Fleet faced one another across the North Sea.

29 The number of submarines in the German U-boat fleet at the start of the war; they sank five British cruisers in the first 10 weeks.

Naval strategies
Admiral John Jellicoe, commander of the Grand Fleet, was intensely conscious that his warships were Britain's only defence against a possible German invasion and must at all costs be preserved.

The High Seas Fleet, commanded at the start of the war by Admiral Friedrich von Ingenohl, was too inferior in size to challenge the British to a battle. Ingenohl's strategy was to wear down the Royal Navy in piecemeal engagements until British naval forces were sufficiently weakened to be defeated in a culminating battle.

The British offered the German navy a suitable opportunity in late August 1914. Commanders at the British naval base at the North Sea port of Harwich planned an operation off the German coast at Heligoland. British submarines were deployed as bait to lure German patrol boats under the guns of a force of destroyers and light cruisers, but once German cruisers arrived on the scene the Royal Navy ships took a battering. They were saved by a squadron of British battlecruisers, commanded by Vice Admiral David Beatty, which emerged from the mist to outgun all the other vessels. Three German light cruisers were sunk in the confrontation.

Contact mine
Attached to the seabed by a chain, contact mines detonated when a ship struck one of their spikes. German mines sank a greater tonnage of British warships than any other weapon.

The Royal Navy could claim a clear victory. Yet the British were beginning to sustain worrying losses to mines and submarines. On 22 September, a single German submarine, the *U-9*, sank three British cruisers patrolling off the Dutch coast, killing almost 1,500 sailors.

Even worse for Jellicoe, in October the super-dreadnought HMS *Audacious*, one of Britain's most powerful warships, was sunk by a

4 m (160 in) gun

Battle of Heligoland Bight
British sailors watch as fire rages on board the stricken German light cruiser *Mainz* on 28 August 1914. Fought in German home waters, the battle was a clear-cut victory for Britain's Royal Navy.

TECHNOLOGY

DESTROYERS

The workhorses of every navy, destroyers were built in large numbers in 1914–18. Small, fast, and versatile, they fulfilled a wide range of functions from coastal defence to minelaying and anti-submarine warfare. No battleships or battlecruisers would go to sea without destroyers to defend them against submarine attacks. Later in the war, they defended merchant convoys.

Destroyers' guns were too light to exchange salvoes with the heaviest vessels in an enemy's fleet, but destroyers were often highly effective in other ways, such as attacking with torpedoes. Destroyer commanders earned a reputation for acting with bold aggression and independence.

contact mine off the coast of Ireland. It was clear that the Royal Navy was not equipped to deal with minesweeping or anti-submarine warfare.

British blockades

The threat posed to his most important warships by mines and submarines forced Jellicoe to curtail operations in the North Sea. He could still impose a naval blockade on Germany from a distance by controlling the entrance to the English Channel and the passage between Scotland and Norway. These distant blockades, however, allowed the German fleet to attempt surprise sorties into the North Sea.

On 16 December, a German battlecruiser squadron under Rear Admiral Franz von Hipper bombarded the English east coast towns of Scarborough, Whitby, and Hartlepool. British naval intelligence had given warning of the sortie but the Grand Fleet failed to intercept Hipper's raiders. The bombardment caused more than 700 casualties, including 137 people killed, mostly civilians. In Britain, it aroused public indignation against German brutality, but also outrage at the failure of the Royal Navy to defend the country.

By the end of 1914, it was clear that naval enthusiasts, especially British ones, were not going to have the war they had expected.

Rapid advances in technology transformed naval warfare at the end of 1914.

NEW DEVELOPMENTS

The German navy deployed **airships for reconnaissance** and the Royal Navy used **float aircraft**, winched over the side of a ship to take off from the sea. The first raid by seaplanes on a shore target was the Royal Naval Air Service's attack on airship sheds at the **German port of Cuxhaven** on Christmas Day 1914. Meanwhile, another sortie by German battlecruisers led to the **Battle of Dogger Bank 124–25 >>** in early 1915.

U-BOAT ATTACKS

In February 1915, Germany initiated its first phase of **unrestricted submarine warfare**, leading to the **sinking of the cruise liner *Lusitania* 126–27 >>** in the following May, **antagonizing the USA**.

SHALL THIS CONTINUE?

JOIN THE NAVY

NAVY LEAGUE PITTSBURGH

ANCHOR BANK BUILDING

AMERICAN NAVY RECRUITMENT POSTER, 1917

Recoil cylinder   Sighting telescope   Gunshield   Elevation and tracking mechanism

Shell loading tray

Pedestal gun platform

British quick-firing naval gun
The 100 mm Mark IV, introduced in 1911, armed most Royal Navy destroyers in World War I. On 5 November 1914, this Mark IV gun mounted on HMS *Lance* fired Britain's first shot in the war, aimed at a German minelayer.

Queen of the Royal Navy
The HMS *Queen Elizabeth* was one of Britain's first super-dreadnoughts. Entering service in 1915, it was fuelled by oil instead of coal and armed with eight 381 mm (15 in) guns, which could hit an enemy ship at a range of 25 km (16 miles).

Coronel and the Falklands

In the early months of the war, the Allies faced a potential threat to seaborne trade from enemy cruisers. It was defused, but only after serious setbacks and through the deployment of large-scale naval forces to track down and destroy German warships.

Almost half the world's merchant shipping was owned by Britain and its dominions. Britain depended on seaborne imports for 60 per cent of its food, as well as essential strategic goods such as rubber and oil. Worldwide sea lanes were potentially hard to defend, and attacks on them by German warships posed a serious threat to Britain's ability to wage war. The only significant force of German warships at large on the world's oceans was the East Asiatic Cruiser Squadron, commanded by Admiral Graf Maximilian von Spee. The squadron consisted of the powerful armoured cruisers SMS *Scharnhorst* and *Gneisenau* and the light cruisers SMS *Emden*, *Leipzig*, and *Nürnberg*. Its base was at Tsingtao in China, but when war broke out the cruisers were scattered across the Pacific. Assembling his ships in the German-ruled Mariana Islands, Spee decided to head east towards South America, away from the Japanese navy, Britain's ally. The *Emden*, commanded by Captain Karl von Müller, was sent to the Indian Ocean.

The unexpected appearance of the *Emden* in an ocean rich in Allied merchant shipping caused mayhem. Operating with scrupulous respect for the rules of war, Müller stopped and sank 16 British merchant

Australian cap
This cap was worn by stoker John Robb of the Royal Australian Navy. Robb was one of the crew of the HMAS *Sydney* when it captured the German cruiser *Emden* at the Cocos Islands on 9 November 1914.

◀◀ BEFORE

Britain was well aware that its dominant position in world commerce and its heavy dependence on imports made its merchant ships a target for Germany.

ROYAL NAVY BLOCKADES
The **German navy** faced problems in mounting a commerce-raiding campaign. The Royal Navy established a **blockade of the English Channel and North Sea ◀◀ 78–79** from the first day of the war. German ships at loose elsewhere had difficulty obtaining coal, which was readily available to Britain and France through their empires.

GERMAN THREATS
Britain had already been **threatened by two German light cruisers**. In the Indian Ocean, the SMS *Königsberg* had been troublesome until trapped by the Royal Navy in the East African Rufiji delta in late October 1914 **◀◀ 76–77**. In the Caribbean, the SMS *Karlsruhe* had **sunk 16 merchant ships**. German hopes for the *Karlsruhe* were dashed, however, when it suffered a catastrophic internal explosion off Barbados on 4 November.

Gun damage
Emden's bell shows the effects of the bombardment from *Sydney*'s guns. *Emden*'s captain beached the ship to avoid sinking, but its sailors suffered almost 200 casualties.

> " Enemy **cruisers** cannot **live** in the ocean for any length of time. "
>
> WINSTON CHURCHILL, FIRST LORD OF THE ADMIRALTY, 1914

ships and a dozen vessels from other nations, each time allowing the crew and passengers to disembark and ensuring their safety.

Müller also carried out a number of daring raids against significant Allied shore targets, such as destroying oil-storage facilities at Madras in India and sinking a Russian light cruiser and a French destroyer in an attack on the port of Penang in British Malaya (now Malaysia).

With 60 Allied warships scouring the ocean, the raider's career could not continue indefinitely. On 9 November 1914, the Australian light cruiser HMAS *Sydney*, commanded by Captain John Glossop, encountered *Emden* at

100,000 The approximate tonnage of shipping sunk by the German raider *Emden* in the Indian Ocean.

Direction Island in the Cocos Islands. *Sydney*'s 152 mm guns outranged *Emden*'s lighter armament and Müller was battered into submission.

By the time Müller surrendered, 130 of his crew had been killed and many others injured. This was a famous first victory for the recently established Royal Australian Navy.

The impact of *Emden*'s solo operation suggests Spee's other cruisers might have caused havoc had they dispersed. Instead, Spee kept them together, a decision that seemed justified when he encountered the British at Coronel, off the coast of Chile.

Catastrophe off Chile
The Battle of Coronel, on 1 November, was a disaster for the Royal Navy. Rear Admiral Sir Christopher Cradock had been ordered to sail from the South Atlantic into the Pacific to search for the German cruisers, although none of his squadron of four ships was a match for the *Scharnhorst* or *Gneisenau*. The German cruiser squadron had been augmented by the light cruiser *Dresden*, until then in the Caribbean. Despite facing superior forces, Cradock felt it his duty to attack. The Germans sank the armoured cruisers *Good Hope* and *Monmouth* with relentless accuracy. The crews, who were mostly reservists or young boys, went down with their ships, as did Admiral Cradock. The other two British vessels escaped, although the light cruiser *Glasgow* was badly damaged.

"All round... were **floating bodies...** terribly mangled."
A.D. DUCKWORTH, ASSISTANT PAYMASTER, HMS "INVINCIBLE"

Desperate for vengeance, the British Admiralty responded by sending the battlecruisers HMS *Invincible* and *Inflexible*, commanded by Vice Admiral Frederick Sturdee, to join the hunt for Spee. Gathering up the five cruisers of the South Atlantic Squadron along the way, Sturdee steamed to Port Stanley

Victor of the Falklands
Sir Frederick Sturdee commanded the British ships that won the Battle of the Falklands against Spee's cruisers in December 1914. Sturdee's ships had much greater firepower.

in the Falkland Islands, where he stopped to take on coal. Meanwhile, Spee had rounded Cape Horn into the South Atlantic. He headed for the Falklands, intending to raid its wireless station and coal stocks.

The Battle of the Falklands
On 8 December, Spee's leading ships approached Port Stanley and, to their surprise, were fired upon. Realizing the harbour was full of unidentified warships, Spee fled out to sea.

The encounter was as much a surprise to the British as the Germans, but once Sturdee reached the sea the outcome was never in doubt. The British battlecruisers were faster than the German ships and had superior guns and armour. The *Scharnhorst* and *Gneisenau* fought a gallant delaying action, attempting to cover the escape of the light cruisers, but both were sunk. The *Scharnhorst* went down with all hands, including Spee. Some 200 crew were rescued from the *Gneisenau*. Only one German ship, the *Dresden*, escaped the British pursuit.

The Battle of the Falklands was a powerful assertion of the Royal Navy's dominance, and ended any serious threat to Allied merchant shipping from German surface vessels for the duration of the war.

German warships take flight
Admiral Graf von Spee's cruiser squadron flees from British pursuit in the South Atlantic during the Battle of the Falklands. More than 1,800 German sailors lost their lives in the battle, in which two armoured cruisers and two light cruisers were sunk.

AFTER »

In the course of 1915, scattered German surface raiders were put out of action, while submarines took over the role of attacking merchant shipping.

GERMAN CHANGE OF TACTICS
The light cruiser *Dresden*, which had escaped destruction at the Battle of the Falklands, remained at sea until March 1915, when it was **captured by British ships** at an island off the Chilean coast. In April 1915, the SS *Kronprinz Wilhelm*, an ocean liner converted into an auxiliary cruiser at the outbreak of war, **sought refuge** in the neutral USA after running short of coal and other supplies. Meanwhile, **German submarines** around the British Isles and in the Mediterranean proved more effective than surface raiders in **threatening seaborne trade**.

COAL, THE MAIN FUEL FOR SHIPS

« BEFORE

Before World War I, China and the Pacific were areas in which the imperialist ambitions of the European powers, the USA, and Japan clashed.

DESIGNS ON CHINA
From the mid-19th century, the Chinese state was riven by political factionalism. Taking advantage of this, the foreign powers obtained **"concessions" in China** – territory over which they exercised effective control. This process was accelerated by joint foreign military intervention in China in 1900, in response to the **Boxer Rebellion** against Western imperialism. A **revolution** in 1911 led to the end of Qing imperial rule and the founding of a highly unstable republic.

JAPANESE AMBITIONS
Japan had emerged as an aggressive regional power from the late 19th century. Its military **victories over China** in 1894–95 and Russia in 1904–05 whetted its ambitions to become a world power. In 1902, **Japan signed an alliance with Britain**, based at the time on mutual hostility towards Russia.

War in the East

The European states that went to war in 1914 were imperialist powers with global interests, and their conflict had worldwide impact. Military operations spread to China and islands in the Pacific as outposts of the German Empire were overrun.

British concerns about German naval power were the factor that first brought East Asia into the war. The German navy's East Asiatic Squadron was based at Tsingtao (now Qingdao) on China's Shantung peninsula, a German-ruled concession. Worried about the threat this posed to its merchant shipping, Britain looked to its Japanese ally for support.

Japan was an expansionist power engaged in long-term empire-building and only too ready for a chance to extend its influence in China and the Pacific. By the time Japan declared war on Germany on 23 August, it was already planning a seaborne expedition to capture Tsingtao. Britain assembled a token force of 1,500 soldiers from its concession at Tientsin (now Tianjin) to join the Japanese force. However, the German East Asiatic Squadron had decided not to defend Tsingtao and embarked on a far-flung naval campaign in the South Atlantic.

The Japanese first landed at Lungkow Bay, 130 km (80 miles) north of Tsingtao, where they set up a supply base. Their main landing followed at Laoshan Bay, 25 km (18 miles) east of

> "It would **shame** me more **to surrender Tsingtao to the Japanese** than Berlin to the Russians."
>
> KAISER WILHELM II, SEPTEMBER 1914

Japanese soldiers at Tsingtao, China
The crew of a Japanese siege howitzer waits for instructions during the attack on German-controlled Tsingtao in November 1914. Tsingtao held out for only a week after the big guns started firing.

the port, on 18 September. These landings on Chinese territory violated Chinese neutrality, but foreign powers were too accustomed to trampling over China for this to worry them.

Tsingtao falls to the Allies

While Japanese warships blockaded Tsingtao, land forces made slow progress in adverse weather. It was 31 October before the port was fully under siege. The German defence of Tsingtao was led by its governor, Alfred Meyer-Waldeck. He had only 4,000 soldiers and marines at his disposal but had some powerful guns, originally intended to repel an attack by sea.

The Japanese bombarded the city for a week and then mounted an infantry assault that penetrated the German defences. On 7 November, short of ammunition, Meyer-Waldeck asked for a ceasefire so that surrender terms could be negotiated. The Germans had lost about 500 men, compared with some 240 Japanese dead and a dozen British. The Germans who surrendered were held as prisoners in Japan until 1920.

German New Guinea
Local troops trained by a few German reservists were the only forces available to defend Kaiser Wilhelmsland. They were unable to mount any real resistance to an Australian occupation force.

Japan's objective was not so much to contribute to the defeat of Germany as to develop its interests in China. In January 1915, Japan presented the Chinese government with the 21 Demands, chiefly designed to extend its influence in Manchuria and Inner Mongolia. The Japanese also intended to keep hold of Tsingtao.

Carving up the Pacific

Japan was now able to seize German possessions in the Pacific. In the absence of the German East Asia Squadron, which had left for the South Atlantic, the Mariana, Marshall, and Caroline islands were easily occupied.

For the governments of Australia and New Zealand, Japanese expansion across the Pacific was highly unwelcome. These British dominions feared Japan and harboured their own colonial ambitions. Despite agreeing to send troops to aid Britain's war effort, they found the resources to seize

96,000 The number of Chinese labourers working for the Allies in France at the end of the war.

defenceless German possessions south of the equator, with New Zealand taking Samoa at the end of August.

The following month, an Australian occupation of Kaiser Wilhelmsland (now part of Papua New Guinea) led to the surrender of the Bismarck Archipelago and the Solomon Islands. Phosphate-rich Nauru was seized by the Australians in mid-November.

Eastern agendas

By the end of 1914, the war in East Asia and the Pacific was over. China and Japan, however, sought advantage from further participation in the European conflict. The Chinese hoped cooperation with the Allies might end reparation payments imposed after the anti-imperialist Boxer Rebellion and lead to the return of Tsingtao.

From 1916, Chinese workers were recruited by Britain and France on a large scale and sent to Europe.

Although not combatants, about 2,000 died labouring on the Western Front, the victims of enemy action, accidents, or disease. The Chinese eventually declared war on Germany in August 1917 – a politically controversial overseas commitment unprecedented in Chinese history. Although China had nothing militarily to offer the Allies, Japan was able to send destroyers to help the Allied navies fight U-boats in the Mediterranean.

AFTER

World War I had a profound impact on East Asia, despite the region's limited involvement in the fighting.

POSTWAR REPERCUSSIONS
At the **Paris Peace Conference 334–35 »** after the war, it was revealed that the Allies had promised the Japanese Tsingtao in return for naval aid in the Mediterranean. The news triggered **mass protests in China** beginning on 4 May 1919. The **May Fourth Movement** became a radical new departure in Chinese politics, leading to the growth of the Chinese Communist Party.

THWARTED JAPAN
Japan was also discontented with the result of the war. Although Japan kept the Pacific islands it had gained, it was forced to **hand back Tsingtao to China** in 1922. Also, Japan's proposal to make **racial equality** a founding principle of the **League of Nations** was rejected by its white allies.

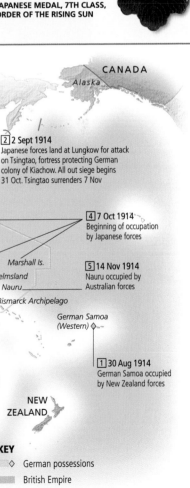

JAPANESE MEDAL, 7TH CLASS, ORDER OF THE RISING SUN

War in the Pacific

In August 1914, Germany's possessions in the Pacific consisted of a naval base at Tsingtao, part of New Guinea, and a scattering of islands. These quickly fell to superior Allied forces after Japan entered the war.

2 **2 Sept 1914**
Japanese forces land at Lungkow for attack on Tsingtao, fortress protecting German colony of Kiachow. All out siege begins 31 Oct. Tsingtao surrenders 7 Nov

4 **7 Oct 1914**
Beginning of occupation by Japanese forces

5 **14 Nov 1914**
Nauru occupied by Australian forces

3 **11 Sept 1914**
Occupation of Kaiser Wilhelmsland by Australian forces begins. German capitulation 17 Sept

1 **30 Aug 1914**
German Samoa occupied by New Zealand forces

RUSSIAN EMPIRE
CANADA
Alaska
MONGOLIA
CHINA
TIBET
JAPAN
Tsingtao
INDIA
PACIFIC OCEAN
Philippine Is. (U.S.)
Mariana Is.
SIAM
FRENCH INDOCHINA
Guam
Yap
Caroline Is. Kaiser Wilhelmsland
Marshall Is.
MALAYA
Nauru
INDIAN OCEAN
DUTCH EAST INDIES
Bismarck Archipelago
PAPUA
German Samoa (Western)
AUSTRALIA
NEW ZEALAND

KEY
◇ German possessions
British Empire
Russian Empire
Japan and possessions
◇ USA and possessions
French possessions
✸ Major siege

3

STALEMATE

1915

While the combatant states mobilized resources for a long conflict, the trench lines of the Western Front became a symbol of the military deadlock. New weapons such as airships, submarines, and poison gas added to the horror of war but did nothing to end it.

Chlorine gas is used by the Germans during the Second Battle of Ypres in April 1915. It is the first large-scale combat use of poison gas in the war, but chemical warfare is soon employed by both sides.

During the Battle of Dogger Bank in January, the British sink the German warship SMS *Blücher*, resulting in the loss of more than 700 men. The rest of the German fleet make it safely home.

Statues of an "iron warrior", as depicted in this propaganda poster, are erected in towns in Germany to raise funds for the war. People are allowed to drive nails into the statue in return for a donation.

Der eiserne Wehrmann

EUROPE

FAEROE ISLANDS
(Denmark)

NORWAY

SWEDEN

North
Sea

DENMARK

Baltic Sea

BRITAIN

NETH.

GERMANY

RUSSIAN
EMPIRE

BEL. LUX.

FRANCE

AUSTRIA-
HUNGARY

SWITZ.

ITALY

ROMANIA

SERBIA

MONT.

BULGARIA

Black Sea

ALB.

GREECE

OTTOMAN
EMPIRE

DODECANESE
(Italy)

CYPRUS
(Britain)

PORTUGAL

SPAIN

Mediterranean Sea

MOROCCO
(France)

ALGERIA
(France)

TUNISIA
(France)

LIBYA
(Italy)

EGYPT
(Britain)

NORWAY

SWEDEN

BRITAIN

ATLANTIC
OCEAN

GERMANY

FRANCE

AUSTRIA-
HUNGARY

ITALY

RUSSIAN EMPIRE

Black Sea

Caspian Sea

PORTUGAL

SPAIN

OTTOMAN
EMPIRE

PERSIA

AFGHANISTAN

SPANISH MOROCCO

TUNISIA

CYPRUS

MOROCCO

ALGERIA

LIBYA

EGYPT

KUWAIT

BAHRAIN
QATAR

TIB
(autono

NEPAL

RIO DE ORO

NEJD
(Saudi)

TRUCIAL
OMAN

INDI

HEJAZ

OMAN

FRENCH WEST AFRICA

ANGLO-
EGYPTIAN
SUDAN
(British mandate)

HADHRAMAUT

ADEN PROTECTORATE

GAMBIA

PORTUGUESE GUINEA

TOGO

FRENCH
EQUATORIAL
AFRICA

ERITREA

FRENCH SOMALILAND

SIERRA LEONE

NIGERIA

BRITISH
SOMALILAND

CEYL

LIBERIA

CAMEROON

ABYSSINIA

ITALIAN
SOMALILAND

GOLD
COAST

RIO MUNI
(Spain)

FRENCH
CONGO

BELGIAN
CONGO

BRITISH EAST
AFRICA

NORTHERN
RHODESIA

ANGOLA

GERMAN EAST
AFRICA

INDIAN

OCEAN

MADAGASCAR

GERMAN
SOUTHWEST
AFRICA

BECHUANA-
LAND

SOUTHERN
RHODESIA

PORTUGUESE
EAST
AFRICA

UNION OF
SOUTH AFRICA

Serbia is stabbed in the back by Bulgaria while defending itself against Germany and Austria-Hungary. This is a broadly accurate caricature of the situation in the Balkans in October 1915.

Armenian refugees flee from Turkey. The country's Armenian minority is subjected to attacks and forced deportation that result in deaths on a massive scale.

T he failure of either side to achieve a victory in 1914 left the combatants facing a long war. On the Western Front, in France and Belgium, armies were immobilized in trench lines. Offensives consistently failed in the face of overwhelming defensive firepower. On the Eastern Front, Germany and Austria-Hungary inflicted defeats on Russia in a war of large-scale manoeuvre, but the Russians sacrificed territory in strategic withdrawals and kept fighting.

Only Serbia was decisively beaten, attacked in overwhelming force by Germany, Austria-Hungary, and Bulgaria. The search for an alternative to the deadlock in the trenches led Britain to initiate an attack on Turkey at the Dardanelles. But when Allied troops, including Australians and New Zealanders, landed at Gallipoli they found themselves bogged down in trench warfare just as frustrating and destructive as that on the Western Front. The entry of Italy into the

John McCrae, a field surgeon with the Canadian Expeditionary Force, writes his well-known poem "In Flanders Fields", based on First Ypres in October 1914.

The transatlantic liner *Lusitania* sails from New York in May 1915. The ship is sunk by a German U-boat off Ireland, killing 1,198 people, including 128 American citizens, outraging US public opinion.

CANADA

UNITED STATES OF AMERICA

MEXICO

BRITISH HONDURAS

CUBA

DOMINICAN REPUBLIC

VIRGIN ISLANDS

LEEWARD ISLANDS

HAITI

GUATEMALA

EL SALVADOR

HONDURAS

NICARAGUA

COSTA RICA

CANAL ZONE

PANAMA

COLOMBIA

VENEZUELA

ECUADOR

PERU

WINDWARD ISLANDS

BARBADOS

TRINIDAD AND TOBAGO

BRITISH GUIANA

DUTCH GUIANA

FRENCH GUIANA

BRAZIL

BOLIVIA

PARAGUAY

CHILE

URUGUAY

ARGENTINA

FALKLAND ISLANDS

ATLANTIC OCEAN

PACIFIC OCEAN

Hawaiian Islands

Christmas Island

French Polynesia

CHINA

JAPANESE EMPIRE

FRENCH INDOCHINA

PHILIPPINE ISLANDS

BRITISH NORTH BORNEO

BRUNEI

SARAWAK

MALAYA

DUTCH EAST INDIES

PORTUGUESE TIMOR

Mariana Islands

GUAM

Marshall Islands

GERMAN PACIFIC TERRITORIES

Caroline Islands

Gilbert Islands

Nauru

Bismarck Archipelago

KAISER WILHELMSLAND

PAPUA

Solomon Islands

Ellice Islands

Cook Islands

German Samoa (Western)

New Hebrides

Fiji

Tonga

New Caledonia

AUSTRALIA

Muslim Indian soldiers are executed after a mutiny against the British in Singapore in February 1915. Most Indian troops serve loyally, ignoring calls from nationalists for a revolt against the imperial power.

THE WORLD IN DECEMBER 1915

- The Central Powers
- Central Powers conquests to Dec 1915
- Allied states
- Allied conquests to Dec 1915
- Neutral states
- — Frontiers Jul 1914

war on the Allied side opened a new front in which the same stalemate prevailed. The Germans hoped to achieve a decisive breakthrough by the use of poison gas, but this proved indecisive. The war expanded into the air and under the sea. German airships raided London and Paris, and German U-boats attacked Allied merchant shipping, the sinking of the liner *Lusitania* bringing sharp protests from the US government.

The combatant countries strove to mobilize their economies and industries for total war and achieved dramatic growth in output of munitions. But more cannon, shells, machine-guns, and bullets translated into higher death tolls at the front. The death toll among civilians also mounted, notably in the expulsion and massacre of Armenians in Turkey and the sufferings of the conquered Serbs in the final months of 1915.

TIMELINE 1915

Trench stalemate in the West ▪ **Liner _Lusitania_ sunk** ▪ Poison gas used ▪
Zeppelin bombings begin ▪ Italy and Bulgaria enter the war ▪ **Allied landings at Gallipoli** ▪ Russian retreat in Poland ▪ **Serbia defeated**

JANUARY

3 JANUARY
In Belgium, Cardinal Mercier is arrested for protesting against the German occupation.

8 JANUARY
On the Western Front, the French attack at Soissons but are repelled by a German counter-offensive.

14 JANUARY
South African forces occupy Swakopmund in German South West Africa.

18 JANUARY
In East Africa, Schutztruppe led by Colonel Lettow-Vorbeck defeat the British at Jassin.

19 JANUARY
The first Zeppelin raid is carried out against the British mainland.

24 JANUARY
British naval victory at the Battle of Dogger Bank, but the Germans escape serious loss.

31 JANUARY
Germans make experimental use of poison gas at Bolimov in Galicia.

FEBRUARY

3 FEBRUARY
British forces in Egypt defeat a Turkish attack on the Suez Canal.

4 FEBRUARY
Germany announces a submarine campaign against merchant shipping in British waters in response to British naval blockade.

7 FEBRUARY
Russian and German forces clash in the Second Battle of the Masurian Lakes, which continues until 21 February.

15 FEBRUARY
British Indian troops in Singapore stage a mutiny.

17 FEBRUARY
Austria-Hungary launches an offensive against the Russians in the Carpathians.

19 FEBRUARY
British and French warships bombard Turkish forts at the entrance to the Dardanelles.

22 FEBRUARY
German artillery bombardment causes heavy damage to historic Reims cathedral.

⌃ Engine room of a German U-boat

MARCH

10 MARCH
British launch an offensive at Neuve Chapelle, but it is called off after three days. The failure is blamed on a shortage of shells.

18 MARCH
British and French warships fail to force a passage through the Dardanelles to Constantinople, resulting in the loss of three battleships.

22 MARCH
The Austro-Hungarian fortress of Przemysl surrenders to the Russians after a siege lasting 133 days. Zeppelins carry out their first bombing raid on Paris.

Boys Come over here you're wanted

« Australian recruitment poster

APRIL

22 APRIL
German offensive starts the Second Battle of Ypres. The Germans use chlorine gas in an attempt to achieve a breakthrough.

24 APRIL
Turkish government begins widespread arrests of Armenians after Armenian rebels seize the city of Van.

25 APRIL
Allied troops land on the Gallipoli peninsula, seeking to win control of the Dardanelles.

26 APRIL
By signing the Treaty of London, Italy agrees to join the war on the Allied side.

» Life belt from the RMS _Lusitania_

MAY

2 MAY
Germany and Austria-Hungary launch the Gorlice-Tarnow Offensive in Poland.

7 MAY
A German U-boat sinks the liner _Lusitania_, killing 1,200 people including US citizens.

25 MAY
Coalition government is formed in Britain. David Lloyd George is made minister of munitions.

LUSITANIA

« Italy enters the war

29 MAY
Turkish authorities begin mass deportation of Armenians.

31 MAY
First German Zeppelin raid on London.

JUNE

⌃ A downed Zeppelin

7 JUNE
A British aircraft shoots down a German Zeppelin airship over Belgium.

9 JUNE
US Secretary of State William Jennings Bryan, opposed to President Wilson's policy on Germany, resigns.

22 JUNE
Austria-Hungary retakes the city of Lemberg (Lvov) as the Russians retreat in Galicia.

23 JUNE
Fighting begins between Italy and Austria-Hungary at the First Battle of the Isonzo.

28 JUNE
Allied troops at Gallipoli launch a failed attack on Turkish defences at Achi Baba.

> "The horrible part… is the slow **lingering death** of those who are **gassed.** I saw some hundred **poor fellows… slowly drowning** with water in their lungs…"

GENERAL JOHN CHARTERIS, WRITING AFTER THE FIRST USE OF CHLORINE GAS, 28 APRIL 1915

JULY	AUGUST	SEPTEMBER	OCTOBER	NOVEMBER	DECEMBER

9 JULY
German forces in Southwest Africa surrender.

22 JULY
Russian forces begin a full-scale retreat from Poland.

1 AUGUST
Start of the "Fokker Scourge" – German monoplanes dominating the skies over the Western Front.

5 AUGUST
German forces capture Warsaw.

1 SEPTEMBER
In response to US pressure, Germany halts unrestricted submarine warfare.

6 SEPTEMBER
Bulgaria agrees to join the war on the side of the Central Powers.

6 OCTOBER
German and Austro-Hungarian forces launch an invasion of Serbia, taking Belgrade.

11 OCTOBER
Bulgarian forces invade Serbia from the east.

5 NOVEMBER
The Central Powers capture Nis in Serbia, establishing a direct rail connection between Germany and Turkey.

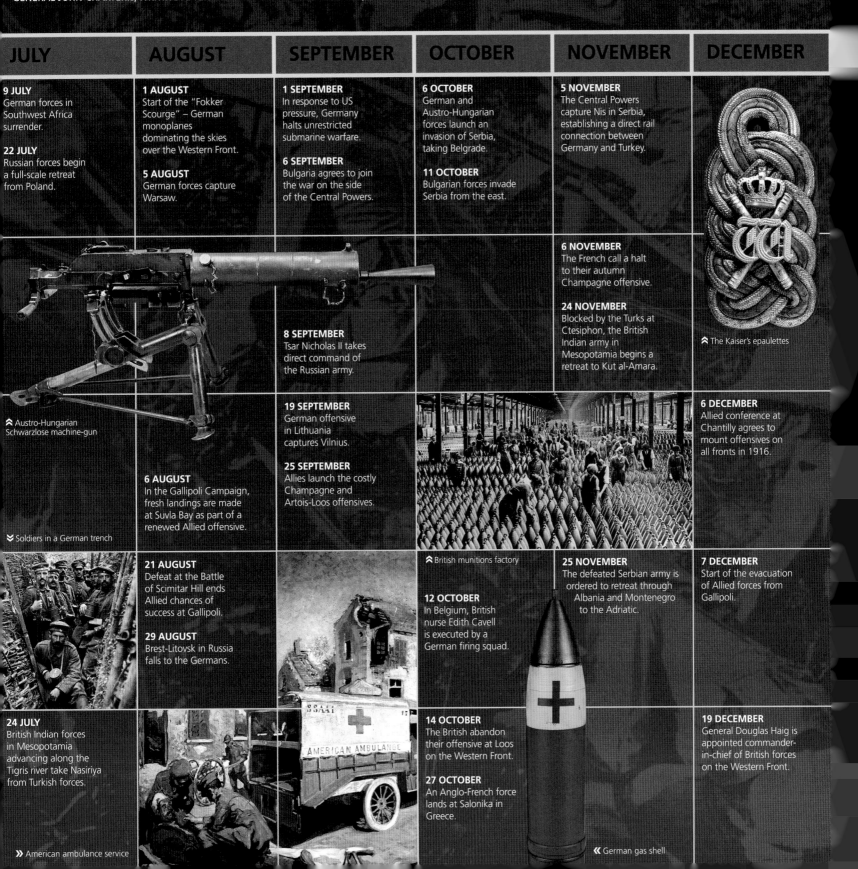

⌃ The Kaiser's epaulettes

8 SEPTEMBER
Tsar Nicholas II takes direct command of the Russian army.

6 NOVEMBER
The French call a halt to their autumn Champagne offensive.

24 NOVEMBER
Blocked by the Turks at Ctesiphon, the British Indian army in Mesopotamia begins a retreat to Kut al-Amara.

⌃ Austro-Hungarian Schwarzlose machine-gun

19 SEPTEMBER
German offensive in Lithuania captures Vilnius.

25 SEPTEMBER
Allies launch the costly Champagne and Artois-Loos offensives.

6 DECEMBER
Allied conference at Chantilly agrees to mount offensives on all fronts in 1916.

6 AUGUST
In the Gallipoli Campaign, fresh landings are made at Suvla Bay as part of a renewed Allied offensive.

⌄ Soldiers in a German trench

⌃ British munitions factory

21 AUGUST
Defeat at the Battle of Scimitar Hill ends Allied chances of success at Gallipoli.

29 AUGUST
Brest-Litovsk in Russia falls to the Germans.

12 OCTOBER
In Belgium, British nurse Edith Cavell is executed by a German firing squad.

25 NOVEMBER
The defeated Serbian army is ordered to retreat through Albania and Montenegro to the Adriatic.

7 DECEMBER
Start of the evacuation of Allied forces from Gallipoli.

24 JULY
British Indian forces in Mesopotamia advancing along the Tigris river take Nasiriya from Turkish forces.

⌄ American ambulance service

AMERICAN AMBULANCE

14 OCTOBER
The British abandon their offensive at Loos on the Western Front.

27 OCTOBER
An Anglo-French force lands at Salonika in Greece.

« German gas shell

19 DECEMBER
General Douglas Haig is appointed commander-in-chief of British forces on the Western Front.

Munitions production
Women work alongside men to manufacture shells in a British munitions factory. Combatant states achieved a massive expansion in output by intervening to direct businesses and labour.

Mobilizing Resources

By the start of 1915, illusions of a quick victory had evaporated. Combatant powers faced a prolonged conflict that would consume vast resources – states that failed to meet the demands of total war would not survive.

ВСЕ ДЛЯ ВОЙНЫ!

ПОДПИСЫВАЙТЕСЬ НА 5½%

ВОЕННЫЙ ЗАЕМЪ.

Women at work
A Russian wartime poster shows a woman engaged in skilled industrial work. Shortages of labour forced countries to employ women in factory jobs from which they had previously been excluded, as well as in areas such as transport and administration.

Governments on all sides had to increase production in key industries if they were to sustain mass armies in the field. They largely relied on private businesses to supply the goods, inducing them to cooperate through government control of raw materials, labour, and contracts.

For the Central Powers, Britain's naval blockade presented a particular problem. By preventing the import of key raw materials, the blockade threatened the ability of German and Austro-Hungarian war industries to continue functioning. The German War Ministry set up a War Materials Department under businessman Walther Rathenau to ensure that industries fulfilling military orders received the necessary supplies. The resources of occupied Belgium and northern France, including coal mines and factories, were fully exploited.

Germany was also fortunate in having strong links between industry and scientific research and the world's most developed chemicals industry.

> **55 PER CENT The proportion of the German industrial workforce made up of women in 1918.**

This facilitated the development of synthetic substitutes for materials that could no longer be imported. Crucially, the nitrates required for making high explosives were synthesized through the work of scientist Fritz Haber.

Maximizing production

At the opposite extreme from Germany, less industrialized Russia was slow to respond to problems in supplying its army. The setting up of a War Industries Committee improved Russia's supply situation during 1915 – most soldiers had rifles, and guns had shells – but the armies still depended on voluntary contributions organized by *zemstvos* (Russian provincial governments) for most of their clothing and medical supplies.

Britain and France had access to raw materials and industrial imports from across the world, as long as sea lanes could be kept open. Nevertheless, in 1915 their armies suffered from shortages of munitions and equipment. In Britain, a scandal over shell shortages, luridly worked up in the press, led to Conservative and Labour politicians entering a coalition government with the Liberals in spring 1915. The Liberal politician David Lloyd George was appointed to head a new Ministry of Munitions. His vigorous interventionism achieved a striking increase in output.

All combatant countries were hard-pressed to meet the conflicting labour demands of army, industry, and agriculture. France was soon obliged to transfer skilled workers back from the military front to the factories. By the end of 1915, Britain had abandoned enrolling volunteers indiscriminately, and had launched a national registry to establish which men should be reserved for vital industrial jobs.

The employment of women in traditionally male jobs was essential to war production. Munitions factories took hundreds of thousands of women, who performed dangerous tasks such as filling shells with explosives. Women who had been shop workers or in domestic service now drove buses and trams.

Many women also found employment as office workers in the expanding government bureaucracies – Britain's Ministry of Munitions had a workforce of 650,000 by the war's end. The number of British women employed in commerce and industry increased from 3 million to 5 million during the war. By 1918, women made up more than half of Germany's industrial workforce.

Money to finance the war effort was found through increased taxes and government borrowing on a massive scale. Patriotic appeals brought in loans from the public in the form of war bonds. As governments pumped money into their economies to promote industry, they struggled to hold down the consequent inflation.

The inequalities of war

Some people were definitely better off in the war, including industrialists who secured lucrative armaments contracts and working-class women who found better-paid jobs, while others suffered hardship. In 1915, social solidarity still held, but discontent surfaced in accusations of profiteering by businessmen and demands for fairness in the sharing of sacrifice.

AFTER »

The combatant countries achieved extraordinary growth in war production, but at mounting financial and social cost.

WEAPONS INDUSTRY
Britain raised its **production of explosives** from 24,000 tonnes in 1915 to almost 186,000 tonnes in 1917. Its **output of machine-guns** over the same period rose from 6,100 to almost 80,000. Before the war, an air industry barely existed, but in 1915 **French factories manufactured** 7,000 **aero engines**, rising to 17,000 in 1916 – all for military use. **Germany** had produced 43,200 **rifles** in 1914; in 1916 it made 3 million. German **production of explosives** multiplied tenfold between 1914 and 1917.

COUNTING THE COST
The financial cost of the war effort was staggering. In Germany, Britain, and France, government **expenditure rose** around 500 per cent between 1914 and 1917. Devoting vast resources to the war also had an impact on **food production**, reducing the labour available for farm work and creating shortages of tools, fertilizers, and horses.

BEFORE

At the onset of war, military authorities and governments in all combatant countries took sweeping powers to suspend basic civil rights.

EMERGENCY MEASURES
In France, Germany, and Austria-Hungary, **siege regulations** were invoked, giving the army powers to requisition property, censor the press, and try civilians in military courts. In Britain, the **Defence of the Realm Act** (DORA) licensed the government to commandeer economic resources and **suppress opposition to the war**. Everywhere horses were requisitioned and railways taken out of private control.

Despite draconian powers, combatant countries were **ill-prepared to run a long war**. The first four months of fighting exhausted their stocks of munitions. **Russia was running out of artillery shells** by September 1914, and by the end of the year all combatants found operations limited by shell shortages.

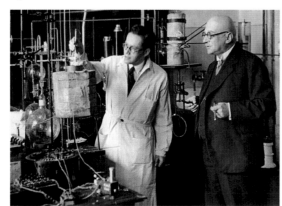

Chemical warrior
German scientist Fritz Haber (right) epitomized the contribution of science to the war, creating synthetic substitutes for strategic materials and poison gas for the battlefield.

Trench Warfare

" It is a wild scene… **Filth and rubbish** everywhere, graves built into the defences … **troops of enormous rats…"**

WINSTON CHURCHILL, LETTER FROM THE TRENCHES AT LAVENTIE, FRANCE, 23 NOVEMBER 1915

B y 1914, trenches were a common aspect of warfare, reflecting the straightforward need for soldiers on the front line to protect themselves against enemy fire. Standard military manuals provided instructions for digging trenches, and armies had equipment for doing so. But there was no precedent for the scale and duration of the trench warfare that was such a feature of World War I.

By the end of 1915, there was a more or less continuous line of trenches stretching 740 km (460 miles) across Europe, from the Belgian coast to Switzerland, and a somewhat less continuous line in the east extending for 1,300 km (800 miles) from the Baltic to the Carpathians. All the other fronts in the war – in northern Italy, Gallipoli in Turkey, Palestine, and the Caucasus – had their own trench systems. At first, trenches were considered to be a temporary,

Over the top at Gallipoli
Allied soldiers advance during the Dardanelles campaign in 1915–16. The terrain at Gallipoli made entrenchment difficult and troops suffered from diseases in the insanitary conditions.

necessary measure. Eventually, some of them became home for thousands of troops for years.

The essentials of any trench were simple. It had to be deep enough for a man to stand, without his head presenting a target for enemy snipers. It also had to be narrow so that it was not an easy target for an enemy shell or mortar. It was better if it wasn't straight. Frequent kinks, which the British called "traverses", stopped blast, shrapnel, or fire sweeping the entire length of the trench. It needed a firestep, a raised platform, in its front wall, so that soldiers could step up to shoot over the top if the enemy attacked.

Trench systems
Where the ground was sodden, as it regularly was in parts of Flanders in Belgium, trenches had to be shallow to avoid flooding, with a parapet of earth and sandbags built up in front. Where the ground was dry and firm, as at the Somme, trenches could be provided with deep underground

German entrenching tool
In trench warfare, the short-handled entrenching spade became as important a piece of military equipment as the rifle. Soldiers of all armies spent long hours of backbreaking labour digging, repairing, and extending trench systems.

bunkers to protect troops against shellfire. In some places, however, defences never progressed beyond a single trench fronted by a few strands of barbed wire.

Trench systems of formidable complexity developed over time. Saps (short trenches) were dug forwards into No Man's Land between the opposing trenches. Parallel lines of support and reserve trenches were dug behind the front line, and a maze of communication trenches linked the front line to the rear. On the Western Front, the Germans eventually constructed complex defensive systems 15 km (9 miles) across, with a series of trenches, disguised machine-gun emplacements, and cunningly sited strongpoints that were reinforced with concrete fortifications.

Life in the trenches
Conditions on the front varied. French trenches provided notoriously poor living conditions. The Germans, by contrast, built dry and warm concrete bunkers and even installed electric lighting for some troops.

Life in the trenches could range from tolerable to almost unbearable. On a quiet sector of the front, daily routines might carry a man through months of the war with only limited danger. Enemies separated by no more than 100–200 m (100–200 yd) of No Man's Land adopted a system of live-and-let-live as the path to mutual survival. A day typically began with "stand to" at

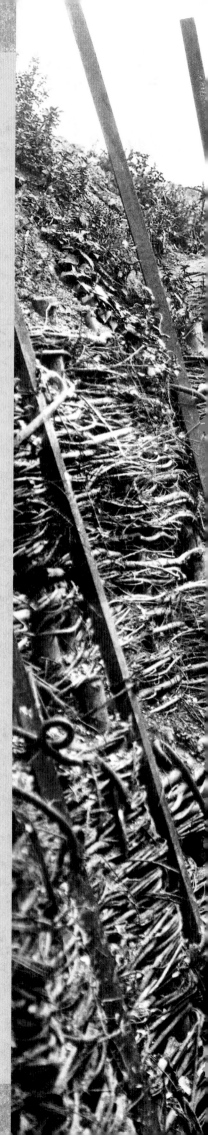

dawn, often the occasion for a ritualistic exchange of fire expected to hurt no one. Then rations were brought up from the rear. Tasks such as cleaning weapons and maintaining or extending trenches filled the day until "stand down" at dusk. Night was a time for repairing barbed wire or moving troops and equipment.

On an active front, commanders insisted on constant harassment of the enemy. Front line units suffered

5,000 The average number of British casualties per month in the trenches of the Ypres salient in 1916, when no major battle was fought.

a grinding attrition of casualties from sniper fire, mortars, or artillery. At night, patrols were sent out into No Man's Land or raids were mounted against enemy trenches, producing heavy casualties for both sides.

Few soldiers went "over the top" in a major offensive more than once or twice. When they did, it was an experience they would never forget. Observation of the enemy, either through periscopes or at advanced listening posts thrust forward into No Man's Land, was a 24-hour-a-day task, and any soldier who fell asleep on sentry duty was severely punished. Soldiers on the Western Front would typically spend less than a week on the front line, before being rotated to the reserve line or the rear, where they laboured on exhausting tasks such as carrying ammunition to the front line.

Lice, rats, and "trench foot"

Infestation with lice was almost universal in the trenches, which also swarmed with well-fed rats. Sometimes corpses and body parts became embedded in trench walls, as it was often too dangerous to retrieve them. Latrine facilities could be primitive. On the Western Front, troops were usually adequately clothed and fed, but such was not the case on other fronts. Extreme weather could turn the trench experience into a nightmare. In the summer heat at Gallipoli, troops were tortured by thirst and racked by disease. In Flanders, heavy rain flooded trenches, turning the battle area into a quagmire; troops standing for days in deep water suffered "trench foot", which could lead to gangrene and amputation.

German trench

This trench has been dug into soft earth, so the walls are "revetted" with wattle to hold them firm. A duckboard of wooden slats has been laid to provide a mud-free walkway.

TIMELINE

- **September 1914** German Chief of the General Staff General Helmuth von Moltke orders forces retreating from the Marne to "fortify and defend" a line at the Aisne river. Entrenched German troops halt the advance of British and French forces, who dig their own improvised trenches.

- **December 1914** With armies entrenched across the Western Front, there is widespread fraternization between German and Allied troops on Christmas Day.

- **January 1915** German Chief of the General Staff General Erich von Falkenhayn orders troops on the Western Front to make their trench lines defensible against superior forces, leading to stalemate.

- **April 1915** The Germans introduce poison gas during the Second Battle of Ypres. Gas becomes a fixed feature of trench warfare on the Western Front.

- **April 1915** Allied troops landing at Gallipoli, Turkey, find themselves forced to entrench under unfavourable conditions. They are unable to make significant progress against Turkish defensive positions.

BISCUIT RATIONS TURNED INTO A FRAME

- **June 1916** Russian General Alexei Brusilov drives Austro-Hungarian forces out of their trench lines and advances 80 km (50 miles).

- **July 1916** German troops in concrete bunkers survive a prolonged Allied bombardment to emerge and cut down attacking soldiers on the first day of the Somme offensive.

- **February–March 1917** German forces on the Western Front between Arras and Soissons withdraw to newly prepared defensive positions (the Hindenburg Line).

- **September 1917** A German offensive against the Russians at Riga shows the effectiveness of using specialist assault troops to penetrate trench systems in depth.

- **November 1917** A British offensive at Cambrai uses massed tanks to overcome soldiers in German trenches, but without decisive effect.

- **March 1918** The German Spring Offensive ends the stalemate on the Western Front.

- **September–October 1918** Allied forces break through the Hindenburg Line.

Life in the Trenches

Life in the trenches varied according to sectors, fronts, the time of year, and local weather conditions. It was, however, far from pleasant. Soldiers on all sides lived under the threat of death from either sniper or shell. Vermin, such as rats and lice, were numerous; trenches would flood in wet weather; and men suffered frostbite in the freezing cold. Those serving also had to contend with the extreme tedium of trench warfare, which was largely static.

"I am still stuck in this trench and so far as I know not likely to be relieved for some days, as I've had a week of it and the regulation dose is four days… I haven't washed or had my clothes off at all, and my average sleep has been two and a half hours in the twenty-four. I don' think I've started to crawl yet, but I don't suppose I should notice if I had… My men are awfully cheery; they are the best souls in the world… although I've lost a good many lately… But there are points in the life that appeal to me vastly, the contrast for instance: the long, lazy, hot days, when no work is done, and any part of the body that protrudes above the trench is most swiftly blown off; the uncanny, shrieking, hard-fought nights with their bizarre and beastly experiences, their constant crack and thunder, their stealthy seeking for advantage, and regardless seizure of it, and in the middle of it all perhaps a song sang round a brazier, a joke or two yelled against the noise of shells and rifles until the sentries' warning."

CAPTAIN EDWIN GERALD YENNING, ROYAL SUSSEX REGIMENT, LETTER TO HIS SISTER, 20 JUNE 1915

"There is something inexpressibly sad and full of renunciation in this stationary warfare. Life would be so easy if we could march, as they do in Russia, march along into the blue distance in the morning light… But here we burrow deep into the earth. There is a candle burning even now in our dug-out, though it is bright daylight outside. Close by, the lads are filling sandbags with which tonight they will stop in our parapets. Everything is quiet just now. The enemy is waiting for nightfall; because he knows that then we shall be working at our farthest-forward position. So there is no real activity except in the dark."

LETTER FROM ALFRED VAETH, 12 SEPTEMBER 1915

The tedium of the trenches
German soldiers read and write letters in a trench in June 1915. Stalemate on the Western Front meant there were often long lulls in the fighting, and soldiers frequently complained of boredom.

BEFORE

The fighting of 1914 left the opposing armies on the Western Front entrenched from the north coast of Belgium to the Swiss border.

LINES ARE DRAWN
The **Allied side of the line** was manned along most of its length by the French. A sector in Flanders and northern France was held by British troops. The **British First Army** was opposite **Neuve Chapelle** and the **Second Army** was at **Ypres** ≪ 60–61.

KING ALBERT I OF BELGIUM

Belgian and French forces held the sector nearest to the coast. The French and Belgian desire to liberate their territories influenced the Allies in favour of an **offensive strategy**.

Failure on the Western Front

In early 1915, Allied operations – the First Champagne Offensive and the Battle of Neuve Chapelle – revealed the problems generals would face in trench warfare on the Western Front. Taking the offensive resulted in heavy losses but minimal gains.

By the end of 1914, a new phase had opened on the Western Front – the stalemate of the trenches. But that is not how it appeared to French commander General Joseph Joffre at the time. Joffre was still planning strategic manoeuvres. He envisaged the German armies, which were pushed forwards in a great arc between Verdun and Lille, being forced to withdraw by Allied advances from Champagne to the south and Artois in the north. He planned for his armies to break through into Belgium, threatening the Germans with encirclement.

Joffre began the campaign against German trenches on the Champagne front in late December 1914. Known as the First Champagne Offensive, it lasted into March 1915. German trench lines were primitive compared with what they would later become. Usually, a single, narrow front-line trench was packed with troops under orders to hold their position at all costs. If the trench was lost, German reserves counterattacked with ferocity to retake the position.

In almost continuous fighting at Champagne, the French army suffered about 90,000 casualties. German losses were probably similar. In the small strips of ground that were fought and refought over, villages were shelled to obliteration. The French advance gained a maximum 3 km (2 miles) of territory.

The Western Front in 1915

A line of trenches snaked across Belgium and northeast France. The key battles of 1915 occurred in Flanders and Artois in the north and Champagne further south, with the French and British mostly on the offensive.

Joffre was already planning an offensive in Artois while the fighting in Champagne raged on. Artois was the junction between the French and British sectors, and British commander Field Marshal Sir John French, eager to shake his troops out of the morale-sapping routines of the trenches, agreed to a joint offensive. Conditions were ripe: the Germans had begun moving large numbers of their best troops to the Eastern Front for an attempt at a decisive blow against Russia.

However, Britain had also begun to think there might be better military opportunities elsewhere. In mid-February, British troops intended for France were diverted to the attack on Turkey at Gallipoli. Joffre had been promised that British forces would take over French responsibilities along the line from Ypres north to the coast. Now that this offer was withdrawn, Joffre cancelled the joint operation at Artois. Perhaps eager to show his Allies what he could do on his own, French decided to go ahead with a limited British attack at Neuve Chapelle.

The Battle of Neuve Chapelle

Well planned and prepared, the Neuve Chapelle operation's aim was to capture Aubers Ridge, a modest eminence in mostly flat country that gave a distinct advantage to the side

> **In the initial attack at Neuve Chapelle, British and Indian forces outnumbered the opposing German troops by five to one.**

that held it. The route to the ridge passed through the ruined village of Neuve Chapelle. The attack was entrusted to the First Army under General Douglas Haig, a rising star who had performed well as a corps commander in the First Battle of Ypres.

The British made innovative use of aerial photography to map the German defences, which were thinly manned and poorly constructed – the wet ground had forced both sides to build parapets upwards rather than dig downwards for shelter.

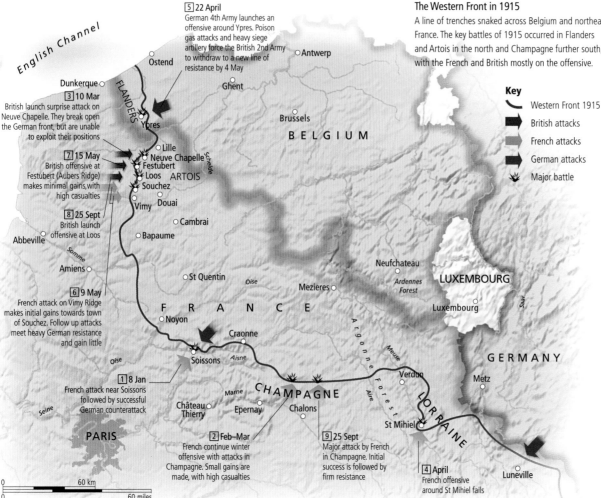

5 22 April
German 4th Army launches an offensive around Ypres. Poison gas attacks and heavy siege artillery force the British 2nd Army to withdraw to a new line of resistance by 4 May

3 10 Mar
British launch surprise attack on Neuve Chapelle. They break open the German front, but are unable to exploit their positions

7 15 May
British offensive at Festubert (Aubers Ridge) makes minimal gains, with high casualties

8 25 Sept
British launch offensive at Loos

6 9 May
French attack on Vimy Ridge makes initial gains towards town of Souchez. Follow up attacks meet heavy German resistance and gain little

1 8 Jan
French attack near Soissons followed by successful German counterattack

Key
~ Western Front 1915
➤ British attacks
➤ French attacks
➤ German attacks
✷ Major battle

2 Feb–Mar
French continue winter offensive with attacks in Champagne. Small gains are made, with high casualties

9 25 Sept
Major attack by French in Champagne. Initial success is followed by firm resistance

4 April
French offensive around St Mihiel fails

0 — 60 km
0 — 60 miles

Battle supplies at Neuve Chapelle
Joseph Gray's painting, *A Ration Party of the 4th Black Watch at the Battle of Neuve Chapelle 1915*, shows battle supplies being brought up under cover of darkness. Progress across the war-torn battlefield was hazardous.

Sixty thousand men and their equipment were moved forward at night without alerting the Germans. The attack came as a surprise for the Germans. At 7:30am on 10 March, some 500 guns opened up a ferocious attack. The German barbed wire was cut and the trench line devastated. In most places, the British troops, which included the Gurkhas and Sikhs of two Indian divisions, were able to cross No Man's Land and occupy the German line almost without loss.

Lost opportunity

Haig had envisaged that initial success would be followed by a rapid push forward, with cavalry eventually riding through into open country.

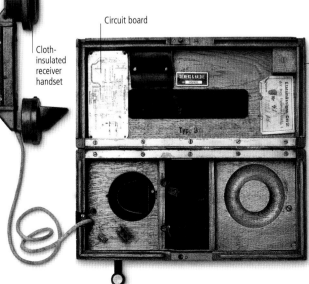

Circuit board

Cloth-insulated receiver handset

Brown Bakelite cabinet box

SIEMENS & HALSKE

Type D

German field telephone
The only equipment for communication between commanders or artillery and advancing troops was the portable field telephone. Its main disadvantage was that its wire could be severed by shellfire.

But confusion reigned. On one flank of the British advance a few German machine-guns inflicted heavy casualties and halted progress. Units lost their way in the devastated terrain.

Communications also broke down. Reports on the situation at the front took hours to reach Haig's headquarters, and orders took further hours to travel in the opposite direction. While the British wasted time, the Germans brought in reserves to block the opening in the line and reinforce flanking positions. By nightfall, the opportunity was lost.

The last stage of the battle followed what was to become a familiar pattern. On 11 March, the German commander, Crown Prince Rupprecht, mounted a counterattack. The British had moved machine-guns into advanced positions and it was the turn of the Germans to fall in large numbers. When fighting subsided on 13 March, losses on the opposing sides were not dissimilar – 11,700 British and 8,600 Germans dead, wounded, or taken prisoner. The British had gained less than 2 sq km (1 sq mile) of territory.

AFTER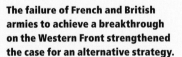

The failure of French and British armies to achieve a breakthrough on the Western Front strengthened the case for an alternative strategy.

GALLIPOLI
The **Gallipoli landings 110–11 ≫** in late April 1915 were intended to exploit the weakness of Turkey and the strength of Allied naval power. But Gallipoli proved no more effective than offensives on the Western Front and also ended in trench warfare.

SECOND BATTLE OF YPRES
Germany made one effort at a Western Front offensive in April–May 1915, at the **Second Battle of Ypres 102–05 ≫**, but otherwise stayed on the defensive while achieving major successes on the **Eastern Front** against Russia and Romania **194–95 ≫**. In the autumn, the Allies launched major offensives in the **Champagne and Artois** sectors, with appalling loss of life.

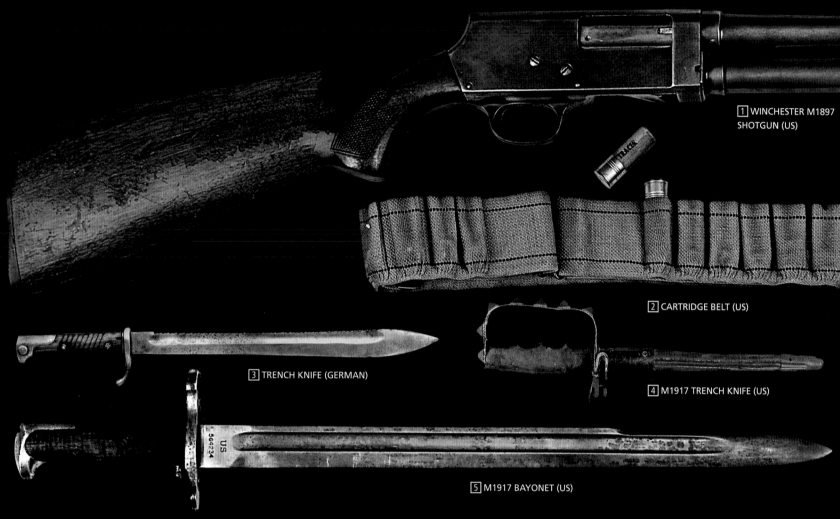

1 WINCHESTER M1897 SHOTGUN (US)

2 CARTRIDGE BELT (US)

3 TRENCH KNIFE (GERMAN)

4 M1917 TRENCH KNIFE (US)

5 M1917 BAYONET (US)

Trench Fighting
Equipment

Trench warfare demanded its own weaponry, as opposing armies fought at very close range. Grenades and mortars were important while night-time raids on enemy trenches required silent equipment.

1 Winchester M1897 shotgun (US) Known as the "trench sweeper", this model sprayed lead pellets and was brutally effective in confined spaces. 2 Cartridge belt (US) This was used to hold buckshot pellets for shotguns. 3 Trench knife (German) Short, sharp, and quiet, knives were essential trench weapons. 4 M1917 trench knife (US) This model combined a knife and a knuckle-duster. 5 M1917 bayonet (US) At 43 cm (17 in) in length, this bayonet was often too long for confined trench combat. 6 Wooden club (British) Soldiers on all sides created home-made weapons. 7 Nail club (British) The hobnails in this club allowed the wielder to inflict serious injury. 8 Metal club (British) Clubs were useful for dispatching foes during stealthy trench raids. 9 Spiked club (British) Designs such as this one had a leather strap to secure the weapon to the wielder's wrist. 10 Kommandantur Lille flare pistol (German) Flares were shot into the air to send signals or to illuminate No Man's Land. 11 Flare pistol cartridges (German) Flares were produced using magnesium. 12 Webley & Scott MK VI revolver (British) In 1915, this became the standard side arm for British troops. 13 Folding shovel (Italian) Intended for digging, shovels were also used as weapons. 14 Wire cutters (British) These were vital for creating passages through barbed wire. 15 M1910 wire cutters (US) These were standard issue to US infantry and cavalry. 16 M1915 hand grenade (German) This grenade was quickly mass-produced. A time delay before exploding allowed the enemy to throw it back. 17 M1915 disk grenade (German) This was a "percussion" grenade, meaning that it exploded on impact. 18 Grenade P1 (French) Also a percussion grenade, this model was known as the "pear" or "spoon". 19 Stokes mortar bomb (British) Up to 30 of these bombs could be fired per minute, at a range of 1,100 m (1,200 yd). 20 No.1 grenade (British) The streamers on this grenade ensured the explosive head landed first. 21 Periscope (British) Periscopes were used by all armies to enable safe observation of enemy trenches.

13 FOLDING SHOVEL (ITALIAN)

14 WIRE CUTTERS (BRITISH)

10 KOMMANDANTUR LILLE FLARE
PISTOL (GERMAN)

11 FLARE PISTOL
CARTRIDGES (GERMAN)

7 NAIL CLUB
(BRITISH)

12 WEBLEY & SCOTT MK
VI REVOLVER (BRITISH)

6 WOODEN
CLUB (BRITISH)

16 M1915
HAND
GRENADE
(GERMAN)

9 SPIKED
CLUB (BRITISH)

8 METAL
CLUB (BRITISH)

S.T. HOW
MK I I

LACH
SK

20/1

15 M1910 WIRE
CUTTERS (US)

17 M1915
DISK GRENADE
(GERMAN)

18 GRENADE P1 (FRENCH)

19 STOKES MORTAR
BOMB (BRITISH)

20 NO.1 GRENADE
(BRITISH)

21 PE
(BRIT

« BEFORE

In spring 1915, the Germans were preparing a major offensive against Russia, but the development of a new weapon also tempted them to attack on the Western Front.

FIRST BATTLE OF YPRES

In November 1914, the **Allies** had gained the Ypres salient in the **First Battle of Ypres** **« 60–61**. Their line of trenches, curving to the east of the Belgian town, was overlooked by **German** positions on higher ground. The trenches on the left of the salient were held by French territorials and colonial troops, with the British Second Army, including the First Canadian Division, holding the front and right.

GERMAN STRATEGY

The **German forces** in the sector were **outnumbered by the Allies**, because German Chief of the General Staff Erich von Falkenhayn had transferred troops to the Eastern Front for the **Gorlice-Tarnow offensive 134–35 »**. Falkenhayn's strategy was to stand on the defensive in the West while attacking in the East.

From late 1914, Germany's **scientists** had begun developing the **poison gas chlorine 104–05 »** for military use. The Ypres salient was identified as a suitable location for an experimental **gas attack**.

POET (1872–1918)

JOHN McCRAE

Canadian doctor and poet John McCrae enlisted as a field surgeon in the Canadian Artillery in 1914. He was in charge of a field hospital during the Second Battle of Ypres. The death of a friend in that battle inspired him to write *In Flanders Fields*, one of the war's most famous poems. Published in Britain in December 1915, it was an instant success with its appeal from the dead to the living to "Take up our quarrel with the foe". McCrae died of pneumonia at Boulogne in France in January 1918. He was buried in the Commonwealth War Graves Commission cemetery at Withereux, just along the coast.

Second Ypres

The Second Battle of Ypres has a sinister place in the history of warfare as the first battle to feature the use of chlorine gas. Germany's secret weapon caused initial shock and panic, but Allied troops quickly learned to cope with this new horror of war.

The Germans surprised the Allies with their chlorine gas attack at Ypres, even though their preparations were slow and clumsy. Their plan was for gas released from pressurized cylinders to be blown across Allied lines by the wind. Some 5,700 cylinders, each weighing about 40 kg (88 lb), were manhandled into position at the front and then buried under a layer of earth.

The cylinders were in place by early April, but a long wait ensued because the wind was in the wrong direction. During the delay, Allied interrogation of German prisoners and a deserter produced detailed accounts of the deployment of the cylinders, but the information was not taken seriously by Allied military intelligence.

On the afternoon of 22 April, with a breeze at last blowing steadily from behind their lines, Germany's special gas troops opened the cylinders. A yellow-green cloud drifted across No Man's Land towards trenches held by French Zouaves, from across France's North African colonies, and Algerian riflemen. Those in the frontline had little chance of escape. If they stayed in the trenches, they were killed by the chlorine in their lungs. If they climbed out, they were exposed to artillery and machine-gun fire.

As the gas rolled towards the rear, troops fled in panic, many choking and with eyes streaming. Meanwhile, German troops issued with respirators as protection advanced into a gap 6 km (4 miles) wide in the Allied line.

Fortunately for the Allies, their superiority in numbers prevented the Germans from fully exploiting their breakthrough. Allied reserves were brought up to block the

> **SALIENT A sector of the battlefield that protrudes into hostile territory, so that it is surrounded by the enemy on three sides.**

AFTER

FRENCH MUNITIONS FACTORY, OCTOBER 1915

SHELL SHORTAGE

In Britain, a political crisis, known as the "shell scandal", was precipitated when senior commanders told journalists they were short of shells. Along with the failure of the **Gallipoli landings 110–113 》**, this provoked the formation of a **coalition government** in late May 1915, with David Lloyd George as Minister of Munitions.

ALLIES DEVELOP POISON GAS

Germany's use of poison further **harmed its reputation**, especially in the USA. While denouncing German immorality, the **Allies set about developing** their own **chemical weapons**. The British made a first attempt to use chlorine gas released from cylinders at the **Battle of Loos 142–43 》** in September 1915. The British, French, and Germans made **extensive use of gas-filled artillery shells**.

---

gap and launch counterattacks. A Canadian Scottish battalion led a frontal assault on a position known as Kitchener's Wood. It succeeded in taking it, but at the expense of 75 per cent casualties.

Fog of chlorine

Allied troops quckly found an improvised answer to the worst effects of chlorine was a wet pad placed over the mouth – at first usually soaked in urine, which neutralized the poison. Thus prepared, Canadian troops subjected to gassing on 24 April did not panic, and the German assault ran into fierce resistance. But the line broke where the gas attack was densest, and at the end of the day the Canadians were

ordered to retreat. On 1 May, it was the turn of the British Dorset Regiment, who were attacked with chlorine at a position known as Hill 60. The men stood on the firesteps of their trenches in a fog of chlorine, shooting blindly at advancing German infantry, stopping only when disabled by poisoned lungs. By then it was clear that the Germans had increased the horror of the war without finding a solution to the trench stalemate.

German gas mask

In preparation for the use of chlorine gas, the Germans issued their own troops with primitive masks and respirators. Despite taking this precaution, some German soldiers were victims of poison gas at Second Ypres.

The Canadians at Ypres

Canadian troops received a baptism of fire at Second Ypres. This painting, *The Second Battle of Ypres*, by the official war artist Richard Jack, shows hard-pressed Canadians repelling a German assault.

German troops continued to have the upper hand, and gained ground piecemeal. The town of Ypres was reduced to rubble by German shelling.

> **6** **out of 10 Canadians who fought at the Second Battle of Ypres were killed, wounded, or taken prisoner.**

As the size of the salient shrank, Allied troops became dangerously crowded, making a tempting target for German artillery. Commander of the British Second Army, General Sir Horace Smith-Dorrien, advocated some tactical withdrawals to improve the defensive position. Annoyed by this suggestion, British commander-in-chief Field Marshal Sir John French used it as a pretext to replace Smith-Dorrien with General Herbert Plumer – who promptly made the necessary tactical

withdrawals in any case. In continued fighting through May, the Germans advanced to within 3 km (2 miles) of Ypres, where a new front line was stabilized from 25 May. The battle was then deemed to have ended.

Anglo-French offensive

As the fighting at Ypres continued, an Allied offensive was launched further south. On 9 May, after a five-day preliminary bombardment by 1,200 guns, the French Ninth Army attacked in Artois, between Arras and Lens. The British First Army, under General Douglas Haig, mounted a supporting attack towards Aubers Ridge, in the same sector as the earlier Battle of Neuve Chapelle. French General Philippe Pétain, commanding a corps, made a breakthrough to the crest of Vimy Ridge, but was then driven back by counterattacking German reserves. A renewal of the offensive on 15 May enabled the British to take the village of Festubert – an insignificant gain for heavy losses. By June, exhaustion dictated a general subsidence of fighting on the Western Front.

Chemical Warfare

"Men were **caught by fumes** and in **dreadful agony,** coughing and vomiting, **rolling on the ground…**"

SECOND LIEUTENANT ERNEST SHEPHARD, DORSET REGIMENT, WITNESS OF A GAS ATTACK, 1 MAY 1915

German gas shell
Gas shells contained a liquid that vaporized when the shell burst. Markings indicated the mix of chemicals inside – for the Germans, green indicated chlorine; yellow, mustard gas; and blue, diphenylchlorarsine, a vomiting agent.

The development of the chemical industry in the 19th century raised the possibility of using its products for military purposes. In an attempt to prevent this from happening, in 1899 the major powers signed the Hague Convention, which, among other restrictions, banned the use of gas shells.

It was widely assumed that the Convention did not cover irritant tear gas, which by 1914 was being used by French police for riot control. Some small tear gas projectiles were probably used by the French army in the early months of the war, allowing the Germans to claim later that France had initiated chemical warfare. Like Germany's own use of irritant gas in 1914, however, this was small-scale and ineffectual.

The decision to develop gas as a major weapon was taken by Germany in the autumn of 1914. Worried by the shortage of high explosive shells and their ineffectiveness against entrenched troops, the German high command accepted a proposal from Carl Duisberg, head of the German chemical giant Bayer, to explore the mass production of poison gases for use in battle.

Developing chemical weapons

Some of Germany's most distinguished scientists, including Fritz Haber, head of the Kaiser Wilhelm Institute in Berlin, were involved in the project. Haber suggested releasing chlorine gas from cylinders – a way around the shell shortage – and experimented with finding the required density of gas for optimal effect.

The gas programme was criticized by some senior German commanders, notably Prince Rupprecht of Bavaria. He argued that it was morally distasteful, would blacken Germany's reputation, and would lead the Allies to develop their own gas weapons. Haber insisted that killing a man with gas was morally no different from

Gas attack
German special gas troops, known to other soldiers as *Stinktruppe*, release chlorine gas. The cylinders containing the gas were unstable, leading to many injuries among the soldiers deploying them.

killing him with explosives, and that the Allies would never be able to match Germany's chemical industry, the most advanced in the world.

On 22 April 1915, chlorine from Haber's gas cylinders, supervised by the scientist in person, enveloped a section of the Allied line at Ypres, killing large numbers of soldiers and driving the rest into panicked retreat. Two weaknesses of gas as a weapon quickly became apparent. Firstly, the cylinders could be used only when the wind was

88,500
The estimated number of deaths caused by poison gas in World War I, including around 56,000 Russians killed by gas.

80
The percentage of gas-induced deaths caused by phosgene, by far the deadliest of the gases used in World War I.

blowing in the right direction – a serious problem for the Germans on the Western Front, where the prevailing wind was against them. Secondly, improvised but fairly effective gas masks appeared within days of the first chlorine attack.

Nonetheless, the Allies perceived poison gas as an essential new weapon and were soon manufacturing their own gas in large quantities. The leading French scientist Victor Grignard competed with the German chemists to develop a deadlier gas, phosgene. Often used in combination with chlorine and tear gas, phosgene and its derivative diphosgene came into widespread use in 1916.

By this time, shells fired by mortars and artillery guns replaced cylinders as the normal delivery system, reducing dependence on wind direction. The British

British gas hood
From summer 1915, British troops wore gas hoods known as smoke helmets. This PH Helmet has a double layer of cloth impregnated with anti-gas chemicals, glass eyepieces, and a one-way valve mouthpiece.

Masks for all
An Allied soldier wears a box respirator, with its one-piece rubberized mask and goggles, while his horse has cover for its nose and mouth. Later horse gas masks included protection for the eyes.

invented a special mortar known as a Livens Projector that hurled an entire gas cylinder into enemy positions.

Masks, bags, and respirators
Counter-measures to protect the troops improved as the use of gas became standard. Chlorine was initially rendered non-lethal by a simple damp pad over the mouth and nose, ideally steeped in bicarbonate of soda. The introduction of "smoke helmets" – hoods of chemically impregnated flannel – soon offered even better protection. Chlorine and phosgene worked by attacking the lungs. This effect was negated when troops were issued with box respirators, which filtered the air, making it breathable. When attached to a rubberized headpiece, as in the British Small Box Respirator (SBR), this became the ultimate in anti-gas protection.

Nothing offered a complete defence against mustard gas, introduced by the Germans at Passchendaele in 1917, because it affected the skin as well as the lungs and eyes. Foul in its effects – blistering skin, causing temporary or permanent blindness and painful internal damage – it was utterly disabling but rarely deadly. It lingered on the battlefield as an oily deposit, creating no-go areas for weeks. It took the Allies a year to develop their own mustard gas, which they employed liberally in the final stages of the war.

190,000
The number of tons of chemicals estimated to have been manufactured for military use in World War I, including 94,000 tons of chlorine and 37,000 tons of phosgene. About 99,000 tons were produced by Germany.

Soldiers hated poison gas. It was not an effective killer, but it was useful as a means of spreading panic. The bell that warned of a gas attack was followed by a desperate fumbling to put on masks. A man caught without his mask – or not issued with one, as was frequently the case in the Russian army – experienced terror. In retrospect, most military commanders judged that the use of poison gas had made life worse for all troops, to no decisive effect.

TIMELINE

- **1899** The Hague Convention, signed by the major powers, bans the military use of projectiles diffusing "asphyxiating and deleterious gases".

- **August–October 1914** The French and Germans make limited and largely unnoticed use of tear gas on the Western Front.

- **October 1914** Germans investigate chemical weapons as a way of attacking troops.

- **December 1914** Fritz Haber heads the chemicals section of the Prussian War Ministry.

- **January 1915** Attacking the Russians at the Battle of Bolimov in Poland, the Germans fire 18,000 shells containing xylyl bromide, a toxic tear gas, but it fails to work in cold conditions.

- **April 1915** The Germans use chlorine gas against the British and French at the Second Battle of Ypres.

- **May 1915** Germany uses poison gas against Russian soldiers, causing a high death rate among unprotected troops.

EARLY GAS MASK

- **September 1915** The British make their first use of poison gas at the Battle of Loos, releasing chlorine gas from canisters.

- **October 1915** The Germans make the first documented use of phosgene, mixed with chlorine, against French troops in Champagne.

- **February 1916** The Battle of Verdun begins. Both sides make wide use of phosgene shells.

- **April 1916** The small box respirator is introduced for British troops.

- **June 1916** The Germans fire large numbers of diphosgene shells at the Battle of Verdun.

- **September 1917** The Germans deploy mustard gas for the first time at the Third Battle of Ypres (Passchendaele).

- **November 1917** The Allies use a stock of German mustard gas shells, captured at Cambrai, against the Germans.

- **April 1918** The USA begins development of a new chemical weapon, Lewisite, but it is not ready by the war's end.

- **September–October 1918** The Allies deploy mustard gas in successful offensives against the Hindenburg Line, the German defence system in northern France.

- **1919** The Treaty of Versailles bans Germany from possessing chemical weapons.

- **June 1925** The Geneva Protocol bans the use of chemical or biological weapons; it is signed by some, but not all, major powers. The USA fails to adhere to it.

- **1939–45** Despite both sides in World War II processing and developing poison gases and nerve gases, chemical weapons are used only by the Japanese against the Chinese.

> "I wish people… could see a **case of mustard gas** – the poor things **burned and blistered** with **blind eyes.**"
>
> VERA BRITTAIN, NURSE AT ÉTAPLES IN 1918, IN HER MEMOIR "A TESTAMENT OF YOUTH"

Italy Enters the War

In May 1915, Italy declared war on Austria-Hungary in a bid to gain territory. This fateful decision committed the Italians to a conflict in which half a million of their soldiers would die, beginning at the Isonzo Front in June 1915.

« BEFORE

Since 1882, Italy had been a member of the Triple Alliance with Germany and Austria-Hungary. At the outbreak of war, it declared neutrality.

ITALY'S STANCE
Italy's alliance with Austria-Hungary and Germany had always been **unpopular in Italy**, since most Italians regarded Austria-Hungary as their traditional enemy.

War with Turkey in 1911–12 had revealed the weakness of Italy's armed forces and put a heavy strain on the economy. In 1914, anti-war sentiment was strong.

Italy aspired to the status of a major European power, despite an inadequate level of economic development. It had territorial ambitions in the Mediterranean, the Balkans, and Africa, as well as around its northeastern border, where a substantial number of Italians lived under Austro-Hungarian rule.

When war broke out in August 1914, the Italian prime minister, Antonio Salandra, saw the conflict as an opportunity to fulfil these aspirations. He adopted an attitude that he dubbed *sacro egoismo* ("sacred self-interest"), which meant offering to join the side that promised Italy the best deal. Germany urged Austria-Hungary to cede some disputed territory to Italy in exchange for Italian entry into the war, but the Austro-Hungarians were reluctant to comply. They grudgingly agreed to offer it the Trentino region in March 1915, but this was too little too late.

The Treaty of London
By spring 1915, the Italian government was leaning heavily towards the Allies, who were promising Italy substantial territory in enemy countries if it entered the war on their side. Allied negotiators held out the prospect of

Supporting the troops
The front page of the French newspaper *Le Petit Journal*, published on 6 June 1915, depicts Italian crowds cheering as their troops depart for war.

Italy expanding its borders to include South Tyrol and the Trentino, Trieste, and part of the Dalmatian coast. They also proposed an Italian protectorate over Albania, recognition of Italian control of the Dodecanese islands, colonies in Africa, and a share in a future carve-up of the Ottoman Empire. This was enough to persuade Salandra

Italian Alpine regiment
Italy's elite mountain warfare troops, the Alpini, are photographed on a glacier in the Alps in 1915. The Alpine battalions played an important role in the war – most of the Austrian front followed the course of the high mountains between Italy and Austria.

and his foreign minister, Giorgio Sonnino, to sign the Treaty of London with the Allies on 26 April.

Under the terms of the treaty, which remained secret, Italy had to declare war on the Central Powers within a month. This was not easily done. In early May, neutralists in the Italian parliament voted Salandra out of office, but King Victor Emmanuel III, who was pro-war, reinstated him. Italian nationalists, including the prominent poet Gabriele d'Annunzio, mounted a passionate propaganda campaign in favour of joining the war.

On 23 May, Italy declared war on Austria-Hungary. Despite Italy's promise in the Treaty of London, its declaration of war on Germany did not follow until 1916. Austria-Hungary was faced with the task of sustaining a war on three fronts – against Russia, Serbia, and Italy – which could have quickly proved disastrous. But the timing of Italy's declaration of war was fortuitous for Austria-Hungary because at that very moment the successful

Distinctive headgear
The Italian Bersaglieri Corps was a highly regarded light infantry formation. Their wide-brimmed hats were decorated with black capercaillie feathers.

Gorlice-Tarnow Campaign was relieving the pressure on Austro-Hungarian forces fighting the Russians on the Eastern Front.

The Isonzo Campaign
Defending their 600 km (370 mile) border with Italy would have been difficult for the Austro-Hungarian army had it not been for the terrain. Most of the frontier consisted of impassable

mountain peaks, except in the Trentino, where the mountain barrier was traversed by a number of passes. Italian Chief of Staff Luigi Cadorna chose to concentrate his forces at the eastern end of the border, where the Isonzo valley offered a corridor into Austro-Hungarian territory.

The Isonzo was no easy option for the Italians, however, for the Austro-Hungarian forces occupied defensive positions – some blasted out of rock with dynamite – on the ridges, blocking progress from the coastal plain and at the northern end of the valley.

Cadorna opened the First Battle of the Isonzo with an offensive on 23 June. The Italian armies were short of heavy artillery. Their best troops, such as the Alpini and the Bersaglieri, were impressive, but many others were poorly trained peasant conscripts from southern Italy who had little emotional connection with the north of the country.

The initial Isonzo offensive failed, despite the Austro-Hungarians being outnumbered by the Italians, as did three more Isonzo offensives before the end of 1915. Italy lost around

217 The number of Italian generals sacked by Chief of Staff Luigi Cadorna between June 1915 and October 1917.

27,000 soldiers in the four battles, and the ground gained was minimal. Losses on the Austro-Hungarian side were also heavy. Shells exploding on the rocky terrain showered sharp rock fragments over a wide area, causing more casualties per shell than in the soft soil of France.

The Austro-Hungarians clung on to their defensive positions and were gradually reinforced. Cadorna, a much feared commander, dismissed many of his generals and imposed brutal discipline on troops, but he had no tactical or strategic solution to the stalemate on the Isonzo Front.

> **"**Blessed are those in their twenties… who are **hungry and thirsty** for **glory,** for they shall be fulfilled.**"**
>
> GABRIELE D'ANNUNZIO, PRO-WAR SPEECH IN GENOA, 4 MAY 1915

AFTER

The deadlock on the Italian front lasted for almost two and a half years, until it was ended by a victory for the Central Powers at Caporetto (now Kobarid in Slovenia).

GAINS AND LOSSES
Austria-Hungary's position was strengthened by the **defeat of Serbia 140–41 ≫** in the winter of 1915–16. This allowed the Austro-Hungarians to mount an initially successful **offensive at Asiago** in the Trentino in May 1916, although without decisive results. The Italians achieved a limited victory at **Gorizia** (the Sixth Battle of the Isonzo) in August 1916 after Austria-Hungary diverted troops to respond to the **Russian Brusilov offensive 174–75 ≫**.

DEFEAT AT CAPORETTO
The Italians renewed their Isonzo Campaign in spring 1917, advancing to within 15 km (9 miles) of Trieste in June. They reached the **Eleventh Battle of the Isonzo** in September 1917. In October, a joint German and Austro-Hungarian offensive shattered the Italian line at **Caporetto 248–49 ≫**.

ITALIAN POET (1863–1938)

GABRIELE D'ANNUNZIO

Italian poet and nationalist Gabriele d'Annunzio campaigned in favour of Italy going to war in 1915, and maintained a high profile throughout the conflict. He took part in a daring, if futile, naval raid on the Austro-Hungarian port of Bakar and, in August 1918, led an air squadron on a 1,100-km (700-mile) flight to Vienna, dropping propaganda leaflets on the Austrian capital. After the war, D'Annunzio protested against the treatment of Italy in the peace treaty and led a private army to occupy the disputed port of Fiume (now Rijeka in Croatia), which he held for over a year.

Anzac Troops

"You are going out to **fight for Australia... strive** to keep a **fit man** and **do your duty.**"

CHARLES GREENWOOD OF VICTORIA, LETTER TO HIS SON, AUGUST 1918

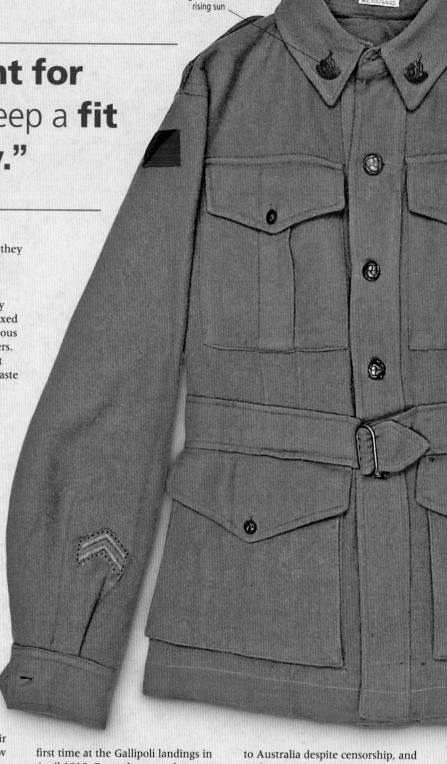

Turndown collar with bronze insignia of the rising sun

In 1914, Australia and New Zealand were self-governing colonies within the British Empire. At the outbreak of war, they unhesitatingly joined the war against Germany in solidarity with what most of their white population regarded as "the mother country".

An appeal for volunteers to serve in Europe met an enthusiastic response. Although the colonies' armies were tiny, all male Australians and New Zealanders had received basic military training.

Both countries were sparsely populated, with Australians numbering almost 5 million and New Zealanders about a million – yet they provided a remarkably high number of soldiers in the course of the war, with some 416,000 enlisting in Australia and 124,000 in New Zealand, including a Maori contingent. In October 1914, the first convoys of the Australian Imperial Force and the New Zealand Expeditionary Force assembled on Australia's west coast, from where they sailed to Egypt.

60 PER CENT of Australians serving on the Western Front were killed or wounded.

53 PER CENT of New Zealand troops serving on the Western Front were killed or wounded.

Fearsome reputation

The New Zealanders were primarily farmers, the Australians a more mixed group, with city dwellers as numerous as men from the outback and miners. They had in common a tough spirit of independence and a distinct distaste for formal discipline and normal military etiquette. Lodged in training camps alongside the Egyptian pyramids, the Anzac troops soon developed a fearsome reputation among British officers and the Egyptian civilian population.

It was in Egypt that they were designated the Australian and New Zealand Army Corps, soon conveniently abbreviated to Anzac. A British officer, General Sir William Birdwood, was given command of the corps. It was a good appointment because he won the enduring respect of the Anzac soldiers, a unique achievement for a senior British commander. In contrast, General Sir Alexander Godley, who led the New Zealanders throughout the war, was savagely disliked. Friction over the quality of British generals and their perceived carelessness with the lives of colonial troops became acute after Anzac soldiers entered action for the

General Sir John Monash

One of the most respected Allied generals of the war, Monash was an Australian of German Jewish origin. From May 1918, he commanded the Australian Corps, the largest corps on the Western Front.

first time at the Gallipoli landings in April 1915. From the start, the Australians and New Zealanders showed themselves to be resourceful, dauntless fighters under some of the worst conditions experienced anywhere in the war.

But frustration and discontent soared as the campaign became bogged down in stalemate. News of heavy casualties suffered in ill-conceived attacks, such as the bayonet charges ordered by Godley at the Nek in August, fed back to Australia despite censorship, and enthusiasm for volunteering faltered. New Zealand introduced conscription in mid-1916, but Australians rejected it in two referendums.

The Gallipoli Campaign would ever after define World War I for Australians and New Zealanders, yet it was merely the beginning of their soldiers' contribution to the war.

After Gallipoli, some Anzac troops stayed in the Mediterranean, forming a mounted division to fight the Turks

Australian service tunic

Soldiers were issued with a distinctive khaki tunic made of Australian wool. A thoroughly practical garment, it was a looser fit than the standard British tunic and had four large external pockets at the front.

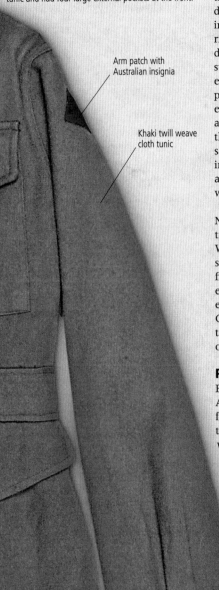

Arm patch with Australian insignia

Khaki twill weave cloth tunic

in the Sinai and Palestine. Because they did not correspond to the British notion of proper cavalry, these troops were designated as "mounted infantry", carrying only rifle and bayonet and denied the cavalryman's sword until nearly the end of the war. Their performance was eventually recognized as outstanding and they enjoyed the satisfaction of riding into both Jerusalem and Damascus by the war's end.

Most Australian and New Zealand troops transferred to the Western Front, serving in France from spring 1916. Fighting in some of the fiercest actions of the trench war, they earned a reputation as elite troops, especially feared and respected by the Germans, while remaining critical of the British high command's acceptance of the need for heavy losses.

Peaceful penetration

By spring 1918, the now independent Australian Corps had become a focus for the development of new battle tactics, dubbed "peaceful penetration", which were designed to exploit the potential of artillery and tanks as offensive weapons and minimize infantry casualties.

Finally under Australian command, with General John Monash leading the corps from May 1918, they spearheaded

Recruitment poster

A wartime poster encourages young Australians to join the troops at Gallipoli. The Australian Imperial Force consisted entirely of volunteers, but it became more difficult to attract new recruits as the war went on.

key attacks in the Hundred Days Offensive that finally won the war on the Western Front.

Some 330,000 Australians and over 90,000 New Zealanders served in the war overseas. About 60,000 Australians and 17,000 New Zealand soldiers were killed. An experience that was never to be forgotten in the histories of the two countries, World War I accelerated a nascent sense of independent nationhood.

New Zealand hat

This khaki felt hat was worn by a soldier in the New Zealand Cyclist Corps. Bicycles were a useful source of mobility in World War I and Anzac cyclists made a significant contribution in a support role.

New Zealand Cyclist Corps badge

November–December 1914 Troops of the Australian Imperial Force and the New Zealand Expeditionary Force sail for Egypt, where they are trained and organized into the Anzac Corps under General Sir William Birdwood.

April–May 1915 The Anzac troops take a leading part in the landings at Gallipoli, Turkey, on 25 April, now celebrated as Anzac Day. They defend a foothold on Anzac Cove against fierce Turkish counterattacks.

August 1915 An attempted breakout from Anzac Cove leads to heavy Australian and New Zealand casualties at Lone Pine, the Nek, and Sari Bair.

December 1915 Australian and New Zealand forces are evacuated from Anzac Cove at the end of the failed Gallipoli Campaign and returned to Egypt, where I and II Anzac Corps are formed.

March 1916 The Anzac Mounted Division is formed in Egypt; the Australians and New Zealanders go on to serve with distinction as light cavalry in the campaigns against Turkey in Palestine and Syria.

March–April 1916 The two Anzac corps are transferred to Europe, and the first Australian and New Zealand troops take up position in the trenches on the Western Front.

LONE PINE ANZAC CEMETERY, GALLIPOLI

July–September 1916 Anzac troops participate in the Battle of the Somme. The Australians suffer heavy losses in the capture and defence of Pozières (23 July–7 August).

June 1917 New Zealand and Australian divisions are prominent in the successful Battle of Messines on the Flanders front.

September–October 1917 Australian and New Zealand soldiers suffer heavy casualties in the Battle of Passchendaele, fought in the rain and mud of Flanders.

December 1917 The five Australian divisions form the Australian Corps under General Birdwood and the New Zealand Division becomes part of British XXII Corps under General Alexander Godley.

July 1918 Under the command of General John Monash, the Australian Corps mounts a successful offensive on the Western Front at Le Hamel (4 July).

August–November 1918 The Australian Corps spearheads a British offensive at Amiens, beginning the war-winning Hundred Days Offensive.

" **Somewhere between the landing at Anzac and the end of the Battle of the Somme, New Zealand** very definitely **became a nation.** "

ORMOND BURTON, NEW ZEALAND STRETCHER-BEARER AND INFANTRYMAN, LATER PACIFIST

BEFORE

Turkey's decision to enter the war on the side of Germany in October 1914 led Britain and France to consider ways of attacking the Turks.

TURKISH TARGETS
The narrow channel of the **Dardanelles** gave sea access from the Mediterranean to the Turkish capital, Constantinople, and from there to the Black Sea and Russia's southern coast. British Admiralty chief **Winston Churchill** sent ships to **bombard Turkish forts** at the mouth of the Dardanelles within days of **Turkey joining the war ‹‹ 74–75**.

DIVERSIONARY TACTIC
Churchill's suggestion for further attacks on the Dardenelles was blocked by the British War Council until the start of 1915, when the **Russians**, hard-pressed by Turkish forces in the Caucasus, asked their **Western allies** to mount a **diversionary attack**. The idea of attacking the Dardanelles was then revived, attracting support as an **alternative** to the **costly fighting** on the **Western Front**.

BRITISH POLITICIAN (1874–1965)

WINSTON CHURCHILL

At the start of World War I, Churchill was a prominent member of Britain's Liberal government. As First Lord of the Admiralty, in command of the Royal Navy, he took the blame for early setbacks in British naval operations and for the fiasco at Gallipoli. Relegated to a minor government post in May 1915, he resigned in November to serve as an infantry officer on the Western Front. In July 1917, he returned to government as an energetic Minister of Munitions. Gallipoli was continually cited against Churchill until it was overshadowed by his performance as British prime minister in World War II.

The Gallipoli Campaign

The Allies initially attempted a naval breakthrough in the Dardanelles straits. When this failed, they embarked upon a land campaign on Turkey's Gallipoli peninsula – a disastrous operation that was a harrowing initiation for Australian and New Zealand troops.

The idea for an attack on the Dardanelles appealed to British politicians, who wanted large gains at small cost. An Allied naval force, they thought, would break through to Constantinople (modern Istanbul), where the threat of its guns would force Turkey to surrender, opening up a sea route to Russia.

But Winston Churchill, the minister responsible for the Admiralty, the prime advocate of the operation, ignored one detail: the Royal Navy did not believe it could be done. The Dardanelles was blocked by minefields and defended by a series of forts and German mobile howitzers.

On 19 February, British Admiral Sackville Carden opened the naval attack. He had a sizeable Anglo-French fleet, including Britain's super-dreadnought HMS *Queen Elizabeth*, but the rest were "pre-dreadnoughts" – dating from before HMS *Dreadnought*, launched in 1906, set a new standard for warships. Their only minesweepers were trawlers fitted with mine-clearing equipment. By 25 February, the Turks had been driven from forts at the entrance to the straits, but beyond that progress had stalled.

In the second week of March, British Minister for War Lord Kitchener ordered landings on the Gallipoli peninsula. The

Turkish hand grenade
The 73 mm (2.8 in) Tufenjieff hand grenade was much used by the Turkish army in trench warfare at Gallipoli. Activated by lighting the rope fuse, it was then lobbed at the enemy.

British 29th Division and the Australian and New Zealand Army Corps (Anzac) were to assemble, along with a French colonial division, at the Greek island of Lemnos, under General Sir Ian Hamilton.

Destroyed by mines
Meanwhile, the naval bid to breech the Dardanelles reached its climax. On 18 March, Admiral John de Robeck sent his battleships forward. Four French pre-dreadnoughts engaged in a close-range duel with forts flanking the Narrows, while the trawlers cleared the mines. After one of the French battleships was beached to avoid sinking, Robeck ordered the others to withdraw. In the process, the French battleship *Bouvet* struck

Shore bombardment
HMS *Cornwallis*, here bombarding Turkish positions, was present at Gallipoli from February 1915 to the evacuation of troops in December.

a mine and sank, taking 639 of its crew with it. Then a British battlecruiser and two British pre-dreadnoughts struck mines. There would be no further attempt at a naval breakthrough.

The task of the army landing force was to take the Turkish positions defending the straits, after which the mines could be cleared and the navy

Landing plans
The Allies intended Anzac troops to cut across the Gallipoli peninsula while other British troops advanced from Cape Helles. They expected to capture the peninsula in a few days.

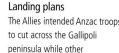

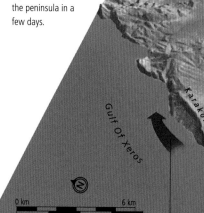

Gulf Of Xeros

Diversionary attack by Royal Naval Division

> **"If the Fleet gets through, Constantinople will fall… and you will have won not a battle, but the war."**
>
> LORD KITCHENER, MINISTER FOR WAR, MARCH 1915

sail through in peace. Hamilton had little information on the terrain of the area or on Turkish defensive positions.

Allied landings

A plan was hastily put together for the British 29th Division to land on beaches, coded S, V, W, X, and Y, at Cape Helles, the peninsula's southern tip. The Anzac troops were to land at an undefended cove further north, while the French staged a diversionary landing on the Asiatic shore.

On the morning of 25 April, Robeck's warships appeared off Gallipoli. As they bombarded the shore, the troops

18,000 The number of Allied soldiers who came ashore on the first day of the Gallipoli landings, 25 April 1915.

12,000 The number of Anzac troops who landed at Gallipoli the same day.

disembarked into rowing boats, towed to shore in lines behind steam pinnaces (small naval boats). At W Beach on Cape Helles, the Lancashire Fusiliers suffered more than 50 per cent casualties, coming under rifle and machine-gun fire as they approached the shore and then finding their way blocked by barbed wire. At nearby V Beach, Turkish machine-guns killed hundreds of British soldiers coming ashore on gangplanks from the troopship SS *River Clyde*. Despite the losses, all the beaches were taken.

Death trap
Australian and New Zealand soldiers move among the dead and wounded on the beach at Anzac Cove. The landing site turned into a trap from which the troops could never break out.

Unfortunately, the Anzac troops had come ashore in the wrong place. They found themselves crowded into a small curve of beach enclosed by ridges and ravines – later known as Anzac Cove. There were no Turkish forces, but reaching the top of Sari Bair Ridge 3 km (2 miles) inland was a daunting physical challenge. As Anzac troops clawed their way towards the summit,

a Turkish counterattack was under way. The Turkish army and its chief German adviser, General Otto Liman von Sanders, had known an attack was coming but not where the landings would be made.

As soon as the naval bombardment began on 25 April, General Mustafa Kemal marched his Turkish 19th Division towards the sound of the

guns. He reached Sari Bair Ridge in time to fire down on Anzac troops caught in mid-climb. After a week's fighting failed to drive the Australians and New Zealanders back into the sea, Kemal ordered his men to dig trenches. The rest of the Cape Helles landings suffered the same fate, bogging down in early May in front of Krithia, just a few miles inland.

»

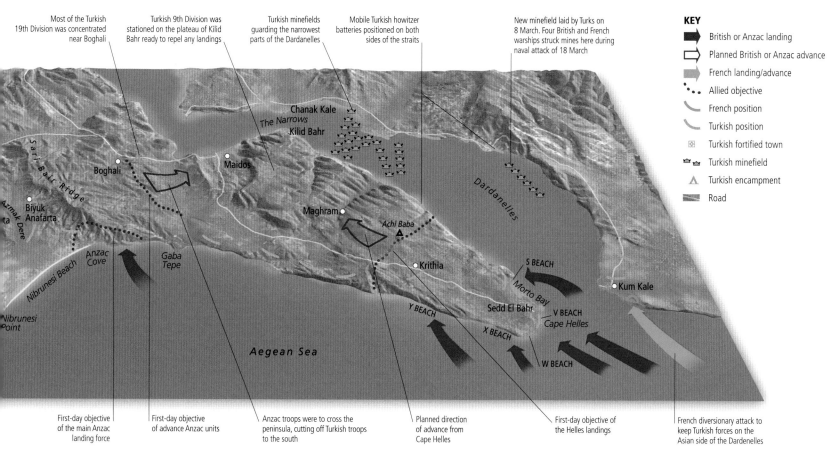

Most of the Turkish 19th Division was concentrated near Boghali

Turkish 9th Division was stationed on the plateau of Kilid Bahr ready to repel any landings

Turkish minefields guarding the narrowest parts of the Dardanelles

Mobile Turkish howitzer batteries positioned on both sides of the straits

New minefield laid by Turks on 8 March. Four British and French warships struck mines here during naval attack of 18 March

KEY

- British or Anzac landing
- Planned British or Anzac advance
- French landing/advance
- Allied objective
- French position
- Turkish position
- Turkish fortified town
- Turkish minefield
- Turkish encampment
- Road

Chanak Kale
The Narrows
Kilid Bahr
Maidos
Boghali
Sari Bair Ridge
Biyuk Anafarta
Azmak Dere
Anzac Cove
Gaba Tepe
Nibrunesi Beach
Nibrunesi Point
Maghram
Achi Baba
Dardanelles
Krithia
S BEACH
Morto Bay
Sedd El Bahr
Kum Kale
Y BEACH
V BEACH
Cape Helles
X BEACH
W BEACH

Aegean Sea

First-day objective of the main Anzac landing force

First-day objective of advance Anzac units

Anzac troops were to cross the peninsula, cutting off Turkish troops to the south

Planned direction of advance from Cape Helles

First-day objective of the Helles landings

French diversionary attack to keep Turkish forces on the Asian side of the Dardanelles

TURKISH GENERAL (1881–1938)

MUSTAFA KEMAL ATATÜRK

An officer in Turkey's wars in Libya and the Balkans before World War I, Mustafa Kemal was a divisional commander at Gallipoli, where his performance made him a national hero. After the war, he led a Turkish national revival, driving the Greek out of Anatolia in 1921–22 and replacing the Ottoman Empire with a Turkish Republic, with himself as president. From 1934, he was known as "Atatürk" – father of the Turks. He introduced many reforms including the emancipation of women, banning traditional Islamic dress, and replacing Arabic script with the Western alphabet.

An assault at Achi Baba in mid-July was a costly failure. Meanwhile, the ground forces lost the back-up support of naval guns as the warships were withdrawn in the face of attacks by German U-boats.

The failure of the Gallipoli landings was a factor influencing a change in British government in May 1915. Churchill, the person most publicly identified with the Dardanelles Campaign, lost control of the Admiralty.

While France continually pushed for all resources to be focused on the Western Front, Britain was not

Anzac push to capture Sari Bair Ridge and various diversionary attacks to keep other Turkish forces occupied.

The landings at Suvla Bay took place on 6 August 1915. Some 20,000 men came ashore easily against only light opposition, but inert leadership from the elderly commander of the Suvla force, General Frederick Stopford, left the soldiers waiting on the beaches while Kemal organized a swift and vigorous counterattack.

>> Spring mutated into an unbearably hot summer without significant movement. Trenches and bunkers swarmed with flies feasting on unburied corpses, and dysentery decimated the ranks. Anzac troops carrying food, water, and ammunition up from the beach to men perched on the rocky slopes passed the wounded and dead being carried down in the opposite direction.

On 19 May, Kemal launched a mass attack at Anzac Cove, attempting to swamp the Anzac positions with sheer numbers. It ended in 13,000 of his men

being killed or wounded. The heaps of corpses in No Man's Land were so unbearable that a temporary truce was negotiated so that the dead on both sides could be buried.

Renewed offensives

In June and July, the British who were entrenched in the north of Cape Helles, now supported by the French on their right flank, attempted new offensives. Reinforced by Gurkhas and newly arrived Territorials, the Allies succeeded in gaining a certain amount of ground to no decisive effect.

6 The number of Victoria Crosses awarded to the Lancashire Fusiliers in the contested landing at W Beach, Gallipoli, on 25 April 1915.

7 The number of Victoria Crosses awarded to Australians for their role in the Battle of Lone Pine, on 6–10 August 1915.

prepared to accept a humiliating defeat. Fresh divisions were found for General Hamilton, who was ordered to break the deadlock. A plan was devised for new landings at Suvla Bay, north of Anzac Cove, to coincide with a major

Close-quarter battles

Meanwhile, Anzac troops engaged in some of the fiercest fighting of the war. A mere diversionary attack by the Australians at Lone Pine developed into an epic close-quarter struggle when the attackers broke into the Turkish trench system. Fighting with grenades and bayonets in a warren of tunnels and bunkers, the Australians

Turkish rifle
The Turkish army ordered large numbers of 9.5 mm Mauser rifles and carbines in 1888 and some were still in use in World War I, alongside 7.65 mm Mausers. Most Turkish equipment was supplied by Germany.

eventually took the position, winning an astonishing seven Victoria Crosses.

In the main Sidi Bair offensive, New Zealanders captured the ridge of Chanuk Bair in two days of savage combat, only to be driven off again by artillery fire and a Turkish counterattack. Australian troops designated to attack another key objective, Hill 971, became lost in the maze of ridges and gullies and never found their target.

In a notorious incident on 7 August, at a ridge known as the Nek, soldiers of the Australian Light Horse, fighting as infantry, were thrown forward in

repeated futile frontal assaults ordered by General Alexander Godley. They suffered more than 60 per cent casualties. By 10 August, stalemate had resumed. On 21 August, the British attempted to reignite the campaign with attacks against Scimitar Hill from Suvla Bay and Hill 60 from Anzac Cove, but the frontal charges against prepared Turkish positions, poorly supported by artillery, ended in failure.

Disease and hardship
There was no more serious fighting at Gallipoli, but the terrible losses continued. Disease took a heavy toll on troops in the trenches. They were poorly supplied with food and drink and had very limited medical support. The excessive heat of the Turkish summer was followed by deadly floods and blizzards in the autumn and winter months.

Complaints about the state of the troops and the quality of command, especially from Australia, led to Hamilton's dismissal in October. His

British artillery in action
A British 60-pounder heavy field gun bombards Turkish trenches at Cape Helles. The gun required a crew of ten men, who could fire two rounds per minute to a range of over 9,000 m (10,000 yd).

Kitchener at Gallipoli
British Minister for War Lord Kitchener visits the trenches at Gallipoli in November 1915 to view the situation at first hand. The evacuation of Allied forces began the following month.

successor, General Sir Charles Monro, took a swift look at the situation and recommended withdrawal. His view did not win easy acceptance in London, where bold spirits were pushing for a new attempt at a naval breakthrough in the Dardanelles. After visiting Gallipoli, Kitchener put an end to such fantasies and proposed evacuation of Suvla Bay and Anzac Cove.

Allied evacuation
On 7 December, the British cabinet ordered the evacuation of all troops from Gallipoli. This tricky operation

was carried out with skill and efficiency. More than 100,000 troops were embarked from Suvla Bay and Anzac Cove between 10 and 20 December, followed by the remaining 35,000 from Cape Helles by 9 January 1916. This logistical feat was the most successful episode in the whole campaign.

" Accept this **honourable desire** of ours and **make our bayonets sharper** so we may **destroy our enemy!**"

HASSAN ETHEM, TURKISH SOLDIER, PRAYER, 1915

AFTER

More than 44,000 Allied troops died at Gallipoli. The Turkish death toll was much higher, with possibly as many as 90,000 killed in the successful defence of their country.

LASTING EFFECTS
The British and French suffered far more casualties at Gallipoli than the Australians and New Zealanders, but the campaign would always have a **special significance** in the history of the

colonies and on their road to becoming **independent nations**. The campaign also had a marked emotional **significance for Turkey**, a country evolving from a multinational empire into a nation state. Militarily its effect was to allow Turkey to fight on for three more years. The **Allied failure** encouraged **Bulgaria to enter the war** on the side of the Central Powers in October 1915, sealing the **fate of Serbia 140–41 »**.

TURKISH ARMY UNIFORM

Battle of Lone Pine

On 6 August 1915, the First Australian Division made a diversionary attack at Lone Pine to support the Allied landings at Suvla Bay, Gallipoli. While the initial assault succeeded in capturing the Turkish trenches, the Australians soon faced waves of Turkish counterattacks. Lone Pine developed into a brutal, five-day, close-quarter battle ending in up to 3,000 Australian and 7,000 Turkish casualties.

"We reached the Turkish lines and found the first trench covered in with logs and branches… There was a partial check, some men fired in through the loopholes, others tried to pull the logs apart. Out runs our officer, old Dickie Seldon, waving a revolver, 'This won't do men! On! On! On!'

I slid down into the trench… The Turks ran round a corner and got into a large cave place… Captain Milson took command… and asked if we would follow him. We all said 'yes' so he threw a bomb and dashed across. A dozen Turks shot him and he fell dead… I was next and as I ran I threw my rifle into the possie and pulled the trigger. I suppose they had never got time to load… but no one followed and I was there alone with no bombs and only my rifle.

I felt a little dickie I can tell you… Whack! Like a sledgehammer on the head and down I went across Milson's body and several Turks, some of whom were only wounded, and groaned and squirmed from time to time. I bled pretty freely and then I got a crack on the shoulder from a shrapnel pellet, which hurt badly…

Soon I heard someone call behind me 'Hullo Australia' and I crawled down the trench and found Seldon with one eye shot out, but still going, leading a party, and I explained the position to him and he sent me away to a temporary dressing station while he went and fixed up the Turks… I got my head bandaged and a drink of rum… I picked up a rifle and… went on… to dig in the now captured trench."

HUGH ANDERSON, FIRST BRIGADE, AUSTRALIAN IMPERIAL FORCE, IN A LETTER TO HIS PARENTS

Anzac troops at Gallipoli
The Gallipoli Campaign of 1915, the first major engagement of Anzac troops in the war, was a series of fierce battles lasting more than eight months. It resulted in thousands of casualties on both sides.

« BEFORE

Russia and Ottoman Turkey were multinational empires. Where their territory met in the Caucasus, Armenians lived on both sides of the border.

ARMENIAN NATIONALISM
The Christian Armenians in Turkey had a history of **conflict** with the Ottoman Empire's **Muslim rulers**. In the 1890s, Armenian **nationalist agitation** provided a pretext for Turkey's **massacres** of thousands of Armenians. In August 1914, the Turkish government asked Armenian representatives, gathered at Erzurum in eastern Turkey, to agree to **incite rebellion against Russian rule** in the Caucasus in case of war. The Armenians, tempted by Russian offers of **autonomy**, rejected the proposal. After Turkey entered World War I, the Caucasus and eastern Anatolia became a **war zone**.

Armenian refugees
In September 1915, thousands of Armenians from villages in southern Turkey were taken aboard warships of the French Mediterranean fleet. The refugees were carried to Port Said in Egypt.

The Armenian Massacre

The massacre and deportation of Turkey's Armenian population took place against a background of fighting between Turkish and Russian forces on the Caucasus front. It has been described by some as the first genocide of the 20th century.

During Turkey's disastrous offensive in the Caucasus in the winter of 1915, Armenians fought as conscripts in the armies of both Turkey and Russia. However, the Russian forces also included units of Armenian volunteers who were fighting for the liberation of Armenians from Turkish rule. Russia was happy to encourage an Armenian revolt against Turkey, in the same way as the Turks hoped for an uprising by Turkic peoples and Muslim Kurds living in the Russian Empire.

The Turkish army suffered a major defeat on the Caucasus front at Sarikamish between December 1914 and January 1915. The Turkish War Minister Enver Pasha, who commanded the Turkish forces in person, blamed his humiliating defeat on Armenian treachery. In February,

he ordered all Armenians serving in the Turkish army to be disarmed and transferred to labour battalions.

Ethnic resentments

Meanwhile, the situation in eastern Anatolia was confused and unstable. Ethnic tensions had become acute. Much of the region's population consisted of Muslims who, having been displaced from the Russian-ruled Caucasus in the 19th century, bitterly resented the Christian, allegedly pro-Russian, Armenians.

The Kurds, another element in the region's ethnic mix, also nourished a hatred of the Armenian population. Incidents of attacks on Armenians proliferated. Turkish soldiers, ill-fed, undisciplined, and demoralized, murdered Armenians and looted their villages. The Armenian nationalists

fighting alongside the Russians also committed atrocities in Muslim villages that fell into their hands.

The situation came to a head in April 1915, when the Armenian population in the eastern Turkish city of Van, which was under threat from Russian forces, rose in armed revolt against its Turkish governor. On 19 April, the Armenians seized control of the town and held it against Turkish counterattacks until the Russians arrived. In the Armenian view,

Kurdish horsemen
Turkey's Caucasus campaigns against Russia included Kurdish light cavalry. Kurds engaged in much casual killing of Armenians, their tradional enemy, during the deportations of 1915–16.

the fighters in Van were acting in self-defence, forestalling a planned Turkish massacre of the male population. To the Turks, it was confirmation that the Armenians constituted a disloyal minority that could undermine their war effort.

Mass deportations

On 24 April, as the Allies were beginning their landings at Gallipoli, Turkish Interior Minister Talaat Pasha ordered the arrest of some 250 members of the Armenian urban elite living in Constantinople. It was in effect a public declaration that the Armenians constituted an internal enemy. Several hundred more prominent Armenians were detained over the following weeks. It took until 29 May for an outright attack on Turkey's Armenian population to be enshrined in law. The Tehcir ("deportation") law authorized the

600,000 The estimated number of Armenians killed in the deportation and massacres, according to some historians. Other scholars put the figure at around 1.3 million.

relocation of anyone considered to be a threat to the country's defences. The law gave the Turkish military authorities a free hand to embark upon the mass deportation of Armenians from Anatolia. The measure was presented as a necessary response to a wartime emergency but it also embodied the long-held attitudes of extreme Turkish nationalists in the government. Men such as Talaat Pasha and Enver Pasha were happy to see Anatolia, popularly regarded as a Turkish heartland, "cleansed" of an alien minority. They had no intention of allowing the Armenians ever to return.

Death and disease

The Armenians were ordered to be deported from Anatolia to Syria and Iraq. The deportations were carried out in a brutal manner that ensured a massive death toll.

Army commanders had specific instructions "to crush without mercy … all resistance".

The clearance of a village often began with the massacre of its male population, considered a potential source of such "resistance", so that the deportees on the roads towards Syria were mostly women and children. These refugees were given no time to prepare for the arduous journey before setting out. Food supplies were inadequate or nonexistent. En route, the Armenians came under attack from hostile Kurds, against whom they were defenceless. Walter Geddes, an American businessman who was travelling in eastern Turkey at the time, described seeing deportees "actually dying of thirst", and young girls "so exhausted they had fallen on

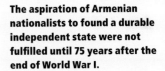

Russian military hat
In winter, Russian soldiers wore a sheepskin *papakha*. Such hats were vital in the freezing conditons of the Caucasus.

the road… with their already swollen faces exposed to the sun". For most of the refugees who reached camps in Syria, there awaited a slow and painful death through disease, hardship, or malnutrition.

The Allies, kept informed of the deportation chiefly by neutral Americans in Turkey, lodged vigorous protests but did almost nothing to intervene. A small number of Armenians on the coast were carried to safety on Allied warships.

Several hundred thousand Armenians took refuge in Russian-held territory, but their fate turned out to be little better than that of the deportees in Syria, with half of them dying of diseases such as cholera and typhus before the war's end.

Shortages at the front

Meanwhile, fighting on the Caucasus front continued. But Russian forces, led by General Nikolai Yudenich, were hampered by a shortage of military supplies. They could attempt only limited action through 1915, consolidating their position west of Lake Van. In the first half of 1916, Yudenich went on to the offensive in Anatolia, capturing the fortress town of Erzurum and the port of Trabzon in February. By then the area's Armenians had vanished.

AFTER »

The aspiration of Armenian nationalists to found a durable independent state were not fulfilled until 75 years after the end of World War I.

HOPES DESTROYED

The **Bolshevik Revolution** of 1917 ended the Russian invasion of Anatolia and allowed the **Turks to invade the Caucasus**, fighting the Armenians who had declared a republic there. Part of Anatolia was granted to Armenia by the **Treaty of Sèvres**, which was imposed on Turkey after World War I. However, a successful **military campaign** by **Turkish nationalists** in 1920 and the **Bolshevik occupation** of Russian Armenia swiftly **destroyed the Armenian republic**.

NATIONHOOD AT LAST

An **independent Armenia** was finally created after the **collapse of the Soviet Union** in 1991. Debate continues as to whether the Armenian massacre of 1915–16 constitutes "genocide", a label that Turkey has always denied.

GENOCIDE MEMORIAL, YEREVAN, ARMENIA

" As the exiles moved, they left… another caravan – that of dead and unburied bodies."

HENRY MORGENTHAU, US AMBASSADOR TO TURKEY IN WORLD WAR I, DESCRIBING THE ARMENIAN DEPORTATIONS

In the Service of Empire

"Don't be grieved at **my death,** because I shall **die arms in hand...** This is the most happy death that anyone can die."

INDAR SINGH, SIKH SOLDIER, WRITING HOME FROM FRANCE, SEPTEMBER 1916

West African soldiers
Newly arrived troops of the Tirailleurs Sénégalais pose for the camera on the Western Front at the time of the First Battle of the Marne.

Before World War I, large areas of Africa and Asia were ruled by the European powers. Lacking sufficient resources to police, defend, and expand their empires with troops sent out from home, the mother countries recruited soldiers locally, either as volunteers or conscripts. Placed under European command, these colonial troops usually proved loyal, providing that such matters as dietary customs and religious observances were respected.

The colonial authorities preferred to recruit from ethnic groups thought to display a traditional warrior spirit. In British-ruled India, Sikhs, Nepalese Gurkhas, and Punjabis were the main source of recruits. The French found soldiers in North Africa, where Berbers and Arabs from Algeria, Morocco, and Tunisia supplied the Tirailleurs. Also of high repute among French colonial troops were the Tirailleurs Sénégalais, drawn from all parts of French West Africa.

Summoning the troops

That colonial forces might be of use in a European war was by no means obvious. When, in 1910, French General Charles Mangin argued the case for black troops from the colonies supplementing France's conscript army in a future European conflict, his views were considered interesting but controversial by fellow militarists.

In the event, the demands of World War I led to the exploitation of every resource the combatant countries had available. Troops from French North Africa were shipped across to France as soon as war was declared. The Tirailleurs Sénégalais followed later, along with soldiers from Madagascar and French Indochina. In total, about

Indian troops in France
Turbanned lancers of the British Indian Army ride along a French rural road near Amiens in autumn 1914. The Indians generally received a warm and enthusiastic welcome from the French people.

200,000 Algerians, Moroccans, and Tunisians fought on the Western Front and at Gallipoli, along with more than 160,000 West African troops. The West Africans were engaged in some of the harshest fighting of the war, and about 30,000 died in the conflict.

> **TIRAILLEURS A French term for lightly armed skirmishers or riflemen. It was applied indiscriminately to all locally recruited French colonial troops.**

The French colonies also helped in the production of munitions. Some 50,000 Vietnamese and 13,000 Chinese from French Indochina worked in French munitions factories. Tens of thousands of Chinese labourers, recruited by the British and the French, were brought to perform support work on the Western Front.

The Indian Army

Britain could call on troops from its self-governing, white-ruled colonies – Canada, Australia, New Zealand, and South Africa – but India was a potentially much larger source of manpower. The regular army of India numbered around 155,000 soldiers at the beginning of the war. These were organized into divisions, each of which included a battalion of British troops alongside the Indian battalions.

Primarily intended for use on India's northern frontier or for suppressing internal revolts, the Indian Army was short of modern weapons and equipment, and its officers were not used to the demands of European warfare. The standard of its troops at the start of the war was high, but the quality was diluted by the rapid expansion in numbers.

An Indian expeditionary force of two infantry divisions and a cavalry division reached France in time to take part in the fighting in Flanders from October 1914. When the war descended into the stalemate of trench warfare, they proved a valuable addition to Britain's overstretched and depleted front-line forces, and they fought bravely at Neuve Chapelle, the Second Battle of Ypres, and Loos. The Germans especially feared the Gurkhas because of their skill at mounting silent raids across No Man's Land with their sharp-edged kukris (knives with a curved blade).

Transferred to Mesopotamia

By autumn 1915, the morale of Indian troops in France was in serious decline, mostly because of a loss of vital cohesion. Heavy casualties resulted

French colonial troops
A company of Tirailleurs Annamites – infantry from French Indochina – wait for action after joining the Allied forces at Salonika, Greece, late in the war. The diversity of troops underlined the global nature of the conflict.

in troops fighting in fragmented formations under unfamiliar officers. By December 1915, all Indian infantry were being transferred from the Western Front to Mesopotamia, where it was thought they would be more used to the terrain and hot climate.

In total, 1.25 million Indian soldiers contributed to the British war effort. More than 70,000 were killed in the service of the Empire.

The question of loyalty

A large proportion of the colonial troops employed by both France and Britain were Muslim. The entry of Turkey into the war in October 1914 raised the possibility of such troops being asked to fight fellow Muslims. In fact, Turkey's call for all Muslims to join in a jihad against the Allies had little effect. There were rare instances of soldiers refusing to fight – such as when the 15th Lancers in Basra would not march on Baghdad in February 1916 – but on the whole, Muslim soldiers fought the Turks without reservation, whether at Gallipoli, in Mesopotamia, or in Palestine.

For their personal honour, the honour of their regiments, and their meagre pay, they served the empires to the end.

" **Gurkhas** had **crawled** far behind enemy lines… and dealt out **destruction** with their kukris before **being killed.**"

CAPTAIN R.F.E. LAIDLAW, AT GULLY RAVINE, GALLIPOLI, JUNE 1915

KEY MOMENT
THE SINGAPORE MUTINY

Early in the war, Germany backed an attempt by an Indian nationalist group, the Ghadar Party, to promote an anti-British mutiny in the Indian Army. Ghadar agents achieved influence over the Muslim Indian Fifth Light Infantry garrisoned in Singapore. Falsely informed that they were to be sent to fight Muslim Turkey, the regiment mutinied on 15 February 1915. More than

40 British soldiers and European civilians were killed. German prisoners were offered arms, but they refused to join the mutineers. Marines and sailors from British, French, and Russian ships combined to suppress the mutiny. A court martial condemned 47 of the mutineers to death by firing squad. The executions took place in public at Outram Prison.

TIMELINE

1904 Commander-in-chief of the British Indian Army, Lord Kitchener, reorganizes the force to create a field army of 10 divisions.

1910 French General Charles Mangin publishes his book *La Force Noire* advocating the use of colonial troops to defend France in the event of a European war.

August 1914 French colonial troops from Africa are ferried to France at the outbreak of war and take part in the first battles on the Western Front.

1 September 1914 Indian troops land at Mombasa in British East Africa for a campaign against German East Africa; they suffer a defeat at the Battle of Tanga on 5 November.

26 September 1914 Indian Expeditionary Force A lands in France to join the British Expeditionary Force on the Western Front.

October 1914 Indian troops see action for the first time on the Western Front, at La Bassée.

5 November 1914 Indian Army Force D lands in Mesopotamia (Iraq) and goes on to occupy Basra on 3 November.

11 November 1914 Ottoman Sultan Mehmed V calls on all Muslim subjects of Britain and France to join a jihad against the colonial powers.

GURKHA KUKRI

February 1915 Indian infantry stage a mutiny against their British officers in Singapore. The mutiny is quickly suppressed.

March 1915 On the Western Front, two Indian divisions play a prominent part in the failed British offensive at Neuve Chapelle.

22 April 1915 French colonial troops are among the casualties in the first poison gas attack on the Western Front at Second Ypres. Some break rank in panic.

April 1915 British Indian troops and French colonial soldiers, the Tirailleurs Sénégalais, take part in the Gallipoli landings.

November 1915 The Indian Corps is withdrawn from the Western Front and transferred to Mesopotamia.

30 April 1916 Indian troops of the Sixth (Poona) Division surrender to the Turks at the siege of Kut al-Amara in Mesopotamia.

24 October 1916 During the Battle of Verdun, French colonial troops perform outstandingly in the retaking of Fort Douaumont.

March 1917–October 1918 A large contingent of Indian troops takes part in the successful British campaign against Turkey in Palestine.

June 1918 The British Cabinet approves a proposal by Secretary of State for India, Edwin Montagu, for an increased measure of representative government in India.

French colonial cavalry
The Spahis were Arab and Berber cavalry regiments, brought from French North Africa to fight in France at the start of the war. Their appearance attracted the photographer Jules Gervais-Courtellemont, who took this colour autochrome image in 1915.

Turkish–German cooperation
A unit of Bavarian artillery struggles forwards to aid the Turks in their campaign in Mesopotamia. Movement of troops and equipment was difficult, especially during seasonal floods along the Tigris and Euphrates rivers.

« BEFORE

The Ottoman sultan's call for a Muslim holy war against the British Empire in November 1914 was a direct challenge to Britain's position in India and the Middle East.

FAILURE TO STIR REVOLT
Turkish and German plans **to carry the war** through **Persia to Afghanistan** and Muslim areas of **northern India** came to nothing. **Egypt also failed to rise up** against British rule, even when the Turks

100 MILLION The estimated number of Muslims living under British rule in 1914. This was more than a third of the world's entire Muslim population at the time.

attacked the **Suez Canal « 75** in February 1915. The situation inside **Persia was precarious**, with Russia, Britain, and Germany vying to extend their influence there. In November 1914, an expeditionary force from British India **occupied Basra** in southern Mesopotamia to strengthen the British position in the oil-rich Persian Gulf.

Disaster in Mesopotamia

In 1915, British Indian forces advanced from Basra towards Baghdad in an overt display of imperial authority. But the prestige of the British Empire suffered a humiliating blow when British forces had to surrender to the Turks at Kut al-Amara in April 1916.

The operation in Mesopotamia was launched and controlled by the British Government of India in Calcutta. Initially only a few thousand troops of the Indian Army were landed at the mouth of the Shatt al-Arab waterway, in southern Mesopotamia, and their mission was limited. They were to establish a defensible position and prevent any Turkish interference with British-owned oilfields across the border in southern Persia (now Iran).

The need for a "forward defence" led to the occupation first of the port of Basra and then of Qurna, further north at the junction of the Tigris and Euphrates rivers. Unlike the British

authorities in Cairo, the Government of India felt no inclination to encourage an Arab revolt against the Turks. Local Arab irregulars thus sided with Turkish forces in a vigorous counterattack in April 1915. This was repulsed by entrenched Anglo-Indian troops at Shaiba outside Basra.

A newly appointed commander of the expeditionary force, the ambitious General Sir John Nixon, took this defensive victory as a springboard for the occupation of the whole of southern Mesopotamia as far north as Nasiriya and Amara, expanding the campaign well beyond its original goals. Given the Allies' setbacks against

the Turks in the Gallipoli Campaign, the conquest of Mesopotamia was seen as a way for Britain to reassert its prestige in the eyes of its Muslim subject peoples.

The Anglo-Indian advance
Despite doubts expressed by the War Office in London, Nixon was authorized by the Government of India to advance troops first to Kut al-Amara, reached in late September, and then onwards towards the historic Muslim city of Baghdad. While Nixon stayed in Basra, the troops on the ground were commanded by General Sir Charles Townshend, an officer with

"We drink river water... Except for the barren, naked plain there is nothing to see... our hope is in God alone."

ABDUL RAUF KHAN, 21ST COMBINED FIELD AMBULANCE, MESOPOTAMIA, LETTER, 7 MARCH 1916

an experience of colonial warfare in India, including holding the fort at Chitral against a rebel siege. However, Townshend was not confident in his mission. Every step towards Baghdad extended the overstretched supply line that linked him to the base at Basra. Moreover, men were decimated by disease and debilitated by the heat.

The Turkish forces

As Townshend's forces advanced up the Tigris, accompanied by river gunboats, Turkish forces prepared to defend Baghdad. Under the command of Ottoman General Khalil Pasha and German veteran Baron Colmar von der Goltz, the Turks dug into trenches at Ctesiphon south of Baghdad. The commander on the ground was Nur ud-Din Pasha.

Townshend attacked the Turkish position on 22 November. The front-line trench was taken and then held against Turkish counterattacks, but by 25 November Townshend had only 4,500 men fit enough to fight – less than half his original force. He decided to withdraw back down the Tigris to Kut al-Amara.

The Anglo-Indian force reached Kut in poor condition. They had been harassed en route by Arab tribesmen. The many sick and wounded lacked adequate medical care. Townshend had only a hazy notion of the state of his food supplies, but decided to sit tight and await relief rather than

Decorated water flask
A British soldier's water bottle is engraved with scenes from the Mesopotamian Campaign. Lack of clean drinking water was a major cause of illness for the troops operating in what is now Iraq.

continue the withdrawal to Basra. On 7 December, Nur ud-Din's forces arrived and, after failing to take Kut by assault, settled into trenches for a siege.

In Basra, the British reorganized. Nixon was dismissed and a new Tigris Corps was created to mount

a relief effort. Plagued by problems of transport and logistics – there were no proper roads or railways, and the river seemed always either too low or in flood – British relief forces pushed northwards from Basra. They were repeatedly repelled by determined Turkish troops, who were dug into defensive positions south of Kut.

Meanwhile, inside Kut conditions were quickly deteriorating. Disease and lack of food reduced the garrison to a pitiable condition. Mules and horses were slaughtered for meat. Morale collapsed and relations between the British officers and their Indian soldiers rapidly deteriorated. An attempt at breakout was out of the question; Townshend was unable even to mount harassing attacks against the Turkish siege trenches.

Forced to surrender

On 22 April, the last British relief expedition was brought to a halt 16 km (10 miles) from Kut. Four days later, Townshend opened negotiations with Khalil Pasha, proposing to pay for his force to be paroled. This improbable offer was refused and on 29 April Townshend surrendered. Some 10,000 British and Indian troops passed into Turkish hands. Their treatment was harsh, with about 4,000 dying in captivity. Townshend, meanwhile, was allowed to live in a comfortable house near Istanbul for the rest of the war.

Townshend at Kut al-Amara
An officer in the British Indian Army, General Sir Charles Townshend commanded the Sixth Indian Division in the Mesopotamian Campaign from April 1915 to the surrender at the siege of Kut a year later.

AFTER »

Viewing the surrender at Kut as a blow to its prestige, Britain devoted much time and many resources to the capture of Mesopotamia.

RETAKING KUT

In summer 1916, London took over control of the Mesopotamian Campaign from the Indian Government. Basra's **port facilities were expanded, roads and railways built**, and **modern weaponry** supplied. Under General Sir Stanley Maude, **British forces retook Kut al-Amara** in February 1917 and **occupied Baghdad** in March. After Maude died of cholera in November, the British effort was scaled down. The British **occupied the oil town of Mosul** at the end of the war.

TURKISH BUGLE

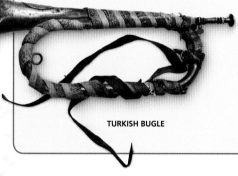

War in Egypt and Mesopotamia
British forces repelled a Turkish attack on Egypt at the Suez Canal, but in Mesopotamia a British advance was stopped by the Turks at Ctesiphon and then forced back to the garrison at Kut al-Amara.

KEY

➡ British offensive	▮➡	British retreat
➡ Turkish offensive	▯➡	Turkish retreat
✹ Battle or siege	＼	Oil pipeline
┄┄ Major railway		

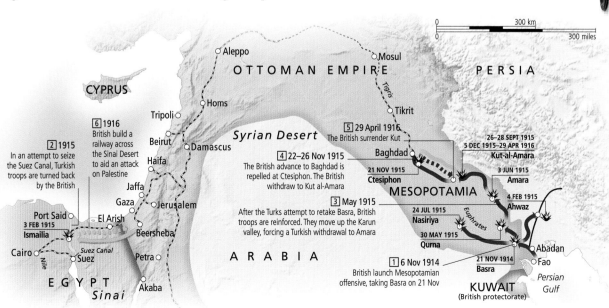

Britain's Royal Navy had experienced a mixed start to the war in 1914, with a number of successes offset by humiliating setbacks.

BRITISH ERRORS

In August 1914, Britain made the mistake of allowing the **German warships** SMS *Goeben* and SMS *Breslau* to sail to **Constantinople** ≪ 74–75, helping to **bring Turkey into the war** on the German side. Britain also lost ships to German submarines and mines and suffered a **defeat in the Pacific at Coronel** ≪ 83 in November. For the British public, the worst incident came on 16 December when **German battlecruisers shelled** towns on the **east coast of England**.

NAVAL BLOCKADE

The British had recorded **victories** at **Heligoland Bight** in the North Sea, on 28 August 1914, and at the **Battle of the Falkland Islands** ≪ 83 in the South Atlantic, on 8 December. **Germany** remained **under British naval blockade** and its High Seas Fleet was unable to leave port for fear of **destruction** by the Royal Navy's Grand Fleet.

TURKISH SWORD BAYONET

The Battle of Dogger Bank

In January 1915, the stand-off between the British and German fleets in the North Sea flared into battle at Dogger Bank. Vice-Admiral Franz von Hipper's German battlecruisers were met by a British force under Vice-Admiral David Beatty and narrowly avoided a major defeat.

German naval strategy was built on the hope of eroding Britain's naval superiority through piecemeal destruction of warships, especially by mines and submarines. To avoid this, the Royal Navy did not attempt a "close blockade" of the German coast, which would have put British ships at risk, but used its control of the exits from the North Sea (around Scotland in the north and Dover and Dunkirk in the south) to maintain a "distant blockade" of Germany.

In principle, this strategy left the German surface fleet free to sortie into the North Sea at will. However, if German warships left port, the Royal Navy aimed to drive them back home or, preferably, destroy them. The British Admiralty had a secret weapon in this cat-and-mouse game. Naval intelligence under Admiral Reginald "Blinker" Hall had obtained German naval code books and set up listening posts to monitor the radio traffic of German ships. By 1915, the codebreakers in Hall's Room 40 at the Admiralty in London could warn of a sortie before the German ships had left port.

German aims

On 23 January 1915, Vice-Admiral Franz von Hipper, who had led a raid on English coastal towns in December, was ordered to take his fleet into the North Sea to attack British trawlers and patrol boats at Dogger Bank, a shallow area 100 km (62 miles) off England's east coast. Hipper had three battlecruisers – his flagship SMS *Seydlitz* leading *Moltke* and *Derfflinger* – plus destroyers and light cruisers.

German commander
Admiral Franz von Hipper, the commander of the battlecruisers of 1 Scouting Group, led the German squadron that fought the British at Dogger Bank.

Battlecruisers were the stars of naval warfare, with guns as heavy as those on battleships but with more speed.

When Room 40 informed the Admiralty that Hipper was setting to sea, Vice-Admiral David Beatty was ordered to lead the Royal Navy's response. Leaving the Scottish port of Rosyth, he steamed south with five battlecruisers – his flagship HMS *Lion* leading *Tiger*, *Princess Royal*, *Indomitable*, and *New Zealand* – joining up with light cruisers and destroyers at Harwich.

Sinking of SMS *Blücher*
German sailors scramble to escape from the cruiser *Blücher* as it capsizes at the end of the battle. There were only 234 survivors out of a crew of more than 1,000 men.

Battlecruiser HMS *Lion*
The flagship at the Battle of Dogger Bank, HMS *Lion* was, like other battlecruisers, fast and heavily armed, but it proved vulnerable to well-directed German shells.

Shortly after 7am on 24 January, the outlying ships of the opposing forces exchanged fire. Hipper quickly realized he had fallen into a trap and turned for home at full speed. Beatty led the chase in the fast-moving *Lion*, with his other battlecruisers trying to keep up. Leading the German fleet on board the *Seydlitz*, Hipper was hampered by the need to keep in touch with his slower ships, especially the out-of-date armoured cruiser *Blücher*.

Gaining on the Germans, the British battlecruisers opened fire shortly before 9am. The range was extreme – more than 18 km (11 miles) – and the ships were moving at maximum speed, so hits were infrequent. At 9:43am, the *Lion* landed the first major blow, exploding *Seydlitz's* two aft turrets with an armour-penetrating shell. More than 160 men were killed, and a worse disaster was averted only through the heroism of a German sailor, Wilhelm Heidkamp, who flooded the magazines to protect them from fire. *Blücher* also took a battering and fell further behind the rest of the German force.

Missed opportunity

The British, however, failed to distribute their fire evenly between the German ships. The battlecruisers *Moltke* and *Derfflinger* were untouched and, as the range shortened, their shells hit the *Lion* with increasing frequency. By 10:45, Beatty's flagship was so battered it came to a stop. The battlecruiser *Tiger* was also badly damaged.

From the British point of view, the battle that had opened so promisingly degenerated into a mess. Beatty first ordered an unnecessary turn to avoid a nonexistent U-boat and then, using flag signals instead of radio, failed to convey his order for the pursuit to be resumed with all speed. Instead, Beatty's subordinates concentrated the fire of their four battlecruisers on the *Blücher*, which Hipper had resolved to abandon to its fate. The *Blücher* finally capsized and sank, while Hipper led his battlecruisers safely back to port.

The crippled *Lion* was towed back to Rosyth, where it received a hero's welcome. The battle had, after all, been a demonstration of British naval strength. But Beatty had fumbled an opportunity to inflict a crushing defeat on the German navy.

The British and German navies drew very different conclusions from their experience of the Battle of Dogger Bank.

SUBMARINE WARFARE

Kaiser Wilhelm II was appalled by the risk that had been taken with his precious warships and **banned further sorties**, not relenting until the following year. The commander of the German High Seas Fleet, Admiral Friedrich von Ingenohl, was replaced by Hugo von Pohl, who

THE IMPERIAL GERMAN NAVY FLAG

in February 1917 gave the order to adopt **unrestricted submarine warfare 220–21 ≫** against Allied shipping.

THE BATTLE OF JUTLAND

To counter **superior German gunnery,** the British concluded they must increase their rate of fire at the expense of safety procedures. This led to many deaths at the **Battle of Jutland 170–71 ≫**.

"The **ship was capsizing...** men **fell or ran** down her side **into the water...**"

PAYMASTER HUGH MILLER ON THE CRUISER HMS ARETHUSA, DESCRIBING THE SINKING OF THE BLÜCHER

After its defeat at the Battle of the Falklands, the German navy started using submarines to attack Allied shipping.

CHANGE OF STRATEGY

Germany's **submarines** were initially intended for use in coastal defence and to sink British warships. The German navy planned to use surface commerce raiders against **Allied merchant shipping**. However, after Germany's decisive defeat at the **Battle of the Falkland Islands << 83** in December 1914, its ability to threaten Allied commerce with surface vessels was curtailed.

NORTH SEA WAR ZONE

While trade to Britain was unimpeded, the Royal Navy maintained a **maritime blockade** of Germany. In November 1914,

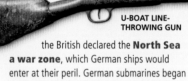

U-BOAT LINE-THROWING GUN

the British declared the **North Sea a war zone**, which German ships would enter at their peril. German submarines began **attacks** against British merchant shipping. The first merchant ship destroyed by a German U-boat was the steamship SS *Glitra*, sunk off Norway on 20 October 1914.

The Sinking of the *Lusitania*

In February 1915, Germany launched a campaign of submarine attacks against Allied shipping off the British coastline. This led to the notorious sinking of the transatlantic liner *Lusitania* and set the Germans on course for a confrontation with the United States.

Germany began discussing the possibility of a systematic submarine campaign against merchant shipping in the late autumn of 1914. The U-boat fleet numbered only a few dozen boats, but they were proving capable of attacks on merchant ships in the North Sea. Submarine commanders were respecting accepted "prize rules", which meant they had to surface, stop a ship, and allow its crew and passengers to disembark before sinking it. If a more intensive campaign was to be mounted, U-boats would need permission to attack without warning, firing torpedoes while submerged. The risk of outraging neutral opinion in doing this, especially in the USA, was outweighed by the need for a more effective response to Britain's naval blockade.

Easy prey

On 4 February 1915, Germany announced that Allied merchant ships in waters around Britain and Ireland were liable to be sunk and it would be impossible "to avert the danger thereby threatened to crew and passengers".

About 20 U-boats were dispatched to seek suitable targets. With no convoy system in place, isolated merchant ships were easy prey. On 22 April, the German embassy in Washington, D.C. published a warning to passengers intending to cross the Atlantic on the British liner *Lusitania*, reminding them that ships entering the war zone around the British Isles

1.9 The average number of merchant ships being sunk by U-boats every day by August 1915.

were liable to be destroyed. Nevertheless, on 1 May, the liner left New York for Liverpool with almost 2,000 people on board. In the hold was a small amount of military cargo, chiefly rifle ammunition.

On the afternoon of 7 May, Captain Walther Schwieger, commanding the submarine *U-20*, sighted the *Lusitania* off the south coast of Ireland. The U-boat was too slow to mount a pursuit, especially when it was submerged to attack, but the liner turned into its path. Schwieger struck the *Lusitania* with a single torpedo in the centre of the ship. Desperate attempts to launch the ship's lifeboats were cut short when the liner sank only 18 minutes after being hit.

The death toll of 1,198 comprised 785 passengers and 413 crew. Almost 100 of the victims were children, and 128 were US citizens. Germany tried in

Final voyage
The Cunard liner *Lusitania* leaves New York on what was to be its last voyage, on 1 May 1915. Launched in 1906, it was awarded the coveted Blue Riband the following year for the fastest crossing of the Atlantic.

Lusitania relic

This lifebelt from the ship is fitted with canvas breeches. The liner had the equipment to evacuate all its passengers and crew, but only six of its 48 lifeboats were launched successfully before the ship sank.

AFTER »

The German U-boat campaign continued through 1915 and into early 1916, further antagonizing the USA.

AMERICA ENTERS THE WAR
On 19 August 1915, a German U-boat sank the **White Star liner *Arabic***, killing 44 people, including three Americans. On the same day, a U-boat was sunk by the British **Q-ship *Baralong*** and all the survivors were executed. President Wilson, more concerned by the *Arabic* sinking, obtained a German pledge to avoid further attacks on passenger ships. However, in March 1916, a U-boat sank the ferry *Sussex* in the English Channel.

Germany was temporarily deterred from submarine warfare by hostility in the USA. Renewed attacks in February 1917 led to the **USA joining the war 212–13 »**.

LUSITANIA COMMEMORATIVE MEDAL

vain to argue that the *Lusitania* was a legitimate target. To most people in Allied and neutral countries, the sinking appeared straightforward mass murder. There were riots in cities in Britain and its dominions, with German-owned shops looted. The worst disorders occurred in the city of Liverpool, where many of the crew had lived.

The US president, Woodrow Wilson, responded to the attack with a series of indignant notes to the German government, in which the sinking was denounced as illegal and counter to "the rights of humanity". Germany was left in little doubt that if it continued attacking unarmed merchant ships – especially passenger ships – without warning, then the USA might be provoked into entering the war.

The submarine campaign was not immediately suspended, but U-boat commanders were ordered to take care in choosing targets and follow prize rules where possible.

British tactics

To counter the submarine campaign, Britain's merchant ships flew the flags of neutral countries, knowing that U-boats had orders to avoid sinking neutral ships. Merchant captains were encouraged to fight back if stopped by a U-boat in accordance with prize rules, a form of self-defence that outraged the Germans.

In summer 1915, the Royal Navy began fitting innocent-looking merchant steamers with hidden guns. These Q-ships, as they were called, lured U-boats into making a surface attack and then blasted them out of the sea. This tactic encouraged the Germans to make submerged attacks without warning, which the British could then denounce as immoral.

> "We can **no longer remain neutral spectators...** Our position… is being assessed by mankind."
>
> AMERICAN ENVOY COLONEL EDWARD HOUSE, TELEGRAM TO PRESIDENT WOODROW WILSON, 7 MAY 1915

Wartime Posters

Propaganda posters were used by all the combatant nations for a number of different purposes – to inspire patriotism, convince volunteers to enlist, or persuade civilians to give financial aid through schemes such as war bonds.

1 CALL TO CONTINUE THE WAR (RUSSIAN)

2 WARTIME THRIFT (FRENCH)

1 A **Russian soldier** unfurls a banner that reads, "War until victory". After the overthrow of the Tsar in March 1917, Russia's new Provisional Government attempted to keep Russia in the war. **2** A **French poster** explains the importance of agricultural production to the war effort; the caption reads, "I'm a brave War Hen. I don't eat much and I produce a lot." **3 British men** are urged to join the army or face the guilt of non-participation in this recruitment poster. Conscription, introduced in Britain in 1916, reduced the need for such campaigns. **4 American women** in this Home Front poster, published in 1918, are encouraged to take up war work in the factories. **5** A **German poster** advertises the unveiling of a wooden knight monument at Königsberg. Nails could be driven into such statues by members of the public in exchange for donations to support the war effort. **6 Designed for Australia's** last recruitment campaign in 1918, this poster appeals for volunteers. Australia did not introduce conscription at any point during the war. **7 Italian civilians are urged** to buy war bonds to support the soldiers serving at the front. **8 This poster advertises** a German U-Boat propaganda film released in

early 1917. U-Boat captains were often portrayed as daring heroes in German propaganda. **9 Advertising an exhibition** of aircraft and captured war material, this German poster shows a plummeting British biplane. **10 Appealing to** German **patriotism**, this poster depicts the battle against British tanks. It urges German civilians to support the fight by subscribing to a war bond. **11 An Austro-Hungarian poster** shows a 16th-century soldier waving a flag bearing the Habsburg coat of arms. **12 This Australian propaganda poster** shows a blood-soaked beast wearing a *pickelhaube*, the distinctive German helmet. The beast grasps a globe, showing it to be vulnerable to the expansionist ambitions of Germany. **13 Germany is depicted** as a thuggish ape in this US poster. The image played on perceptions of Germany's wartime barbarism. **14 Men are encouraged** to join the US Tank Corps in this recruitment poster. The Tank Corps first went into combat in September 1918. **15 American posters** often showed Uncle Sam, the national personification. This one is based on a British poster design featuring Lord Kitchener striking a similar pose.

5 THE IRON WARRIOR (GERMAN)

8 THE U-BOATS ARE OUT! (GERMAN)

9 WAR BOOTY (GERMAN)

10 CALL TO BUY WAR BONDS (GERMAN)

11 SUBSCRIBE TO THE WAR LOAN (AUSTRO-HUNGARIAN)

Daddy, what did YOU do in the Great War?

3 DADDY WHAT DID YOU DO
IN THE GREAT WAR? (BRITISH)

For
EVERY
FIGHTER
a
WOMAN
WORKER

CARE
for
HER
through *The* YWCA

UNITED
WAR
WORK
CAMPAIGN

4 WOMEN WORKERS (US)

The TRUMPET CALL

NORMAN LINDSAY

W.A. Gullick Gov' Printer, Sydney.

6 RECRUITMENT POSTER (AUSTRALIAN)

*Fate tutti
il vostro dovere!*

LE SOTTOSCRIZIONI AL PRESTITO SI RICEVONO PRESSO IL

CREDITO ITALIANO

7 EVERYONE MUST DO THEIR DUTY! (ITALIAN)

?

12 ANTI-GERMAN PROPAGANDA
(AUSTRALIAN)

DESTROY
THIS MAD BRUTE

ENLIST

13 CALL TO DESTROY GERMANY (US)

TREAT'EM
ROUGH!

JOIN THE
TANKS
United States Tank Corps.

14 TANK CORPS RECRUITMENT (US)

I WANT YOU
FOR U.S. ARMY
NEAREST RECRUITING STATION

15 I WANT YOU (US)

Pro-war march
The Preparedness Movement campaigned for the neutral USA to expand its military forces. It attracted those Americans who wanted their country to fulfil the role of a great power.

America and the European War

« BEFORE

In the early 20th century, the USA was a fast-growing economic power, with a rapidly expanding population.

OVERSEAS INVOLVEMENT
The USA had **limited experience of military involvement** overseas. The Americans had fought a brief one-sided war against Spain in 1898, which left them **in possession of the Philippines**, where they conducted a vicious counter-insurgency campaign against Filipinos seeking independence. They also intervened in Central America and the Caribbean, including in **Nicaragua** from 1912 and **Haiti** from 1915.

THE US PRESIDENCY
In 1912, **Woodrow Wilson 214–15 »**, a Democrat, was elected president. During his first two years in office he was preoccupied with economic and social reforms. He was also distracted by the death of his wife in the first week of the war.

When war broke out, American President Woodrow Wilson declared the USA neutral. But Americans soon found themselves drawn towards involvement, whether through economic interests, the ties of sentiment, or outrage at the aggressive actions of combatant countries.

The initial decision to avoid involvement in the war was uncontroversial in the United States. The USA traditionally avoided what Founding Father Thomas Jefferson had dubbed "entangling alliances" with foreign powers.

Although the USA had a population of about 100 million in 1914, its army was small, with fewer than 100,000 troops, a third of the size of the army of Belgium. The USA did, however, have a strong modern navy, reflecting the recognized need for defence of the country's shores and trade routes, as well as concern for the international prestige possession of a fleet conferred.

The natural decision for a non-militarist country with no vital interests at stake, neutrality also avoided a potentially difficult confrontation between ethnic and US identities. The USA's governing elite was mainly of British stock, but approximately 10 per cent of Americans were of German origin, and Scandinavian immigrants also tended to identify with Germany. Those most hostile to the Allied cause were the Irish Americans, who were inclined to be more anti-British than the Irish in Ireland.

German provocations
During the first year of the war, the USA shifted from non-involvement towards support for Britain and France. Germany alienated US opinion by its mistreatment of the Belgians at the start of the war. Other German actions, such as the bombing of European cities

Torpedo factory
A US naval workshop manufactures torpedoes for its navy. The industrial capacity of the USA was vital to the Allies in their struggle against Germany, even before the USA entered the war.

by Zeppelins and the first use of poison gas created an image of Germany as a militarist aggressor. Nonetheless, President Wilson's Secretary of State in 1914, William Jennings Bryan, was determined to maintain US neutrality and non-involvement. He was outraged by the British naval blockade of Germany, which interfered with the USA's right of free trade. On the other hand, the British were courteous, listened politely to American concerns, paid compensation for confiscated goods, and did not kill Americans.

Germany had no means of blockading Britain except by using submarines. The U-boat sinking of the liner RMS *Lusitania* in May 1915, with heavy American loss of life, tipped the balance of US public opinion – and Wilson's personal stance – against Germany. The pacifistic Bryan was replaced by Robert Lansing as Secretary of State. Lansing adopted "benevolent neutrality" – still aiming to keep the USA out of the war if possible but backing the Allies.

Financial motives

The USA also had a strong economic interest in the Allied war effort. It had a third of the world's industrial capacity, as well as being a major producer of food and raw materials. The Central Powers and the Allies wanted to draw on these immense resources. German agents worked at purchasing vital goods and routing them through neutral countries to avoid the British naval blockade, but their efforts had limited success.

The British and French were able to place orders and ship goods at will. Initially this was funded by selling off

$2.3 BILLION The sum lent by US banks to the Allies by April 1917.

$27 MILLION The sum lent by US banks to Germany by the same date.

British assets in the USA, but from 1915 American banks were authorized to supply massive loans to finance trade with the Allies – money they knew they would never see again if the Allies lost the war.

Business boomed, with US exports rising to double their pre-war level by the end of 1915 and share prices on Wall Street going up by 80 per cent. German agents in the USA mounted a campaign of sabotage, such as setting fire to ships and warehouses, to inhibit the supply of war material to the Allies. The British intelligence services made sure the US authorities were kept informed of these illegal activities. Franz von Papen, the military attaché at the German embassy in Washington, was expelled in December 1915 for promoting sabotage attacks.

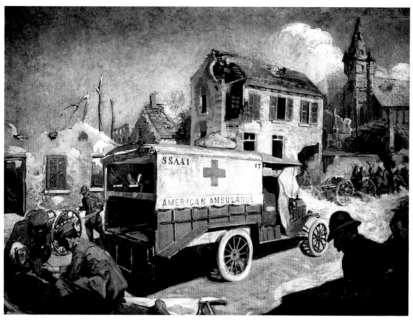

To the rescue
American volunteers drove ambulances from the start of the war, helping British, Belgian, and French troops. This painting by Victor White shows the American Field Service aiding a wounded soldier at Cappy-sur-Somme.

Meanwhile, many individual American volunteers had been actively involved in the European war from its earliest stages. In 1914, the expatriate colony of Americans resident in Paris embraced the French cause. They set up the American Field Service, which became a valued source of medical support for Allied forces in the field. Those Americans with a taste for combat joined the French Foreign Legion, including the Harvard-educated poet Alan Seeger, who wrote one of the war's most famous poems, *I Have a Rendezvous with Death*, before being killed on the Western Front. American volunteers flew as pilots in French air units, forming the Lafayette Escadrille (Squadron) that fought in the skies over Verdun in 1916.

Tension builds

In 1915, pro- and anti-war argument raged. The Preparedness Movement, led by former US Chief of the General Staff General Leonard Wood and former President Teddy Roosevelt, argued that the USA needed to make ready for war by introducing universal military service. It argued that

AFTER

In the US presidential elections of 1916, Wilson was re-elected as "the man who kept us out of the war". But this stance didn't last.

THE USA DECLARES WAR
Wilson's preferred role was as a mediator. He sent his envoy, "Colonel" Edward House, to European capitals to **seek a peace settlement**, but in vain. Meanwhile, evidence of hostile German intent mounted, including the **Zimmermann Telegram 212–13 ›** of January 1917 encouraging Mexico to attack the USA. Congress declared war in April 1917 after Germany adopted **unrestricted submarine warfare**, which affected US shipping.

WARTIME PROPAGANDA POSTER

conscription would unite the nation's ethnically fragmented population. This stance was opposed by anti-war groups, notably socialists, women's groups, and church organizations.

The consequence of contradictory pressures was a compromise: the National Defense Act of December 1915. The army was to double in size, but there would be no conscription, and the National Guard was to be enlarged. The outcome was seen as a defeat for the Preparedness Movement and a victory for those who wanted to keep the USA out of the war.

FIGHTER PILOT (1894–1961)

EUGENE BULLARD

The world's first black fighter pilot, Eugene Bullard was born in Columbus, Georgia. He left the USA as a teenager and emigrated first to Britain and then to France. In 1914, he joined the French Foreign Legion and saw action as an infantryman on the Western Front, for which he was awarded the Croix de Guerre. In 1917, Bullard learned to fly and joined the Lafayette Escadrille Squadron, American volunteers serving in the French air service. He flew on combat missions between August and November 1917. His fellow American pilots joined the US Army after the USA entered the war, but Bullard was rejected on account of his colour.

"There is such a thing as a nation being so right it does not need to convince others by force that it is right."

WOODROW WILSON, US PRESIDENT, SPEECH IN PHILADELPHIA, 10 MAY 1915

Airship firebomb
This incendiary bomb was dropped by Zeppelin *LZ38* in the first airship raid on London on 31 May 1915. Too small to cause much damage, the bomb was released by hand out of the airship's gondola.

« **BEFORE**

Count Ferdinand von Zeppelin, a former German cavalry officer, developed his first airship, *LZ1*, in 1900. "Zeppelin" became a generic term for all lighter-than-air craft.

MILITARY POTENTIAL
The possibility of **airships attacking cities with bombs** was widely imagined before World War I – appearing, for example, in H.G. Wells's 1908 fantasy novel *The War in the Air* – and was discussed by senior German commanders.

Germany had acquired a dozen metal-framed **Zeppelin** and wooden-framed **Schütte-Lanz** rigid airships by the outbreak of the war. Other combatants used a range of rigid airships and non-rigid airships known as "blimps", but Germany was well ahead of them in this field.

Yarmouth raided
The east coast port of Great Yarmouth was hit in the first German airship raid on Britain on 19 January 1915. Four people were killed in the attack by two German navy Zeppelins, *L3* and *L4*.

The Zeppelin Raids

In 1915, Germany mounted bombing raids using Zeppelin and Schütte-Lanz airships against Paris, London, and other cities. Although limited in effect, the night-time attacks of these giant aircraft made an indelible impression on the people who witnessed them.

Deployed by the German army and navy from the start of the war, airships proved effective in a naval reconnaissance role, and the idea of also using them to bomb targets in Britain fascinated German military commanders. Kaiser Wilhelm had qualms about authorizing bombing raids on Britain, but was led by stages to lift restrictions on airship operations.

Mounting a bombing campaign was, however, no easy matter. The airships' huge bulk and slow speed – the largest were 200 m (650 ft) long and travelled at 80–95 kph (50–60 mph) – made them vulnerable to being shot down. To prevent this, attacks were made at night, but this posed a challenge to navigators, especially after Britain and France introduced blackouts. In addition, airships required favourable weather. Many missions were aborted because of poor weather or operating problems such as engine failure.

Bombing Britain
The campaign against Britain began with attacks on England's east coast towns from January 1915. London was bombed for the first time on 31 May and raids later spread to the Midlands and northeast England. Captain Peter Strasser, head of the German navy's airship fleet, imagined Britain being overcome by "extensive destruction of cities, factory complexes, dockyards…". But Germany never had many airships – 16 took part in the largest raid of the war – and their bombload was modest. In total, 51 German airship raids on Britain are estimated to have killed 556 people, and damage to buildings and other infrastructure was limited. The moral impact was out of all proportion to the material effect. British civilians felt fear and outrage at being attacked in their

> **71** **The number of people killed in the war's deadliest airship raid on London, on 31 October 1915. One bomb struck London's Lyceum theatre, killing or injuring 37 people.**

homes. Politicians responded to public opinion by switching resources from the Western Front to home defence. Fighter aircraft were brought back from the front to intercept the raiders, and London was ringed with searchlights and anti-aircraft guns in an effort to repel the airships.

Air attacks were mounted, with some success, against Zeppelin sheds in Belgium and Germany. Through 1916, the airships faced more losses. In February, two were shot down by anti-aircraft fire over the French city of Nancy. In June, an airship returning from an abortive raid on Britain was destroyed over Belgium when a British pilot dropped bombs on its gas bag.

Deflated and defeated
The development of incendiary rounds made it easier for aeroplanes to attack airships. On the night of 2 September, Lieutenant William Leefe Robinson, flying a BE2c biplane, shot down airship *SL11* within sight of London. By the year's end, five more airships had been shot down over Britain by ground fire or pursuit aircraft.

These were unsustainable losses for Germany. Refusing to abandon the campaign, the German navy lightened its airships to make them "height-climbers", operating at altitudes that aeroplanes could not reach. This made them invulnerable to enemy action but problematic for their crews, who were

Zeppelin look-out
The captain (left) looks out of the side of a gondola under the airship's gas bag, while a coxswain steers the craft. Operating an airship was a complex business, typically requiring at least 16 crew.

flying at over 4,900 m (16,000 ft) in unheated, unpressurized craft. Five "height-climbers" were lost on a single mission against Britain in October 1917. The airship bombing campaign had in effect been defeated.

AFTER »

Aeroplanes began to replace airships in bombing campaigns against Britain, though airships were still sometimes used to transport supplies.

REPLACED BY PLANES
Germany revitalized its bombing campaign against Britain and France in summer 1917 by using **Gotha aeroplanes** instead of airships **232–33 »**, inflicting more damage at lower cost. Occasional **airship raids on Britain** continued until August 1918, when German naval airship chief **Peter Strasser** was **killed** in an attack across the North Sea.

BANNED BY VERSAILLES
Germany was banned from possessing military airships after the war under the terms of the **Treaty of Versailles 338–39 »**, but in the 1920s it resumed its lead in commercial lighter-than-air flights. By World War II, all countries had abandoned airships as impractical.

Zeppelin downed by an aircraft
This painting, *Lieutenant Warneford's Great Exploit* by F. Gordon, depicts the first German airship to be destroyed by an Allied aircraft. Warneford, of the Royal Navy Air Service and flying a Morane-Saulnier monoplane, bombed the airship over Belgium.

Campaigns on the Eastern Front

In 1915, the overstretched Russian armies fought a series of disastrous battles, from the Baltic to the Carpathians. By contrast, the Austro-German Gorlice-Tarnow offensive was one of the most successful campaigns of the whole war.

In early 1915, the Russians and the Central Powers had more or less symmetrical plans for offensives. Russia aimed to strike against East Prussia in the north and through the Carpathian Mountains into Hungary in the south. Field Marshal Hindenburg and General Ludendorff planned a German offensive at the Masurian Lakes in East Prussia, to coincide with an Austro-Hungarian offensive in the Carpathians.

The Central Powers struck first. At the Second Battle of the Masurian Lakes, launched in a snowstorm on 7 February, Hindenburg and Ludendorff attempted to trap the Russian Tenth Army with a vast pincer movement. One Russian corps, finding itself encircled, surrendered en masse in the Augustow Forest, but the rest of the Tenth Army escaped, and the front restabilized.

On the Carpathian front, in March, Austria-Hungary was rocked by the fall of the fortress of Przemysl and its 120,000-strong garrison after a Russian siege lasting 133 days. Neither side made much progress in fighting in the

The Eastern Front in 1915

Between the Gorlice-Tarnow offensive on 2 May and the end of September 1915, the Russians suffered a series of severe reverses, obliging them to abandon Poland and Lithuania to German and Austro-Hungarian forces.

high Carpathian passes. Considering that Russian soldiers had been short of every form of equipment, from rifles, bullets, and shells to boots and overcoats, they had put up a creditable performance on both fronts.

The Gorlice-Tarnow offensive

Animosity between German Chief of the General Staff Erich von Falkenhayn and the Hindenburg–Ludendorff partnership shaped the next moves. Rejecting Hindenburg's and Ludendorff's pleas for an offensive in

BEFORE

The fighting on the Eastern Front in 1914 had produced no decisive result. The Russians suffered defeats against the Germans but won victories over Austria-Hungary.

FOCUS ON THE EAST

Field Marshal Paul von Hindenburg and his Chief of Staff Erich Ludendorff, in East Prussia, argued for maximum resources to **knock Russia out of the war**. German Chief of the General Staff Erich von Falkenhayn did not believe Russia could be easily defeated, but agreed to stand on the **defensive** on the **Western Front** and **transfer troops** to **the East**.

RUSSIAN GAINS AND LOSSES

By the start of 1915, Russia had pushed the Austro-Hungarians back to the Carpathian Mountains and was **besieging** the Galician fortress of **Przemysl** ≪ **71**. The Russians had **defeated Turkish forces** at **Sarikamish** ≪ **75** on the Caucasus front. They had, however, been forced to **pull back** behind Lodz in Russian Poland ≪ **70–71**.

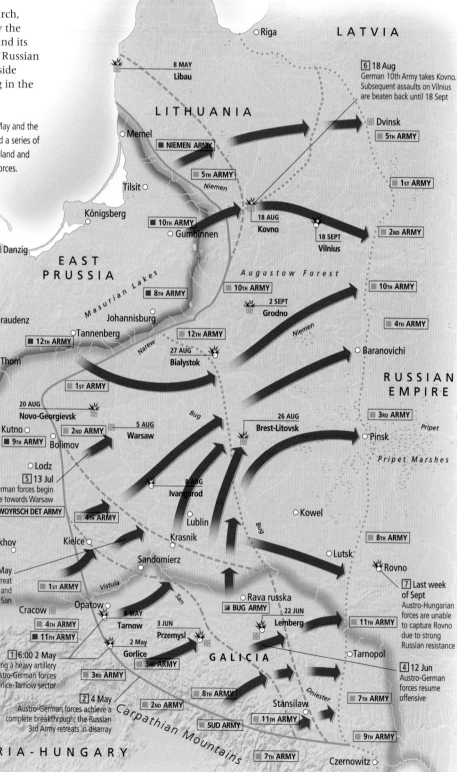

KEY
- ⊠ Major fort/fortified town
- ▪ Austro-Hungarian army
- ▪ German army
- ▪ Russian army
- ➤ Austro-German movements
- ⌒ Russian positions 1 May
- ⌒ Russian positions 1 Jun
- ⌒ Russian positions 13 Jul
- ⌒ Russian positions 15 Aug
- ⌒ Russian positions 30 Sept
- 24 SEPT Date of capture by Austro-Germans
- ✺ Major battle

6 18 Aug
German 10th Army takes Kovno. Subsequent assaults on Vilnius are beaten back until 18 Sept

5 13 Jul
Austro-German forces begin advance towards Warsaw

3 15 May
Despite Russian resistance, the retreat continues. By 1 Jun Austrians and Germans are established east of the San

1 6:00 2 May
Following a heavy artillery bombardment, Austro-German forces attack in the Gorlice-Tarnow sector

2 4 May
Austro-German forces achieve a complete breakthrough; the Russian 3rd Army retreats in disarray

4 12 Jun
Austro-German forces resume offensive

7 Last week of Sept
Austro-Hungarian forces are unable to capture Rovno due to strong Russian resistance

0   100 km
0   100 miles

East Prussia, Falkenhayn concentrated his resources on a new Eleventh Army under General August von Mackensen in northern Galicia. Mackensen was also given effective command of the Austro-Hungarian Fourth Army.

On 2 May, this Austro-German force launched an offensive between Gorlice and Tarnow, in the gap between the Carpathians and the Vistula river. The Russian Third Army holding the sector was woefully ill-prepared. A four-hour artillery bombardment destroyed poorly constructed trenches and drove the Russian infantry into headlong flight. Neither the Russian system of command nor their railway network was capable of a rapid movement of reserves to block the breakthrough. By 10 May, the Russians had retreated to the San river, which was crossed by Austro-German forces a week later. Tens of thousands of Russian soldiers, reduced to fighting with bayonets due to lack of ammunition, surrendered.

Russian counterattacks failed and on 3 June Przemysl was retaken by Austria-Hungary. The retreat of the Russian Third Army forced the armies to its south to pull back as well. By early July, most of Galicia was in the hands of the Central Powers.

Russian retreat

Hindenburg and Ludendorff scorned Falkenhayn's breakthrough, arguing that in driving the Russians back he was missing the chance to encircle and destroy them. They envisaged an offensive from East Prussia to the Pripet Marshes that would cut off the Russian armies in Poland. Falkenhayn instead

The Germans conquer Vilnius
A poster celebrates Germany's final success against the Russians in 1915 – the capture of Vilnius, capital of the Russian Baltic province of Lithuania. Hindenburg and Ludendorff are given pride of place in the centre.

Khaki wool

Reversible shoulder strap with rank and unit number

Brass buckle plate

Russian tunic
The Russian army modernized its uniform after its defeat in the Russo-Japanese War of 1904–05. Soldiers entered World War I wearing a khaki version of the 19th-century pullover shirt-tunic, the *gymnasterka*.

authorized Mackensen to continue his advance, turning northeast across the Vistula towards Brest-Litovsk. Hindenburg and Ludendorff were reduced to a supporting role, commanding offensives from East Prussia into Lithuania and the north of the Polish salient.

For their part, the Russians were determined not to be encircled and were ready to sacrifice territory to keep their armies intact. The Germans advanced across Poland in July and August, but they were slowed by the poor roads and lack of railways. The Russians withdrew in front of them. This became known as the Great Retreat. As they withdrew, the Russian troops adopted scorched-earth tactics. Crops were burned, animals killed, bridges blown, and buildings destroyed. A policy of denying resources to the

enemy spilled over into looting and attacks on civilians, especially Jews. Hundreds of thousands of refugees were driven in front of the retreating armies. No provision was made for this displaced population, who ended up starving in Russian towns.

The Russian commanders achieved their objective as a defensive line was stabilized in September, but a blow had been delivered to the Russian Empire.

Imperial visitor
Tsar Nicholas II (second from left) visits the front in May 1915. In September 1915, Nicholas took over from his uncle, Grand Duke Nikolai (far right) as commander-in-chief of the Russian forces.

> " No **cartridges**, no shells. **Bloody fighting** and difficult **marches day after day.**"
>
> RUSSIAN GENERAL ANTON DENIKIN, IN HIS MEMOIRS, "OCHERKI"

AFTER ≫

Despite suffering casualties of between one and two million in the battles of 1915, including hundreds of thousands of soldiers taken prisoner, Russia was prepared to fight on.

TSAR NICHOLAS TAKES CHARGE
On 1 September 1915, **Tsar Nicholas II** assumed supreme **command of the Russian armies**. This ensured he would be personally identified with any future military reverses. Meanwhile, the **poor state of supply** to the troops at the front was popularly blamed on **corruption and treachery** at the tsarist court and in the government. In fact, a surprising **improvement in arms production** meant that Russia's armies were equipped to continue the war in 1916, with mixed success.

CONQUEST OF SERBIA
In the last months of 1915, Germany and Austria-Hungary turned their attention to the **conquest of Serbia 140–41 ≫**. While this was under way, Falkenhayn took the decision to **divert resources from the Eastern Front** for a major offensive against the French at **Verdun 154–55 ≫**. This prevented Field Marshal Hindenburg and General Ludendorff from pursuing an offensive strategy and allowed the **Russians** to regain the initiative with the **Brusilov offensive 174–75 ≫** in the summer of 1916.

War horses
A Russian field gun is hauled across a stream on the Eastern Front. Horses were used for combat and logistical purposes. Millions of them died from injuries, accidents, exhaustion, or neglect.

Machine-Guns

Machine-guns were heavy and limited in number at the outbreak of war, but they were highly effective in defensive roles. As the war progressed, lighter models capable of accompanying infantry assaults were introduced.

1 **Lewis gun (British)** From its adoption in 1915, the Lewis gun remained the standard British infantry light machine-gun throughout the war. It was also mounted on Allied aircraft. 2 **Lewis gun drum magazine (British)** The Lewis gun's distinctive circular magazine came in two sizes: this version held 47 rounds, the other 97. 3 **Hotchkiss M1914 (French)** Nearly 50,000 of these tripod-mounted heavy machine-guns were delivered to the French army during the course of the war. 4 **Schwarzlose M7/12 (Austro-Hungarian)** Adopted in 1907, this model had just 10 working parts, which reduced the likelihood of mechanical failure. Captured models were used by both the Russians and Italians. 5 **Schwarzlose M7/12 ammunition (Austro-Hungarian)** This weapon was fed via a 250-round ammunition belt and could fire up to 500 rounds per minute. 6 **Vickers gun (British)** Usually operated by a team of six men, the Vickers gun was effective but unwieldy. It was replaced by the Lewis gun from late 1915. 7 **Ammunition belt** Made of fabric and brass, this device fed cartridges into many different types of machine-guns (as seen on No.10). 8 **MG 08/15 (German)** A hurried attempt to produce a light machine-gun, the sledge-mounted MG 08 was modified by the addition of a bipod, gunstock, and pistol grip. This helped to improve its portability, but it remained relatively heavy. 9 **Browning M1918 automatic rifle (US)** Introduced late in 1918, this model was designed to be operated by a single soldier. It was light enough to be fired from the hip as troops advanced on enemy positions. 10 **Pulemyot Maxima 1910 (Russian)** A highly durable and reliable machine-gun, this model remained in service with the Russian army until World War II. 11 **Chauchat M1915 (French)** The principal French light machine-gun, the Chauchat gained a reputation for unreliability; mud and grit would enter the weapon through its open-sided magazine, which often caused it to jam. 12 **Browning M1917 (US)** Due to delays in production this heavy machine-gun did not see service until the final months of the war. It could fire around 450 rounds per minute.

3 HOTCHKISS M1914 (FRENCH)

7 AMMUNITION BELT

10 PULEMYOT MAXIMA 1910 (RUSSIAN)

1 LEWIS GUN
(BRITISH)

2 LEWIS GUN DRUM
MAGAZINE (BRITISH)

4 SCHWARZLOSE M7/12
(AUSTRO-HUNGARIAN)

5 SCHWARZLOSE M7/12
AMMUNITION
(AUSTRO-HUNGARIAN)

6 VICKERS GUN (BRITISH)

8 MG 08/15 (GERMAN)

9 BROWNING M1918
AUTOMATIC RIFLE (US)

11 CHAUCHAT M1915 (FRENCH)

12 BROWNING
M1917 (US)

139

BEFORE

Although World War I started with Austria-Hungary's declaration of war against Serbia, by 1915 the Serbian front had become a backwater.

THE SERBIAN FRONT
After Serbia's successful resistance against **invasion by Austro-Hungarian forces** ‹‹ 68–69 in the first months of the war, fighting subsided. Austria-Hungary did **not** have the resources to defeat Serbia while also fighting Russia and, from May 1915, Italy.

BULGARIA'S STANCE
Serbia's neutral neighbour **Bulgaria** had lost territory to Serbia, Greece, Turkey, and Romania in the **Second Balkan War** of 1913. It was courted both by the Allies and the Central Powers. Allied failure against **Turkey at Gallipoli** ‹‹ 110–13 and the **Russian retreat from Poland** ‹‹ 52–3 influenced Bulgaria's leaders to form an alliance with the **Central Powers**.

Serbia Crushed

The defeat of Serbia in the final months of 1915 completed a year of almost unrelieved military failure for the Allies. About a quarter of the Serbian population is thought to have died in the course of the war, mostly from hardship and disease.

In September 1915, negotiations between the Central Powers and Bulgaria were brought to a successful conclusion. In return for a promise of substantial territorial gains, the Bulgarians signed the Pless Convention on 6 September, agreeing to join in an invasion of Serbia within 35 days. Unimpressed by the performance of Austro-Hungarian forces, they stipulated that the invasion must include German troops and be under German command.

This was not to the liking of Austro-Hungarian Chief of Staff General Conrad von Hötzendorf, who was increasingly worried by German dominance, but it suited German Chief of the General Staff Erich von Falkenhayn. He wanted a swift defeat of Serbia that would bind Bulgaria into an alliance with the Central Powers and open up a direct line of communication between Germany and Turkey.

Invasion of Serbia
German and Austro-Hungarian forces under the command of General August von Mackensen launched the offensive on 6 October. Their main thrust was directed southwards

King Peter I of Serbia
Born in 1844, King Peter passed executive power to his son, Crown Prince Alexander, shortly before the start of the war. The king remained a focus for Serbian loyalty and stayed with the army through the retreat of 1915.

across the Danube. The river was in spate but the crossing was achieved with the support of heavy artillery and the guns of Austro-Hungarian gunboats. The Serbian forces were in poor shape. As well as being outnumbered and short of weapons and munitions, they had been decimated by a typhus epidemic. The capital, Belgrade, had already fallen by the time the Bulgarian army attacked across Serbia's eastern border on 11 October. Under its experienced

Serbia attacked
An illustration in the French magazine *Le Petit Journal* shows Serbia defending itself against Austria-Hungary's Emperor Franz Joseph and Kaiser Wilhelm II of Germany while being stabbed in the back by Bulgaria.

HONGRIE

DANUBE BELGRADE

ROUM

SERBIE

NISCH

BULGARIE

SOFIA

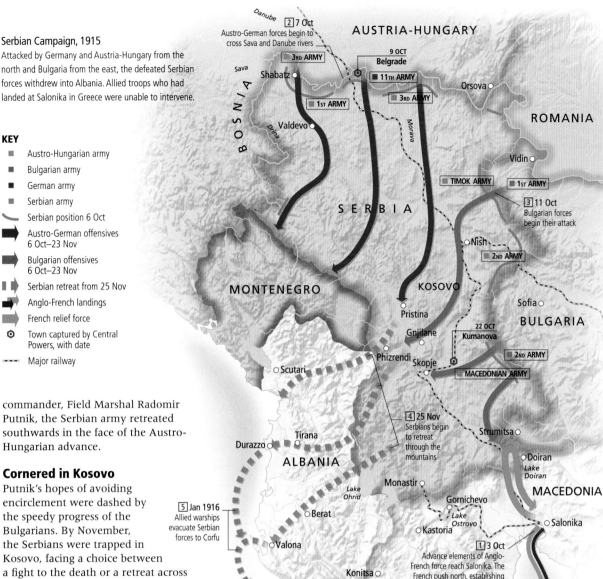

Serbian Campaign, 1915

Attacked by Germany and Austria-Hungary from the north and Bulgaria from the east, the defeated Serbian forces withdrew into Albania. Allied troops who had landed at Salonika in Greece were unable to intervene.

KEY

- ■ Austro-Hungarian army
- ■ Bulgarian army
- ■ German army
- ■ Serbian army
- ⌒ Serbian position 6 Oct
- ➡ Austro-German offensives 6 Oct–23 Nov
- ➡ Bulgarian offensives 6 Oct–23 Nov
- ❚❚ Serbian retreat from 25 Nov
- ➡ Anglo-French landings
- ➡ French relief force
- ◎ Town captured by Central Powers, with date
- ---- Major railway

Map labels:
AUSTRIA-HUNGARY
Danube
2 7 Oct Austro-German forces begin to cross Sava and Danube rivers
Sava
3RD ARMY
Shabatz
9 OCT Belgrade
11TH ARMY
3RD ARMY
Orsova
1ST ARMY
Valdevo
Drina
Morava
ROMANIA
BOSNIA
Vidin
TIMOK ARMY
1ST ARMY
SERBIA
3 11 Oct Bulgarian forces begin their attack
Nish
2ND ARMY
MONTENEGRO
KOSOVO
Sofia
BULGARIA
Pristina
Gnjilane
22 OCT Kumanova
Phizrendi
Skopje
2ND ARMY
Scutari
MACEDONIAN ARMY
4 25 Nov Serbians begin to retreat through the mountains
Tirana
Strumitsa
Durazzo
ALBANIA
Doiran
Lake Doiran
5 Jan 1916 Allied warships evacuate Serbian forces to Corfu
Lake Ohrid
Monastir
MACEDONIA
Berat
Gornichevo
Lake Ostrovo
Salonika
Valona
Kastoria
1 3 Oct Advance elements of Anglo-French force reach Salonika. The French push north, establishing position in Doiran area. Under increasing Bulgarian pressure, Doiran position is abandoned on 3 Dec
Konitsa
CORFU
GREECE
0 ___ 100 km
0 ___ 100 miles

commander, Field Marshal Radomir Putnik, the Serbian army retreated southwards in the face of the Austro-Hungarian advance.

Cornered in Kosovo

Putnik's hopes of avoiding encirclement were dashed by the speedy progress of the Bulgarians. By November, the Serbians were trapped in Kosovo, facing a choice between a fight to the death or a retreat across the mountains.

Serbia might have hoped for some assistance from the Allies, but none was forthcoming. Only three days before the launch of the Austro-German invasion, advanced parties of an Anglo-French force, known in France as the Army of the Orient, had landed at Salonika in neutral Greece, from where they were to proceed by rail to Serbia. But their arrival provoked a political crisis in Greece. The prime minister, Eleftherios Venizelos, who had invited the Allied troops, was dismissed by the country's pro-German King Constantine. The Allies suddenly found themselves unwelcome.

Under the command of General Maurice Sarrail, some 45,000 French troops advanced across Macedonia into southern Serbia. After brief clashes with the Bulgarians they withdrew again to Salonika.

Flight through the mountains

In the last week of November, Putnik ordered a general retreat across the mountains to the Adriatic. Some

Curved mouth of pipe

Soldier's pipe
The underused Allied troops at Salonika had plenty of time on their hands. This pipe was carved by a British private in the Durham Light Infantry.

200,000 soldiers and civilians set off on this trek, including the Serbian government and the 71-year-old King Peter, carried in a sedan chair. The roads were deep in snow and temperatures were far below freezing. Thousands died of exposure. Although bad weather dissuaded enemy forces from mounting a pursuit, Albanian warlords attacked the Serbians passing through their territory.

The survivors reached the Adriatic coast after about three weeks. From there they were evacuated by Allied transport ships, chiefly to the Greek island of Corfu. But the island had no

adequate food or shelter for a sudden influx of 140,000 military and civilian refugees.

The Germans made no attempt to continue the Serbian Campaign towards Salonika, where the Army of the Orient was in a potentially perilous position. Falkenhayn decided to leave the Balkan front dormant while he turned his attention to an offensive against the French at Verdun.

Bulgaria was satisfied with its victory over the Serbs. Austria-Hungary, however, was not – Conrad disliked the fact that it had been

Serbians flee
The winter retreat of the Serbian army through the mountains into Albania was a nightmare of hardship. At least 50,000 Serbian soldiers and civilians died on the journey to the Adriatic coast.

AFTER »

There were outbreaks of revolt in Serbia against harsh rule by Austro-Hungarian and Bulgarian occupation forces, but the Balkan front remained largely inactive until 1918.

PARTIAL WITHDRAWAL
In autumn 1916, Allied forces from Salonika, including Serbian troops, advanced across the border from Greece and **forced the Bulgarians to withdraw** from part of southern Serbia. No further progress was made in 1917, as the Allies focused on persuading Greece to join the war, a goal achieved in June 1917. **Serbia was liberated** by an Allied offensive launched in September 1918. The **Corfu Declaration** of July 1917 foreshadowed the creation of the Serbian-led postwar state of Yugoslavia.

> "We **slowly creep** toward the sheer cliffs… **step by step** on the compacted **snow**."

JOSIP JERAS, SERBIAN REFUGEE, DIARY ENTRY, DECEMBER 1915

achieved under German command. Relations between Austro-Hungarian and German leaders deteriorated and cooperation declined. Meanwhile, Corfu became the seat of a Serbian government-in-exile, complete with parliament. Much of the Serbian army joined the Allied forces in Salonika, waiting for the chance to wage a war of national liberation.

The **Artois-Loos Offensive**

In September 1915, the Allied offensives in Champagne and Artois resulted in over 300,000 Allied casualties, including large numbers of British volunteers. The failure of Britain's contribution to the offensives led to the sacking of its commander-in-chief.

BEFORE

At a conference held at Chantilly on 7 July 1915, the Allied countries agreed that they must take action together to put maximum pressure on the Central Powers.

OPPORTUNITY FOR THE ALLIES
With **Russia** suffering **severe setbacks in Poland ≪ 70–71**, and **Italy** engaged in **offensives on the Isonzo ≪ 106–07**, France and Britain realized they needed to mount a major **offensive** on the **Western Front**. However, they knew that **attacking the German trenches** was unlikely to achieve a breakthrough, as failures earlier in the year, both in **Artois and Champagne ≪ 142–43**, had confirmed. A window of opportunity arose when large numbers of German soldiers were **transferred to the east** for the **onslaught against Russia**, leaving their troops on the Western Front **heavily outnumbered** by the Allies.

French commander-in-chief General Joseph Joffre's long-held plan for cracking the German trench system was to mount major offensives in Artois and Champagne, on the northern and southern flanks of the salient occupied by the German army in France. Joffre and British commander-in-chief Field Marshal Sir John French had a clear idea how the campaign might be won. Heavy artillery bombardment would devastate German trenches, allowing infantry to occupy the enemy front line, after which reserves would be brought through to continue the offensive in depth.

Whether the commanders really expected to succeed is doubtful. Apart from the need to support Allies on other fronts, Joffre justified the offensives as essential to maintain morale. Otherwise, he said, "our troops will little by little lose their physical and moral qualities". British Minister for War Lord Kitchener told his commander-in-chief Sir John French, "We must do our utmost to help the French, even though by so doing, we suffer very heavy losses indeed."

The plan unfolds

The British, reinforced by the first volunteer troops of Kitchener's New Armies, held most of the Artois front with a single French army on their right. French forces were concentrated on the Champagne front, where they outnumbered the German defenders by three to one. Joffre assembled over 2,000 artillery pieces for the

Hard hat
Introduced in autumn 1915, the French Adrian helmet was the first steel helmet issued to troops of any country in World War I. Its light steel offered protection against shrapnel.

French troops at Artois
Zouaves (French light infantry) from North Africa in the Artois sector of the front. By this stage, they had abandoned their traditional uniforms, but had not yet been issued with steel helmets.

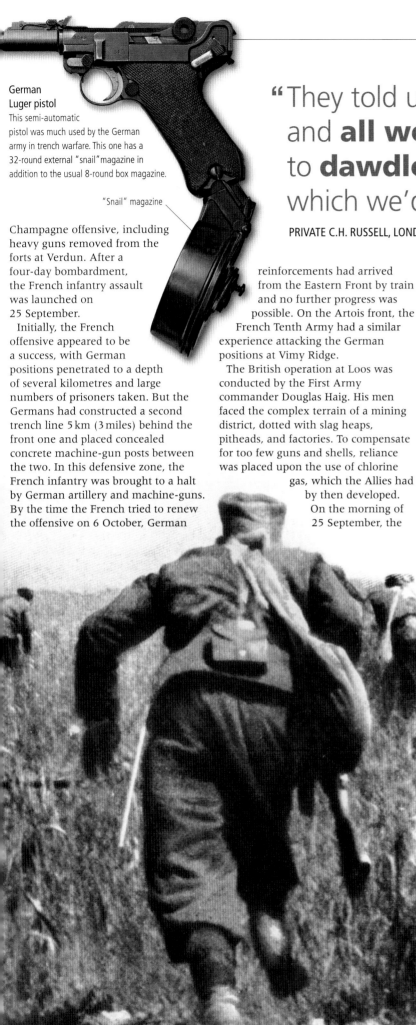

German Luger pistol
This semi-automatic pistol was much used by the German army in trench warfare. This one has a 32-round external "snail" magazine in addition to the usual 8-round box magazine.

"Snail" magazine

"They told us it would be a bit of cake and all we'd got to do for this attack was to dawdle along and take these trenches which we'd find pulverized by our guns."

PRIVATE C.H. RUSSELL, LONDON SCOTTISH REGIMENT AT LOOS

Champagne offensive, including heavy guns removed from the forts at Verdun. After a four-day bombardment, the French infantry assault was launched on 25 September.

Initially, the French offensive appeared to be a success, with German positions penetrated to a depth of several kilometres and large numbers of prisoners taken. But the Germans had constructed a second trench line 5 km (3 miles) behind the front one and placed concealed concrete machine-gun posts between the two. In this defensive zone, the French infantry was brought to a halt by German artillery and machine-guns. By the time the French tried to renew the offensive on 6 October, German

reinforcements had arrived from the Eastern Front by train and no further progress was possible. On the Artois front, the French Tenth Army had a similar experience attacking the German positions at Vimy Ridge.

The British operation at Loos was conducted by the First Army commander Douglas Haig. His men faced the complex terrain of a mining district, dotted with slag heaps, pitheads, and factories. To compensate for too few guns and shells, reliance was placed upon the use of chlorine gas, which the Allies had by then developed.

On the morning of 25 September, the gas cylinders were opened, despite the changeable wind direction, while smoke candles provided a screen for advancing infantry. Some of the gas blew back into British trenches, causing chaos and a number of casualties, but it helped weaken the German defences.

Launched at 6:30am, the British attack was highly successful in its southern sector. Soldiers from the Territorial Army broke through to capture Loos and reach the outskirts of Lens, before being held up by German

320,000 The approximate number of Allied casualties incurred in the Artois and Champagne offensives in the autumn of 1915.

100,000 The approximate number of German casualties in the battles.

machine-guns. By 9:30am, Haig was appealing to Field Marshal Sir John French for reserves to be rushed forward to exploit the opening. Decision-making was slow, however, and the reserves – two divisions of Kitchener's volunteer New Army troops – were too far away. Marching along the cobbled roads, unrested and unfed, they were not in a position to join the fighting until the following day. By then, the Germans were holding their second line of defence. The New Army divisions marched forwards without artillery support into the fire of German machine-guns.

Attributing blame
About 8,000 out of 15,000 men were killed or wounded before a withdrawal, with many of them caught in uncut barbed wire. The British then endured German counterattacks that ended hopes of further progress. Among the victims was John Kipling, the 18-year-old son of the author Rudyard Kipling. He had been shot in the face during the Irish Guards' defence of a chalk pit.

After the offensive was abandoned, Haig made sure that Sir John French was held responsible for not bringing up reserves, which was in turn blamed for the failure of the offensive. In mid-December, French was sacked and Haig was appointed to take his place.

Allied commanders
General Haig talks to General Joffre while Sir John French strides alongside. By October 1915, Haig was the rising star among British commanders.

AFTER ››

The failure of the autumn offensives in Artois and Champagne brought no fundamental change in Allied strategy or tactics, although political consensus in France was put under strain.

COORDINATED PLAN
A second **inter-Allied conference** at Chantilly in December 1915 agreed that **coordinated offensives** should be mounted on the different fronts – Western, Eastern, and Italian – in 1916, to **dissuade the Germans from shifting troops** from one front to another. German Chief of the General Staff **General Erich von Falkenhayn** had his own plans, however. He intended to launch a **major offensive** on the **Western Front** at Verdun 154–55 ›› that would drive the French out of the war.

FRENCH SUPPORT WOBBLES
The heavy losses incurred in Artois and Champagne put **strain upon the "union sacrée"** (sacred union) of French political parties in support of the war effort. At the end of October 1915, however, a **new coalition government** under Aristide Briand reaffirmed the shaky political consensus.

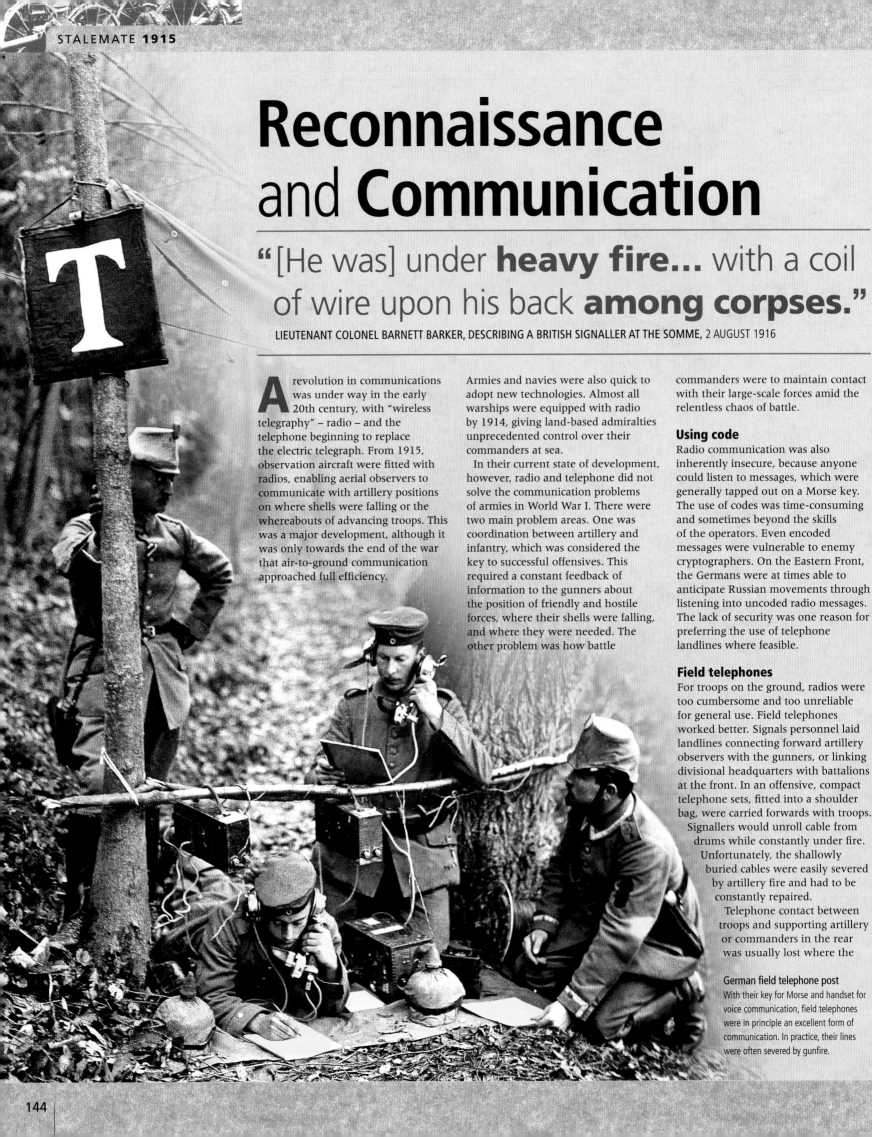

Reconnaissance and Communication

"[He was] under **heavy fire...** with a coil of wire upon his back **among corpses.**"

LIEUTENANT COLONEL BARNETT BARKER, DESCRIBING A BRITISH SIGNALLER AT THE SOMME, 2 AUGUST 1916

A revolution in communications was under way in the early 20th century, with "wireless telegraphy" – radio – and the telephone beginning to replace the electric telegraph. From 1915, observation aircraft were fitted with radios, enabling aerial observers to communicate with artillery positions on where shells were falling or the whereabouts of advancing troops. This was a major development, although it was only towards the end of the war that air-to-ground communication approached full efficiency.

Armies and navies were also quick to adopt new technologies. Almost all warships were equipped with radio by 1914, giving land-based admiralties unprecedented control over their commanders at sea.

In their current state of development, however, radio and telephone did not solve the communication problems of armies in World War I. There were two main problem areas. One was coordination between artillery and infantry, which was considered the key to successful offensives. This required a constant feedback of information to the gunners about the position of friendly and hostile forces, where their shells were falling, and where they were needed. The other problem was how battle commanders were to maintain contact with their large-scale forces amid the relentless chaos of battle.

Using code

Radio communication was also inherently insecure, because anyone could listen to messages, which were generally tapped out on a Morse key. The use of codes was time-consuming and sometimes beyond the skills of the operators. Even encoded messages were vulnerable to enemy cryptographers. On the Eastern Front, the Germans were at times able to anticipate Russian movements through listening into uncoded radio messages. The lack of security was one reason for preferring the use of telephone landlines where feasible.

Field telephones

For troops on the ground, radios were too cumbersome and too unreliable for general use. Field telephones worked better. Signals personnel laid landlines connecting forward artillery observers with the gunners, or linking divisional headquarters with battalions at the front. In an offensive, compact telephone sets, fitted into a shoulder bag, were carried forwards with troops. Signallers would unroll cable from drums while constantly under fire. Unfortunately, the shallowly buried cables were easily severed by artillery fire and had to be constantly repaired.

Telephone contact between troops and supporting artillery or commanders in the rear was usually lost where the

German field telephone post

With their key for Morse and handset for voice communication, field telephones were in principle an excellent form of communication. In practice, their lines were often severed by gunfire.

Communications rocket

Small rockets were sometimes used to send messages. This slender black metal rocket has a hollow nose compartment into which a written message could be concealed.

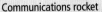

fighting was fiercest. In the heat of battle, communication often depended on courageous runners carrying written messages back and forth through the storm of shelling and machine-gun fire. This was a slow means of communication and depended upon the man surviving his hazardous journey, which often he did not.

Reconnaissance

The use of aircraft revolutionized reconnaissance in World War I. Although observation from aircraft was initially distrusted as a novelty by generals, it rapidly became apparent that making the best use of this new method of reconnaissance would have a military advantage. It was superior to cavalry, whose role it had traditionally been to locate enemy forces and report back on their movements.

As early as the end of August 1914, French commander General Joseph Joffre was urging his armies to "imitate the enemy in the use of aeroplanes". At sea, aerial reconnaissance from planes and airships soon proved their worth as a way of looking beyond the horizon.

An eye on the enemy

On the Western Front from 1915, observation from aircraft or fixed balloons provided information on enemy positions and gave vital feedback to artillery on where their shells were falling. Balloons were tethered behind the front line as observation platforms at a height of about 900 m (3,000 ft), with the balloon crews communicating with ground staff via a telephone cable.

Aircraft were sent on missions over the enemy trenches. While the pilot dodged anti-aircraft fire and attacks by enemy fighters, his colleague, the aerial observer, mapped troop movements and scribbled notes on what was happening below.

Observers' impressionistic sketches and reports were soon rendered redundant by aerial photography. Equipped with box cameras, slow-moving aircraft trundled at low altitude back and forth over enemy positions, an inviting target for enemy fire. Interpreting the resulting aerial photographs required considerable skill, but intelligence officers soon became adept at building up composite images of enemy trench systems and gun emplacements.

Animal messengers

Where humans could not carry messages, animals were sometimes used. Dogs were employed on all fronts. Fast and agile, they could leap barbed wire, with messages in a tube attached to their collars. Carrier pigeons were also a common means of communication. An estimated half a million pigeons were used by the combatant nations, with some birds achieving fame for voyaging through heavy gunfire.

Aerial photography

An observer in a German reconnaissance aircraft takes an aerial photograph. The camera's photographic plates had to be changed manually each time a photograph was taken.

Visual communication was another option. Semaphore flags and flashing lights were used, although they generally put the exposed signaller at too much risk. Limited communication could also be achieved through prearranged coded signals. Hard-pressed troops fired a particular coloured flare or rocket, for example, to call for an artillery bombardment

> **95** PER CENT The estimated success rate of pigeons carrying messages in World War I.

in response to an enemy raid or counterattack. Rockets were also used to carry written messages.

None of this solved the fundamental problem of command and control of offensives. Commanders at headquarters in the rear were supposed to receive a flow of information, analyse it, and distribute appropriate orders. But once their forces had begun an offensive, the generals mostly had little idea where the men were and little hope of directing a coherent response to a rapidly changing situation.

Carrier pigeons

A basket of homing pigeons was standard equipment for signallers in World War I. A pigeon that carried messages out of Fort Vaux during the Battle of Verdun was awarded the Légion d'honneur.

TIMELINE

■ **1792** The Chappe telegraph, a visual semaphore system, establishes long-distance military communication across France.

■ **1794** The French Revolutionary army uses a balloon for observation at the Battle of Fleurus, the first aerial reconnaissance.

■ **1837** American Samuel Morse patents his version of the electric telegraph, developing a practical code for transmitting messages.

■ **1854** The British Telegraph Detachment makes the first military use of the electric telegraph in the Crimean War.

AUTOMATIC TELEGRAPH TRANSMITTER, 1858

■ **1876** Alexander Graham Bell wins the race to patent a telephone, transmitting voice messages along a line.

■ **1896** Guglielmo Marconi invents the first commercially viable long-distance wireless telegraph, or radio.

■ **1904–05** The Japanese army uses field telephones and its navy employs radio on warships in the Russo-Japanese War.

■ **1911** European armies begin experimenting with the use of aircraft for reconnaissance.

■ **August 1914** Aerial reconnaissance and intercepted radio messages help the Germans encircle and destroy a Russian force at Tannenberg.

■ **September 1914** Aerial observation of the movement of German armies helps the Allies to mount a successful counterattack at the First Battle of the Marne.

■ **1915** Aerial photography is introduced on the Western Front, and some reconnaissance aircraft are equipped with radios.

■ **1915–18** German airships conducting night bombing raids are guided to their targets by a radio navigation system.

■ **May 1916** Interception of German naval radio transmissions allows the Royal Navy to attack German warships at the Battle of Jutland.

■ **June 1916** French troops who are besieged inside Fort Vaux during the Battle of Verdun communicate with the outside world using carrier pigeons.

■ **1918** Germany introduces the Rumpler C.VII reconnaissance aircraft, taking photographs with an automatic camera at high altitude.

■ **August–November 1918** In their final Hundred Days Offensive, the Allied armies make increasing use of radios.

4

YEAR
OF BATTLES
1916

The vast attritional battles at Verdun and the Somme exacted an unprecedented death toll for trivial gains. The war effort also strained the social and political cohesion of the warring countries, forcing political change and stirring revolt,

YEAR OF BATTLES

Dublin's Easter Rising against British rule in Ireland fails. Fourteen of the rebels, celebrated in this painting, are executed. The Irish nationalists had hoped for German support for their uprising, but little was forthcoming.

In the Battle of Verdun, Fort Douaumont is a key objective of the German offensive. It is captured by the Germans in February 1916 but retaken by a French assault after eight months' fighting.

The Battle of Jutland, fought in the North Sea, is the only encounter between the main British and German fleets in World War I. Britain's Royal Navy suffers the heavier losses, but the German warships have to flee for home to escape destruction.

EUROPE

FAEROE ISLANDS (Denmark)

NORWAY

SWEDEN

North Sea

DENMARK

Baltic Sea

BRITAIN

NETH.

GERMANY

RUSSIAN EMPIRE

BEL.

LUX.

FRANCE

SWITZ.

AUSTRIA-HUNGARY

ROMANIA

MONT.

SERBIA

BULGARIA

Black Sea

ALB.

ITALY

PORTUGAL

SPAIN

GREECE

OTTOMAN EMPIRE

Mediterranean Sea

DODECANESE (Italy)

ALGERIA (France)

TUNISIA (France)

CYPRUS (Britain)

MOROCCO (France)

LIBYA (Italy)

EGYPT (Britain)

ICELAND

NORWAY

SWEDEN

BRITAIN

GERMANY

ATLANTIC OCEAN

FRANCE

AUSTRIA-HUNGARY

ITALY

RUSSIAN EMPIRE

Black Sea

Caspian Sea

PORTUGAL

SPAIN

SPANISH MOROCCO

MOROCCO

TUNISIA

OTTOMAN EMPIRE

CYPRUS

PERSIA

AFGHANISTAN

TIB... (autono... NEPAL

ALGERIA

LIBYA

EGYPT

KUWAIT

BAHRAIN

QATAR

NEJD (Saudi)

TRUCIAL OMAN

OMAN

INDIA

RIO DE ORO

ANGLO-EGYPTIAN SUDAN (British mandate)

HADHRAMAUT

ADEN PROTECTORATE

FRENCH WEST AFRICA

GAMBIA

PORTUGUESE GUINEA

TOGO

FRENCH EQUATORIAL AFRICA

ERITREA

FRENCH SOMALILAND

SIERRA LEONE

NIGERIA

ABYSSINIA

BRITISH SOMALILAND

LIBERIA

GOLD COAST

CAMEROON

ITALIAN SOMALILAND

RIO MUNI (Spain)

FRENCH CONGO

BELGIAN CONGO

BRITISH EAST AFRICA

GERMAN EAST AFRICA

INDIAN OCEAN

Food shortages are acute in Germany during the hard winter of 1916. Like many other countries, Germany is hit by shortages and malnutrition in the course of the war, leading to a sharp increase in civilian death rates.

ANGOLA

NORTHERN RHODESIA

SOUTHERN RHODESIA

MADAGASCAR

GERMAN SOUTH WEST AFRICA

BECHUANA-LAND

PORTUGUESE EAST AFRICA

UNION OF SOUTH AFRICA

On the first day of the Somme Offensive on 1 July 1916 almost 20,000 British troops are killed, making it the most costly single day in the history of the British army. Here, British soldiers bound for the Somme raise a cheer for the camera.

The Arab Revolt against Turkey's Ottoman Empire is led by Emir Feisal and T.E. Lawrence. Arab irregulars function as guerrilla fighters, attacking railways and garrisons.

During 1916, the scale of the war effort and the vast sacrifice of life it entailed began to push some combatant states towards the brink of collapse. In February, Germany launched a large-scale offensive against the French at Verdun, hoping to drive France out of the war either by a demoralizing defeat or sheer reduction in its military manpower. The British, having trained a mass citizen army since the start of the war, led an offensive of similar scale at the Somme from July, partly to relieve presssure on Verdun. Both Verdun and the Somme, however, became scenes of epic slaughter in which fighting lasted for months, and death tolls mounted into hundreds of thousands. Despite the introduction of tanks and the beginning of air combat between fighter squadrons, neither battle achieved any significant objective except the killing of large numbers of soldiers on both sides.

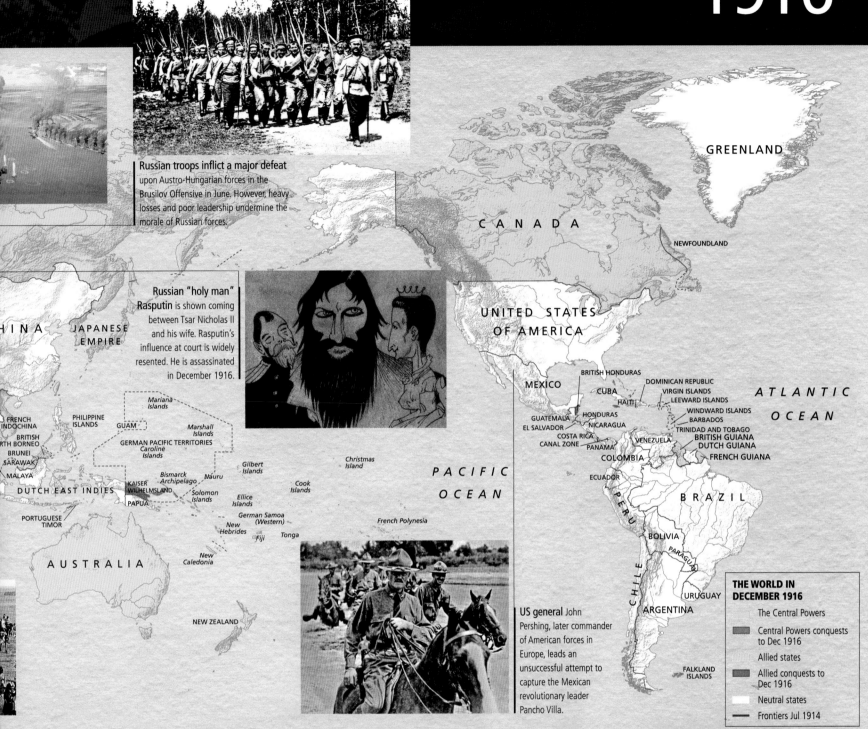

Russian troops inflict a major defeat upon Austro-Hungarian forces in the Brusilov Offensive in June. However, heavy losses and poor leadership undermine the morale of Russian forces.

Russian "holy man" Rasputin is shown coming between Tsar Nicholas II and his wife. Rasputin's influence at court is widely resented. He is assassinated in December 1916.

US general John Pershing, later commander of American forces in Europe, leads an unsuccessful attempt to capture the Mexican revolutionary leader Pancho Villa.

THE WORLD IN DECEMBER 1916

- The Central Powers
- Central Powers conquests to Dec 1916
- Allied states
- Allied conquests to Dec 1916
- Neutral states
- Frontiers Jul 1914

On the Eastern Front, Russia recorded a major victory against Austria-Hungary in an offensive masterminded by General Aleksei Brusilov in June. The victory had no decisive outcome, however. Both Russia and Austria-Hungary continued to fight, but their imperial regimes tottered under the pressure of war. Austria-Hungary was threatened by rising nationalism among its Slav minorities, and in Russia discontent at all levels of society focused upon incompetence and scandals at the tsarist court. Revolts broke out in the Ottoman Empire, where Arabs rose up against the Turks, and in Ireland where Catholic nationalists rebelled against British rule. In Germany, however, Field Marshal Paul von Hindenburg and General Erich Ludendorff took a firm hold on the direction of the war. Despite severe food shortages in German cities that fuelled popular discontent, the military leadership geared up for a drive for victory at any cost.

TIMELINE 1916

Battle of Verdun ▪ Naval battle at Jutland ▪ **Russian Brusilov Offensive** ▪

Arab revolt against Turkey ▪ **Somme Offensive** ▪ Irish Easter Uprising ▪

Tanks first used in combat ▪ Romania enters the war

JANUARY	FEBRUARY	MARCH	APRIL	MAY	JUNE

9 JANUARY
Final evacuation of Allied troops ends the Gallipoli Campaign.

10 JANUARY
Russians launch an offensive against Turkish forces in the Caucasus.

16 FEBRUARY
Russians capture Erzurum in eastern Turkey.

18 FEBRUARY
German colonial forces in Cameroon, West Africa, surrender.

6 MARCH
Germans extend their Verdun offensive to the west bank of the Meuse river.

9 MARCH
Germany declares war on Portugal.

9 APRIL
Fresh German offensive at Verdun fails to break French resistance.

20 APRIL
Under American pressure, Germany again restricts submarine warfare.

2 MAY
General Robert Nivelle takes over field command of French forces at Verdun.

≫ Russian Mosin-Nagant revolver

21 FEBRUARY
German troops open an offensive against the French at Verdun.

« French temporary grave marker

4 MAY
Germany suspends unrestricted submarine warfare in order to appease the USA.

14 MAY
Austria-Hungary takes the offensive on the Trentino front in Italy.

4 JUNE
Russian General Brusilov launches an offensive in Galicia. It is initially successful.

18 JANUARY
Mass evacuation of defeated Serbian troops from the Albanian coast to Corfu begins.

24 JANUARY
Admiral Reinhard Scheer is appointed commander of the German High Seas fleet.

24 FEBRUARY
General Philippe Pétain takes command of the defence of Verdun.

25 FEBRUARY
The Germans capture Fort Douaumont, the key French fortress at Verdun.

≫ General Phillipe Pétain

≫ A nurse tends to a badly wounded soldier

12 MARCH
Italians resume their offensive against Austria-Hungary on the Isonzo front.

24 APRIL
In Dublin, Irish Republicans attempt an uprising against British rule; it is crushed by the British army after a week.

15 MAY
Germans seize Le Mort Homme ridge, a key position in the French defence of Verdun.

31 MAY
The British and German fleets clash in the largest naval battle of the war at Jutland, but it is indecisive.

25 JANUARY
Invaded by Austro-Hungarian forces, Montenegro surrenders.

27 JANUARY
The Military Service Act allows conscription to be introduced in Britain.

18 MARCH
Russians launch an offensive against German forces at Lake Naroch in Belarus. It is a disastrous failure.

25 APRIL
German warships bombard the English east coast ports of Lowestoft and Yarmouth.

≫ German Fahrpanzer, mobile artillery piece

5 JUNE
British Minister for War Lord Kitchener dies at sea.

29 JANUARY
First experimental trial of tanks is held in Britain.

24 MARCH
British passenger ferry SS Sussex is torpedoed by a U-boat in the English Channel after Germans resume unrestricted submarine warfare.

30 APRIL
The British Indian garrison of Kut al-Amara surrenders to the Turks.

7 JUNE
At Verdun, Germans capture Fort Vaux.

10 JUNE
Arab forces loyal to Sherif Hussein attack the Turkish garrison at Mecca, launching the Arab Revolt.

≫ British Victoria Cross awarded for bravery at Jutland

150

> "Anguish makes me wonder when and how this **gigantic, unprecedented struggle** will end… I wonder if it won't just finish for **lack of men left to fight.**"

LIEUTENANT ALFRED JOUBAIRE, DIARY ENTRY 22 MAY 1916, AT VERDUN

JULY	AUGUST	SEPTEMBER	OCTOBER	NOVEMBER	DECEMBER

2 SEPTEMBER
The Central Powers invade Romania. For the first time, a German airship attacking London at night is shot down by a British fighter aircraft.

« British soldiers head to the Somme battlefield

1 OCTOBER
At the Somme, British forces attack the Ancre Heights.

3 OCTOBER
Raid on London by five German airships kills 71 civilians.

2 NOVEMBER
At Verdun, the French retake Fort Vaux.

5 NOVEMBER
Germany announces its intention to create an independent Polish state.

3 DECEMBER
Arab rebels defend the port of Yenbo against Turkish attack.

1 JULY
The British, with French support, launch a major offensive at the Somme. Britain loses almost 20,000 men on the first day.

9 AUGUST
Italian troops take Gorizia from Austria-Hungary.

27 AUGUST
Romania declares war on the Central Powers and invades Hungary.

15 SEPTEMBER
Tanks are used for the first time by the British at Flers-Courcelette, in a renewal of the offensive at the Somme.

4 OCTOBER
Allied troops attack the Bulgarians in a push towards Monastir in Macedonia.

⌃ British Sopwith Pup

10 OCTOBER
Romanian forces are driven out of all Austro-Hungarian territory they have occupied.

7 NOVEMBER
Woodrow Wilson is re-elected President of the United States.

13 NOVEMBER
British launch final attacks at the Somme. Snow halts the offensive five days later.

6 DECEMBER
David Lloyd George becomes British prime minister. The Central Powers occupy Bucharest.

12 DECEMBER
Nivelle replaces Joffre as French commander-in-chief.

⌃ The Krupp arms factory

13 JULY
British achieve a limited breakthrough at the Somme with a surprise night attack at Longueval Ridge.

29 AUGUST
Falkenhayn is sacked as German Chief of the General Staff and replaced by Hindenburg and Ludendorff, who propose a programme for total war.

23 SEPTEMBER
Germans begin construction of the Hindenburg Line.

24 OCTOBER
French counterattack at Verdun commanded by General Nivelle recaptures Fort Douaumont from the Germans.

25 OCTOBER
German and Bulgarian troops take the Romanian Black Sea port of Constanza.

18 DECEMBER
Battle of Verdun ends in French victory. President Wilson circulates a Peace Note, asking countries to state their war aims.

29 DECEMBER
Rasputin, believed to be an evil influence at the tsarist court, is assassinated.

14 JULY
French launch counterattack at Verdun.

23 JULY
At the Somme, Australian troops begin fight for Pozières.

On les aura !

2ᴱ EMPRUNT DE LA DÉFENSE NATIONALE
Souscrivez

« French propaganda poster

28 OCTOBER
Pilot Oswald Boelcke, Germany's first fighter "ace", is killed in action over the Western Front.

21 NOVEMBER
Austro-Hungarian Emperor Franz-Joseph dies. He is succeeded by Charles I.

» David Lloyd George

Facing Deadlock

In 1916, the combatant countries were trapped in a war they could neither stop nor win. They needed to find either a basis for peace negotiations or a route to military victory, but neither strategy nor diplomacy could supply a way out of the paralyzing deadlock.

Aerial camera
Photo-reconnaissance was typical of a number of technical innovations in the war – ingenious and useful, but unable to break the military stalemate of trench warfare.

BEFORE

During 1915, both sides in the war had made efforts to break the prevailing stalemate, but without lasting effect.

FAILED ALLIED OFFENSIVES
In the **trench warfare ≪ 94–95** on the Western Front, the Allies failed to achieve a breakthrough, while the Germans established defensive positions of increasing strength and depth. Hopes that **landings of Anzac and other Allied troops at Gallipoli ≪ 110–13** might knock Turkey out of the war proved false. Italy's entry into the war on the Allied side opened a new front without bringing significant progress.

ANZAC HELMET

EASTERN FRONT BREAKTHROUGHS
The Central Powers could point to more substantial successes. Between May and September 1915, they drove the **Russians out of most of Poland ≪ 134–35**, after which they tempted Bulgaria into the war and **conquered Serbia ≪ 140–41**. These were striking victories, but they fell short of **Germany's goal** to knock at least one of the three major Allied powers – France, Russia, or Britain – out of the war.

The war had started with the expectation that a series of swift and decisive battles would be followed by victory for one side or the other. By 1916, the prospect of this happening seemed remote, if not impossible. Instead, the war had become a contest of endurance, to be won by maximizing the losses and hardships imposed on the enemy.

General Erich von Falkenhayn, German Chief of the General Staff until August 1916, identified Britain as Germany's main enemy. His decision to attack the French at Verdun in February 1916 was based on the idea that France might be induced to surrender and that, without its French ally, Britain would have to withdraw from the conflict.

The Allies based their strategy for 1916 on mounting simultaneous offensives on all fronts to put maximum pressure on the Central Powers. But enormous losses in battle through the year brought no progress towards ending the war.

Economic pressure
A British-led trade blockade of the Central Powers was seen by some British politicians and strategists as

Fighters turn farmers
British soldiers of the Seaforth Highlanders help French peasants gather their potato crop in 1916. Disrupted food supplies contributed to a rise in civilian deaths in countries on both sides in the war.

an alternative to the slaughter of the trenches, but it was slow to take effect. Through 1916, Britain applied mounting pressure on neutral states to limit trade with Germany and its allies. In February 1916, Portugal was induced to intern German and Austro-Hungarian ships in port at Lisbon, leading to Germany also declaring war on the Portuguese, adding another country to the ranks of the Allies. But the growing shortages of food and raw materials in Germany and Austria-Hungary, although painful for the people, failed to derail the Central Powers' war effort.

Peace initiatives
Given the vast scale of the suffering and the threat the war was posing to the survival of political and social systems in Europe, peace might have been expected to come to the forefront of the political agenda. Indeed, on 12 December 1916, German Chancellor Bethmann-Hollweg did make a public peace offer to the Allies, the first peace initiative since the start of the war. But it was too unrealistic to be a serious

> "We must hope to **hold our ground** till the **end of 1916** and finish up with a **decisive victory.**"
>
> FIELD MARSHAL PAUL VON HINDENBURG, 8 SEPTEMBER 1916

GERMAN CHIEF OF THE GENERAL STAFF (1861–1922)
ERICH VON FALKENHAYN

As Prussian War Minister during the crisis of July 1914, General Falkenhayn bore a measure of responsibility for starting World War I. Six weeks into the war, he took command as German Chief of the General Staff. Enjoying the confidence of the Kaiser, he resisted the political scheming of Field Marshal Hindenburg and General Ludendorff, keeping a personal grip on strategy until undermined by the failure of his offensive against France at Verdun. After his fall from power in August 1916, he dutifully accepted relegation to lower command, performing effectively as head of the Ninth Army in the Romanian Campaign and then of the German-Turkish Yilderim Force in Palestine.

gesture. The proposal demanded Allied acceptance of the current military situation, with German forces remaining in control of large areas outside Germany's borders. An essential objective, permanent German control of Belgium and northeast France, was clearly unacceptable to the British and French. The German leadership had also become committed to the goal of long-term domination of Central Europe, including the

15 **MILLION The number of troops on all sides killed, wounded, taken prisoner or missing in 1916. Some 1.4 million of these were German.**

Germanization of Poland. This also ruled out any compromise with the Russians. The German "peace offer" was in effect a call for the Allies to accept defeat.

US mediation

President Woodrow Wilson also pursued a peace initiative as an uninvited mediator in Europe in 1916. His "peace note", issued six days after Bethmann-Hollweg's offer, called on all sides to make a statement of war aims as a prelude to negotiations. This was also doomed to failure, for the Allies were no more able than Germany to pursue a compromise. In the event of

Belgian soldiers on the Western Front
Disagreement about the future of Belgium – whose soldiers were still fighting alongside the Allies in 1916 despite their country being occupied by Germany – stood in the way of any possible peace agreement.

an Allied victory, they had secretly agreed to allow Russia to take control of Constantinople (Istanbul) and to permit Italy to make territorial gains at the expense of Austria-Hungary.

War escalates

From the end of August 1916, the rise to power of Field Marshal Paul von Hindenburg and General Erich Ludendorff led Germany to adopt a risky strategy to break the deadlock. Military victory was to be achieved

through state control of industry, labour, and resources to maximize the war effort, and unrestricted submarine warfare, even though this was likely to bring the USA into the war in support of the Allies. Germany planned to defeat Russia while standing on the defensive in the West, and then launch a decisive offensive in the West before American troops had time to arrive in Europe. It was a plan that ensured the war would be fought remorselessly to its conclusion, one way or the other.

AFTER

The pattern of the war shifted in 1917, with the USA entering the war and Russia leaving it.

RUSSIA BACKS OUT
Russia was the first major power to collapse under the pressure of war. The **abdication of Tsar Nicholas II 210–11 ≫** in March 1917 was followed by the **Bolshevik seizure of power 252–53 ≫** in November. Austria-Hungary was also in difficulty, treated as a subordinate by Germany and facing demands for independence from **Slav nationalists 168–69 ≫**. Emperor Charles, who succeeded Franz Joseph in November 1916, put out **peace feelers** in March 1917.

FRESH HOPE
Unrestricted submarine warfare by Germany in April 1917 led to the **US entering the war 212–13 ≫**. This gave hope to Britain and France, who suffered heavy losses on the Western Front in 1917, with the French army racked by mutinies after the **Nivelle Offensive 224–25 ≫**.

German firepower at Verdun
Howitzer of the First Bavarian Foot Artillery fires on French defences. Heavy artillery prepared the way for specially trained assault troops. The French were poorly prepared for this onslaught.

 BEFORE

In 1916, the historic fortress town of Verdun, standing on the Meuse river, was an exposed lightly held outpost of France's eastern defences.

FORTIFIED CITY
In the late 19th century, concentric rings of **modern forts** armoured in steel and concrete had been built around Verdun as part of a defensive line following the Franco-Prussian War. In 1914, the initial fighting **came to a halt at trench lines** outside the fortified perimeter. Verdun was left surrounded by German-held territory on three sides and supplied along **inadequate road and rail links** to the rear.

STRIPPED OF ARTILLERY
Verdun was a quiet sector of the front. French commander-in-chief General **Joseph Joffre** « **56–57** resisted pressure to strengthen its trench line, which was recognized as weak. In autumn 1915, believing the fortresses outdated, Joffre **stripped the Verdun forts** of most of their guns and garrisons to feed his **Champagne offensive** « **142–43**. In December 1915, Verdun was identified by German Chief of the General Staff General Erich von Falkenhayn as the **ideal target** for a powerful blow against France.

The **German** **Offensive** at **Verdun**

On 21 February 1916, German forces attacked the French in front of Verdun, launching one of the bloodiest battles of the entire war. The success of the initial German offensive was soon turned to stalemate by a stubborn French defence.

German Chief of the General Staff Erich von Falkenhayn viewed the Verdun operation – Germany's only major offensive on the Western Front between 1914 and 1918 – as an attack on France's will to fight. French morale would be hit by the loss of Verdun or by the huge losses sustained in defending it.

Massive firepower
The offensive was entrusted to Germany's Fifth Army, commanded by Crown Prince Wilhelm, but Falkenhayn kept overall control of the battle. Through January and early February 1916, a huge concentration of artillery was built up opposite Verdun, on the east bank of the Meuse.

It included 1,200 guns, ranging from giant 420 mm howitzers to 77 mm field guns, and 2.5 million shells. French aerial reconnaissance over the sector was hampered by German fighter planes. Nonetheless, hints of the German preparations filtered through to French intelligence.

Bad weather forced the Germans to postpone the offensive, originally scheduled for 10 February. This gave the French time to send in two divisions as reinforcements, but they

Verdun fortress
An aerial photo shows Fort Douaumont, which was taken by German infantry in February 1916. Like other Verdun forts, most of its structure was underground, with its main guns in rotating retractable turrets.

"The forces of France will **bleed to death...** whether we... **reach our goal or not.**"

GENERAL FALKENHAYN, MEMORANDUM TO KAISER WILHELM II, 25 DECEMBER 1915

were still outnumbered by two to one. The offensive opened on the morning of 21 February with a bombardment lasting seven hours. The French forward positions were battered relentlessly. To the rear, French artillery batteries were eliminated, and communication and supply links cut. The German infantry attacked in the late afternoon, the specially trained troops using grenades and flamethrowers to clear French soldiers from their dugouts and bunkers.

By 23 February, French battalions in the forward defences were reduced to a half or third of their initial strength and were running out of ammunition and food. The Germans pressed forward through the outer trench zone towards the forts around Verdun. On 25 February, Fort Douaumont, the largest fort, was taken by the 24th Brandenburg Regiment.

Steel helmet
During the Battle of Verdun, German troops were issued with a steel helmet, the Stahlhelm, to replace their leather Pickelhaube headgear. The Stahlhelm gave better protection and led to fewer head wounds.

Before the German offensive, General Joseph Joffre had viewed Verdun as indefensible. Military logic dictated that, if attacked in strength, French troops should withdraw to the west of the Meuse. Politically, however, this was impossible. One of the dead in the early fighting was Colonel Émile Driant, a politician and writer as well as an army officer, who had vigorously criticized Joffre's neglect of the defences at Verdun. He was now a martyr whose heroic death could be laid at Joffre's door. If Verdun fell, Joffre would be blamed. Wishing to avert this, Joffre sent his deputy, General Noel de Castelnau, to assess the situation. Castelnau duly decided that Verdun must be held at all costs.

Last-ditch defence

On 25 February, the day on which Fort Douaumont fell, General Philippe Pétain took command of the forces at Verdun. As someone who didn't subscribe to the widespread French belief in the inherent superiority of attack over defence, he turned out to be the ideal person to lead the defence.

Pétain's first step was to cancel costly infantry counterattacks and focus on artillery as the means to stop the German advance. Guns on the west

> **POILUS The popular term used for French soldiers, literally meaning "hairy ones" or "shaggy ones", a reference to the bushy beards and moustaches favoured by French troops.**

bank of the Meuse, still in French hands, were used to batter the Germans on the east bank. The issue of supply was vigorously addressed. As French forces built up – soon half a million French soldiers and 200,000 horses were in the salient – a road was made to carry the supplies they needed to keep them fighting. It was known as La Voie Sacrée – the Sacred Way.

Afraid that the soldiers' morale would crack under the strain of the Verdun battlefield, with its unprecedented

Vital supply line
Trucks and soldiers follow La Voie Sacrée (Sacred Way), the road that kept Verdun supplied with men and munitions through 10 months of fighting. Troops going up to the front passed the wounded coming down.

density of shelling, Pétain instituted strict troop rotation. In principle, no soldier was to spend more than eight days at the front. By early March, Pétain had restored morale and the stubborn French "poilus" brought the Germans to a halt. Falkenhayn released reserves for an attack on the west bank of the Meuse, but again the French held out, defending a ridge between their positions at Côte 304 and Le Mort Homme. Verdun had been saved, but the battle went on.

AFTER

> **By early March, Germany's best chance of a breakthrough at Verdun had gone but their offensive continued to put extreme pressure upon the French army until July 1916.**

THE SOMME
Because of the French commitment at Verdun, the **Somme operation 180–85 »**, planned by France and Britain for summer 1916, became a predominantly British offensive. It was launched on 1 July, earlier than British commander General Douglas Haig wanted, in order to draw German troops away from Verdun. In this it succeeded. Germany was also distracted by the **Russian Brusilov Offensive 174–75 »**. Fighting at **Verdun continued** until December 1916, ending in a **series of French counter-offensives** under Pétain's successor, General Robert Nivelle **224–25 »**.

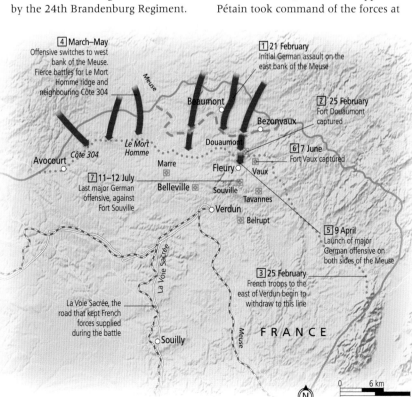

4 March–May
Offensive switches to west bank of the Meuse. Fierce battles for Le Mort Homme ridge and neighbouring Côte 304

Meuse

Beaumont

1 21 February
Initial German assault on the east bank of the Meuse

Bezonvaux

2 25 February
Fort Douaumont captured

Le Mort Homme

Douaumont

Côte 304

Avocourt

Marre

Fleury

Vaux

6 7 June
Fort Vaux captured

7 11–12 July
Last major German offensive, against Fort Souville

Belleville

Souville

Tavannes

Verdun

Belrupt

5 9 April
Launch of major German offensive on both sides of the Meuse

La Voie Sacrée

La Voie Sacrée, the road that kept French forces supplied during the battle

3 25 February
French troops to the east of Verdun begin to withdraw to this line

Souilly

Meuse

FRANCE

German offensives at Verdun

An initial German offensive east of the Marne was followed by further offensives on both sides of the river. The French position continued to deteriorate slowly until July, when France regained the initiative.

KEY
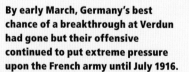 German attack
— French front line 21 Feb 1916
– – French front line 24 Feb 1916
· · · French front line 9 Apr 1916
⊡ French fort
▭▭▭ Railway

0   6 km
0   6 miles

N

Verdun

The German army began its offensive at Verdun with a nine-hour-long artillery bombardment. Such was its ferocity that many French soldiers were buried alive in their trenches. In the afternoon, the German assault troops began their advance. The French conducted a tenacious defence and gradually mounted successful counterattacks. The fighting continued for a further 10 months at a terrible cost – almost 650,000 French and German soldiers were killed.

"Thousands of projectiles are flying in all directions, some whistling, others howling, others moaning low, and all uniting in one infernal roar. From time to time, an aerial torpedo passes, making a noise like a gigantic motor car. With a tremendous thud, a giant shell bursts quite close to our observation post, breaking the telephone wire and interrupting all communication with our batteries.

A man gets out at once for repairs, crawling along on his stomach through all this place of bursting mines and shells. It seems quite impossible that he should escape in the rain of shell, which exceeds anything imaginable; there was never such a bombardment in war… Finally, he reaches a less stormy spot, mends his wires, and then, as it would be madness to try to return, settles down in a big crater for the storm to pass.

Beyond, in the valley, dark masses are moving over the snow-covered ground. It is German infantry advancing in packed formation… They look like a big grey carpet being unrolled over the country… and as they deploy, fresh troops come pouring in.

There is a whistle over our heads. It is our first shell. It falls right in the middle of the enemy infantry… Through glass we can see men maddened, men covered with earth and blood, falling one upon the other.

When the first wave of the assault is decimated, the ground is dotted with heaps of corpses, but the second wave is already pressing on. Once more our shells carve awful gaps in their ranks… Then our heavy artillery bursts forth in fury. The whole valley is turned into a volcano, and its exit is stopped by the barrier of the slain."

ANONYMOUS FRENCH STAFF OFFICER, DESCRIBING THE FIRST GERMAN ATTACK AT VERDUN

Bombardment
French infantry struggle under shellfire during the Battle of Verdun. In an impressive logistical feat, the Germans had moved up over 1,000 artillery pieces in preparation for their offensive.

FRENCH COMMANDER Born 1856 Died 1951

Philippe Pétain

"I am **taking command.** Inform your troops. Keep up your **courage.**"

PÉTAIN'S MESSAGE TO THE GENERALS, VERDUN, 26 FEBRUARY 1916

One of the most controversial figures in modern French history, Philippe Pétain was born into a farming family in the village of Cauchy-à-la-Tour in northern France. In the long peace in Europe between the Franco-Prussian War and World War I, he pursued a dull but solid army career, taking 35 years to reach the rank of colonel. His humble family background was advantageous for promotion in Republican France, which was keen to dilute the aristocratic composition of the officer corps, but his attitudes marked him out as unfashionable.

Cautious character
Pétain lacked the optimism considered essential in a general. In the lectures that he delivered at the French war college, he emphasized the battlefield dominance of artillery, scorning the belief that the attacking spirit of infantry could outweigh firepower. Such views were considered heresy. By 1914, Pétain was 58 years old and could expect to advance no further in his career.

Rapid promotion
The war changed everything, however. Commanding troops in action for the first time, Pétain proved level-headed, reliable, and decisive. In the torrent of sackings and promotions that were

Soldier and political leader
Pétain came to prominence as a general in World War I. His simplicity of dress expressed his identification with the ordinary soldier.

part of French commander-in-chief Joseph Joffre's response to the German invasion of France, he advanced in just two months from being a colonel in charge of a brigade to a general in command of a corps.

Battlefield successes
Pétain's star continued to rise after the onset of trench warfare. In the Artois offensive of May 1915, his corps penetrated the German lines to a depth of 5 km (3 miles) on the first day, before being driven back by counterattacks. Joffre was impressed, and by the time of the autumn offensive in Champagne, Pétain had an army under his command.

Pétain insisted on making meticulous preparations for an offensive, including a preliminary bombardment. Through 1915, however, he seemed as ready as any other commander on the Western Front to sacrifice soldiers' lives for limited gains.

When the Germans launched their offensive at Verdun in February 1916, Pétain was chosen to command the defence not because of any special characteristics he possessed, but simply because he was available. He travelled to Verdun on 25 February, learning of the fall of Fort Douaumont when he arrived. He instantly imposed himself upon a chaotic situation. Subordinate commanders were urged to use artillery to stop the Germans, only counterattacking with infantry where tactical advantage was to be gained.

Famous three
The pre-eminent French generals of World War I were Joseph Joffre, Ferdinand Foch, and Philippe Pétain. All three were honoured as Marshals of France.

Meeting the troops
Pétain visits a group of French Territorials at soup time. He was unusual among World War I generals for his habit of talking with the ordinary troops on the ground.

Maintaining supplies was recognized as vital by Pétain, and he tackled the problem energetically. Sensing that morale would collapse if men were exposed for too long to the horrors of the artillery-saturated battlefield, he instituted an eight-day rotation of units at the front. His orders of the day were delivered plainly, without bombast. He spoke to the soldiers, handed out medals, and visited the wounded – a kind of direct contact scrupulously avoided by most of the other World War I generals.

Sidelined by Joffre
A national hero after the defence of Verdun, Pétain was less admired in France's ruling circles, where his approach was perceived as negative. To Joffre, his readiness to cede

of firmness and understanding in this, punishing ringleaders but making concessions on matters such as leave and food, which were very important to the troops. Above all, he let the men know there would be no more wastage of lives in futile, overly ambitious offensives. The French army was placed on a predominantly passive footing, waiting, Pétain said, for "the tanks and the Americans".

Morale and discipline were duly restored, as the French performance in the great battles of 1918 would show. Once again, however, Pétain was not judged to be the man for the top job.

In spring 1918, it was General Ferdinand Foch, the fiercest advocate of offensive warfare, who was made Allied Supreme Commander. Pétain was considered too defeatist and anti-British for the job, although he was still an effective commander-in-chief of the French forces.

After World War I
In the decades after the war, Pétain was actively engaged in shaping French military policy. Faced with spending cuts that weakened the French army, he embraced a defensive strategy and construction of the Maginot Line fortifications along the border with Germany.

At some point, his native pessimism and bitter experience of war tipped over into defeatism. Brought into government in World War II to stiffen resolve, he advocated an armistice in June 1940 during the German invasion of France. As head of the collaborationist Vichy regime, he saw himself as restoring order to France, purging it of the vices that had brought about its downfall. Instead, he became an accomplice in crimes against Jews and resistance fighters.

In 1945, aged 89, Pétain was convicted of treason and sentenced to life imprisonment by a French court. He died in prison six years later.

> ## "Upon the day when France had to **choose** between **ruin** and **reason,** Pétain was promoted."
> CHARLES DE GAULLE, ON PÉTAIN BECOMING COMMANDER-IN-CHIEF IN MAY 1917

ground and his reluctance to order counterattacks at Verdun were unacceptable. Unable to sack a man who had become the embodiment of French resistance, in April 1916 Joffre promoted him to command the Army Group controlling the Verdun sector, formally increasing his authority but in practice removing him from front-line responsibility.

Pétain suffered another rebuff when the optimistic General Robert Nivelle was promoted over his head to succeed Joffre as commander-in-chief in December. However, in May 1917, Pétain was appointed to replace Nivelle in order to deal with widespread mutinies following the failure of the Nivelle Offensive at Chemin des Dames. Pétain showed a mixture

Liberation of Alsace
Pétain visits an area of Alsace retaken from the Germans in October 1917. He became a focus for conservative patriotism in the postwar years, trusted by many because of his reputation as a humane general who cared about his men.

FRENCH POSTER DURING THE VICHY REGIME

TIMELINE

- **1856** Born at Cauchy-à-la-Tour in the Pas de Calais region, northern France.
- **1876** Joins the army, later entering the Saint-Cyr Military Academy.
- **1911** Promoted to colonel. Commands the 33rd infantry regiment.
- **August–October 1914** Earns rapid promotion in the first phase of World War I, commanding a division at the First Battle of the Marne. He is made a corps commander in October.
- **May 1915** Leads his corps in the spring offensive in Artois, winning promotion to command of the Second Army in June.
- **September–October 1915** Leads the Second Army in the failed Champagne offensive.
- **February–March 1916** Mounts a defence of Verdun and prevents a German breakthrough.
- **April 1916** Relieved of control of Verdun by promotion to command of Army Group Centre.
- **May 1917** Appointed commander-in-chief as mutinies sweep the French army in the wake of the Nivelle Offensive. Restores order.
- **March 1918** In the German Spring Offensive, Pétain is subordinated to Ferdinand Foch.
- **November 1918** Given the honorary rank of Marshal of France.
- **February 1922** Appointed Inspector General of the Army, a post he holds until 1931.
- **September 1925** Commands the French forces sent to suppress the Riff Rebellion in Morocco.
- **February–November 1934** During a political crisis in France, accepts a government post as Minister of War.
- **June 1940** Appointed prime minister. With France facing defeat by Germany, he agrees an armistice.
- **July 1940** Becomes head of state of the French government at Vichy.
- **August 1945** After the liberation of France, he is tried and sentenced to death for treason, later commuted to life imprisonment.
- **1951** Dies in prison on the Ile d'Yeu.

The **French Fight Back** at **Verdun**

From spring through to winter 1916, the German and French armies remained locked in combat at Verdun, expending hundreds of thousands of lives in a sustained battle. In the end, France could claim a defensive victory, but a huge price had been paid.

BEFORE

Initial German success at Verdun was halted when French commander Philippe Pétain took up the reins.

FRENCH AND GERMAN POSITIONS
The **German offensive at Verdun** « **154–55** in February 1916 was fought to a standstill in early March. **Pétain** depended on artillery fire to hold back the German infantry. The most effective gun positions were on the west bank of the Meuse and they were ready

259 The number of French infantry regiments (out of a total of 330) that fought at some point at Verdun, because of Pétain's system of troop rotation.

to repel German troops attempting to advance on the east bank. On 6 March, the **Germans launched a second offensive**, this time on the west bank.

SACRED CAUSE
The patriotic press in France turned the battle for Verdun into a sacred cause. The narrow French supply route to the battlefield, dubbed **La Voie Sacrée** (Sacred Way) by the press, carried 50,000 tonnes of ammunition and 90,000 men to the front every week.

> "I thought: if you **haven't seen Verdun** you **haven't seen anything** of **war**."
>
> PRIVATE J. AYOUN, FRENCH SOLDIER, 1916

B attles on the Western Front defied the generals' efforts to impose a shape and sense of purpose on the fighting. German Chief of the General Staff Erich von Falkenhayn's decision to use a reserve corps to launch an offensive on the west bank of the Meuse in early March was logical: French guns were savaging his troops on the east bank.

But the new offensive immediately turned into a stalemated struggle for control of a ridge stretching between two key French positions, Le Mort Homme and Côte 304. Unable to take the crest of the ridge, the attempted German advance bogged down. Falkenhayn tried again on 9 April, launching simultaneous attacks both east and west of the river using massive artillery support. The German guns exhausted 17 trainloads of shells.

This onslaught sorely tried French morale, prompting General Pétain to end his order that day with the phrase "*On les aura!*" – "We shall have them!". Whether encouraged or not by this optimism, the French held firm.

Battle of the generals

In May, the Germans took Côte 304 and Le Mort Homme after an artillery bombardment that in places reduced the height of the ridge by 7 m (23 ft).

View of the battlefield
German soldiers use periscopes at an observation post on Côte 304, a ridge on the west bank of the Meuse wrested from the French in April–May 1916.

Yet this only brought them up against the next French defensive line at the Bois Bourrus. Falkenhayn was urged by Crown Prince Wilhelm, commander of the German Fifth Army at Verdun, to call off the battle, but the German Chief of Staff had become too closely identified with Verdun to admit it had been a failure. Meanwhile, on the French side, Pétain's cautious posture was frustrating commander-in-chief General Joseph Joffre.

The saving of Verdun in February 1916 had made Pétain a national hero, but Joffre removed him from control on the battlefield by promoting him to the command of the Army Group overseeing Verdun. On 19 April, General Robert Nivelle, who shared Joffre's belief in attack, took over front-line responsibility, with General Charles Mangin in command of a division. The French infantry was soon being thrown forwards in the wasteful manner Pétain had avoided.

The fight for the forts

On 22 May, Mangin led a brave attempt to retake Fort Douaumont. Its failure, at the cost of many lives,

had a seriously detrimental effect on French morale, and the troops nicknamed Mangin "the Butcher".

Ten days later, the Germans mounted a full-scale assault on Fort Vaux. Its heroic defence by Major Sylvain-Eugène Raynal and his small garrison was one of the minor epics of the war. German infantry broke into the building on 1 June, but the French held out in a maze of tunnels and corridors, communicating with the outside world by pigeon. They resisted poison gas and flamethrowers, but eventually succumbed to thirst, surrendering on 7 June with their water supply exhausted.

Battle raged in the air as well as on the ground. It was over Verdun that combat between fighter aircraft was invented, with ace pilots such as the Germans Max Immelmann and Oswald Boelcke and the French elite of the *Cigognes* (Storks) squadron contesting command of the air.

Turning point

On the whole, the aerial battle was won by the French, but on the ground the Germans held the upper hand into early July. On 23 June, they captured Fleury, within 5 km (3 miles) of Verdun, provoking Nivelle to end his order of the day with the phrase: "*Ils ne passeront pas!*" ("They shall not

162,440 The estimated number of French soldiers killed at Verdun.

143,000 The estimated number of German dead at Verdun.

pass!"). On 11 July, using diphosgene gas for the first time, the Germans attempted to storm Fort Souville. This was a desperate moment for the French troops who successfully repulsed the attack. By then, however, the tide had already turned in favour of the French, because of events elsewhere.

Falkenhayn had been forced to transfer troops to the Eastern Front in response to the crisis caused by the Russian Brusilov offensive in June. The launch of the British-led Somme

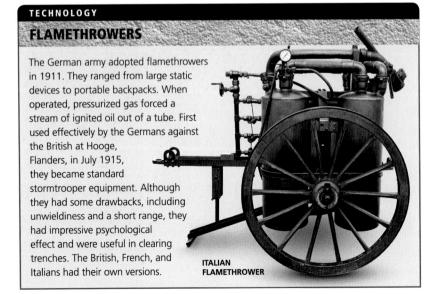

ITALIAN FLAMETHROWER

On les aura !

2^E EMPRUNT
DE
LA DÉFENSE NATIONALE

Souscrivez

DEVAMBEZ IMP PARIS

offensive on 1 July made continuing the concentration of German forces at Verdun impossible. Falkenhayn's great offensive had failed and he paid the price, losing his job as Chief of the General Staff on 27 August.

French success

On the French side, Nivelle was now the rising star. With Mangin, he retook Fort Douaumont on 24 October in a lightning attack that combined artillery and infantry. Fort Vaux was recaptured nine days later. By the time the battle ended in December, the French had returned roughly to their position before it began. For this, some 300,000 French and German soldiers had died.

Boosting French morale

This war bond poster designed by French illustrator Jules-Abel Faivre combines a classic image of the French infantryman with General Pétain's famous morale-boosting order of the day for 10 April 1916: *"On les aura!"* ("We shall have them!").

AFTER »

The enormous number of French and German casualties at Verdun strained morale and resources on both sides.

CHANGES AT THE TOP
His reputation sky-high after his successes in the later stages of the battle, **Nivelle replaced Joffre** as French commander-in-chief in December 1916. The over-ambitious offensive he launched the following spring led to **widespread mutinies in the French army 224–25 »**. The Germans did not launch another Western Front offensive until March 1918. **Verdun** was remembered by the **French** as **their greatest sacrifice** of the war. Remains of French and German soldiers fill the **Douaumont Ossuary**, a memorial completed on the Verdun battlefield in 1932.

DOUAUMONT OSSUARY

> " Certainly, **humanity has gone mad!** It must be mad to do what it's doing. **Such slaughter!** Such scenes of **horror and carnage!**"

LIEUTENANT ALFRED JOUBAIRE, DIARY ENTRY AT VERDUN, 22 MAY 1916

Fort Douaumont today
One in a ring of fortresses around Verdun, Fort Douaumont was much fought over during the 1916 Battle of Verdun. Captured by the Germans in February, it was retaken by the French in October.

« BEFORE

The outbreak of World War I occurred at a critical moment in Irish history, as Britain prepared to grant the country Home Rule.

RELIGIOUS DIVIDE

In 1914, the British parliament had passed a bill giving Ireland an **elected assembly with limited powers**. Welcomed by most Irish Catholics, it was opposed by Ulster Protestants, who armed a militia, the **Ulster Volunteer Force** (UVF), to resist it. The Catholics responded by forming the **Irish Volunteers**. When Britain entered World War I, a political truce was agreed with Ireland. **Home Rule** was enacted but deferred until the end of the war. The **UVF became the 36th (Ulster) Division** of the British Army. Many **Irish Catholics also joined the British Army**, with most forming part of the 16th (Irish) Division **« 33**.

IRISH NATIONALIST (1868–1916)
JAMES CONNOLLY

Born and raised in Edinburgh by Irish Catholic parents, James Connolly moved to Ireland as young married man, taking up the position of secretary for the Dublin Socialist Club in 1896. After a spell in the USA from 1903–06, he returned to Dublin, setting up the Citizen Army to protect trade unionists in 1913. He joined with the Irish nationalists in January 1916 and played a leading role in the Easter Rising. Gravely wounded in the fighting, he was condemned to death by a British military tribunal. On 12 May, he was taken from hospital in a military ambulance to the execution yard in Dublin's Kilmainham Jail. Unable to stand, he was tied to a chair so that he could be shot.

The **Easter Rising**

An armed rebellion against British rule in Ireland, the Easter Rising attracted little public support and was swiftly suppressed. The execution of the rebel leaders, however, outraged Irish Catholics and strengthened the Republican cause.

Rebels' gun

In 1914, before the outbreak of war, Germany had supplied the Catholic Irish Volunteers with Model 1871 Mauser rifles. Many of these were used by Irish rebels against British soldiers during the Easter Rising.

W orld War I divided opinion in Catholic Ireland. A majority of people supported John Redmond, the leader of the Irish Party in the Westminster parliament, who called for the Irish to back the British war effort in return for Home Rule, which granted limited independence. A minority rejected Redmond's stance, seeing the war as an opportunity to shake off British rule completely.

The Irish Volunteer militia reflected this split, with a minority of its members advocating that it reject Redmond's proposal and prepare for a future rebellion. As well as the anti-Redmond Volunteers, radical nationalist organizations included the secretive Irish Republican Brotherhood (IRB), with Patrick Pearse as its main spokesman, and the trade union-based Citizen Army, led by the socialist James Connolly. There was broad agreement among them that a rising should be attempted but disagreement about its aims. The IRB felt a "glorious failure" would serve the cause, but others, such as the Irish Volunteers' chief of staff Eoin MacNeill, wanted German support for a fight to defeat the British.

German backing

Roger Casement, a former British diplomat and a critic of colonialism, became the Irish nationalists' key link with the Germans. Casement failed to find recruits for a rebel brigade among Irish soldiers in German prisoner-of-war camps, nor would Germany send forces to invade Ireland. The Germans did, however, promise to ship arms to the Irish rebels.

In January 1916, IRB leaders and Connolly agreed to stage an uprising on Easter Sunday, 23 April. The IRB had taken over key positions in the Volunteers, but did not control the

116 The number of British soldiers killed in the course of the uprising.

318 The number of Irish rebels and civilians who died.

organization. Their plan depended on drawing the mass of Volunteers into the rebellion, since their own followers numbered only a few thousand, chiefly in Dublin. MacNeill was induced to issue the Volunteers with orders for a nationwide uprising.

In the event, all the plans went awry. The promised arms shipment from Germany arrived at the Kerry coast on

Men of the Easter Rising

This painting shows the 14 Irish rebels executed for their part in the Easter Rising in Dublin. A 15th Irish nationalist, Thomas Kent, was also executed in May 1916 for killing a policeman in Cork.

the steamer SMS *Aud* on 20 April but there were no Volunteers to unload it. Trapped by the Royal Navy, the *Aud* was scuttled to avoid capture. Casement landed in Ireland from a German submarine and was instantly arrested (the British hanged him as a traitor the following August). Faced with a potential fiasco, MacNeill revoked the order for an uprising. Pearse, Connolly, and their colleagues, however, decided to go ahead.

The uprising

On Easter Monday, a day later than planned, about 1,600 armed rebels seized control of key buildings in Dublin. Standing on the steps of the General Post Office, which the rebels had taken as their headquarters, Pearse read out a proclamation on behalf of "the Provisional Government of the Irish Republic".

Dubliners reacted with initial bemusement, followed by a wave of looting as police withdrew from the streets. In the rest of Ireland, there were isolated uprisings, but most Volunteers followed MacNeill's order to stay at home. The British response was delayed by a lack of troops on the spot. Few of the soldiers garrisoning Dublin had ammunition for their rifles.

On 26 April, troop reinforcements arrived from England. Soldiers of the Sherwood Foresters, marching into the

"In the name of God and of the dead generations from which she receives her old tradition of nationhood, Ireland… strikes for her freedom."

PATRICK PEARSE, PROCLAMATION OF THE PROVISIONAL GOVERNMENT OF THE IRISH REPUBLIC, 24 APRIL 1916

After the fighting
Dubliners walk through the ruins of the city's General Post Office after the suppression of the Easter Rising. Used as the rebel headquarters, the building was destroyed by British artillery fire.

city from the port of Kingstown, came under fire from rebels at Mount Street Bridge on the Grand Canal. Ordered to make repeated frontal assaults across the bridge, the British soldiers suffered 240 casualties.

Failure and the firing squad

Further British losses occurred when rebel positions were attacked by infantry, but mostly the British relied on artillery, shelling buildings held by the rebels until they became untenable. Driven from the burning General Post Office building on 29 April, Pearse ordered a surrender. The fighting ceased the following day.

As the rebels had conspired with Britain's enemies in time of war, harsh retribution was inevitable. Martial law was imposed under General Sir John Maxwell, and 15 Irish nationalists were executed in early May. Among those who faced the firing squad were Pearse and James Connolly. The executions outraged the Irish Catholics and won wider public support for republicanism than had ever existed before.

The British were not insensitive to the need for reconciliation. Almost 1,500 nationalists sent to internment camps following the uprising were released at the end of the year. Most death sentences were commuted, with those spared including the American-born future Irish leader Éamon de Valera. The alienation of Irish Catholic opinion would nonetheless prove fatal to the continuance of British rule in Ireland.

AFTER »

Political developments after World War I led to the formation of the Irish Free State in the south of Ireland, while parts of the north stayed British.

THE RISE OF SINN FEIN
Sinn Fein emerged as a unifying organization for Irish nationalists. In the general election held after the war, Sinn Fein achieved a **landslide victory** in Catholic areas and set up a parliament in Dublin. Sinn Fein's military arm, the **Irish Republican Army** (IRA), fought an independence war against Britain masterminded by Michael Collins. In 1922, the **Irish Free State** was founded, while Protestant-dominated Northern Ireland remained part of the UK.

FORGOTTEN ROLE
The contribution that many Irish Catholics had made to the war effort was forgotten. In Northern Ireland, the service of **Protestant soldiers at the Somme** was contrasted with **Catholic rebels** who had "stabbed Britain in the back". This prejudice still lingers on a century later.

MICHAEL COLLINS

165

Intelligence and Espionage

" The number of agents of the **German Secret Police...** working in our midst… are believed to be over **five thousand.**"

WILLIAM LE QUEUX, "SPIES OF THE KAISER", 1909

Before World War I, tension between the European powers fuelled anxieties that foreign agents and traitors could undermine national security. States developed organizations dedicated to gathering foreign intelligence and protecting

military secrets. Much of the concern about espionage was exaggerated, but agents were undoubtedly employed to sketch foreign naval ports and other military installations, or to search wastepaper baskets for war plans. When war broke out, however, signals

intelligence – the interception of enemy messages – proved more fruitful. Although the experts of the French Deuxième Bureau were noted for their codebreaking skills, the most spectacular intelligence coups of the war were the work of the

British Naval Intelligence Division under the command of Admiral Reginald "Blinker" Hall. Captured German code books – notably those seized by the Russians from the cruiser SMS *Magdeburg* in the Baltic in late August 1914 – allowed Hall's codebreakers in Room 40, the British Navy's secret intelligence room, to read the German navy's radio traffic. The information gathered permitted the interception of the German High Seas Fleet at Jutland in 1916.

Of even greater importance was the decoding of diplomatic messages. Since Britain had cut the undersea cables linking Germany to the outside world, the Germans had no safe way of communicating with their embassies. In January 1917, a message from the German Foreign Minister, Arthur Zimmermann, to the embassy in Mexico was decoded by Room 40 and passed on to the American

Military communications
French soldiers man the switchboard at a military headquarters on the Western Front. The communications on which armies and navies depended were inherently insecure.

INVISIBLE INK KIT

BUTTONS WITH CODED TEXT

HIDDEN CAMERA

Spy kit
German spy agents employed a range of equipment to record and convey information. An invisible ink kit like this one was found among Mata Hari's possessions when she was arrested.

government. Its instructions to the German ambassador to lure Mexico into attacking the USA helped bring America into the war against Germany.

Secret agents
Attempts to run spies in enemy countries had limited success. The Netherlands and Switzerland, neutral countries on the edge of the conflict, became hotbeds of espionage activity where rival intelligence agencies operated freely. The advantage of employing "neutrals" as agents was that they were generally free to cross borders into enemy territory.

However, counter-intelligence organizations exercising surveillance over foreigners and reading letters and telegrams generally picked up such agents quite swiftly. A total of 235 Allied agents were convicted of espionage by the Germans, without any notable intelligence emerging from their activities. France had a full-blown

spy scandal in 1917 when evidence emerged of payments made by German agents to anti-war elements in the country, notably the left-wing journal *Le Bonnet Rouge*. Among those arrested and executed, the best remembered is the dancer Mata Hari, whose alleged

11
The number of people in Britain executed for spying for Germany in the course of World War I.

use of exotic charms to extract secrets from French officers appealed to the public's taste for the sensational.

Resistance networks
The activity of resistance networks in German-occupied Belgium and northern France was of far more practical importance than the work of secret agents. Groups such as the White Lady network based in the Belgian city of Liège, for example,

provided the Allies with valuable information on the movement of German troop trains. Typed encrypted reports were either smuggled across the border into the Netherlands or sent to France across German lines by carrier pigeon.

The Belgian resistance movement, much of which was operated by Catholic priests and nuns, also smuggled people out of the country, including Allied prisoners of war and Belgians of military age wanting to join the Belgian army fighting in Flanders. The executions of Edith Cavell and Philippe Baucq attracted world attention to these activities, but they

Mata Hari
Dutch exotic dancer Mata Hari was executed by firing squad by the French in October 1917 for being a German agent. France's wartime spy mania was then at its height.

were only two among hundreds of resisters killed by the German occupation forces.

In Russia, the belief that key figures in the tsarist court were German agents undermined confidence in the regime. After the revolution that overthrew the Tsar in March 1917, Germany actively supported anti-war revolutionaries, including the Bolshevik Vladimir Ilyich Lenin, who was provided with money and a train to bring him home from exile in Switzerland. After Lenin seized power the following November, Allied agents plotted against the Bolshevik regime. Their only achievement, however, was to stimulate Bolshevik paranoia and secret police activity.

RESISTANCE WORKER (1865–1915)
EDITH CAVELL

A British nurse working in Belgium before the war, Edith Cavell stayed there under the German occupation. A high-minded humanitarian, she became involved with a resistance network run by an architect called Philippe Baucq, helping wounded Allied soldiers or prisoners of war escape to Britain via the Netherlands. When the network was betrayed to the Germans, Cavell was arrested, tried, and shot. Cavell's execution was a propaganda gift to the Allies, causing outrage in Britain and the USA. Her reported last words included the famous phrase: "Patriotism is not enough."

TIMELINE

1894 French officer Captain Alfred Dreyfus is arrested for allegedly passing secrets to Germany. After his sentence to life imprisonment, his case becomes a dividing point in French politics.

CONTEMPORARY PORTRAYAL OF ALFRED DREYFUS

1906 After the political triumph of his supporters, Dreyfus is fully exonerated and reinstated in the army.

1907 The French Deuxième Bureau, first created in 1871, is reactivated to gather military intelligence abroad.

1909 The British government creates a secret service bureau to gather intelligence abroad and counter foreign spies in Britain.

May 1913 Colonel Alfred Redel, former head of Austrian counter-intelligence, commits suicide after being exposed as a double-agent working for Russia.

October 1914 British Naval Intelligence establishes Room 40, devoted to the decoding of intercepted German naval radio messages.

6 November 1914 German agent Carl Lody is shot in the Tower of London.

12 October 1915 British nurse Edith Cavell and four Belgian resisters, including Philippe Baucq, are executed by a German firing squad.

January 1917 British Room 40 cryptographers reveal German plans to induce Mexico to wage war against the USA.

June 1917 The Espionage Act is passed in the USA, suppressing opposition to the war.

July 1917 French anti-war magazine *Le Bonnet Rouge*, allegedly funded by German agents, is suppressed.

15 October 1917 Dancer Mata Hari is executed for espionage at Vincennes in France.

November 1917 Louis Malvy, a former minister in the French government, is arrested over alleged contacts with Germany.

17 April 1918 Paul Bolo, a German agent in France, is executed by firing squad.

Lancers on parade
Polish Uhlan lancers serving in the Austro-Hungarian army parade in Warsaw on the founding of the Polish Regency Council in October 1917. Regency Poland was a client state of the Central Powers.

« **BEFORE**

In 1914, Russia and Austria-Hungary were multinational empires. Their large Slavic populations had long-nourished hopes of independence.

DIVISION OF POLAND
Poland had been partitioned between Russia, Austria, and Prussia in the 18th century. Most Poles came under Russian rule, with a large population in Austrian-ruled Galicia. Substantial numbers also dwelt in Silesia and East Prussia, in Germany. There were **major uprisings** in Russian Poland in 1830 and 1863, suppressed by tsarist forces. The **struggle for Polish independence** was recognized as a just cause by liberal opinion across Europe.

AUSTRO-HUNGARIAN PACT
In 1867, the **Austrian Empire**, ruled by ethnic Germans, made a **power-sharing deal** with its **Hungarian population** to resist the nationalist aspirations of its Slav peoples – Czechs and Slovaks, Poles and Ruthenians, Serbs, Croats, and Slovenes. By 1914, Slav groups were a disruptive element in Austro-Hungarian politics.

Slav Nationalism

World War I gave the subject Slavs a chance to fight for independence. But which side they should take in the war was not always clear. Soldiers from oppressed Slav peoples in various European countries served both the Allies and the Central Powers.

The assassination of Archduke Franz Ferdinand by Bosnian Serbs wishing to shake off Austro-Hungarian rule triggered World War I. Yet the nationalist aspirations of Serbs and other Slav peoples became a side issue once the major powers went to war. Instead of rising up against their ruling empires, the impulse of the subject Slavs was to support them in the conflict. This enthusiasm rapidly waned, however, and mounting Slav disaffection was accompanied by the efforts of nationalist leaders to exploit the opportunity offered by the war.

The Polish position
Poland stood out as a country with a long-established claim to nationhood, but also as the principal battleground

between Russia and the Central Powers. The leading Polish nationalists were split over their attitude to the war. The anti-Russian Josef Pilsudski sided with Austria-Hungary, while followers of the more pragmatic Roman Dmowski favoured Russia, on the grounds that it offered

protection against German domination and was allied to the democratic Western powers.

At the start of World War I, Pilsudski led a personal militia from Galicia into Russian Poland, where he was surprised not to be greeted as a liberator. He was soon integrated into the Austro-Hungarian army, leading a brigade of the Polish Legions that he had helped to found. The Polish Legions proved their fighting quality in the costly combat on the Eastern Front, notably at the Battle of Kostiuchnowka in July 1916.

Polish Adrian helmet
Soldiers in the Polish Army in France wore the French Adrian helmet with its distinctive emblem. This force entered the fighting on the Western Front halfway through 1918.

> "Only the **sword** now carries any **weight** in the balance for the **destiny of a nation.**"
>
> JOSEF PILSUDSKI, 1914

POSTER (1918) FOR POLAND'S INDEPENDENCE

NEW NATIONS

In Poland, **independence** was declared on 11 November 1918. The Poles fought a major war against the Soviet Union before frontiers were finalized in 1922. **Czechoslovakia** became independent on 18 October 1918, with Tomas Masaryk its first president. On 1 December 1918, South Slavs joined with Serbia to form the **Kingdom of Serbs, Croats and Slovenes**, later renamed Yugoslavia.

future of Poland, but in November 1916 Germany declared its intention to found an independent Polish state. This gradually came into existence through 1917 – it was proclaimed a kingdom and governed, in the absence of a king, by a Regency Council – but its lack of genuine independence was clearly apparent.

In July 1917, Pilsudski was arrested by the Germans after urging the Polish Legions to reject an oath swearing loyalty to Germany.

Meanwhile, the revolution in Russia in March 1917 and the espousal of Polish independence as a war aim by the Allies ended any hope of the Central Powers winning Polish support. On the Western Front, a Polish Legion, recognized by the French as the "Polish Army", was formed from Polish emigrants to the USA and Canada. It fought in the epic battles of 1918.

Czechs and Slovaks

The idea that Czechs and Slovaks, Slav minorities in Austria and Hungary respectively, might make common cause had been mooted before World War I. It took solid shape in 1916 when Czech nationalists Edvard Benes and Tomas Masaryk and Slovak nationalist Milan Stefanik created the Czechoslovak National Council in Paris.

These leaders worked tirelessly to attract Allied support for their cause. Benes and Masaryk, who were both academics, established contact with Allied leaders, while Stefanik sought to create Czechoslovak Legions, primarily from prisoners of war or deserters from the Austro-Hungarian army. The Czechoslovak Legion in Russia distinguished itself in the Kerensky Offensive of summer 1917, fighting at the Battle of Zborov. It was later drawn into the Russian Civil War. Czechs and Slovaks also fought with the Allies in France and Italy.

Czech soldiers

The Czech and Slovak volunteers who joined the French Foreign Legion served on the Western Front from 1915. They later formed an autonomous Czechoslovak Legion fighting alongside the French army.

Croats, Serbs, and Slovenes

While some South Slavs in Austria-Hungary – Croats, Serbs, and Slovenes – fought in the Austro-Hungarian army, others identified with an already independent combatant country, Serbia. In 1916, after the conquest of Serbia by the Central Powers, the Serbian parliament in exile in Corfu called for the creation of a kingdom of South Slavs. After the war, the new states came into being as the Kingdom of Serbs, Croats and Slovenes, the union of the three peoples cemented by Allied pressure.

On the whole, Polish popular opinion was initially more in favour of Russia, with Poles in Galicia often aiding advancing Russian forces, but the oppressive behaviour of these forces soon swung attitudes the other way. In fact, Polish civilians suffered at the hands of all the combatants. Before the Central Powers conquered most of Russian Poland in 1915, the country was devastated and partially depopulated by the "scorched earth" policy deployed by the retreating Russian soldiers. It was then ruthlessly exploited by Germany and Austria-Hungary as a source of food and forced labour.

There were sharp disagreements between the German and Austro-Hungarian governments over the

JOSEF PILSUDSKI

Born in Russian Poland, Polish nationalist Josef Pilsudski was twice imprisoned by the Russian authorities for his subversive activities. From 1914, he led the Polish Legions fighting for Austria-Hungary against Russia. He collaborated with the Central Powers until July 1917, when he was imprisoned in Magdeburg, Germany, after refusing to swear an oath of loyalty to the German Kaiser. At the end of the war, Pilsudski proclaimed Polish independence, becoming modern Poland's first head of state on 22 November 1918.

BEFORE

Germany was desperate to break the naval blockade imposed by Britain's Royal Navy, which controlled the sea routes through the North Sea and the English Channel.

NORTH SEA SORTIES

For a year after the British success at the **Battle of Dogger Bank ≪ 124–25** in January 1915, the German High Seas Fleet stayed in port. In January 1916, however, the fleet received a new commander-in-chief, Vice-Admiral **Reinhard Scheer**.

An aggressive commander, Scheer ordered sorties into the North Sea in March and in April and **bombarded the English east coast towns** of Lowestoft and Great Yarmouth. Scheer's aim was to lure the Royal Navy into combat on his own terms and sink enough of its warships to undermine Britain's long-held naval superiority.

Battle of Jutland from the air

An artist's impression shows ships steaming in line, the formation that optimized chances for firing on the enemy. Much of the battle was fought at long range, with some guns hitting targets 16 km (10 miles) away.

The **Battle** of **Jutland**

The only full-scale encounter between the German and British fleets in World War I took place in the North Sea at the end of May 1916. A staggering 250 warships, including some of the world's largest battleships, fought a dramatic running battle, but with no decisive result.

On 30 May 1916, Admiral Sir John Jellicoe, commander of the Royal Navy's Grand Fleet, was informed by the Admiralty that the German High Seas Fleet was preparing to go to sea the following day. The information, from signals intelligence and the Admiralty's Room 40 cryptographers, was short on detail but sufficient for action.

The Battlecruiser Fleet, based in the Firth of Forth in Scotland, and commanded by Vice-Admiral Sir David Beatty, was dispatched towards the waters off Denmark's Jutland peninsula in the expected path of the German sortie. There, it was to be joined by the overwhelming might of Jellicoe's Grand Fleet steaming from Scapa Flow in the Orkneys. If Beatty encountered the German High Seas Fleet, he was to lead it to Jellicoe, who would destroy it with his far superior weight of guns.

On 31 May, the German fleet steamed northwards with its battlecruisers, commanded by Vice-Admiral Franz von Hipper, in the lead, and Admiral Scheer's main fleet following.

Mighty confrontation

Hipper's forces comprised 99 warships, including 16 modern battleships and five battlecruisers. The British had 151 warships at sea, including 28 battleships and nine battlecruisers. Scheer's position was precarious. Bad

Award for heroism

This Victoria Cross was awarded to Jack Cornwell, a 16-year-old Boy Seaman. He was mortally wounded while serving aboard HMS *Chester*, but even so remained standing at his post.

"There seems to be **something wrong** with our **bloody ships** today."

VICE-ADMIRAL SIR DAVID BEATTY, AT JUTLAND, 31 MAY 1916

weather prevented the Germans from using airships for reconnaissance. The British, for their part, did not make best use of their intelligence, as little of the information had reached Jellicoe.

It was a surprise to both sides when their battlecruiser forces made contact in the early afternoon. Hipper quickly

9 The number of survivors from the 1,275-man crew of the battlecruiser *Queen Mary*.

2 The number of survivors from the 1,019-man crew of the battlecruiser *Indefatigable*.

turned southwards to draw Beatty towards Scheer's main force. Beatty gave chase. He had more battlecruisers than Hipper and four of the latest Queen Elizabeth class battleships in

support. However, the battleships lagged behind, and the exchange of fire between the rival battlecruisers quickly turned to Germany's advantage. German gunnery was accurate and the British battlecruisers had insufficient armour.

Tactical mistakes

The Royal Navy had also neglected to protect their stock of weapons against fire. In quick succession the battlecruisers *Indefatigable* and *Queen Mary* exploded and sank. There were only 11 survivors from two crews totalling over 2,000 men. Beatty's flagship the *Lion* was also badly hit, only narrowly avoiding the same fate.

When Scheer arrived on the scene with his main force, he sensed a chance for a major victory. Beatty's surviving battlecruisers fled to the north, while the four battleships, slow to pick up the manoeuvre, faced Scheer's pursuit from the rear. The British continued to lose ships in the confused fighting.

Meanwhile, Jellicoe was drawing close to the battle area. Only hazily aware of the situation ahead of him, he deployed his ships in line of battle. At 6:30pm, the rival fleets emerged from thickening mist. Scheer was taken by surprise. Facing a formidable line of British warships 10km (6 miles) long across his bows, he turned behind a smokescreen and headed towards home.

High explosives
Armour-piercing shells, such as this British example, were used by both fleets at Jutland. Inadequately armoured British battlecruisers proved vulnerable to shellfire, a defect exploited by German gunners.

Jellicoe now had a great opportunity. If he could cut off the German line of escape and force Scheer to fight, the High Seas Fleet would be destroyed.

As a cautious man burdened with heavy responsibilities, however, Jellicoe was aware of the great risks this action entailed. He feared that in the heat of pursuit his best ships might be decimated by German submarines, torpedo boats, or mines.

As Scheer manoeuvred desperately in search of an escape route, the battleships of the Grand Fleet twice had the Germans under their guns, and inflicted heavy damage.

German escape

At a crucial juncture, however, German torpedo boats launched a covering attack that caused Jellicoe to turn away from the pursuit. The British admiral was in any case convinced that, as night fell, he could position his fleet across the German route home and bring them to battle at daylight. Instead, under cover of darkness, Scheer cut behind Jellicoe's battleships and forced a passage through the destroyers and cruisers at the rear of the British line.

There was fierce fighting through the night. Among the ships sunk was the German pre-dreadnought battleship SMS *Pommern*, hit by torpedoes from a British destroyer. All hands were lost.

When day broke, Jellicoe learned that the bulk of the German fleet had slipped past him and was almost home.

The British lost 14 ships at Jutland, which was five more than Germany, but strategically the indecisive outcome worked in Britain's favour.

ASSESSING THE DAMAGE

The Royal Navy still maintained an unshakeable **superiority in surface warships** – immediately after the Battle of Jutland the British had 24 battleships ready to sail, while only 10 German battleships were in a seaworthy condition. Scheer **continued to mount occasional sorties** into the

6,094 The number of British sailors killed at Jutland, compared with 2,551 German dead.

North Sea – the next in August 1916 and the last in April 1918 – but without resulting in significant combat.

In the wake of Jutland, Scheer pressed for the **resumption of unrestricted submarine warfare** as the only truly valid naval response to the British blockade. This measure was adopted in February 1917, posing severe problems for the Royal Navy and effectively bringing **America into the war 212–13 »**.

America into the war 212–13 »

BRITISH ADMIRAL (1859–1935)

JOHN JELLICOE

Admiral Sir John Jellicoe was appointed commander of the Royal Navy's Grand Fleet at the outbreak of war. His defensive approach made strategic sense but did not satisfy the British public's demand for dashing victories. In the words of Sir Winston Churchill, then Lord of the Admiralty, he was perceived as "the only man on either side who could lose the war in an afternoon".

In November 1916, Jellicoe was promoted to the post of First Sea Lord, and effectively sidelined. In December 1917, he was sacked.

"Everything in the **ship went quiet,** the floor of the turret was **bulged up** and the guns were **absolutely useless.**"

PETTY OFFICER ERNEST FRANCIS, ON BOARD HMS QUEEN MARY

On Board the SMS *Derfflinger*

Later nicknamed Iron Dog by British sailors, the *Derfflinger* participated in the sinking of two Royal Navy vessels, the *Queen Mary* and *Invincible*, during the course of the Battle of Jutland. But it did not escape unscathed. The *Derfflinger* received the highest casualty rate of any ship not sunk, with 157 men killed and 26 wounded, and was under repair for nearly five months after the battle.

"I selected a target and fired as rapidly as possible… And all the time we were steaming at full speed into this inferno, offering a splendid target to the enemy… Salvo after salvo fell around us, hit after hit struck our ship.

A 38 cm [15 in] shell pierced the armour of the 'Caesar' turret and exploded inside. The brave turret commander, Lieutenant Commander von Boltenstern, had both his legs torn off and with him nearly the whole gun crew was killed… The burning cartridge-cases emitted great tongues of flame which shot up out of the turrets as high as a house… another shell pierced the roof of the 'Dora' turret… and exploded. The same horrors ensued. With the exception of one single man, who was thrown by the concussion through the turret entrance, the whole turret crew of eighty men… were killed instantly. From both after-turrets great flames were now spurting, mingled with clouds of yellow smoke, two ghastly pyres.

…The enemy had got our range excellently… A terrific roar, a tremendous explosion and then darkness in which we felt a colossal blow. The whole conning tower seemed to be hurled into the air… and then to flutter trembling into its former position. A heavy shell had struck the fore-control about 50 cm [20 in] in front of me. The shell exploded, but failed to pierce the thick armour… Poisonous greenish-yellow gases poured through the apertures into our control.

I called out: 'Down gas masks!' and immediately every man pulled down his gas mask over his face… We could scarcely see anything of the enemy, who were disposed in a great semicircle around us. All we could see was the great reddish-gold flames spurting from the guns."

COMMANDER GEORG VON HASE, FIRST GUNNERY OFFICER ON THE SMS DERFFLINGER, FROM HIS BOOK "KIEL AND JUTLAND", 1921

The Battle of Jutland

During the course of the battle, SMS *Derfflinger* was hit 17 times by heavy calibre shells and nine times by secondary guns. The ferocity of its engagement with the British fleet is captured in this painting by German artist Claus Bergen.

BEFORE

Despite massive losses of men and territory in campaigns on the Eastern Front in 1915, Russia was committed to a major offensive in 1916.

DIVERSIONARY ATTACKS

At the **Chantilly Conference** in December 1915, the Allies had pledged to launch diversionary offensives if one of their number came under pressure. When **Germany attacked** the **French at Verdun** in February 1916 《 **154–55**, France appealed to Russia for assistance. Russian commanders agreed to **launch an attack towards Vilnius** at the northern end of the Eastern Front in March 1916.

RUSSIAN FAILURE

Russian supplies of equipment had greatly improved, and thanks to the arrival of fresh conscripts and the **transfer of German troops to Verdun**, the Russians had a large numerical advantage. But the **Lake Naroch offensive**, on 18 March, was a **disaster**. Russia lost 100,000 men compared with German casualties of 20,000. The little ground gained was retaken by the Germans in April.

RUSSIAN GENERAL (1853–1926)

ALEKSEI BRUSILOV

Russian General Aleksei Brusilov came from an aristocratic family with a long tradition of military service. He performed well when leading the Eighth Army in Galicia in 1914–15, before sealing his reputation with the success of his 1916 summer offensive. Disillusioned with the incompetence of the tsarist regime, he encouraged Nicholas II to abdicate in March 1917. Appointed commander-in-chief under Russia's Provisional Government, he failed to repeat the success of his 1916 offensive. In spite of his aristocratic roots, he sympathized with the common man and supported the Bolsheviks in the Russian Civil War.

The Brusilov Offensive

Russia's most successful operation of the war was the superbly prepared offensive launched by General Aleksei Brusilov in June 1916. It drove Austro-Hungarian forces back across a wide front and dealt a mortal blow to the tottering Austro-Hungarian Empire.

In mid-April 1916, Russia's senior commanders held a meeting with their commander-in-chief Tsar Nicholas II to discuss military plans for the summer. The Tsar and his Chief of Staff, General Mikhail Alexeev, were committed to a summer offensive that would coincide with an Allied attack at the Somme on the Western Front.

The generals commanding the northern sector of the Russian front, chosen as the location for the offensive, were appalled at the prospect of leading an attack they believed could not succeed. Only when promised large-scale reinforcements did they agree to the plan. To their surprise, General Brusilov, who was commanding the Southwest Army Group facing Austro-Hungarian forces in Galicia, also volunteered to mount an offensive. Since he was not asking for reinforcements, Alexeev allowed him to go ahead, viewing his operation as a harmless diversion from the main Russian attack in the north.

Brusilov had made a careful study of available trench warfare techniques and analysed the reasons for previous failures. The offensive tactics so far adopted by Russia had been based on concentrating a large mass of infantry and artillery upon a small sector of the front. This sledgehammer approach, he concluded, produced small initial gains at heavy cost, before enemy reserves delivered crushing counterattacks.

New Russian tactics

Brusilov planned an offensive delivered by four armies at points across his entire front, thus preventing the enemy from concentrating reserves at any point. He intended to seize enemy trenches without using substantial numerical superiority of infantry or artillery. Aerial reconnaissance would be used to locate Austro-Hungarian artillery batteries, and other key targets for the Russian guns, which were for once adequately supplied with shells.

> "The great **heart** of the country was **beating** in **sympathy** with the **well-loved soldiers** of my **victorious armies.**"

ALEKSEI BRUSILOV, "A SOLDIER'S NOTEBOOK, 1914–18"

Russian soldiers

The infantry of the Tsarist armies, here photographed marching in 1916, were better supplied than before and capable of fighting well if properly led. However, morale among Russian forces remained precarious.

Soldiers were thoroughly trained for the operation and, unlike in the previous year, all had rifles. Saps (short trenches) were dug forward into No Man's Land to serve as launch pads for surprise attacks. Further back, huge dugouts were excavated to shelter reserves within range of enemy guns.

The offensive begins

Launched on 4 June, the offensive was a total surprise to Austro-Hungarian forces. The preliminary bombardment was brief and accurate. Waves of Russian infantry occupied enemy front-line trenches with only light casualties. Brusilov then poured in his reserves to sustain the offensive.

Unable to mount a viable resistance, the Austro-Hungarians were soon falling back in disarray. Their fortified position at Lutsk fell in two days. Within a week, Russian forces had advanced up to 65 km (40 miles) from their start lines. Austro-Hungarian

500,000 The number of Russian casualties, including prisoners of war, in the Brusilov Offensive from June to September 1916.

1,000,000 The number of Austro-Hungarian casualties during the offensive, including some 400,000 troops who were taken prisoner.

soldiers surrendered in vast numbers – some 200,000 prisoners were taken during the first nine days alone.

Austro-Hungarian Chief of the General staff Conrad von Hötzendorff was forced to transfer troops from the Italian front and plead for help from Germany. Heavily engaged at Verdun and aware of an imminent Allied offensive on the Somme, the Germans had limited support to offer.

By mid-June, supply and transport problems had halted the Russian advance, but an Austro-Hungarian and German counterattack largely failed. Brusilov was able to renew his offensive in July, achieving further advances – Russian troops at the southern end of the front reached the Carpathians.

But these gains were made at mounting cost. The glow of triumph for the Russians gradually faded. Brusilov's efforts were poorly supported by

Moisin-Nagant revolver
Introduced into service in 1895, the seven-shot Moisin-Nagant revolver was the standard sidearm of the Russian army in World War I. It remained in use in the Soviet Union until 1952.

Russian central command and the generals to the north. The arrival of increasing numbers of German troops stiffened defences, so that Russian gains diminished and losses increased. By the time the offensive petered out in the autumn, Russian troops were suffering as many casualties as their enemies.

Austria-Hungary was the chief loser in the fighting. From September 1916, the Germans took command of Austro-Hungarian forces on the Eastern Front. Without control of its own army, Austria-Hungary had effectively ceased to be a fully independent country.

Austro-Hungarian helmet
Steel helmets like this one, worn by Austro-Hungarian troops in the later years of World War I, were variants of the German Stalhelm. Like the Stalhelm, they sharply reduced deaths from head wounds caused by shrapnel.

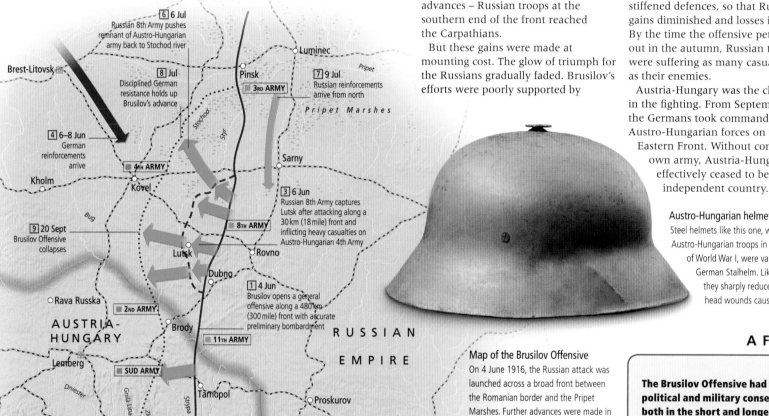

Map of the Brusilov Offensive
On 4 June 1916, the Russian attack was launched across a broad front between the Romanian border and the Pripet Marshes. Further advances were made in July and August, but by mid-September German and Austro-Hungarian troops had stabilized a defensive line.

KEY
- Austro-Hungarian army
- Russian army
- Austro-German lines 4 June
- Austro-German lines 10 June
- Austro-German lines 20 Sept
- Russian advance
- Russian reinforcements
- German reinforcements
- Fortified city
- Main railway

AFTER ≫

The Brusilov Offensive had important political and military consequences both in the short and longer term.

ROMANIA ENTERS THE WAR
The setback on the Eastern Front contributed to the **resignation of** German Chief of the General Staff General Erich von **Falkenhayn** at the end of August 1916. At the same time, the Russian successes persuaded **Romania to enter the war 194–95 ≫** against the Central Powers – an ill-advised decision as the country was **swiftly defeated**. In Russia, the strain of the war led to popular discontent and the **overthrow of the tsarist regime 210–11 ≫** in March 1917. In Austria-Hungary, Emperor **Franz Joseph died** in November 1916 and was succeeded by Emperor Charles I, who began a vain search for a peace agreement with the Allies.

« BEFORE

In all its military conflicts before World War I, Britain had relied upon a small professional army.

THE TERRITORIAL FORCE

The British government realized that a European conflict was a strong possibility, but **conscription** was considered politically unacceptable. Richard Haldane, Minister for War 1905–1912, sought other ways in which to **boost** Britain's **military capacity**. He consolidated existing bodies of part-time soldiers – militia and volunteer forces – into the **Territorial Force**, primarily intended for home defence. A **Special Reserve** also offered training to other men, who would provide **reinforcement** to regular regiments if a major war broke out.

BRITISH ARMY
RECRUITMENT POSTER

BRITONS
"WANTS
YOU"
JOIN YOUR COUNTRY'S ARMY!
GOD SAVE THE KING
Reproduced by permission of LONDON OPINION

Kitchener's Armies

In August 1914, the newly appointed British Minister for War, Lord Kitchener, appealed for volunteers to form a New Army. More than two million men from all walks of life responded to the call, giving Britain its first mass citizen army by the summer of 1916.

Military service had become commonplace in continental Europe before 1914, but in Britain only a small minority of men knew how to fire a rifle or appear on parade.

When Lord Kitchener entered the British government as Minister for War in August 1914, he startled his political colleagues by stating that the war would last three years, rather than the three months generally predicted. He voiced his contempt of the piecemeal state of British military preparations, commenting: "Did they consider when they went headlong into a war like this, that they were without an army, and without any preparation to equip one?"

Kitchener had no faith in the part-time Territorial Force, which might have been used as the basis for a mass army. Instead, on 6 August, he launched an appeal for volunteers to form a "New Army" of 100,000 men. This number soon proved far too modest. By October, four more New Armies had been authorized.

Recruitment posters featuring Kitchener's face became so well known in Britain that the New Armies would always be known unofficially as Kitchener's Armies.

The recruitment process

From the start, there were queues outside recruiting offices. The authorities struggled to find enough recruiting officers, clerks, and doctors to carry out the process of selection and enrolment. By early September, 33,000 men were enrolling per day – at a time when the entire British forces deployed in France numbered around

Medical check-up

Potential soldiers had to pass a medical before being accepted into the British Army. Early in the war, 40 per cent of would-be conscripts failed the test, so standards were lowered.

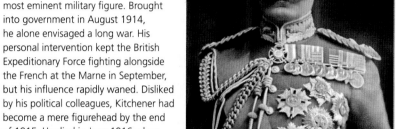

"We stood... **stripped to the nude...** a **medical officer** gave us a swift **examination.**"

PRIVATE PERCY CRONER, DESCRIBING A RECRUITING OFFICE, DECEMBER 1914

100,000. New battalions were formed by local initiatives that allowed men from the same area or workplace to serve together. Lord Derby, promoting such a formation in Liverpool, called it "a battalion of pals... in which friends from the same office will fight shoulder to shoulder". There were battalions of stockbrokers and of footballers, battalions based on public schools and on Lads' Clubs (working class youth clubs), battalions of postal workers, and of artists.

The drawback of this system, made so apparent by the Somme Offensive in July 1916, was that friends who fought together also often died together. Battalions suffering heavy losses brought irreparable grief to the communities from which they were drawn.

Wooden rifles

Training and equipping the New Armies was a long and difficult process. To begin with, the volunteers lacked everything from uniforms and rifles to a decent place to sleep. They were still practising drill with wooden rifles in Britain while Territorial formations were proving their worth in France – Kitchener's initial doubts about the Territorial Force having been overridden by necessity.

Lack of noncommissioned officers (NCOs) – highly experienced soldiers who rose to corporal or sergeant level through the ranks – was a serious problem for the New Armies. Volunteers found themselves in the hands of the inexperienced or the antiquated – a mix of youthful officers from the pre-war university and public school Officer Training Corps and

aged sergeant-majors, the veterans of 19th-century imperial conflicts with no experience of modern warfare.

Into battle

Morale on the whole survived intact through the lengthy period of training, and the first New Army volunteers to go into battle, at Loos in France in September 1915, did so in good spirits. Senior British commanders had little confidence in these troops, who came from a stratum of society – clerks and factory workers – they considered unlikely to yield decent military material. In reality, the men showed no lack of courage or fighting spirit, but their training was an inadequate preparation for the realities of the Western Front.

White feathers

Social pressure on men to volunteer was intense. The White Feather movement, for example, encouraged women to present this traditional symbol of cowardice to any man of military age who was not in uniform.

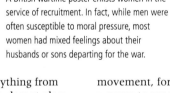

Female ambivalence
A British wartime poster enlists women in the service of recruitment. In fact, while men were often susceptible to moral pressure, most women had mixed feelings about their husbands or sons departing for the war.

HERBERT KITCHENER

Lord Kitchener, a successful general in various imperial campaigns, was Britain's most eminent military figure. Brought into government in August 1914, he alone envisaged a long war. His personal intervention kept the British Expeditionary Force fighting alongside the French at the Marne in September, but his influence rapidly waned. Disliked by his political colleagues, Kitchener had become a mere figurehead by the end of 1915. He died in June 1916 when the warship carrying him on a visit to Russia was sunk by a mine.

Nonetheless, volunteering tailed off in 1915 as enthusiasm for the war faded. The British government also needed to

5.7 MILLION The number of British men who served in the army in World War I, a quarter of the adult male population.

2.4 MILLION The number of men in the British Army who were volunteers.

rationalize the recruitment process, so that men doing essential work – for example, in war industries such as mining – could be kept out of the army.

In October 1915, the British government tried a last-ditch alternative to conscription, a national registration scheme that invited all men of military age to "assent" to serve if called upon. But this also failed to attract enough recruits, and in January 1916 conscription was introduced. Nonetheless, it was largely as a result of Kitchener's call for volunteers that, by summer 1916, Britain had around two million men on the Western Front. Many of them would lose their lives during the bloody Somme campaign.

AFTER »

Conscription was extended twice after its introduction. Men could claim exemption on conscientious grounds, but few did so.

EXTENDING CONSCRIPTION

The **Military Service Act** of January 1916 introduced **conscription** for unmarried men aged 18 to 41. It was extended to married men in the following April. The upper age limit was eventually increased to 51. Men whose work was vital to the war effort were **excluded**. Conscription was not extended to Ireland.

CONSCIENTIOUS OBJECTORS

Conscripts could **apply for exemption**. Most appeals were based on domestic hardship, such as the need to look after an elderly relative. About 16,000 "conscientious objectors" claimed exemption on grounds of principle or religious belief. Most agreed to serve as non-combatants, such as stretcher-bearers. Some 1,500 men who refused any kind of service were punished and imprisoned.

On the way to the Somme

Soldiers of the Worcestershire Regiment, on their way to the front on 28 June 1916, display high spirits. Many of them were to die in the Somme Offensive launched three days later.

BRITISH GENERAL Born 1861 Died 1929

Douglas Haig

"With our **backs to the wall...** each one of us **must fight** on **to the end.**"

DOUGLAS HAIG, SPECIAL ORDER OF THE DAY, 11 APRIL 1918

In popular culture, Field Marshal Sir Douglas Haig is often portrayed as the epitome of military leadership at its worst – a man who sent hundreds of thousands of brave soldiers to their deaths in unimaginative assaults for trivial objectives. Few military historians, on the other hand, now regard Haig with such scorn. As British commander-in-chief on the Western Front through the last three years of the war, he grappled with at times seemingly insurmountable problems and, in the end, led his armies to victory.

Haig's headquarters
The Château de Beaurepaire at Montreuil, in northern France, was Haig's headquarters on the Western Front. Based far from the horrors of the trenches, he was criticized for being remote from the realities of warfare.

Haig was from a wealthy background, but not a member of the landed aristocracy that dominated his chosen arm of the military, the cavalry. He rose to senior command largely on merit, becoming a major-general by the age of 42.

Modernizing force
British Minister for War Richard Haldane chose Haig to play a key role in the modernization of the British Army from 1906, including the shaping of the British Expeditionary Force (BEF). When the BEF went to France in August 1914, Haig's

Controversial general
Although showered with honours, Douglas Haig was a commander whose reputation has always been contested. He was known for being distant and arrogant.

appointment as one of the commanders of the two corps was a matter of course.

Haig was ruthlessly ambitious. Promoted to commander of the new First Army in December 1914, he led the British offensive at the Battle of Loos in the autumn of 1915. When this ended in failure, he ensured the blame fell on his commander-in-chief, Field Marshal Sir John French, for not moving reserves in on time.

Having engineered French's downfall, Haig became commander-in-chief himself in December 1915. In his view, the war could only be won by victory on the Western Front. Like most commanders of his day, he believed in the superiority of the offensive and in the importance of fighting spirit. He insisted on a policy of constant raids. His aim was to use massed artillery and infantry to achieve a breakthrough that could be exploited by the cavalry riding through into open country. Attrition was a means to this end, wearing down enemy forces until they eventually cracked.

Haig was a keen supporter of innovations in tactics and technology.

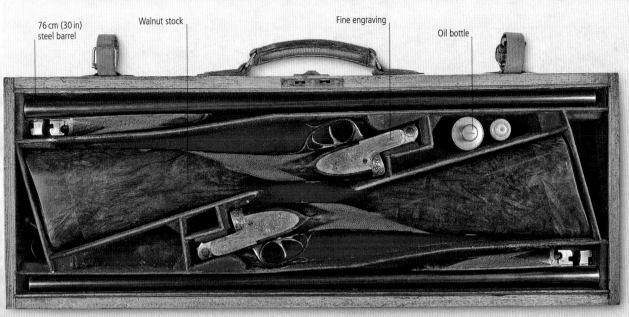

76 cm (30 in) steel barrel — Walnut stock — Fine engraving — Oil bottle

Haig's shotguns
A pair of 12-bore shotguns owned by Haig and made by J. Purdey & Sons was auctioned for £15,000 in 2011. The case is impressed with the initials "D.H.", and the brass escutcheon is engraved "7th Hussars".

He encouraged improvements in coordination between artillery and infantry, pressed for maximum use of aircraft, and was enthusiastic about the deployment of tanks. At the same time, he firmly believed in the importance of cavalry in modern warfare and in the need for cavalrymen to fight in the traditional manner, with sabre and lance.

High stakes
As commander of the largest army Britain had ever put into the field, Haig will always be judged by his offensives at the Somme in 1916 and Passchendaele (Third Ypres) in 1917. Fought at huge cost in lives, they failed to achieve major breakthroughs. Haig was sustained through these epic conflicts by his staunch belief in his eventual success. His optimism remained unshakeable – he wrote in his diary after the first day of the Somme that the casualties "could not be considered severe".

Always glimpsing success just around the corner, Haig continued the battles long after they had irremediably failed, driving men forward in renewed attacks for diminishing returns. On the other hand, no alternative to fighting in this way was available, if fighting was to take place at all.

Battles with Lloyd George
Haig's relations with David Lloyd George, British prime minister from December 1916, were based on mutual distrust. Lloyd George wanted an end to what appeared to be senseless slaughter. Yet he not only failed to offer an alternative to the continuing fighting on the Western Front but also failed to find any general prepared to take Haig's place.

The last man standing
In the crisis of spring 1918, when German offensives threatened to win

> "To **throw away men's lives** when there is no reasonable chance of advantage **is criminal.**"
>
> B.H. LIDDELL HART, "THE REAL WAR, 1914–18"

the war, Haig cooperated resolutely with his Allies, accepting subordination to General Ferdinand Foch. His order of the day on 11 April, calling for a fight "to the last man", showed surprising eloquence for a notably reserved commander.

Watching over the Legion
Earl Haig visits the British Legion factory making remembrance poppies at Richmond, Surrey, in 1926. After the war, Haig devoted time and energy to upholding the interests of ex-servicemen.

But Haig was not considered to have the popular touch. As a commander, he neither spoke to the men directly nor visited the wounded – apparently their terrible injuries upset him too much.

Both his private comments during the war, however, and his founding of the Haig Fund and British Legion to support ex-servicemen afterwards, suggest respect and concern for the ordinary soldier. His offensives cost many lives. Whether this sacrifice contributed proportionately to the Allies' eventual victory remains a matter for debate.

TIMELINE

1861 Born in Edinburgh to a family of famous whisky distillers.

1884–85 Attends the Royal Military College at Sandhurst and becomes a cavalry officer.

1898 Commands a squadron of cavalry in the Anglo-Egyptian army that defeats Mahdist rebels at Omdurman in Sudan.

1899–1902 Serves as a staff officer and commander of cavalry in the Boer War in South Africa.

1905 Marries Dorothy Vivian, a lady-in-waiting to Queen Alexandra.

1906 Appointed Director of Military Training at the War Office.

August 1914 Given command of I Corps, one of the two corps of the British Expeditionary Force (BEF).

October–December 1914 After leading I Corps at the First Battle of Ypres, Haig is given command of the new First Army in December.

March 1915 Commands the First Army at the Battle of Neuve Chapelle.

September–October 1915 Commands the British offensive at Loos. Blames its failure on Field Marshal Sir John French.

December 1915 Replaces French as commander-in-chief of the BEF.

July–November 1916 Directs the offensive at the Somme, which costs 420,000 British and Commonwealth casualties.

July–November 1917 Oversees the British offensive at Passchendaele (Third Ypres), in which British and Commonwealth casualties total around 260,000.

April 1918 Faced with a German breakthrough on the Western Front, Haig urges his men to fight with their "backs to the wall".

STATUE OF EARL HAIG

August–November 1918 Presides over British successes in the Hundred Days offensives.

1919 Raised to the British peerage as Earl Haig.

1921 Founds the Haig Fund for ex-servicemen and helps establish the British Legion ex-servicemen's organization.

1928 Dies of natural causes and is accorded a state funeral.

« BEFORE

As the point where French and British sectors of the Western Front met, the Somme was considered a good place to launch an Anglo-French offensive.

JOINT ACTION

A major offensive at the Somme was first proposed in December 1915. Plans were altered after the Germans attacked the French at **Verdun << 154–55** in February 1916. Instead of an Anglo-French operation, it became a British offensive with French support. General **Sir Douglas Haig << 178–79** wanted to delay the offensive until August, but the French insisted it go ahead sooner, to relieve the pressure on Verdun.

The Somme Offensive

The first day of the Somme Offensive, 1 July 1916, saw the heaviest loss of life in a single day's fighting in British military history. This was only the beginning of a sustained slaughter that eventually caused over a million casualties.

The German defences on the stretch of front chosen for the Allied Somme Offensive were among the strongest on the whole Western Front. The German front line consisted of a complex of trenches and fortified strongpoints with deep dugouts to shelter troops from artillery fire. A good distance behind this, there was a second defensive line, and in places a third behind that. The British plan to overcome these formidable defences relied upon a prolonged and heavy preliminary bombardment.

The plan and its execution

While the British engineers dug under the German lines to lay mines, and cut their barbed wire, the artillery was expected to demolish the German trenches and stun or kill the defenders. It would be the job of the infantry to move across from the British trenches and occupy the devastated defences.

British commander-in-chief General Sir Douglas Haig then envisaged cavalry breaking through into open country, over the German line. General Sir Henry Rawlinson, commanding the British Fourth Army, which had the

largest role in the offensive, thought in terms of a more gradual advance that would chew its way through the German defences in a series of "bites".

Haig and Rawlinson were both too optimistic. The British artillery was not adequate to the task it was set. Although it had more than 1,000 guns, these were spread too thinly across a broad front. What's more, in the rush to manufacture shells, quality had been neglected, and about a third of the 1.5 million shells fired failed to

Welsh at the Somme
The 38th (Welsh) Division attacked German positions at Mametz Wood on 10 July. Fighting at close quarters with bayonets, they succeeded in capturing the wood on 12 July, but at a cost of 4,000 casualties. This painting by Christopher Williams depicts the episode.

explode. German soldiers sat in their bunkers, profoundly shaken but safe, through eight days of preliminary bombardment. The wire in front of their trenches remained mostly uncut.

Over the top
At 7:30am on 1 July, the British infantry began their assault. Many were battalions of Kitchener's New Armies entering battle for the first time. Rawlinson had issued the order that infantry were to advance at walking pace in evenly spaced lines. Many experienced officers ignored this, filtering men forward into No Man's Land in preparation for a dash to the enemy wire or exploiting cover to move soldiers forward in small groups.

Thousands of soldiers, however, did emerge from their trenches to form up in lines and walk steadily forward behind their officers. Ahead of them

500,000 The number of British troops assembled for the offensive.

150,000 The number of French troops assembled. They were deployed on the southern flank of the British.

the British artillery attempted to provide a creeping barrage – landing shells just ahead of the advancing infantry – but coordination was clumsy and the barrage lifted too soon. Once the shells had stopped falling, the Germans emerged from their dugouts and manned the machine-guns.

The slaughtered
Blocked by intact wire, bombarded by German artillery, and cut down by machine-guns, the British infantry were massacred at many points along the line. Out of 720 Accrington Pals, a battalion of the East Lancashire Regiment sent to attack a strongpoint at Serre, 584 were killed, wounded, or missing by 8am. Of the 780 men of the Newfoundland Regiment attacking Beaumont Hamel, only 68 survived unscathed.

The Grimsby Chums, a battalion of the Lincolnshire Regiment, advanced in the La Boisselle sector where a huge mine created the Lochnagar crater. Most of the Chums advanced no further than the crater, where they were trapped under heavy fire. Their casualties numbered 502 officers and men out of a total of 600.

The role of mines
Lochnagar crater near La Boisselle is a reminder of the first day of the Somme. Ninety metres (330 ft) in diameter, it was created by a mine detonated by British engineers just before the troops went "over the top".

Some parts of the offensive were a relative success. To the south of the British, the French progressed to take most of their objectives, supported by a greater density of artillery. Alongside the French, the troops at the southern end of the British sector captured the village of Mametz, occupying Fricourt the following day. Further north, the 36th (Ulster) Division broke through the German front line and penetrated the strongpoint of the Schwaben Redoubt but were halted in front of Thiepval and forced to pull back.

Over the next days a few more objectives were achieved – La Boiselle was taken on 7 July, and Mametz Wood on 12 July. In other places, there were minimal gains, or none.

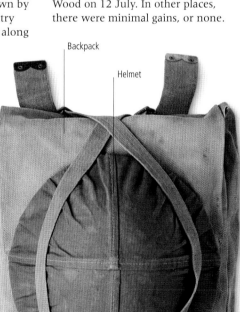

Backpack

Helmet

AFTER ≫

The British Army suffered 57,470 casualties on the first day at the Somme, including 19,240 dead. British commanders refused to accept that a military disaster had occurred.

A STILL FROM A 1916 DOCUMENTARY FILM COMMEMORATING THE SOMME OFFENSIVE

NO TURNING BACK
After the initial battle, General Rawlinson said: "I do not think that the percentage of losses is excessive." Urged on by the French, the British **continued attacks** through another five months 184–85 ≫. On the German side, Chief of the General Staff General Erich von Falkenhayn was forced to **abandon his offensive at Verdun** and **transfer troops to the Somme**. In that sense, the Somme operation achieved its objective.

PUBLIC REACTION
The heavy losses at the Somme **could not be disguised** from the British public, but the press made every effort to present the offensive as a success. A **documentary film of the battle**, released in August 1916, attracted large audiences. Including both real and re-enacted footage, it succeeded in depicting some of the horrors of the war, while being carefully slanted to boost morale.

Backpack and helmet
The soldiers who attacked on the first day of the Somme were heavily burdened with equipment, such as this backpack and helmet, which formed part of the kit of a British infantryman.

The **First Day** of the **Somme**

The 1 July 1916 marked the start of the Battle of the Somme. The costliest day in the history of the British Army, it resulted in nearly 58,000 casualties, including 19,240 dead. The day's enduring image is of heavily burdened infantrymen trudging across No Man's Land being mowed down in their thousands by German machine-guns.

Friday 30 June, 1916

"My dearest Mother and Dad,

I'm writing this letter the day before the most important moment in my life... The day has almost dawned when I shall really do my little bit [for] the cause of civilization. Tomorrow morning I shall take my men – men whom I have got to love, and who, I think, have got to love me – over the top to do our bit in the first attack in which the London Territorials have taken part as a whole unit.

I'm sure you will be very pleased to hear that I'm going over with the Westminsters. The old regiment has been given the most ticklish task in the whole of the Division; and I am very proud of my section... my two particular machine-guns have been given the two most advanced, and therefore most important, positions of all – an honour that is coveted by many.

I took my Communion yesterday with dozens of others who are going over tomorrow... I have a strong feeling that I shall come through safely; but nevertheless, should it be God's holy will to call me away, I am quite prepared to go... and you, dear Mother and Dad, will know that I died doing my duty to my God, my Country, and my King. I ask that you look upon it as an honour...

I wish I had time to write more, but time presses... I fear I must close now. Au revoir... fondest love to all those I love so dearly...

Your devoted and happy son,
Jack"

SECOND LIEUTENANT JOHN SHERWIN ENGALL, 16TH LONDON REGIMENT, A LETTER WRITTEN HOME ON THE DAY BEFORE THE START OF THE SOMME OFFENSIVE. ENGALL WAS KILLED IN ACTION THE FOLLOWING DAY.

Preparing for the Somme
A unit of British troops moves towards the start line for an offensive on the Somme in July 1916. The Battle of the Somme was one of the bloodiest in World War I.

Attrition on the Somme

As a result of the British failure to achieve a decisive breakthrough in July 1916, the Battle of the Somme degenerated into an attritional struggle on a vast scale. By November, British troops were still fighting to take some of the objectives set for the first day of the offensive.

« BEFORE

Launched on 1 July 1916, the British and French offensive at the Somme achieved limited initial gains.

DIVERSION FROM VERDUN
Allied commanders were resolved to continue the Somme Offensive, partly because it was effective in relieving German pressure on the **French at Verdun « 154–55**. German Chief of the General Staff Erich von Falkenhayn responded to the Somme Offensive by insisting on **immediate counterattacks** to regain any ground lost. The first of these German counterattacks was made on 2 July.

LIMITED GAINS
In the **opening phase of the battle « 180–81**, the Allies made progress in the southern part of the front, where French troops advanced up to 10 km (6 miles) and British forces also made gains. Further north, however, the **British ground to a halt** on the Albert-Bapaume road and in front of German defences at Thiepval, Beaumont Hamel, and Serre.

After the initial offensive, the fighting at the Somme became a series of local attacks and counterattacks over several months, aimed at capturing or recovering places – hills, woods, small towns – held as strongpoints or offering a perceived tactical advantage. Losses were consistently heavy on both sides.

The Allies had marginally the better of the fighting. Aided by command of the air, which enabled aircraft to pinpoint targets, the British artillery became far more effective. Cooperation between the infantry and the gunners enabled soldiers to advance close behind a creeping barrage that suppressed German defences.

Attacking British troops also became better at using light machine-guns, grenades, and mortars. In spite of these improvements, however, gains were small and hard won in the face of tenacious German resistance.

At first, British generals still seriously contemplated a breakthrough. On 14 July, the Fourth Army commander, General Sir Henry Rawlinson, planned an offensive to take the German second line defences on Longueval Ridge and push cavalry through the opening. Troops prepared for a night attack, with those involved in the initial assault taking up position in No Man's Land close to the German line. After a brief but intense artillery bombardment, the troops rushed forward at dawn to capture the pulverized trenches.

Initial success was followed by disappointment. Cavalry moved forward too slowly to exploit the opening and key objectives were not taken, including Delville Wood, which only fell to South African troops after a two-week struggle.

German counterattacks

The Germans poured large numbers of troops and guns into the Somme to resist the Allied pressure. Their orders were to hold positions to the last man and regain lost ground at whatever cost. The savage fighting this entailed was exhibited at the village of Pozières on the Albert-Bapaume road. Australian troops broke into the fortified village on 23 July, but fighting continued for a fortnight as the Germans first refused to give up the part of the position they still held and then mounted fierce counterattacks.

> **6.5** MILLION **The number of shells fired by British artillery at the Somme in the two months from 15 July to 14 September 1916.**

> "Among the living **lay the dead...** One company after another had been shoved into the drum fire and **steadily annihilated.**"
>
> ERNST JÜNGER, GERMAN LIEUTENANT, IN HIS MEMOIR "STORM OF STEEL"

TECHNOLOGY

MK I TANK

The British Mark I (Mk I) was the first operational tank. Developed to support attacking infantry in trench warfare, it was designed to advance across broken ground at walking speed.

Most Mk Is had 6-pounder naval guns mounted in sponsons (projections in which the gunners sat) on each side of the hull, although some carried only machine-guns. A crew of eight was required to operate the vehicle, which they did in great discomfort. The interior of the tank was hot, noisy, and filled with fumes. Steering was achieved using a complex system of gears, operated by two of the crew.

Mk Is were not as invincible as they first appeared. They frequently suffered mechanical breakdown and were vulnerable to artillery fire, armour-piercing rifle ammunition, and grenades.

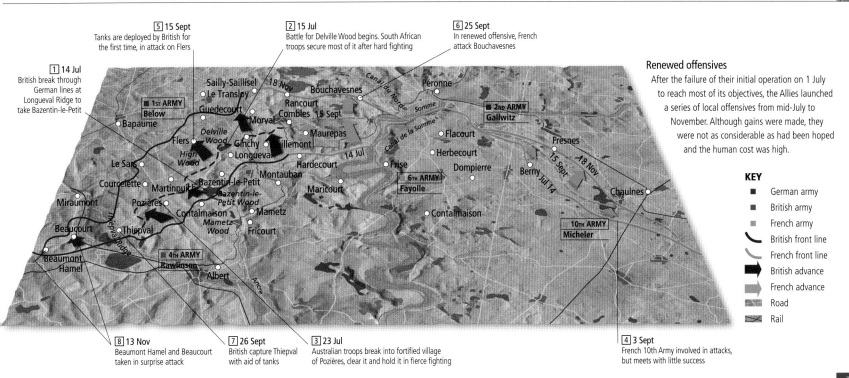

5 15 Sept
Tanks are deployed by British for the first time, in attack on Flers

1 14 Jul
British break through German lines at Longueval Ridge to take Bazentin-le-Petit

2 15 Jul
Battle for Delville Wood begins. South African troops secure most of it after hard fighting

6 25 Sept
In renewed offensive, French attack Bouchavesnes

8 13 Nov
Beaumont Hamel and Beaucourt taken in surprise attack

7 26 Sept
British capture Thiepval with aid of tanks

3 23 Jul
Australian troops break into fortified village of Pozières, clear it and hold it in fierce fighting

4 3 Sept
French 10th Army involved in attacks, but meets with little success

Renewed offensives

After the failure of their initial operation on 1 July to reach most of its objectives, the Allies launched a series of local offensives from mid-July to November. Although gains were made, they were not as considerable as had been hoped and the human cost was high.

KEY

- ■ German army
- ■ British army
- ■ French army
- British front line
- French front line
- ◄ British advance
- ◄ French advance
- Road
- Rail

The Australians ended up in possession of Pozières, but at the cost of 23,000 casualties – similar to their losses in the entire Gallipoli operation.

The first use of tanks

On 15 September, a new element entered the battle when the British deployed 32 Mark I tanks for an attack at Flers-Courcelette. The commander-in-chief, Sir Douglas Haig, chose to employ the tanks despite their crews being inadequately prepared and too few vehicles being available for decisive effect. The appearance of these armoured monsters certainly had a psychological effect on German soldiers, but most of the tanks quickly broke down, became stuck in shell holes, or were taken out by enemy artillery. A few tanks led infantry in the capture of the village of Flers, however, and Haig was impressed.

As summer moved into autumn, rain reduced the battle zone to mud. The British continued to creep forward, taking German positions that had been first-day objectives – from Thiepval, occupied on 26 September, to Beaumont Hamel, seized on 13 November. The Battle of the Somme ended on 18 November. By then, snow was falling and even Haig could see that no purpose could be served by continuing. Allied troops had gained at most 12 km (7.5 miles).

AFTER »

The fighting at the Somme caused an estimated 420,000 British, 200,000 French, and 500,000 German casualties. These massive losses led to a rethink on both sides of the conflict.

BRITISH AND COMMONWEALTH CEMETERY, POZIÈRES

GERMAN AND ALLIED REACTIONS

Taking over supreme command in September 1916, Field Marshal Paul von Hindenburg and General Erich Ludendorff decided to **construct a new fortified line** that was shorter and easier to defend. In February–March 1917, the Germans withdrew from the Somme to the **Hindenburg Line**.

In spite of criticism of Haig's strategy, the British attacked again at **Arras 226–27 »** in April 1917. Haig also asked for mass production of **tanks**. These had a big impact at **Cambrai 248–49 »** in November 1917.

REMEMBERING THE DEAD

After the war, the remains of the men who fell at the Somme were reburied in dedicated **war cemeteries**, such as the one at Pozières, where so many Australian soldiers died.

Crossing the battleground

Troops of a British supply train cross an area devastated by shelling during the Battle of the Somme. Conditions steadily deteriorated as the fighting was prolonged and the weather worsened.

Medical Treatment

"It is… always like this in a **field hospital.** Just **ambulances** rolling in, and **dirty, dying men…** "

AMERICAN NURSE ELLEN LA MOTTE, "THE BACKWASH OF WAR", 1934

In the century before World War I, the provision of decent care for soldiers at war had become a recognized humanitarian issue as well as a practical concern for army commanders. By World War I, wounded combatants on all sides were treated by dedicated army medical services, who had increasingly modern medical techniques.

Hygiene and sanitation

The mobilization of millions of men meant a daunting task for preventive medicine. The static, overcrowded conditions of trench warfare were an obvious breeding ground for disease. Yet when combatants combined inoculation against epidemic diseases such as typhoid with strictly enforced measures to ensure good hygiene and sanitation – as did British and German forces on the Western Front – disease levels were remarkably low. Where hygiene and sanitation broke down, as they did among British troops at Gallipoli and among the Russians on the Eastern Front, the ensuing epidemics killed thousands.

Trench fever, a disease spread by lice, defied attempts to suppress it. Other persistent medical problems were trench foot, caused by damp, and frostbite, both severely disabling conditions that could lead to amputation.

The outbreak of "Spanish influenza" in the last year of the war – inexplicable and untreatable by medicine at the time – caused large-scale losses among soldiers that continued into peacetime.

From first aid to amputation

To deal with combat casualties, a coordinated system was needed that stretched from the battlefield back to base hospitals far from the front.

The German army entered the war with such a system in place; other countries caught up under the pressure of the war. Treatment started with first aid on the battlefield. Officers and men often carried field dressings and painkillers, sometimes including morphine tablets. Stretcher-bearers braved fire to bring the wounded to an advanced dressing station, where they were sorted – hopeless cases were left to die, those superficially wounded were directed back to their units. The seriously wounded were loaded on to ambulances and taken to a casualty clearing station, a set of tents or huts where emergency treatment, including surgery, was carried out. During a major battle, a clearing station might handle more than a thousand cases a day. The wounded were then

19 MILLION The number of men wounded in all armies during World War I.

transferred to a base hospital by train.

Wounded men's chances of survival depended upon the speed and efficiency of the medical evacuation process and the quality of care they

Tending to the wounded

A nurse cares for a badly wounded soldier at a hospital in Antwerp, Belgium, early on in the war. Many soldiers expressed profound gratitude for the nursing care they received.

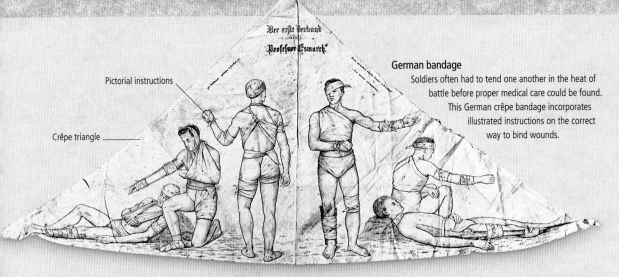

German bandage
Soldiers often had to tend one another in the heat of battle before proper medical care could be found. This German crêpe bandage incorporates illustrated instructions on the correct way to bind wounds.

Pictorial instructions

Crêpe triangle

TIMELINE

1854 British nurse Florence Nightingale's interventions to improve sanitation and medical facilities in the Crimean War lead to major developments in military hospitals and nursing.

1854–56 French military surgeons widen the use of chloroform as an anaesthetic during the Crimean War.

1862 During the American Civil War, Dr Jonathan Letterman, surgeon-general of the Army of the Potomac, pioneers the use of a field ambulance service to evacuate casualties.

1864 The Red Cross is established, inspired by the Swiss businessman Henri Dunant.

1870–71 During the Franco-Prussian War, German military surgeons employ antiseptics, sharply reducing post-operative death rates.

1899–1902 In the Boer War in South Africa, British troops suffer 13,000 deaths from disease due to poor hygiene and failure to boil drinking water. This compares with 8,000 deaths in combat.

1904–05 At war with Russia, Japan greatly reduces losses to disease through use of antitoxins and good hygiene. Russia becomes the first country to recognize battle stress as a medical problem to be treated by psychiatry.

1909 In Britain, the Voluntary Aid Detachment (VAD) nursing organization is established.

1911 The US Army introduces compulsory typhoid vaccination for all recruits.

1914 The use of sodium citrate is shown to prevent coagulation (clotting) in blood transfusions. It is widely used during the war.

1915 The Gallipoli operation is a medical disaster for the British Army, which fails to maintain good hygiene, supply clean water, or evacuate the wounded efficiently by sea.

received during it. Providing timely tetanus jabs, for example, reduced the rate of tetanus infection among British wounded from around a third in 1914 to almost zero by the war's end.

World War I weaponry caused wounds that were appalling in both number and severity. Field surgeons, operating for up to 16 hours a day during a major offensive, resorted freely to amputation of limbs as the best hope for many of the wounded.

The use of anaesthetics was long-established and, by the later stages of the war, procedures to limit post-operative infection were as effective as could be achieved in the absence of antibiotics, which were not available

500,000 The estimated number of amputations performed during the course of World War I.

until World War II. A major innovation was the widespread use of blood transfusion, a life-saving procedure that became a practical proposition through the use of anti-coagulants and refrigeration, allowing blood to be

stored instead of transferred person-to-person. The prevalence of facial wounds saw progress in plastic surgery. Specialist hospitals were established for the reconstruction of faces. American surgeons in particular made advances in this field, although permanent disfigurement remained the fate of thousands.

Shell shock
Casualties suffered mental as well as physical trauma. Psychiatric medicine was becoming increasingly accepted in the early 20th century, and disturbed behaviour as a result of combat stress was recognized as a medical problem. The German army was broadly up to date with this modern thinking, but to many British and French army commanders "shell-shock" seemed a sign of weakness. It is not true that men suffering mental collapse were routinely executed as cowards, although there

were probably a few cases of this. As the war went on, all combatants established psychiatric wards and hospitals. The US army had 263

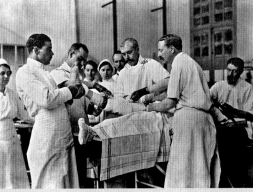

Wartime surgery
By 1914, operations had a reasonable success rate. During the last stages of the war, more than nine out of ten wounded men survived.

military psychiatrists in France in 1918. Therapy ranged from analysis of in-depth mental problems to crude electric-shock treatment.

Tending the wounded
Nurses were among the heroes of the conflict. Established bodies of military nurses were too small to cope with the scale of the war so there was a demand for volunteers such as the British Voluntary Aid Detachment (VAD) nurses or the 3,000 women who became Nursing Sisters in the Canadian Army.

Often from sheltered backgrounds, they coped astonishingly well with the task of tending severely wounded men. Women such as British VAD nurse Vera Brittain and American Ellen La Motte wrote some of the most eloquent testimonies of the war.

Red Cross symbol

Horsedrawn ambulance
At the start of the war, all ambulances were horse-drawn, but large numbers of motor ambulances were introduced later on. The Red Cross symbol was universally recognized, but did not stop ambulances coming under fire.

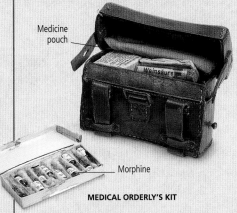

Medicine pouch

Morphine

MEDICAL ORDERLY'S KIT

1916 The British Medical Corps records treating 2.65 million sick and wounded men during the course of the year.

1917 William Rivers pioneers shell-shock treatment.

1918 The US Army's medical service grows to a staff of 295,000, from 5,000 in June 1917.

1943 Mass production of penicillin provides the first effective antibiotics for use in World War II.

Dogfights and Aces

Air combat developed as an offshoot of trench warfare and had the same high death rates as the war on the ground. But the myth of ace fighter pilots as "knights of the air" engaged in chivalrous combat fulfilled a popular need for heroes in a grim industrialized war.

Fold-up collar

Goggles with tinted glass

Long flying coat

Sheepskin-lined flying boots

Rubber soles for secure grip

British pilot's clothing
Flying in an open cockpit, a World War I airman needed warm, head-to-toe clothing. This also offered a degree of protection if the aircraft caught fire, the most feared hazard of aerial combat.

BEFORE

The rival armies entered World War I with about 500 aircraft between them. The planes were flimsy and not armed for aerial combat.

RECONNAISSANCE ROLE
Aircraft had been used in war by the Italians in **Libya in 1911** and by the **Balkan states in the wars of 1912–13**. They had proved capable of attacking ground targets with grenades or small bombs, but the major European armies were interested in their potential for **reconnaissance ≪ 144–45**.

THE FIRST SHOT
At the start of the war, pilots had a supporting role. Their job was to **ferry observers**, who outranked them, on reconnaissance missions. On their own initiative, some observers carried pistols or carbines to **shoot at any enemy aircraft** they encountered. This proved ineffectual, but on 5 October 1914 a French observer **shot down a German aircraft** using a Hotchkiss machine-gun.

Most armies used aircraft during World War I. In trench warfare from 1915, generals found them invaluable for observing enemy lines and liaising with artillery.

Fighter aircraft developed later in order to shoot down enemy reconnaissance and bomber planes. But mounting a machine-gun on a propeller-driven plane was not easy. One solution, exemplified by the British Vickers "Gunbus", was to place the propeller behind the pilot while an observer with a machine-gun sat in a balcony in the nose of the aircraft.

Solo fighter planes
Single-seat aircraft with a front propeller performed much better. The introduction of the interrupter gear – allowing bullets to pass through a spinning propeller – enabled the German Fokker Eindecker monoplane to dominate the skies over France in the winter of 1915–16.

The Allies responded with their own solo fighters. The French Nieuport 11 "Bébé" biplane, introduced in early 1916, had a machine-gun mounted on its upper wing to fire over the

TECHNOLOGY
INTERRUPTER GEAR

The first man to fire a machine-gun through the arc of his spinning propeller was French pilot Roland Garros in April 1915. Garros had metal plates fitted to the propeller blades to deflect any bullets that struck them.

Anthony Fokker, a Dutch aircraft designer working for the Germans, trumped this by fitting his Eindecker monoplane with an interrupter gear. This device, which had been patented before World War I, synchronized the fire of the machine-gun with the rotation of the propeller, so the bullets passed through the arc without hitting the blades. This allowed the pilot simply to aim his aircraft at the target and fire, in effect making the solo fighter pilot possible.

Flying helmet with face mask

Sheepskin gauntlets

Warm wool lining

Map case

propeller. It was operated by the pilot pulling a chord. The Allies developed their own interrupter gear, using both wing-mounted guns and guns firing through the propeller. Once both sides had fighter aircraft, pilots fought one another as well as destroying reconnaissance craft.

Initially lone hunters, they were later grouped into squadrons. By summer 1915, German pilot Oswald Boelcke had formulated basic principles of air combat, such as to attack out of the sun and to open fire only at close range. He taught them to other pilots, including the top German fighter pilot Manfred von Richthofen, popularly known as the Red Baron.

Air aces
Air combat proved to be an activity at which a few individuals excelled, achieving multiple "kills" while their colleagues scored few or none. The German and French armies established a system for allotting "ace" status to pilots who shot down a certain number of enemy aircraft. The British army resisted a formal "ace" system, but the press celebrated the most successful fighter pilots. Men such as Charles Nungesser in France, Albert Ball in Britain, Billy Bishop in Canada, and Eddie Rickenbacker in the USA were glamorized as "knights of the air".

Deadly dogfights
From 1916 onwards, a struggle for air supremacy accompanied the great battles on the ground. As well as duelling with other aircraft in "dogfights", pilots were instructed to attack ground troops and observation balloons, activities that exposed them to ground fire. Squadrons suffered flying accidents and mechanical failure as well as actual combat. Airmen had no parachutes until the Germans began to issue them in 1918.

The strain on elite fighter squadrons such as the French Cigognes ("Storks") and Richthofen's Jagdgeschwader 1 (the "Flying Circus") was immense. The pilots were mostly young and few lived long – when British ace Albert Ball died in 1917 he was just 20 years old. During the Battle of Arras in spring 1917, the life expectancy of newly trained British pilots was two weeks.

Neither side was able to establish permanent air supremacy, for the advantage changed hands as new aircraft were introduced. The British and French won the production battle, however, manufacturing almost three times as many aircraft as Germany did in 1917.

Father of air combat
One of Germany's first air aces, Oswald Boelcke (centre) formalized the principles of aerial combat and founded the first elite fighter squadron. He was killed in action in October 1916.

French fighter ace
Rejected as too frail to serve in the infantry, French fighter pilot Captain Georges Guynemer became a national hero as a pilot in the elite Cigognes squadrons. He was killed in action in September 1917, aged 22.

AFTER

By the last year of the war, about 8,000 aircraft were deployed by all combatants, more than 40 per cent of them fighters.

FIGHTING ANOTHER DAY
About 15,000 airmen were killed in the war. Some fighter pilots who survived went on to have notable postwar careers, including **Hermann Goering**, a member of Manfred von Richthofen's "Flying Circus". He became a leading figure in Adolf Hitler's Nazi regime.

In April 1918, Britain was the first country to create an independent air force, placing its army and navy aircraft under the control of the **Royal Air Force**. Germany was forbidden an air force under the **Treaty of Versailles 338–39 »**, but Hitler re-established it as the Luftwaffe in 1935.

Dogfight in France
Aerial combat over the Western Front was typically fought by biplanes with fixed undercarriages. In this painting by English painter William Wyllie, an aircraft has burst into flames, a fate feared by pilots.

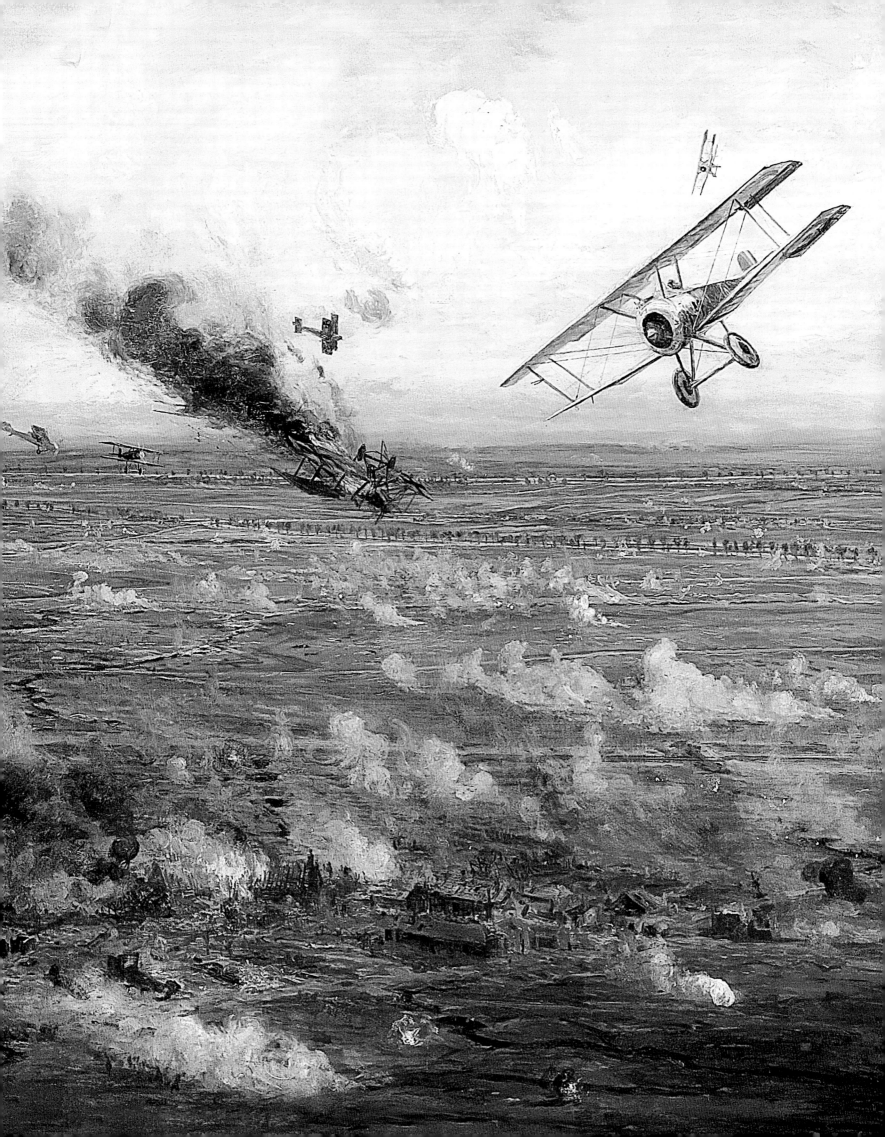

Warplanes

World War I was the first conflict in which aircraft were used on a large scale. They were initially unarmed and used for observation, but advances in technology soon saw the development of fighters, bombers, and ground-attack planes.

1 **Bristol F.2B Fighter (British)** This two-seat reconnaissance and fighter biplane was popularly known as the Brisfit or Biff. 2 **Avro 504K (British)** Primarily a training aircraft, this plane was also used as an emergency home defence fighter against German bombers. 3 **Airco DH.9A (British)** This two-seat light bomber, which saw front-line service from July 1918, flew in missions against German railways, aerodromes, and industrial centres. 4 **Sopwith Camel (British)** Introduced to the skies over the Western Front in 1917, Camels are credited with shooting down 1,294 enemy planes, more than any other Allied aircraft. 5 **Sopwith Baby (British)** This single-seat seaplane was used as a naval scout and bomber aircraft. 6 **Sopwith Pup (British)** On 2 August 1917, a Pup became the first aircraft to land aboard a moving ship, the HMS *Furious*.

7 **Caudron G.3 (French)** Used early in the war for reconnaissance and later as a training aircraft, the Caudron G.3 was withdrawn from front-line operations in mid-1916. 8 **Spad S.XIII (Belgian)** This French-designed S.XIII was flown by the Belgian 10th Squadron. It was used by the Belgian airforce from March 1918. 9 **Hanriot HD.1 (Belgian)** Rejected by French squadrons, the HD.1 fighter was used successfully by Belgian pilots from 1916. 10 **Fokker D.VII (German)** This Fokker design, which entered service in May 1918, was highly regarded as a fighter. 11 **LVG C.VI (German)** This two-seat reconnaissance plane, which entered front-line service in mid-1918, was armed with two machine-guns. 12 **Albatros D.V (German)** The final development of the Albatros D series, the D.V was the standard German fighter aircraft in 1917.

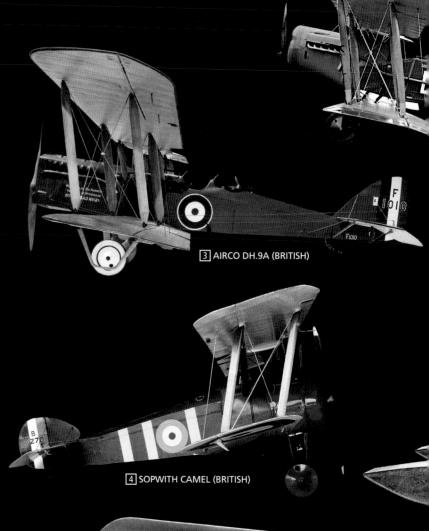

3 AIRCO DH.9A (BRITISH)

4 SOPWITH CAMEL (BRITISH)

7 CAUDRON G.3 (FRENCH)

8 SPAD S.XIII (BELGIAN)

11 LVG C.VI (GERMAN)

1 BRISTOL F.2B FIGHTER (BRITISH)

2 AVRO 504K (BRITISH)

5 SOPWITH BABY (BRITISH)

6 SOPWITH PUP (BRITISH)

9 HANRIOT HD.1 (BELGIAN)

10 FOKKER D.VII (GERMAN)

12 ALBATROS D.V (GERMAN)

The **Romanian Campaign**

In August 1916, Romania entered the war on the side of the Allies. It was an unfortunate move, based on poor assessment of the success of the Brusilov Offensive. By December, most of Romania was occupied by the Central Powers.

Romanian horseman
In 1916, Romania's army was large but poorly trained and ill-equipped compared with its German opponent. This Romanian cavalryman carries a lance.

The Romanians signed a treaty with Allied negotiators in Bucharest on 17 August 1916. In return for entering the war, Romania would be allowed to annex Transylvania, Bukovina, and other territories, chiefly at the expense of Hungary. As part of the Bucharest agreement, the Allies promised military action in support of Romanian forces.

« BEFORE

The Kingdom of Romania was an ally of Germany and Austria-Hungary before World War I, but it chose to remain neutral at the outbreak of war.

TERRITORIAL AMBITIONS
Romania was connected to Germany through its **royal family**, who were Hohenzollerns. However, it nursed **ambitions to annex Transylvania and Bukovina**, territories in Austria-Hungary with a large ethnic Romanian population. Romania fought against Bulgaria in the **Second Balkan War** in 1913, gaining a substantial slice of Bulgarian territory.

INITIAL NEUTRALITY
Although Romania's King Carol I was **bound to the Central Powers** by a secret treaty signed in 1883, popular opinion was hostile to Austria-Hungary. The king thus opted for neutrality in August 1914. Romania joined the war in summer 1916, when the success of the **Brusilov Offensive « 174–75** opened the prospect of defeating Austria-Hungary.

Russia would renew its offensive on the Austro-Hungarian front while British, French, and other Allied forces attacked Bulgaria from their base at Salonika in northern Greece.

Romania goes to war
With these assurances, Romania declared war on the Central Powers on 27 August. The Romanian conscript army, numbering some 650,000, had an impressive reputation gained against the Bulgarians in the Second Balkan War of 1913. The troops were, however, short of equipment, with outdated rifles, few machine-guns, and little artillery.

Romanian strategy focused on fulfilling its territorial ambitions. Advancing through inadequately

1,100 The length in kilometres (680 miles) of the border that Romania had to defend in 1916. It was as long as the entire Russian front from the Baltic to Romania.

550,000 The number of Romanians who died in World War I, comprising 220,000 military and 330,000 civilian fatalities.

defended mountain passes into Hungary, Romanian forces occupied eastern Transylvania. Had they done this a few months earlier, when the Russian Brusilov Offensive was succeeding, it might have contributed to the collapse of Austria-Hungary. But by September, Russian operations were

running out of steam and the Germans, under their new Chief of the General Staff Field Marshal Paul von Hindenburg, were able to intervene to shore up their Austro-Hungarian ally. Hindenburg's predecessor as Chief of the General Staff, General Erich von Falkenhayn, was sent to take overall command of operations against Romania, while also leading the German Ninth Army in Transylvania.

The experienced Field Marshal August von Mackensen was sent to Bulgaria to command a combined force of Bulgarian and German troops on the Danube front opposite Romania's southern border. They were later joined by Turkish troops carried by ship across the Black Sea.

Problems mount
Romania's allies failed to provide the promised military support. The Russians regarded the Romanian front as a distraction, and the assistance they provided was limited and slow. Initially, just 50,000 Russian troops were sent to stiffen the Romanian army.

The planned offensive from Salonika, under French General Maurice Sarrail, was pre-empted by German and Bulgarian attacks in southern Serbia and eastern Greece in August. Outmanoeuvred, Sarrail achieved only a limited advance when he launched his offensive in September, crawling forward to force the Bulgarians out of Monastir (modern-day Bitola in Macedonia) by mid-November.

Left exposed to an invasion from Bulgaria and to counterattacks in Transylvania, Romania was soon in difficulty. Mackensen led his forces from Bulgaria into Romania's Dobruja province on 1 September. To meet the threat, the Romanians transferred

GERMAN GENERAL (1849–1945)

AUGUST VON MACKENSEN

August von Mackensen began his military service with the Prussian Life Hussars – in later life, he often wore their death's head emblem. Leading a corps at the outbreak of World War I, he was given command of an army in November 1914. He performed outstandingly in campaigns in Poland and was promoted to field marshal in June 1915. He was engaged in occupied Romania from 1916 until the end of the war, overseeing the exploitation of Romanian resources for the German war effort.

The Romanian Campaign
Romanian troops advancing into Transylvania were counterattacked by German and Austro-Hungarian forces, while Mackensen's Danube Army pushed into Dobruja.

KEY

- ■ Austro-Hungarian army
- ■ Bulgarian army
- ■ German army
- ■ Romanian army
- ➡ Romanian offensive into Transylvania 27 Aug–18 Sept 1916
- ➡ Austro-German advance through Wallachia and Moldavia 18 Sept 1916–7 Jan 1917
- ➡ Danube Army advance through Dobruja 1 Sept 1916/7 Jan 1917
- ◟ Central Powers front in Transylvania 18 Sept 1916
- ◟ Central Powers front in Dobruja 23 Sept 1916
- ◞ Romanian positions 26 Nov 1916
- ◞ Central Powers front 7 Jan 1917
- ◎ Town captured by Central Powers, with date
- ⌁ Major railway

Map labels:
AUSTRIA-HUNGARY · RUSSIAN EMPIRE · TRANSYLVANIA · MOLDAVIA · WALLACHIA · ROMANIA · SERBIA · BULGARIA · DOBRUJA · Black Sea · Prut · Maros · Sereth · Aluta · Jiu · Arges · Danube

Klausenburg · Jassy · Schossburg · Berlad · Hermannstadt · Hatseg · Focsani · Galatz · Isman · Mehadia · Orsova · Campolung · Ploesti · Bucharest · Cernavoda · Constanza · Craiova · Turtukai · Silistria · Rustuchuk · Sistova · Varna

4TH ARMY · 1ST ARMY · 9TH ARMY · 1ST ARMY · 2ND ARMY · 3RD ARMY · DANUBE Mackensen

3 18 Sept Falkenhayn launches counterattack, forcing Romanians back through Vulcan Pass on 10 Nov
1 27 Aug Romanians begin advance into Transylvania
14 OCT Campolung
Predeal Pass
7 1 Dec Falkenhayn's superior forces defeat Romanian attacks from Bucharest area
6 DEC Bucharest
25 OCT Cernavoda
25 OCT Constanza
21 NOV Craiova
6 SEPT Turtukai
9 SEPT Silistria
5 20 Oct Mackensen's forces begin advance to Constanza and Cernavoda
4 23 Sept Front stabilized
6 23 Nov Danube Army begins advance on Bucharest
2 1 Sept Combined army of Bulgarians and Germans crosses border
Vulcan Pass

150,000 troops from Transylvania to the Danube in mid-September, and attempted an ambitious counter-offensive at the end of the month, including crossing the Danube to attack Mackensen's army from the rear.

March on Bucharest
Disrupted by adverse weather conditions, the river crossing proved a chaotic failure and was abandoned on 3 October. Falkenhayn then launched the German Ninth Army and the Austro-Hungarian First Army in an offensive against the Romanian forces in Transylvania, bursting through the Vulcan Pass into Wallachia. Falkenhayn's and Mackensen's armies advanced on the Romanian capital, Bucharest, from the south and west. The city fell on 6 December.
The Romanians had lost more than 300,000 men, a large proportion of them taken prisoner. The survivors retreated north into Moldavia, behind the Sereth river. British agents tried to destroy the oil installations at Ploesti,

> "We will march into **battle** with the irresistible elan of a **people** firmly **confident** in its destiny."
>
> PROCLAMATION BY ROMANIAN KING FERDINAND I, 28 AUGUST 1916

56 km (35 miles) north of Bucharest, but these fell into German hands, as did the Black Sea port of Constanza.
Hampered by bad roads and winter weather, the Germans and their allies failed to mount an effective pursuit. As fighting died down for the winter elsewhere on the Eastern Front, Russia belatedly began transferring forces to Romania from the end of October. Most did not arrive until December, in time to stabilize a defensive line that left most of Romania occupied by the Central Powers.

Under occupation
Mackensen was installed as military governor of the area of Romania controlled by the Central Powers. His main task was to ensure that supplies of grain, oil, and other materials flowed to Germany. As a consequence, many Romanians suffered from malnutrition. Around half a million of them are estimated to have died of hardships and deficiencies.

AFTER »

With most of its territory occupied by the Central Powers, from the start of 1917 Romania was subjected to economic exploitation.

ROMANIAN CURRENCY UNDER GERMAN OCCUPANCY

CONTINUING THE FIGHT
Holding Moldavia, the Romanian army fought well alongside the Russians, but their efforts were undermined by the failure of the **Russian Kerensky Offensive 234–35** ». German attacks on Moldavia were repulsed, but the **Bolshevik Revolution 252–53** » and the **Russian Civil War** left them isolated. After an armistice with Germany in December 1917, the Romanian government accepted **punitive peace terms** in May 1918. Romania nominally re-entered the war on the Allied side on 10 November 1918.

Bucharest occupied
German, Turkish, Austro-Hungarian, and Bulgarian soldiers are photographed in the Romanian capital, Bucharest, in 1917. The military occupation was to prove a bitter experience for the Romanian people.

195

The **Arab Revolt**

In June 1916, Hussein bin Ali, Sherif of Mecca, proclaimed an Arab revolt against the rule of Ottoman Turkey. This triggered a guerrilla campaign that contributed significantly to Turkey's defeat, which in turn led to the division of the Middle East by the Allied powers.

S herif Hussein, head of Arabia's Hashemite clan, was a prestigious Islamic figure, claiming descent from the Prophet Muhammad and controlling Islam's holiest city, Mecca. His power base, the Hejaz region on Arabia's Red Sea coast, was part of Turkey's Ottoman Empire, its cities garrisoned by Ottoman soldiers.

After Turkey entered the war in autumn 1914, relations with its Arab subjects deteriorated. Food shortages and growing hardship stimulated discontent, which was brutally surpressed.

In October 1915, Hussein obtained a promise from Sir Henry MacMahon, the British high commissioner

Rebel warrior
Emir Feisal, the military leader of the Arab Revolt, was a member of the Hashemite clan, dominant in the Hejaz region of western Arabia. Feisal collaborated closely with British intelligence officer T.E. Lawrence.

in Egypt, that Britain would broadly support Arab independence from Arabia north to Syria and east to Mesopotamia. Hussein proposed to rule this vast area as an Arab king.

Call to arms

Sherif Hussein launched his revolt in June 1916. Although it called for the support of "all brother Muslims", at

first it seemed unlikely to be more than a local disturbance. Supplied with British rifles, the rebels overcame the Ottoman garrison in Mecca and seized the port of Jeddah with the support of Britain's Royal Navy, but they failed to take the second holy city of Medina.

Meanwhile, an advance by British troops from Egypt across the Sinai Desert, timed to coincide with the

Barrel

Rear sling swivel aids accuracy

Cocking lever

revolt, made slow progress. Turkish reinforcements were sent to Arabia from Syria along the Hejaz railway.

Lawrence of Arabia

In November 1916, Lieutenant Colonel T.E. Lawrence, a British intelligence officer, was sent to establish relations with Hussein's son, Emir Feisal, who was leading a force of chiefly Bedouin irregulars around the port of Yenbo (in modern-day Saudi Arabia). In December, with British naval support,

> **IRREGULARS Combatants who do not belong to any formal army. They often favour guerrilla tactics, such as raids, ambushes, and sabotage.**

Lawrence and Feisal repulsed a Turkish counterattack at Yenbo, and in January mounted a bold operation to seize the port of Wejh, 300 km (190 miles) north.
Feisal and Lawrence understood the importance of spreading the revolt beyond the Hejaz region. Feisal's

British rifle
The Martini-Henry rifle, a veteran of 19th-century colonial wars, was among the weaponry supplied by Britain to arm the Arab rebels. The Martini-Henry was prized for its accuracy and reliability.

irregulars ranged across northern Arabia, carrying out guerrilla attacks on targets such as the Hejaz railway and evading the Turkish troops sent to counter them. In July 1917, they captured the Red Sea port of Aqaba (in modern-day Jordan), overrunning the defences with a camel charge. Aqaba became an important base for landing British supplies from Egypt.
As the British Army from Egypt advanced to fight the Turks in southern Palestine, the Arab irregulars operated on their eastern flank, raiding northwards into Syria.

Secret agreement

While militarily the Arab Revolt gathered momentum, political developments were running counter to Sherif Hussein's aspirations. From November 1915, two Middle East experts, the French diplomat François Georges-Picot and the British adviser Sir Mark Sykes, held discussions in London to define French and British spheres of influence in the region.
The secret Sykes-Picot Agreement of May 1916 allotted Syria and Lebanon to France and the rest of the region to Britain, except for Palestine, which was to be shared between Britain, France, and Russia. Although the agreement allowed for the creation of Arab kingdoms in these spheres of influence, it clearly ran counter to Britain's understanding with Sherif Hussein.
The situation was further complicated in November 1917 when British Foreign Secretary Arthur Balfour publicly declared British support for the Zionist project of a "national home for the Jewish people" in Palestine.

Sense of betrayal

The Balfour Declaration and the Sykes-Picot Agreement, made public by the Bolsheviks after their seizure of power in Russia in November 1917,

Arab forces at Yenbo
This photograph of Arab irregulars outside the Red Sea port of Yenbo was taken by T.E. Lawrence in December 1916. Bedouin tribesmen formed a major part of the rebel forces.

Turkish artillery
A Turkish field gun in action in Palestine in 1918. Highly mobile Arab rebels supported the British Army as it took on the Ottoman main force.

seriously shook Arab confidence in their alliance with Britain. Emir Feisal discreetly contacted the Turks to see if they would provide a better deal. However, further evolution of the murky political situation was pre-empted by Allied military successes in Palestine and Mesopotamia. Feisal's forces, continuing to operate beyond the right flank of the British Army in Palestine, captured the important rail junction of Dera in September 1918. With Australian cavalry, they occupied the Syrian capital, Damascus, before the war's end.

> The dissolution of the Ottoman Empire after World War I only partially satisfied the nationalist aspirations of the Arabs, leading to further conflicts in the future.

ARAB HOPES DASHED
Emir Feisal attended the **Paris Peace Conference 334–35 »** in 1919 as the Arab representative, but returned frustrated. In March 1920, with popular support, he declared himself **king of Syria and Palestine**, but was deposed by French troops in the following June. **Britain and France were then authorized** by the newly formed League of Nations to **rule most Arab areas** of the former Ottoman Empire, including Syria, Lebanon, Palestine, and Mesopotamia.

THE FUTURE OF PALESTINE
In 1921, Britain made **Feisal king of the new state of Iraq**, which roughly corresponded to the former Mesopotamia. The British also turned the eastern part of Palestine into the **Kingdom of Transjordan** (later known as Jordan) under a Hashemite ruler. The **rest of Palestine** remained under **direct British control**. By the 1930s, it had turned into an arena of conflict between Jewish settlers, Palestinian Arabs, and the British authorities.

> **" God has vouchsafed the land an opportunity to rise in revolt... to seize her independence."**
>
> SHERIF HUSSEIN, PROCLAMATION OF THE ARAB REVOLT, 27 JUNE 1916

BRITISH ARMY INTELLIGENCE OFFICER (1888–1935)

T.E. LAWRENCE

Popularly known as "Lawrence of Arabia", Thomas Edward Lawrence was an archaeologist working in the Middle East when the war broke out. Employed as a British Army intelligence officer in Cairo because of his knowledge of the region, he was sent to Arabia in 1916.
Lawrence acted as a liaison officer with Emir Feisal's Arab rebels, helping develop the strategy and tactics for a guerrilla war against Ottoman forces. Lawrence identified with the cause of Arab nationalism and acted as Feisal's adviser at the Peace Conference in 1919. He wrote a highly coloured account of his experiences in *The Seven Pillars of Wisdom* (1922).

« **BEFORE**

The outbreak of war stimulated a wave of social and political solidarity in the combatant countries. However, this mood did not last when the prospect of a swift victory receded.

RESOLVE WEAKENS
The sacrifices demanded of people in the states at war were extreme. By the end of 1915, for example, around **640,000 French soldiers** had been **killed** in the conflict. Civilians had also found themselves exposed to mounting hardships as governments **mobilized** their full **resources**. In Germany, the need to conserve supplies of animal feed had led to the **mass slaughter of livestock** in 1914–15, exacerbating the food shortages of 1916. The **political truce** that had prevailed at the beginning of the war began to **break down**.

TEMPORARY GRAVE MARKER, FRANCE

GRIGORI RASPUTIN

A peasant by birth, Grigori Rasputin was a Russian monk who gained access to the court of Tsar Nicholas II. His apparent ability to suppress the haemophilia of the Tsar's son, Alexis, won him the trust of Nicholas's German-born wife, Alexandra, who acted as regent when Tsar Nicholas went off to lead the Russian army. By 1916, Rasputin's relationship with Alexandra was the subject of scurrilous rumours. On 16 December 1916, he was murdered by a group of noblemen and monarchists, who believed he was bringing the regime into disrepute.

The **Strains** of **War**

Throughout 1916, many people in the warring states of Europe faced mounting economic hardship. Governments struggled to maintain social cohesion. States that could not cope with the demands of war faced the threat of revolution.

For many civilians in Germany and Austria-Hungary, the experience of the war centred on their daily struggle to find enough to eat. Inevitably, the Central Powers blamed their acute food shortages on the Allied economic blockade. From the start of the war, Britain included foodstuffs among the items that its Royal Navy banned from entering Germany. But Germany and Austria-Hungary were large agricultural producers and not heavily dependent on seaborne imports of staple foods. The blockade contributed to shortages, but a steep fall in domestic agricultural output was also a factor. This was partly caused by the transfer of labour from agriculture to the army and factories, and partly by a shortage of fertilizers, due to chemicals being diverted to make high explosives.

Germany's black market
From 1915, Germans were eating "K-bread" made chiefly of potatoes. Ersatz (substitute) products replaced many items, including coffee, butter, and sausages. The German government introduced rationing and created various agencies to enforce controls on food production and prices. The effect of these was often counter-productive and a black market flourished.

Germany's harvest in 1916 was a disaster. There followed the "Turnip Winter", named after the only food many people could obtain. The official ration allowed 100 g (3.5 oz) of meat and one egg a week, but these were often unobtainable. Germans with money to buy goods on the black market or contacts in the countryside could eat, but poor people in urban areas suffered malnutrition.

The food situation in Germany was at its worst in the winter of 1916–17, although shortages, soup kitchens, and food queues were a permanent fact throughout wartime life. There were

Misery of war
An elderly woman is taken ill while queuing for food in Germany in 1916. German civilians suffered from malnutrition in the course of the war, as did people in other countries, including Russia and Austria-Hungary.

occasional food riots and strikes in Berlin, Vienna, and other cities, and a perception that sacrifices were not being fairly shared. Support grew for anti-war socialists, and for separatism among Austria-Hungary's minorities.

Social disintegration
Russia's problems were more acute than those of the Central Powers because its less developed economy and inefficient administration could not cope with the strains the war imposed. Well-meaning liberals from Russia's professional, business, and landowning classes set up a voluntary organization, the Zemstvo Union, to run some aspects of the war. These included military supply and food relief for the hungry. They were, however, often obstructed by officials, who regarded them as subversives. The Duma, the Russian parliament representing liberal opinion, was rarely summoned to sit and had no power. Through 1916,

> **WINDSOR The name adopted by the British royal family in July 1917, to replace its original Germanic name Saxe-Coburg-Gotha.**

shortages of food became acute in Russian cities and the rail network began to break down for lack of fuel. In the countryside, where men and horses had been taken off to the army, women were yoked to ploughs to till the soil. In factories, strikes erupted as price inflation ran ahead of wages, making scarce food unaffordable for many. Meanwhile, among Russia's aristocracy and administrative class, flagrant corruption was widespread, as was conspicuous consumption of luxury goods.

Under these difficult circumstances, Russia's tsarist regime could not hold the allegiance of the common people or the middle classes. Increasingly, blame was pinned on German elements within the court. Popular

> **" The women who stood in queues...** spoke more about their **children's hunger** than about the **death of their husbands."**
>
> ERNST GLAESER, GERMAN AUTHOR, DESCRIBING GERMANY IN WORLD WAR I

discontent had already found expression in anti-German riots in 1915. Tsar Nicholas's wife, Tsarina Alexandra, was of German origin and some of the Tsar's ministers had Germanic names.

Changing the name of the capital from the Germanic St Petersburg to the Russian Petrograd was not enough to stem rumours that a pro-German clique around Alexandra was subverting the war effort and deliberately starving the people. The mysterious Rasputin, a powerful influence on the Tsarina, was viewed as a sinister force at court. His assassination in December 1916 did nothing to halt the deterioration of

Female labour
Women haul clay to a brick-making plant in Wales. Although female workers won better pay and status during the war, many of the jobs they performed involved exhausting and monotonous physical labour.

a political situation in which both liberals and the urban and rural working populations were aligned against the regime.

Sharing the pain
Britain, France, and Italy suffered less severe shortages than other countries. But their governments had difficulty persuading people that sacrifices were being fairly shared. Profiteering by businessmen running war industries aroused anger. In France, disillusion was widespread when Henri Barbusse's anti-war novel *Le Feu* (Under Fire) was published in 1916.

In Britain, in spite of the increasing frequency of workers' strikes, a large measure of political and social solidarity was maintained. First Herbert Asquith and then David Lloyd George led coalition governments supported by the Conservative, Liberal, and Labour parties.

The first state to collapse under the strain of war was Russia, but there was also unrest in France.

RUSSIAN TURMOIL
The **overthrow of the Tsar 210–11 »** in March 1917 was followed by the **Bolshevik seizure of power 252–53 »** in October 1917. The upheaval in Russia offered inspiration to would-be revolutionaries in other countries. In **Germany**, many socialists saw **no reason to continue the war** once the

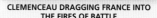

CLEMENCEAU DRAGGING FRANCE INTO THE FIRES OF BATTLE

tsarist regime, which they had feared, had been overthrown. In 1917, Germany's new USPD (Independent Social Democratic Party) **campaigned to end the war**.

FRENCH MUTINIES
In France, the failure of the **Nivelle Offensive 224–25 »** led to **army mutinies** in spring 1917. **Industrial strikes** in France also suggested the continuation of the war might be in doubt. Instead, the appointment of **Georges Clemenceau** as prime minister in November 1917 brought a reassertion of France's will to fight.

BRITISH PRIME MINISTER Born 1863 Died 1945

David Lloyd George

"The predominant **task...** is the **vigorous prosecution** of the war to a **triumphant conclusion.**"

DAVID LLOYD GEORGE, SPEECH, DECEMBER 1916

Although he was not raised in poverty, David Lloyd George was considered to be a man of the people. Born in Manchester, he grew up in rural Wales with his mother and her brother, shoemaker and Baptist minister Richard Lloyd. His father had died when Lloyd George was a year old, so he adopted his uncle's surname of Lloyd along with his own, George.

Through talent, hard work, and ambition, he became first a successful solicitor and then, in 1890, at the age of 27, the youngest member of the House of Commons at the time. He soon earned a reputation as a fiery radical, denouncing the hereditary privileges of the aristocracy and the militarism of the British Empire. As a leading member of Liberal governments from 1906 he was at the forefront of social and political reform and known for the emotional eloquence of his speeches.

On a personal level, Lloyd George was no stranger to scandal. His secretary, Frances Stevenson, was his mistress, and in 1913 he was caught up in allegations of insider share trading in Marconi's Wireless Telegraph Company. As prime minister, he sold honours and peerages for cash.

Britain's war leader
As prime minister from December 1916, David Lloyd George provided decisive leadership for wartime Britain. His lowly origins and radical credentials helped him win vital popular backing for the war effort.

Master orator
Lloyd George addresses a crowd at the unveiling of a war memorial in London in October 1927. He was a powerful orator, described by many as exercising an almost hypnotic grip upon his audience.

Lloyd George was instinctively aligned with the anti-war tradition of the Liberal Party. However, during the Agadir crisis of 1911, when a visit by the German Kaiser to the Moroccan port was perceived as provocative by France and Britain, Lloyd George made a prominent speech advocating war if it was necessary to preserve Britain's vital interests and prestige.

Driving force

The German invasion of Belgium in August 1914 overcame any hesitations Lloyd George had about supporting the declaration of war. He established himself as the leading figure in a drive to mobilize the economy and, in May 1915, was the natural choice to head a new Ministry of Munitions. He bullied and bribed businessmen into turning factories over to war production, achieving an impressive increase of output. As an acknowledged radical,

he was able to win acceptance from trade unions for "dilution" – the use of unskilled workers and women to do jobs previously restricted to skilled male workers.

Unlike old-fashioned Liberals such as Prime Minister Herbert Asquith, Lloyd George had no scruples about government interference in business or violation of individual freedoms. In December 1916, he won the support of the Conservative and Labour parties to replace Asquith as prime minister, splitting the Liberal Party.

He set about establishing a small war cabinet and expanded government control of national life in order to boost the war effort. Many areas of the economy, such as coal mining and merchant shipping, were taken over by the state for the duration of the war. New ministries were created to direct food production and labour.

Relations with the generals

Lloyd George was not always so successful in imposing his will on the generals conducting the war. Instinctively anti-militarist, he distrusted generals, while they regarded him as militarily ignorant. He sought an alternative to the slaughter on the Western Front, advocating a diversion of resources to Salonika or Italy. This was opposed by General Sir William Robertson, the Chief of the Imperial General Staff, and Field Marshal Douglas Haig commanding British forces in France. Lloyd George tried to undermine the generals, eventually ridding himself of Robertson in February 1918, but Haig proved immovable.

In his war memoirs, published in 1933, Lloyd George presents himself as the man consistently humane and right while the military leaders were brutal and foolish. But some of his claims – for example, to have been solely responsible for the introduction of the convoy system at sea in April 1917 – are now widely contested. He

has been blamed for withholding troops from the Western Front in early 1918, as part of his private war with Haig, leaving the British Army vulnerable to the German Spring Offensive.

Postwar career

Lloyd George won the postwar general election of 1918 partly by promising to make Germany pay reparations and to prosecute German war criminals, including the Kaiser. At the Paris Peace Conference in 1919, however, he tried to steer a course between French Prime Minister Georges Clemenceau's desire to permanently disable Germany and the idealism of US President Woodrow Wilson.

In domestic affairs he aspired to continue his pre-war radical reforms – he had set up a Ministry for Reconstruction as early as 1917 – but as the leader of a predominantly Conservative coalition had little scope for action. He returned to leadership of the Liberal Party from 1924, but that

Commemorative jug
An earthenware jug celebrating Lloyd George's wartime premiership bears text in Welsh as well as English. Lloyd George is the only Welshman to have held the post of British prime minister.

once great movement never recovered from the split he had engineered in 1916. In the run-up to World War II, Lloyd George admired Hitler's forceful leadership and favoured seeking peace in 1940. As a result, he had become an isolated figure in British public life by the time he died in 1945.

Juggling his allies
A wartime caricature presents Lloyd George as a circus strongman juggling his French, Russian, and Italian allies. His skill at diplomacy was never equal to his grasp of domestic policy issues.

> **"I** never believed in **costly frontal attacks** either in **war or politics,** if there were **a way round."**
>
> DAVID LLOYD GEORGE, "WAR MEMOIRS", 1934

TIMELINE

- **January 1863** David George is born of Welsh parents in Manchester, England.
- **1884** Becomes a solicitor. Marries Margaret Owen, a farmer's daughter, four years later.
- **1890** Enters parliament as Liberal Member of Parliament for Carnarvon in North Wales.
- **1899–1902** Is a critic of British involvement in the Boer War in South Africa.
- **1906** Enters government for the first time as president of the Board of Trade.
- **1908** Becomes Chancellor of the Exchequer, a post he holds until 1915. He introduces old age pensions and unemployment insurance.
- **August 1914** Supports a British declaration of war in support of Belgium, preventing a major split in the cabinet.
- **May 1915** Appointed Minister of Munitions after the "shell scandal" and achieves a rapid expansion of war production.
- **June 1916** On the death of Lord Kitchener, Lloyd George becomes Minister for War.
- **December 1916** Becomes prime minister at the head of a coalition government, establishing a five-man war cabinet.
- **April 1917** Backs the adoption of a convoy system to counter German U-boats.
- **July 1917** Reluctantly acquiesces in General Douglas Haig's offensive at Passchendaele.
- **January 1918** Makes a firm statement of Britain's commitment to democracy and national self-determination as war aims.
- **December 1918** Wins a landslide victory in a general election at the end of the war.
- **1919** Represents Britain at the Paris Peace Conference.
- **1922** His coalition with the Conservatives collapses and he falls from power.
- **1936** Visits Germany and meets with Nazi dictator Adolf Hitler.
- **1940** Refuses the offer of a place in Winston Churchill's wartime government.
- **1943** A widower from 1941, he marries Frances Stevenson, his mistress since 1913.
- **1945** Dies shortly after being elevated to the peerage as Earl Lloyd-George of Dwyfor.

LLOYD GEORGE AND FRANCES STEVENSON AT THEIR WEDDING, 1943

Germany's New Order

From August 1916, the German war effort came under the control of the Third Supreme Command, spearheaded by Field Marshal Paul von Hindenburg and General Erich Ludendorff. Together, they began laying the foundations for a German-dominated Europe.

Chief of the General Staff Paul von Hindenburg and Quartermaster-General Erich Ludendorff exercised joint power over Germany's Third Supreme Command (Hindenburg being the third German Chief of the General Staff to lead the war). They controlled German military strategy and also dictated economic and diplomatic policies. Kaiser Wilhelm II was barely consulted on policy, and the Chancellor, who headed the civilian government, depended on the approval of the Supreme Command. German military and business leaders worked closely together, pursuing the same nationalist and expansionist agenda.

The war machine

The policies of the Third Supreme Command grew partly out of an immediate need to cope with the war situation, including shortages of labour, raw materials, and food. To maximize war production, the Third Supreme Command sought total state direction of the German economy, controlling the allocation of raw materials and taking powers to order workers into war industries. One of the ways in which it raised money for the war effort was to invite people to pin money and pledges to invest in war bonds on wooden statues of Hindenburg erected in German towns and cities.

Substantial increases in production were achieved, although organization of the war economy fell short of the level of efficiency to which it aspired. For example, in 1917 output of rifles and machine-guns hugely exceeded the army's requirements but production of steel, a vital war material, fell. Profits for business

were not controlled and manufacturers connected with the military regime made fortunes.

Inevitably, priority lay with meeting the immediate needs of the war effort. Conquered territories were plundered of food and raw materials.

Employing the labour of conquered peoples was also seen as essential, with the German workforce depleted by the demand for soldiers. From 1914, the work of prisoners of war, chiefly Russians, was invaluable to the German war effort. The Third Supreme Commander pressed to maximize the supply of workers from conquered territories. Thousands of Poles were deported to Germany and put to work. When the policy was applied in occupied Belgium in the autumn of 1916, protests organized by trade unions and by the influential Belgian spokesman Cardinal Mercier led to the deportations being halted in 1917.

German nationalism

The Supreme Command also reflected a broader vision of the future of Europe and Germany's place within it, articulated by German nationalists. They argued that Slavs were inherently inferior to Germans and that Germany had a historic "civilizing mission" in the east. In his influential book *Mitteleuropa* (Central Europe), published in 1915, the politician Friedrich Naumann envisaged Germany permanently dominating a swathe of Europe from the Baltic to the Black Sea.

Forced labour
Russian soldiers captured by the Germans work under armed guard. The labour of millions of such prisoners of war was essential to the war economies of the Central Powers.

Supreme commanders
German Chief of the General Staff Hindenburg is followed by his Quartermaster-General Ludendorff. As joint leaders of the Third Supreme Command they installed a virtual military dictatorship in Germany.

Some areas were to be emptied of their existing population and colonized by German settlers, others were to be placed under puppet governments and economically exploited. This vision was endorsed by Austria's German rulers – who intended to take control of the Balkan Slavs and of northern Italy – as well as by Germany itself, whose main interests lay in Poland, Ukraine, and the Baltic states. The Hungarians would exercise control over Croatian Slavs.

Conquered territories

Attempts were made to implement aspects of the "Mitteleuropa plan". In 1914–15, for example, victories

« BEFORE

Germany entered World War I without clear war aims, but its leaders were soon tempted by the idea of creating a German-dominated Europe.

EXPANSIONIST PLANS
In September 1914, the German Chancellor drafted a plan for the **annexation** of Belgium, the Netherlands, and northern France and the **economic exploitation** of states in Central Europe. Though not officially adopted, this programme represented government thinking. The **battles of 1914–16** left Germany and Austria-Hungary in temporary control of parts of France, Belgium, the Balkans, and Eastern Europe.

BELGIAN MILITARY PIN

Krupp arms factory
Most German artillery was manufactured by the steel manufacturer Krupp. The owners of such businesses worked in close collaboration with the military leadership to maximize production.

" The naked truth is… **every deported worker is another soldier** for the **German army.**"

CARDINAL MERCIER, PROTESTING AGAINST DEPORTATIONS FROM BELGIUM, 7 NOVEMBER 1916

AFTER »

In 1918, Germany fulfilled some of its ambitions in the east and came close to victory on the Western Front.

POISED TO WIN

Revolutions and military **collapse in Russia** opened the way for Germany to impose the **Brest-Litovsk Peace Treaty 276–77 »** on the Russians in March 1918. The treaty gave Germany control of nominally independent countries from Ukraine in the south to the Baltic states in the north. In May 1918, **Romania** was also forced to sign a treaty giving Germany ownership of its oil wells. **German offensives** on the Western Front in spring 1918 **282–83 »**, however, failed to achieve victory before the **arrival of American troops** in large numbers.

GERMAN LUGER PISTOL

on the Eastern Front brought large areas around the Baltic under the administration of "Ober Ost" – German Supreme Command in the East – which was then headed by Hindenburg and Ludendorff.

One of Ludendorff's initiatives was a programme of Germanization, sending German teachers into local schools, in preparation for the future mass arrival of German colonists. General Hans von Beseler, the Governor-General of German-occupied Poland from 1915, promoted a scheme to shift two million Poles and Jews out of a broad strip of Polish territory bordering Germany and replace them with German settlers – a programme that had become official German policy by March 1918.

As well as the Mitteleuropa plan for the east, the long-term ambitions of Germany's military leadership included the annexation of much of Belgium and part of northern France.

The Legacy

This New Order long predated the more familiar Nationalist Socialist New Order of the 1930s. Hitler tried to reconstruct a larger and more deadly version of the area controlled by Austria-Hungary and Germany by 1917–18. His Third Reich also practised the economic exploitation and ethnic cleansing envisaged by Hindenburg and Ludendorff.

Financing the U-boat campaign

A poster encourages Germans to invest in war bonds. It explains that the money will be used to build U-boats, which will relieve the pressure on German soldiers by sinking Allied ships.

ME9828

DEVIL

5
REVOLUTION AND DISILLUSION
1917

Swept by revolution, Russia became the first
major combatant to leave the war. Though
weakened by years of conflict, and uncertain
of victory, the other powers continued
the struggle. The USA, provoked by
German submarine warfare, finally joined
the side of the Allies.

REVOLUTION AND DISILLUSION

Opposition to war and the desire for peace, expressed by these British demonstrators in May 1917, strengthens as the conflict drags on. Governments in most combatant countries, however, maintain sufficient popular support to keep the war effort going.

Kaiser Wilhelm II studies maps with Germany's military leaders Field Marshal Paul von Hindenburg and General Erich Ludendorff. The German leadership ignores a pro-peace vote in Germany's parliament, the Reichstag.

EUROPE

FAEROE ISLANDS (Denmark)
NORWAY
SWEDEN
Baltic Sea
North Sea
DENMARK
BRITAIN
NETH.
GERMANY
SOVIET RUSSIA
BEL. LUX.
FRANCE
SWITZ.
AUSTRIA-HUNGARY
ITALY
ROMANIA
MONT. SERBIA BULGARIA
ALB.
Black Sea
PORTUGAL
SPAIN
GREECE
OTTOMAN EMPIRE
Mediterranean Sea
DODECANESE (Italy)
CYPRUS (Britain)
MOROCCO (France)
ALGERIA (France)
TUNISIA (France)
LIBYA (Italy)
EGYPT (Britain)

BRITAIN
GERMANY
ATLANTIC OCEAN
FRANCE
AUSTRIA-HUNGARY
SOVIET RUSSIA
PORTUGAL
SPAIN
ITALY
Black Sea
OTTOMAN EMPIRE
Caspian Sea
PERSIA
AFGHANISTAN
SPANISH MOROCCO
MOROCCO
CYPRUS
TI (auto NEPAL
RIO DE ORO
ALGERIA
LIBYA
EGYPT
KUWAIT
BAHRAIN
QATAR
NEJD (Saudi)
TRUCIAL OMAN
OMAN
IND
FRENCH WEST AFRICA
ANGLO-EGYPTIAN SUDAN
HADHRAMAUT
ADEN PROTECTORATE
GAMBIA
PORTUGUESE GUINEA
TOGO
FRENCH EQUATORIAL AFRICA
ERITREA
FRENCH SOMALILAND
SIERRA LEONE
NIGERIA
ABYSSINIA
BRITISH SOMALILAND
LIBERIA
GOLD COAST
CAMEROON
ITALIAN SOMALILAND
RIO MUNI (Spain)
FRENCH CONGO
BELGIAN CONGO
BRITISH EAST AFRICA
GERMAN EAST AFRICA
INDIAN OCEAN
NORTHERN RHODESIA
ANGOLA
MADAGASCAR
GERMAN SOUTHWEST AFRICA
BECHUANA-LAND
SOUTHERN RHODESIA
PORTUGUESE EAST AFRICA
UNION OF SOUTH AFRICA

German U-boats step up their assaults on Allied merchant shipping, but disaster for Britain is averted by its introduction of convoys in April 1917.

The Third Battle of Ypres, a British-led offensive in Flanders in September 1917, is hampered by appalling weather conditions and mud. The battle came to be known by the name of its final objective, Passchendaele.

Illustrirte Zeitung
Unsere U-Boote
Verlag J.J.Weber, Leipzig

In East Africa in October 1917, German General Paul von Lettow-Vorbeck's guerrilla campaign against British forces achieves a notable victory over South African-led troops at Mahiwa.

The pattern of the war underwent fundamental changes in 1917. The German resumption of unrestricted submarine warfare in February provoked the USA to declare war on Germany in April. German leaders had anticipated this but gambled that they could win the war before American manpower could be brought to bear. Meanwhile, in Russia, a revolution overthrew Tsar Nicholas II. A provisional government sought to revive the Russian war effort as a patriotic struggle in defence of new-won freedoms. Instead, the Russian army disintegrated after a last summer offensive. The Bolsheviks, led by Vladimir Ilyich Lenin, seized power in November and sought an armistice with the Central Powers.

On the Western Front, the Germans stood on the defensive throughout the year. In April, after the failure of an offensive commanded by General Robert Nivelle, much of the French

1917

ЗАЕМЪ СВОБОДЫ

ВОЙНА до ПОБѢДЫ

Russia's provisional government, taking power after the fall of the Tsar in March 1917, calls for Russia to continue the war "until victory". By the year's end, the Bolsheviks have seized power and concluded an armistice.

The Canadian Corps capture Vimy Ridge from the Germans in a famous assault in the Battle of Arras in April 1917. Overall, however, the Battle of Arras was a failure for the Allies.

The USA enters the war after President Woodrow Wilson gains approval from Congress. The USA formally declares war on Germany on 6 April 1917.

CANADA

UNITED STATES OF AMERICA

CHINA

JAPANESE EMPIRE

FRENCH INDOCHINA

PHILIPPINE ISLANDS

BRITISH NORTH BORNEO

BRUNEI

SARAWAK

MALAYA

DUTCH EAST INDIES

PORTUGUESE TIMOR

Mariana Islands

GUAM

Marshall Islands

GERMAN PACIFIC TERRITORIES

Caroline Islands

KAISER WILHELMSLAND

PAPUA

Bismarck Archipelago

Nauru

Solomon Islands

Gilbert Islands

Ellice Islands

Hawaiian Islands

Christmas Island

Cook Islands

German Samoa (Western)

Tonga

French Polynesia

New Hebrides

Fiji

New Caledonia

AUSTRALIA

NEW ZEALAND

PACIFIC OCEAN

MEXICO

BRITISH HONDURAS

CUBA

HAITI

DOMINICAN REPUBLIC

VIRGIN ISLANDS

LEEWARD ISLANDS

GUATEMALA

EL SALVADOR

HONDURAS

NICARAGUA

COSTA RICA

CANAL ZONE

PANAMA

WINDWARD ISLANDS

BARBADOS

TRINIDAD AND TOBAGO

BRITISH GUIANA

DUTCH GUIANA

FRENCH GUIANA

VENEZUELA

COLOMBIA

ECUADOR

PERU

BRAZIL

BOLIVIA

PARAGUAY

CHILE

ARGENTINA

URUGUAY

FALKLAND ISLANDS

ATLANTIC OCEAN

French colonial troops employed in the war include these Tirailleurs Annamites, infantry from French Indochina. The colonies are an important source of manpower for Britain and France. Germany has no comparable resource.

THE WORLD IN DECEMBER 1917

The Central Powers

Central Powers conquests to Dec 1917

Allied states

Allied conquests to Dec 1917

Neutral states

Frontiers Jul 1914

army mutinied. Discipline was restored by a new commander-in-chief, General Philippe Pétain, and the appointment of Georges Clemenceau as prime minister stopped defeatism among French civilians. The British army took over the main burden on the Western Front. Operations such as the capture of Vimy Ridge in April and Messines Ridge in June showed a fresh tactical sophistication, but British troops suffered disillusion in terrible fighting at Passchendaele in the autumn.

Overall, outside Russia commitment to continuing the war held firm. In Italy, the shock of a major defeat at Caporetto strengthened rather than weakened national solidarity. On both sides, however, voices were raised in favour of reaching a compromise peace, notably in a resolution voted by the German Reichstag in July. But the collapse of Russia only confirmed the German military leadership in its unswerving pursuit of victory.

TIMELINE 1917

Unrestricted submarine warfare ▪ Revolution in Russia ▪ The USA enters
the war ▪ French army mutinies ▪ Slaughter at Passchendaele ▪ Italian defeat at
Caporetto ▪ British take Jerusalem ▪ Armistice on the Eastern Front

JANUARY

9 JANUARY
German military and political leaders agree to resume unrestricted submarine warfare.

16 JANUARY
German Foreign Secretary Arthur Zimmermann sends a telegram promising Mexico US territory in return for an alliance. It is intercepted by the British.

≫ German anti-war propaganda

20 JANUARY
The Romanian front stabilizes at the Sereth river.

22 JANUARY
US President Wilson makes a speech calling for peace without victors or vanquished.

FEBRUARY

≫ German submariner's badge

1 FEBRUARY
Germany resumes unrestricted submarine warfare, causing the USA to break off diplomatic relations.

21 FEBRUARY
On the Western Front, the Germans begin Operation Alberich, a tactical withdrawal to the Hindenburg Line defences.

24 FEBRUARY
British forces retake Kut in Mesopotamia.

26 FEBRUARY
President Wilson asks Congress for permission to arm US merchant ships.

MARCH

1 MARCH
The Zimmermann telegram is publicized in the US press, outraging public opinion.

8 MARCH
Revolution begins in Russia as protesters take to the streets of Petrograd.

11 MARCH
British forces capture Baghdad.

15 MARCH
Tsar Nicholas II abdicates as revolution grips Russia. A Provisional Government takes power.

26 MARCH
British Empire forces fail to break through Turkish defences in the First Battle of Gaza in Palestine.

31 MARCH
German U-boats sink almost a million tons of merchant shipping in two months.

APRIL

3 APRIL
Bolshevik leader Vladimir Ilyich Lenin returns to Russia.

6 APRIL
The USA declares war on Germany.

≫ Lenin in Petrograd

9 APRIL
British launch offensive at Arras. Canadians take Vimy Ridge.

16 APRIL
Start of the Nivelle Offensive. Its failure leads to mutinies in the French army.

MAY

≫ French 1893 Lebel rifle

15 MAY
Pétain replaces Nivelle as French commander-in-chief. He ends mutinies in the French army.

16 MAY
Battle of Arras ends with small gains for the British.

19 MAY
General Pershing is appointed to command the American Expeditionary Force.

JUNE

4 JUNE
General Brusilov is appointed Russian army commander-in-chief.

7 JUNE
At Ypres, the British blow up German positions on Messines Ridge, as a prelude to a successful offensive.

11 JUNE
King Constantine of Greece abdicates under pressure from the Allies.

13 JUNE
German Gotha bombers raid London in daylight, killing 162 people.

≫ Detonator

25 JUNE
First troops of the American Expeditionary Force arrive in Europe.

29 JUNE
Greece declares war on the Central Powers.

≪ Canadian soldiers at Vimy Ridge

"Enormous **masses of ammunition,** such as the human mind had never imagined… were **hurled on the bodies of men** scattered in **mud-filled shellholes.**"

GERMAN GENERAL ERICH LUDENDORFF, DESCRIBING PASSCHENDAELE, AUTUMN 1917

JULY	AUGUST	SEPTEMBER	OCTOBER	NOVEMBER	DECEMBER
1 JULY The Kerensky Offensive, the last Russian offensive of the war, begins. It ends in disastrous failure.	**1 AUGUST** General Kornilov takes over from Brusilov as Russian commander-in-chief. **6 AUGUST** Central Powers launch successful offensive against Romanians in Moldavia.	**3 SEPTEMBER** Germans commanded by General Hutier capture Riga from the Russians in an attack that uses new "infiltration tactics".		**6 NOVEMBER** Turkish forces abandon Gaza, allowing the British to advance into Palestine. **7 NOVEMBER** The Bolsheviks seize power in Petrograd, setting up a government of people's commissars.	**4 DECEMBER** Battle of Cambrai ends with most of the early British gains lost. **7 DECEMBER** The USA declares war on Austria-Hungary.
⌃ Austro-Hungarian troops		**9 SEPTEMBER** General Kornilov is accused of attempting a coup and dismissed as Russian commander-in-chief. Kerensky arms workers' militias, the Red Guard.		**9 NOVEMBER** Italian Chief of Staff General Luigi Cadorna is replaced by General Diaz. The Allies form a Supreme War Council to coordinate strategy.	⌄ Appealing for tank crews
6 JULY Arab irregulars capture the Red Sea port of Aqaba from the Turks.	**10 AUGUST** British Ypres offensive is renewed towards the Gheluvelt plateau, but little progress is made. A further attack on 16 August also fails. **14 AUGUST** China declares war on the Central Powers.	**16 SEPTEMBER** Colonel T.E. Lawrence leads an Arab attack on the Hejaz railway in Arabia. **20 SEPTEMBER** At Ypres, British, Australian, and New Zealand forces attack with some success at the Menin Road.	⌃ Mata Hari **12 OCTOBER** At Ypres, Australian troops lead a failed attempt to take Passchendaele Ridge. **15 OCTOBER** In France, exotic dancer Mata Hari is shot as a German spy.	**10 NOVEMBER** The third Battle of Ypres ends with Passchendaele in British hands. **15 NOVEMBER** Georges Clemenceau is appointed French prime minister.	TREAT'EM ROUGH! JOIN THE TANKS United States Tank Corps
16–19 JULY Popular disturbances in Petrograd, the July Days, are suppressed. Lenin flees to Finland to avoid arrest. **17 JULY** British royal family changes its name from Saxe-Coburg and Gotha to Windsor.		**26 SEPTEMBER** British Ypres offensive continues with a successful attack at Polygon Wood.	**24 OCTOBER** An Austro-German breakthrough at Caporetto drives the Italian army into chaotic retreat. **26 OCTOBER** Canadian troops spearhead the final assault on Passchendaele Ridge.		**8 DECEMBER** French and British troops arrive in Italy to help stabilize a defensive line at the Piave river. **9 DECEMBER** Romania signs an armistice with the Central Powers.
19 JULY German Reichstag votes for a Peace Resolution. **31 JULY** The British launch a major offensive in Flanders, beginning the Third Battle of Ypres.			**30 OCTOBER** Vittorio Orlando becomes Italian prime minister. **31 OCTOBER** The British attack Turkish defences at Gaza and Beersheba in Palestine. ⌞ US recruitment office	⌃ General Luigi Cadorna **20 NOVEMBER** A British offensive at Cambrai using massed tanks achieves a short-lived breakthrough. **26 NOVEMBER** The Russian Bolshevik government asks for an armistice.	**11 DECEMBER** General Allenby leads the formal entry of British forces into the holy city of Jerusalem. **15 DECEMBER** Bolshevik Russia and Germany sign an armistice at Brest-Litovsk.

≪ BEFORE

At the start of the war, Russia's social and political problems were briefly forgotten, but divisions reopened as military disasters and economic hardship unfolded.

STRING OF DEFEATS

Russia suffered a series of military setbacks from its **defeat at Tannenberg ≪ 64–65** in August 1914 to the **Great Retreat from Poland ≪ 70–71** in summer 1915. Although the **Brusilov Offensive ≪ 174–75** in summer 1916 was initially a major victory, it did not bring an end to the war any closer.

ROLE OF RASPUTIN

Distrust of Russia's rulers centred on alleged treachery at court. With **Tsar Nicholas II away at the front** commanding the Russian army, suspicions fell on his German-born wife, **Alexandra**, and her associate, the mystic **Rasputin**. In December 1916, Rasputin was murdered by noblemen trying to restore the reputation of the monarchy.

CARTOON OF NICHOLAS II, RASPUTIN, AND ALEXANDRA

The **Tsar Overthrown**

In March 1917, Russia's tsarist regime was toppled – partly for its failure to cope with the demands of modern warfare. The Provisional Government that took its place struggled to reinvigorate the Russian war effort while also holding off pressure for more radical change.

B y early 1917, popular hostility towards the tsarist regime was widespread. In the army and navy, morale was poor and there were several mutinies. In the factories, workers staged strikes as wages fell behind the rapidly rising prices. In the countryside, peasants hoarded food and coveted the estates of landowners.

Educated Russians also resented the regime. Middle-class politicians in the Duma (the Russian parliament) despaired of the incompetence of the tsarist administration, which made fighting an effective war impossible.

The people revolt

The Russian capital, Petrograd (St Petersburg), was especially hard hit by shortages of food and fuel. Its population had expanded rapidly during the war and keeping the urban masses supplied was beyond the capacity of the railway system, which was crippled by a lack of coal. On 8 March 1917 (23 February according to the Julian calendar, then in use in Russia), demonstrators celebrating International Women's Day

were joined on the streets of the capital by striking factory workers. Protests focused on the shortage of bread.

By 11 March, the city's factories were at a standstill and demonstrators numbered hundreds of thousands. When soldiers garrisoning Petrograd were ordered to suppress the protests, most refused and joined the revolt.

Tsar Nicholas II, who had left Petrograd for military headquarters just before the uprising, attempted to return to the capital. But on

15 March, on the advice of his senior generals and ministers, he abdicated in favour of his brother, Grand Duke Michael. The Grand Duke, however, declined to take the throne until a new constitution was agreed.

In effect, Russia's monarchy was at an end. Nicholas sought exile in Britain, but King George V was advised that the former tsar's presence might provoke unrest among the British working class, and so refused to receive him. Nicholas thus remained under house arrest, with his family, at the Alexander Palace at Tsarskoe Selo.

In the absence of a tsar, a group of politicians from

Revolution in Petrograd
Russian workers and soldiers demonstrate in front of St Isaac's Cathedral in Petrograd (St Petersburg). The popular uprising led to the downfall of the tsarist regime in March 1917.

Imprisoned at the palace
Tsar Nicholas II is held under guard at the royal palace in Tsarskoe Selo after his abdication in March 1917. Under the Provisional Government, the imperial family was well treated. This changed under the Bolsheviks.

the Duma, led by Prince Giorgi Lvov, formed the Provisional Government to restore order and prepare democratic elections to a Constituent Assembly. At the same time – and in the same building, the Tauride Palace – a Soviet (council) of Workers' and Soldiers' Deputies, elected in Petrograd's factories and barracks, was established as a rival centre of authority to the new government.

Impact on the war
The Provisional Government was dominated by conservatives and liberals, the Soviet by socialists. Neither intended to abandon the war. In fact, the members of the Provisional Government had become disillusioned

with the tsarist regime because of its failure to pursue the war effort with proper vigour.

The Petrograd Soviet voted in favour of a "just peace" and sought links with German socialists, but was also opposed to German militarism. Joseph Stalin, a member of the extreme socialist Bolshevik Party, wrote that "revolutionary soldiers and officers who have overthrown the yoke of tsarism" would not leave their trenches while German soldiers were "still obeying their emperor".

Initially, soldiers serving at the front were not involved in the revolution. But reverberations of the political upheaval inevitably reached the trenches. The Petrograd Soviet's first act was to circulate an order on military discipline. Order No. 1 called on soldiers to elect committees to represent their units and attacked Russian military practice, such as the requirement to address senior officers as "your excellency".

The order was intended just for Petrograd and explicitly upheld officers' authority at the front. But that authority was called into question as soldiers' committees asserted their right to be consulted. In a well-meaning gesture of liberalism, the Provisional Government abolished the death penalty, removing an important deterrent to

The arrival of Lenin
This romanticized painting by V. Lyubimov portrays Lenin returning from exile in April 1917. Lenin's followers were surprised by his determination to press for an immediate socialist revolution.

mutiny and desertion. Instead of being fired with a fresh determination to fight in defence of the revolution, soldiers succumbed to war weariness. Insubordination and even attacks on officers were common, and the rate of desertion rose sharply.

At first, the fall of the Tsar was welcomed by Russia's allies in the war. It removed the political embarrassment of being tied to an illiberal regime and potentially promised a reinvigoration of the Russian war effort. For the Central Powers, it increased the difficulty of maintaining support for

> **5.5 MILLION** The number of Russian soldiers killed, missing, or taken prisoner by October 1916.

the war. Liberals and socialists in Germany and Austria-Hungary had backed the war chiefly because of their fear of tsarist Russia. Now they saw no reason for the conflict to continue.

The return of Lenin
Germany's military leaders responded cautiously to the developments in Russia. They held back from launching offensives on the Eastern Front, where an unofficial truce mostly prevailed through spring 1917, and sought a political victory through encouraging Russian anti-war sentiment.

As part of this policy, the Germans provided a train to carry anti-war Russian revolutionary socialists living in exile in Switzerland back to Petrograd. They also gave them money. Among those transported across Germany in the "sealed train" – a train not subject to passport or customs controls – was exiled Bolshevik Party leader Vladimir Ilyich Lenin. Arriving in Petrograd on 16 April, Lenin

shocked even his extremist followers by declaring the imminent transformation of the "imperialist war" into a "worldwide socialist revolution". For the moment, Lenin was isolated, but the failure of the Provisional Government to carry out political and land reforms or end food shortages and inflation left it dangerously short of popular support.

AFTER »

Further military losses brought a Bolshevik government to power in Russia. By the end of 1917, it had agreed an armistice with Germany.

KERENSKY OFFENSIVE
Alexander Kerensky dominated Russia's Provisional Government from May 1917, but the **Kerensky Offensive 234–35 »**, launched in July, was a disaster. The Russian army disintegrated and in November the **Bolsheviks seized power 252–53 »**.

ARMISTICE
The Bolsheviks agreed an **armistice** in December 1917 and signed the **Brest-Litovsk Peace Treaty 276–77 »** in March 1918. Russia was then devastated by a **civil war**. The **Tsar** and his family were **executed 300–01 »** by the Bolshevik secret police **Cheka**, in July 1918.

CHEKA BADGE

Wilson calls for war
On 2 April 1917, US President Woodrow Wilson asked Congress for a declaration of war on Germany. He argued that the world had to be "made safe for democracy".

America Enters the War

On 6 April 1917, the USA formally declared war on Germany. This was in resonse to Germany's resumption of unrestricted submarine warfare and other provocations, including a plot to promote a Mexican invasion of the USA.

On 7 November 1916, President Woodrow Wilson was re-elected for a second term as "the man who kept [America] out of the war". Nonetheless, Wilson was well aware that the USA might easily be sucked into the European conflict. He had made it clear to Germany that the USA would regard a resumption of unrestricted submarine attacks on US shipping as a cause for war.

Wilson was also angry about the activities of German agents operating in the USA, including suspected sabotage attacks against factories involved in the supply of war material to Allied countries. The Black Tom Island explosion in Jersey City in July 1916, for example – which even damaged the Statue of Liberty –

> **UNRESTRICTED SUBMARINE WARFARE**
> The sinking of merchant ships by submarines without warning and without allowing the crews to disembark first.

may have been the work of anti-British Irish or Indian nationalists, but it was blamed on the Germans.

Presidential Peace Note
Wilson favoured the role of peaceful mediator. A month after his return to office, he circulated a Peace Note to the European combatants, inviting them to state their war aims as a prelude to entering into negotiations. However, this gesture was overtaken by events. In January 1917, Germany announced its decision to resume an unrestricted submarine campaign against merchant shipping.

In response, on 4 February, the USA broke off diplomatic relations with Germany. Wilson still hoped to avoid

was confronted with the story, he admitted its truth.

The publication of the Zimmermann telegram in the US press caused widespread outrage. Even those Americans who had tended to favour the Central Powers – German and Swedish immigrants, and Irish Americans hostile to Britain – could not tolerate a foreign conspiracy to seize US territory.

The overthrow of the tsarist regime in Russia removed another block to US entry into the war, as it meant that the conflict could be presented as a struggle between liberal democracies on one side and authoritarian militarist empires on the other.

The number of merchant ships sunk by German U-boats mounted through February and March 1917. On 2 April,

Black Tom Island explosion
In July 1916, an explosion devastated Black Tom Island, a munitions depot in New Jersey, destroying military equipment destined for Britain and France. German agents were blamed for this act of sabotage.

America intended to fight not to ensure the victory of one group of European countries over another, but to ensure the triumph of moral and political principles that would sort out Europe's problems once and for all.

massacres in Belgium « 42–43 in 1914, the first use of poison gas « 102–03, the bombing of civilians by airships « 132–33, and the execution of British nurse Edith Cavell « 166–67.

the German U-boat campaign in May 1915, especially the sinking of the liner RMS *Lusitania* « 126–27, in which 128 Americans died. Further protests after the U-boat attack on the British passenger ferry SS *Sussex* in March 1916 forced the Germans to limit U-boat warfare.

BEFORE

America's initial reaction to the outbreak of war in Europe was to maintain neutrality. Over time, an anti-German bias developed.

PROVOCATIVE PROPAGANDA
A number of German actions allowed Allied propagandists to portray the Germans as uncivilized militarists. These included

U-BOAT ATTACKS
American public opinion was influenced by the German U-boat campaign in May 1915, especially the sinking of the liner RMS *Lusitania* « 126–27, in which 128 Americans died. Further protests after the U-boat attack on the British passenger ferry SS *Sussex* in March 1916 forced the Germans to limit U-boat warfare. The USA remained neutral, but its **banks and factories** supported the Allied war effort.

> "It is a **fearful thing** to lead this great peaceful **people into war...** But the right is **more precious** than peace..."
> PRESIDENT WOODROW WILSON, ADDRESS TO CONGRESS, 2 APRIL 1917

full-scale war, asking Congress to authorize the arming of merchant ships for self-defence.

The Zimmermann telegram
An earlier event now also threatened to draw America into war. On 16 January 1917, German foreign secretary Arthur Zimmermann had sent a coded cable to the German embassy in Mexico. The ambassador was instructed to offer Mexico a military alliance in the event of war between Germany and the USA. The Mexicans would be rewarded with Texas, New Mexico, and Arizona. This cable was intercepted by British naval intelligence and decrypted by the Admiralty's Room 40 codebreakers.

In February, the British leaked the telegram to the US government. At first, the Americans were inclined to think it a fake, but when Zimmermann

Wilson addressed both houses of Congress, laying out his case for war. He asserted that Germany had already in effect opened hostilities against the USA through submarine attacks on its shipping. As well as invoking self-defence, he declared a moral crusade to cleanse the world of autocracy. American arms were to guarantee future peace.

Associate Power
War was officially declared four days later, on 6 April, after being approved by Congress. The USA entered the war not as one of the Allies but as an Associate Power, maintaining a distance that was meant to protect it against the corrupting effects of European entanglements.

AFTER

It took over a year to convert the USA's declaration of war in April 1917 into substantial practical action in Europe.

ASSEMBLING AN ARMY
The US government immediately decided to send an **American Expeditionary Force** (AEF) to Europe under **General Jack Pershing**. A small number of US troops began arriving in Europe in summer 1917, but a mass **conscript army 216–17 »** had to be recruited and trained from scratch. American soldiers **did not enter the fighting in France** until spring 1918.

TRICKED BY BRITAIN
There was little opposition in the USA to the decision to go to war. The small minority who did oppose it faced punishment under the **Espionage Act** of June 1917. After the war, however, opinions changed, with many Americans feeling they had been **tricked** into taking part by **British propaganda**.

US SOLDIERS' MANUAL

US PRESIDENT Born 1856 Died 1924

Woodrow Wilson

> "The **world** must be **made safe** for **democracy.** Its peace must be planted upon… **political liberty.**"
>
> PRESIDENT WOODROW WILSON, ADDRESS TO CONGRESS, 2 APRIL 1917

It is ironic that Woodrow Wilson should have been the president to lead the USA into a world war. Brought up in the American South during and after the Civil War (1861–65), he was acutely aware of the devastation that armed conflict brings. His sober nature, Presbyterian upbringing, and academic studies in law, made him opposed to the settlement of disputes by force. He rejected contemporary theories that

Speaking to the common man
President Woodrow Wilson addresses a crowd in 1914. When Wilson was inspired by a cause, he believed in touring the country to explain it in person.

saw victory in war as an invigorating instance of the "survival of the fittest". Wilson could only bring himself to lead the USA into war by proclaiming the American war effort a crusade for the principle of democracy and a fight for a just and lasting peace.

Non-intervention

A late entrant into politics after an academic career, Wilson was at midpoint in his first term as president when the European war erupted in August 1914. Relatively uninterested in foreign affairs, and with his attention focused on domestic social and economic reforms, he declared US neutrality on 19 August.

But Wilson was not a pacifist. Once the liner RMS *Lusitania* was sunk by a German submarine in May 1915, with the loss of 128 American lives, he realized that US involvement in the war was only a matter of time.

This perception gave urgency to his efforts to promote a peace settlement through his envoy Colonel Edward House, who was first sent to Europe in 1915. At the same time, Wilson issued stern warnings to Germany on its use of submarine warfare.

Attempt at mediation

During Wilson's campaign for re-election as president in 1916, his publicists used the slogan: "The man who kept [America] out of the war." However, Wilson was well aware that his role might suddenly reverse.

After re-election, in December 1916 he made a final gesture of mediation with a Peace Note sent to the combatant governments on both sides. Addressing the Senate, on

Principled statesman
An academic from a Presbyterian background, President Woodrow Wilson took a high-principled approach to foreign policy. He rejected the idea of war as the pursuit of national interest or territorial gain.

214

22 January 1917, he spoke in favour of "peace without victory". But the German resumption of unrestricted submarine warfare that month, in which merchant ships were sunk without warning, forced his hand.

Marching into Europe

Although Wilson was initially reluctant to enter the war, he was thorough and absolute in its pursuit once the decision was taken. His speech to Congress on 2 April 1917, requesting approval for a declaration of war, represented his intention to fight for the purest motives. America was going to march into Europe and remake the continent in accordance with principles of democracy and justice that would end war forever. Justified by such ends, he introduced compulsory military service, and banned criticism of the war.

Wilson never agreed a joint policy with the Allies. The USA would fight its own war for aims that the president expressed in the Fourteen Points

Stars and Stripes Forever
A poster dating from the peak period of Wilson's popularity during the war depicts him as the natural successor of America's greatest presidents, George Washington and Abraham Lincoln.

that he declared in front of Congress in January 1918. Widely publicized by American propagandists, Wilson's principles, stressing justice for all, including minorities, gave hope to millions of people worldwide who were desperate for peace and freedom.

Wilson's idealism and even-handed tone concealed his commitment to overthrowing German militarism, which he blamed for causing the war. His apparent fairness encouraged the German leadership to believe they might be able to avoid punitive peace terms in their negotiations with Wilson in October 1917. But when the Germans asked him for an armistice based on the Fourteen Points, Wilson instead joined forces with the British and French in imposing crushing armistice terms on Germany.

Hero's welcome
When Wilson visited Europe in December 1918 he was cheered, adored, and idolized. A great weight of expectation lay upon him, but he was not in any position to dictate his own

> " ... unless **justice** be **done** to others it will **not be done** to us."
>
> WOODROW WILSON, FOURTEEN POINTS SPEECH, 8 JANUARY 1918

peace terms. Forced to compromise with the interests of the other victors at the Paris Peace Conference, he settled for establishing the League of Nations as a future mechanism for maintaining peace. Returning to the USA, he toured the country delivering speeches to sell the idea of the League.

At that crucial moment, Wilson's health collapsed. Crippled by a stroke, he struggled to complete his term of office. Whether as a fit man he could have persuaded Congress to sign up for the League of Nations and the peace treaty will never be known, but in the event it accepted neither. Wilson's health never recovered and he died in 1924.

Visit to France
Wilson's motorcade passes through the streets of Paris on his first visit to Europe in December 1918. He was greeted as a saviour by the populations of the victorious Allied countries.

TIMELINE

- **December 1856** Born in Staunton, Virginia, the son of a minister in the Presbyterian Church. His family moves to Augusta, Georgia, in the following year.
- **1879** Graduates from Princeton University, New Jersey.
- **1883** Studies for a doctorate in history and political science at Johns Hopkins University, Maryland, taking his PhD in 1886.
- **1885** Marries Ellen Louise Axson, daughter of a Presbyterian minister.
- **1890** Becomes professor of jurisprudence and political science at Princeton.
- **1902** Appointed president of Princeton, a post that he holds until 1910.
- **November 1910** Elected Democratic governor of New Jersey with a reformist agenda.
- **November 1912** Elected as 28th President of the USA with 41.8 per cent of the popular vote, aided by a split in the Republican vote.
- **August 1914** His wife dies in the same week as the outbreak of war in Europe. Declares the USA strictly neutral.
- **May 1915** Protests strongly to Germany over the U-boat sinking of the liner RMS *Lusitania*.
- **December 1915** Marries his second wife, Edith Bolling Galt. Expands US armed forces through the National Defense Act.
- **April 1916** Threatens to break off diplomatic relations with Germany after the U-boat sinking of the British passenger ferry SS *Sussex*.
- **November 1916** Wins a second term of office in a close-fought presidential election.
- **December 1916** Sends a Peace Note to the combatants in Europe, inviting them to state their war aims.
- **2 April 1917** Asks Congress for approval of a declaration of war on Germany.
- **January 1918** Issues the Fourteen Points, intended as a programme for a just peace.
- **October 1918** Refuses German peace advances based on acceptance of continued rule of the Kaiser and military leadership.
- **December 1918** Visits France and Britain after the Armistice, receiving a hero's welcome.
- **June 1919** Attends the Paris Peace Conference, in which his principles are compromised by European political realities.
- **September–October 1919** Campaigns in the USA for acceptance of the League of Nations, but his health breaks down and he suffers a stroke.
- **December 1920** Awarded the Nobel Peace Prize for 1919.
- **1924** Dies on 3 February at his townhouse in Washington, DC.

WILSON'S IMAGE ON THE $100,000 BANKNOTE

Organizing America for War

When the USA entered the war on 6 April 1917, it was unprepared for a major conflict. To create a mass army and organize resources for the war effort, radical measures were needed, involving an unprecedented expansion of government and the sacrifice of basic freedoms.

The immediate task of the US government after its decision to go to war was to create a new national army. Its existing regular force was inadequate for the demands of a major European war.

President Woodrow Wilson had publicly stated his opposition to conscription as late as February 1917, and he remained briefly committed to the volunteer principle even after war was declared. Many of his Democrat supporters in the southern and western states regarded compulsory military service as an unacceptable offence against the liberty of the individual.

Introducing the draft

Volunteers were slow to come forward – just 97,000 had enlisted by the end of April 1917 – and so Wilson soon succumbed to the argument that conscription, as well as being fairer, would make it easier to balance the demands of the military against industry's need for skilled workers.

The Selective Service Act, passed on 18 May 1917, required all male American citizens aged 21 to 31 to register for the draft by 5 June (the age range later became 18 to 45). Local boards then had to decide who should be drafted. Federal or state officials and workers in designated industries were exempted, as were men whose family circumstances were deemed to require their presence at home. Only members of recognized pacifist religious group such as Quakers were exempted from the draft on grounds of conscience.

Honor Roll
Du Bois
Smith
O'Brien
Cejka
Haucke
Pappandrikopolous
Andrassi
Villotto
Levy
Turovich
Kowalski
Chriczanevicz
Knutson
Gonzales

Victory Liberty Loan

Liberty bonds

Investing in government bonds to raise money for the war was presented as a patriotic duty of all US citizens. This poster, with its diverse list of names, urges all ethnic groups to support the war.

ON THE JOB FOR VICTORY
UNITED STATES SHIPPING BOARD   EMERGENCY FLEET CORPORATION

Once inducted, draftees were fed into a training programme for which new army camps were established across the USA. Volunteers continued to join the regular army, as well as supplying sailors for the navy.

Racial segregation

Black Americans were drafted in disproportionately high numbers. All the American armed services were strictly segregated. Plans to field 16 black infantry combat divisions were scaled back after riots involving black soldiers in Houston, Texas, in August 1917, provoked racist fears about the consequences of arming African Americans. The majority of black draftees were assigned to supply units, involved in delivering and maintaining equipment, and limited to performing menial jobs as cooks or labourers. However, two black infantry divisions eventually saw combat in France.

Building ships for the war

A poster publicizes the vital role of shipbuilding in the American war effort. Under the US Shipping Board's Emergency Fleet Corporation, American shipyards vastly expanded output during the course of the war.

The Committee on Public Information, a government propaganda body headed by popular journalist George Creel was entrusted with selling the war to the American people. Creel enlisted the help of the media and sent public speakers across the nation to rouse patriotic sentiment. He also flooded the country with provocative propaganda posters.

Silencing dissent

Only a small number of Americans actively opposed the war or the draft, but the government took harsh measures against this minority. The Espionage Act of June 1917, reinforced by the Sedition Act in May 1918, gave

> **"Lead this people** into war and they'll **forget** there ever was such a thing as **tolerance. To fight** you must be **brutal and ruthless..."**
>
> PRESIDENT WOODROW WILSON, PRIVATE CONVERSATION, 1 APRIL 1917

Joining the army

Drafted men queue to be issued with their uniforms at Camp Travis in San Antonio, Texas. Almost 3 million Americans were drafted in World War I. Equipping and training this mass army was a formidable task.

the authorities sweeping powers to suppress dissent. The Socialist Party of America and the Industrial Workers of the World movement (popularly known as the "Wobblies") were targeted for harsh punishments. The Socialist Party's leader, Eugene Debs, for example, was sentenced to ten years in prison in 1918 for making speeches criticizing the draft.

Economic factors

Organizing the war effort also involved unprecedented federal intervention in the economy. The War Industries Board under

Bernard Baruch drove the production of munitions through cooperation with big business. Railways were taken under federal control and so were shipyards. Federal boards were set up to oversee production, and the consumption of food and fuel. Not all war industry developed smoothly – aircraft production failed to develop – but output was mostly impressive. The tonnage of ships completed multiplied fivefold between 1916 and 1918.

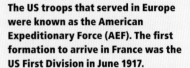

US Navy uniform for women

In 1917, the US Navy started enlisting women to perform support duties. Previously, the only women in the military services were nurses.

The government found it politically impossible to raise money for the war effort through extra taxes. Instead, it depended on patriotic appeals to invest in "liberty bonds". Some $21 billion was raised in this way.

Inevitably, the war had an impact on everyday life. There was little formal rationing, but patriotic Americans were urged to observe "meatless", "gasless", and "wheatless" days. Labour shortages drew more women into factory work and opened new job opportunities for African Americans, some 400,000 of whom migrated from the rural south to northern cities such as Chicago and New York between 1916 and 1918. For Americans of German origin, the war brought suspicion and occasional incidents of persecution.

AFTER ›››

The US troops that served in Europe were known as the American Expeditionary Force (AEF). The first formation to arrive in France was the US First Division in June 1917.

READY FOR BATTLE

Through 1917, First Division was joined by other formations, including the 42nd "Rainbow" Division of National Guardsmen. But it was not until spring 1918 that **General Jack Pershing 310–11 ››**, commander of the AEF, felt he had sufficient troops to enter battle. By the war's end some **2.8 million American soldiers had been sent to France**. About 116,000 died on military service, half of them killed by the influenza epidemic of 1918–19. The Espionage Act was a permanent legacy of the war, remaining in use in the USA into the 21st century.

Peace Initiatives and War Aims

By 1917, the destructiveness of the war and the lack of any prospect of military victory had led to war weariness. Combatant states were under pressure to end the slaughter, and those determined to continue had to clarify their goals if they were to maintain popular support.

« BEFORE

Few people in the combatant countries had openly opposed the war in the early years of the conflict.

FORCES FOR PEACE
In Germany, **revolutionary socialists** Karl Liebknecht and Rosa Luxemburg were imprisoned for anti-war agitation in summer 1916. In Britain, notable pacifists included Scottish socialist **Keir Hardie** and philosopher **Bertrand Russell**. Anti-war **feminists** met at an International Congress of Women at the Hague in the Netherlands in 1915. At government level, Germany offered **peace negotiations** in December 1916, but these were tantamount to the Allies accepting a German victory.

I n July 1917, British Army lieutenant Siegfried Sassoon issued a statement protesting against the war. He claimed it was "being deliberately prolonged by those who have the power to end it" and that the conflict had changed from "a war of defence and liberation" into "a war of aggression and conquest". Sassoon's personal protest – which had no practical effect – expressed an increasingly common feeling in all the countries involved in the conflict.

Evidence of mounting disaffection was widespread, from mutinies in the French army in May 1917 to industrial strikes in all combatant countries.

Anti-war forces
Opposition to the war had two main strands. Revolutionary socialists, such as the Russian Bolsheviks and the Spartacists, led by Rosa Luxemburg and Karl Liebknecht in Germany, saw the war as a capitalist swindle imposed on the international working class.

Moderate socialists and liberals, in contrast, were prepared to support the war as long as it was fought for national defence or idealistic goals, but not if it was for conquest. For many Germans, the overthrow of the tsarist regime in Russia in March 1917 ended the main threat to Germany and thus took away the justification for the war. In July 1917, Social Democrats and centre parties in the Reichstag, Germany's parliament, passed a resolution calling for "a peace of understanding and… reconciliation".

In the same month, an attempt by socialists to hold an international peace conference in Stockholm, Sweden, was sabotaged by the refusal of combatant countries, including France and Britain, to issue delegates with passports.

The seizure of power by revolutionary Bolsheviks in Russia in November 1917 gave the Bolshevik leader, Vladimir Ilyich Lenin, a platform for expounding the Bolsheviks' views on the war. He urged combatant countries to pursue a "just and democratic peace" without annexations or indemnities.

Peace broker
It was partly in order to seize back the moral high ground from Lenin that US President Woodrow Wilson launched his Fourteen Points peace programme in January 1918, in which he envisaged a postwar world based on the principles of democracy and national self-determination.

The British, French, and Italians had reservations about some of Wilson's points, but broadly endorsed the American aims. This did not, however, make peace negotiations any more likely. Ignoring the Reichstag, the German military leadership intended to dominate Europe, with virtual

Pope Benedict XV
In 1916 and 1917, the pope launched a series of peace initiatives, arguing for an agreement placing "the moral force of right" above "the material force of arms". His initiatives were scorned by both sides.

annexation of Belgium and control of Poland. The Allies had demands that went beyond evicting German troops from territory occupied during the war – France, for example, required the return of Alsace-Lorraine, annexed by Germany in the Franco-Prussian War.

Emperor Charles of Austria, however, was interested in peace. He viewed the war as a disaster that threatened the survival of his country. But his secret approach to the French government in March 1917 was fruitless, as he was incapable of a foreign policy independent of his German allies.

AFTER »

The first peace negotiations of the war were held between Russia and the Central Powers at Brest-Litovsk, in December 1917. Their outcome was a brutal, imposed agreement.

BREST-LITOVSK TREATY
In March 1918, Russia, under duress, signed the **Brest-Litovsk Treaty 276–77 »**, in which it lost territory containing about 30 per cent of its population. Germany also imposed a **harsh peace on Romania** in May. Exploitative and annexationist, these treaties were taken by the Allies as an example of the terms they could expect if they were defeated.

THE TABLES TURN
In October 1918, facing defeat, Germany sought an **armistice** on the basis of President Woodrow Wilson's **Fourteen Points 322–33 »**. By then, anti-war feeling was rampant in Austria-Hungary and Germany. In Allied countries on the verge of victory, support for the war revived.

British conscientious objectors
In May 1917, Britain's Independent Labour Party (ILP) mounted a demonstration in support of conscientious objectors held in Dartmoor prison. While the Labour Party backed the war, the minority ILP opposed it.

The dead vote for peace
An image from a 1917 German Social Democrat satirical magazine, *Der Wahre Jacob*, is captioned: "Those in favour of a negotiated peace, raise your hands." The scale of the deaths made it hard to accept that the war might have been fought in vain.

The **U-boat Onslaught**

A campaign of unrestricted submarine warfare launched against Allied merchant shipping from February 1917 almost won the war for Germany. The adoption of a convoy system by the Royal Navy cut Allied shipping losses, but the submarine menace was never overcome.

BEFORE

The German submarine campaign against Allied merchant shipping in February 1915 was in response to the British naval blockade of Germany.

U-BOAT ATTACKS
Initially, Germany had only 20 U-boats, but they achieved considerable success. In May 1915, the submarine *U-20* **sank the liner RMS *Lusitania* ≪ 126–27**, causing the deaths of 1,198 passengers and crew and provoking a protest from the US government. In May 1916, after US objections to an attack on the British passenger ferry **SS *Sussex***, Germany suspended submarine warfare, but it resumed restricted operations in October.

SINKING OF THE *LUSITANIA*

On 22 December 1916, Admiral Henning von Holtzendorff, the German navy's Chief of Staff, sent a memorandum to Kaiser Wilhelm II arguing for unrestricted submarine warfare. The U-boat campaign had been a subject of intense debate among Germany's political and military leaders since early in the war, its negative impact on relations with neutral countries such as the USA balanced against its effectiveness as a weapon against Allied trade.

In late 1916, German U-boats were sinking a considerable number of merchant ships, but their operations were hampered by restrictions such as allowing crews to disembark first, to appease neutral states. Holtzendorff argued that such restrictions should be lifted and U-boats permitted to sink any ship bound for British ports without any warning. Since Britain was utterly dependent on food imports,

the British could be starved into submission in six months. At a meeting on 8 January 1917, the proposal for unrestricted submarine warfare was adopted by the German military leadership, although they knew it would almost certainly lead to war with the USA.

Forcing Britain to its knees
Germany had greatly expanded its submarine fleet since the start of the war and had 148 U-boats available

to begin the campaign in February 1917. The initial results were horrifyingly impressive. Holtzendorff had calculated that sinking 600,000 tons of merchant shipping a month would force Britain to its knees. Operating as lone hunters, the U-boats spread out across crowded shipping lanes and picked off any vessels that came into view. The most successful commanders were sinking several ships a day.

The British Admiralty's response, under First Sea Lord Admiral John Jellicoe, was to order the Royal Navy to hunt down the U-boats and destroy them. But this was impossible. The navy had developed hydrophones to

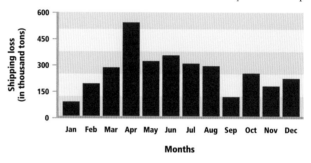

British merchant shipping losses to U-boats in 1917
German unrestricted submarine warfare increased attacks on merchant ships from February to April. The adoption of a convoy system in May reduced sinkings to a sustainable level.

> **"Submarine warfare** is… the **right way to end this war** victoriously…"
> ADMIRAL HENNING VON HOLTZENDORFF, MEMORANDUM, 22 DECEMBER 1916

listen for submarines underwater, and depth charges to destroy them once they were found, but submerged U-boats could rarely be located accurately enough to give any chance of a kill. Only nine U-boats were sunk from February through April 1917 – paltry losses that German shipyards could easily make up.

The convoy solution

While bizarre solutions such as training circus sea lions to detect U-boats were explored with enthusiasm, Jellicoe and the Admiralty staff resisted the introduction of a convoy system – merchant ships sailing together, protected by the Royal Navy – on the grounds that warships could not be spared as escorts.

In late April, with Britain facing disaster, Jellicoe approved a trial

German U-boat heroes
An illustration in a German wartime magazine presents a dramatic image of a heroic U-boat crew in action. Casualties were heavy, with half of all German submarines lost in the course of the war.

German U-boat gun
U-boats were typically armed with one or two deck guns for use on the surface. These guns, such as the 10.5 cm (4.1 in) shown here, were very effective with high rates of fire.

Barrel
Gunsight
Breech
Gunner's seat

convoy. It proved successful, with 16 merchant ships reaching port without loss. Introduction of the convoy system was slow – about half of all merchant ships were travelling in convoys by the end of 1917 – but it saved Britain from defeat. U-boats found convoys more difficult to locate than the same number of vessels scattered across the sea and far more dangerous to approach and attack.

By the second half of 1917, monthly merchant shipping losses had fallen to an average of 400,000 tons and U-boat losses had risen to between five and ten a month. Use of convoys increased through 1918 as the number of escort vessels rose, including American destroyers.

Nets and mines
The Allies never overcame the German U-boat menace. Large-scale resources were devoted to creating and patrolling anti-submarine barriers across the

Dover Straits and between Scotland and Norway. Comprising underwater nets and mines, these barriers presented an obstacle to U-boats, but with patience they could pass through safely. Increasing British use of air patrols, mostly with blimps (non-rigid airships), also made life more difficult for the German submarines, forcing them to submerge, which they could do for only short periods.

Yet in summer 1918, the U-boat campaign was still in full swing. In a notorious incident in June, a Canadian hospital ship, HMHS *Llandovery Castle*, was sunk by *U-86* and the survivors were fired on in their lifeboats. Long-range U-boats were deployed across the Atlantic, sinking ships in US coastal waters. As late as 10 October 1918, with the end of the war in sight, the mailboat RMS *Leinster* was torpedoed outside Dublin Bay, killing over 500 people.

In all, 5,000 Allied merchant ships were sunk by German U-boats during the war, set against 178 U-boats destroyed in combat.

Underwater raider
A German U-boat rises to the surface during a patrol. The range of submarines increased during the course of the war – by 1918, they could cross the Atlantic to operate in American coastal waters.

AFTER »

The U-boat campaign had many consequences. As well as drawing the USA into the war, it was a major preoccupation for Allied strategists.

ALLIED RESPONSE
The desire to attack U-boat bases on the coast of Flanders was a major motive for the British-led offensive at **Passchendaele (Third Ypres) 240–43 »** in July to November 1917. The U-boat bases were also targeted unsuccessfully from the sea by the Royal Navy in the **Zeebrugge Raid 292–93 »** in April 1918. The U-boat campaign had an impact on British food supplies, causing inflation to rise and some rationing in spring 1918, but there were never serious food shortages in Britain.

SUBMARINE BAN
After the war, Germany was **banned from possessing submarines** under the terms of the **Treaty of Versailles 338–39 »**. Over time, the Germans circumvented this restriction and Britain accepted the existence of a U-boat fleet in the 1935 Anglo-German Naval Agreement.

GERMAN GENERAL Born 1865 Died 1937

Erich Ludendorff

"Basically, **this war** comes down simply **to killing one another.**"

GENERAL ERICH LUDENDORFF, APRIL 1917

The son of an undistinguished Prussian landowner – lowly origins by the standards of the German officer corps – Erich Ludendorff made a brilliant career in the peacetime army through hard work and intelligence. He was appointed to a position on the General Staff, where he became an expert on war planning and mobilization.

Considered abrasive and arrogant by his fellow officers, he made no effort to ingratiate himself. He showed his indifference to conventional opinion by marrying a divorcee with four children. Although a consummate military professional, he also lacked the traditional soldier's respect for hierarchical authority. Shortly before the war, convinced that limits on

military spending were crippling the German army, he conspired with nationalist politicians to press for a change in policy. His outspoken criticisms outraged his superiors and he was sacked from the General Staff.

Man of action
When war broke out, Ludendorff was in command of an infantry brigade, a relatively lowly position. But his experience on the General Staff meant that he was also a leading expert on the Schlieffen Plan, Germany's initial war strategy. As such, he was immediately switched to a role on the staff of the Second Army, spearheading the invasion of Belgium. Entering combat for the first time at

Tough leader
Energetic and arrogant, General Ludendorff never troubled to make himself liked. He antagonized army colleagues and the Kaiser, but he was clear-sighted and determined.

Ludendorff Donation Fund
A postcard publicizes a charitable fund for servicemen disabled in the war. Set up in spring 1918, the fund borrowed Ludendorff's name for credibility, though he made little effort himself to aid crippled soldiers.

Liège, he led a bold push into the city and demanded the surrender of its citadel by hammering on the door.

German Chief of the General Staff Helmuth von Moltke then chose Ludendorff to defend Germany from a Russian invasion. He was sent to East Prussia to take over as Chief of Staff of the Eighth Army, meeting his new army commander, Field Marshal Paul von Hindenburg, on the train.

Victory at Tannenberg made Hindenburg and Ludendorff national heroes. They remained inseparably linked until the last weeks of the war.

Battle with Falkenhayn

Ludendorff remained on the Eastern Front until August 1916, proving outstanding as a staff officer, especially in his use of railways for rapid troop movements. However, his effectiveness was limited by his hostile relationship with Moltke's successor, Erich von Falkenhayn. Given the right resources, Ludendorff believed he could destroy the Russian armies and force Russia to make peace. But Falkenhayn did not agree. In January 1915, Ludendorff tried to have Falkenhayn dismissed, but Kaiser Wilhelm, who disliked Ludendorff, kept Falkenhayn in place.

Falkenhayn relegated Ludendorff to the command of subsidiary operations. Ludendorff plotted against him, cultivating the support of nationalist politicians and industrialists unhappy with the progress of the war. In August 1916, Falkenhayn lost the struggle and the Kaiser reluctantly appointed Hindenburg as head of the Third Supreme Command, with Ludendorff choosing his own designation as Quartermaster-General.

Joint war leaders
Ludendorff is portrayed at a planning session with Field Marshal Paul von Hindenburg in a painting by H. Vogel. Ludendorff and Hindenburg were men of contrasting character, but they shared broadly similar attitudes.

> ## "[He] changed the **defensive war** into a war of **conquest.**"
>

By mid-1917, Ludendorff was close to acting as a military dictator. He subordinated the civilian government to the military and ignored both the Reichstag (German government) and the Kaiser. His policy was to wage total war for total victory, and he sought to mobilize the entire resources of the German nation and its conquered territories for the war effort.

A believer in Germany's "civilizing mission" in the east, his plans for Poland and other Slav areas included ruthless economic exploitation and the deportation of populations to make way for German settlers. Such thinking lay behind the peace terms imposed on Russia and Romania in spring 1918.

Wild gambles

Ludendorff brought clarity to German military thinking, notably in the withdrawal to the Hindenburg Line in spring 1917, which sacrificed territory to make the German position on the Western Front more defensible. But his overall strategy was a gamble. Both the adoption of unrestricted submarine warfare in January 1917 and the massive Spring Offensive on the Western Front in 1918 were high-risk throws of the dice that failed.

The final stage of the war showed Ludendorff at his worst. Convinced from August 1918 that victory was no longer possible, he became increasingly erratic in his behaviour. At the end of September, he insisted that the civilian government seek an armistice, but a month later advocated a fight to the finish. When he issued orders to the army that ran counter to official policy, the Kaiser forced him to resign.

As soon as the war was over, Ludendorff began constructing the myth that the German army had been undermined by socialists and Jews. He became active in nationalist extremist politics, backing attempts to overthrow the Weimar Republic, including Adolf Hitler's failed putsch in 1923. Ludendorff was never a popular figure, however. He was marginalized while Hindenburg rose to be German president. By the 1930s, Ludendorff had no time for Hitler or for any political figure, instead pursuing his own campaign against Jews and Christians, especially Jesuits, whom he blamed for the ills of Germany and the world.

Allying with Hitler

Ludendorff poses with Adolf Hitler and other participants in the failed Beer Hall Putsch in Munich in 1923. Ludendorff's support of the Nazi Party was only temporary, but it gave Hitler credibility in Germany.

TIMELINE

April 1865 Born the son of a modest landowner near Posen, then in Prussia, now in Poland.

1885 Commissioned as an infantry lieutenant in the German army.

1894 As a staff officer, he earns a reputation for ability and drive.

1905 Joins the General Staff in Berlin, in charge of developing the Schlieffen Plan.

1909 Marries divorced mother-of-four Margarethe Pernet.

1913 After pushing for an expansion of the German army, he is sacked from the General Staff and returned to regimental duties.

August 1914 Appointed Deputy Chief of Staff to the Second German Army, he is celebrated for his role in the capture of Liège. Transferred to East Prussia as Chief of Staff to Field Marshal Paul von Hindenburg, he participates in the defeat of the Russians at Tannenberg.

September 1914 His reputation is enhanced by success in the Battle of the Masurian Lakes.

September 1915 Commands the offensive that captures Vilnius in Lithuania.

August 1916 As Quartermaster-General in the Third Supreme Command, he becomes joint leader of the German war effort with Hindenburg.

January 1917 Supports the resumption of unrestricted submarine warfare as part of a strategy aimed at achieving total victory.

July 1917 Engineers the fall of German Chancellor Bethmann-Hollweg.

March 1918 Directs the German Spring Offensives designed to win the war on the Western Front.

29 September 1918 Urges an armistice in response to the imminent collapse of Germany and its allies.

26 October 1918 After trying to reverse the pursuit of an armistice, he is forced to resign.

November 1918 Flees into exile and writes his memoirs, blaming German defeat on a "stab in the back" by socialists and Jews.

1920 Returning to Germany, he supports the failed Kapp Putsch, an attempted coup to overthrow the democratic government.

1923 Participates in the failed Beer Hall Putsch in Munich led by Adolf Hitler.

1925 Stands for election as German president, and attracts 1.1 per cent of the vote.

1926 Divorces his first wife and marries Mathilde von Kemnitz, with whom he founds the esoteric Society for the Knowledge of God.

December 1937 Dies aged 72. Hitler attends his state funeral.

ERICH AND MATHILDE LUDENDORFF

BEFORE

Through 1915 and 1916, fighting on the Western Front had degenerated into a war of attrition in which the French army suffered particularly heavy losses.

FRENCH DECISION
The **Battle of Verdun ‹‹ 154–55**, fought in 1916, resulted in 380,000 French casualties. In its later stages, however, a number of German-held positions were **captured in attacks** mounted by **General Robert Nivelle ‹‹ 160–61**. In December 1916, Nivelle replaced **General Joseph Joffre** as the French commander-in-chief and persuaded the French and British prime ministers, Aristide Briand and David Lloyd George, to **back his plans for a major offensive**. The British commander-in-chief, **Douglas Haig**, reluctantly agreed to mount a diversionary attack at **Arras 226–27 ››**.

The **Nivelle Offensive**

In spring 1917, a new French commander-in-chief, General Robert Nivelle, promised that the Allies could win the war with a swift and decisive breakthrough on the Western Front. When his offensive failed, the French army was paralysed by widespread mutinies.

General Robert Nivelle won political support for his offensive in April 1917 by telling French leaders what they wanted to hear: that victory on the Western Front could be achieved quickly and without heavy loss of life. He planned an offensive at the Aisne river between Soissons and Reims, centring on the Chemin des Dames ridge. He envisaged a breakthrough within 48 hours. A creeping barrage of artillery fire – advancing in tandem with the infantry assault – would clear a path through the German defences. Infantry and cavalry would then pour through the gap.

The Hindenburg Line
In March, French preparations were thrown into confusion by the withdrawal of German forces from the Somme to the newly built fortifications of the Hindenburg Line. The Germans laid waste to the French territory they were abandoning, ruining farms and villages, destroying railways and bridges, and leaving booby-trap devices to maim or kill the unwary.

In the face of this German defensive move, the French needed time to reconsider their strategy. But Nivelle insisted the offensive should go ahead.

Scorched earth
In April 1917, French troops advanced across country devastated by the Germans during their withdrawal to the Hindenburg Line. The French gained more ground from the voluntary German withdrawal than from the Nivelle Offensive.

FRENCH GENERAL (1856–1924)

ROBERT NIVELLE

French General Robert Nivelle was an artillery officer who rose from colonel to army commander in the first two years of the war. Brought in by General Joseph Joffre to replace General Philippe Pétain at Verdun in May 1916, Nivelle achieved notable successes through the intelligent use of artillery in support of infantry assaults. Charming, confident, and persuasive, he was appointed French commander-in-chief in December 1916, promising to repeat these victories on a much larger scale. At the Aisne river in April 1917, his costly offensive failed to fulfil the high expectations he had raised. Sacked in May 1917, he was sent to spend the rest of the war in Africa. He retired from the military in 1922 and died in 1924.

The Western Front, January to May 1917

The German withdrawal to the fortifications of the Hindenburg Line changed the shape of the Western Front. The British attack at Arras and the French Nivelle Offensive on the Aisne made only limited gains.

KEY

- ■ British army
- ▪ French army
- ■ German army
- ⌣ Western Front, early 1917
- ‑ ⋅ Hindenburg Line, 5 April
- ➡ German withdrawal to Hindenburg Line, 15 March–5 April
- ➡ British Arras Offensive
- ➡ French Nivelle Offensive
- ┈┈ Major railway

0 ——— 50 km
0 ——— 50 miles

1 9 Apr
Canadians of the 3rd Army capture Vimy Ridge

2 9 Apr
British subsidiary attack commences in Arras area. Offensive temporarily halted 15 Apr

3 16 Apr
French attack in Chemin des Dames area (Nivelle Offensive). The offensive ends 9 May after heavy French losses and limited gains

French Lebel rifle

The standard French infantry gun throughout the war was the 1893 bolt-action Lebel rifle, firing an 8 mm round. However, many French soldiers preferred the less common 1915 Berthier rifle.

Battle commences

After a 10-day preliminary barrage, the infantry went "over the top" on 16 April. Their progress was slow. The creeping barrage, meant to advance just ahead of the infantry, instead pushed far beyond them.

Without artillery support, French soldiers suffered heavy losses to machine-gun fire and German artillery bombardment. Lapses in French security had enabled the Germans to acquire detailed knowledge of the planned offensive, and they had strengthened the depth of their defences to meet it. French Schneider CA1 tanks, used for the first time, became stuck or broke down and were reduced to burning wrecks by German artillery. As the advance stalled, troops coming forward to exploit the breakthrough were caught in a vast traffic jam behind the front.

The Nivelle Offensive was not an outright military disaster for the French. They took 28,000 German prisoners, captured some German guns, and gained around 500 m (600 yd) of territory. But by the time the operation was abandoned on 9 May, the French army had suffered another 120,000 casualties and the anticipated breakthrough had not been achieved. The cost of the offensive outweighed the gains, and Nivelle was sacked.

500 The approximate number of death sentences handed down to the ringleaders of the French army mutinies. Fewer than 50 executions were carried out.

French mutinies

After the offensive, morale crumbled among the French troops. By the end of May 1917, widespread mutinies had swept the army. Thousands of troops quit front-line duties. Nine infantry divisions were almost completely out of action, another 45 considerably affected. Soldiers made it clear they would continue to defend France, but they rejected any further futile offensives and called for improvements in conditions.

General Philippe Pétain replaced Nivelle as commander-in-chief. Pétain made personal visits to army divisions to assure them there would be no more rash offensives. While the ringleaders of the mutinies were court-martialled, measures were introduced to improve the rations and leave. By July, a fragile order had been restored to the French army.

AFTER »

By the end of the Nivelle Offensive, about one million French soldiers had been killed in the war. Yet French commitment to the conflict survived.

CLEMENCEAU CRACKS DOWN

The army mutinies of May 1917 were linked to an **upsurge of "defeatism"** in France. Anti-war French socialists tried to attend a **peace conference** in Stockholm, but were refused passports. There were widespread **strikes** in industry. After a period of political in-fighting, **Georges Clemenceau** was appointed prime minister in November 1917. Unswervingly committed to the war, he cracked down on those who disagreed with it.

BRITAIN TAKES THE LEAD

In the wake of the mutinies, the French army refrained from major offensives. Although it carried out an effective limited offensive on the **Aisne** in October 1917, the British took over the leading Allied role on the Western Front, notably at **Passchendaele (Third Battle of Ypres) 240–43 »**.

The Battle of Arras

Launched in April 1917, the British offensive at Arras is best remembered for the outstanding achievement of Canadian troops in taking Vimy Ridge. Overall, however, it was a failure, despite the improving performance by British infantry and artillery.

<< BEFORE

The Battle of Arras was undertaken by the British to support a French offensive on the Aisne river.

ANGLO-FRENCH COLLABORATION
In early 1917, French commander-in-chief Robert Nivelle claimed he could achieve a breakthrough at the **Aisne river** **<< 224–25**. British commander Field Marshal Douglas Haig agreed to support Nivelle by making diversionary attacks at Arras and Vimy Ridge. **Canadian troops 230–31 >>** were chosen to lead the assault on Vimy Ridge. They had already participated in the **Battle of Neuve Chapelle**, the **Second Battle of Ypres**, and the **Somme**.

THE HINDENBURG LINE
Meanwhile, in March 1917, the Germans withdrew to the **Hindenburg Line**, a series of fortifications they had built in northeastern France, and **abandoned** the area between **Arras and the Aisne << 224–25**.

The British Army had learned many lessons in the nine months since the disastrous first day of the Somme. The attack at Arras was still preceded by a five-day artillery bombardment, which sacrificed the element of surprise, but it was far more effective than at the Somme. The British gunners could identify the exact positions of German batteries by using sound-ranging techniques, which analysed the sounds of the guns, and "flash-spotting" – observing the flashes when enemy guns were discharged.

The British also had shells with new "graze" fuses that exploded on touching barbed wire, enabling the artillery bombardment to clear the wire in front of enemy trenches more effectively. Meanwhile, engineers excavated tunnels leading to the British front line, linking up existing caves and quarries into an underground system, so thousands of soldiers could assemble in forward positions unobserved by the enemy on high ground. Saps (short trenches) were dug into No Man's Land to provide jumping-off points from which to rush the enemy trenches.

Dawn attack
The offensive was launched at dawn on 9 April, a bitterly cold Easter Monday, amid sleet and flurries of snow. Through good coordination with the artillery, the infantry were able to advance as close as 50 m (50 yd) behind the creeping barrage laid down by the gunners, who mixed gas shells with high explosives for maximum effect.

Four divisions of the Canadian Corps were tasked with seizing Vimy Ridge, an obstacle that had resisted all previous attacks. Well trained and led, the Canadians had taken the crest of the ridge by late afternoon and were looking down on retreating Germans on the plain beyond. There were further advances by the British Third Army on the Canadians' right.

> **4,070** The average number of British and Commonwealth troops killed each day during the 38 days of the Battle of Arras.

German grenade launcher
Designed specifically for trench warfare, the launcher could hurl grenades into an enemy trench from the other side of No Man's Land. Grenades had become vital infantry weapons by 1917.

Fragmentation grenade

Elevation scale

Base plate

Once through the German front line British infantry advanced in places to a depth of over 5 km (3 miles), using flexible small-unit tactics to surround and overcome fortified strongpoints and machine-gun nests. About 9,000 German prisoners were taken on the first day and many guns were captured.

The Germans were partly undone by their own tactics. The German army had adopted the principle of "defence in depth". This meant that front-line positions were to be relatively lightly held, with counterattack forces rushing forward from the rear to retake ground once the enemy attack lost momentum. But at Arras the counterattacking reserves were held

too far back, leaving outnumbered, unsupported German front-line troops to suffer grievous losses.

False hope

The appearance of a major British victory soon proved ill-founded. General Edmund Allenby, commanding the Third Army, was slow to seize the opportunity to press on with the advance, then over-optimistic when it was too late. On 11 April, he told his men they were pursuing a defeated enemy and brought forward the cavalry to exploit the breakthrough.

> ## "No one could have foreseen that the… offensive would gain ground so quickly."
>
> CROWN PRINCE RUPPRECHT, GERMAN COMMANDER, DIARY ENTRY, 10 APRIL 1917

By that time, however, German reserves were arriving and progress stalled. At the southern end of the line, Australian troops sent to attack at Bullecourt on 10–11 April were caught up in a confused slaughter that recalled the Somme. Artillery was inadequate, barbed wire was uncut, and tanks arrived too late to forge a path for the Anzac infantry. The attack failed and the Australians suffered their heaviest single-day losses of the war.

Meanwhile, a savage air battle raged overhead. The British Royal Flying Corps, commanded by General Hugh Trenchard, was relentlessly active in support of the army, carrying out photo-reconnaissance, acting as aerial observers for the artillery, and attacking ground targets. German anti-aircraft fire and fighter aircraft, including Baron Manfred von Richthofen's squadron, took a heavy toll on the inferior British aircraft. Heavy losses of aircrew led to novice British pilots being thrown into combat with little chance of survival.

Lost cause

British commander-in-chief Field Marshal Douglas Haig insisted on continuing the Arras operation into May as a gesture of support for the French, who were heavily engaged in the Nivelle Offensive to the south. British casualties mounted sharply for insignificant gains. By the time the operation was halted on 16 May, the British Army had suffered more than 150,000 casualties, including 11,000 Canadians. German losses probably numbered around 130,000.

Advance at Vimy
Canadian soldiers cross captured ground at Vimy Ridge. One man (second left, foreground) is carrying a Lewis gun, a light machine-gun that was a useful addition to infantry firepower.

Bloody April
Britain's Royal Flying Corps lost 245 aircraft in the battle for air superiority fought over Arras in April 1917. Outclassed by German planes and by pilots such as Manfred von Richthofen, the British called it "Bloody April".

AFTER »

The Battle of Arras and the French Nivelle Offensive marked a shift in the balance between British and French forces on the Western Front.

BRITAIN STEPS UP
The British Army had acted as a junior partner in the alliance with the French since 1914. However, after the failure of the **Nivelle Offensive** « **224–25** and the subsequent **mutinies in the French army**, Britain took leading responsibility for offensive operations. After a success at Messines in June 1917, Haig launched a large-scale offensive at the **Ypres** salient at the end of July. Continuing until November, the notorious bloodbath that followed became known as the **Battle of Passchendaele 240–43** ».

BRITISH WATER BOTTLE

GERMANY IMPROVES DEFENCE
The Germans reflected hard upon their initial setbacks at Arras and Vimy Ridge, **refining their strategy of defence in depth** to improve its effectiveness.

Field of shells
A soldier stands amid spent shell cases in France. Vast quantities of shells were fired in the preliminary bombardments of major offensives, including some 2.7 million shells at the Battle of Arras in April 1917.

Canadians in the War

"Whenever the **Germans** found the **Canadian Corps** coming into the line, they **prepared for the worst.**"

BRITISH PRIME MINISTER DAVID LLOYD GEORGE, "WAR MEMOIRS"

Infantryman's cap
The badge on this soldier's service cap identifies the wearer as Canadian. This headgear would have been worn in combat until 1916, when steel Brodie helmets were adopted by British and Commonwealth troops.

A British dominion with a population of 7.2 million, Canada entered the war in solidarity with Britain in August 1914. This was unsurprising – the English-speaking majority had a strong sense of British identity and the attitude of the Canadian prime minister, Robert Borden, was pro-British.

Canada had a tiny regular army of around 3,000 men, backed up by a larger part-time militia. Borden ordered the formation of a volunteer Canadian Expeditionary Force (CEF), with an initial strength of one division, to serve with the British Army. By October 1914, 32,000 volunteers had enrolled, many of them British-born immigrants. There was also a privately raised regiment, Princess Patricia's Canadian Light Infantry, named after the daughter of the Duke of Connaught and Strathearn, the Governor General of Canada. It recruited men with previous military experience. The Newfoundland Regiment was another separate formation, as the British colony of Newfoundland was not at that time part of Canada.

Arriving in Europe
A large troop convoy carried the Canadians across the Atlantic to Britain, where they were sent to a training camp on Salisbury Plain and placed under the command of a British officer, General Edwin Alderson.

In February 1915, the troops crossed to France. After very limited experience of the trenches, in April they found themselves in the path of a German offensive at Ypres in which chlorine gas was used for the first time. The Canadians displayed immense courage under gas attack and then in a series of brutal

Battle of the Somme
Canadian infantry climb out of a trench during the fighting at the Somme in October 1916. More than 400,000 Canadians served in Europe in World War I.

engagements that kept Ypres out of German hands. Their system of command, however, was considered poor, as was their equipment. Their Canadian-made Ross rifles were inferior to the British Lee-Enfields.

Fresh volunteers continued to arrive from Canada, allowing the formation of a Canadian Corps in September 1915, into which the Princess Patricia's infantry were soon integrated. But this expansion was accompanied by bitter disputes between the Canadian government and General Alderson, who was determined to ditch the Ross rifle and sack some incompetent Canadian officers. In 1916, the Lee-Enfield rifle superseded the Ross, while Alderson was replaced by another British officer, General Julian Byng.

Battle triumphs

Byng was a popular and effective commander. With the aid of rapidly promoted Canadian General Arthur Currie, who commanded First Division, he made the Canadians into an elite formation. The Corps was permeated from top to bottom by an attitude of self-improvement. Their performance in every action was subjected to detailed analysis, with lessons learned and necessary changes applied. During the Battle of the Somme, the Canadians became openly critical of some senior British generals, whom they regarded as too wasteful of men's lives.

In April 1917, entrusted with the task of assaulting the previously impregnable Vimy Ridge in the Battle of Arras, the Canadian Corps showed outstanding preparation and execution of a set-piece attack. It earned Byng promotion to command of an army, leaving Currie to take over leadership of the Canadian Corps.

In October 1917, British commander-in-chief Field Marshal Douglas Haig chose the Canadian Corps to take Passchendaele in the Third Battle of Ypres. The Canadians did not let Haig down, although Currie was

60,661 The number of Canadian soldiers who died in World War I.

172,000 The number of Canadian soldiers who were injured.

unconvinced that the achievement was worth the heavy casualties it cost. Again in August 1918, the Canadians were switched from Flanders to Amiens in France to spearhead a decisive offensive, the move disguised from the Germans who had learned to see the presence of Canadian troops as a sign of an imminent attack.

An unbroken sequence of Canadian successes continued through the Hundred Days Offensives that ended the war, from Amiens to the crossing of the Canal du Nord and the final capture of Mons in Belgium. A Canadian private, George Price, is traditionally regarded as the last British and Commonwealth soldier to be killed in the war. He died just two minutes before the Armistice came into effect.

Canadians at home were proud of the performance of their troops. They also found a hero in the air, Billy Bishop from Ontario, one of the war's most famous ace pilots in the British Royal

Canadian hero

A bankrupt businessman and part-time militia officer at the start of the war, Arthur Currie developed into a skilful and humane general, leading his troops to many of their finest victories.

Canadian war bonds
A wartime poster appeals for citizens of the "land of the beaver" to help the war effort.

Flying Corps. But the war was not uncontentious. Prime Minister Borden's decision to introduce conscription revealed the lack of support for the war among French Canadians, who responded with rioting in spring 1918. In practice, the CEF remained almost entirely a volunteer force to the war's end.

Return to Canada

There was a regrettable postscript to Canada's involvement in World War I. The slow speed and perceived unfairness of demobilization – priority might depend on a soldier's marital status, length of service, or peacetime job – led to serious disturbances at Canadian army camps in Britain in 1919. In one incident five soldiers were killed as order was restored. Yet when they did finally return home, as the official history of the Canadian Expeditionary Force says, the soldiers "brought back with them a pride of nationhood that they had not known before".

TIMELINE

- **August 1914** The Canadian government sets out to raise a volunteer expeditionary force.
- **October 1914** The Canadian Expeditionary Force (CEF) is shipped to Britain.
- **January 1915** Princess Patricia's Light Infantry is the first Canadian regiment to be deployed in France.
- **March 1915** Troops of the CEF's First Division take up position at the front line on the Western Front.
- **April 1915** At the Second Battle of Ypres, Canadians are among the first troops to be exposed to a poison gas attack.
- **September 1915** The Canadian Corps is formed, initially with two divisions.
- **December 1915** A Third Canadian Division is formed. (A fourth is added in August 1916.)
- **June 1916** The Canadians fight a fierce defensive battle to hold Mont Sorrel on the Ypres salient against a German attack.
- **1 July 1916** The Newfoundland Regiment is decimated on the first day of the Battle of the Somme.
- **September–November 1916** The Canadian Corps fights at the Battle of the Somme, including at Flers-Courcelette, Thiepval, and the Ancre Heights.
- **9 April 1917** At the Battle of Arras, the four divisions of the Canadian Corps take Vimy Ridge from the Germans.
- **June 1917** Canadian General Currie is given command of the Canadian Corps.
- **August 1917** A new Military Service Act introduces conscription for all Canadian men aged 20–45.
- **15–25 August 1917** The Canadian Corps takes Hill 70, overlooking the French city of Lens.
- **26 October–10 November 1917** The Canadians are given the leading role in the final stage of the Battle of Passchendaele.
- **March–April 1918** At least five people are killed in anti-conscription riots among French Canadians in Quebec.
- **8 August 1918** Together with the Australians, the Canadians inflict a heavy defeat on the Germans at Amiens.
- **2 September 1918** Canadians break through the Drocourt-Quéant Line, part of the German Hindenburg Line defensive system.
- **27 September 1918** Canadian troops cross the Canal du Nord, also part of the Hindenburg Line.
- **11 November 1918** Canadians liberate Mons in Belgium. Canadian soldier George Price is killed two minutes before the Armistice.

GRAVE OF GEORGE PRICE

The **German Bomber Offensive**

From spring 1917, Germany launched bombing raids against British cities. While attacks were countered by fighter aircraft and anti-aircraft guns, harassed citizens learned to live with blackouts and air-raid warnings.

Gotha heavy bomber
Flown by a three-man crew, German Gotha bombers had a wingspan of around 24 m (78 ft) and carried up to ten 50 kg (110 lb) bombs. They were the mainstay of the German bombing offensive.

Until 1915, the limitations of aircraft meant that only airships could carry out long-range bombing missions.

BIRTH OF BOMBER AIRCRAFT
German **airships** launched the **first strategic bombing campaign** « **132–33** against British and French cities in 1915. By 1917, German **airship losses** had become **unsustainable** in the face of fighter aircraft armed with explosive darts and incendiary rounds. Meanwhile, the first large **bomber aircraft**, the Russian Ilya Muromets and Italian Caproni Ca1, had entered service in 1915. By 1917, the Germans had developed their own **multi-engine bombers**, the Gotha and the Zeppelin-Staaken "Giant".

ANTI-ZEPPELIN DART

Britain was the primary target for German strategic bombing. Germany's leaders believed that an effective bombing campaign, especially against London, might undermine civilian morale and lead to popular pressure on the British government to make peace. By spring 1917, Germany had assembled a fleet of Gotha G.IV bombers at airfields in occupied Belgium. With two Mercedes engines, the Gotha was able to carry a 500 kg (1,100 lb) bombload.

On 25 May, 21 Gothas attacked the English Channel port of Folkestone and a nearby army camp in broad daylight, killing 95 people and injuring another 260. At noon on 13 June, the Gothas struck London. Fourteen aircraft appeared over the city without warning, dropping bombs around Liverpool Street Station. The population was so ill-prepared that people ran out into the streets to see the aircraft rather than taking cover. Among the 162 people killed were 18 children in a school classroom.

The British government responded to popular anger by diverting fighter aircraft from the Western Front to home defence. But when flying in formation, Gothas could defend themselves quite well against attack by fighter aircraft by using interlocking machine-gun fire so that their arcs of fire overlapped. Nevertheless, after nimble Sopwith Camel fighters were added to the British defences in the summer of 1917, the Germans were forced to operate by night.

152
The number of attacks on Britain by German Gotha and "Giant" bombers between May 1917 and May 1918. They killed 857 people and injured 2,508.

Enter the Giants
From September 1917, the German Gothas were joined by a smaller number of Zeppelin-Staaken "Giants". These extraordinary aircraft had four engines and a wingspan of 42 m (138 ft) – larger than most World War II bombers. The Gothas and Giants carried out night raids through to May 1918, with London, Paris, and the Channel ports regular targets.

In response to the raids, the Allies established an aircraft observation system so that fighter aircraft could intercept the bombers, and civilians could be given time to seek shelter. In January 1918, a bomb penetrated a basement shelter in central London, killing 38 people inside.

Hit and miss
Flying Gothas and Giants to a target city with a blackout in force was difficult, although by emitting radio signals the pilots could pinpoint their position from radio stations on the ground. Many missions were aborted because of bad weather, and mechanical failures accounted for many losses. In the last major raid on London on 19 May 1918, 43 German bombers took off from

Belgium, but nine failed to reach the English coast and only 19 penetrated London's outer defences. The raid nonetheless caused substantial damage, killing 49 people and injuring 177. Germany then abandoned strategic bombing to dedicate its aircraft to the support of the German army in France.

Effect on Britain
The scale of the German bomber offensive was very limited, causing civilian deaths in the hundreds rather than thousands, but countering it tied down British aircraft and guns. British morale was shaken by the failure of the government to protect civilians from attack. South African statesman Jan Smuts, a member of the British War Cabinet, headed an inquiry into air defence in summer 1917. His report recommended amalgamating the separate army and navy air corps into an independent Royal Air Force. This was done in April 1918.

In the course of 1918, the Allies stepped up their efforts to bomb industrial cities in Germany.

STRATEGIC BOMBING
In June 1918, Britain's newly created **Royal Air Force** set up the **Independent Air Force**, a fleet of bomber aircraft based at Nancy in France. Commanded by General Hugh Trenchard, it was tasked with mounting a strategic bombing campaign **against German industrial cities 294–95 »**, although it mainly performed **tactical bombing** in support of the army, striking targets such as airfields and munitions dumps. Before the war ended, both British and French bombers carried out **night raids** on cities such as Cologne, Frankfurt, and Mannheim.

TECHNOLOGY
ANTI-AIRCRAFT GUNS

During World War I, quick-firing guns were developed for an anti-aircraft role. They mostly fired shrapnel shells, but high-explosive and incendiary rounds were also used. Hitting an aircraft flying at around 130 kmh (80 mph) was difficult. Techniques were devised for estimating the altitude of an aircraft, so that shells could be set to explode at the right height. Methods also had to be found to compute an aircraft's speed and course. In the absence of accuracy, dense fire from massed gun batteries was most effective. From summer 1917, German planes sent to bomb London had to penetrate a ring of anti-aircraft batteries and searchlights.

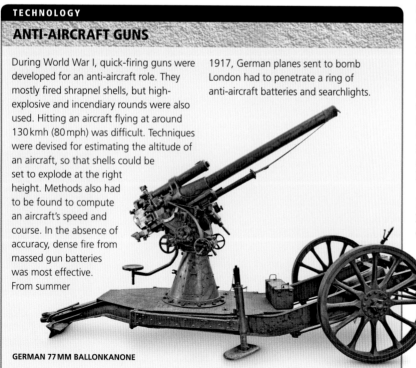

GERMAN 77 MM BALLONKANONE

Manning a Giant
Airmen on a Zeppelin-Staaken "Giant" bomber had to climb around the outside of the craft while it was in flight to man the machine-guns and monitor the engines. The crew of seven included two mechanics.

The **Kerensky Offensive**

The Provisional Government that replaced Russia's tsarist regime in March 1917 was eager to step up the country's war effort. But its attempt to revive popular support for the war failed and the defeat of an ambitious offensive led to the disintegration of the Russian army.

War for the revolution
A poster issued by the Russian Provisional Government in 1917 urges the Russian people to continue the war. It cautions against allowing the freedom won in the revolution to be crushed by German militarism.

The Russian decision to launch a major offensive in summer 1917 was a huge gamble. In the ranks of the army, morale and discipline were close to collapse. Soldiers' committees, set up in the wake of the revolution, contested the authority of unpopular officers. In the capital, Petrograd (St Petersburg), anti-war feeling was rife. The Provisional Government, in contrast, was fully committed to playing its part in the Allied war effort. It was receiving substantial funding from Britain and France, in return for which the Russian army was expected to undertake major military operations.

In May 1917, the Provisional Government shifted to the left, with more representatives of socialist parties. Alexander Kerensky, until then the only socialist member of the government, became minister for war. One of his first acts was to appoint General Alexei Brusilov as army commander-in-chief. Not only had Brusilov commanded Russia's most successful offensive of the war the previous year, but he was also broadly in sympathy with the revolution, seeking to work with soldiers' committees rather than against them.

Planned offensive

Kerensky and Brusilov agreed to mount an offensive that could be presented as a liberation struggle, turning the revolutionary energies of the Russian people against German imperialism. It would, they hoped, restore army morale and unite the people behind the government.

Kerensky toured the trenches making stirring speeches that celebrated the Russian army as the freest military force in the world. The Russian middle classes, enthused by patriotism, formed volunteer units and also headed for the front. Female volunteers were allowed to form Women's Battalions of Death, combat units that were meant to shame men into continuing the fight.

Tired of war

The notion that Russian soldiers might fight with greater enthusiasm for the revolution than they had for the Tsar was wildly over-optimistic. Disaffection among ordinary soldiers was deep-rooted. On many sectors of the front, mutinies and desertion were common. Bolshevik Party propaganda advocating immediate peace found a ready audience in the trenches. Most soldiers were tired of a war that seemed pointless. Mainly peasants, they wanted to go back to their villages to farm the plots of land promised to them by the new government.

Brusilov focused the offensive in Galicia, the scene of his great success the previous year, with subsidiary attacks in the centre and north of the Russian front. The scale of the operation was smaller than in 1916 because many units were not in usable shape. Launched on 1 July, after a two-day preliminary bombardment,

<< **BEFORE**

In summer 1916, the Russian army achieved its greatest success of the war in the Brusilov Offensive, but then political upheaval ensued.

RUSSIAN TURMOIL
General Alexei Brusilov inflicted a heavy **defeat** upon the **Austro-Hungarian army** in Galicia in June 1916 << **174–75**, but fighting continued into the autumn, by which time Russian losses were severe. The **defeat** of **Romania by Germany** in August–December 1916 << **194–95** further weakened Russia's military position. The hardships endured by Russian soldiers and civilians, and distrust of the tsarist regime, led to an **uprising in Petrograd** (St Petersburg) in March 1917 and the **abdication of Tsar Nicholas II** << **210–11**. A **Provisional Government** took over the Russian war effort, but its authority was contested by the Petrograd Soviet (council), representing revolutionary soldiers, sailors, and workers.

RUSSIAN POLITICIAN (1881–1970)

ALEXANDER KERENSKY

After the revolution of March 1917, Russian socialist politician Alexander Kerensky was a prominent member both of the Petrograd Soviet and the Provisional Government. Russian minister for war from May, he mounted a failed summer offensive that broke the Russian army. He became the Russian prime minister in July 1917 and army commander-in-chief in August, but he could not control the disintegrating political situation. His attempt to claim leadership of the revolution failed and the Bolsheviks overthrew him in November. Kerensky spent the rest of his life in exile in France and the USA.

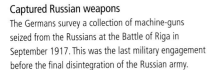

Captured Russian weapons

The Germans survey a collection of machine-guns seized from the Russians at the Battle of Riga in September 1917. This was the last military engagement before the final disintegration of the Russian army.

the offensive made some initial gains, with several kilometres of ground taken. The Germans, however, had already transferred divisions from the Western Front to meet the well-publicized attack.

The Russian advance stalled after two days. In many places, reserves refused orders to relieve the front-line troops. As the German and Austro-Hungarian counterattack got under way, Russian troops fled in a chaotic retreat that degenerated into mass desertion.

Spiralling crisis

Military disaster at the front was accompanied by political disturbances in Petrograd, known as the July Days. Demonstrators calling for the overthrow of the Provisional Government were suppressed by Kerensky with the aid of loyal military units. The Bolsheviks were blamed for the

protests, and their leader, Vladimir Ilyich Lenin, fled to Finland to avoid imprisonment. Tightening his grip on power, Kerensky became prime minister, while Brusilov, paying the price for the failed offensive, was replaced as commander-in-chief by General Lavr Kornilov.

Kornilov took command of Russia's disintegrating army. On 1 September, the German General Oskar von Hutier

launched an offensive at Riga, on the Baltic, using new infiltration tactics. The German forces easily defeated the demoralized Russians, taking Riga in just two days.

The battle at Riga was the last serious fighting on the Eastern Front. Hutier's forces began advancing on Petrograd, but quickly realized it was pointless. The Russian state and its army were falling apart.

The failure of the Kerensky Offensive helped send Russia into a political and social meltdown.

PRESSURE ON KERENSKY
After the Russian defeat at Riga, **Kerensky dismissed General Kornilov**, who was alleged to have been planning a military coup. To defend himself, Kerensky relied on the armed support of revolutionary workers and soldiers in Petrograd. He released Bolshevik leaders from prison, including **Leon Trotsky**.

THE ROAD TO CIVIL WAR
In November, the **Bolsheviks ousted Kerensky** and set up a **revolutionary government**. They sought an armistice with Germany and accepted a punitive **peace treaty** at **Brest-Litovsk 252–53 》** in March 1918. **Civil war** then broke out between the anti-Bolshevik White and the Bolshevik Red armies.

BOLSHEVIK BANNER

Advance in Galicia

Russian soldiers run past a church in the Galicia region, the main site of the Kerensky Offensive in July 1917. The Russian attacks quickly ran out of momentum and were repulsed by German and Austro-Hungarian troops.

The **Revolutionary Army**

When the Kerensky Offensive began to fail, Russian morale plummeted and the army started to disintegrate. Some troops refused to fight and soldiers' committees questioned whether officers should be obeyed.

"Since you could not fight bravely and beat the enemy for the old regime, under the threat of being shot, surely you will not now hesitate... to defend our freedom and exalt our great Revolution.

We will be ready then to sacrifice ourselves, to defend at whatever cost that which we have won, and, where it may be necessary, to hurl ourselves upon the enemy and crush him.

Then all hail to Mother Russia, and long may she live. And hail to our Provisional Government, and our War Minister, Kerensky, whose hope is in us. And I, comrade soldiers and officers, vouch for it to them that we will honourably, faithfully, and gallantly fulfil our duty. **"**

COMMANDER-IN-CHIEF ALEXEI BRUSILOV'S ADDRESS TO THE RUSSIAN ARMY BEFORE THE OPENING OF THE KERENSKY OFFENSIVE, 1 JULY 1917

"At 10 o'clock, July 19th, the 607th Mlynoff Regiment... left their trenches voluntarily and retired, with the result that the neighbouring units had to retire also. This gave the enemy the opportunity for developing his success.

Our failure is explained to a considerable degree by the fact that under the influence of the extremists (Bolsheviks) several detachments, having received the command to support the attacked detachments, held meetings and discussed the advisability of obeying the order, whereupon some of the regiments refused to obey the military command. The efforts of the commanders and committees to arouse the men to the fulfilment of the commands were fruitless.**"**

BRUSILOV'S OFFICIAL REPORT, 21 JULY 1917

Russian army disintegrates
A Russian soldier attacks a retreating comrade near Ternopil, Ukraine, in July 1917. In the face of the German counter-offensive, the Russian army began a rapid and chaotic retreat. Ternopil fell on 26 July, and Riga, in the north, was captured in early September.

Messines Ridge

The Battle of Messines Ridge in June 1917 is chiefly remembered for the massive explosions that destroyed German positions at the start of the British attack. It was an outstanding offensive success for the British Army, and a rare instance of German defenders suffering the heavier losses.

« BEFORE

The First and Second battles of Ypres in 1914 and 1915 left the British holding a salient, facing German troops entrenched on higher ground.

ALLIED FAILURES
From early 1916, British commander-in-chief **Field Marshal Douglas Haig « 178–79** favoured an offensive at the **Ypres salient**, but the need to cooperate with the French led to operations at the **Somme « 180–83** and **Arras « 226–27**. The failure of the French **Nivelle Offensive « 224–25** in spring 1917 and subsequent **mutinies** in the French army left the British to pursue their own plans. Haig envisaged a major offensive at Ypres, in preparation for which the British Second Army would seize Messines Ridge.

In early May 1917, British Second Army commander General Herbert Plumer, commander in the Ypres salient since 1915, was ordered to prepare an operation to take the low German-held ridge stretching from Messines to Wystchaete and a position known as Hill 60, 5 km (3 miles) southeast of Ypres. This would strengthen the British position south of Ypres as the prelude to a larger Flanders offensive further north. Plumer had proposed an attack on Messines as early as January 1916.

The underground war
By 1917, preparations were well advanced for destroying the German defences with buried explosives. The waterlogged ground in Flanders was on the whole unsuitable for tunnelling, but at Messines British Royal Engineers had found a usable layer of blue clay

Mining at Messines
Tunnellers at work under the Ypres salient. Excavation was hard and dangerous, and often done by candlelight in a slurry of mud. The tunnellers made as little noise as possible for fear of betraying their location to the enemy.

at a depth of 25–30 m (80–100 ft). Through 1916, around 30,000 British, Australian, Canadian, and New Zealand soldiers – a combination of military engineers and infantrymen who were miners in civilian life – had dug tunnels under the German-held ridge. At the end of each tunnel they hollowed out a chamber to hold explosives.

The work of tunnelling was arduous, despite the availability of portable oxygen tanks, electric light, and eventually mechanical diggers. The task was made more difficult by German counter-measures to locate and blow up the British tunnels. The British also listened for the Germans and mounted counterattacks, digging tunnels at lesser depth to intercept the German tunnellers. Occasionally, miners would break into an enemy tunnel, and hand-to-hand combat ensued. In August 1916, the German tunnellers had a major success in this underground war, when they broke into a British chamber and destroyed it.

More than 20 British tunnels remained undetected. The chambers were packed with explosives, much of

> **8,000** The estimated length in metres (26,000 ft) of the tunnels dug under Messines Ridge by British and Commonwealth engineers.

it in metal containers to protect against the wet conditions. Because tunnelling subsided towards the end of 1916, the Germans on Messines Ridge became complacent. By spring 1917, they had stopped worrying about mines.

Supply lines
General Plumer was a methodical commander with a reputation for being careful with his soldiers' lives. He had new light railways constructed behind the British lines to bring up ammunition and other supplies. Because thirst was a constant problem for troops in battle, pipelines were laid

On Messines Ridge
Gunner F.J. Mears, who served with the British artillery in France during the war, painted this picture of soldiers on Messines Ridge. The trees lining the road have been stripped bare by shellfire.

to ensure a supply of water at the front. An impressive concentration of artillery was assembled along a 16 km (10 mile) front, with 2,200 guns to support an infantry assault.

Defences organized in depth

The German defences presented a formidable challenge. By 1917, the German army had greatly refined its defensive tactics. Instead of facing a line of trenches, Allied soldiers were met with defences organized in depth. At Messines, this meant four systems of trenches, machine-gun emplacements, and concrete pillboxes, backed by further positions. The Germans accepted that an attack would break into these defences, but counterattack forces held at the rear were to come forward once the enemy onslaught lost momentum and drive the attackers back with heavy losses.

Messines Ridge was held by a corps of the German Fourth Army commanded by General Maximilian

von Laffert. He chose to maintain unusually large numbers of troops in his front two lines, a decision the Germans came to regret.

On 21 May, the British guns began a devastatingly effective preliminary bombardment that lasted for 17 days.

Plunger to activate

Explosives detonator
Most of the equipment used for digging mines and setting off explosive charges was identical to that employed by civilian miners and engineers. Nineteen charges were detonated almost simultaneously at Messines.

Electrical contact

Explosive box

Leather strap

The success of the Battle of Messines boosted British morale and encouraged Field Marshal Haig's plans for a full-scale offensive in Flanders.

PASSCHENDAELE
Haig launched the **Third Battle of Ypres 240–45 »**, known as the Battle of Passchendaele, on 31 July 1917. Continuing through to November, this turned into a vast attritional struggle without decisive result.

POSTWAR MESSINES
At least two of the buried **mines** at Messines remained **unexploded** after the end of the war. One of them erupted in 1955, fortunately killing only a cow. Since 1998, Messines has been the site of the **Irish Peace Tower**, commemorating Catholic and Protestant Irish soldiers who died in World War I.

THE IRISH PEACE TOWER AT MESSINES

Precisely targeted with the assistance of reconnaissance aircraft, British firepower destroyed a large part of the German artillery. German infantry positions were laid to waste. Front-line troops could not be relieved or supplied and ran short of food and water.

Walls of fire
The British attack was launched on 7 June. At 3:10am, just before dawn, the mines in 19 of the chambers under Messines Ridge were exploded by the engineers. The mines ranged from 7,700 kg (17,000 lb) to over 43,000 kg (95,000 lb) of explosives. Eyewitnesses

fire over their heads. The soldiers engaged in the assault were chiefly Australians and New Zealanders of the Anzac Corps, who captured Messines village, and Irish soldiers of the 16th Irish and 36th Ulster divisions. Formed in 1914 around the Catholic National Volunteers and the Protestant Ulster Volunteer Force respectively, militias that had been close to fighting one another in a civil war, the Irish forces advanced side by side, taking the village of Wystchaete.

Reserves were fed forward in the afternoon to capture further objectives and consolidate the gains. German

"Out of the **dark ridges** of Messines and Wystchaete… **gushed out and up…** volumes of **scarlet flame.**"
PHILIP GIBBS, WAR CORRESPONDENT, DESCRIBING THE EXPLOSIONS ON 7 JUNE 1917

described sheets of flame, clouds of smoke, and the ground shaking like an earthquake. The sound of the explosions was heard in London, over 160 km (100 miles) away.

As many as 10,000 German soldiers may have been killed in the eruption. Dazed survivors wandered towards the British lines to surrender. British troops advanced almost unopposed to occupy the German forward positions and prepared to assault the second line.

At 7am, after a considerable delay, the second stage of the assault opened. Troops advanced close behind a creeping artillery barrage, with massed machine-guns providing supporting

counterattacks were slow to materialize and were mishandled, with British artillery fire making it hard for the German troops to get forward.

Plumer's plan had been to seize and hold limited objectives, rather than achieve a total breakthrough. Fighting continued until 14 June, by which time the British were in possession of the ground they had sought to gain, dominating the Gheluvelt plateau.

The Germans had lost an estimated 25,000 men, including 7,000 taken prisoner, compared with British losses of 17,000 – a rare instance of the attritional balance favouring the side on the offensive.

Third Ypres

The Third Battle of Ypres, often known as Passchendaele, was a British-led offensive that became notorious for the suffering endured by the troops. Begun in pursuit of valid objectives, it degenerated into an attritional struggle fought by soldiers floundering in mud.

BEFORE

British commander-in-chief Field Marshal Douglas Haig had long wanted to mount a major offensive in Flanders. In summer 1917, he decided the time to attack had arrived.

PRESSURE MOUNTS
The **First and Second battles of Ypres**
《 60–61, 102–03 in 1914 and 1915 had left the British dug into a salient around the ruined Belgian town. After the failure of the French **Nivelle Offensive**
《 224–25 in spring 1917, Haig began planning a major operation at Ypres that would relieve pressure on the French and support offensives by Britain's Italian and Russian allies.

BADGE MARKING ALLIED COOPERATION

RECENT VICTORY
The success of new British tactics at the **Battle of Messines Ridge** **《 238–39** in June 1917 encouraged Haig's offensive plans.

British plans for an offensive at the Ypres salient in summer 1917 were bold and strategically coherent. The declared aim was to capture ports in occupied Belgium that were being used as bases for German U-boat attacks on British merchant shipping.

Supported by the French, the British intended to break through the German defences in front of Ypres, and then join up with other British troops to make an amphibious landing on the Belgian coast behind the German lines. From the outset, however, British commander-in-chief Field Marshal Douglas Haig evaded commitment to the second part of the plan, arguing that an offensive at Ypres alone might crack the morale of the German army. Haig believed German resources were strained to breaking point, owing to its commitments on other fronts.

British Prime Minister David Lloyd George tried to oppose plans for an offensive at Ypres, but his suggestions for alternative uses of military resources, such as transferring troops to Italy, carried little weight. Backed by the Chief of the Imperial General Staff, General William Robertson, Haig was allowed to go ahead, although Lloyd George only grudgingly withdrew his veto.

> **4.25 MILLION** The number of shells fired by **British artillery in the two-week preliminary bombardment at Third Ypres.**

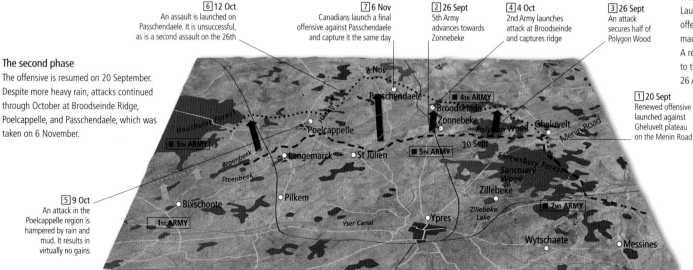

2 10 Aug After a two-week break in the fighting because of heavy rain, the British launch an attack against the Langemarck-Gheluvelt line. Langemarck is taken

3 22 Aug On the right, British 5th Army makes little progress and is halted on the Menin Road

1 3:50am 31 July Offensive is launched at dawn. Gains are made on Bixschoote, Pilkem and St Julien ridges to north of Ypres

The second phase
The offensive is resumed on 20 September. Despite more heavy rain, attacks continued through October at Broodseinde Ridge, Poelcappelle, and Passchendaele, which was taken on 6 November.

6 12 Oct An assault is launched on Passchendaele. It is unsuccessful, as is a second assault on the 26th

7 6 Nov Canadians launch a final offensive against Passchendaele and capture it the same day

2 26 Sept 5th Army advances towards Zonnebeke

4 4 Oct 2nd Army launches attack at Broodseinde and captures ridge

3 26 Sept An attack secures half of Polygon Wood

5 9 Oct An attack in the Poelcappelle region is hampered by rain and mud. It results in virtually no gains

The first phase
Launched on 31 July 1917, the Allied offensive, led by the British Fifth Army, made initial gains but lost momentum. A renewed attack in mid-August led to the capture of Langemarck. By 26 August, the operation had stalled.

1 20 Sept Renewed offensive launched against Gheluvelt plateau on the Menin Road

KEY
- ■ British army
- ▪ French army
- ▪ German army
- ➡ British advance
- ➡ French advance
- ⤷ British front line
- ⟋ French front line
- ▰ Road
- ▰ Railway

Battling the mud
British troops haul a gun through mud during the Third Battle of Ypres in September 1917. The appalling conditions under which men had to fight – the result of heavy rain and shelling – were the worst in the war.

> " It looked as though some **appalling earthquake** had **torn the earth apart…** In the midst of this **men** just had to **hang on.**"
>
> LIEUTENANT COLONEL SÜSSENBERGER, COMMANDING AN INFANTRY COMPANY AT THIRD YPRES

At the Ypres salient, the Germans held the higher ground and had spent almost three years organizing their defences in depth. Haig assigned the lead role in attacking this position to the British Fifth Army commanded by General Hubert Gough, a thrusting cavalry officer. Gough planned to advance 6,000 m (6,000 yd) on the first day, to reach the third line of German defences.

Hurricane of fire

In preparation for the assault, some 3,000 guns bombarded the German positions for a fortnight, firing four times the number of shells expended in preparation for the Somme Offensive the previous year. The damage inflicted on German positions was considerable. The bombardment rose to a climax in the early hours of 31 July. German General Hermann von Kuhl described the bombardment as "a hurricane of fire" in which "the whole earth of Flanders rocked".

Advancing behind a creeping barrage of artillery, the Allied infantry went "over the top" at dawn. They made considerable gains in places, with the British Guards Division, for example, progressing some 4,000 m (4,000 yd). Tanks aided the infantry, lumbering forward over reasonably dry ground. But in accordance with their doctrine of "flexible defence", the Germans had held back their main strength for counterattacks, which soon began to have an impact on exhausted Allied troops. It also started to rain. Ground churned up by massed artillery fire turned to deep mud punctuated by water-filled shell craters. Wounded men from both sides crawled into these craters for shelter. As the water rose, the most seriously injured drowned.

By 3 August, the initial offensive had petered out far short of its objectives. The maximum advance in some sectors was just 500 m (500 yd). Haig reported to the British War Cabinet that the operation had so far been "highly satisfactory" and losses had been "slight" – in fact, there were around 35,000 Allied casualties in four days.

Crown Prince Rupprecht, the German Army Group commander at Ypres, also described himself as "very satisfied" with the results of the fighting, despite similar losses on the German side.

Renewed attack

After a two-week pause, the British resumed their offensive with attacks at Langemarck and the Gheluvelt plateau. To the south, the Canadian Corps assaulted a position known as Hill 70 outside the town of Lens. Their aim was to stop the Germans transferring troops to Ypres.

7,800 The number of British Fifth Army soldiers killed during the opening of the offensive at Third Ypres, between 31 July and 3 August 1917.

Fore sight

Barrel

Pan magazine

Cocking handle

Lewis gun
The British Army's standard light machine-gun, the Lewis gun was issued to every infantry section by 1917. In action, the barrel was enclosed in an aluminium tube for air-cooling.

Nach Passchendaele

German road sign
This road sign, "Towards Passchendaele", was erected by the German army. The village was the objective of the British offensive during the final stages of Third Ypres.

>> The Canadian operation went well. Hill 70 was taken and then held against large-scale German counterattacks. Gough's attacks, in contrast, were inadequate in planning and execution, achieving small gains for high losses. At the end of August, Haig sidelined Gough and his Fifth Army, and handed chief responsibility for the Ypres offensive to General Hubert Plumer and the Second Army, the victors at Messines Ridge in June.

Plumer had a clear strategy for the battle. There would be a series of rigorously prepared attacks, each designed to take a limited objective that would then be held against counterattacks. The strategy was called "bite and hold".

Plumer relaunched the offensive at the Menin Road on 20 September and followed up with successful attacks on

The wasteland
After the conclusion of the fighting at Passchendaele in November 1917, the landscape was a wasteland of mud and water-filled shell craters. For many people, Passchendaele symbolized the futility of war.

Polygon Wood on 26 September and Broodseinde Ridge on 4 October. Each attack was carried out in a limited sector with massive artillery support – guns firing both high explosive and gas shells. The infantry had plentiful Lewis guns and rifle grenades among its armoury. The ground was firm enough for tanks to move forward.

The advance was halted before the infantry outran their artillery support, so that German attempts at counterattacks ran into a curtain of shellfire. Overhead, Allied aircraft, defying German anti-aircraft guns, spotted targets for the artillery and machine-gunned German positions.

The Germans suffered notably heavy losses at Broodseinde, where German troops massed in the front line in preparation for an attack of their own were bombarded by British artillery. Large numbers of Germans were taken prisoner, reinforcing Haig's belief that German morale was approaching breaking point.

Waist-deep in mud
After 4 October, however, the weather changed. A return to heavy rain made the ground a sea of mud. Troops struggled to move forward along duckboards – wooden paths laid by engineers over the muddy morass. Where the duckboards ended, men could find themselves waist-deep in mud. Artillery could only be brought up along narrow plank roads, and engineers had to build platforms for the guns to stop them sinking.

In these appalling conditions, renewed attacks at Poelcappelle on 9 October and towards Passchendaele Ridge three days later were a failure. The Australians and New Zealanders suffered particularly heavy casualties. Their artillery support was inadequate because guns could not be manoeuvred into position. Many shells were simply absorbed into the deep mud without exploding. Floundering troops were cut down by flanking machine-gun fire from German concrete pillboxes.

For the New Zealand forces, 9 October was the costliest day of the entire war, with 2,700 casualties trapped in front of uncut barbed wire at Poelcappelle. The Australian Third Division, under General John Monash, experienced even heavier losses attacking at Passchendaele on 12 October.

The first attack on Passchendaele was a costly debacle for British and Commonwealth forces. Meanwhile, the Germans were under almost intolerable pressure. Crown Prince Rupprecht was seriously considering a full-scale withdrawal from positions in front of Ypres.

In reality, however, the British offensive had worn itself out. Germans reinforcements were arriving from the Eastern Front, where the Russian army had ceased to be a serious threat. The Germans also had increasing supplies of mustard gas shells. Above all, the terrible mud made a decisive Allied breakthrough unthinkable.

The last push

Although the British had abandoned plans for an amphibious landing behind German lines, Haig would not give up on his offensive. The morale of many units of the British Army had been badly shaken, so Haig turned to the Canadian Corps. He bullied and pleaded with its commander, General Arthur Currie, to lead a final push to take Passchendaele.

Despite expressing coherent objections to the proposed operation, which he believed would be too costly

Identity tag
General John Monash was considered an outstanding Australian commander. He led a division at Third Ypres and later commanded all Australian forces on the Western Front.

to justify any advantage it might bring, Currie finally succumbed to pressure from Haig and accepted the task, with the promise of extra artillery.

The Canadian-led assault on Passchendaele proceeded methodically in three phases. On 26 October, a limited advance broke through key German defensive positions; further advances were made on 30 October; and on 6 November the ruins of Passchendaele fell to the Canadians. It cost 16,000 casualties to take the village. A final

assault on 10 November cleared the ridge of its remaining German presence and brought Third Ypres to a close.

The final count

There is no certainty about the casualty figures on either side in the battle, but it is probable that, between 31 July and 10 November, about 70,000 British and Commonwealth soldiers died at Third Ypres, with another 200,000 wounded or taken prisoner. German losses are even harder to establish, but they may have been broadly similar to Allied casualties.

The battle in the mud was severely demoralizing for soldiers on both sides, but perhaps especially for the British, many of whom learned a bitter distrust of their high command. The distinguished military historian John Keegan wrote: "On the Somme [Haig] had sent the flower of British youth to death or mutilation; at Passchendaele he had tipped the survivors into the slough of despond."

By the end of Third Ypres, the course of the war was being altered by events elsewhere.

MIXED FORTUNES

On the Western Front, the British achieved a shortlived breakthrough at **Cambrai 248–49 »** in November, ending Allied offensive operations for the winter. In March 1918, the German army launched the first of a series of offensives that, among other gains, **retook Passchendaele**.

DEVELOPMENTS IN ITALY AND RUSSIA

On the Italian front, German and Austrian forces achieved a **breakthrough at Caporetto 246–47 »** in the last week of October 1917. Haig was forced to transfer troops from the Western Front to Italy. In Russia, the **Bolsheviks 252–53 »** under Vladimir Ilyich Lenin seized power during the last days of Third Ypres. Lenin sought an **armistice with the Central Powers**.

ITALIAN FARINA HELMET

"The **British army lost its** spirit of **optimism,** and there was a **sense of deadly depression** among the **officers and men...**"

PHILIP GIBBS, WAR CORRESPONDENT, ON THE AFTERMATH OF THIRD YPRES

Recording Third Ypres
This image in chalk of action on the Ypres salient, entitled *Shellburst, Zillebeke*, was made by official British war artist Paul Nash in 1917. Nash recorded the bleak conditions in which the men had to fight.

《 BEFORE

After Italy entered the war on the Allied side in May 1915, Italian and Austro-Hungarian forces were locked in a prolonged stalemate.

ALPINE WARFARE
The fighting took place in the area between Italy and Austria-Hungary, with active sectors in **Trentino** province to the north and at the **Isonzo river** to the east. Apart from an Austro-Hungarian attack at **Asiago in Trentino** in May 1916, the Italians took the offensive. Repeated Italian assaults in the Isonzo sector achieved no decisive result. In January 1917, after the **Ninth Battle of the Isonzo**, the Italians requested support from British and French forces, but none could be spared. Offensives continued through 1917, with the **Eleventh Battle of the Isonzo** in August.

RELIEF FOR GERMANY
Meanwhile, the collapse of the Russian army after the **Kerensky Offensive 《 234–235** reduced the number of German troops required on the Eastern Front.

Italian Disaster at Caporetto

The overwhelming victory of German and Austro-Hungarian forces at the Battle of Caporetto in October 1917 brought a sudden and spectacular end to more than two years of stalemate and attrition on the Italian front. It failed, however, to knock Italy out of the war.

The fighting on the Italian front was often conducted in terrible conditions. The Isonzo sector, on the modern border between Italy and Slovenia, consisted of barren limestone cliffs where soldiers survived in caves or makeshift shelters.

Repeated Italian offensives had brought high losses for both sides. The Eleventh Battle of the Isonzo, from August to September 1917, resulted in almost 150,000 Italian casualties and more than 100,000 Austro-Hungarian losses. Austrian Emperor Charles I and his senior commanders believed their

forces on the Isonzo were close to breaking point and would not survive another defensive battle.

In line with the military thinking of the time, the Austro-Hungarians decided that the best solution was to take the offensive. The emperor asked the Germans to take over from Austro-Hungarian troops on the Eastern Front so that his forces could mount an attack on Italy. However, German military leaders doubted the competence of the Austro-Hungarian army and were keen to extend their own influence. They insisted on

sending German troops to the Italian front and created a new combined German and Austro-Hungarian army, under German command.

German build-up
The Austro-German Fourteenth Army, commanded by General Otto von Below, was concentrated in a sector of the Isonzo front opposite the town of Caporetto (now Kobarid, Slovenia), where Italian positions were lightly held. German mountain troops were brought in, including the elite Bavarian Alpenkorps in which

> "The farther we **penetrated** into the **hostile zone** of defence… the **easier the fighting.**"
>
> LIEUTENANT ERWIN ROMMEL, GERMAN COMPANY COMMANDER AT CAPORETTO

Army in retreat
Demoralized Italian soldiers withdraw towards the Piave river after the breakthrough of German and Austro-Hungarian forces at Caporetto. In some places, the Italian retreat degenerated into a disorderly rout.

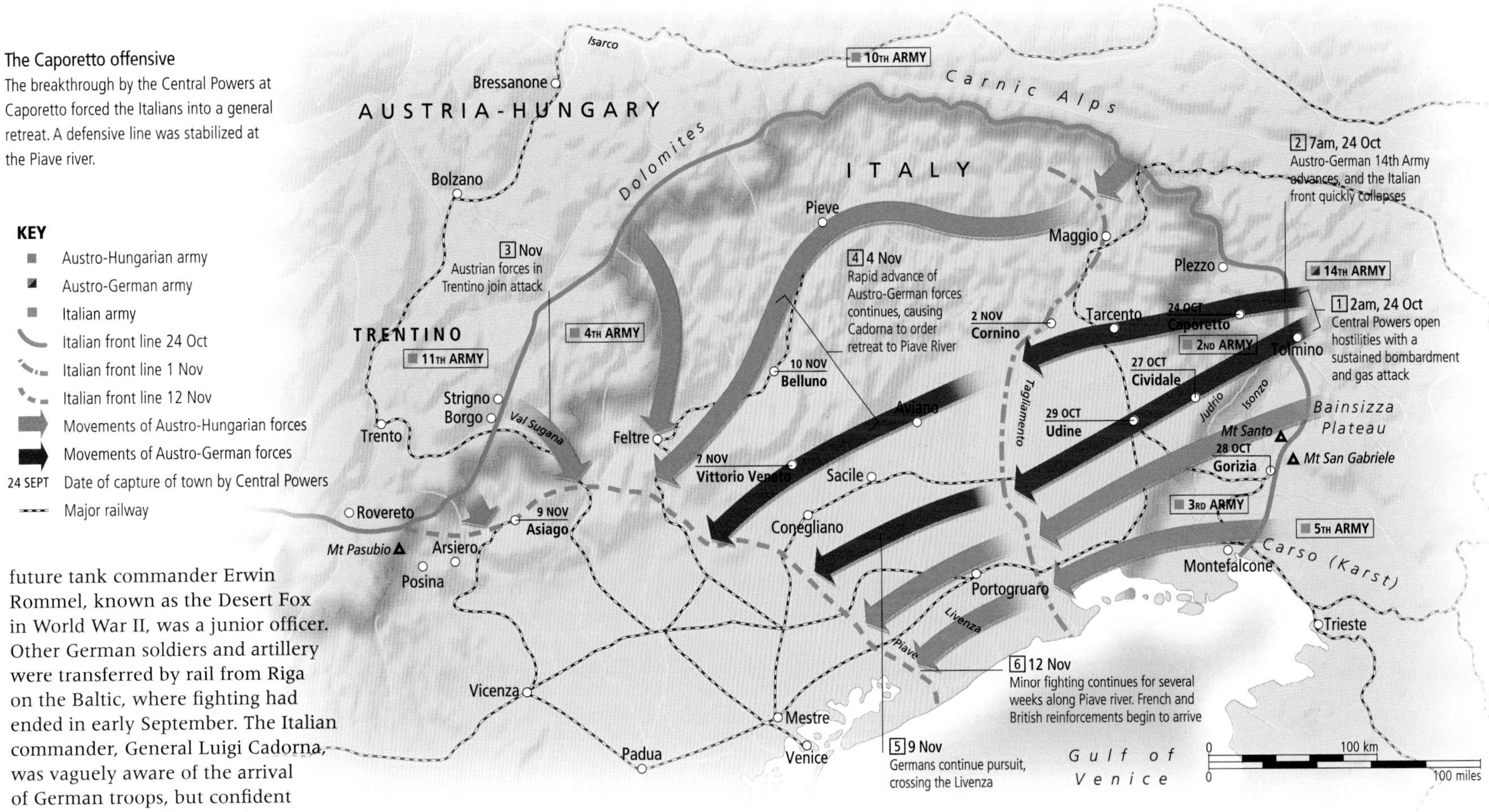

The Caporetto offensive

The breakthrough by the Central Powers at Caporetto forced the Italians into a general retreat. A defensive line was stabilized at the Piave river.

KEY

- ■ Austro-Hungarian army
- ▨ Austro-German army
- ■ Italian army
- ⟍ Italian front line 24 Oct
- ⟍ Italian front line 1 Nov
- ⟍ Italian front line 12 Nov
- ➤ Movements of Austro-Hungarian forces
- ➤ Movements of Austro-German forces
- 24 SEPT Date of capture of town by Central Powers
- ---- Major railway

(map labels)

Isarco · Bressanone · AUSTRIA-HUNGARY · Carnic Alps · 10TH ARMY · Dolomites · Bolzano · ITALY · Pieve · Maggio · 2 7am, 24 Oct Austro-German 14th Army advances, and the Italian front quickly collapses · Plezzo · 14TH ARMY · 3 Nov Austrian forces in Trentino join attack · 4 ARMY · 4 4 Nov Rapid advance of Austro-German forces continues, causing Cadorna to order retreat to Piave River · Tarcento · 24 OCT Caporetto · 1 2am, 24 Oct Central Powers open hostilities with a sustained bombardment and gas attack · 2 NOV Cornino · 2ND ARMY · Tolmino · TRENTINO · 11TH ARMY · 10 NOV Belluno · 27 OCT Cividale · Isonzo · Bainsizza Plateau · Strigno · Aviano · 29 OCT Udine · Mt Santo ▲ · Borgo · Feltre · Val Sugana · Tagliamento · 28 OCT Gorizia · ▲ Mt San Gabriele · Trento · 7 NOV Vittorio Veneto · Sacile · 3RD ARMY · Rovereto · 9 NOV Asiago · Conegliano · 5TH ARMY · Mt Pasubio ▲ · Arsiero · Montefalcone · Carso (Karst) · Posina · Portogruaro · Trieste · Livenza · Vicenza · Piave · 6 12 Nov Minor fighting continues for several weeks along Piave river. French and British reinforcements begin to arrive · Mestre · Gulf of Venice · Padua · Venice · 5 9 Nov Germans continue pursuit, crossing the Livenza · 0 100 km · 0 100 miles

future tank commander Erwin Rommel, known as the Desert Fox in World War II, was a junior officer. Other German soldiers and artillery were transferred by rail from Riga on the Baltic, where fighting had ended in early September. The Italian commander, General Luigi Cadorna, was vaguely aware of the arrival of German troops, but confident of the strength of his own forces. The bulk of Italian troops were kept in vulnerable forward positions.

Italian collapse

Moving at night, the Austro-German forces reached their attack positions undetected. In the early hours of 24 October they unleashed a furious bombardment, first with gas shells and then high explosives. At 7am, the infantry assault began. The Germans used newly adopted "infiltration tactics", penetrating in depth without halting to secure their flanks or take out Italian strong points.

Italian commander

General Luigi Cadorna, the Italian commander-in-chief from the outset of the war, was considered an unimaginative tactician. He was dismissed from his position in the wake of the disaster at Caporetto.

As the Fourteenth Army advanced, Italian morale and discipline collapsed. Hundreds of thousands of Italian soldiers simply fled towards the rear. Others surrendered en masse. Cadorna struggled to turn this rout into an orderly retreat to the Tagliamento river. Fleeing Italian soldiers were shot by officers attempting to restore order. The pursuit by Austro-German forces slowed as problems with transport mounted. They crossed the Tagliamento in early November, forcing Cadorna to order a further withdrawal to the Piave river.

Aftermath

Beyond the Piave, a formidable obstacle, the Italians held a defensive line. The Central Powers had advanced some 130 km (80 miles) in less than a fortnight. About 250,000 Italian soldiers were taken prisoner, and 30,000 were killed or wounded.

Instead of causing Italy to fall apart, the defeat succeeded in overcoming political and social divisions, as the country rallied to defend itself. A new Italian government came to power under Prime Minister Vittorio Orlando in late October. Orlando successfully appealed to his allies for military

Elite Italian uniform

This uniform, with its roll-neck sweater, was issued to Italy's elite Arditi assault troops. Most Italian troops wore varieties of grey-green uniforms and a version of the French Adrian helmet.

(labels: Steel helmet · Regimental badge)

support, and British and French divisions were soon arriving in Italy. Cadorna paid the price of defeat. He was sacked on 8 November and the cautious General Armando Diaz became the new commander-in-chief.

AFTER

In the aftermath of Caporetto, Italy's weak position was matched by that of Austria-Hungary.

CONTINUING THE WAR

An immediate consequence of Caporetto was the creation of an **Allied Supreme War Council** to coordinate strategy. It also led the **USA to declare war on Austria-Hungary** in December 1917, seven months after it had done so against Germany.

The new Italian commander-in-chief, General Armando Diaz, restored morale by improving his troops' **living conditions** and refraining from costly offensives. At home, the Orlando government cracked down on anti-war elements in Italy. **German troops** were soon **withdrawn** from the Italian front in preparation **for offensives on the Western Front in spring 1918 278–79 ≫**.

ITALIAN VICTORY

Both Italy and Austria-Hungary were **reluctant to resume offensive action**. In June 1918, Austro-Hungarian forces attacked across the Piave river and in the Trentino, but the operation failed. The Italians did not return to the offensive until October 1918, when **Austria-Hungary** was on the **verge of collapse**. Italy's **Vittorio Veneto Offensive 318–19 ≫** regained much of the ground lost a year earlier.

False Dawn at Cambrai

In November 1917, the British launched an offensive against the German Hindenburg Line in front of Cambrai in northern France. Led by tanks and making innovative use of artillery, the operation achieved a shortlived breakthrough.

The proposal for an operation at Cambrai originated with the British Tank Corps. Its commander, Brigadier-General Hugh Elles, and his Chief of Staff Colonel John Fuller were keen to show what tanks could achieve if deployed as a mass shock force rather than scattered among infantry. As tanks easily became bogged down in soft ground, they identified Cambrai, where the land was firm, dry, and chalky, as a suitable location for an attack.

Elles presented the proposal for a tank raid to General Julian Byng, who had commanded the Canadian Corps in the taking of Vimy Ridge in April 1917. As commander of the British Third Army from July 1917, Byng was responsible for the Cambrai sector. At the same time, he was approached by a divisional artillery commander, General Hugh Tudor, who wanted to try some new tactics involving artillery. British gunners had been working on ways to achieve accurate "predicted fire". A variety of factors had previously made it impossible to hit distant targets reliably without firing many preliminary ranging shots, which inevitably put the enemy on alert. Tudor believed it was now possible for guns to hit their targets without this "pre-registration" and to gain surprise by delaying opening fire until the tanks and infantry were

Transporting tanks
British tanks await movement by rail to Cambrai. Each tank carries fascines – bundles of brushwood to bridge trenches and ditches.

ready to go forward. Dispensing with a prolonged preliminary bombardment also avoided churning up the ground ahead of the tanks.

Attempt at a breakthrough
British commander-in-chief Field Marshal Douglas Haig approved the operation on 13 October. The Cambrai attack had been conceived as a "raid", because the Tank Corps commanders knew their machines were too mechanically unreliable for a sustained offensive. By November, however, it had evolved into an ambitious attempt at a breakthrough, with two cavalry divisions on hand to ride into the open country beyond the German lines. The German defences in front of Cambrai formed part of the Siegfriedstellung, a sector of the Hindenburg Line to which German troops had withdrawn from the Somme in spring 1917.

> ## "Surprise and rapidity... are of the utmost importance."
> BRITISH THIRD ARMY ORDERS FOR THE BATTLE OF CAMBRAI, 13 NOVEMBER 1917

◄◄ BEFORE

The second half of 1917 was a time of setbacks for the Allies on most fronts, but British generals remained committed to the offensive.

GAINS AND LOSSES
On the Eastern Front, the failure of the **Kerensky Offensive ‹‹ 234–35** in the summer of 1917 was followed by the collapse of the Russian army and the **Bolshevik seizure of power ‹‹ 252–53**. In Italy, the Austro-German breakthrough at **Caporetto ‹‹ 246–47** in late October put the Italian army to flight. On the Western Front, the British achieved success with an **offensive at Messines ‹‹ 238–39** in June. A British-led offensive at **Ypres ‹‹ 240–45**, at the end of July, resulted in high casualties and small gains, ending with the Allies capturing **Passchendaele Ridge** in early November.

THE TANK CORPS
The British were the first to use tanks, during the **Battle of the Somme ‹‹ 180–85** in September 1916. In July 1917, a **Tank Corps** was formed. Used to support infantry, tanks had proved useful but not decisive. At Third Ypres (Passchendaele), they were often unable to operate on the soft, muddy terrain.

ME 9828

DEVIL

Track tensioner

Metal crawler track plate

The British Mark IV tank
Introduced in 1917, the Mk IV existed in two versions. The "male", shown here, had six-pounder guns in sponsons (gun turrets) on its flanks, while the "female" was armed exclusively with machine-guns.

"Tanks were all over the place, some noses up, some afire."

WAR DIARY OF E BATTALION, TANK CORPS, AT FLESQUIÈRES, 20 NOVEMBER 1917

Physically the defences were strong. Barbed wire entanglements hundreds of metres deep fronted three lines of trenches and fortified positions reaching to a depth of 6 km (4 miles). But the sector was only lightly garrisoned by two German divisions with very limited artillery support.

The British plan depended upon surprise. Tanks and artillery were moved into position at night. Aircraft flew up and down the front to mask the noise of the tank engines. The entire strength of the Tank Corps and 1,000 artillery pieces were in position by 20 November without the Germans realizing it.

Steel plate armoured hull

A hurricane artillery bombardment began at 6:20am, followed by the advance of 300 Mk IV tanks. Clanking forward at walking pace, they crushed the German wire and crossed the trenches. Infantry followed, some with their rifles slung over their shoulders and smoking cigarettes. In places there were hardly any British casualties. Some infantry divisions had advanced more than 5 km (3 miles) by midday.

Generally, the stunned Germans surrendered without a fight. The exception was at Flesquières, in the centre of the attack. Here, a German artillery general, Oskar von Watter, ordered his men to roll forward field guns and pick off the tanks as they came over a ridge. With the supporting infantry of 51st Highland Division too far behind the tanks,

28 tanks were lost and the advance was halted. By the end of the day, some British forces had crossed the St Quentin Canal and the path into the rear of the German defences was open, but cavalry failed to exploit the brief opportunity for a breakthrough.

Hollow victory

After the horrors of Passchendaele, the initial success at Cambrai was trumpeted by the British as a victory. But by the end of the first day 179 tanks were out of action, 65 destroyed by the Germans, and the rest broken down or ditched. Haig insisted that the offensive continue, but it became bogged down in a struggle for Bourlon Wood, 6 km (4 miles) west of Cambrai.

By 30 November, German commanders had moved fresh troops to Cambrai and organized a counter-offensive. The British advance had

Moving artillery
German soldiers move a 75 mm Skoda field gun forward on the Western Front. During the Battle of Cambrai, artillery pieces were hauled out of gun pits to engage the British tanks with direct fire at close range.

Sponson with 6-pounder gun

476 The number of British tanks deployed at the Battle of Cambrai. Of these, 378 were fighting tanks while the rest performed support roles.

created a salient. The Germans attacked it from the north and south. They were trying out their own new tactics, using stormtroopers – elite assault forces trained in infiltration tactics. Launched against tired British soldiers insufficiently prepared for defence, the German counterattacks broke through on the southern flank, until halted by the British Guards Division.

By the end of the first week in December, the battle was over. The British retained their hold on one section of the Hindenburg Line but had lost ground elsewhere. The number of casualties was around 45,000 on each side. After the hopes raised on 20 November, it was another severe disappointment for Britain.

AFTER

The Battle of Cambrai showed that new technology and tactics were making it possible to overcome even strong defences on the Western Front. This pointed the way to more mobile warfare.

CAMBRAI REVISITED

German assault tactics employing **stormtroopers 274–75 »** created major breakthroughs in their spring offensives in 1918, leaving Cambrai far behind German lines. The Allies returned to Cambrai in October 1918, when it was taken by Canadian troops during the **Hundred Days Offensive** that ended the war.

NEW MILITARY THEORIES

British and French tanks played a significant role in Allied operations in 1918. After the war, the Battle of Cambrai became a reference point for military theorists advocating **the use of tanks** as the primary **shock force in modern warfare**.

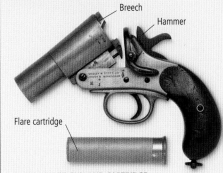
Breech

Hammer

Flare cartridge

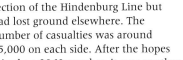

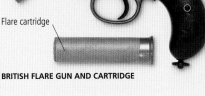

BRITISH FLARE GUN AND CARTRIDGE

Tank Warfare

" A **huge grey object** reared itself into view and slowly, very slowly, **it crawled along...** It was **a tank.**"

CANADIAN PRIVATE DONALD FRASER, JOURNAL ENTRY, 15 SEPTEMBER 1916

Like most inventions, the tank has complex and disputed origins. The idea of an armoured motor vehicle capable of operating across difficult terrain was developed by imaginative fiction writers and military officers early in the 20th century. The development of tractors with caterpillar tracks for agricultural use also drew interest from armies seeking vehicles to pull heavy artillery.

After the outbreak of World War I several officers, including Colonel Jean Baptiste Estienne in France and Colonel Ernest Swinton in Britain, understood the potential value of an all-terrain armoured vehicle on the Western Front. By early 1915, the idea had attracted the support of some powerful figures, including the British First Lord of the Admiralty, Winston Churchill, who headed a Landships Committee set up in February 1915. The stalemate on the Western Front added urgency to the quest for a vehicle that could forge a path through barbed wire and possibly cross enemy trenches.

Development proceeded haltingly, with many setbacks, but by 1916 both Britain and France had arrived at

prototypes of a tracked armoured vehicle. The British used the code name "tank" to disguise the nature of the experimental machines they were developing.

The first tanks to arrive at the front were British Mk Is, delivered to the Somme in late August 1916. British commander-in-chief General Douglas Haig was keen to use them

British Whippet tank
Officially designated the Medium Mk A, the Whippet was armed with four Hotchkiss machine-guns, providing all-round fire from a fixed turret. It was powered by two engines originally designed for buses, achieving a speed of 13 kph (8 mph).

immediately, believing they might "add very greatly to the prospect of success" in an offensive he had planned at Flers-Courcelette on 15 September. Haig rejected the argument that he should wait until more tanks were available and then launch them in a mass surprise attack.

Tanks in battle

Forty-nine tanks were available at Flers-Courcelette. The general handling the offensive, Henry Rawlinson, was dubious about the value of the new machines and scattered them among his infantry. Mechanical failures combined with inexperienced crews contributed to an inauspicious debut. Only 32 of the tanks managed to reach their start line, 25 actually entered combat, and nine penetrated German positions, aiding in

5,500 The approximate number of tanks manufactured by Britain and France during World War I.

20 The total number of tanks manufactured by Germany during World War I.

the capture of Flers village. However, Haig was enthused by their negative impact on German morale and requested delivery of a thousand tanks of improved design.

The Germans were in fact not greatly impressed by tanks and devoted very limited resources to producing a

version of their own. Only a handful of German A7V tanks eventually entered service in 1918. Enormous vehicles with a crew of 18, they had almost no impact on the war.

Further developments

From 1917 onwards, tanks became a standard feature of British and French operations. The British developed the Mk IV and Mk V, versions of the original Mk I heavy tank that had been somewhat improved in armour, speed, and reliability. The first French models to enter service, the Schneider CA1 and its rival, the Saint-Chamond, were also heavy tanks, mounting 75 mm armament.

The French largely sidelined these models in 1918 and adopted the Renault FT, a light tank that marked a leap forward in design, since it had a rotating gun turret. Relatively cheap and easy to produce, the FT was manufactured in larger quantities than any other World War I tank and was used in massed formations.

More than 3,500 Renault FTs were produced in the course of the war, for the American army as well as the French. The British also built a lighter tank, the Whippet, that gave good service in 1918, racing along at over 13 kph (8 mph).

Tank crews had, on the whole, a tough experience of war. The inside of a tank was always uncomfortably

ANTI-TANK WARFARE

Barrel

Trigger

Bipod

Artillery was effective against tanks, although achieving a direct hit was a challenge. Infantry attacked tanks with grenades and mortars, but found rifle fire largely ineffective. The Germans introduced K bullets, armour-piercing ammunition fired from a standard Mauser rifle, but these rounds were countered by improved tank armour. In 1918, the first purpose-built anti-tank rifle, the Mauser T-Gewehr, was deployed. Firing a 13 mm round, it was derived from big-game hunters' "elephant guns". Its recoil could break the collarbone of the soldier firing it.

> "The **tanks appeared** not one at a time but in **whole lines** kilometres in length!"

HEINZ GUDERIAN, GERMAN OFFICER, DESCRIBING THE BATTLE OF CAMBRAI, 20 NOVEMBER 1917

hot and filled with engine fumes. The machine shook and the noise inside was deafening. Visibility was restricted and so was communication with the outside world. There were no radios in fighting tanks – the vehicles carried pigeons into battle for sending messages to the rear. The heavy tanks were so slow they sometimes had difficulty keeping pace with the troops advancing on foot.

Forging forwards

Tanks were in no sense wonder weapons that could win the war on their own, but they did play a part in ending the stalemate of trench warfare. They provided invaluable assistance to the infantry, clearing a path through layers of barbed wire and attacking strongpoints such as machine-gun posts. Deep mud, as at

British tank crew helmet and mask
When bullets struck a tank's armour, shards of metal sometimes flew off the inside of the hull, causing severe wounds. British tank crews were issued with helmets and face masks to protect against this hazard.

Third Ypres in autumn 1917, stopped the tanks, but they usually succeeded in forging a path across cratered ground and over trenches.

The British tank offensive, which briefly broke through at Cambrai in November 1917, demonstrated how effective tanks could be when used in conjunction with infantry and artillery. But it also showed that World War I tanks were not fast enough for the kind of mobile warfare that would occur in World War II.

Leather skull cap

Leather visor

Chainmail mouthpiece

Mk IV tank at Cambrai
A British Mk IV tank is manoeuvred over a trench at Cambrai in November 1917. Slow-moving and prone to mechanical failure, the armoured vehicles could only be effective as part of a combined arms operation with infantry and artillery.

TIMELINE

- **November 1904** American inventor Benjamin Holt demonstrates a working tracked tractor.
- **August 1914** French Colonel Jean Baptiste Estienne calls for the development of an all-terrain vehicle armed with a 75mm gun.
- **February 1915** The British government establishes the Landships Committee to investigate production of an armoured vehicle.

A CATERPILLAR TRACTOR

- **May 1915** In France, arms manufacturer Schneider begins development of an armoured vehicle based on a Holt tractor.
- **January 1916** Demonstration of the British Mk I tank, then known as Big Willie.
- **February 1916** The French army orders production of 400 Schneider CA1 tanks.
- **15 September 1916** Tanks are sent into combat for the first time by the British at Flers-Courcelette during the Somme Offensive.
- **16 April 1917** The French deploy Schneider CA1 tanks during the Nivelle Offensive.
- **May 1917** The British Mk IV heavy tank goes into production.
- **27 July 1917** The British Tank Corps is formed.
- **20 November 1917** British Mk IV tanks lead a shortlived breakthrough at Cambrai.
- **December 1917** The first British Whippet medium tanks are delivered to the Tank Corps.
- **21 March 1918** Germany's only operational World War I tank, the A7V, goes into combat.
- **24 April 1918** The first tank-on-tank combat occurs at Villers-Bretonneux, near Amiens.
- **31 May 1918** The French Renault FT light tank enters combat at the Fôret de Retz.
- **8 August 1918** The British Army employs about 600 tanks in the Amiens offensive.
- **12 September 1918** American tank units enter combat at the Battle of St Mihiel; they use French-supplied Renault FTs.
- **November 1918** The Anglo-American Mk VIII Liberty tank is about to enter service when the war ends.

FRENCH RENAULT FT LIGHT TANK

The **Bolshevik Revolution**

By autumn 1917, the Russian war effort had largely disintegrated. The revolutionary Bolshevik Party – soon to be renamed the Communist Party – seized power in Russia in November and immediately pursued an armistice with the Central Powers.

Russia's Provisional Government, led by Alexander Kerensky, was in a perilous situation in September 1917. The country was in a state of upheaval, with strikes in factories, peasants seizing land, and widespread looting. The newly appointed commander-in-chief of the Russian army, General Lavr Kornilov, demanded authorization to restore discipline by a series of tough measures, including the suppression of soldiers' committees and the disbanding of rebellious regiments. Kerensky agreed with the need to restore order but feared that Kornilov intended to seize power and institute military rule.

On 9 September, Kerensky accused Kornilov of planning a coup and dismissed him from his post. Kornilov responded by rebelling against the government. Fearing an advance on the capital by Kornilov's troops, the Petrograd soviet joined Kerensky in organizing a defence of the capital. Bolshevik leaders imprisoned after the July Days, including Leon Trotsky, were released and arms were distributed to Petrograd factory workers, who formed Red Guard militias alongside pro-revolutionary soldiers and sailors. Kornilov was quickly arrested and the affair fizzled out, but the Red Guards kept their guns.

In the wake of the Kornilov affair, Trotsky was elected chairman of the Petrograd soviet, which was now dominated by the Bolsheviks. Lenin remained in hiding in Finland, to which he had fled after the July Days, but from there urged the overthrow of the Provisional Government. Meanwhile, Kerensky attempted to send the soldiers of the Petrograd garrison to the front. The soldiers mutinied.

The Bolsheviks seize power

With the Provisional Government defenceless, Lenin returned to Petrograd. A Military Revolutionary Committee dominated by Trotsky set about seizing power. On 6 November,

Red Guard armband
Members of the Red Guard paramilitary units set up during the revolution wore red armbands. They fought in the early part of the Russian Civil War, but were eventually replaced by the Red Army.

key points in the city, including the railway station, telephone exchange, and post office were taken over by revolutionary soldiers and Red Guards.

The Winter Palace, the seat of the Provisional Government, was defended by just a unit of female soldiers and Cossack cavalry. On the night of 7 November, the cruiser *Aurora*, in the hands of its sailors, fired a blank round across the Neva river to signal an attack on the Winter Palace. There was no resistance. Kerensky had already slipped out of the building and fled.

Barrel |

Mobile firepower
A machine-gun is mounted on a horse-drawn carriage for deployment on the streets of Petrograd by the Bolsheviks during the Russian Revolution. In the event, very little fighting took place in the capital.

Lenin proclaimed a Bolshevik government of People's Commissars, with himself as Chairman and Trotsky as Commissar for Foreign Affairs. On 8 November, addressing the All-Russian Congress of Soviets in Petrograd, he issued an appeal for an immediate end to the war. He called on the combatant powers to negotiate a peace "without annexations or indemnities". He also appealed to the working classes in Germany, Britain, and France to rise in revolution against their "imperialist governments".

Minority rule

Lenin's revolutionary government held sway in a limited area, with Petrograd and Moscow key bases. The Bolsheviks were in a minority even in the Congress of Soviets, and when a democratically elected Constituent Assembly met in January 1918 just 175 of its 703 deputies were

Bolsheviks. Lenin closed it down after a day. The installation of a Russian government committed to ending the war was a disaster for the Allies. They not only lost their eastern ally but were also deeply embarrassed by the Bolsheviks' revelation of "secret treaties", found in Russian archives,

showing the territorial gains that the Allies had hoped to achieve from the war. Germany, in contrast, was keen to respond to Russian peace feelers. The Central Powers agreed an armistice with the Bolsheviks on 16 December, ending the fighting on Germany's Eastern Front.

Women's Battalion of Death

Female volunteers formed combat units of the Russian army during 1917, adopting names such as "Battalion of Death" or "Shock Battalion". Several hundred of these women were assigned to defend the Winter Palace against the Bolsheviks.

AFTER »

The Bolshevik Revolution marked the beginning of a traumatic period in Russian history.

FROM WORLD WAR TO CIVIL WAR
Trotsky was entrusted with negotiating the **peace agreement** with the Central Powers. The punitive treaty dictated by Germany at **Brest-Litovsk 276–77** » in March 1918 deprived Russia of a large part of its territory.

Immediately after the revolution, **civil war** broke out between the pro-Bolshevik Red and the anti-Bolshevik White armies in Russia, with **Allied forces intervening 300–301** » on the side of the Whites.

ANTI-BOLSHEVISM POSTER

Box seat

Footboard

Shaft

Mounting step

Wooden wheel

" The **government** considers it the **greatest** of **crimes against humanity** to continue this war."

BOLSHEVIK DECREE ON PEACE, 8 NOVEMBER 1917

German colonial troops
A field gun is manned by European and African soldiers of the East African Schutztruppe. Black troops, known as Askaris, formed the majority of fighting men on both sides.

« **BEFORE**

The Allies occupied all of Germany's African colonies in the war, but met stiff resistance in German East Africa.

CROSS-BORDER RAIDS
German colonial forces under Lieutenant Colonel Paul von Lettow-Vorbeck launched cross-border raids into British colonies from German East Africa in September 1914. In November, a division from British India was defeated by Lettow-Vorbeck's forces at **Tanga** (in modern-day Tanzania) **« 76–77**.

REINFORCEMENTS ON BOTH SIDES
After the **conquest of German South West Africa** (Namibia) in July 1915, many South African troops joined the East African campaign. Meanwhile, sailors from the German cruiser SMS *Königsberg*, destroyed by the Royal Navy in East Africa's **Rufiji delta « 76–77**, escaped capture to join Lettow-Vorbeck's forces.

ASKARI CAP

Guerrilla War in East Africa

The guerilla campaign mounted by German colonial troops in East Africa tied down substantial Allied forces at very little cost to Germany. Although just a sideshow in the context of the wider war, it was a catastrophe for the local African population.

German East Africa – mainland Tanzania, Rwanda, and Burundi – had an area of around 1 million sq km (386,000 sq miles). In 1914, its European population numbered barely 5,000. German rule was maintained by a defence force, the Schutztruppe, consisting of about 2,500 Askaris (black African troops) under the command of a few German officers. The colony was bordered by British, Belgian, and Portuguese colonies with an equally sparse white population.

When war broke out in Europe in 1914, the commander-in-chief of the Schutztruppe, Lieutenant-Colonel Paul von Lettow-Vorbeck, saw it as his duty to contribute to the wider German war

effort by engaging Germany's enemies wherever and whenever possible. This was to be the rationale for a campaign

> **40,000** **The number of black African porters who died of hardship and disease in British service during the East African campaign.**

that began in September 1914 and continued throughout the war

In January 1915, Lettow-Vorbeck, pursuing this policy of aggression, had attacked the British Indian garrison at Jassin on the border between German East Africa and British East Africa, forcing the soldiers to surrender. This

had proved a hollow victory, however, since Lettow-Vorbeck lost several key officers in the attack and used up a large quantity of ammunition, which was in short supply. He was obliged to change his tactics, carrying out repeated cross-border raids, ambushing trains and destroying bridges, but avoiding battle. The Uganda railway, a key transport link in British East Africa, was a particularly vulnerable target.

The indomitable Schutztruppe
In 1916, the British embarked upon a major campaign to occupy German East Africa and defeat the Schutztruppe once and for all. South African General Jan Smuts was sent to lead the

"Our track is **marked** by **death, plundering,** and **evacuated villages."**

DR LUDWIG DEPPE, A MEDICAL OFFICER IN EAST AFRICA, DESCRIBING THE GERMAN SCHUTZTRUPPE OFFENSIVE

campaign, taking a substantial body of South African mounted troops. Along with the predominantly black soldiers of the King's African Rifles and British Indian troops, this gave Smuts a force of around 25,000 men.

Meanwhile, Lettow-Vorbeck had built up his Schutztruppe to around 15,000 combat troops, including several thousand Germans from the settler population and sailors from the abandoned cruiser SMS *Königsberg*, destroyed by the Royal Navy in the Rufiji delta the previous year.

Attack and counterattack

From March 1916, Smuts dispatched columns into German East Africa, while attacks were also mounted by the Belgians across the border from the Congo. Lettow-Vorbeck was unable to prevent Smuts taking the colony's two railways and occupying the administrative capital, Dar es Salaam, by September. The British success was, however largely illusory. Mounting ambushes and counterattacks, Lettow-Vorbeck inflicted losses on Smuts's forces in a number of small-scale encounters in which the Schutztruppe achieved local superiority.

The South Africans' dependence on horses proved disastrous, since most of the animals died of disease carried by the tsetse fly. The South African troops suffered from malaria and dysentery, and many units were soon reduced to a fraction of their original strength.

In January 1917, Smuts left East Africa claiming a victory, but Lettow-Vorbeck had withdrawn his forces south to the Rufiji river region and was in no sense beaten.

Overcoming obstacles

In 1917, the British increased the proportion of black troops deployed in East Africa, in the belief that they would be best able to tolerate the climate and withstand disease. A Nigerian brigade was sent from West Africa and more soldiers were recruited locally into the King's African Rifles. The British also sought to benefit from improved technology, bringing in a number of reconnaissance aircraft and making use of radio. With horses ruled out by the prevalence of tsetse fly, motor trucks were imported for transport, though the shortage of roads of even the most basic kind limited their effectiveness.

Local conditions forced both sides in East Africa to campaign in a similar fashion. The Schutztruppe and their opponents operated in self-sufficient columns on foot, depending on thousands of forcibly recruited African porters to carry their supplies.

Lettow-Vorbeck's soldiers resupplied themselves by capturing British equipment and living off the land. Like locusts, their passage through a fertile zone left a food shortage in its wake. Troops on both sides would systematically destroy crops to deny them to the enemy, condemning the local villagers to starvation.

Pursuit through Africa

Despite the difficulty of simply surviving as fugitive forces in a largely hostile environment, Lettow-Vorbeck's columns continued to seize the initiative. From February to October 1917, a column of about 500 Schutztruppe, initially led by Captain Max Wintgens and then by Captain Heinrich Naumann, forged their way northwards across East Africa from Lake Nyasa to Mount Kilimanjaro. Pursued by thousands of British and Belgian troops, it was eventually forced to surrender.

Even when harried by superior forces, Lettow-Vorbeck sought any

Officer's sword

This sword belonged to a German Schutztruppe officer in World War I. Swords were not generally worn on active service except by cavalry, but they retained their ceremonial function.

Sharkskin grip

Folded guard

opportunity to inflict a defeat. In October 1917, the new British commander-in-chief, South African General Jacob van Deventer, sent Nigerian troops to attack the Schutztruppe at Mahiwa in the south of German East Africa. Poorly led, they were outmanoeuvred and encircled. A British relief attempt failed, but the Nigerians eventually escaped through a gap in the German lines. Mahiwa was a humiliating defeat for the British, although the Schutztruppe could ill afford the casualties it also suffered.

Reports of Lettow-Vorbeck's exploits aroused great enthusiasm in Germany. In November 1917, an ambitious

> **2,500** The number of British casualties, out of a force of 5,000, at the Battle of Mahiwa in October 1917. German casualties numbered about 500, a third of the original German force.

attempt was made to supply the Schutztruppe with ammunition by flying Zeppelin airship *L-59* 6,500 km (4,000 miles) from Bulgaria to East Africa. The airship reached Sudan before the mission was called off because of a false report that Lettow-Vorbeck had been defeated.

In fact, with a force that had dwindled to 2,000 men, Lettow-Vorbeck continued to evade capture through the last year of the war. After a long trek through the Portuguese colony of Mozambique, where he found easy targets for raiding, he led his men back into German East Africa in September 1918. Lettow-Vorbeck surrendered, still undefeated, on 25 November after belatedly receiving news of the armistice.

PAUL VON LETTOW-VORBECK

Before World War I, German officer Paul von Lettow-Vorbeck saw action in colonial wars in China and German South West Africa (Namibia). He was appointed commander of the defence force in German East Africa in April 1914. After defeating British Indian troops at Tanga in November, he sustained a guerrilla campaign undefeated for four years. A strict disciplinarian, he shared the hardship of his troops and won their loyalty. He was hero-worshipped in Germany and admired even by his enemies as a skilful if ruthless opponent. After his return to Germany at the end of the war, he was dismissed from the army for involvement in a failed coup in 1920.

AFTER »

In the peace settlement at the end of the war, Germany lost its entire colonial empire, including all of its African possessions.

DIVIDING GERMAN EAST AFRICA

After the war, Britain and Belgium divided **German East Africa** between them. Their colonial rule was legally sanctioned by the grant of mandates from the League of Nations in 1922. The bulk of the former German colony became British-ruled Tanganyika, while the Belgians took over Rwanda and Burundi.

ASKARI MONUMENT, NEAR HAMBURG

WEST AND SOUTH WEST AFRICA

The German colonies of **Togoland** (now Togo) and **Kamerun** were divided between Britain and France under the mandate system. The mandate to rule **German South-West Africa** (Namibia) was given to South Africa. Most of these countries became independent in the 1950s and 60s. Namibia remained under South African control until 1990.

« BEFORE

The shape of the naval war in the Mediterranean slowly became clear once Italy and Turkey decided to become combatants.

AREAS OF RESPONSIBILITY

Britain and France agreed before the war that the **French navy** would take responsibility for the **Mediterranean**, while Britain's **Royal Navy** concentrated on the **English Channel and North Sea**. **Italy's** decision to **enter the war « 106–07** on the Allied side in 1915 was a relief for the Allied navies.

TURKISH CRUISER MIDILLI

THE NAVIES OF THE CENTRAL POWERS

In August 1914, the only two German warships in the Mediterranean, SMS *Goeben* and *Breslau*, escaped pursuit by entering Turkish waters, an incident that contributed to **Turkey entering the war « 74–75** as an ally of the **Central Powers**. *Goeben* and *Breslau* became part of the Turkish navy. Austria-Hungary had a navy based at ports in the **Adriatic**.

Naval War in the Mediterranean

Naval control of the Mediterranean was vital to Allied land operations in the area and to maintaining communications with the British and French overseas empires. Despite their overwhelming naval superiority, the Allies had a tough fight to keep their sea lanes open.

From the start of the war, the surface warships of the Central Powers could not challenge Allied naval supremacy in the Mediterranean. Operating from British bases in Malta, Gibraltar, and Alexandria in Egypt, and from ports in southern France and French Algeria, the Allied navies forced Austria-Hungary to confine its fleet to the Adriatic.

Intervention in Greece

Allied naval power could also exert considerable influence in the countries around the Mediterranean, as demonstrated in Greece. Although Greece was officially neutral, the Greek people were divided, some supporting the pro-Allied politician Eleftherios Venizelos, others the pro-German king, Constantine I. In October 1915, Venizelos had invited Allied troops to land at Salonika in northern Greece, in order that they might proceed to Serbia to assist it in fighting the Central Powers. This move by Venizelos provoked a confrontation between Venizelists and royalists in Greece.

Allied naval power was used to intervene in the crisis. During 1916 and 1917, mostly French warships blockaded Greek ports, threatened to bombard cities, and even fired upon the royal palace. These actions eventually drove the king to abdicate and brought Greece into the war on the Allied side in June 1917.

The U-boat menace

If Allied naval supremacy could not be challenged on the surface of the sea, it was a different story underwater. Early in the war the Austro-Hungarian navy made effective use of its submarines against Allied warships that were maintaining a blockade of the Adriatic. The French battleship *Jean Bart*, flagship of Admiral Augustin Boué de Lapeyrère, French commander in the

Torpedo boat commander
Italy's most celebrated naval hero of World War I was Luigi Rizzo. Commanding a motor torpedo boat, Rizzo sank the Austro-Hungarian dreadnought SMS *Szent István* on 10 June 1918.

Mediterranean, was badly damaged by a torpedo in December 1914. Another Austro-Hungarian U-boat sank the French armoured cruiser *Léon Gambetta*, with heavy loss of life, in April 1915.

German U-boats began arriving in the Mediterranean in response to the Allied landings on Turkey's Gallipoli Peninsula in the spring of 1915. Based at Constantinople and in the Adriatic, they not only sank Allied warships but also merchant shipping. Connecting the Atlantic to the Suez Canal, the Mediterranean was a major trade route offering a multiplicity of targets for

Allied warships in Malta
Ships of the British and French Mediterranean fleets lie at anchor in the Grand Harbour in Malta in 1916. A British territory, Malta was a vital link in the Allied chain of naval bases.

Italian attack
The *Fàa di Bruno*, an armoured barge fitted with two heavy guns, was used for land bombardment in support of ground troops. Here, it is assisted by an Italian seaplane.

U-boats. Sinkings for the Allies reached crisis level in 1916, when more than 400 merchant ships went down.

The Otranto barrage
In an attempt to block U-boat operations from Adriatic ports, the Allies created the Otranto barrage between the Italian coast at Brindisi and the island of Corfu. This consisted of a line of trawlers with "indicator nets" designed to detect submarines. If a U-boat was discovered, the trawlers would radio warships for support. In practice, U-boats slipped through the barrage with ease. It did, however, give the Austro-Hungarian navy a chance to mount hit-and-run raids on the trawlers. One raid, headed by Captain Miklos Horthy, led to a naval battle in May 1917 when Allied warships damaged Horthy's cruiser SMS *Novara*.

Losses of merchant ships to German U-boats in the Mediterranean peaked at 1.5 million tons in 1917, falling to half that level by 1918. The belated introduction of escorted convoys from spring 1917 helped reduce Allied losses, but a shortage of escort vessels remained a problem. Britain's ally Japan responded to an urgent request for assistance by sending 14 destroyers to the Mediterranean for convoy escort duties. The use of aircraft on anti-submarine patrols and the towing of manned kite balloons (blimps) behind convoys for aerial observation also inhibited U-boat operations.

The Allies eventually got their revenge for the embarrassment caused to them when the two German warships SMS *Goeben* and *Breslau* evaded pursuit at the start of the war by sailing into Turkish waters. Given to Turkey by Germany, and renamed *Yavuz Sultan Selim* and *Midilli*, the two ships sailed from Constantinople into the Aegean Sea in January 1918, attacking British destroyers and monitors off the island of Imbros.

Attempting to return to base, however, they ran into a minefield. *Midilli* was sunk and *Yavuz Sultan Selim* disabled.

Skirmishes in the Adriatic
The Italian and Austro-Hungarian navies fought around the shores of the Adriatic. The Austro-Hungarian fleet bombarded the Italian coast in 1915, causing heavy civilian casualties at the port of Ancona. The Italians raided the Austro-Hungarian naval bases at Trieste, Cattaro, and Pola by sea and by air. Italian patriots were elated when their small motor torpedo boats sank the Austro-Hungarian battleships *Wien* in December 1917 and *Szent Istvan* in June 1918. On 1 November 1918, an Italian "human torpedo" midget submarine penetrated Pola harbour, placed a limpet mine on the hull of the Austro-Hungarian dreadnought *Viribus Unitis*, and sank it.

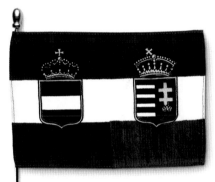

Austro-Hungarian flag
Although Austria and Hungary are now landlocked countries, in 1914 they had ports on the Adriatic coast and strong naval traditions. The Austro-Hungarian navy boasted four dreadnought battleships, as well as submarines.

"We **sped down** the **Aegean** and **encountered** the **U-boat** that **dogged** us so relentlessly."
TROOPER REGINALD C. HUGGINS, EAST RIDING OF YORKSHIRE IMPERIAL YEOMANRY

AFTER »

The armistice between Turkey and the Allies, negotiated on 30 October 1918, resulted in the Allied occupation of Constantinople.

CLEARING THE DARDANELLES
Under the **terms of the armistice 316–17 »** at the end of October, Turkey had to **clear a passage** through the heavily mined Dardanelles for Allied ships. By mid-November 1918, a **line of Allied warships** was anchored off Constantinople. The British commander in the Mediterranean, Admiral Sir John de Robeck, supervised a **military occupation** of the city in 1920.
Meanwhile, the **disintegration of Austria-Hungary 320–21 »** at the end of the war left both Austria and Hungary without access to the sea. The Austro-Hungarian ports devolved either to Italy or to Yugoslavia.

BEFORE

Germany's ally Ottoman Turkey was fighting Russia in the Caucasus and against the British in Mesopotamia (Iraq) and Palestine.

THE BRITISH THREAT

In 1917, pressure on Turkey on the **Caucasus front** was relieved by the **revolutionary upheavals in Russia**. In Mesopotamia, Britain recovered from its defeat at the **Siege of Kut ≪ 122–23** and took Baghdad in March, continuing to press northwards through the rest of the year. In **Palestine**, the Turks were threatened by the **Arab Revolt ≪ 196–97** and by a British expeditionary force advancing across the Sinai from Egypt.

CARTOON DEPICTING TURKEY VERSUS BRITAIN

From **Gaza** to **Jerusalem**

Between October and December 1917, British and Commonwealth forces, assisted by Arab irregulars, mounted a successful campaign against Turkish forces in Palestine. The Turks were forced to abandon the holy city of Jerusalem to British occupation.

In March 1917, the British Egyptian Expeditionary Force, commanded by General Archibald Murray, had advanced across the Sinai Desert and was poised to break into Palestine. Its route lay through a line from Gaza on the coast to Beersheba, 50 km (30 miles) inland, lightly held by Turkish troops and their German advisers. However, the British were finding it difficult to cope with the desert terrain. Water shortages meant offensives had to be swiftly concluded before portable supplies ran out.

On 26 March, British troops succeeded in penetrating Gaza in a surprise assault but were then withdrawn because of fear of a Turkish counterattack. A second British attack

Camel ambulance
Medical orderlies of an Australian field ambulance prepare to load a wounded soldier on to a camel's back. Camels were often the most practical transport in desert terrain.

on Gaza on 17 April faced much stronger resistance and was repelled. Murray was relieved of command and replaced by General Edmund Allenby.

The new commander was given substantial reinforcements so he could satisfy British Prime Minister David Lloyd George's demand to take Jerusalem by Christmas. The expanded forces were reorganized and Arab forces, led by Emir Feisal and Colonel T.E. Lawrence, were supplied with money and equipment.

The opposing side was also preparing for a fight, but the Germans and Turks had problems at command level. General Erich von Falkenhayn, former German Chief of the General Staff, had been sent to Turkey to head the German-Turkish Yildirim ("Thunderbolt") Army, originally

> "They were an **awe-inspiring sight,** galloping through the **red haze...** the dying **sun glinting** on bayonet points."

AUSTRALIAN TROOPER ION IDRIESS, DESCRIBING THE CAVALRY CHARGE AT BEERSHEBA

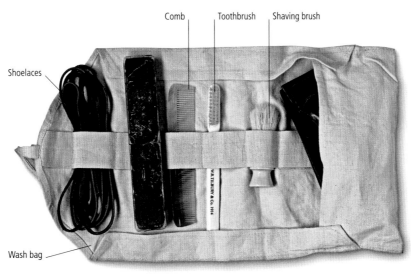

Comb Toothbrush Shaving brush

Shoelaces

Wash bag

British wash kit
This standard kit was carried by British soldiers in World War I. Care for basic hygiene on the Palestine front was difficult because of the lack of water, but it was also essential for survival.

AFTER

By the end of 1917, Ottoman Turkey was in a perilous situation, dependent for survival, both militarily and economically, on aid from Germany.

THREE-PRONGED ATTACK
The collapse of Russia after the **Bolshevik Revolution ‹‹ 252–53** allowed Turkish forces to advance at will on the Caucasus front, but this **could not disguise their weakness** elsewhere. Through 1918, delayed and distracted by crucial battles on the Western Front, the **British prepared a** three-pronged offensive, **to attack Turkey** from Palestine and Syria, from northern Mesopotamia, and through Bulgaria from their base at Salonika in northern Greece.

ARMISTICE WITH TURKEY
The **defeat of German and Turkish forces in Palestine** in September 1918 and the fall of Damascus and Beirut to the Allies in early October sufficed to persuade Turkey to **negotiate an armistice 316–17 ››**. The fighting officially stopped on 30 October.

intended to intervene in Mesopotamia. The British build-up opposite the Gaza–Beersheba line led Falkenhayn to take his troops to Palestine instead, where he assumed overall command of German and Turkish forces. Yet his arrogance offended the Turks, and General Mustafa Kemal, commander of the Turkish Seventh Army at Gaza, left on sick leave rather than serve under him.

Meanwhile, Allenby planned his offensive with care. He devised an intelligent deception operation to make the enemy believe he intended to renew the attack on Gaza, while

670 The number of years Jerusalem had been under continuous Muslim rule before the British occupation of the city in 1917.

Yeomanry Mounted Division
James Beadle's painting depicts the British Yeomanry Mounted Division charging Turkish positions at El Mughar Ridge in November 1917. Cavalry played a major role in the Palestine campaign.

actually sending the bulk of his forces to attack Beersheba at the other end of the Turkish line. While Gaza was subjected to a six-day artillery bombardment, British troops moved to new positions 40 km (25 miles) distant. A contingent of the Royal Flying Corps flew combat patrols to block the Germans from carrying out aerial reconnaissance over British lines.

The British advance
The offensive was launched on the morning of 31 October. While infantry struggled forward, cutting a path through barbed wire, Australian and New Zealand cavalry executed a daring flanking movement to approach the Turkish defences from the north and east. The speed and unexpectedness of the cavalry charge by the Australian Fourth Light Horse Brigade carried them through Turkish trench lines and into Beersheba by nightfall. The whole Turkish line quickly became indefensible. By 6 November, Gaza was also in British hands.

With Feisal and Lawrence's Arab forces operating in the desert on his right flank, Allenby pressed forward determinedly. The Turkish Seventh and Eighth armies retreated in front of him to a new defensive line southwest of Jerusalem. These formations arrived much depleted by troops deserting or surrendering to the British.

Capturing Jerusalem
From 10 November, fighting resumed in earnest. After a British cavalry charge helped infantry capture fortified villages at El Mughar Ridge, Junction Station was taken, cutting Turkish rail links with Jerusalem. The Turkish Eighth Army withdrew northwards, leaving the Seventh Army to defend the holy city. The advance of British troops was then slowed by the onset of winter rains. Falkenhayn's Yildirim Army came into action in late

November, delivering a dangerous counterattack against a position lightly held by British cavalry. It soon proved, however, to be no more than a delaying action.

On the night of 6–7 December, a British surprise attack in heavy rain broke through the Turkish defences on the outskirts of Jerusalem. Commanders on both sides accepted there would be no fighting in the city itself, and Turkish troops were allowed to withdraw to the north. The British took possession of Jerusalem on 11 December, fulfilling Lloyd

George's wish for the city to be in British hands by Christmas. The capture of Jerusalem was a boost to British morale and a severe blow to Turkish prestige. Militarily, however, it was the start of a long pause in British offensive operations, which would not resume until September 1918.

Allenby enters Jerusalem
General Allenby strides through Jerusalem's Jaffa Gate on 11 December 1917. Although a cavalry officer, Allenby chose to enter the conquered holy city on foot as a mark of respect.

Recording the War

"I am **a messenger** who will **bring back word** from **the men...** It will have a **bitter truth...**"

BRITISH OFFICIAL WAR ARTIST PAUL NASH, IN A LETTER DATED 13 NOVEMBER 1917

The efforts of hundreds of gifted and brave artists and photographers produced an impressive visual record of World War I. Some worked with official backing from government agencies, others followed a private impulse to capture their observations and experiences on the battlefield. All had at best an ambivalent relationship with the military authorities, who viewed both mediums as a potential security risk open to abuse by spies.

Military and propaganda uses were found for soldiers with artistic training, from inventing camouflage schemes to producing sketches of enemy positions for intelligence purposes, but their wider talents were at best only tolerated by armies as a trench pastime. Civilian governments, in contrast, saw art and photography as vital tools in their propaganda campaigns to drum up support for the war on the home front and publicize their cause abroad.

War photography

As the war raged on, more long-term goals emerged, with authorities in some countries consciously preparing a visual record of the conflict for future generations. Officially sponsored photography and art became the norm, eventually leading to the founding of institutions such as Britain's Imperial War Museum and the Australian War Memorial.

By 1914, technology had improved and war photography became easier. Cameras were smaller and lighter, with shutter speeds capable of capturing rapid movement. Photographers worked with a range of

equipment – both hand-held cameras and tripods, glass plates or roll film, and panoramic cameras. Most pictures were black and white, but colour shots of trench life were taken, notably by Germany's Hans Hildenbrand.

In 1914, Germany was the world's technical leader in photography and had the best grasp of its propaganda value. Some 50 photographers were embedded with its forces, compared to 35 with the French. The British military authorities lagged behind. It was not until spring

1916 that a British photographer was allowed on to the Western Front. Eventually, however, some of the finest images were made by Britain's Ernest Brooks and John Brooke, Canada's William Rider-Rider, and Australia's Frank Hurley.

Lost in print

Inevitably, given the danger and technical difficulty involved, few photographs were taken in the thick of action. When they were, the results

were mostly disappointing – indistinct images of small figures advancing across featureless ground. To meet the demand for exciting combat shots, photographers resorted to fakery, either staging action for the camera or retouching photographs in the studio.

Illustrated newspapers and magazines were the main market for war pictures. Image quality was poor, and detail all but lost in reproduction. One reason for the prevalence of soldiers silhouetted against the sky in World War I photographs is that such pictures showed up well even when they were badly printed.

Although the aim was to promote the war effort, and some of those published were fatuously cheerful, photographers often succeeded in conveying the tough conditions under which troops were fighting, hinting at their sufferings. Some subjects were, however, only covered by soldiers taking amateur images with their own box cameras. The fraternization between enemy

Lens

Lens

Stereoscopic camera and glass slide
Some World War I photographers used twin-lensed stereoscopic cameras that enabled them to capture three-dimensional images. The glass slides had to be seen through a special viewer.

A war artist's tools

This paintbox and set of brushes was used by British artist John Nash during World War I. Nash served for a year as a soldier on the Western Front before being appointed an official war artist in January 1918, a move that probably saved his life.

Brush case

Mixing palette

Paintbrush

troops during the Christmas truce in 1914, for example, was recorded in this way, and so was the frequent spectacle of hideously mutilated corpses – which was censored from the official record.

Artistic expression

The role of the war artist in World War I was complex and subtle. The painting of heroic battle scenes and vignettes of military life was an established genre and during the war painters and illustrators represented the drama of cavalry charges and close-quarters infantry combat. Although demand for this kind of work never ceased, there was an uncomfortable awareness that it did not represent the reality of the industrialized warfare to which soldiers at the front were being subjected.

From the outset of the war many artists found themselves faced with the reality of combat, serving either as conscripts or volunteers in their national armies. They included members of innovative modernist groups – Cubists, Futurists, Vorticists, Expressionists – who had been challenging traditional forms of representation in the pre-war period. Their

responses to the experience of the conflict were varied and individualistic. French Cubist Fernand Léger, for example, found inspiration in the shapes of gun barrels, whereas German Expressionist Otto Dix ironically entitled a 1915 painting of himself in uniform, *Self-Portrait as a Target*.

In 1916, when two serving British soldiers, C.R.W. Nevinson and Eric Kennington, exhibited determinedly unheroic paintings based on their own experiences at the front, they caused a considerable sensation in Britain. In the same year, the French government mounted an exhibition of soldiers' paintings in Paris.

Official sponsorship of war artists, practised in all countries, reached the scale of a major cultural project in Britain from 1916. Established artists such as the American John Singer Sargent and Irish painter William Orpen were sent to the front to record the war, while young painters already serving in the army were plucked from the trenches and adopted as official artists. Friction between

> **40,000** The number of photographs taken by the official British, Australian, and Canadian war photographers during World War I.

individual artistic goals and official requirements was never entirely absent. Nonetheless, artists were allowed to present their own views of the war, however grim, in their own style, however radical. Artists receiving official commissions included modernists such as Percy Wyndham Lewis, leader of the Vorticist movement, as well as traditionalists like Sargent. Many war painters continued to produce commemorative works long after the war's end.

Motion pictures

As well as painting and photography, the relatively new medium of motion pictures was applied to recording the war. All combatant countries produced newsreels for public exhibition in cinemas. Probably the most ambitious project was the British documentary *The Battle of the Somme*. Shot by Geoffrey Malins and John McDowell, it included a considerable amount of authentic footage shot during the 1916 Somme Offensive and is considered to be the first full-length documentary film. America's entry into the conflict gave a substantial boost to the task of recording of the war on moving film, with cameramen from the US Signal Corps shooting thousands of reels on their hand-cranked cameras. Although they include a large proportion of re-enactment in action sequences, these black-and-white films remain a valuable testimony.

Fallen men

First exhibited in May 1918, British war artist William Orpen's *Dead Germans in a Trench* is an unflinching depiction of the horrors of war. If the painting had shown fallen Allied soldiers, Orpen would not have been allowed to exhibit such a picture.

Glass slide

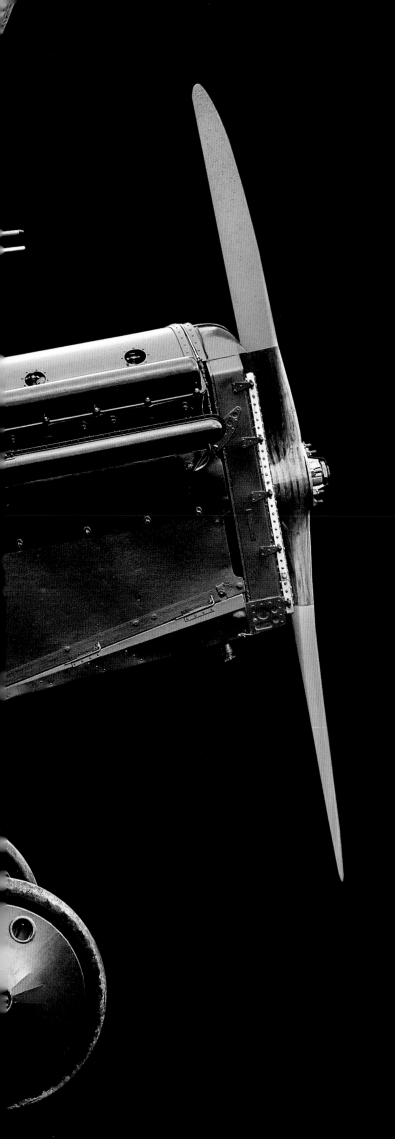

6

VICTORY
AND DEFEAT
1918

In spring 1918, Germany attempted to win
the war with a series of offensives on the
Western Front. But large numbers of newly
arrived American troops helped defeat the
German armies, and Germany was forced to
sign an armistice before the year's end.

VICTORY AND DEFEAT

Celebrations in Paris on Armistice Day, 11 November 1918, express relief at the ending of the war and satisfaction in victory. Most people hope it will be "a war to end wars".

Germany's defeat against the Allies is depicted in this French poster. By November 1918, the countries at war with Germany include China, Brazil, Siam (now Thailand), and Cuba.

Strategic bombing of enemy cities is a significant part of military strategy on both sides by 1918. The Italian Caproni Ca4 was one of the largest bomber aircraft used in the war.

EUROPE

The fall of the Kaiser and the declaration of a German republic in November 1918 is accompanied by street battles in Berlin. The new government shoulders responsibility for the Armistice.

The defeat of Bulgaria in September 1918 leaves Austria-Hungary and Germany open to invasion by Allied forces from the Balkans.

B y early 1918, Germany had won the war on its Eastern Front. Russia had to sign the Treaty of Brest Litovsk — a ruthlessly punitive treaty that opened the way for German domination and exploitation of Central and Eastern Europe. Transferring troops from the Eastern to the Western Front, the Germans gambled on a massive offensive to win the war before newly arrived US troops were committed to combat. Launched on 21 March, the Michael Offensive, part of a wider Spring Offensive, achieved a breakthrough on the Somme front and was a severe shock to the Allies.

The offensive did not, however, achieve its larger objectives. The Allies tightened the coordination between their armies and continued to fight. A series of German follow-up offensives in Flanders and at the Aisne river achieved further breakthroughs, but by June the German army was running out of steam.

The Allies intervene in the Russian Civil War from 1918, initially in the hope of reviving Russia's war effort. Here, Allied troops supporting White anti-Bolshevik troops march through Vladivostok, a port on Russia's Pacific coast.

US troops achieve a victory at the St Mihiel Salient in September 1918. The 2 million US servicemen sent to Europe play an essential role in the defeat of the Central Powers.

An Australian propaganda poster shows Germany as a grasping bloodthirsty beast with global ambitions. Such simplistic and exaggerated views of the German enemy fell out of favour in Allied countries after the war ended.

CANADA

UNITED STATES OF AMERICA

MEXICO

CHINA

JAPANESE EMPIRE

FRENCH INDOCHINA

PHILIPPINE ISLANDS

BRITISH NORTH BORNEO

BRUNEI

SARAWAK

MALAYA

DUTCH EAST INDIES

PORTUGUESE TIMOR

AUSTRALIA

NEW ZEALAND

GUAM

GERMAN PACIFIC TERRITORIES

Mariana Islands

Marshall Islands

Caroline Islands

Bismarck Archipelago

Nauru

KAISER WILHELMSLAND

PAPUA

Solomon Islands

Gilbert Islands

Ellice Islands

New Hebrides

New Caledonia

Fiji

Tonga

German Samoa (Western)

Cook Islands

Hawaiian Islands

Christmas Island

French Polynesia

PACIFIC OCEAN

BRITISH HONDURAS

CUBA

HAITI

DOMINICAN REPUBLIC

VIRGIN ISLANDS

LEEWARD ISLANDS

WINDWARD ISLANDS

BARBADOS

TRINIDAD AND TOBAGO

GUATEMALA

EL SALVADOR

HONDURAS

NICARAGUA

COSTA RICA

CANAL ZONE

PANAMA

VENEZUELA

COLOMBIA

ECUADOR

PERU

BOLIVIA

CHILE

PARAGUAY

ARGENTINA

URUGUAY

BRAZIL

BRITISH GUIANA

DUTCH GUIANA

FRENCH GUIANA

ATLANTIC OCEAN

FALKLAND ISLANDS

THE WORLD 11 NOVEMBER 1918

The Central Powers

Central Powers conquests to 11 Nov 1918

Allied states

Allied conquests to 11 Nov 1918

Neutral states

Frontiers Jul 1914

In July, the French led a successful counter-offensive at the Marne, supported by US troops. On 8 August, British and Commonwealth forces achieved a striking victory at Amiens. From then on, the Allies launched an unbroken series of offensives, climaxing in the breach of the German Hindenburg Line at the end of September.

While German troops continued to fight hard on the Western

Austria-Hungary all surrendered to the Allies. From late October, mutinies and revolutionary uprisings broke out in German cities. On 9 November, Kaiser Wilhelm II was deposed and Germany became a republic. Two days later, the Germans reluctantly accepted rigorous armistice terms and the fighting stopped. There were wild celebrations in the victor countries, while the defeated were immersed in political

TIMELINE 1918

Peace of Brest-Litovsk ▪ **German Spring Offensives** ▪ US troops enter the war ▪ **Allies turn the tide** ▪ Hindenburg Line breached ▪ **Germany's allies defeated** ▪ Kaiser overthrown ▪ **Germans sign an armistice**

JANUARY

8 JANUARY
US President Wilson presents a Fourteen-Point peace programme to Congress.

14 JANUARY
Former French prime minister Joseph Caillaux is arrested for treason for supporting a negotiated peace.

16 JANUARY
Vienna and Budapest are rocked by riots against food shortages.

24 JANUARY
Rejecting German peace terms, Russia's Bolshevik government adopts the stance of "no war, no peace".

28 JANUARY
Strikes in German cities in protest at the continuation of the war.

FEBRUARY

≫ The Russian bear in search of peace

10 FEBRUARY
The Bolshevik delegation walks out of peace talks with the Central Powers.

18 FEBRUARY
Germany resumes military operations against Russia, advancing unopposed into Russian territory.

24 FEBRUARY
At Lenin's insistence, the Bolshevik government reluctantly agrees to accept German peace terms.

≪ Manfred von Richthofen

MARCH

3 MARCH
Russia signs the Treaty of Brest-Litovsk with the Central Powers.

21 MARCH
Germans launch the Michael Offensive against the British Fifth Army on the Western Front and achieve a major breakthrough.

23 MARCH
Paris comes under bombardment from a long-range German railway gun.

26 MARCH
French General Ferdinand Foch is given coordinating powers over Allied armies on the Western Front.

28 MARCH
German offensive fails to take Arras in the face of stiff British resistance.

APRIL

1 APRIL
British army and navy aircraft are unified in the independent Royal Air Force.

4 APRIL
The Michael Offensive peters out as Allied defensive line stabilizes.

8 APRIL
Slav nationalists meeting in Rome demand right to form nation states.

9 APRIL
The Germans launch the Lys Offensive in Flanders, driving the Allies into retreat.

21 APRIL
German air "ace" Baron von Richthofen (the Red Baron) is shot down and killed over the Somme.

≫ German and Austro-Hungarian prisoners of war head home

≫ Gas mask

23 APRIL
The British Royal Navy raids the ports of Zeebrugge and Ostende in an attempt to halt U-boat operations.

29 APRIL
Germany suspends the Lys Offensive without reaching strategic targets.

MAY

Kladderadatsch
Der liebenswürdige Hindenburg

≫ Field Marshal Paul von Hindenburg deals with Field Marshal Douglas Haig.

7 MAY
Romania signs a punitive peace treaty imposed by the Central Powers.

27 MAY
Germans launch an offensive at the Aisne river that forces the Allies into another withdrawal.

28 MAY
US troops see their first major action at the Battle of Cantigny.

30 MAY
German forces advancing from the Aisne reach the Marne.

JUNE

3 JUNE
US and French forces begin the defence of Belleau Wood. The German advance on the Marne front is halted.

8 JUNE
French General Franchet d'Esperay takes command of Allied forces at Salonika in Greece.

9 JUNE
German offensive at Matz achieves limited gains and is quickly abandoned.

10 JUNE
Austria-Hungary launches an offensive in Italy at the Piave river. By 15 June it has failed.

≫ US marine fights a German at the Battle of Bellau Wood

"Already this was **a different world...** The war was over; a new age was beginning; but **the dead were dead** and **would never return."**

BRITISH NURSE VERA BRITTAIN, REMEMBERING ARMISTICE DAY 1918

JULY	AUGUST	SEPTEMBER	OCTOBER	NOVEMBER	DECEMBER

1 JULY
President Wilson announces that one million US troops have been sent to Europe.

15 JULY
Start of the Second Battle of the Marne. A German offensive is halted by 17 July.

16 JULY
Tsar Nicholas II and his family are murdered by the Bolsheviks at Ekaterinburg.

18 JULY
In the Second Battle of the Marne, French and US forces launch a successful counter-offensive, using large numbers of tanks.

31 JULY
Allied intervention force in Russia takes the northern port of Arkhangelsk.

8 AUGUST
Successful British offensive at Amiens in France is dubbed the "blackest day of the German army".

Gemeinde Eibau.
Lebensmittel-Karte.
Name: R. Stecker.
Eibau, Nr. 323.

» German ration card

10 AUGUST
General Pershing announces the formation of the US First Army.

⌃ French Renault FT tank

22 AUGUST
In a renewed offensive north of Amiens, British troops take the town of Albert.

29 AUGUST
New Zealand troops occupy Bapaume.

2–3 SEPTEMBER
Canadian forces make first successful assault on the Hindenburg Line defences at Drocourt-Quéant.

12 SEPTEMBER
The US First Army goes into action at the St Mihiel salient.

15 SEPTEMBER
The Allied army at Salonika launches the Vardar offensive against Bulgaria.

19 SEPTEMBER
Turkish forces suffer a crushing defeat at the Battle of Megiddo in Palestine.

26 SEPTEMBER
Americans and French launch the Meuse-Argonne offensive.

27 SEPTEMBER
Canadians penetrate the Hindenburg Line at the Canal du Nord.

28 SEPTEMBER
British troops cross the St Quentin Canal.

29 SEPTEMBER
Bulgaria agrees an armistice with the Allies.

⌃ German Stahlhelm, with camouflage

⌃ US General John Pershing

1 OCTOBER
Damascus is captured by Australian and Arab forces.

3 OCTOBER
Prince Max von Baden becomes German chancellor and seeks an armistice.

10 OCTOBER
German U-boat sinks an Irish ferry, killing 500 people.

14 OCTOBER
Belgian King Albert leads a major Allied advance in Flanders.

24 OCTOBER
Successful Italian offensive at Vittorio Veneto begins.

26 OCTOBER
Ludendorff is forced to resign after opposing German acceptance of an armistice.

29 OCTOBER
Mutiny breaks out in the German navy, triggering uprisings in German cities.

30 OCTOBER
Turkey signs an armistice at Mudros.

3 NOVEMBER
Austria-Hungary signs an armistice.

9 NOVEMBER
Kaiser Wilhelm II abdicates and flees to the Netherlands. Germany is declared a republic.

⌃ The German delegation arrives to sign the Armistice

11 NOVEMBER
A German delegation signs an armistice; fighting stops at 11am. Emperor Charles I renounces his powers as ruler of Austria-Hungary.

⌃ Grave of the last British and Commonwealth soldier to be killed in the war

22 NOVEMBER
Belgian King Albert re-enters Brussels.

25 NOVEMBER
German forces in East Africa surrender after learning of the Armistice.

1 DECEMBER
Kingdom of Serbs, Croats and Slovenes declares independence.

13 DECEMBER
President Wilson arrives in France for the Paris Peace Conference.

14 DECEMBER
Coalition led by David Lloyd George wins a large majority in British general election.

BEFORE

Combatant countries entered the war in a spirit of national unity, but the pressures of a long conflict brought social and political strains.

POPULAR DISILLUSION
In the course of 1917, an uprising that began with protests over food shortages and inflation **overthrew the tsarist regime** in Russia and a **Bolshevik revolutionary government << 252–53** later seized power. Germany and Austria-Hungary experienced disturbances provoked by **acute food shortages << 198–99** in the winter of 1916–17, known in Germany as the **Turnip Winter**.

BOLSHEVIK MILITARY PATROL

Home Fronts

Soldiers on the battlefields often complained that people at home failed to share their bitter experience of war. But by 1918, few civilians in any of the combatant countries were immune to the impact of the war, and raising their morale had become a crucial issue for governments.

The combatant states had a rich fund of patriotism to draw upon, but as the conflict continued into its fourth year, war-weariness began to spread. For many in Germany and Austria-Hungary, constant food and fuel shortages made daily existence a struggle for survival.

By early 1918, official rations in Vienna, allowed 70 g (2.5 oz) of potatoes per person a day and 23 g (0.8 oz) of meat. Mobile soup kitchens regularly fed about one in five of the city's population with a thin gruel. In summer 1918, tens of thousands of Viennese children were evacuated into rural areas, where they received food in return for supplying farm labour.

Living standards
Conditions in Germany were little better. Short of food and living in unheated buildings through the winter, Germans suffered a steep rise in deaths from tuberculosis and other diseases associated with poverty, damp, and malnutrition. At the same time, working hours were increased to meet the rising demands of war production. German women, who were often undernourished, were forced into factory jobs, where overtime and Sunday working were compulsory and safety standards were poor. After work, they would stand for hours in food queues. German troops on leave from the front were demoralized by the poor state of their families.

Conditions in the Allied countries were never quite as bad. By spring 1918, Britain had introduced rationing for sugar, tea, butter, and meat, but this was in order to put a stop to panic buying rather than because of food shortages. The government introduced a range of practical measures, such as encouraging the setting up of factory canteens and subsidizing wheat prices, which helped keep the British population decently fed.

Citizens of London and Paris endured the inconvenience of blackouts and occasional air raids. From March 1918, Parisians were bombarded by long-range German shellfire. Although few civilians were killed by enemy action, it brought the war home and had a psychological effect.

Private profits
The authorities in combatant states knew they needed to persuade their populations that sacrifices were being evenly shared. All countries, however, adopted policies in which state

British strike meeting
Striking transport workers hold a meeting at Mitcham Green in London in 1918. In general, British trade unions supported the war, and strikes were about low pay and job status rather than the conflict itself.

> "As for the **mood of** the **people**, the **heroic** attitude has entirely **disappeared**. Now one sees **faces** like masks, **blue with cold** and **drawn by hunger**."

PRINCESS BLÜCHER, DESCRIBING BERLIN, DIARY ENTRY, FEBRUARY 1917

direction of the economy went hand in hand with private enterprise. The profits made by industrialists and traders became a widespread source of popular anger on both sides in the war. In Germany and Austria-Hungary, government attempts to control prices and food supplies led to a thriving black market. Wealthy city dwellers, for example, would take trips to the country to buy meat direct from farmers at well over the official fixed price. Police action failed to stop such trading, allowing the well-off to eat while others went hungry.

Controlling labour

In most countries, state measures designed to increase output provoked popular opposition. People resented attempts to stop them from choosing their place of work, and they resisted the drafting of unskilled men and women into skilled jobs. Above all, discontent focused on rising prices and rents, with workers demanding pay rises to maintain their living standards.

1,400 The estimated daily calorific intake for German adults in 1918, down from over 3,000 calories in 1914.

5.9 MILLION The number of working days lost to strike action in Britain in 1918.

Governments tried to persuade trade unions to support the war effort, thus giving them a respectability they had not previously possessed. But even if union leaders supported government policies, workers at factory level often opposed them, so strikes were still widespread. Labour unrest was common not only in Europe, but also in Australia and the USA.

During the last years of the war, Britain experienced more strikes than any other combatant country, with over 900,000 British workers engaging in some form of industrial action during 1918. However, with a handful of exceptions, such as on "Red Clydeside" in Glasgow, anti-war socialism had little impact on Britain's war effort.

In France, politicized strikes were brought to an end by vigorous repressive action after Georges Clemenceau became prime minister in November 1917. In Germany and Austria-Hungary, on the other hand, popular anger over difficult working and living conditions took on a

German ration coupons
Food ration cards were issued in Germany from the early stages of the war. Supplies of many staple goods were limited and officially customers could only buy them on production of these coupons.

dangerously revolutionary flavour, particularly in the wake of the Bolshevik Revolution in Russia.

Urgent demands

In mid-January 1918, Austria-Hungary was swept by strikes after further reductions in food rations. At the same time, about a million workers went on strike in Berlin and other German cities. They demanded more food, an end to the black market, and the

prosecution of profiteers. They also wanted the country's leaders to introduce democratic reforms and end the war. The strikes were quickly suppressed. Ringleaders were arrested or drafted into the army and sent to the front. Few concessions were made. The waves of strikes left little doubt, however, that in the longer term only military victory could avert some form of revolutionary upheaval in Germany and Austria-Hungary.

Ersatz products
Unable to import goods by sea, the German population had to put up with substitute ersatz products. Coffee was made from roasted acorns, tea from common weeds, and soap from a range of chemicals and abrasives.

"COFFEE"

"SOAP"

"TEA"

While malnutrition encouraged the rapid spread of a deadly form of influenza, demands for democratic reforms led to a widening of suffrage, including votes for women in Britain, the USA, Germany, and Austria.

SPANISH FLU
One effect of wartime hardship was to **weaken resistance** to the virulent **"Spanish flu"** of 1918. The pandemic is thought to have killed around 400,000 Germans, a similar number of French, 250,000 British, and possibly as many as 650,000 Americans.

ANNE J. CURRY, THE FIRST US WOMAN TO VOTE

VOTES FOR WOMEN
Some measures taken to secure support for the war became **permanent**. In Britain, for example, the **Representation of the People Act**, passed by the House of Commons in February 1918, **tripled the size of the electorate**, enfranchising all men over 21 and most women over 30. Women were also given the vote in Germany and Austria.

In the **USA**, President Woodrow Wilson agreed in 1918 to enshrine **votes for women** in the US Constitution, a move ratified by the 19th Amendment to the Constitution in 1920.

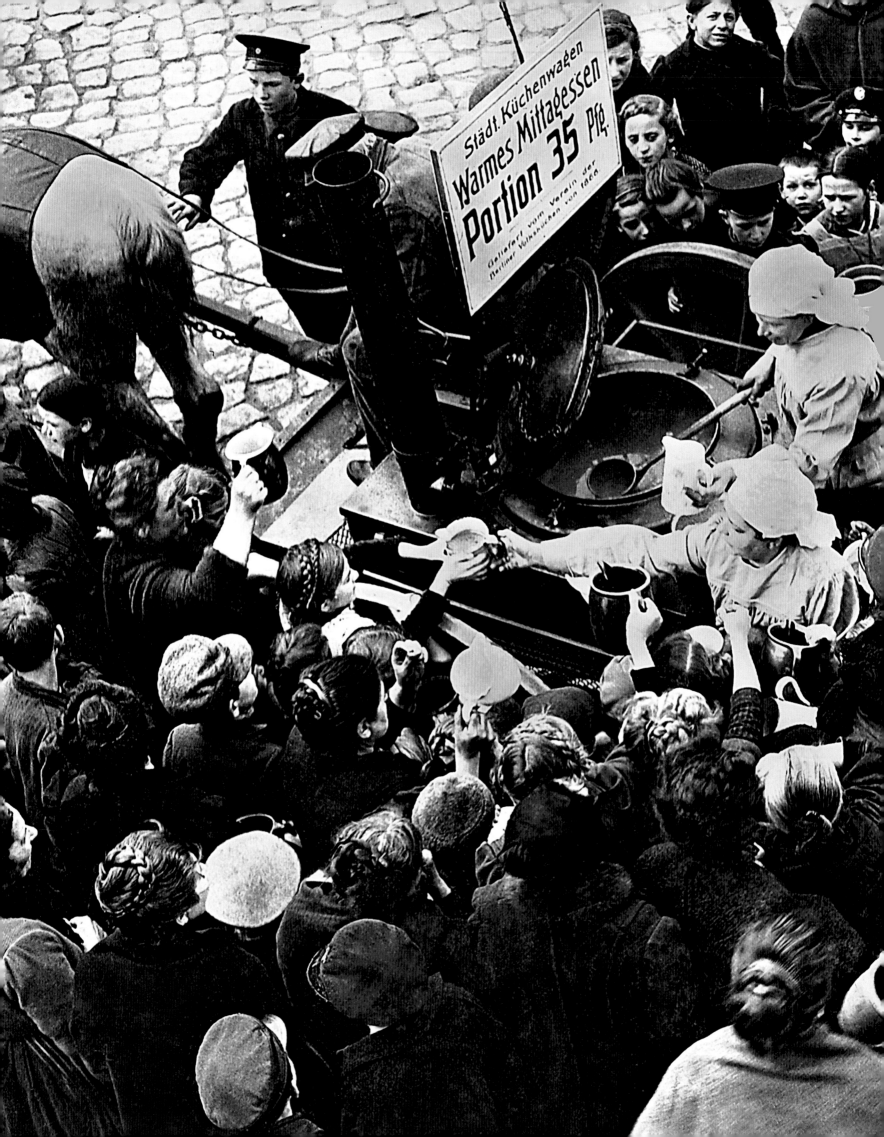

Hunger on the Home Front

By the end of 1917, there was a marked deterioration in the living conditions of Germany's civilian populace. The drain on resources caused by war on multiple fronts and the Allied naval blockade was compounded by the harsh winter of 1916–17. Shortages of food, fuel, soap, and other items left those who could not pay for black market goods struggling to survive. Some estimates place the death toll due to malnutrition-related disease at more than 700,000 during the course of the war.

"Among the three hundred applicants for food there was not one who had had enough to eat in weeks. In the case of the younger women and the children, the skin was drawn hard to the bones and bloodless. Eyes had fallen deeper into the sockets. From the lips, all colour was gone, and the tufts of hair that fell over parchmented foreheads seemed dull and famished, a sign that the nervous vigour of the body was departing with the physical strength."

GEORGE ABEL SCHREINER, US JOURNALIST, FROM "THE IRON RATION: THREE YEARS IN WARRING CENTRAL EUROPE"

"At long last, there's butter, flour, and chocolate in the house. But not much of it, only two small squares of chocolate each! It has been so long, it brings back memories of breakfasts before the war. We are having a hard time. It is very cold, which increases your appetite. My older brothers go to work in thick boots to keep their feet warm. But we have faith in France and God, and comfort ourselves with the thought that over in Germany they are almost as unhappy as we are. There is famine in Berlin, Dresden, and Bavaria. I hope they all die!"

AYVES CONGAR, FRENCH CIVILIAN, FROM "JOURNAL DE LA GUERRE 1914–1918"

Civilians crowd around a municipal kitchen cart on the streets of Berlin, in 1918
People in urban areas were most affected by acute food shortages and profiteering, leaving Germany's government unable to maintain morale on the home front.

Trench Warfare Transformed

In 1918, after three years of trench stalemate, a degree of mobility was restored to the fighting on the Western Front. The adoption of innovative tactics and new technology allowed armies to take the offensive with a good chance of success.

Steel-welded cylinder

Operating lever

World War I generals are often portrayed as unimaginative men who were forever marching their soldiers straight into the fire of enemy machine-guns. In reality, commanders on both sides in the war made constant efforts to improve the performance of their troops. Technological innovations were adopted with enthusiasm and new techniques were developed.

Transforming the battlefield
By 1918, artillery was a refined instrument of war. For set-piece offensives, gunners developed complex firing plans in coordination with infantry assaults. Different kinds of fuse and shell were allotted to various tasks, from cutting barbed wire to destroying enemy artillery batteries.

Assault troops in action
Stormtroopers advance through barbed wire during the German offensive on the Western Front in March 1918. Trained to maintain the momentum of their attack at all costs, these specialist assault troops proved capable of punching holes deep into Allied lines.

A brief but intense "hurricane" bombardment became the usual start to an attack, replacing the prolonged preliminary bombardments practised earlier in the war and restoring an element of surprise. The creeping barrage, introduced by the British and French in 1916, had been perfected so that attacking soldiers had the confidence to advance 50 m (50 yd) behind a protective curtain of shellfire. While this barrage crept forward, other guns would saturate the area behind the enemy front line with high-explosive and gas shells to pre-empt counterattacks.

Defensive artillery fire was effectively suppressed by the accurate shelling of enemy batteries. This was achieved through well-honed techniques for identifying their exact position, such as aerial reconnaissance, sound location, and "flash-spotting" – observing the flashes from the muzzles of the guns.

By 1918, infantry tactics had none of the crudity seen earlier in the war. Armed with light machine-guns,

Portable flamethrower
The fuel tank of a German flamethrower was carried on a soldier's back while a comrade operated the firing tube. Flamethrowers were frequently used by stormtroopers as part of their shock assault equipment.

grenades, rifle grenades, and mortars, as well as rifles and bayonets, infantry sought to push forward at speed in small units. Official British infantry tactics from 1917 emphasized the platoon – around 40 soldiers – as the

" We **crossed a battered tangle of wire** without difficulty and at a jump were over the front line."

ERNST JÜNGER, STORMTROOPER COMMANDER, IN HIS MEMOIR "STORM OF STEEL"

essential unit of combat, with one part of the unit pinning down the enemy defenders with suppressive fire while the other moved to attack.

Stormtrooper tactics

The Germans began developing specialist assault infantry from 1915. The success of an assault detachment under Captain Willy Rohr evolved into the creation of stormtrooper battalions as elite formations of shock troops. Stormtroopers were armed with light and heavy machine-guns, mortars, and flamethrowers, as well as light artillery pieces. Their role was to spearhead attacks, breaking through weak points and then penetrating in depth to capture enemy guns. German infantry would follow on to deal with strongpoints that had been bypassed.

These "infiltration tactics", usually preceded by a hurricane barrage of artillery, were employed successfully by General Oskar von Hutier's Eighth Army at Riga in September 1917. They are often referred to as Hutier tactics.

Combined attack

Aircraft were used increasingly in a ground-attack role in support of infantry. Advancing stormtroopers could expect close air support from Halberstadt aircraft or all-metal Junkers J4s. But the Allies made the best progress in combined air and land attacks. By the second half of 1918, they could field numerous tanks and

ground-attack aircraft, as well as artillery, in tight cooperation with infantry. Australian forces coined the term "peaceful penetration" to describe an assault in which the coordinated use of artillery, tanks, and aircraft as a shock force allowed infantry to occupy ground with relatively few casualties.

The Germans in particular still created defences in depth. They were prepared to sacrifice front-line troops to draw their enemy into a zone of concealed machine-gun nests and further trench lines, where they could then be engaged by counterattack troops.

Poor communication

Despite the progress made in tactics and technology, offensive operations on the Western Front in 1918 were still plagued with difficulties. Without effective mobile radios, communication was always a problem for troops on the offensive. The German stormtroopers could achieve a breakthrough in depth but they could not speed up Germany's creaky supply system, which mostly depended on horsedrawn carts, or the movement of heavy artillery across war-torn ground. It remained true that a

defender could move in reserves to block a breakthrough more quickly than the attacker could exploit it.

Time to rethink

The Allies achieved a string of successes from August 1918 by abandoning the pursuit of a breakthrough and adopting a step-by-step approach – biting small chunks out of the German defences and then holding them against counterattacks, taking care to stay within range of supporting artillery. They consolidated a series of limited gains that progressively pushed the enemy line back towards Germany. The war was no longer static, but it was still hard, slow, and exhausting.

British postcard
A wartime comic postcard depicts, with a good deal of exaggeration, the fear inspired in German troops by British heavy tanks. The Byng Boys were popular music hall entertainers of the day.

AFTER

A lull in the fighting on the Western Front ended when the Germans launched the Michael Offensive on 21 March 1918.

THE SEARCH FOR VICTORY
Spearheaded by **stormtroopers 274–75 》**, the German army achieved **breakthrough offensives** from March through to June, but **not decisive victory**. From August 1918, aided by large numbers of American troops, the Allies began a new campaign of **offensives** that achieved an unbroken series of **military successes** lasting to the war's end in November.

After the war, the stormtrooper principle of shock attack in depth combined with the use of tanks and aircraft created the German "Blitzkrieg" tactics used in World War II.

Camouflage suit
Among wartime innovations was the development of the art of camouflage. This camouflage outfit was worn by a British sniper seeking to fire on German troops from a concealed position.

Hood with face mask

Hand-painted linen

Sniper's mitten

Stormtrooper Equipment

The German stormtroopers (Sturmtruppen) were elite soldiers specially trained in trench infiltration tactics. As rapidly moving assault troops, they required their kit and weaponry to be quick to deploy, highly portable, and easily accessible inside the confined conditions of an enemy trench.

1 **Gas mask** features a screw-fitted air filter and plastic goggles. 2 **M1917 Stahlhelm Helmet** The distinctive German helmet was introduced in 1916. The 1917 model saw improvements to the liner. 3 **Death's head badge** The *totenkopf* (death's head) symbol, originally used by cavalry in the Prussian army, was adopted by some stormtroopers during the offensives in 1918. 4 **Spoon and fork** Stromtroopers often had to eat quickly in lulls between fighting; they carried the necessary utensils. 5 **Battery-operated torch** It was important for assault troops to see into dug-outs and other dark spaces within trenches. 6 **Tunic** Many soldiers would cover their epaulettes with a strip of cloth, so the enemy could not identify their regiment. The top medal indicates the soldier has been wounded, the bottom one is an Iron Cross First Class. 7 **Bergmann MP18/I** Introduced in 1918, this was the first practical submachine-gun employed in combat. At least 5,000 were used before the end of the war. 8 **Mauser KAR 98AZ** This carbine was preferred by stromtroopers over the Gewehr 98 rifle, as its shorter length made it more effective in trench warfare. 9 **Equipment belt** Items clipped to the belt included a water bottle, ammunition pouches, bayonet, axe, and bread bag. 10 **Books** A military pass, a *schiessbuch* ("shooting book" to record marksmanship training), a German-French dictionary, and a paybook. 11 **Stick grenade** The *stielhandgranate*, introduced by Germany in 1915, was called the "potato masher" by British troops. 12 **Assault pack** This backpack holds a shovel, used to entrench and as a weapon. It also contains a *zeltbahn*, a rain poncho that doubled as a tent. 13 **Puttee** These strips of cloth were wound around the leg, acting as support. 14 **Trousers** Three-quarter-length trousers with knee patches were worn by stormtroopers in 1918. 15 **Trench knife** Knives were used in hand-to-hand combat during assaults on trenches.

1 GAS MASK

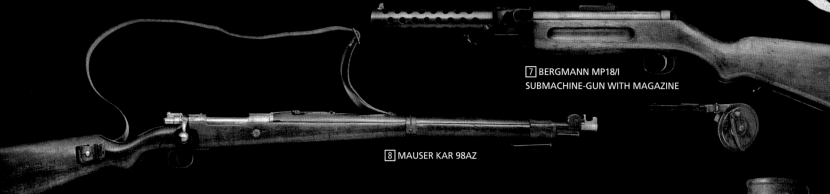

7 BERGMANN MP18/I SUBMACHINE-GUN WITH MAGAZINE

8 MAUSER KAR 98AZ

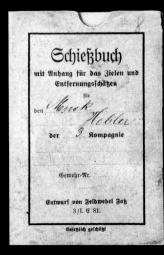

10 BOOKS

11 STICK GRENADE

2 M1917
STAHLHELM HELMET

3 DEATH'S
HEAD BADGE

4 SPOON
AND FORK

5 BATTERY-OPERATED TORCH

6 TUNIC

9 EQUIPMENT BELT

12 ASSAULT
PACK

13 PUTTEE

14 TROUSERS

15 TRENCH KNIFE

German **Victory** in the **East**

An armistice was agreed between Russia and the Central Powers in December 1917, but the Russian Bolshevik government stalled negotiations over the terms of the peace. The Bolsheviks finally accepted German terms in the Treaty of Brest-Litovsk in March 1918.

BEFORE

The strain of fighting for three years against Germany, Austria-Hungary, and Ottoman Turkey eventually proved too much for the Russian Empire. A political, social, and military collapse followed during the course of 1917.

RUSSIAN BEAR IN SEARCH OF PEACE

TURMOIL IN RUSSIA
Russia's **tsarist regime was overthrown** ❮❮ **210–11** in March 1917. The Provisional Government attempted to revitalize the Russian war effort, but the failure of the **Kerensky Offensive** ❮❮ **234–35** led to the disintegration of the Russian army. In November 1917, revolutionary Bolsheviks seized power in Russia and called for an end to the war. By that time, German and Austro-Hungarian troops had **occupied large areas of the former Russian Empire**, including Poland.

On 13 November 1917, Leon Trotsky, Commissar (minister) for Foreign Affairs in the Russian Bolshevik government, contacted the German High Command to request an armistice as a prelude to peace negotiations. Talks with the Central Powers were held at Brest-Litovsk, a German regional headquarters in modern-day Belarus. Having no diplomatic corps, the Bolsheviks sent a delegation of revolutionary activists and token representatives of Russian society – workers, soldiers, sailors, peasants, and women. An armistice, initially for one month, was announced on 15 December. Further progress towards a peace agreement, however, raised deeply divisive issues.

54 PER CENT of the former Russian Empire's industrial enterprises and 89 per cent of its coal mines were lost to Germany under the terms of the Treaty of Brest-Litovsk of March 1918.

Peace at any price
Militarily weak and facing starvation in its cities, Austria-Hungary was prepared to renounce all territorial gains in the interest of achieving a swift agreement. In contrast, Germany's military leaders, Field Marshal Paul von Hindenburg and General Erich Ludendorff, were determined to treat Russia as a defeated enemy and impose harsh peace terms. Germany's civilian government, sensitive to support within the Reichstag (German parliament) for less punitive terms, pursued a more nuanced approach. In the end, however, Hindenburg and Ludendorff prevailed.

On the Russian side, the Bolsheviks were in a weak negotiating position. They were struggling to hold on to power and were facing the beginnings of a civil war. In parts of the former Russian Empire, notably Ukraine and Finland, anti-Bolshevik nationalists were asserting independence. The Russian army had disintegrated and the new Red Army was not yet a credible fighting force. The Bolsheviks' only hope lay in the spread of revolution. They believed that if they could spin out the negotiations at Brest-Litovsk, workers' revolutions might overthrow the governments of Germany, Austria-Hungary, and other countries, and bring other socialist regimes to power.

Taking over leadership of the Bolshevik delegation at Brest-Litovsk in January 1918, Trotsky adopted a stance summed up in the slogan: "Neither war nor peace". He would neither accept Germany's peace terms nor resume the fighting.

On 9 February, Germany and its allies presented an ultimatum: the Bolsheviks must either agree peace terms or the Central Powers would resume hostilities. On 10 February, Trotsky broke off negotiations. The Bolshevik leadership was split. The largest faction favoured launching a revolutionary people's war against the Central Powers. Lenin, however, believed it was necessary to accept the German terms. He argued that the alternative was

Negotiating table
In December 1917, Prince Leopold of Bavaria, supreme commander of German forces on the Eastern Front, signed an armistice with the Bolsheviks at Brest-Litovsk.

Helping the Finns
German medical orderlies aid a wounded Finnish soldier. The Germans intervened in support of anti-Bolshevik forces in the civil war fought in Finland from January to May 1918.

to see the Bolshevik government overthrown by the German army and the revolution snuffed out. On 18 February, while the Bolsheviks hesitated, the Germans took the offensive. Meeting no resistance, German troops pushed deep into Ukraine, Belarus, the Donetz basin, and the Crimea, advancing up to 50 km (30 miles) a day.

Fearing an imminent attack on the Russian capital, Petrograd, by German and anti-Bolshevik Finnish forces, the Bolshevik government accepted German terms on 23 February. These were harsher than those they had previously rejected. A peace treaty

was signed at Brest-Litovsk on 3 March. Russia lost almost all its European territories. Ukraine, Poland, Finland, Estonia, Latvia, and Lithuania became nominally independent states under effective German control. Turkey was awarded territory in the Caucasus. The areas lost were especially populous and prosperous, accounting for a third of Russia's pre-war population and more than half its industry.

Impact on Germany
Along with a punitive peace imposed on Romania in May, the Brest-Litovsk treaty was a triumph for the Central Powers. But the victory in the east proved less valuable to the German war effort than had been expected. The

greatest gain was the transfer of German troops to the Western Front from late 1917, but over a million soldiers were still needed as occupation forces in the east. Their task of extracting resources from the conquered territories – such as the oil-producing city of Baku (in modern-day Azerbaijan) – and sending them to Germany was hindered by wrecked transport networks.

There was also continued fighting. In Finland, for example, German troops helped right-wing nationalists defeat socialists in a civil war. In Ukraine, the exploitative policies of the German military governor, Field Marshal Hermann von Eichhorn, provoked armed uprisings among the peasant population. The occupation forces also had to be fed, further reducing the quantities of goods that trickled back to Germany and Austria-Hungary.

Russian losses
Between the armistice of December 1917 and the signing of the Brest-Litovsk Treaty in March 1918, the armies of the Central Powers occupied a vast swathe of the former Russian Empire.

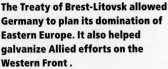

KEY
Armistice line 15 Dec 1917
Line set by treaty of Brest-Litovsk 3 Mar 1918

Prisoners return
German and Austro-Hungarian prisoners of war, released by the Russians under the terms of the Treaty of Brest-Litovsk, arrive by train in the German-occupied city of Kiev in spring 1918.

AFTER

The Treaty of Brest-Litovsk allowed Germany to plan its domination of Eastern Europe. It also helped galvanize Allied efforts on the Western Front.

THE SPRING OFFENSIVES
For the Allies, the Brest-Litovsk Treaty ended any hopes of a negotiated "just peace" by showing that Germany's leadership was intent upon **military conquest**. Eighteen days after the signing of the treaty, the Germans launched a string of **offensives on the Western Front**, employing the extra forces transferred from the East. The campaign, known as the Spring Offensive, began with the Michael Offensive on 21 March **278–79 >>**. Germany's intention was to win the war before **US troops** could be drafted to Europe in substantial numbers. The strategy began well but **ultimately failed 282–83 >>**.

THE FUTURE OF EUROPE
Germany's defeat in November 1918 left the **Brest-Litovsk Treaty null and void** and Germany withdrew its army from the lands it had occupied. Instead, the future shape of Central and Eastern Europe was determined by the outcome of the **Russian Civil War** and **other conflicts 342–43 >>** that continued into the early 1920s.

Slow progress
A German column advances during the Spring Offensive in 1918. The reliance on horse-drawn supply wagons meant that, even after the Germans achieved a breakthrough, further progress was slow.

The **Michael Offensive**

On 21 March 1918, Germany launched a massive offensive on the Western Front in a bold bid to win the war. Known as the Spring Offensive – *Kaisersschlacht* (Kaiser's Battle) to the Germans – it achieved spectacular early successes, beginning with the Michael Offensive.

« BEFORE

Germany saw spring 1918 as an opportunity for victory before US troops arrived in large numbers.

DEFEAT OF RUSSIA
Germany's adoption of unrestricted **submarine warfare** had brought the **USA into the war ‹‹ 212–13** in April 1917 without achieving the victory the German navy had hoped for. While the Americans recruited and trained a mass army, the **defeat of Russia ‹‹ 276–77** enabled Germany to transfer elite troops from the Eastern to the Western Front.

NEW TACTICS
French and British **offensives in 1917** failed to break the **stalemate of trench warfare**. The German high command believed that new infiltration tactics held the key to successful offensive action.

TRENCH PERISCOPE

G eneral Erich Ludendorff gave the order to prepare for the Michael Offensive on 21 January 1918. His aim was to exploit a temporary advantage in the number of German divisions opposing those of the Allies on the Western Front. Peace with Bolshevik Russia had allowed him to transfer 50 divisions from the east, including many infantry troops trained in infiltration tactics.

German artillery, under the direction of General Georg Bruchmüller, was meticulously prepared for an initial artillery barrage that would destroy enemy command and communications, gun batteries, and trench systems with accurate fire of devastating power. Ludendorff focused on achieving a breakthrough, leaving objectives vague. "We will punch a hole," he said. "For the rest, we will see."

The attack was to take place on a sector of the front held by the British Fifth and Third armies between Arras and St Quentin. Only 26 British divisions manned the 90 km (56 mile)

Strap

Glass eye piece

Rubberized canvas

Mouth piece

Flexible hose

Box filter

British gas mask
The small box respirator was used by British forces as anti-gas protection from 1916. By filtering gas from the air to make it breathable, the respirator saved lives, but it was uncomfortable to wear and had limited visibility.

sector. By March, they were facing 63 German divisions. The British Fifth Army, commanded by General Hubert Gough, was particularly thinly spread in the southern part of the sector, where it had been sent to recuperate from heavy losses incurred at Passchendaele the previous year.

The Germans attack
The Allies knew a German offensive was likely, but failed to identify where or when the blow would fall. The opening of the attack on the morning

"We could see the Germans swarming over the ridge... pouring towards us in an endless torrent."

BRITISH PRIVATE FREDERICK NOAKES, THIRD COLDSTREAM GUARDS, DESCRIBING THE GERMAN ADVANCE ON 26 MARCH 1918

of 21 March was shocking in its intensity. The bombardment was unleashed at 4:20am, involving 6,000 artillery pieces and 3,000 mortars. It savaged the British defences. Phosgene and tear gas shells were mixed with the high explosives, and British soldiers struggled to put on gas masks in time.

At around 9am, the German infantry advanced. Spearheaded by elite stormtrooper battalions, the grey-clad troops emerged from dense morning mist to fall upon the British in their devastated trenches. In places, British resistance crumbled, and large numbers of bewildered soldiers surrendered. Entire battalions were lost as front-line positions were overrun by German troops.

General Oskar von Hutier's Eighteenth Army broke through the British Fifth Army's defences, advancing up to 20 km (12 miles) by 22 March. Further north, the better-organized British Third Army under General Julian Byng gave ground only grudgingly but was forced to withdraw to keep in touch with the retreating Fifth Army. Hutier continued to set the pace for the German advance, reaching Montdidier, 65 km (40 miles) from his starting point, on 27 March. In

Germany, the Kaiser announced a school holiday in celebration of victory.

Down but not out

The Allies were, however, by no means beaten. In response to the crisis, rapid changes were made in command. On 26 March, French General Ferdinand Foch was entrusted with coordinating the action of the Allied armies, a role soon formalized as the Supreme Commander of the Allied Armies. This gave Foch authority over the French army commander-in-chief, General Philippe Pétain, who had been failing to act in support of the retreating British.

Meanwhile, on the ground, the German advance quickly began to run out of steam. This was partly the result of poor transport and supply, worsened by the war-torn terrain, but also because of a lack of discipline among the troops. Long subjected to Germany's food shortages, the German soldiers turned aside to feast on the

> **21,000** The number of British soldiers who were taken prisoner on 21 March 1918, the first day of the Michael Offensive.

food and alcohol they discovered in abandoned British stores and the cellars of French farmhouses.

Brought to a standstill

By 28 March, Hutier's Eighteenth Army had come to a temporary halt. Ludendorff attempted to relaunch the offensive with an attack by nine fresh divisions against the British Third Army in front of Arras. Despite using the same tactics that proved so successful a week earlier, the Germans failed to make any impression on the well-entrenched defenders. By 5 April, the German Second Army, commanded by General Georg von der Marwitz, had been stopped by British and

Australian troops at Villers-Bretonneaux, 16 km (10 miles) short of its objective, Amiens.

In two weeks, the German army had suffered 250,000 casualties, including a large percentage of its elite stormtroopers, without achieving the decisive victory it needed. The Allies had experienced a shock, but were still in position to continue the fight.

THE PARIS GUN

On 23 March 1918, the Germans opened a long-range bombardment of Paris using a specially adapted gun. Mounted on a railcar, it fired on the city from a distance of 120 km (74 miles). Based on a Krupp 380 mm gun, its barrel was lengthened and lined, reducing it to 210 mm calibre. Its shells reached a height of 40 km (25 miles) at the top of their trajectory, becoming the first man-made objects to enter the stratosphere. Technical problems made bombardment intermittent. Paris was struck by 320 shells before an Allied offensive forced the gun's withdrawal in August. About 250 Parisians were killed by the shelling and 620 were injured.

German A7V "Wotan" tank
The Germans first used their A7V tank on the opening day of the Michael Offensive. Manned by 18 soldiers, the Wotan was too slow and cumbersome to be effective, and only 20 entered service.

AFTER

The Michael Offensive was followed by a succession of other German offensives, each seeking the decisive blow that would win the war.

KEEPING UP THE PRESSURE
Ludendorff had planned **subsidiary offensives** in support of the Michael Offensive, and these now became major operations in their own right. On 9 April 1918, the Germans launched the **Lys Offensive in Flanders**. As in the Michael Offensive, spectacular initial success was soon followed by a loss of momentum, leaving German forces far short of their strategic objectives. The French bore the brunt of the **next German offensive**, at the **Aisne river** on 27 May.

SECOND BATTLE OF THE MARNE
By early June, the Germans had reached the Marne, 90 km (56 miles) from Paris, but US troops were beginning to enter combat **284–85 »**. A final German offensive in mid-July was rebuffed by a French-led counter-offensive at the **Second Battle of the Marne 286–87 »**. By then, Germany's chance of winning the war had evaporated.

The Opening of the Michael Offensive

On the morning of 21 March, the Germans launched the first in a series of assaults that aimed to split and then destroy Allied forces on the Western Front. Following an intense preliminary bombardment, and aided by foggy conditions, stormtroopers began to puncture holes in the Allied line. Before midday, British forces in the north were in headlong retreat.

"Turmoil and confusion are everywhere. Troops, baggage, and all the litter of war… Where are we going? No one knows. Where's the 8th? Where's the 7th? Where is any regiment? Officers claim us… Loaded like pack-mules we move on, march, deploy, circle, get lost, dig in, get moved on… and at dawn we are still digging in. At noon the attack opens up on us. Casualties are heavy… Lieutenant W calls for volunteers to go to headquarters for help. I set off, and take a boy with me who is badly hit in the head. The area we cross is swept by rifle and machine-gun fire… the boy is in pain. 'Here they come!' he cries… He is right, the first wave is almost on top of us… 'Up!' I say, 'and take your helmet off'. The German in front of me… raises his rifle and takes aim… For ten seconds we remain so… then he beckons and we approach… We go back to the rear of the German line, passing through successive waves of troops going forward. More prisoners join us… what a crowd: hundreds, perhaps thousands, French and English. A long column stretches down the road before us and behind us… on we go into Germany. Adventure is at an end; henceforth we are prisoners."

ENGLISH PRIVATE ALFRED GROSCH WAS CAPTURED AT LA FÈRE DURING THE OPENING STAGES OF THE MICHAEL OFFENSIVE

The German advance
Soldiers of the German 18th Army advance through smoke and gunfire as they overrun Allied lines near the Somme. The Germans achieved early success as they encountered inadequately prepared defensive positions.

The German Search for Victory

In April and May 1918, warfare on a vast scale raged across the Western Front. At times, the series of German offensives appeared to bring the Allies to the brink of defeat. In the end, however, Germany's desperate bid for victory failed.

German mortar shell
Mortars made a substantial contribution to bombardments in preparation for a ground attack. This 21 cm German mortar shell was capable of blowing up an entire section of a trench.

By the start of April 1918, it was clear that the German Michael Offensive launched on 21 March had failed to inflict a decisive defeat upon the Allies. It had nonetheless gained territory and placed the British Army, in particular, under immense strain. Seeking to capitalize on this advantage, General Ludendorff ordered a fresh offensive, shifting the point of attack to the mostly British-held sector of Flanders. The site of some of the fiercest fighting of the war, including the Battle of Neuve Chapelle, the three battles of Ypres, and the Battle of Messines, the Flanders sector was crucial to Britain because it defended the Channel ports. A German breakthrough would threaten to cut the transport link between the British Army in France and its home bases.

Resuming the offensive

Codenamed Operation Georgette, and known as the Battle of the Lys, the German offensive in Flanders opened on 9 April with an attack by the Sixth Army in the area of Neuve Chapelle. As in the Michael Offensive, the Germans unleashed a powerful onslaught against a relatively weak defensive sector. The full brunt of the initial attack was borne by the Second Portuguese Division, commanded by

« BEFORE

From autumn 1916, Field Marshal Paul von Hindenburg and General Erich Ludendorff pursued a German military victory at all costs.

USA MOBILIZES

By resuming **unrestricted submarine warfare « 220–21** from February 1917, the Germans drew the USA into the war. American troops would not, however, be ready to fight in large numbers until summer 1918. Meanwhile, **Russia underwent a revolution** and dropped out of the war, signing a humiliating **peace treaty** with the Central Powers at **Brest-Litovsk « 276–77**.

GERMAN ARMOUR

NEW OFFENSIVES

Freed from the need to fight a war on two fronts, the Germans concentrated on the Western Front, **gambling on winning the war** before US troops took the field. Germany's devastating **Michael Offensive « 278–79**, launched on 21 March 1918, forced an **Allied retreat** and **virtually destroyed the British Fifth Army**. It did not, however, achieve the knockout blow to the Allies that Hindenburg and Ludendorff were seeking.

50 The number of German divisions transferred from the Eastern Front to the Western Front after the defeat of Russia.

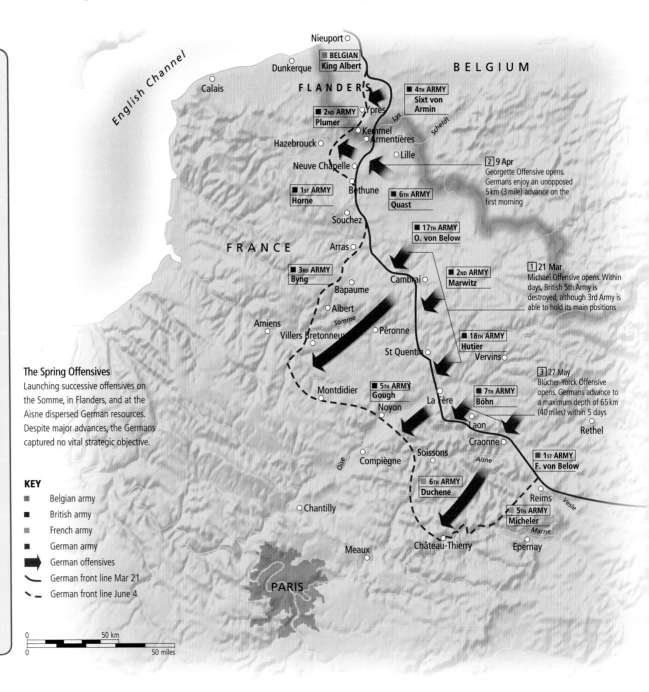

The Spring Offensives
Launching successive offensives on the Somme, in Flanders, and at the Aisne dispersed German resources. Despite major advances, the Germans captured no vital strategic objective.

KEY
- ■ Belgian army
- ■ British army
- ■ French army
- ■ German army
- ➤ German offensives
- ⌒ German front line Mar 21
- ⌒ German front line June 4

Map labels:
- Nieuport
- BELGIAN King Albert
- Dunkerque
- BELGIUM
- Calais
- FLANDERS
- 4TH ARMY Sixt von Armin
- 2ND ARMY Plumer
- Ypres
- Lys
- Scheldt
- Kemmel
- Armentières
- Hazebrouck
- Lille
- 2 9 Apr / Georgette Offensive opens. Germans enjoy an unopposed 5 km (3 mile) advance on the first morning
- Neuve Chapelle
- 1ST ARMY Horne
- Béthune
- 6TH ARMY Quast
- Souchez
- 17TH ARMY O. von Below
- FRANCE
- Arras
- 3RD ARMY Byng
- Cambrai
- 2ND ARMY Marwitz
- Bapaume
- 1 21 Mar / Michael Offensive opens. Within days, British 5th Army is destroyed, although 3rd Army is able to hold its main positions
- Albert
- Amiens
- Somme
- Péronne
- 18TH ARMY Hutier
- Villers Bretonneux
- St Quentin
- Vervins
- 3 27 May / Blücher-Yorck Offensive opens. Germans advance to a maximum depth of 65 km (40 miles) within 5 days
- 5TH ARMY Gough
- Montdidier
- La Fère
- 7TH ARMY Böhn
- Noyon
- Laon
- Rethel
- Craonne
- Oise
- Compiègne
- Soissons
- Aisne
- 1ST ARMY F. von Below
- 6TH ARMY Duchene
- Reims
- Vesle
- Chantilly
- 5TH ARMY Micheler
- Marne
- Meaux
- Château-Thierry
- Epernay
- English Channel
- PARIS

0 ____ 50 km
0 ____ 50 miles

General Manuel Gomes da Costa. Portugal had entered the war in 1916 and a Portuguese Expeditionary Force had been deployed with British forces on the Western Front since summer 1917. Poorly led and suffering from low morale, the Portuguese troops were about to be relieved of front-line duties when the German offensive began. Stunned by a perfectly orchestrated German bombardment, the Portuguese faced German infantry in the morning fog. Despite individual acts of heroism, Gomes da Costa's troops put up little resistance. Some 7,000 Portuguese were taken prisoner and a similar number were killed or wounded.

Crisis for the British

The British 55th Division held its position to the south of the Portuguese, but to the north the British were forced to retreat, losing the town of Armentières on the second day of the battle. This was followed by further losses as the German Fourth Army launched the second phase of the offensive at the Ypres salient. Held by the British Second Army under General Herbert Plumer, this ground had become sacred to the British through the sheer scale of the sacrifice that had taken place there. Now Plumer was forced to abandon Messines Ridge and Passchendaele, withdrawing to a defensive line on the very outskirts of Ypres itself.

On 11 April, British commander-in-chief Field Marshal Douglas Haig's order of the day called for a fight in defence of "the safety of our homes

> ## "There is **no course**... but to **fight it out.** Every **position** must be **held...** there must be **no retirement."**
>
> FIELD MARSHAL DOUGLAS HAIG, ORDER OF THE DAY, 11 APRIL 1918

and the freedom of mankind". Haig's rhetoric drew a mixed response from war-weary British soldiers, but it did express the enduring resolve of senior Allied commanders at a crucial moment of the war. Instead of falling apart, the Allies pulled together.

Foch takes charge

On 14 April, the British formally acknowledged French General Ferdinand Foch as Supreme Commander of the Allied Armies on the Western Front. Although Foch was slow to respond to appeals from Haig for reinforcements, rightly fearing an imminent German offensive against a French-held sector of the front, he eventually sent French troops to relieve exhausted British formations.

The Belgian army, on the British left, also stepped up its efforts.

By the third week in April, the Flanders offensive had degenerated into a series of local engagements in which stubborn defence by Allied troops slowed German progress to a crawl. Neither the French Channel port of Dunkerque nor the vital rail junction of Hazebrouck were seriously threatened. Further south, on 25 April, a German attack towards Amiens failed to take the city.

Still seeking the elusive decisive victory, Ludendorff gathered German strength for yet another major offensive, codenamed Blücher-Yorck, in May. Instead of reinforcing the effort in Flanders, he chose to attack at the Aisne river in northern France, held by the French Sixth Army. Some 6,000 guns and two million shells were

Prisoners of war

The Germans display Portuguese prisoners in Flanders in April 1918. The Portuguese were about to be relieved by British troops when they came under attack.

assembled for the initial bombardment, undetected by the Allies. The main weight of the attack was to fall upon the Chemin des Dames Ridge, captured by the French in May 1917. It was defended by British soldiers who had been transferred to this quiet sector from Flanders for a period of rest and recuperation. Crowded into forward positions in poorly organized trenches, the British were decimated by the German initial bombardment on the 27 May and then overrun by stormtroopers.

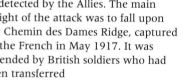

50,000 The number of Allied soldiers taken prisoner by the Germans in the Aisne Offensive between 27 and 30 May 1918.

Allied troops retreated across the Aisne pursued by the Germans. A German advance of 15 km (9 miles) on the first day was maintained over the following week. By 3 June, the Germans had reached the Marne river. With Paris apparently under threat, France experienced the same sense of crisis that Britain had in April. Few people then recognized the truth – that the German offensives had failed to achieve any decisive objective.

Britain takes a beating

A cartoon published in a German magazine during the Lys Offensive in April 1918 shows Field Marshal Hindenburg thrashing British commander-in-chief Douglas Haig.

AFTER

The Germans had hoped to win the war before US troops were engaged. By June 1918, time had run out.

THE TIDE TURNS
The **first Americans entered combat** under overall French command at the Aisne in late May 1918. The following month, US troops were prominently involved at **Belleau Wood**

650,000 The number of American soldiers in France by the start of June 1918.

284–85 ≫ and the **Battle of Matz**. A final German offensive was defeated in July at the **Second Battle of the Marne** **286–87 ≫**. Massive German losses since 21 March **demoralized German troops**, and there was an increasing sense that Germany had lost its strategic purpose. The tide was set to turn on the Western Front.

Hand-to-hand combat
French war artist Lucien Jonas made this image of an American soldier grappling with the enemy in Belleau Wood. The hand-to-hand fighting occurred during the US assault on the wood on 6 June.

The Battle of Belleau Wood

At a crucial point in the war, with German forces advancing on Paris, American troops were thrown into combat for the first time. American marines and army infantry fought with outstanding courage against the Germans at Belleau Wood near the Marne river.

Half a million US soldiers had arrived in France by the start of May 1918. Although some divisions had spent time in trenches on quiet sectors of the front, none had entered battle.

The German breakthrough at the Aisne river on 27 May brought US forces into action for the first time, in support of the French. The next day, elements of the US First Division fought the Germans at Cantigny, 32 km (20 miles) southeast of Amiens.

As the Germans advanced to the Marne river, just 80 km (50 miles) from Paris, French commander-in-chief General Philippe Pétain called upon US assistance again. In response, commander of the American Expeditionary Force (AEF), General Jack Pershing, rushed the US Second and Third divisions to the Marne. Fighting alongside French colonial troops, the Third Division fought a successful holding action against the Germans at Château-Thierry on the Marne on 31 May.

In the first days of June, the Second Division dug in along the front to the left of the Third Division. The division, which included a brigade of marines under Brigadier General James Harbord, took up position opposite Belleau Wood, a few kilometres west of Château-Thierry. On 3–4 June, the Germans attacked in strength but were repelled by the French and Americans. German troops advancing out of Belleau Wood were cut down by marine rifle fire. During this engagement, the marines rejected advice from the French to conduct a tactical withdrawal. Marine Captain Lloyd Williams allegedly responded, "Retreat? Hell, we just got here."

Ferocious combat

The German failure on 4 June was a sign that the offensive launched at the Aisne eight days earlier was stalling. The French identified the moment as ripe for a counterattack and the Americans complied.

The counterattack was launched at dawn on 6 June, with the US Marines and Third Infantry Brigade attacking Belleau Wood and a nearby position known as Hill 142. Although the US troops had already demonstrated their fighting spirit, their shortage of combat experience was now evident. The attacks showed neither the tight cooperation between artillery and infantry nor the sophisticated infantry tactics that the British, French, and Germans had developed during the war. The Americans behaved as soldiers had in 1914, advancing in dense waves across open ground.

The wheatfields were soon thick with dead and wounded US troops, the marines suffering over 1,000 casualties on the day. The Americans nonetheless took Hill 142 and penetrated the German defences in Belleau Wood, engaging the enemy at close quarters.

Allied successes

The bloody battle for Belleau Wood and the nearby villages of Vaux and Bouresche continued for another 20 days, with desperate attacks and counterattacks by both sides. At times, there was hand-to-hand fighting. German troops learned a healthy respect for their US opponents, especially the marines.

Belleau Wood was in American hands on 26 June. By then, US troops had also helped the French repulse the Germans at the Battle of Matz (9–12 June), on the Matz river. The German advance towards Paris had been brought to a halt. With increasing numbers of US troops arriving in France – the size of the AEF passed a million men in July – any serious possibility of Germany winning the war had evaporated.

> **9,777** The total number of US casualties in the fighting from 6 to 26 June 1918, including 1,811 dead.

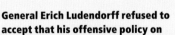

Camouflage helmet
American troops fighting in World War I wore the British Brodie helmet or its US-manufactured equivalent, the M1917.

BEFORE

German offensives in spring 1918 banked on US troops not being fully deployed. In fact, they were ready for action by May.

RECRUITMENT POSTER FOR THE US MARINES

THE AEF IS FORMED
The USA declared war on Germany in April 1917. However, the recruitment and training of an American Expeditionary Force (AEF) proceeded slowly. The AEF's commander, **General Jack Pershing**, wanted a US army to fight as an independent force and resisted pressure to provide units for the British and French armies. The crisis caused by the German **Michael Offensive ‹‹ 278–79** in March 1918 and **subsequent offensives in Flanders** and at the **Aisne ‹‹ 282–83** necessitated a change in US policy.

Witnessing Belleau Wood
The US war correspondent Floyd Gibbons lost an eye while trying to save a wounded soldier at Belleau Wood. The French awarded Gibbons the Croix de Guerre for valour in battle.

AFTER

General Erich Ludendorff refused to accept that his offensive policy on the Western Front had failed.

GERMANY FLOUNDERS
In July, Ludendorff launched yet another ambitious offensive, precipitating the **Second Battle of the Marne 286–87 ››**. The German attack failed and a French-led counter-offensive then turned the tables, forcing the Germans to withdraw from the ground they had won in late May. With limited manpower, Germany could not cope with huge troop losses, a situation made worse by the onset of a deadly **influenza epidemic**. An **Allied offensive at Amiens 304–05 ››** in August proved a success. In September, General Pershing launched the first American-led operation at the St-Mihiel salient **306–07››**, followed by the larger **Battle of Meuse-Argonne 308–09 ››**.

The Second Battle of the Marne

Fought in July 1918, the Second Battle of the Marne was a key turning point in the final phase of the war. A German offensive at Reims was halted and then trumped by a powerful French-led counter-offensive that seized the initiative for the Allies. The scene was set for an Allied drive to victory.

Gun

Renault FT tank
The most successful armoured vehicle of World War I, France's innovative Renault light tank had its main armament in a fully rotating turret. More than 3,500 FTs were manufactured during the war.

Hatch through which the driver looks

Entrance

Caterpillar tracks

By summer 1918, the German high command was beginning to lose touch with the reality of the war. General Erich Ludendorff planned an offensive to encircle the city of Reims in Champagne, 30 km (18 miles) north of the Marne river. His aim was to draw the French into committing their reserves to a defence of the historic city, diverting troops away from Flanders where he then intended to strike a decisive blow. By then such grandiose plans were beyond the capacity of the

Courageous commander
General Henri Gouraud was widely praised for his leadership of the French Fourth Army during the opening defensive phase of the Second Battle of the Marne. Earlier in the war, Gouraud had lost an arm in the fighting at Gallipoli.

German army. It had been severely weakened by heavy losses in offensives since March and was showing increasing signs of declining morale.

On the Allied side, Supreme Commander of the Allied Armies General Ferdinand Foch, buoyed by the arrival of US troops in ever larger numbers, was also planning to take the offensive. Foch prepared an attack on the western side of the salient created

1,143 The number of Allied aircraft used to support the offensive at the Second Battle of the Marne on 18 July 1918.

513 The number of Allied tanks assembled for the 18 July offensive.

by the German advance to the Marne river between May and June. The French Tenth Army was chosen to spearhead the operation, under the command of General Charles Mangin.

The Allies learned about the German offensive plans, chiefly through interrogation of enemy prisoners. The French commander-in-chief General Philippe Pétain wanted a maximum concentration of forces at Reims to

resist the German onslaught, but Foch refused to be deflected from pursuing his own offensive preparations.

Attack on Reims
The Germans attacked first. On 15 July, the First and Third armies struck to the east of Reims while the Seventh Army attacked to the west of the city. The defensive positions were held by the French Fourth Army under the command of General Henri Gouraud on the eastern side and the Sixth Army under General Jean Degoutte in the west. The French armies also had

under their command nine American and two Italian divisions.

The German attack to the east of Reims went badly from the start. Gouraud had prepared his defences in depth, leaving front positions only lightly held. His artillery carried out an effective bombardment of German troops as they assembled for the initial assault. When the Germans rushed forward, they easily overran the French front-line positions, but were brought to a halt in a fiercely defended battle zone to the rear. Gouraud infused the defence with his own ferocity of spirit, calling on his forces to "Kill them, kill them in abundance until they have had enough".

The Germans had had enough on 16 July, when the eastern attack was called off. To the west of Reims, however, it was a different story.

BEFORE

Between March and June 1918, the Germans achieved major advances on the Western Front.

THE SPRING OFFENSIVES
Following the **Michael Offensive** **«278–79**, the Germans launched offensives in Flanders in April and at the **Aisne** **«282–83** in late May, but **failed to pursue a clear strategy**. German losses were heavy and their gains not decisive.

Meanwhile, the Allies made French General **Ferdinand Foch** their supreme commander. In June, US troops fought well at **Belleau Wood** **«284–85**, halting the Germans at the Marne.

BRITISH BINOCULARS

> " American comrades, **I am grateful** for the **blood you... spilled** on... **my country.**"
>
> FRENCH GENERAL CHARLES MANGIN, 7 AUGUST 1918

Rotating turret

Tail

barrage accompanied by tanks. The majority of the troops were French, but the US First and Second divisions spearheaded the assault in the sector around Château-Thierry. Although German machine-gun and artillery fire inflicted heavy casualties, the tanks helped break through defensive positions and Allied aircraft bombed German troops.

Pushed back

The Germans were forced back, retreating some 10 km (6 miles) in the first two days of the offensive. By 22 July, the two US divisions had lost 11,000 men, either killed or wounded, but they had retaken Château-Thierry (lost to the Germans in June) and won the admiration of their French colleagues. The French were also impressed by the performance of African-American troops, assigned to separate formations in the segregated US Army. Regiments of the black 93rd Division performed outstandingly when seconded to French divisions, where they received more respectful treatment than they were used to under US command.

Harlem Hellfighters
The African-American 369th Regiment, known as the Harlem Hellfighters, was seconded to fight under French command at the Marne. The soldiers were issued with French rifles and Adrian helmets.

Through the last week of July, the Germans steadily gave ground and by 3 August had managed an orderly withdrawal across the Aisne river, returning to the positions they had held before their offensive in late May. Ludendorff had been forced to transfer troops south from Flanders to help hold the line against the French advance, ending any prospect of a renewed German offensive towards the Channel ports.

Although Ludendorff publicly disparaged the quality of US troops, in private the German leadership had to face the fact that their presence meant that military victory was no longer an option for Germany. The endgame of the war was about to begin.

German stormtroopers established a bridgehead across the Marne. In the fierce fighting that followed, the US Third Infantry Division earned its nickname "the Rock of the Marne" for standing firm while other troops fell back.

Pétain wanted to transfer troops preparing for the Allied offensive to the defence of Reims, but Foch refused. Aided by the arrival of two British divisions, the Allied position west of Reims had stabilized by 17 July.

Return to the Marne

The German offensive had failed and it was time for the Allied offensive to begin. Foch's aim was to eliminate the large salient created by the German advance from the Aisne to the Marne in late May to early June. The attack was launched on 18 July from positions to the west of the Reims battlefields in the direction of Soissons. Impressive forces had been assembled for the operation, including over 1,000 aircraft and massed tanks, mostly the light Renault FTs. After a brief artillery bombardment, the Allied infantry went "over the top" at dawn, advancing behind a creeping

US troops on the move
Soldiers of the American Expeditionary Force (AEF) move up by truck towards Château-Thierry in preparation for the counterattack at the Marne on 18 July. American manpower altered the balance of forces in the war.

AFTER ≫

The French-led offensive at the Marne was the first in a series of Allied attacks that continued to push the Germans back through 1918.

HONOURED GENERAL
The initial French reaction to the Second Battle of the Marne was **relief that Paris had been saved**. In recognition of his victory, Foch was granted the title of Marshal of France on 6 August 1918, the second French general accorded this honour during World War I. The first was General Joseph Joffre in 1916.

GRAND OFFENSIVE
The Allies resumed offensive operations with an important victory principally won by British and Commonwealth forces at **Amiens 304–05 ≫** on 8 August. From September, Foch orchestrated a simultaneous "Grand Offensive" by Allied armies on different sectors of the Western Front, including American-led operations at **St Mihiel** and **Meuse-Argonne 306–09 ≫** and British-led attacks on the **Hindenburg Line 312–13 ≫**.

Blinded by gas
In this painting entitled *Gassed*, by US artist John Singer Sargent, British infantry are led to a dressing station after a gas attack. Sargent witnessed the scene near Arras on 21 August 1918.

MARSHAL OF FRANCE Born 1851 Died 1929

Ferdinand Foch

"He is the **most courageous man** I have ever met."

BRITISH GENERAL SIR HENRY WILSON, 1920

T he defeat of France by Germany in the Franco-Prussian War of 1870–71 was a formative experience for Ferdinand Foch. It not only gave him his first taste of the army as a volunteer, but also filled him with a lasting fear of German military power.

A love of military history led Foch to study the campaigns of the French Emperor Napoleon I (1769–1821).

Unshaken belief

Marshal Ferdinand Foch was the commander who led the Allies to victory on the Western Front in 1918. He was an aggressive commander, whose military thinking influenced many French officers.

earned him a reputation as an influential military theoretician. At France's War College, the École Supérieure de Guerre, a generation of French officers absorbed Foch's belief that a spirited attack would always overcome defensive firepower. It was a conviction that ultimately cost many Frenchmen their lives.

From desk to battlefield

At the outbreak of war, Foch was a 62-year-old general with no combat experience who had spent most of his career in desk jobs or lecture rooms. Leading XX Corps on the Lorraine front in August 1914, he attracted the favourable attention of French commander-in-chief General Joseph Joffre when he

LE MARÉCHAL FOCH

Front page news

Wearing the uniform of a Marshal of France, Foch was the natural choice for the front page of a French illustrated newspaper in August 1918, the month when the Allied armies turned the tide of the war.

As an officer in the artillery from 1873, Foch belonged to the section of the army most changed by technological progress, but his Napoleonic studies led him to believe troop morale to be the most crucial factor in warfare. He always favoured offence over defence. Commitment to the offensive suited his confident, energetic character, and he never abandoned it.

During the long peace in Europe between 1871 and 1914, Foch's clarity of mind and originality of thought

Awarding medals to Allied soldiers
As Allied Supreme Commander, Foch distributes medals to Belgian soldiers on the Western Front in 1918, watched by King Albert I of Belgium. Foch liked to meet troops and other generals face to face.

prevented a German breakthrough by mounting a successful counterattack at the Trouée de Charmes near Nancy. Sensing that Foch was the man for a crisis, Joffre gave him command of the Ninth Army, a makeshift new formation, and ordered him to plug a gap in the French line south of Reims in what would become the First Battle of the Marne.

Foch again employed counterattack as the best form of defence, motivating exhausted retreating troops to turn and engage the advancing Germans. His bold commitment to attack from an apparently hopeless position appealed to French propagandists and quickly acquired the status of myth. It also commended him to Joffre who, in the wake of the victory on the Marne, would have made Foch his deputy had such a position existed.

Champion of new technology
For Foch, as for other World War I generals, trench warfare imposed a painful learning process. After presiding over costly failed offensives in 1915, he became an advocate of "scientific warfare", seeking to limit infantry losses by more effective use of artillery, aircraft, and later, tanks. He fell from favour after Joffre was sidelined in December 1916, but quickly returned to prominence in spring 1917 as Chief of Staff to the new French commander-in-chief, General Philippe Pétain.

When a Supreme War Council was set up in November 1917 to coordinate Allied action in Italy in the wake of the Caporetto disaster, Foch proved its most effective member. Although speaking no English, he had a good relationship with British commander General Douglas Haig, who preferred Foch to the pessimistic Pétain.

Allied Supreme Commander
In the crisis provoked by the German breakthrough on the Western Front in March 1918, Foch was immediately chosen as the man to coordinate the action of the British and French armies. Although given the title of Allied Supreme Commander in April, he never ran the war directly. Instead, he relied upon his powers of persuasion to encourage the different Allied commanders to coordinate their plans. His intervention to ensure the launch of a counteroffensive at the Second Battle

of the Marne in July, overruling Pétain's defensive instincts, was a turning point in the war.

The drive to victory
Success at the Second Battle of the Marne confirmed Foch's personal authority and allowed him to promote a coherent Allied offensive strategy, even going so far as bending the obdurately independent US General John Pershing to his will. Foch's positive spirit was exactly what the moment required and ensured an unrelenting drive to victory.

Foch pressed for the imposition of tough terms on Germany in the Armistice negotiations that ended the fighting, and protested vigorously against what he regarded as lax peace terms during the Paris Peace Conference in January 1919. He insisted that only permanent French annexation of the Rhineland could guarantee against future German aggression. When the Treaty of Versailles was signed on 28 June 1919, Foch warned, with notable foresight, that it would condemn France to fighting the war all over again.

Signing the Armistice
Foch leads the Allied delegation at the signing of the Armistice on 11 November 1918. The signing took place on his private train in the Forest of Compiègne. Foch insisted that the Germans accept rigorous terms.

> "My **right** is **driven in**; my **left** is **giving way;** the situation is excellent; **I am attacking!**"

ATTRIBUTED TO FOCH AT THE FIRST BATTLE OF THE MARNE, SEPTEMBER 1914

TIMELINE

■ **October 1851** Ferdinand Foch is born on 2 October at Tarbes in southwest France.

■ **1870** Enlists in the infantry on the outbreak of the Franco-Prussian War but fails to see action.

■ **1873** Graduates from the École Polytechnique and artillery training school. Commissioned as an artillery officer.

■ **1895** Appointed as instructor at the École Supérieure de Guerre and becomes a renowned military theorist.

■ **1903–04** Returns to regimental duties and publishes collections of his lectures: *On the Principles of War* and *On the Conduct of War*.

■ **1908** Promoted to the rank of general, he is appointed commander of the École Supérieure de Guerre, a post he holds until 1911.

■ **August 1914** Enters the war as a corps commander in the French Second Army. Performs well during the Battle of the Frontiers on the Lorraine front. His son and son-in-law are killed in separate incidents on 22 August.

■ **September 1914** As commander of the Ninth Army, he plays a vital role in the defeat of the Germans at the First Battle of the Marne.

■ **October–November 1914** Appointed commander of the French armies in northern France. Cooperates with the British in the Race to the Sea and the First Battle of Ypres.

■ **1915–16** As commander of Northern Army Group, he has overall control of French forces at the Second Battle of Ypres, the Artois-Loos Offensive, and the Battle of the Somme.

■ **December 1916** When Nivelle replaces Joffre as French commander-in-chief, Foch is dismissed from his post and sent to the Italian front.

■ **May 1917** New French commander-in-chief Pétain selects Foch as his Chief of Staff.

■ **November 1917** Appointed France's representative on the Allied Supreme War Council.

■ **March 1918** Entrusted with coordinating Allied armies on the Western Front, a role later formalized as Allied Supreme Commander.

■ **July 1918** Masterminds a successful counter-offensive at the Second Battle of the Marne.

■ **August 1918** Granted the honorary title of Marshal of France.

■ **November 1918** Heads the Allied armistice negotiations, which impose strict terms upon Germany.

■ **June 1919** Boycotts the signing of the Treaty of Versailles, which he considers too lenient towards Germany.

■ **March 1929** Dies on 20 March and is buried in Paris alongside his hero, Napoleon I.

STATUE OF FERDINAND FOCH, LONDON

After the raid
A British aerial reconnaissance photograph shows three British cruisers sunk as blockships in the mouth of the Zeebrugge–Bruges canal. The passage of German U-boats through the canal was only briefly obstructed.

« BEFORE

The Battle of Jutland in 1916 was the last significant encounter between British and German surface warships in World War I.

THE WAR ON U-BOATS
Germany adopted **unrestricted submarine warfare** « 220–21 against Allied merchant shipping from February 1917. The U-boats failed to win the war, but Allied shipping losses remained high. The British tried and failed to stop the U-boats breaking into the Atlantic by placing **barrages** across the English Channel and in the North Sea between Britain and Norway.

U-BOAT SUBMARINER'S BADGE

The Zeebrugge Raid

In April 1918, Britain's Royal Navy and Royal Marines made a bold raid on the port of Zeebrugge in German-occupied Belgium. The operation failed to stop the movement of U-boats, but it boosted the morale of the British public, who longed for heroic naval action.

In late 1917, acting Vice-Admiral Roger Keyes, considered one of the British Royal Navy's most capable leaders, was assigned the task of improving the defence of the eastern entrance to the English Channel against German submarines.

Since 1915, a barrage of anti-submarine nets and mines had been maintained between the English and French coasts, but U-boats sailing from Germany's North Sea ports and from bases at Zeebrugge and Ostende in Belgium continued to filter through

this flimsy obstacle at will. To counter these attacks, Keyes increased the number of mines along the barrier, stationed 70 trawlers and drifters (small fishing vessels) as lookouts on the surface, and backed them up with patrols by destroyers (generally used to defend larger warships) based at Dover.

Keyes was incensed when, in mid-February 1918, German destroyers attacked the English Channel barrier by night, sinking eight drifters and trawlers with impunity. There was a possibility that the barrier might

become unsustainable. Keyes responded by pressing for a raid on Zeebrugge and Ostende to stop the movement of U-boats at its source.

Audacious plan
The German submarine pens were situated inland at the Belgian city of Bruges, from where they were moved by canal to the coastal ports and then the open sea. The planned raid would sink "blockships" – vessels that were deliberately sunk to impede the passage of other ships – in the mouths

"Hell was let loose, troops were climbing the scaling ladders on to the mole..."

ROYAL MARINE PRIVATE G. CALVERLEY ON BOARD THE "IRIS"

of the canals, thus denying the U-boats passage to the sea. Inevitably, the Belgian ports would be heavily defended, but the British were convinced that such a raid was feasible.

Various vessels were assembled for the operation, including 19th-century cruisers, ferry boats, motor launches, and submarines. To maintain secrecy, seamen were invited to volunteer for the mission without being told what it entailed.

The plan for the attack on Zeebrugge was complex, ingenious, and fallible. Under cover of a smokescreen, the elderly cruiser HMS *Vindictive* and two ferries would advance to the breakwater at the harbour entrance so marines and seamen could disembark. This landing party would then silence the German guns defending the port, while submarines packed with explosives would demolish the bridge connecting the breakwater to the land, preventing the Germans from sending in reinforcements. Then three antiquated cruisers packed with rubble and concrete would be sunk by their crews at the entrance to the canal. At the same time, a similar plan, involving two blockships, was to be executed at Ostende.

Night attack

After two false starts, when the raids were aborted due to bad weather, Keyes's raiding force set to sea on 22 April, with the admiral sailing on board the destroyer HMS *Warwick*. The Ostende attack was abandoned when it was found that buoys put in place to guide the ships to the port entrance had been destroyed by the Germans, but the raid at Zeebrugge went ahead.

Just after midnight, *Vindictive* and the ferries *Iris* and *Daffodil* approached the breakwater. The sea was lit up by German flares and searchlights, but the ships were hidden by a bank of smoke laid down by British destroyers and motor launches. *Vindictive* emerged

from this protective cloud within a few hundred metres of the breakwater. It was then raked by fire from a whole range of German guns at point-blank range.

Marines and seamen who were crowded onto the deck in preparation for the landing suffered heavy casualties. Some men gallantly mounted ladders on to the breakwater but, pinned down by German machine-guns, they stood no chance of reaching the heavy gun emplacements that were their main objective. One of the British submarines succeeded in blowing up the link between the breakwater and the shore.

Vindictive had been armed with howitzers and mortars to provide additional fire support for the landing party, but its position was soon untenable. After less than an hour, the British ships were forced to withdraw, loaded with dead and wounded seamen.

Despite the failure at the breakwater, the three blockships continued with their mission. Under heavy German fire, *Iphigenia* and *Intrepid* sailed to the mouth of the canal where they were scuttled by their crews as planned – most of the men were picked up by small boats and carried safely back to England. The third blockship, *Thetis*, did not make it to the canal but was sunk short of its target.

Heroic failure

The Zeebrugge raid was a brave but botched operation. More than 200 British servicemen lost their lives and some 400 were wounded or taken prisoner. Even though the raid did not achieve its objective, the courage

of the men who executed it was acknowledged with the award of eight Victoria Crosses.

The Bruges canal was blocked for only two days. The Germans quickly opened a channel for submarines to bypass the blockships, and the effect on the U-boat campaign was imperceptible. Coming at a dark moment in the war, however, with German armies on the offensive in France, the raid was celebrated as a victory by the British.

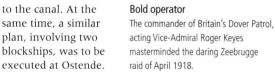

Bold operator
The commander of Britain's Dover Patrol, acting Vice-Admiral Roger Keyes masterminded the daring Zeebrugge raid of April 1918.

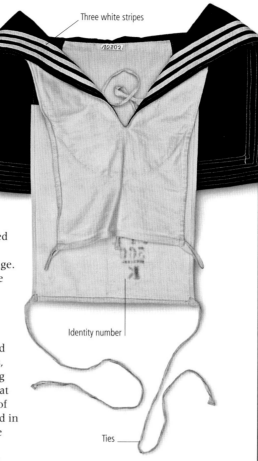

Three white stripes

German naval kit
A detachable collar was part of the uniform worn by a Matrose (seaman), the lowest rank in the German Imperial Navy.

Identity number

Ties

AFTER ≫

The raid had no effect on the shape of the naval war. The Allies could not stop U-boat attacks, and the German surface fleet were unable to break the Royal Navy's blockade.

RENEWED ATTACK
The British **attempt to raid Ostende** was renewed on 9–10 May 1918. HMS *Vindictive*, this time involved as a blockship, was sunk in Ostende harbour. As in the Zeebrugge raid, the effect on the movement of U-boats was limited. The German navy **withdrew its U-boats from Belgium** in September 1918 when the Belgian ports were threatened by advancing Allied armies in Flanders. Submarine operations continued from German ports.

188,000 The number of tons of Allied shipping sunk by U-boats in September 1918.

GERMAN MUTINY
The German High Seas Fleet coincidentally made its last sortie into the North Sea on the same day as the Zeebrugge raid. Attempting to **intercept a convoy off Norway**, it was chased home by the British fleet. The morale of German sailors deteriorated. A naval mutiny triggered **revolutionary upheaval 320–21 ≫** in Germany at the war's end.

Return from Zeebrugge
Badly damaged by gunfire, the cruiser HMS *Vindictive* arrives back in Dover after the Zeebrugge raid. *Vindictive* was sunk as a blockship in an attack on Ostende in the following month.

BEFORE

Aircraft were used for bombing or reconnaissance early in the war. Later, fighter planes were built for combat.

CHANGING ROLE

Britain was the first country to engage in **strategic bombing** by targeting Zeppelin hangars in Cologne and Düsseldorf in September 1914. From 1915, Germany carried out **long-range bombing** of British and French cities **‹‹ 232–33**, a tactic later adopted by the Allies. From 1916, specialist fighter planes, first built to attack aircraft bombing targets behind enemy lines or engage in reconnaissance, **battled for air supremacy ‹‹ 188–89**.

ALTIMETER

Climax of the Air War

By 1918, German airmen were outnumbered and could not stop the Allies winning command of the air. Although the support of army operations remained the principal role of aircraft, late in the war an Allied bombing campaign was launched against German cities.

In the final campaigns of the war, from the German Michael Offensive in March 1918 to the Allied Hundred Days Offensives between August and November, army commanders made aircraft an integral part of their tactics for ending the stalemate of trench warfare. Troops learned to fear being gunned down by low-flying planes, and tactical bombing of targets such as arms dumps, railway stations, and ports hampered the supply of equipment and reinforcement.

Air support was often inhibited by bad weather and did not always work – for example, an attempt by the British to bomb bridges over the Somme during the Battle of Amiens in August 1918 failed. But the use of aircraft contributed

substantially to the return to mobile warfare. Aerial observers, now able to contact ground staff by radio, could report on the movements of ground forces that had penetrated enemy defences in depth. They also enabled artillery fire to be accurately targeted in support of infantry. Late in the war, supplies were dropped from the air to troops advancing at speed.

Fight for supremacy

As the role of aircraft became more important to the war effort, the fiercer the struggle for air superiority became. Air commanders learned the value of raiding enemy airfields as the first blow in an offensive. Ever larger formations were put into the skies over the Western Front – 700 aircraft supported the French counterattack at the Marne in July 1918.

The battle for air superiority was fought in factories as well as in the air. The British aircraft industry, built up from almost nothing during the course of the war, produced over 30,000 aircraft in 1918, while French factories manufactured almost 25,000 planes.

Hampered by shortages of labour and raw materials, Germany produced only 14,000 aircraft during the same period, insufficient to replace its losses in the fighting from spring to autumn 1918.

The entry of the USA into the war was expected to boost Allied aircraft output, but it proved surprisingly difficult to turn US automobile factories into aircraft manufacturers. A mere 1,400 aircraft were produced by the USA during the war and most US pilots flew in British or French machines.

With well-organized squadrons, the Germans achieved air supremacy in spring 1918. They held a slender lead in technology. The introduction of

> **270,000** The number of workers employed in the British aircraft industry by the end of the war.

KEY
- ■ 1914
- ■ 1918

War in the skies

Military aviation expanded rapidly during the war. In August 1914, around 500 aircraft were deployed by all combatants combined. By the end of the war, some 12,000 military aircraft were engaged in active service.

(bar chart: Front-line combat aircraft vs Countries — France, Britain, Germany, Italy, USA)

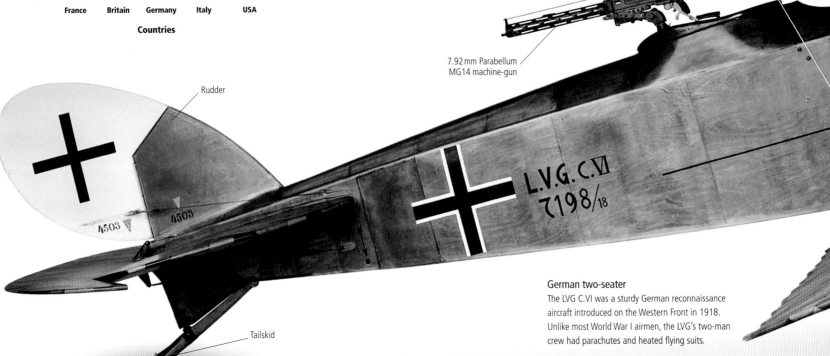

Aileron

7.92 mm Parabellum MG14 machine-gun

Rudder

L.V.G. C.VI
7198/18

4503

4503

Tailskid

German two-seater

The LVG C.VI was a sturdy German reconnaissance aircraft introduced on the Western Front in 1918. Unlike most World War I airmen, the LVG's two-man crew had parachutes and heated flying suits.

Italian triplane bomber
One of the largest bomber aircraft deployed in the war was the Italian three-engine triplane Caproni Ca.4. Although clumsy in appearance, it was able to carry a substantial bombload on long-range missions.

the Fokker D.VII in April gave them a better fighter aircraft than the Allied Sopwith Camels, SE5s or SPAD XIIIs.

The German Rumpler C.VII, also deployed in 1918, was the war's most advanced reconnaissance aircraft. It could fly at 6,000 m (20,000 ft), above Allied fighters, its crew equipped with oxygen and heated flying suits to cope with the high altitude. Germany even issued parachutes, a refinement scorned by Allied commanders, who feared aircrew would jump out of their planes through cowardice.

But nothing could save German forces from the logic of numbers. By summer 1918, they were being overwhelmed by the sheer number of Allied aircraft over the battlefield – 1,500 were deployed at the St Mihiel salient in northeastern France in September. Heavy combat losses meant the quality of German pilots declined as inexperienced pilots were drafted to the front. Growing petrol shortages in Germany curtailed training flights and limited the number of combat missions that could be flown. By autumn 1918, the Allies had achieved indisputable air superiority over the Western Front.

Bombing campaigns
The German bombing campaign against British and French cities, with airships in 1915 and with planes from 1917, ended in spring 1918 with a late flurry of heavy raids on Paris. The German bombers were then reassigned to tactical missions aimed at targets of immediate military value. By then the British had begun preparing their own

> **15,000** The estimated number of airmen of all nationalities killed in the course of the war.

bombing campaign against German cities in the hope of undermining Germany's performance on the battlefield by targeting its industries.

In Britain, the Royal Air Force was established in April 1918 to make air power independent of army and naval commanders, partly with a bombing campaign in mind. In June, the British and French assembled their bomber aircraft in France as an independent air force commanded by General Hugh Trenchard. They began raids deep into Germany with fleets of up to 40 bombers. Large Caproni and Handley Page aircraft attacked by night, and smaller de Havillands and Breguets by day.

As the Germans had already discovered, causing large-scale damage was beyond the capacity of World War I aircraft, but the inhabitants of Mannheim and Frankfurt experienced the terror that had struck London and Paris. Commitment to the strategic bombing campaign was less than total. Trenchard more often used his aircraft to support the Allied armies. Had the Armistice not intervened, however, the Allied bombing campaign would have undoubtedly expanded.

Treaty of Versailles 338–39 »

From 1919, air forces shrank to a fraction of their wartime strength, but belief in the potential of strategic bombing grew.

COVERT FORCE
Under the terms of the 1919 **Treaty of Versailles 338–39 »**, Germany was banned from possessing an air force. Covertly, however, a **shadow air force** was kept in place, with pilots trained in Russia under the terms of the German-Soviet Treaty of Berlin of 1926. After the rise to power of Adolf Hitler in 1933, Germany began a **rapid expansion of military aviation**, formally announcing the founding of the **Luftwaffe** in 1935.

THE CHANGING FACE OF WAR
In 1921, Italian General Giulio Douhet published an influential book, *The Command of the Air*, arguing that a future war could be won through **mass bombing attacks on enemy cities** and industrial facilities. The chief of Britain's Royal Air Force (RAF), Hugh Trenchard, and General Billy Mitchell in the USA were inspired by a similar vision. It led to the development of the **bomber forces** that would devastate cities in **World War II**.

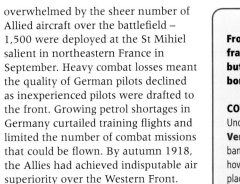

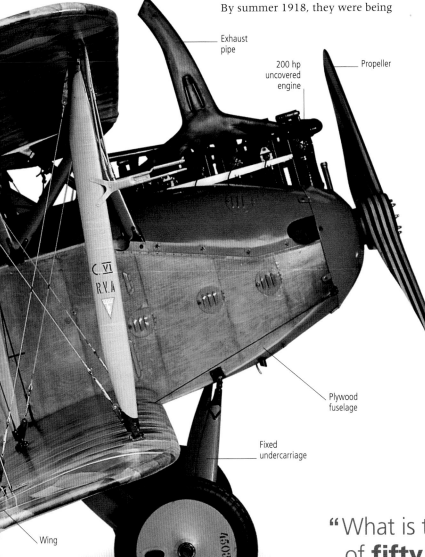

Exhaust pipe

200 hp uncovered engine

Propeller

Plywood fuselage

Fixed undercarriage

Wing

Air Force recruitment poster
A wartime poster encourages men to join Britain's Royal Air Force. The RAF was established as an independent service in April 1918 by amalgamating the Royal Flying Corps and the Royal Naval Air Service.

> "What is the point of **shooting down five** out of **fifty machines?**... The **enemy's** material **superiority** was **dooming us to failure.**"
>
> GERMAN PILOT RUDOLF STARK IN "WINGS OF WAR: AN AIRMAN'S DIARY OF THE LAST YEAR OF WORLD WAR ONE"

Aerial Combat

As fighting continued unabated on the Western Front, a ferocious air battle raged in the skies above, leading to a high casualty rate among pilots. By 1918, some 8,000 aircraft were in action over northern France and Belgium. Successful pilots were glorified by propaganda and the media.

"Suddenly we saw a squadron approaching from the other side... I was nearest to the enemy and attacked the man to the rear... My opponent did not make matters easy for me. He knew the fighting business... he plunged into a cloud and had nearly saved himself. I plunged after him and as luck would have it, found myself close behind him. I fired and he fired without any tangible result. At last I hit him. I noticed a ribbon of white benzine vapour... He was a stubborn fellow and fought until he landed. When he had come to the ground I flew over him at an altitude of about 30 feet in order to ascertain whether I had killed him or not. What did the rascal do? He took his machine-gun and shot holes into my machine.**"**

GERMAN ACE MANFRED VON RICHTHOFEN, FROM HIS AUTOBIOGRAPHY "RED AIR FIGHTER" (1918)

"At 150 yards I pressed my triggers. The tracer bullets cut a streak of living fire into the rear of the Pfalz tail. Raising the nose of my aeroplane slightly, the fiery streak lifted itself like the stream of water pouring from a garden hose... The swerving of its course indicated that its rudder no longer was held by a directing hand. At 2,000 feet above the enemy's lines I pulled up my headlong dive and watched the enemy machine continuing on its course. Curving slightly to the left, the Pfalz circled a little to the south and the next minute crashed into the ground. **"**

AMERICAN ACE EDDIE RICKENBACKER, FROM HIS MEMOIR "FIGHTING THE FLYING CIRCUS" (1919)

Safe return
Ground staff cheer as a German Gotha returns safely from a mission. Aircrew on both sides were worked to the point of exhaustion, often having to make several flights each day for weeks on end.

FIGHTER PILOT Born 1892 Died 1918

Manfred von Richthofen

"Fly... to the **last drop of blood...** the **last beat of the heart.**"

MANFRED VON RICHTHOFEN, TOAST TO HIS FELLOW PILOTS

German pilot Manfred von Richthofen, popularly known as the Red Baron, has proved the most enduringly famous of the World War I fighter aces. He was singled out by German propagandists as a hero whose daring deeds would shine forth in invigorating contrast to the mechanical slaughter of the trenches.

Brought up on an estate in rural Prussia, he developed a passion for hunting from an early age. The hunt would later be his favourite metaphor for air combat, with himself as the hunter and enemy aircraft as his prey. Following family tradition, he entered the Prussian military education system when he was a child.

Medal of honour
After confirmation of his 16th "kill" in January 1917 Richthofen was awarded the Pour le Mérite (Blue Max), Germany's highest military honour. Richthofen eventually scored 80 "kills".

A junior officer in the Uhlan lancers when the war broke out, Richthofen was soon disillusioned by the lack of opportunity for dashing action and transferred to the air service in search of adventure. After serving six months as an observer in a two-seater reconnaissance aircraft, he learned to fly in October 1915.

Courage is the key

Richthofen's skill was as a killer not a pilot – he later wrote that he had shot down 20 aircraft by the time he was comfortable at the controls. He would always disparage complex aerobatics, saying that "one does not need to be a clever pilot" but only "to have the courage to fly in close to the enemy before opening fire".

Assigned to piloting two-seater bombers on the Eastern Front, Richthofen was saved from obscurity in 1916 by a chance acquaintance with Oswald Boelcke, Germany's leading fighter ace. Boelcke chose Richthofen to join his elite Jagdstaffel (Jasta) 2 fighter squadron on the Western Front.

The first theoretician of air combat, Boelcke passed on the basics of this new form of warfare to Richthofen and the other pilots in his squadron. Boelcke's guiding principles included not flying into the sun when attacking an enemy and not opening fire until at close range. Employed against slow-moving Allied reconnaissance aircraft and

The Flying Circus

Albatros aircraft of Richthofen's Jagda 1 fighter wing line up at an airfield in France. Jagda 1 was known as the Flying Circus because of its aircrafts' bright colours. Richthofen himself became known as the Red Baron.

bombers, which were the German fighters' principal targets, these tactics allowed Richthofen to build up a high number of "kills" very quickly.

Flying ace

Richthofen became one of Germany's elite band of pilots on 23 November 1916 when he shot down one of Britain's most successful fighter aces, Major Lanoe Hawker. The British pilot, caught flying an inferior aircraft deep behind German lines, was pursued relentlessly by Richthofen's faster Albatros until the German was close enough to shoot him in the head.

In 1917, Richthofen was given command of his own squadron and then of Germany's first fighter wing, the four squadrons of Jagdgeschwader (Jagda) 1. He excelled as a commander, taking time to teach new pilots how to fight. The Flying Circus, as Jagda 1 came to be called, nurtured many ace

German hero

As well as being Germany's most celebrated pilot, Manfred von Richthofen was an outstanding leader of men. He was depicted by German wartime propaganda as a chivalrous "knight of the sky".

pilots, including Manfred's younger brother, Lothar. It was used as a trouble-shooting formation, sent to whichever sector of the Western Front was thought most crucial at the time.

Combat takes its toll

By spring 1917, with over 50 "kills" to his name, Richthofen was one of the most famous men in Germany. He was invited to meet the Kaiser, and urged to write his memoirs as a morale-boosting tale for the German public. Like all World War I fighter aces, however, he suffered from the nervous strain of combat and the frequent deaths of comrades. On 6 July 1917, he was shot in the head by a Lewis gunner in a British two-seater. Although almost blinded, he managed to land his aircraft safely. However, his health never fully recovered.

The injury occurred at a moment when Germany was losing its technical superiority to a new generation of Allied aircraft. Richthofen informed the German air staff of the "poor morale" of German fighter pilots

due to their "sorry machines". He used his prestige to push for the mass manufacture of the Fokker Dr.1 triplane, which would become his most famous mount, and then for development of the Fokker D7, which became the highest-performing fighter of the war.

By 1918, Richthofen was under pressure to withdraw from combat, since his death would be a heavy blow to German morale. But he refused, stating that it would be despicable to preserve his "valuable life for the nation" while "every poor fellow in the trenches… has to stick it out."

On 21 April, pursuing a potential victim over British lines with uncharacteristic recklessness, Richthofen was shot dead, either by Canadian pilot Roy Brown or by Australian machine-gunners on the ground. He was only 25 years old.

Buried by the enemy

The Australian Flying Corps gave Richthofen a military burial at Bertangles, near Amiens, on 22 April 1918. Some Allied fliers expressed respect for a fallen enemy, others were openly glad he was dead.

TIMELINE

- **3 May 1892** Born into an aristocratic Prussian family near Breslau (now Wroclaw in Poland).

- **1903** Enters military cadet school at the age of 11.

- **1911** Graduates from the Royal Military Academy, joining an Uhlan light cavalry regiment with the rank of lieutenant in 1912.

- **May 1915** Transfers from the cavalry to the German air service, seeing action as an observer on reconnaissance missions.

- **October 1915** After meeting German ace Oswald Boelcke, he begins pilot training, qualifying in early 1916.

- **March 1916** Flies two-seater bomber aircraft at Verdun and on the Eastern Front.

- **August 1916** Becomes a fighter pilot, joining Oswald Boelcke's squadron Jagdstaffel (Jasta) 2 on the Western Front.

- **September 1916** Achieves his first "kills", shooting down two Allied aircraft.

- **October 1916** Witnesses the death of Boelcke in a collision during combat with British aircraft.

- **November 1916** Flying an Albatros D.1, he shoots down the British ace pilot Major Lance Hawker.

- **January 1917** Awarded the Pour le Mérite (Blue Max) for 16 "kills", Richthofen is appointed commander of a fighter squadron, Jasta 11, in northern France.

- **April 1917** Flying an Albatros D.3 fighter, he shoots down 21 Allied aircraft in a month during the Battle of Arras.

- **June 1917** Appointed commander of a flight wing of four squadrons, Jagdgeschwader (Jagda) 1, known as Richthofen's Flying Circus.

- **July 1917** Suffers a serious head wound in combat and has to undergo surgery.

- **August 1917** Returns to command of Jagda 1 during the Third Battle of Ypres, flying the Fokker Dr.1 triplane for the first time.

- **September 1917** Still suffering the effects of his wound, he takes convalescent leave to complete his memoirs, *Der rote Kampfflieger* (The Red Battle Flyer).

- **March–April 1918** Leading Jagda 1 in the German Spring Offensive, Richthofen raises his tally of "kills" to 80.

- **21 April 1918** Richthofen is killed either by ground or air fire while flying over the Somme. Hermann Goering takes over his squadron.

REPLICA OF THE FOKKER DR.1 TRIPLANE

"I approached… and **fired 50 bullets until** the **machine began to burn.**"

MANFRED VON RICHTHOFEN, DESCRIBING HIS LAST "KILL" ON 20 APRIL 1918

Allied Intervention in Russia

From spring 1918, the Allies intervened in Russia in a way that called into question their true motives towards the country. Initially aimed at advancing the war effort against Germany, their actions soon developed into a confused bid to overthrow the Bolshevik regime.

The collapse of Russia was a severe setback for the Allies, because it freed Germany from the need to fight a war on two fronts. The situation in Russia was also dangerously chaotic. The Bolsheviks controlled Petrograd and Moscow, but elsewhere former tsarist officers led "White" armies, a loose affiliation of anti-communist forces, in revolt against Bolshevik rule. Bolshevism was also contested by rival revolutionaries and ethnic groups.

BEFORE

Revolutionary upheaval in Russia in 1917 created a confused situation for Russia's military allies, who were desperate to keep Russia in the war.

BOLSHEVIK REVOLUTION
Tsar Nicholas II was forced to **abdicate** **《 210–11** in March 1917. The Provisional Government that replaced the Tsar pledged to continue the war, and was provided with money and arms by Britain, France, and the USA. The failure of a **Russian summer offensive** was followed by the overthrow of the Provisional Government by **the Bolsheviks 《 252–53** in November.

PEACE TREATY
The Bolsheviks agreed an **armistice** with the Central Powers in December 1917, but peace negotiations proceeded slowly. Allied hopes that the Bolsheviks could be persuaded to resume the war were dashed by the **Brest-Litovsk Peace Treaty** **《 276–77** in March 1918.

PROVISIONAL GOVERNMENT SOLDIER

As early as December 1917, the Allies agreed in principle to intervene in Russia to support any political force prepared to resume the war against Germany, and to protect military supplies stockpiled in Russian ports from falling into German hands. Action was slow to develop, however, partly because of mutual suspicion between the Allies. Japan was best placed to intervene, with troops available to land at the key Russian port of Vladivostok in eastern Russia, but fears of Japanese territorial ambitions made the other Allies hostile to an independent Japanese initiative.

The Czech Legion

By strange accident, the Allies found themselves with a substantial military force caught up in the chaos of post-revolutionary Russia. The Czech Legion was a body of Czech and

13,000 The number of American troops involved in military intervention in Russia.

40,000 The number of British troops sent to Arkhangelsk and Vladivostok.

Slovak soldiers recruited during 1916–17 from the Russian army and prisoners of war or deserters from the Austro-Hungarian army. They intended to fight for the Allies in the hope of being rewarded with national independence once the Central Powers had been defeated.

The Bolshevik government had agreed to allow the Czech Legion to cross Russia to Vladivostok, from where it could sail to France to join other Czechs and Slovaks fighting on the Western Front. Strung out along the Trans-Siberian Railway through

Bolshevik propaganda
Proclaiming that "the enemy is at the gate", a Bolshevik poster calls on the people to fight in defence of the revolution. In 1918, the Bolshevik regime was under siege and seemed unlikely to survive.

May and June 1918, however, elements of the Legion came into conflict with Bolshevik authorities, who tried to disarm them and obstructed their progress. Local clashes developed into full-scale fighting. An organized and motivated force of some 50,000 men, the Czechs and Slovaks soon had control of a substantial area of Russia along the line of the Trans-Siberian Railway and at Vladivostok.

Also in June 1918, substantial numbers of Allied troops began to land in northern Russia. Large stockpiles of munitions, previously sent by Britain to aid their Russian allies, had accumulated at the ports of Murmansk and Arkhangelsk. These were vulnerable to attack by German forces active in Finland. To secure the munitions, a few thousand British and French troops landed at Murmansk and, in July, went on to occupy Arkhangelsk. A subsidiary objective of this operation was to provide an alternative route for the Czech Legion to leave Russia and sail for France.

The British, however, began to toy with an alternative plan for the revival of war on the Eastern Front. They proposed that the Allied forces at Arkhangelsk, the Czech Legion, and the White Army of Admiral Alexander Kolchak, based in Siberia, would join together to overthrow the Bolsheviks and reopen Russia's war with Germany.

KEY MOMENT

THE MURDER OF THE TSAR

From March 1917, former Tsar Nicholas II, his wife Alexandra, and their five children were placed under house arrest – first at a palace in Tsarskoe Selo near Petrograd and then at Tobolsk in Siberia. In April 1918, the Bolshevik authorities moved the family to a house in Ekaterinburg, a town between Tobolsk and Moscow, where they were subjected to petty harassment. By July, Ekaterinburg was

under threat from the anti-Bolshevik forces of the Czech Legion. On 16 July, the Bolsheviks herded the entire family, along with their doctor and servants, into the basement of the house and shot them dead in a clumsily executed massacre. The bodies were buried in secret, the last remains not being discovered and identified until 2008.

" The **strangling of Bolshevism** at its **birth** would have been an **untold blessing** to the human race. "

WINSTON CHURCHILL, SPEECH, 1949

Mixed motives

In summer 1918, Allied intervention in Russia gained momentum. President Woodrow Wilson sent US troops both to Arkhangelsk – a move known as the Polar Bear Expedition – and to Vladivostok. In August, 7,000 Japanese troops poured into Vladivostok, spreading out to occupy a substantial area of eastern Siberia.

The Allies were far from united in their strategy or objectives, however. Contingents of British, French colonial, and Italian troops landing at Vladivostok were ordered to head into central Russia to support a drive by the Czech Legion against the Bolsheviks. The Japanese concentrated on occupying territory in the east, which they hoped to hold on to after the war. The commander of the 8,000 US troops in Vladivostok, General William

Graves, refused to become involved in anti-Bolshevik adventures and concentrated on making the Trans-Siberian Railway fully operational. By autumn 1918, the Bolsheviks had turned their newly founded Red Army into an increasingly effective fighting force. Allied and White Russian troops advancing south from Arkhangelsk faced vigorous Bolshevik counterattacks.

On 11 November 1918, the day of the Armistice between the Central Powers and the Allies on the Western Front, British, Canadian, and US troops were fighting hard to repel a Red Army attack on the Dvina river at Tulgas.

Admiral Kolchak
Backed by foreign forces, Admiral Alexander Kolchak headed an anti-Bolshevik White government based at Omsk in Siberia. In 1920, he was captured by Bolshevik forces and executed.

The end of the war on the Western Front at least clarified the true purpose of Allied intervention in Russia all along – the straightforward support of the White armies seeking to overthrow the Bolsheviks. The French even expanded intervention to a new front by landing troops at Odessa in southern Ukraine to aid White Army forces in December 1918. Allied war-weariness would, however, soon call a halt to such ventures.

AFTER »

Most Allied powers left Russia in early 1919, except for the USA and Japan, which stayed on in Vladivostok.

THE ALLIES DEPART
Under pressure both from the Bolshevik Red Army and war-weary public opinion at home, **Allied forces withdrew** from Murmansk and Arkhangelsk in the first half of 1919. The French left Odessa in April 1919 after a mutiny in their fleet. The **Czech Legion** negotiated an **armistice with the Bolsheviks** and returned to newly independent Czechoslovakia in early 1920. The **intervention at Vladivostok** lasted the longest, with most Allied troops, including the Americans, leaving in 1920. Japanese troops did not withdraw until 1922.

Allied troops in Vladivostok, 1918
French, British, US, and Japanese flags hang from a building in Vladivostok, on Russia's Pacific coast, during a march-past by Allied forces. Various foreign troops occupied the port between 1918 and 1922.

Writers at War

> " My **subject is war** and the pity of war. The **poetry** is in **the pity... All a poet can do** today is **warn.**"

WILFRED OWEN, BRITISH OFFICER AND WAR POET, 1918

The writings of poets and novelists who took part in World War I have shaped popular perception of the war, chiefly through underlining the suffering and waste of life it entailed. From the start of the war, however, many established writers were inspired by patriotism and lined up to serve their country.

In October 1914, for example, 93 leading German intellectuals signed a manifesto defending Germany's invasion of Belgium and declaring "the German army and the German people are one and the same". Novelist Thomas Mann, a future Nobel prize winner, was a prominent supporter of the German cause, asserting the superiority of Prussian militarism as opposed to "the pacifist ideal of civilization". In Britain, at a meeting organized by the government's propaganda bureau in September 1914, prominent authors, including Arthur Conan Doyle, Rudyard Kipling, and H.G. Wells, agreed to write essays and give public lectures in support of the war.

Fired by patriotism

Much of the writing published during the war was the work of individuals employing the time-worn clichés of honour and glory. But it would be wrong to see those who wrote in support of the war effort on both sides as insincere. Many were deeply moved by patriotism and the perceived justice of their country's cause, emotions that only deepened as the death toll mounted. Kipling suffered irreparable grief over the death of his son at the Battle of Loos in 1915, but it did not alter his commitment to Britain winning the war. Even citizens of the initially neutral USA were inspired by the conflict. The US novelist Edith Wharton, living in France when the war broke out, published essays expressing her admiration for the French, whom she described as nobly engaged in a struggle for survival.

Anti-war novel

Henri Barbusse's controversial 1916 novel, *Le Feu* (Under Fire) captured the horrors of trench warfare. It made a big impact in France and was published in English the following year.

L'ŒUVRE de Gustave Téry publie

LE FEU

notes d'un combattant HENRI BARBUSSE

The war poets

For younger writers, the situation was profoundly different because they became actively engaged in the war. The fashionable young English poet Rupert Brooke, who joined up as a junior officer in September 1914, wrote verse that epitomized the high-minded enthusiasm of the first

Wounded novelist
American writer Ernest Hemingway was wounded by shrapnel while serving as an ambulance driver in Italy in 1918. He used his wartime experience in the novel *A Farewell to Arms*.

of their daily lives at the front. An urge grew to testify to the reality of the war and to find a means of expression suitable to its horrors and humiliations. A turning point was marked by the publication of the novel *Le Feu* (Under Fire) by the French author Henri Barbusse in 1916. Defying government censorship, and based on the writer's own experience of the trenches, it provided the first graphic description of the grim conditions and grotesque sufferings at the front.

A number of British soldier-poets were inspired by a similar impulse to record and protest against the sordid reality of the war. The verse of poets

however, only came after the war had ended – Owen was unknown at the time of his death in November 1918.

Looking back

In the 1920s, memoirs and retrospective novels reshaped the way the war was remembered. Not all reflected the disillusion that was widespread in the postwar period – for example, Ernst Jünger's record of his experiences as a German infantry officer, *Storm of Steel*, expressed the excitement of battle as well as its horrors. But more typical was the writing of Czech author Jaroslav Hasek, who forever fixed the image of

Private poet
Most writers serving in the war were officers, but the British-Jewish poet and artist Isaac Rosenberg served as a private. Rosenberg produced this *Self-Portrait in a Steel Helmet* shortly after enlisting in 1915.

TIMELINE

- **5 September 1914** French poet Charles Péguy is killed at the Battle of the Marne.

- **23 April 1915** Seven months after joining the war as a junior officer, English poet Rupert Brooke dies of an infected mosquito bite on his way to the Gallipoli landings.

- **1916** Henri Barbusse's anti-war novel *Le Feu* (Under Fire) wins the Prix Goncourt.

- **March 1916** French modernist poet Guillaume Apollinaire, serving as an officer, suffers a head wound from which he never fully recovers.

- **June 1916** British poet Wilfred Owen joins the Manchester Regiment as a second lieutenant.

- **1917** German novelist Thomas Mann publishes his essay *Reflections of Non-Political Man* in praise of German militarism.

- **July 1917** British officer and poet Siegfried Sassoon publishes an open letter entitled *Finished with the War: A Soldier's Declaration*. In the same month, young American writers John Dos Passos and E.E. Cummings volunteer for ambulance service in France.

- **1 April 1918** British poet Isaac Rosenberg is killed on the Somme.

- **May 1918** Ernest Hemingway signs up as an ambulance driver on the Italian front.

- **4 November 1918** Wilfred Owen is killed in action a week before the end of the war.

- **1920** German officer Ernst Jünger's war memoir *Storm of Steel* is privately published.

- **1928–29** A flood of war memoirs are published in Britain, including Robert Graves's *Goodbye to All That* and Edmund Blunden's *Undertones of War*.

- **1929** Erich Remarque's anti-war novel *All Quiet on the Western Front* is a best-seller.

> # "**Heroes** don't **exist,** only **cattle** for the slaughter and the **butchers** in the general staffs."
>
> JAROSLAV HASEK, "THE GOOD SOLDIER SCHWEIK", 1923

phase of the war. His poems "The Soldier" ("… there's some corner of a foreign field/That is for ever England") and the series *1914*, containing "Peace" ("Now God be thanked who has matched us with his hour…"), were already famous when he died at the age of 27 in April 1915. French poet Guillaume Apollinaire, a volunteer arriving at the front in 1915, wrote "Ah Dieu! que la guerre est jolie…" ("O God! How beautiful war is…") and celebrated the spectacle of shells and flares by night as a superb firework display.

Bitter experience

These attitudes could not survive long experience of trench warfare and the apparently interminable prolongation of the conflict. Like all soldiers, writers in uniform became disgusted at the gap between the patriotic rhetoric published in newspapers and the truth

such as Siegfried Sassoon, Wilfred Owen, Isaac Rosenberg, and Ivor Gurney was later to be seen as a landmark in English literature and the most enduring and moving memorial to the war dead. In particular, Owen's expression of what he called "the pity of war" and his anger at the "old lie" that it was sweet and honourable to die for one's country were to have lasting impact. The triumph of British anti-war poetry,

The Good Soldier
Czech author Jaroslav Hasek created Austria-Hungary's most famous anti-war hero in his absurdist comedy *The Good Soldier Schweik*. This image of the unwittingly subversive Schweik was drawn by cartoonist Josef Lada.

Austria-Hungary's war as a tragic farce in *The Good Soldier Schweik*, a satire published posthumously in 1923. German author Erich Remarque's novel *All Quiet on the Western Front* was the most influential title in a wave of books inspired by a pacifist rejection of the war in the late 1920s and early 1930s. Another example was *Testament of Youth*, the memoirs of Vera Brittain, who served as a nurse on the Western Front and lost a brother and a fiancé in the conflict.

American author Ernest Hemingway, who had served as an ambulance volunteer on the Italian front in 1918, popularized the idea that those for whom the war was a formative experience constituted a "Lost Generation". War had profoundly affected those it touched, and it continued to exert a powerful influence on postwar writers.

ALL QUIET ON THE WESTERN FRONT

- **1933** Vera Brittain, a nurse during the war and a pacifist campaigner, publishes her moving war memoir *Testament of Youth*.

- **May 1933** *All Quiet on the Western Front* is banned and publicly burned by the Nazi regime in Germany.

Turning Point at Amiens

In August 1918, an Allied offensive led by British and Commonwealth troops inflicted a sharp defeat on the Germans at Amiens. This demonstration of their increasing superiority over the enemy forced the Germans to accept that they could no longer hope to win the war.

« BEFORE

By the summer of 1918, the German offensives begun in the spring had lost momentum. American troops were arriving in France in ever increasing numbers.

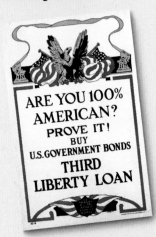

US POSTER PROMOTING LIBERTY LOANS

GERMAN FAILURE

From the **Michael Offensive « 278–79** in March to the May **Artois Offensive « 282–83**, Germany had achieved striking successes. However, the **arrival of US troops**, backed by the country's financial might, changed the strategic balance. By July, the USA had helped the French defeat the last German offensive at the **Second Battle of the Marne « 286–87**.

Allied Supreme Commander General Ferdinand Foch called for a continuous series of offensives to maintain pressure on the Germans after Allied success at the Second Battle of the Marne. At a meeting on 24 July, British commander-in-chief Field Marshal Douglas Haig agreed to Foch's plan. Britain's Fourth Army, commanded by General Henry Rawlinson, supported by the French, was to attack Amiens. The assault would be led by the Australian Corps under General John Monash and the Canadian Corps under General Arthur Currie – the Canadians and Australians being considered the freshest, hardest-fighting troops on the Western Front.

The Australian Corps was already part of the Fourth Army and had carried out a successful attack on German positions at Hamel near Amiens on 4 July. The Canadians, however, were 113 km (70 miles) to the north in Flanders. If the Germans became aware of the Canadian Corps' shift south to Amiens, they would have clear warning of the offensive.

Deceiving the enemy

To hide the movement from observation by German aircraft, the Canadians marched only by night. Two Canadian battalions were left in Flanders and their radio operators kept up a constant stream of traffic to persuade the Germans the Corps was still in place. The deception worked perfectly.

More than 2,000 guns and around 1,800 aircraft were assembled for the attack, but any increase in artillery bombardment or air activity was avoided, leaving the Germans unaware of the troops' presence. More than 500 tanks, including 342 heavy Mark Vs and 72 lighter Whippets, were concealed in the countryside to the rear of the troops, undetected by the enemy. As the tanks moved up to the front under cover of darkness on

Australian boots

These custom-made brown leather ankle boots were worn by an Australian officer at the Battle of Amiens. Australian and Canadian infantry were chosen to spearhead the Amiens offensive.

Allied attacks July to September 1918

From mid-July 1918, the Allies took the offensive, driving the Germans back in a continuous series of assaults that culminated in a coordinated "Grand Offensive" in late September.

KEY

- ■ US army
- ■ Belgian army
- ■ British army
- ■ French army
- ■ German army
- ➡ American offensives
- ➡ British offensives
- ➡ French offensives
- ⊠ Fortified town
- --- Major railway

ALLIED FRONT LINE 18 JUL
- ＼ American sector
- ＼ Belgian sector
- ＼ British sector
- ＼ French sector

ALLIED FRONT LINE 25 SEPT
- •-• American sector
- •-• Belgian sector
- •-• British sector
- •-• French sector

Map labels:
NETHERLANDS · BELGIUM · GERMANY · LUXEMBOURG · FRANCE · English Channel · PARIS

Ostend · Bruges · Antwerp · Nieuport · Ghent · Dunkerque · Brussels · Liège
■ BELGIAN King Albert · Ypres · ■ 4TH ARMY Sixt von Armin
8 28 Sept 4th Battle of Ypres · ■ 2ND ARMY Plumer · FLANDERS
Hazebrouck · Lille · Namur · Meuse
7 27 Sept British 1st and 3rd armies breach Hindenburg Line between Cambrai and St Quentin · ■ 5TH ARMY Birdwood · Festubert · ■ 6TH ARMY Quast · Mons · Charleroi
■ 1ST ARMY Horne · Maubeuge · Aulnoye
4 21 Aug British 3rd Army opens offensive along a 16 km (10-mile) sector. British 4th Army resumes its advance · Arras · Quéant · ■ 17TH ARMY von Below · ■ 2ND ARMY Marwitz
Bapaume · Cambrai · Le Cateau
■ 3RD ARMY Byng · Albert
Amiens · Péronne · St Quentin · Mézières · LUXEMBOURG Luxembourg
■ 4TH ARMY Rawlinson · Chaulnes · La Fère
2 8 Aug 4th Army opens first British offensive, supported by French to the south · Montdidier · ■ 9TH ARMY Eben · ■ 18TH ARMY Hutier · Sedan
■ 1ST ARMY Debeney · Noyon · Laon · ■ 7TH ARMY Boehn · ■ 5TH ARMY Gallwitz · Longwy
■ 3RD ARMY Humbert · Soissons · Vesle · ■ 1ST ARMY Eberhardt · ■ 3RD ARMY Einem · Thionville
3 20 Aug Aisne Heights captured by French 10th Army · ■ 10TH ARMY Mangin · Fère-en-Tardenois · Reims · Mont Blanc · Argonne · Verdun · Metz
Chantilly · ■ 5TH ARMY Berthelot · Château Thierry · ■ 4TH ARMY Gouraud · St Menhould · ■ 1ST ARMY Pershing · Troyon · ■ 19TH ARMY Bothmer
Seine · Chalons · St Mihiel · Bar Le Duc · Nancy
1 18 Jul French launch counterattack to clear Marne salient
6 26 Sept Argonne offensive opens. Slow progress is made over difficult country by French and US forces
5 12 Sept Americans begin attack on the St Mihiel salient. It is cleared by Sept 16

0 ———— 100 km
0 ———— 100 miles

"August 8th was the **blackest day** of the German army in the history of the war."

GENERAL ERICH LUDENDORFF, "MY WAR MEMOIRS 1914–19"

the eve of the attack, the noise of their engines was masked by aircraft flying back and forth overhead.

At 4:20am on 8 August, the British artillery opened a devastating bombardment accurately targeted at all parts of the German defences, from the front-line trenches to the gun batteries at the rear. Taken completely unawares, German troops scarcely had time to man defensive positions before Australian and Canadian troops were upon them, emerging out of mist and smoke.

Attack after attack

Amply supplied with grenades, rifle grenades, and Lewis guns, the Allied troops set about clearing the German trenches. Tanks provided support, trundling forward to take out strongpoints that might have held up the advance. The Germans were outnumbered and stunned by the unexpectedness of the offensive. The second wave of Allied troops, following up the first attack, passed large numbers of German prisoners heading in the opposite direction. By the afternoon of 8 August, the Australians

German prisoners at Amiens

More than 15,000 German soldiers were taken prisoner on the first day of the Battle of Amiens. Their reluctance to fight to the death was a clear sign of the declining morale of the German army.

and Canadians had penetrated the German defences to a depth of about 12 km (7.5 miles).

From that point on, familiar problems accumulated. Supply and communication difficulties slowed the pace of the advance, giving German reserves time to arrive and stiffen their defences. Tanks suffered mechanical failure or were taken out by German anti-tank weapons. After considerable hesitation, Haig and Foch agreed to halt

the attack on 15 August. This was a wise decision. Instead of persisting in the face of mounting casualties and diminishing gains, as had happened before, the Allies would now repeatedly shift the point of assault, holding on to each limited advance.

German reaction

Meanwhile, the German high command was appalled by the readiness of so many German troops to surrender and the worsening balance of forces at the front. Convinced that victory was no longer possible, General Erich Ludendorff offered to resign. His resignation was refused and the German government continued to assure its people of imminent victory. In private, however, the German leadership began looking for a way out of the war.

The British on the offensive

Soldiers advance through German barbed wire as a tank is disabled by artillery fire. For British and Commonwealth troops, the fighting in the summer of 1918 continued to be a brutal experience, with over 20,000 men killed or wounded at Amiens.

AFTER »

The Battle of Amiens marked the beginning of the Hundred Days Offensive, a series of operations that lasted until the end of the war.

THE BRITISH STRIKE
On 21 August, less than a week after the **Amiens operation** was halted, the British Third Army mounted an attack to the north and took the town of Albert. With the aid of the **Fourth Army**, they took Baupaume on 26 August. Meanwhile, General Charles Mangin's French Tenth Army attacked successfully at the Aisne.

1.2 MILLION The number of German soldiers who were killed, wounded, or taken prisoner during the Hundred Days Offensive.

GERMANY WEAKENED
The **American Expeditionary Force** (AEF) saw its first independent action at the **St Mihiel salient 306–07 »** on 12 September. It then attacked, with French support, in the Meuse-Argonne offensive **308–09 »**, part of a wider Allied assault on the German **Hindenburg Line 312–13 »**. Germany was further thwarted when its allies – Austria-Hungary, Turkey, and Bulgaria – were defeated. In October, the German leaders **sought an armistice**.

Taking the St Mihiel Salient

In September 1918, after months of preparation, an American army entered battle in Europe for the first time. The US-led attack on the exposed St Mihiel salient yielded a decisive victory for General Pershing's men – a prelude to much tougher fighting ahead.

n the summer of 1918, 300,000 fresh US troops were arriving in France every month. By August, about one and a half million "doughboys" (an informal term, with unknown origins, for an American soldier) were learning fighting skills.

In training camps or as combatants in American formations, these men served under overall French or British command. After four long years of costly war, the Allies needed infantry in greater numbers. They were happy to supply the Americans with artillery, tanks, transport vehicles, and aircraft, as long as the Americans supplied men. US commander General John Pershing was, however, determined that his troops would not become cannon-fodder for Allied generals to use up. His aim was to build an independent American army and lead it in a battle planned and commanded by Americans. The US First Army was thus created on 10 August 1918.

Pershing agreed with Allied Supreme Commander General Ferdinand Foch that the new army would be used to attack the St Mihiel salient. This was an area south of Verdun that had been held by Germany since 1914. Something of a backwater by this stage of the war, it was not heavily defended and was therefore a tempting target for a quick success.

450 The number of German guns captured by the Americans at the Battle of St Mihiel.

16,000 The number of German troops taken prisoner at the Battle of St Mihiel.

American rage

Pershing and his staff wanted to be more than a sideshow, however, and extended the plan to include a follow-up attack eastwards to the fortress city of Metz. This would cut major transport links and take the fighting to the German border.

More than half a million US soldiers assembled opposite the salient, along with over 50,000 French troops who were to play a supporting role. Planning and organization were well advanced when on 30 August,

Foch went to Pershing's headquarters and declared he had changed his mind. He wanted US forces to abandon the St Mihiel operation and instead cooperate with French forces in a major offensive in the Champagne and Meuse-Argonne regions. A furious row erupted, with Pershing refusing to see his army dispersed to provide units for wider Allied operations. It would fight as "an independent American army" or not at all.

Three days later they reached a compromise. On 12 September, the US First Army would go ahead with its attack on the St Mihiel salient but abandon the advance to Metz. Once the salient was taken, the American force would transfer to the Meuse-Argonne sector, where it would lead an offensive, with French support, from 26 September. Pershing thus kept his army together but was committed to fighting two offensives just a fortnight apart.

By this stage in the war the Germans were being forced back to the strongly

BEFORE

A year and a half separated the USA's declaration of war in April 1917 from the first entry of an independent US army into action in France at St Mihiel.

CHANGE OF PLAN
Appointed commander of the first American Expeditionary Force to be **deployed in France**, General John Pershing sought to assemble, train, and organize an entire mass army before entering combat. But German successes in May 1918 threatened to finish the war before the Americans arrived and this idea had to be modified. Fighting alongside the French armies, US divisions played a major combat role from **Belleau Wood** in June **❮❮ 284–85** through to the Second Battle of the Marne **❮❮ 286–87**.

American ace

Eddie Rickenbacker was the most successful American fighter pilot in World War I. He was awarded the Distinguished Service Cross for exceptional heroism during the St Mihiel offensive.

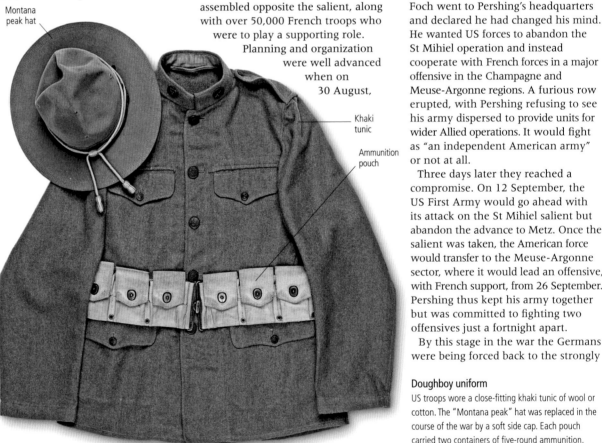

Montana peak hat

Khaki tunic

Ammunition pouch

Doughboy uniform

US troops wore a close-fitting khaki tunic of wool or cotton. The "Montana peak" hat was replaced in the course of the war by a soft side cap. Each pouch carried two containers of five-round ammunition.

FRENCH POSTER WELCOMING THE AMERICANS

"We have developed a type of manhood superior in initiative to that existing abroad which, given equal training, developed a superior soldier."

GENERAL JOHN PERSHING, SPEAKING OF AMERICANS, SEPTEMBER 1918

Battle from the air

This oil painting by an unknown artist was based on an aerial photograph taken during the fighting at St Mihiel. Smoke and gas habitually obscured battlefields on the Western Front, hiding potential targets from artillery or air bombardment.

prepared defensive positions of the Hindenburg Line. Regarding the St Mihiel salient as indefensible, they began preparing a withdrawal as soon as the build-up of US troops in the sector became evident. This further weakened defences that stood no chance of resisting an attack of overwhelming force.

Battle commences

As well as half a million infantry, Pershing had 267 French Renault light tanks – the majority of them with American crews – under the command of Colonel George Patton. The French supplied 3,000 artillery pieces to support the offensive. In the air, General Billy Mitchell, the head of the US Army Air Service, commanded a force of around 1,400 aircraft that included squadrons from other Allied countries as well as American pilots in British- or French-supplied machines. Launched on 12 September, the operation was a precise and effective set-piece attack that took the Germans by surprise.

The battle opened with a four-hour artillery bombardment, followed by the advance of infantry and tanks behind a creeping barrage. American troops had to force a path through barbed wire entanglements, coming under intersecting fire from concealed machine-gun nests, and being threatened by buried mortar bombs strewn as booby traps across their line of advance. Some German soldiers were quick to surrender, but others fought on with great tenacity.

Advances from the south and west brought the salient under American control by 16 September.

The end game

Although they suffered 7,000 casualties, the doughboys had come through their baptism of fire well. Logistical support for the men in the field had not been so successful. Inadequate US staff work had led to huge traffic jams developing behind the lines. Many front-line troops went short of food and water because of serious failings in supplies.

In the euphoria of a first US victory, however, there was no inclination to analyse weaknesses. President Woodrow Wilson cabled his congratulations to Pershing, writing: "The boys have done what we expected of them, and done it the way we most admire."

Victorious American troops

Cheering US soldiers put up a sign dedicating their victory at the St Mihiel salient to President Woodrow Wilson. War-weary Europeans were impressed by the high morale and good physical condition of the men.

AFTER »

Even before the victory at the St Mihiel salient was complete, the USA was preparing for another, larger offensive at the Argonne forest.

PLAN OF ATTACK

The Meuse-Argonne Offensive **308–09** » opened on 26 September 1918, as part of Foch's wider plan for concerted **Allied attacks** to breach the German Hindenburg Line defences **312–13** ». The transfer of troops and equipment from the St Mihiel salient to a new front 97 km (60 miles) distant in ten days was a triumph of logistics. Masterminded by Colonel George Marshall, a future Chief of Staff, the offensive continued until the **Armistice** in November **322–23** », by which time the Americans were close to taking Sedan.

« BEFORE

In August 1918, the Allied armies began a relentless series of attacks. The onslaught, known as the Hundred Days Offensive, comprised a series of battles along the Western Front.

SHEET MUSIC FOR A MARCHING SONG

AMERICAN TROOPS SEE ACTION
Following the victory of **British and Commonwealth** troops at Amiens, in August **« 304–05** the Germans knew they could no longer take the offensive. Instead, they sought to **delay the Allied advance** with a stubborn defence.

Throughout the summer of 1918, ever-increasing numbers of US troops in France **tipped the balance** of forces against Germany. Formally created in August, the American First Army entered combat at the **St Mihiel salient** on 12 September **« 306–07**. After swiftly capturing the salient, the army moved northwards in preparation for the Meuse-Argonne Offensive.

The Meuse-Argonne Offensive

Although mostly forgotten today, the Meuse-Argonne Offensive was the largest battle in the US Army's history, involving 1.2 million troops and lasting 47 days. A brutal struggle against a capable enemy, it was the USA's biggest contribution to Germany's defeat on the Western Front.

The Meuse-Argonne Offensive was a daunting task for which General John Pershing's First Army was inadequately prepared. The Americans were to advance up the west bank of the Meuse river, supported by the French Fourth Army on their left. The forested, hilly terrain was described by US General Hunter Liggett as a "natural fortress". The Germans had improved on nature, creating a formidable defensive network in depth. This was manned by the battle-hardened soldiers of the German Fifth Army under General Max von Gallwitz.

Short on resources
Although 600,000 US soldiers were available for the offensive, most of them had not previously experienced combat and many were poorly trained. The Americans were strong on infantry numbers but remained heavily dependent on the British and French for tanks, artillery, and aircraft. Since the Meuse-Argonne attack was timed to coincide with British and French offensives elsewhere on the front, the Allies had withdrawn equipment and personnel to meet their own needs, leaving Pershing with far fewer tanks and aircraft than for the smaller battle of St Mihiel two weeks earlier.

Battle scarred
US infantry advance through the village of Varennes, taken by 28th "Keystone" Division on the first day of the offensive. The ruins are evidence of the hard fighting that was needed to seize the village.

Launched on 26 September, the Meuse-Argonne Offensive soon ran into trouble. German forward positions were overrun by weight of numbers but US losses were heavy. Inexperienced American officers flung men forwards in frontal attacks only for them to be mown down by machine-gun fire. Pershing was concerned by the poor coordination between artillery and infantry, with some units forced to carry out assaults without any artillery support.

In contrast, German artillery fire, both with explosive and gas shells, was terrifyingly effective, the gunners benefiting from intelligence provided by German observation aircraft, which dominated the sky. US logistical problems meant that, as advances were made, food and ammunition supplies often failed to reach troops engaged in combat on the front. Even the weather was hostile, with persistent rain adversely affecting the US soldiers' morale.

By 28 September, the offensive had bogged down and the Germans were mounting counterattacks. One of these severely mauled the US 35th Division (National Guardsmen from Missouri and Kansas) and forced its withdrawal from battle. Then, poorly-trained African-American troops of the 92nd Division, under the command of indifferent white officers, broke and fled under German fire at Binarville, in the Argonne Forest. This episode later became a point of reference for those who wanted to denigrate the fighting spirit of African-Americans, which was, in fact, amply demonstrated elsewhere in the war.

Pershing regroups
After the battle, Allied Supreme Commander Marshal Ferdinand Foch believed US generals had proved incapable of handling a large-scale offensive and made a move to bring US troops under French command. Pershing, however, clung to his independence. After a pause for reorganization, on 4 October he relaunched the offensive with more experienced troops in the lead.

US SOLDIER (1887–1964)
ALVIN C. YORK

American war hero Alvin C. York came from a poor background in rural Jamestown, Tennessee. In 1917, he requested exemption from the draft on religious grounds, but his application was denied. By the time of the Meuse-Argonne Offensive, York was a corporal in the 82nd Infantry Division. He killed 32 German soldiers with rifle fire, helped capture 132 others, and seized 35 machine-guns during action outside the French village of Châtel-Chéhéry on 8 October 1918.

York was awarded the Medal of Honor for his bravery and, after the war, was promoted as a celebrity. His life story formed the basis for the 1941 film *Sergeant York*, directed by Howard Hawks.

"We were stumbling over dead horses and dead men... shells were bursting all around."
CORPORAL ALVIN C. YORK, DIARY ENTRY, 5 OCTOBER 1918

US troops mostly fought with outstanding courage and enthusiasm, but again the gains were hard-won and losses severe. In one notable episode, six companies of the 77th Division, led by Major Charles Whittlesey, were surrounded by German forces, their only method of keeping in touch with the rest of the army being by carrier pigeon. This "Lost Battalion" held out for six days before it was rescued from encirclement. Only 194 of its original force of 554 men were still fit for action.

Gradually and painfully, progress was made. By 12 October, the Germans had been cleared from the Argonne Forest and US troops were facing the Kriemhilde Stellung, the southernmost part of the Hindenburg Line.

Heroic pigeon
The homing pigeon Cher Ami lost a leg while carrying a message from the "Lost Battalion" through German fire. The pigeon was honoured for its bravery with the Croix de Guerre medal. Its stuffed body is preserved in the Smithsonian Institution in Washington, D.C.

Momentum had again been exhausted, however, and Pershing decided to reorganize his forces. To accommodate increasing numbers of troops – about 1 million by mid-October – he created a new Second Army under General Robert Bullard. At the same time, he transferred command of the First Army to General Liggett, allotting himself a supervisory role.

Liggett was an excellent fighting general. While the desperate attritional struggle continued through the second half of October, he strove to imbue his army with the tactical sophistication it had lacked under Pershing. Infantry were to advance in small units, some firing to cover the movement of others; artillery was to coordinate closely with infantry, providing a creeping barrage behind which they could advance. Tanks and aircraft were to support the infantry.

Hard-won victory

On 1 November, it all came together when an assault by the US V Corps broke the Kriemhilde Stellung. Exploiting their training and experience, the US soldiers crossed the Meuse river and advanced along opposite banks, driving back the German forces. By 9 November, the Americans had progressed 40 km (25 miles) to reach the hills overlooking the city of Sedan. When the Armistice stopped the fighting two days later, Pershing claimed the Meuse-Argonne Offensive as a victory, even if it was achieved at great cost.

AFTER >>

The Americans suffered 122,000 casualties in the Meuse-Argonne Offensive, including 26,277 dead. German losses were on a similar scale.

GERMANY SUCCUMBS

The relentless pressure kept up by the US and supporting French troops in the Meuse-Argonne sector prevented the Germans from reinforcing the **Hindenburg Line** further north. This was **taken by the British and French** in late September and early October 312–13 **>>**.

Along with the defeat of Germany's allies on other fronts – Turkey in Palestine, Bulgaria in Macedonia, and Austria-Hungary in Italy – these German setbacks on the Western Front led Germany to **seek an armistice 322–23 >>** on 11 November. By that time, the American Expeditionary Force (AEF), like other armies on the Western Front, was in the grip of an **influenza epidemic** that would kill 25,000 Americans, compared with a total of 53,000 killed in combat.

Montfaucon in ruins
The village of Montfaucon d'Argonne was held by the Germans from September 1914 until its capture by US forces in September 1918. The remains of a German observation post is on the left of the ruined church.

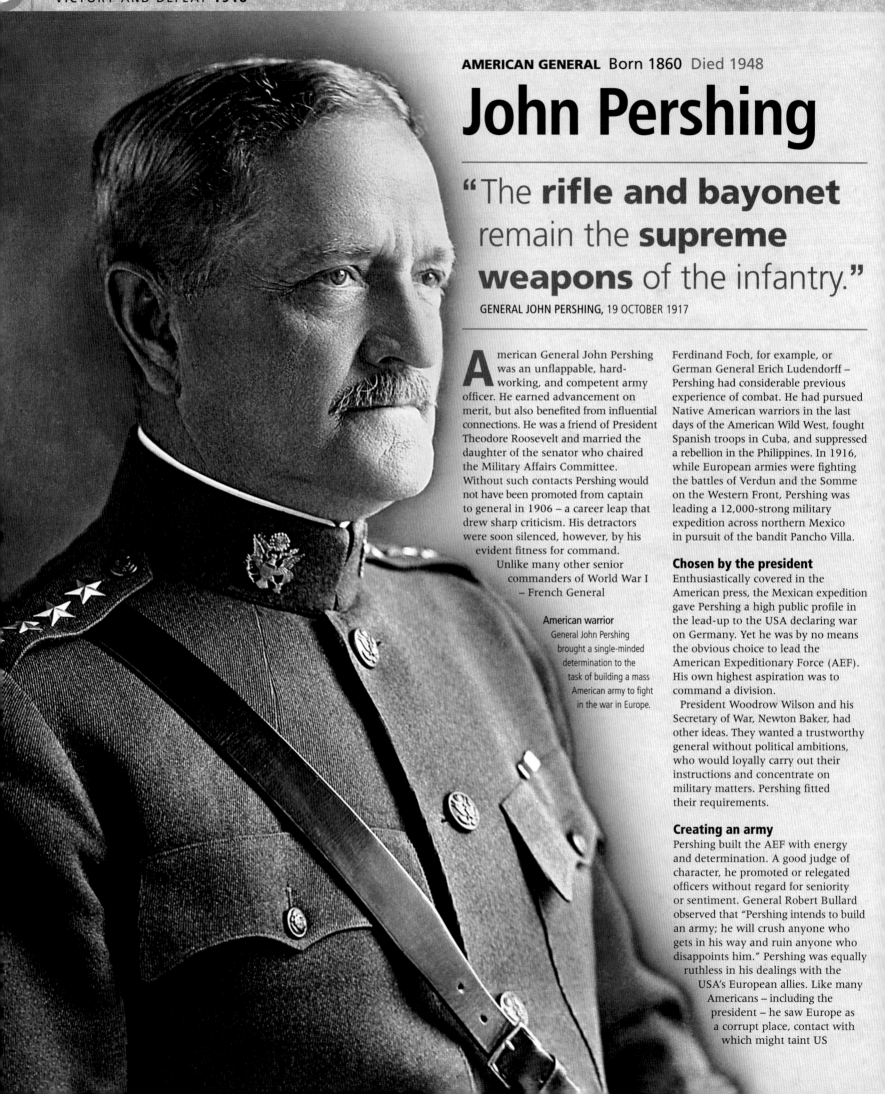

AMERICAN GENERAL Born 1860 Died 1948

John Pershing

"The **rifle and bayonet** remain the **supreme weapons** of the infantry."

GENERAL JOHN PERSHING, 19 OCTOBER 1917

American General John Pershing was an unflappable, hard-working, and competent army officer. He earned advancement on merit, but also benefited from influential connections. He was a friend of President Theodore Roosevelt and married the daughter of the senator who chaired the Military Affairs Committee. Without such contacts Pershing would not have been promoted from captain to general in 1906 – a career leap that drew sharp criticism. His detractors were soon silenced, however, by his evident fitness for command.

Unlike many other senior commanders of World War I – French General

American warrior
General John Pershing brought a single-minded determination to the task of building a mass American army to fight in the war in Europe.

Ferdinand Foch, for example, or German General Erich Ludendorff – Pershing had considerable previous experience of combat. He had pursued Native American warriors in the last days of the American Wild West, fought Spanish troops in Cuba, and suppressed a rebellion in the Philippines. In 1916, while European armies were fighting the battles of Verdun and the Somme on the Western Front, Pershing was leading a 12,000-strong military expedition across northern Mexico in pursuit of the bandit Pancho Villa.

Chosen by the president
Enthusiastically covered in the American press, the Mexican expedition gave Pershing a high public profile in the lead-up to the USA declaring war on Germany. Yet he was by no means the obvious choice to lead the American Expeditionary Force (AEF). His own highest aspiration was to command a division.

President Woodrow Wilson and his Secretary of War, Newton Baker, had other ideas. They wanted a trustworthy general without political ambitions, who would loyally carry out their instructions and concentrate on military matters. Pershing fitted their requirements.

Creating an army
Pershing built the AEF with energy and determination. A good judge of character, he promoted or relegated officers without regard for seniority or sentiment. General Robert Bullard observed that "Pershing intends to build an army; he will crush anyone who gets in his way and ruin anyone who disappoints him." Pershing was equally ruthless in his dealings with the USA's European allies. Like many Americans – including the president – he saw Europe as a corrupt place, contact with which might taint US

Guerrilla expedition
Pershing leads cavalry in pursuit of revolutionary leader Pancho Villa, in Mexico in 1916. Villa had provoked the US incursion by mounting a cross-border raid against the American town of Columbus, New Mexico.

idealism. He fully endorsed his orders from the president, which were to keep US forces "separate and distinct".

Britain and France were desperate for American manpower, but Pershing refused to commit his soldiers piecemeal to the battle and continued with the slow process of building an independent US mass army. Even after Pershing had been forced to bend a little, allowing some US troops to fight as part of larger Allied formations from May 1918, he continued to focus on the ultimate goal – of creating an army that would enter battle under his command. It was a stance that infuriated other Allied commanders, but neither their pleas nor bullying could shake his resolve.

Hard lessons
Unfortunately, Pershing's distrust of Europe extended to its fighting style. Seeing the stalemate of trench warfare as evidence of poor military leadership, he failed to recognize the progress that had been made by 1918 in infantry tactics and combined arms warfare. Ignoring the importance that light machine-guns, grenades, and mortars had assumed in infantry assaults, he continued to preach the pre-eminence of the rifle and bayonet.

US troops did receive training from British and French advisers, but Pershing never appreciated how much they had to learn. He neglected issues such as the importance of close cooperation between infantry and artillery. Lessons that could have been learned on the training ground were instead learned on the battlefield.

When Pershing led the American First Army into battle in September 1918, it marked a triumph of willpower and organization. But World War I battles rarely made generals look good, and Pershing was no exception to this rule. The bloodbath during the opening phase of the Meuse-Argonne Offensive, in particular, brought him little credit. A week into that operation, Foch, as Allied Supreme Commander, would have sacked Pershing had he been able. But George Marshall, an officer on Pershing's staff during the offensive, later recorded his impression of Pershing's unshakeable "determination to force the fighting over all the difficulties and objections" as an incomparable example of leadership under pressure. Pershing's decision to reorganize his forces during the offensive, which involved creating the Second Army and delegating battlefield command to subordinates, was both brave and successful.

Excluded from the peace
When the prospect of an armistice was first mooted in October 1918, Pershing expressed a strong preference for demanding unconditional surrender. This led to his only disagreement with President Wilson and to his exclusion

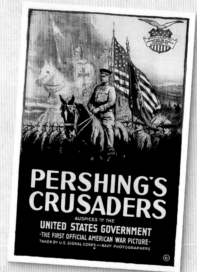

War documentary
Pershing's Crusaders was the first war documentary released by the US Committee of Information in 1918. Its title is indicative of the general's status as a focus for high-flown wartime idealism.

from the Paris Peace Conference. Although laden with honours, Pershing was never especially popular. Proposed as a candidate for the presidency in 1920, he received little support.

Pershing lived long enough to see World War II run its course – a war he blamed on the failure of the Allies to achieve total victory in World War I. He died in Washington, D.C., in 1948.

PERSHING'S TOMBSTONE

Foch and Pershing
Relations between Pershing and Allied Supreme Commander Marshal Ferdinand Foch were often strained. Pershing resisted Foch's attempts to split up his army and place it under French command.

"No commander was ever **privileged** to lead a **finer force.**"

GENERAL JOHN PERSHING, DESCRIBING THE AMERICAN EXPEDITIONARY FORCE, 1931

Attacking the Hindenburg Line

During the last week of September 1918, the Allied armies on the Western Front broke through the formidable fortifications of the Hindenburg Line. A series of offensives demonstrated the Allies' superior tactics and technology, pushing Germany to the brink of military defeat.

« BEFORE

From summer 1918, the balance of forces on the Western Front shifted in favour of the Allies with the arrival of large numbers of US troops.

US SMITH & WESSON REVOLVER

ALLIES ADVANCE
A **French-led counterattack** at the **Marne** « 286–87 in July and a successful offensive by **British and Commonwealth forces** at **Amiens** « 304–05 in August initiated a series of **Allied advances**. Further attacks pushed the Germans back to the Hindenburg Line. Meanwhile, in mid-September, the **US First Army went into action**. With the help of the French, they captured the **St Mihiel Salient** « 306–07 south of Verdun.

The Hindenburg Line was a collective name for a series of linked German defensive positions that stretched from the coast of Belgium to Verdun in northeastern France. Under construction from late 1916, the Wotan, Siegfried, Alberich, Brunhilde, and Kriemhilde Stellungs (positions) were systems of trenches, strongpoints, barbed wire, machine-gun emplacements, and artillery batteries, often 16 km (10 miles) in depth. They incorporated existing features of the landscape, such as ridges, rivers, and canals, to improve their defences. By late summer 1918, the line offered a fallback position for German forces battered by Allied offensives and desperate to stop foreign troops reaching German soil.

Attacking the Hindenburg Line was a daunting prospect. Allied commanders feared a repeat of battles such as the Somme or Third Ypres – stalled offensives with appalling casualty lists. In September, however, under the leadership of Supreme Commander of the Allied Armies Marshal Ferdinand Foch, the decision was taken to mount simultaneous offensives along the entire length of the German line.

Foch adopted the slogan: *"Tout le monde à la bataille"* ("Everyone into battle"). In the northern sector of the front, Belgian King Albert I was given command of an Allied army group to launch an offensive in Flanders. The British were to lead an assault on the Siegfried Stellung, the strongest sector of the line, between Cambrai and St Quentin. In the southeast, the US First Army was entrusted with leading the Franco-US Meuse-Argonne offensive.

The Allies did not have vastly more troops, but their soldiers were better fed and supplied than their opponents. They had thousands of tanks and trucks, whereas the Germans had few motor vehicles of any kind. Allied

> ## "For the **first time** in the war all the **Allied armies...** were **on the move together.**"
> BRITISH OFFICIAL HISTORY OF THE GREAT WAR

aircraft dominated the skies. Above all, the Allies had developed a skill in coordinating artillery and infantry that made a successful assault feasible even against the best organized defences – as long as everything went to plan.

A tough fight
On 26 September, the launch of the Meuse-Argonne operation showed how hard the fighting was going to be, as inexperienced US troops became bogged down in a brutal attritional struggle. The following day, the British Third and First armies attacked at the northern end of the Siegfried Stellung in the direction of Cambrai. The Canadian Corps was given the unenviable task of crossing the Canal du Nord. This half-built waterway was dry along part of its length, but was still a major obstacle, impassable to tanks and dominated by German forces on higher ground. Masterminded by Canadian General Arthur Currie, the assault used massed artillery and machine-gun fire to suppress enemy defences, enabling troops to cross the canal. Combat engineers followed to improvise bridges, while guns were moved forward to support the infantry advancing on the other side.

St Quentin Canal
On 29 September, the British Fourth Army launched an offensive at the St Quentin Canal in the southern sector of the Siegfried Stellung. A formidable obstacle, the canal served as a moat in front of the German defensive position. With steep sides plunging into deep water and mud, lined with barbed wire and covered by German machine-guns, the canal appeared impregnable.

Along one 5-km (3-mile) stretch, however, the waterway passed through a tunnel, offering ground across which an attack could be launched. The Germans had identified

Weapon of destruction
The British used two naval guns mounted on railway carriages for long-range bombardment during the last months of the war. They struck targets such as railway junctions behind the German defences.

this weak spot and concentrated maximum defensive firepower upon it. The main attack across the tunnel was entrusted to Australian troops and two US regiments, under the command of Australian General John Monash. It was a costly failure. The Australians blamed inexperienced US troops, but it was inadequate coordination with artillery that left Allied infantry and tanks unable to advance.

The situation was saved by the action of the British North Midland Division. Ordered to carry out a diversionary attack further south, it devised a plan for soldiers – many of them non-swimmers – to cross the canal, wearing lifejackets borrowed from cross-Channel ferries. Remarkably, the plan worked. German defences were crushed by the weight of artillery and machine-gun fire. The British infantry established a bridgehead on the far bank, capturing 4,000 prisoners. Outflanked, the German troops defending the tunnel crossing had to withdraw and the canal was taken.

Crisis point

With the Siegfried Stellung breached, it appeared as if the German armies might collapse. In Flanders, King Albert's Belgian, French, and

British liberators
Territorials of the Liverpool Irish Regiment march through the French city of Lille, which they had helped liberate from German occupation on 17 October. The British soldiers received a warm welcome from the local people.

British troops broke out of the Ypres salient, retaking Passchendaele in a day. In places, German reserves moving up to the front were jeered at for prolonging a hopeless situation by the soldiers they were relieving. At the end of September, the German high command told its government to seek an immediate armistice.

In October, however, German resistance stiffened. Many machine-gunners were still ready to fight to the death to hold up the Allied advance. The Allies encountered the usual problems in moving supplies, tanks, and artillery forward over broken ground. After a two-week delay on the Flanders front, King Albert relaunched his offensive on 14 October. Lille was taken and so were the Belgian ports from Ostende to Zeebrugge.

Further south, however, Allied forces encountered some of the fiercest fighting of the war at the Battle of Selle (17–26 October). Although an armistice was already being discussed by then, the Allied commanders continued to prepare for further military campaigns into 1919.

Canal crossing
On 27 September 1918, Canadian soldiers moved ammunition forwards across the dry bed of the Canal du Nord. Crossing the canal was an important stage in the Allied attack on the Hindenburg Line.

AFTER »

While the Allies advanced, Germany suffered the collapse of its allies and social upheaval at home.

GERMANY FOUNDERS
At the same time as the Allies attacked the Hindenburg Line, **Bulgaria asked for an armistice** and **Turkey was defeated** by the **British offensive in Palestine 316–17** ». In October, Austria-Hungary began to disintegrate, with different national groups declaring independence. **Italy launched a final offensive** against Austro-Hungarian forces at Vittorio Veneto on 27 October **318–19** ».

ARMISTICE SOUGHT
In Germany, a new **government** installed on 3 October sought a compromise peace deal. While progress towards an armistice stalled, a naval mutiny sparked a revolutionary uprising in Germany that overthrew the monarchy **320–21** ». Germany signed the Armistice on 11 November **322–23** ».

Breaking the Hindenburg Line
Brigadier General J.V. Campbell addresses British
troops of the 137th Brigade (46th Division) from
the Riqueval Bridge after their capture of the
St Quentin Canal in October 1918.

Turkey and Bulgaria Defeated

In 1918, the southern flank of Germany's alliance system unravelled. Defeats for Turkey at Megiddo in Palestine and for Bulgaria in Macedonia left both countries with no choice but to seek an armistice. Germany was no longer capable of military intervention to save its allies.

BEFORE

Turkey entered the war as an ally of the Central Powers in October 1914, as did Bulgaria a year later.

CHANGING FORTUNES
Bulgarian troops helped **defeat Serbia** **《 140–41** in autumn 1915 and **Romania** the following year **《 194–95**. In autumn 1915, Allied forces **landed at Salonika** in northern Greece, across the border from Bulgaria and Serbia. **Greece entered the war** on the Allied side in June 1917.

Although Turkey repulsed Allied landings at **Gallipoli 《 110–15** from April 1915 and was victorious at **Kut al-Amara 《 122–23** in Mesopotamia (modern-day Iraq) in April 1916, it **lost Baghdad** in 1917. In Palestine, British troops led by General Edmund Allenby and Arab rebels led by Emir Feisal and T.E. Lawrence **captured Jerusalem** in December 1917 **《 258–59**.

T.E. LAWRENCE'S *AGAL*

The troops of the multinational Allied army established in the Macedonian region of northern Greece from October 1915 were dubbed the "gardeners of Salonika", because of their relative inactivity. Despite intermittent offensives and counter-offensives, the Macedonian front remained largely passive, with far heavier losses to disease than combat.

The arrival of a new commander, the French General Louis Franchet d'Espèrey, in June 1918 shook the Allied army out of its torpor. His force of French, British, Greek, Serbian, Italian, and Czech troops numbered over half a million. The Bulgarian forces entrenched opposite the Allies were similar in number but had been demoralized by the withdrawal of

Bulgarian troops advance
Infantry of the Bulgarian army walk towards shellfire in Macedonia in 1918. Bulgarian troops used German equipment and often fought under German command.

German military support since spring 1918, when all German resources were redeployed to the Western Front.

Franchet d'Espèrey planned a two-pronged operation. French and Serbian troops would lead a surprise offensive through mountainous southern Serbia, while British and Greek forces attacked further east at Lake Doiran, the site of earlier fighting and well fortified by its Bulgarian defenders.

The French and Serbians launched their attack on 15 September and advanced 30 km (19 miles) in three days. At Lake Doiran, the Bulgarians repulsed the British and Greeks on 18–19 September, inflicting heavy losses on infantry mounting frontal assaults. However, the Bulgarians were immediately forced to withdraw from the Lake Doiran region in an attempt to block the French and Serbian advance from the west. Earlier in the war, German forces would have been swiftly deployed to the Macedonian front to stabilize the situation, but none were now available.

Anti-war demonstrations broke out in Bulgarian towns as the military situation deteriorated. Bulgaria's King Ferdinand I wanted a fight to the death, but his government requested an armistice. This came into force on 30 September. The collapse of Bulgaria

left the Allies free to attack Austria-Hungary to the north or the Turkish capital Constantinople to the east.

March on Anatolia

Meanwhile, British progress in Palestine had been halted by the transfer of troops to the Western Front. Although British General Edmund Allenby had occupied Jerusalem in December 1917, Turkish troops, with German support and under German command, held positions north of the city. While waiting for reinforcements from India, Allenby planned an attack on the coastal plain of western Palestine followed by an advance north through Syria into the Anatolian heartland of Turkey.

On 19 September, he launched his meticulously planned offensive at the Battle of Megiddo. His forces were impressive, with 35,000 infantry supported by the cavalry of the Desert Mounted Corps, 500 artillery pieces, and more than 100 aircraft. The Turkish trenches were overrun by noon on the first day and cavalry broke through, forcing the Turks and Germans to retreat. Over the

90,000 The number of Bulgarian soldiers who were either killed in combat or died of disease in World War I. Around 1.2 million men served in the country's wartime army.

> "We could see the **enemy bolting like rabbits.** We had had orders to go forward… The Bulgars have **broken at last!**"
>
> MAJOR ALFRED BUNDY, MIDDLESEX REGIMENT, 15 SEPTEMBER 1918

TSAR OF BULGARIA (1861–1948)
FERDINAND I

An Austrian aristocrat related to European royalty, Ferdinand was invited to take the vacant throne of Bulgaria in 1887. In 1908, he asserted Bulgaria's full independence from Ottoman Turkey, taking the title of tsar. The Balkan Wars of 1912–13, in which Bulgaria was ultimately on the losing side, left Ferdinand with a bitter hostility to Serbia. In October 1915, he joined the Central Powers to attack the Serbs and win territory in Macedonia. The unpopularity of the war in Bulgaria undermined his authority and he was powerless to prevent his government seeking an armistice in September 1918. He abdicated on 4 October.

following days, fleeing troops were attacked by air and outflanked by pursuing cavalry and armoured cars.

Meanwhile, Arab irregulars led by Emir Feisal and Colonel T.E. Lawrence captured Dera on the eastern side of the River Jordan. At the end of September, Australian horsemen entered Damascus, where they were joined by Feisal's Arabs the following day.

General Mustafa Kemal, commanding the Turkish Seventh Army, strove to establish a defensive line to protect Anatolia, but the situation was hopeless. To the east, in northern Mesopotamia, a British Indian army was occupying the oilfields of Mosul. To the west, only a thin line of Turkish

Turkish hand grenade
The standard Turkish grenade had a five-second fuse, which was lit by a matchhead struck on an abrasive igniter. Shortages of munitions were a problem for the Turks during the later stages of the war.

troops stood between the Allied army in Macedonia and Constantinople. The Young Turks who had led the country into war fell from power and on 14 October a "peace government" was formed under General Ahmed Izzet. An armistice was negotiated on board the British warship HMS *Agamemnon*, off the Greek island of Lemnos, and signed on 30 October.

The defeat of Bulgaria and Turkey sealed the fate of Austria-Hungary and Germany.

IMPACT ON THE WAR
The collapse of Bulgaria left the Central Powers with an **undefended southern front**. The Allies advanced northwards through Serbia, and **captured Belgrade** on 1 November. With no troops available to prevent an Allied invasion of their countries, both Austria-Hungary and Germany **sought a way to end the war**. Austria-Hungary **signed an armistice**

on 3 November, four days after Turkey, and Germany followed suit on 11 November.

TERRITORIAL LOSSES
Bulgaria and Turkey were punished for their support of Germany and Austria-Hungary. Under the terms of the 1919 **Treaty of Neuilly**, Bulgaria ceded Western Thrace to Greece and lost territory to the future Yugoslavia. The Turkish Ottoman Empire was dismembered by the **Treaty of Sèvres** in 1920. A nationalist revolt established a **Turkish Republic** in 1922, which successfully revoked some of the treaty's terms.

FINISH JOMMNY !

GREETINGS FROM THE

SALONIKA ARMY

XMAS - 1918.

BRITISH POSTCARD FROM SALONIKA

Bitter experience
A Bulgarian officer mourns at the graveside of a comrade. Participation in World War I was a catastrophe for Bulgaria, which not only suffered heavy military casualties but also civilian hardship.

Italians ready for action
Occupying a rocky outcrop east of Lake Garda in 1918, these Italian soldiers are better equipped than their Austrian opponents. Their weapons include a Lewis gun, supplied by their allies.

Italy Victorious

In June 1918, the Italians repulsed a major Austro-Hungarian attack at the Battle of the Piave river. The Italian army launched its own offensive at Vittorio Veneto in the last weeks of the war, contributing to the final collapse of Austria-Hungary.

The Austro-German breakthrough at Caporetto in October 1917 had placed major Italian cities, including Venice and Verona, under threat. In June 1918, Austria-Hungary prepared an offensive to capture these prestigious prizes and drive Italy out of the war. According to the plan, troops under Field Marshal Svetozar Boroevic would cross the Piave river, while, further north, Field Marshal Conrad von Hötzendorf advanced from the mountainous Trentino region.

BEFORE

After the Central Powers' victory at Caporetto in October 1917, Italy's leaders worked hard to restore the morale of Italian troops and civilians.

AUSTRIA-HUNGARY WEAKENS
While Italian General Armando Diaz had **restored army morale** after Italy's **defeat at Caporetto ‹‹ 246–47**, in Austria-Hungary food and fuel shortages led to **popular unrest**. In April 1918, Italy hosted a Congress of Oppressed Nationalities in Rome, at which ethnic groups, including Poles, Czechs, Slovaks, and Serbs, asserted a **right to independence** from Austria-Hungary. The Allies sent troops to support the Italians while **German forces** were moved from Italy to the **Western Front**.

POLISH LEADER JÓZEF PILSUDSKI'S UNIFORM

This ambitious plan ignored the change in the relative strength of the opposing armies on the Italian front since Caporetto. The transfer of German troops to fight on the Western Front from spring 1918 left Austria-Hungary reliant on its own forces, which were short of food and weakened by desertions. In addition, formations recruited from Austria-Hungary's Slav minorities had become unreliable. The Italian forces, meanwhile, had been bolstered with Allied troops and equipment. Under the command of General Armando Diaz, they were dug into defensive positions prepared in depth.

Failure on the Piave
On 10 June, Boroevic's Fifth and Sixth armies crossed the Piave river on pontoon bridges and made inroads into Italian defences near the Adriatic coast. Conrad's offensive in the Trentino region followed on 15 June.

Within a week, however, both operations had failed. The bridges across the Piave came under attack from Allied aircraft and many were swept away in the current. The Austro-Hungarian armies came under counterattack. Forced to abandon their bridgehead, they suffered heavy losses as they retreated across the river. In the Trentino region, the Austro-Hungarian onslaught caused panic in the British-held sector of the Asiago, but defensive discipline was soon restored. Conrad's costly frontal assaults barely dented the Allied line before the offensive was called off, just six days after it had begun.

Medal of honour
This bronze war medal, decorated with the helmeted head of Italy's King Victor Emmanuel III, was awarded in 1920 to all Italian soldiers who had served in World War I.

With General Diaz content to sit on the defensive, there was little action on the Italian front through summer 1918. On 9 August, Italian patriots were enthused when the poet and nationalist Gabriele d'Annunzio led an air squadron on a long-distance flight to the Austrian capital Vienna, where it dropped leaflets informing the population that they were losing the war. This was not news to the Austro-Hungarians. The failure of the offensive on the Piave revealed the poor state of Austria-Hungary's armed forces. The collapse of its economy was evident in the malnutrition on the streets of Vienna.

The surrender of Bulgaria in late September left Austria-Hungary exposed to attack through the Balkans. Emperor Charles appealed to US President Woodrow Wilson for a peace deal but was rebuffed. In an attempt to stave off political collapse, on 16 October Charles announced a major reform of the constitution, but various ethnic groups were already setting up their own councils to prepare for independence.

With Austria-Hungary disintegrating, the Italians decided to embark on an offensive that would strengthen their position in future peace negotiations. Diaz planned an advance from Monte Grappa in the north and across the Piave towards the city of Vittorio Veneto. He had 51 Italian divisions, five French and British divisions, and token Czech and US contingents. On paper, the opposing sides were evenly matched, but in reality the Austro-Hungarian divisions were at half strength, short of artillery, and demoralized.

Reviewing the troops
Austro-Hungarian Emperor Charles I meets some of his soldiers. The young emperor tried to improve conditions in the army, such as abolishing flogging, but discontent was rife in the ranks.

The offensive was launched on 24 October. For two days the Austro-Hungarian army fought fiercely, but from 26 October it began to disintegrate. Italian progress was rapid, and Vittorio Veneto fell on 30 October. More than 300,000 Austro-Hungarian soldiers were taken prisoner. An armistice was agreed on 3 November, but the Italians continued to advance for another two days, regaining the territory lost after Caporetto.

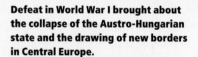

AFTER

Defeat in World War I brought about the collapse of the Austro-Hungarian state and the drawing of new borders in Central Europe.

THE EMPIRE DISINTEGRATES
Austria-Hungary had in effect **ceased to exist** before the Armistice was agreed. The country's Poles joined the **new Polish state**. Czechs and Slovaks declared **Bohemia and Moravia** independent on 18 October 1918. The **South Slavs** – Serbs, Croats, and Slovenes – declared independence on 29 October. Hungary quit the union with Austria. Emperor Charles renounced his role as head of state on 11 November.

TERRITORIAL GAINS
The peace treaty of St-Germain-en-Laye, concluded with Austria in 1919, **reduced Austria to a small republic** of predominantly ethnic Germans. **Italy gained some territory** at Austria's expense, including South Tyrol and Trieste, but less than it had hoped, leaving a legacy of bitterness. By the 1920 **Treaty of Trianon**, Hungary had lost 70 per cent of its pre-war territory to Romania, Czechoslovakia, and Yugoslavia.

> "We all knew that **Italy had been saved,** and we rejoiced together."
>
> HISTORIAN G.M. TREVELYAN, SERVING WITH THE BRITISH RED CROSS AT THE BATTLE OF PIAVE RIVER, JUNE 1918

Mutiny and Revolution

In October 1918, Germany announced it was seeking an armistice. As politicians rushed to introduce democratic reforms, a mutiny in the navy triggered uprisings in German cities. Kaiser Wilhelm was deposed, leaving Germany's new leaders to end the war.

On 29 September, Germany's military leaders, Paul von Hindenburg and Erich Ludendorff, told the German civilian government that it must seek an immediate armistice. This was a brutal shock to the politicians who, like the German people, had been kept in the dark about the true military situation.

To the east, German armies had occupied large areas of the former Russian Empire, and to the west they were still fighting in France and Belgium. But with Allied forces breaking through the Hindenburg Line, Germany's military leadership feared that the Western Front defences were about to collapse. They also knew that their southern flank had become

Revolution in Germany
On 11 November 1918, the French newspaper *Le Petit Journal* announced a revolution in Germany and the abdication of Kaiser Wilhelm II. The Armistice was signed on the morning this report appeared.

« BEFORE

Under the leadership of Field Marshal Paul von Hindenburg and General Erich Ludendorff, Germany sought to establish German dominance in Europe through military victory.

LAST GASP
Germany's **defeat of Russia**, confirmed by the **Treaty of Brest-Litovsk «« 276–77** in March 1918, was followed by a **series of offensives** on the Western Front. These failed to win the war, however, and from August the Germans were driven in retreat, first to the **Hindenburg Line «« 312–13** and then beyond. Germany's allies, Bulgaria, Turkey, and Austria-Hungary, successively sought armistice agreements to exit the war.

indefensible. Germany had no spare soldiers to transfer to the Balkans following the defeat of Bulgaria or to prop up Austria-Hungary.

Search for an exit
Certain that the strategic situation was hopeless, the German Supreme Command sought to escape the consequences of total military defeat by luring the Allies into an armistice. Their main hope lay in US President Woodrow Wilson, who in January 1918 had made an idealistic fourteen-point declaration of war aims. The Fourteen Points seemed to provide the ground for a peace deal that would leave German military forces intact, the Kaiser on his throne, and German territory free of foreign occupation.

Recognizing Wilson's predilection for democracy, the German leaders' first move was to appoint a new chancellor, the moderate conservative Prince Max von Baden, as head of a liberal civilian government. For the first time in its history, the German government was representative of the majority in the Reichstag, including members from the Social Democratic Party (SDP) and from Zentrum, the Catholic party. On 4 October, Prince Max sent a note to President Wilson requesting an armistice and accepting the Fourteen Points as the basis for negotiations.

Wilson initially responded favourably to the German proposal, only requesting that the Germans withdraw their armies from occupied territory as a prelude to an armistice. But a hostile reaction from other Allied leaders and military commanders – including US General John Pershing – as well as public opinion in the USA soon forced Wilson to stiffen his position.

On 10 October, a German U-boat sank the Irish ferry *Leinster*, killing over 500 people. Wilson demanded an immediate end to submarine warfare plus real progress towards democracy in Germany. Prince Max complied, calling off the U-boats and pushing through reforms to make Germany a constitutional monarchy. On 23 October, Wilson made it clear that to obtain an armistice Germany would have to

Germany humiliated
A French poster of 1918 depicts the Kaiser with a broken sword kneeling before the massed flags of the Allies, including the Stars and Stripes.

surrender and the Kaiser would have to be removed. Wilson handed over the task of formulating the precise terms of an armistice to the Allied commanders.

German U-turn
By this time, the German armies had shown they were able to fight on and the prospect of their collapse receded. Hindenburg and Ludendorff reversed their support for an armistice, expressing outrage at Allied terms. On 24 October, ignoring the government, they ordered the German armies to fight to the death. Two days later, after a row with the Kaiser, Ludendorff was replaced by General Wilhelm Groener. Hindenburg remained at his post. Meanwhile, the German people were thrown into confusion by the prospect of defeat. The liberalization of Germany

under Prince Max included the release of political prisoners and the introduction of freedom of speech. Racked by hunger and shortages, German cities seethed with unrest. The left-wing Independent Social Democratic Party, which had deputies in the Reichstag and links with radical shop stewards in factories, advocated

340,000 The estimated number of **German soldiers who surrendered in the last four months of the war.**

the overthrow of the Kaiser. Released from prison in October, Karl Liebknecht and Rosa Luxemburg, leaders of the far-left Spartacus League, agitated for a revolutionary upheaval to found a socialist state.

Naval mutiny
On 28 October, the German Admiralty ordered the High Seas Fleet at Wilhelmshaven to put to sea for a last encounter with the Royal Navy's Grand Fleet. Blockaded in port for most of the war, poorly fed, and alienated by arrogant officers, German sailors were in no mood for a death-or-glory sortie. They

Inciting revolution
Karl Liebknecht, one of the leaders of Germany's Spartacus League, addresses a gathering of soldiers and sailors in Berlin. Liebknecht wanted a Bolshevik-style revolution to make Germany a workers' state.

Schloss Platz.

Fighting on the streets
The streets of Berlin saw fighting between soldiers and civilians on both sides. German army leaders refused to defend the monarchy against armed attack by revolutionaries in the crisis of November 1918.

"The **old and rotten,** the **monarchy has collapsed...** Long live the German **Republic!**"

PHILIPP SCHEIDEMANN, DECLARATION FROM THE REICHSTAG BUILDING, 9 NOVEMBER 1918

refused to sail. The mutiny spread to the port city of Kiel, which was taken over by revolutionary sailors' councils, modelled on the Russian soviets.

Through the first week in November the uprising spread. Workers', soldiers', and sailors' councils took control of cities across Germany. In Munich, Independent Socialists led by Kurt Eisner declared Bavaria a republic. In army units in Germany, officers were disarmed by soldiers and stripped of their insignia. On the Western Front, discipline held and German troops continued fighting.

Germany becomes a republic
On the night of the 7 November, a German delegation travelled through Allied lines for face-to-face armistice negotiations. Before agreement was reached, however, the German Empire ceased to exist. On 9 November, as revolutionary upheaval reached Berlin, Prince Max handed the chancellorship to moderate Social Democrat Friedrich Ebert. Meanwhile, another Social Democrat, Philipp Scheidemann, on his own initiative declared Germany a republic.

Ebert formed a revolutionary government of People's Commissars, drawn from the Social Democrats and Independent Socialists. Kaiser Wilhelm, at the German military headquarters at Spa in Belgium, was informed by Groener that the army would not fight to keep him on the throne. He fled across the border into exile in the neutral Netherlands.

1.45 MILLION The number of working days lost to strikes in Germany in 1918.

Balcony speech
On the afternoon of 9 November 1918, German Social Democrat politician Philipp Scheidemann announced the creation of a German Republic, addressing a crowd from a balcony of the Reichstag building in Berlin.

After the war, a liberal democratic government came to power in Germany but it was undermined by right-wing militarists.

THE WEIMAR REPUBLIC
After the **Armistice 322–33 »**, efforts to turn Germany into a revolutionary socialist state failed. An uprising in Berlin led by the Spartacists was suppressed in January 1919. Germany emerged as the centre-left **Weimar Republic**.

14 The number of years that the German Weimar Republic lasted, before Adolf Hitler was appointed chancellor.

The **Treaty of Versailles 338–39 »** was signed by German delegates under duress in June 1919. Right-wing militarists, including Hindenburg and Ludendorff, **created the myth** that the German army had lost through a **"stab in the back"** by Jews and socialist subversives.

The signing of the Armistice
In a railway carriage in the Fôret de Compiègne, the leader of the German delegation, Matthias Erzberger, faces Marshal Ferdinand Foch across the table on which the Armistice will be signed.

The Armistice

On 11 November 1918, an armistice brought an end to more than four years of slaughter. There were scenes of rejoicing on city streets in the victorious countries, but relief and pride were tempered by grief for the fallen. In the defeated countries, chaos and bitterness reigned.

 BEFORE

In autumn 1918, the deterioration of Germany's military situation and the collapse of its allies forced the country's leaders to seek an armistice.

DEFEAT ON ALL FRONTS
The success of Allied armies on the Western Front culminated in the breaching of the **Hindenburg Line ❮❮ 312–13** in late September. Meanwhile, the **defeat of Bulgaria** left the Allies free to march through the Balkans, with French and Serbian troops reaching Belgrade on 5 November. **Turkey agreed an armistice ❮❮ 316–17** on 30 October. **Austria-Hungary** was **defeated by the Italians ❮❮ 318–19** at Vittorio Veneto and signed an armistice on 3 November. Germany was in the **grip of revolution**, leading to the fall of the Kaiser and the proclamation of a republic on 9 November **❮❮ 320–21**.

On the night of 7 November, a German delegation, headed by the respected politician Matthias Erzberger, was taken to Rethondes in eastern France. Supreme Commander of the Allied Armies Marshal Ferdinand Foch and other Allied officers awaited their arrival on a train in a siding in the Fôret de Compiègne.

The Allies had agreed to present harsh armistice terms. Germany was to withdraw all of its troops from France, Belgium, and Alsace-Lorraine; German territory on the west bank of the Rhine would be occupied by Allied troops, who would also hold bridgeheads across the Rhine; and large quantities of military equipment, surface warships, and submarines were to be handed over to the Allies. The naval blockade of Germany would continue to operate.

Foch was not certain that Germany would accept these terms which, by rendering their country indefensible, effectively constituted a surrender rather than a cessation of hostilities. Allied attacks on the Western Front continued unabated, as did planning for future operations, into 1919.

Opinion among Allied generals was divided. British commander Field Marshal Douglas Haig, impressed by the strength of German resistance, was keen on an immediate end to the fighting. US General John Pershing hoped the Germans would reject the Armistice so that they could be more thoroughly beaten in battle. "What I dread," Pershing said, "is that Germany doesn't know that she is licked."

Any possibility of the Germans rejecting the Armistice terms was annulled by the outbreak of revolution at home. The newly installed government of the German Republic, proclaimed on 9 November, was fully occupied with establishing a hold on power in Berlin.

5,000 The number of locomotive engines that were to be surrendered to the Allies by the Germans under the terms of the Armistice.

On the evening of 10 November, a telegram from the government authorized Erzberger to accept the Allied terms. Around 2am on the morning of 11 November, the German delegation stepped down from their train and walked on planks across muddy ground to Foch's railway carriage. For the following three hours, various points in the Armistice

Cheering for victory
Soldiers of the Irish Guards raise their helmets aloft to cheer the announcement of the Armistice at Maubeuge in northern France.

AFTER »

The Armistice was followed by a peace conference in Paris in 1919, at which the victors discussed the terms to be imposed on the defeated.

THE FALLOUT
The delay in finalizing peace terms slowed the **demobilization of Allied armies**, and soldiers demanded the right to go home. Many civilians in Germany and former Austria-Hungary suffered hardship through the continuing Allied blockade and economic and political dislocation. All countries experienced high death rates from an **influenza pandemic** that in total probably killed more people than the war. The **Treaty of Versailles 338–39 »**, signed by the Germans under protest in June 1919, formally ended the war. Matthias Erzberger was assassinated by German nationalist extremists in 1921 for his "crime" in signing the Armistice.

SPANISH FLU OVERTAKES THE ANGEL OF PEACE

agreement were discussed, but there were no real negotiations. Erzberger read out a statement of protest, concluding: "A people of 70 million are suffering, but they are not dead."

At 5:10am the Armistice was signed by Foch and British First Sea Lord Admiral Rosslyn Wemyss for the Allies, and by Erzberger and three of his colleagues for Germany. It was agreed that, since it was the eleventh day of the eleventh month, hostilities would cease at 11am, to complete the coincidence.

The last shots
The war continued until the last moment. Everywhere Allied troops were advancing. The Belgians had just retaken Ghent, the Canadians Mons,

Thanksgiving Day at Eagle Hut, London. November 28th 1918.

Celebratory feast
The annual Thanksgiving Day celebrations had special significance for Americans in November 1918. As this menu shows, the traditional turkey dinner was served in London to US soldiers who had survived the war.

and the Americans Mézières. There were 11,000 Allied casualties on the morning of 11 November, as officers ordered attacks to seize key points ahead of the ceasefire. Outside Mons, three British soldiers who had survived four years of combat were killed by a burst of machine-gun fire.

Canadian Private George Price is recognized as the last British and Commonwealth fatality of the war, shot dead by a sniper at 10:58.

> ## "No more **slaughter,** no more **maiming,** no more **mud** and **blood,** and no more **killing.**"
>
> BRITISH LIEUTENANT R. G. DIXON, ROYAL ARTILLERY, ON THE ARMISTICE

As the watches of the officers ticked to 11 o'clock, the order was given to cease firing. An uncanny silence fell along the front. Soldiers realized, with amazement, that the war really had stopped. As the guns fell silent, reactions were mixed. At the front there was no fraternization between opposing troops. Allied soldiers still manned their positions, while to the rear reactions ranged from decorous thanksgiving ceremonies to riotous celebrations with the local population.

Public reactions
The most joyous scenes took place in Allied cities. In London's Trafalgar Square, on Broadway in New York, and along the Seine in Paris, crowds danced and sang. Political leaders – Georges Clemenceau in France, David Lloyd George in Britain – made speeches. In some places, such as Chicago in the USA and Melbourne in Australia, celebrations degenerated into disorder. More frequently well-behaved street parties took place, as families waited to be reunited with loved ones.

For many people, in mourning for relatives killed in the fighting or struck down by the deadly influenza epidemic then sweeping the world, the rejoicing seemed inappropriate. The family of the English poet Wilfred Owen

Anglo-American celebrations
In Paris, on 11 November 1918, two British soldiers, an American sailor, and an American nurse celebrate the Armistice together. An apparently interminable conflict had come to a surprisingly sudden end.

received the telegram announcing his death in combat as the bells were ringing for the Armistice. In Belgium, celebration of the German defeat was accompanied by retribution against collaborators and profiteers. Belgian women alleged to have had relationships with German soldiers were forced to walk naked through the streets with their heads shaved, and traders believed to have exploited food shortages for profit had their shops looted and burned.

There was no rejoicing in the defeated countries. In Germany, shock and bitterness were widespread among civilians who had thought their country would win the war and soldiers who could not believe the

German army had been beaten. One corporal, Adolf Hitler, heard the news of the Armistice while in hospital recovering from a gas attack. In his memoirs, *Mein Kampf,* he described his anguish at the realization that four years of fighting had "all been in vain". The reactions of men such as Hitler to the experience of defeat were to become a dangerous factor in postwar German political life.

Victory parade
French civilians and US soldiers celebrate the conclusion of the war. The collapse of the German army led the country's leaders to sign an armistice with the Allies on 11 November 1918.

7
AFTERMATH
1919 – 1923

The postwar peace conference failed to create a new world order based on harmony and justice. While people sought solace in commemorating the fallen, local wars and political conflicts continued and the seeds of another world war were sown.

British dominion. Northern Ireland, dominated by Protestants, remains part of the UK. Civil war breaks out in 1922 between the Irish Free State government and Republicans.

through garbage for fuel and edible refuse. The Allied economic blockade on Germany is maintained until the peace is signed.

1915. Such cemeteries remain places of pilgrimage to the present day.

OPE

AEROE ISLANDS (Denmark)
NORWAY
SWEDEN
FINLAND
ESTONIA
LATVIA
LITHUANIA
North Sea
DENMARK
Baltic Sea
DANZIG (League of Nations Administration)
NETH.
BRITAIN
GER.
BEL.
LUX.
GERMANY
POLAND
USSR
SAAR (League of Nations Administration)
SWITZ.
AUSTRIA
HUNGARY
CZECHOSLOVAKIA
FRANCE
YUGOSLAVIA
ROMANIA
ITALY
BULGARIA
ALB.
Black Sea
SPAIN
Mediterranean Sea
GREECE
TURKEY
DODECANESE (Italy)
ALGERIA (France)
TUNISIA (France)
CYPRUS (Britain)
SYRIA
OCCO nce)
LIBYA (Italy)
EGYPT (Britain)
IRAQ

ICELAND

ATLANTIC OCEAN

NORWAY
SWEDEN
FINLAND
BRITAIN
GERMANY
POLAND
FRANCE
ITALY
USSR
PORTUGAL
SPAIN
Black Sea
TURKEY
SPANISH MOROCCO
MOROCCO
TUNISIA
CYPRUS (French mandate)
SYRIA (French mandate)
PERSIA
AFGHANISTAN
TIB (autor
PALESTINE (British mandate)
IRAQ (British mandate)
ALGERIA
LIBYA
EGYPT
TRANSJORDAN (British mandate)
KUWAIT
BAHRAIN
QATAR
NEPA
RIO DE ORO
NEJD (Saudi)
TRUCIAL OMAN
INDI
FRENCH WEST AFRICA
ANGLO-EGYPTIAN SUDAN (British mandate)
ASIR
YEMEN
OMAN
HADHRAMAUT
GAMBIA
PORTUGUESE GUINEA
CAMEROONS (British mandate)
TOGO (French mandate)
ADEN PROTECTORATE
SIERRA LEONE
NIGERIA
FRENCH EQUATORIAL AFRICA
ERITREA
FRENCH SOMALILAND
LIBERIA
TOGO (British mandate)
GOLD COAST
CAMEROONS (French mandate)
ABYSSINIA
BRITISH SOMALILAND
ITALIAN SOMALILAND
CEY
UGANDA
KENYA
BELGIAN CONGO
TANGANYIKA (British mandate)
ANGOLA
NYASALAND
NORTHERN RHODESIA
INDIA OCEA
SOUTHERN RHODESIA
MADAGASCAR
SOUTH WEST AFRICA (South African mandate)
BECHUANA-LAND
PORTUGUESE EAST AFRICA
UNION OF SOUTH AFRICA

aty of Versailles
een the Allies and Germany is signed ne 1919, watched rowd of onlookers. Most Germans do ept that the peace terms are just.

Polish independence, celebrated in this poster, is achieved in November 1918. The state of Poland, which did not exist before the war, is created from Germany, Russia, and the former Austria-Hungary.

The Paris Peace Conference in January 1919 fails to satisfy the demands of many delegates, including Prince Feisal, who hopes to gain Arab independence.

hroughout World War I, people had been told that their efforts and sacrifices would lead to the building of a better where peace and justice would reign. The Paris Peace rence of 1919 inevitably disappointed these high aspirations. eaty of Versailles imposed on Germany was a compromise that ered the Germans without sufficiently guaranteeing French y. The map of Europe and the Middle East was extensively

redrawn as a result of the collapse of the Russian, Austro-Hungarian, and Ottoman empires. Nationalist movements created new states such as Czechoslovakia, Poland, and Yugoslavia. The peacemakers determined the new borders.

There was much disappointment, even among the victors. Italy did not gain the territory it had expected, while the Arabs saw their part of the former Ottoman Empire divided between Britain and France.

US President **Woodrow Wilson** is the
focus for hopes of a "just peace" in 1919. He
fails to sell the peace treaty to the US Congress
and the American people, with the result that
the USA never joins the League of Nations.

The **Spanish flu pandemic**
is at its peak in 1918–19. It kills
50–100 million people worldwide,
including one in five people in
Samoa. Here the virus is depicted
saddening the angel of peace.

**THE WORLD IN
DECEMBER 1923**
— Frontiers

GREENLAND

CANADA

NEWFOUNDLAND

UNITED STATES
OF AMERICA

MEXICO

BRITISH HONDURAS
CUBA
DOMINICAN REPUBLIC
VIRGIN ISLANDS
HAITI
LEEWARD ISLANDS
WINDWARD ISLANDS
GUATEMALA
HONDURAS
BARBADOS
EL SALVADOR
NICARAGUA
TRINIDAD AND TOBAGO
COSTA RICA
BRITISH GUIANA
CANAL ZONE
VENEZUELA
DUTCH GUIANA
PANAMA
FRENCH GUIANA
COLOMBIA

ECUADOR

PERU

BRAZIL

BOLIVIA

PARAGUAY

CHILE

URUGUAY

ARGENTINA

FALKLAND
ISLANDS

ATLANTIC
OCEAN

PACIFIC
OCEAN

Hawaiian Islands

Mariana
Islands
(Japanese mandate)

Marshall Islands
(Japanese mandate)

Caroline
Islands
(Japanese mandate)

Gilbert
Islands

Christmas
Island

Nauru
(Australian mandate)

Cook
Islands

TERRITORY
OF NEW GUINEA
(Australian mandate)

Solomon
Islands

Ellice
Islands

PAPUA

WESTERN
SAMOA
(New Zealand
mandate)

AMERICAN
SAMOA

French Polynesia

New
Hebrides

Tonga

Fiji

New
Caledonia

AUSTRALIA

NEW
ZEALAND

NGOLIA

HINA

JAPANESE
EMPIRE

FRENCH
INDOCHINA
PHILIPPINE
ISLANDS
GUAM
BRITISH
ORTH BORNEO
BRUNEI
SARAWAK
MALAYA

DUTCH EAST INDIES

PORTUGUESE
TIMOR

Much of the postwar world seethed with discontent and was
immersed in suffering. An influenza pandemic in 1918–19 may have
been the most costly natural disaster ever to strike the human race.
In the former Russian Empire, millions died in civil war and famine
before the establishment of the Communist-ruled Union of Soviet
Socialist Republics (USSR) at the end of 1922. There were wars
between the Irish and British, Poles and Russians, Turks and Greeks,

In 1923, France and Belgium sent troops into Germany to secure
reparations payments imposed by the Versailles Treaty. Ravaged by
hyperinflation and threatened by political extremists, the German
Republic survived to achieve a fragile return to normality by 1924.

The war was obsessively memorialized, but most people hoped
it would never be repeated. German resentment and bitterness,
however, led directly to the outbreak of World War II in 1939.

TIMELINE 1919 – 1923

Paris Peace Conference ▪ **Versailles Peace Treaty** ▪ Remembrance ceremonies ▪
Russian Civil War ▪ Irish independence ▪ **Fascist triumph in Italy** ▪
Turkey becomes a republic ▪ **Ruhr occupied** ▪ German hyperinflation

1919

JANUARY
World is in the grip of Spanish flu pandemic.

15 JANUARY
The Spartacist uprising in Berlin is crushed, ending the attempt to carry out a communist revolution.

18 JANUARY
First plenary session of Paris Peace Conference.

21 JANUARY
Sinn Fein MPs meet in Dublin and proclaim an Irish Republic.

» The Paris Peace Conference

25 JANUARY
Paris Peace Conference agrees in principle to the creation of the League of Nations.

21 MARCH
Communists led by Bela Kun take power in Hungary.

23 MARCH
Benito Mussolini founds the Italian Fascist movement.

23 APRIL
Italian Prime Minister Vittorio Orlando walks out of the peace conference after Italian demands are not met.

4 MAY
Chinese protest against decision to grant Shantung to Japan.

7 MAY
The Allies present peace terms to Germany. They include loss of territory, limits on armed forces, and payment of reparations.

21 JUNE
The German High Seas Fleet is scuttled off the British naval base at Scapa Flow in the Orkneys, in protest at peace terms.

« Protection against Spanish flu

28 JUNE
The Treaty of Versailles is signed in Paris.

19 JULY
The Cenotaph is unveiled in London.

1 AUGUST
In Hungary, Bela Kun's communist regime is overthrown.

11 AUGUST
Founding of German Weimar Republic.

≫ German naval flag

10 SEPTEMBER
The Treaty of St Germain formalizes peace between the Allies and Austria.

19 OCTOBER
In Russia, Red cavalry defeats White army advancing on the city of Tula.

11 NOVEMBER
Ceremonies on the first anniversary of the Armistice begin the tradition of remembrance.

19 NOVEMBER
US Senate fails to ratify the Treaty of Versailles.

27 NOVEMBER
Bulgaria signs the peace treaty of Neuilly with the Allies.

1920

20 JANUARY
Georges Clemenceau resigns as French prime minister and retires from politics.

≫Georges Clemenceau's office seal

8 MARCH
Arab leader Feisal is declared King of Syria.

13 MARCH
Kapp Putsch by paramilitary Freikorps against German government. It collapses five days later.

19 MARCH
US Congress rejects the Versailles Treaty and membership of the League of Nations.

23 APRIL
Mustafa Kemal opens a National Assembly in Ankara in opposition to Ottoman government.

4 JUNE
Treaty of Trianon formalizes peace between the wartime Allies and Hungary.

10 AUGUST
Turkey signs the Treaty of Sèvres, the terms of which include transfers of territory to Greece.

12–25 AUGUST
Bolshevik Russian forces are defeated by the Poles at the Battle of Warsaw.

11 NOVEMBER
Burials of the Unknown Warriors take place in London and Paris.

14 NOVEMBER
Russian Civil War ends with the evacuation of White troops from the Crimea.

⌃ The body of Britain's Unknown Warrior is taken home

15 NOVEMBER
The former port of Danzig is made a free city to give Poland access to the sea.

» A postage stamp from the free city of Danzig

330

> "I have **endeavoured to destroy… that Treaty** which … contains the **vilest oppression** that **peoples** and human beings have **ever… put up with.**"
>
> GERMAN FÜHRER ADOLF HITLER ON THE VERSAILLES TREATY, 28 APRIL 1939

1921

29 JANUARY
An Inter-Allied Reparations Commission decides on the sum of German war reparations. Germany rejects the figure as too high.

29 JULY
Adolf Hitler becomes leader of the small extremist Nazi Party in Germany.

23 AUGUST
The British make Feisal King of Iraq, although the country remains under British control.

18 MARCH
The Treaty of Riga establishes the border between Poland and Bolshevik Russia.

13 SEPTEMBER
Turkish nationalist forces defeat an invading Greek army at the Battle of Sakariya.

5 MAY
The Allies threaten to occupy the Ruhr area of Germany if the Germans reject a revised reparations demand. Germany agrees to pay.

6 DECEMBER
The Anglo-Irish Treaty ends the Irish War of Independence and establishes the Irish Free State.

⌃ Cemetery and memorial at Notre Dame de Lorette, France

29 DECEMBER
USA, France, Britain, Italy, and Japan sign the Washington Treaty limiting the size of their navies.

1922

28 FEBRUARY
Britain ends its protectorate over Egypt, declaring the country independent.

16 APRIL
Treaty of Rapallo normalizes relations between Germany and Russia.

1 NOVEMBER
The Turkish National Assembly abolishes the Ottoman sultanate.

⌃ Greek refugees struggle to flee the city of Smyrna

28 JUNE
Civil war breaks out between the Irish Free State government and Republicans who reject the Anglo-Irish Treaty.

⌄ Poster celebrating the fascist March on Rome

30 AUGUST
Turkish forces defeat the Greeks at the Battle of Dunlupinar.

13 SEPTEMBER
Occupied by Turkish troops, Smyrna (modern-day Izmir) is destroyed by fire.

31 OCTOBER
Fascist leader Mussolini forms a government in Italy after the "March on Rome".

30 DECEMBER
The Union of Soviet Socialist Republics (USSR) is founded.

1923

≪ French troops begin their occupation of the Ruhr

11 JANUARY
French and Belgian troops occupy the Ruhr area of Germany in response to the country's failure to make reparations obligations.

13 AUGUST
Gustav Stresemann becomes German chancellor and begins efforts to end ongoing economic and political crisis.

29 OCTOBER
Turkey is declared a republic.

24 MAY
Irish Civil War ends with surrender of Republican forces opposed to the Anglo-Irish Treaty.

8–9 NOVEMBER
Nazi leader Adolf Hitler, supported by Erich Ludendorff, tries to seize power in the Munich Putsch. The attempted coup fails.

JULY
The value of the German mark collapses through hyperinflation. One US dollar buys 353,000 marks.

⌃ Adolf Hitler

24 JULY
Treaty of Lausanne between Turkey and the wartime Allies replaces the earlier peace treaty of Sèvres.

15 NOVEMBER
Issue of the new Rentenmark ends German hyperinflation. One Rentenmark equals one trillion old marks.

BEFORE

World War I had lasted more than four years and caused the collapse of the Russian, Austro-Hungarian, Ottoman, and German empires.

AUSTRO-HUNGARIAN ANTI-WAR POSTER

NEW WORLD ORDER

A series of **armistices** ended the fighting, notably with Ottoman Turkey **« 316–17** on 30 October 1918, Austria-Hungary **« 318–19** on 3 November, and Germany **« 322–23** on 11 November. New states asserted their independence as the **old empires collapsed**, including Poland, Czechoslovakia, and the Kingdom of Serbs, Croats and Slovenes (later Yugoslavia). In the former Russian Empire, **civil war** was raging.

Devastated World

After the fighting stopped, the world faced a daunting transition to peace. Malnutrition and disease killed millions, while political disorder and continuing armed conflict blocked recovery in many places. Soldiers returning home were disoriented by the experience of war.

World War I cost the lives of almost 10 million military personnel. These included over 2 million Germans, 750,000 British, 62,000 Australians, 65,000 Canadians, 74,000 Indians, and 58,000 Belgians. The French death toll was 1.4 million, about one in 10 of all French males. Almost 117,000 US service personnel died.

Overall, losses were heavily concentrated in younger adult males. In Germany, for example, one in three men who had been aged 19 to 22 when the war started was dead by November 1918. Countless survivors were to varying degrees disabled and most were psychologically scarred.

It is impossible to establish how many civilian deaths were attributable to the effects of the war, although a figure of 6 million has been suggested. Malnutrition and general hardship, which increased the incidence of disease, continued beyond the war's end.

Deadly virus

Whether the flu pandemic raging at the time of the armistice should be considered a consequence of the war is uncertain, although wartime conditions certainly facilitated the spread of the deadly virus known misleadingly as "Spanish flu". Many thousands of soldiers who had survived the fighting died of influenza around the war's end. First recorded in January 1918, the virus killed between 50 and 100 million people worldwide before subsiding in late 1919. The population of Germany, weakened by food shortages, suffered heavily, but so did the well-fed USA. The world's attention was distracted from probably the most deadly pandemic in human history by focusing upon the war and its aftermath. The demobilization of Allied soldiers proceeded slowly and often unfairly, leading to public protests and serious disturbances – including an incident in which five mutinous Canadian soldiers were shot at their army camp in Wales. Implementation of the terms of the Armistice with Germany went ahead. Allied soldiers occupied the Rhineland and German warships and submarines were interned in British ports. Allied prisoners of war were released from their camps and left to find their own way to friendly territory.

Influenza pandemic

The "Spanish flu" that swept the world in 1918–19 mostly affected young adults, like this American soldier. Around 550,000 Americans died in the pandemic.

Extreme nationalism

German soldiers marched home from France, Belgium, Russia, and Ukraine to find their country in the grip of revolutionary turmoil. Seeking an explanation for a defeat they had not expected and could not accept, some of them, such as future dictator

German hardship
Women stoop to salvage food from a rubbish dump in Berlin in the aftermath of the war. Malnutrition was rife and the death toll high.

Adolf Hitler, were drawn into nationalist extremist groups that blamed socialists and Jews for the debacle. Unable to reintegrate in civilian life, many ex-soldiers joined paramilitary organizations called Freikorps. The German government, led by moderate Social Democrats intent on founding a parliamentary democracy, used the Freikorps to crush an attempted communist uprising in Berlin in January 1919. A socialist republic proclaimed in Bavaria, southern Germany, in May 1919 was also brutally suppressed.

Pitiful living conditions
Life remained a miserable struggle for most Germans, who faced poverty, cold, and hunger, induced by political chaos and the effects of the Allied naval blockade, which under the terms of the Armistice was maintained until a final peace agreement was signed.

It was a similar picture in other countries shattered by the war. In the Turkish capital Constantinople (Istanbul), typhus was rampant, food scarce, fuel unobtainable, and transport

at a standstill. In the former Austro-Hungarian and Russian empires, the condition of many people was pitiful.

New conflicts
There were outbreaks of fighting as new states sought to establish their borders – for example, between Poland and Czechoslovakia. In Hungary, a communist revolutionary, Bela Kun, seized power in March 1919 and proclaimed a Soviet Republic. He was overthrown by an invasion of Romanian and Czechoslovak forces, which allowed Hungarian Admiral Miklos Horthy to take power.

The victor countries were not immune to conflict and disorder. Italy was swept by riots and strikes. In the USA, the authorities made widespread arrests of anarchists and socialists in the "Red Scare" from April 1919. The British Empire was challenged by revolts in Ireland, Egypt, and India. Meanwhile, Belgium and France faced the daunting challenge of reconstruction in the war-devastated zone of the Western Front, with its ruined or obliterated towns and villages, wrecked factories

and mines, gas-poisoned soil, and dangerous litter of unexploded munitions. Even neutral countries such as Norway and the Netherlands were stalked by hunger.

The establishment of the American Relief Administration in February 1919, to provide food aid to Europe, was an attempt at a civilized international response to the catastrophe. But mostly individuals and states had to seek their own way back to normality.

Leaders of the victorious powers gathered for a conference in Paris in January 1919, leading to the agreement of a series of treaties to formally end the war.

SEEDS OF FUTURE CONFLICT
The crucial peace agreement with Germany, the **Versailles Treaty 338–39 》**, was signed in June 1919. Accepted by the Germans under duress, it included provision for **substantial reparations payments.** The German Weimar Republic was formally created in August 1919, but Germany continued to be racked by **civil conflict and hyperinflation** until 1924. In Italy, discontent with the outcome of the war was a major factor in the rise to power of **Benito Mussolini's Fascist Party** in 1922. In places, warfare continued into the 1920s, notably in the **Russian Civil War** and the **Greco-Turkish War 342–43 》**.

Clearing the ruins
German prisoners of war are set to work clearing debris in the ruined French town of Béthune in 1919. It took about seven years to return the devastated areas of northeastern France to normality.

> "We have won the war. Now we will **have to win the peace.** That may **prove harder.**"

FRENCH PREMIER GEORGES CLEMENCEAU, 11 NOVEMBER 1918

GERMAN DICTATOR (1889–1945)
ADOLF HITLER

The future German dictator Adolf Hitler was Austrian. He moved to Munich in Germany as a young man, joining the German army as a volunteer in August 1914. After the war, he drifted into nationalist politics, and in 1921 became leader of the small Nazi Party.

In 1923, his attempt to seize power in the Munich Putsch failed. After a spell in prison, he built up mass support by arguing that all Germany's ills were due to the Treaty of Versailles. Taking power in 1933, he sought to reverse the result of World War I, eventually leading Germany to catastrophic defeat in World War II.

The **Paris Peace Conference**

In January 1919, world leaders met for a peace conference in Paris. Hopes were high for the creation of a new and better world that would justify the sacrifice of the war. The conference ended in disillusion, however, as the participants haggled over conflicting interests.

BEFORE

Wartime agreements between Allied countries and public statements by political leaders set the complex agenda for the peace conference.

QUEST FOR NATIONHOOD
US President Woodrow Wilson had declared that the war would **"make the world safe for democracy"** **≪ 212–13**. Britain and France had agreed with the Americans to allow national groups such as the Poles to form **independent states ≪ 168–69**. But Italy expected to gain territory in Dalmatia, which had a mainly Slav population. The **Arabs** had been promised **independence ≪ 196–97**, contradicting an Anglo-French agreement to share former Turkish land and British **promises to Jewish Zionists**.

ITALIAN POLITICIAN (1860–1952)
VITTORIO ORLANDO

A law professor and politician from Sicily, Vittorio Orlando was Italy's minister of the interior before being appointed prime minister in the wake of the Caporetto disaster in 1917. His firm leadership secured a degree of national unity in support of the war effort. At the peace conference, he staged a walkout in protest at the treatment of Italy, but Italian nationalists still condemned him for failing to secure territorial expansion. They forced his resignation in June 1919.

The Paris Peace Conference was a vast, unwieldy event. Thirty-two states were represented, each with its entourage of diplomats, advisers, and secretaries. The most significant absentees were the defeated powers, who were not invited, and Bolshevik Russia. The leaders of all the major Allied states attended in person – David Lloyd George for Britain, Georges Clemenceau for France, Italian premier Vittorio Orlando, and US president Woodrow Wilson. The first US president to travel abroad on official business, Wilson was greeted in Europe by adoring crowds.

Initially, the most important issues at the conference were discussed by a Council of Ten, consisting of two representatives from each of the five major powers – the USA, Britain, France, Italy, and Japan. By March, this had been ditched in favour of a Council of Four – Wilson, Lloyd George, Clemenceau, and Orlando.

The League of Nations
The European Allies had broadly accepted the principle of a "just peace" based on democracy and national self-determination, as proposed by President Wilson. Lloyd George and Clemenceau both supported Wilson's idea for an international organization, the League of Nations, to preserve future peace. But each representative was there to promote his country's interests and ambitions. Victors expected to be rewarded for their war effort and compensated for their losses. Many were soon disappointed.

Japan proposed that the League support racial equality between members, but this was rejected.

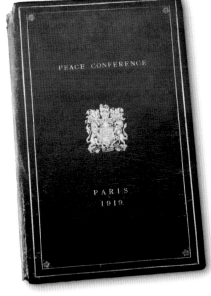

Record of the talks
This writing case was used by David Lloyd George at the Paris Peace Conference in 1919. The British prime minister found himself mediating between French leader Clemenceau and US President Wilson.

In compensation, the Japanese were told they could keep control of Tsingtao in China, seized from the Germans during the war. This outraged the Chinese, who felt they had gained nothing by supporting the Allied cause. Meanwhile, the Arabs who had fought alongside British troops against Turkey found the British and French intent on dividing Mesopotamia (Iraq), Palestine, and Syria between themselves.

Disputed borders
The peacemakers are sometimes said to have redrawn the borders of Europe, but except for the crucial case of Germany, most changes were decided elsewhere. Poland, Czechoslovakia, and the Kingdom of Serbs, Croats and Slovenes (Yugoslavia) had already declared

Arab representatives
Prince Feisal and his delegation, including British officer T.E. Lawrence (to the right of Feisal), at the conference. Having supported the Allies against Turkey, the Arabs expected to be rewarded with independence.

independence. The peacemakers could only intervene over the detail of borders, and sometimes, as in the case of Poland's eastern frontier, their decisions were later ignored.

Much time was spent discussing the fate of Fiume (Rijeka), which Italy and Yugoslavia both claimed. In April, Orlando walked out of the conference after his allies refused to back Italy. The frustration of its territorial ambitions fuelled discontent in the country in the postwar period. Overall, attempts to

> **NATIONAL SELF-DETERMINATION**
> **The right of ethnic groups to form independent nation-states instead of living under foreign rule.**

match borders to ethnicity revealed how impossible it was to apply self-determination to Europe's complex web of people.

A series of peace treaties were signed with the defeated powers: the Treaty of Versailles with Germany in June 1918, the Treaty of St Germain with Austria in September, the Treaty of Neuilly with Bulgaria in November, the Treaty of Sèvres with Turkey in April 1920, and the Treaty of Trianon with Hungary the following June. The treaties were complex, detailed, and partially ineffectual. The compromises between justice and revenge, and idealism and self-interest, left grounds for resentment, fuelling hostility and conflict for decades to come.

AFTER

In the 1920s and 30s, two of the peace treaties were nullified. Some of the disputes were settled by force.

BROKEN PROMISES
The **Treaty of Versailles 338–39 ≫** with Germany included provision for reparations that the Germans had difficulty in paying. The treaty was overturned by the Nazi regime from 1933. The **Treaty of Sèvres**, signed with Ottoman Turkey, was invalidated by the overthrow of the Sultan and success of Turkish Republican forces in a war with Greece. The **Treaty of Lausanne**, far more favourable to Turkey, replaced it in July 1923.

SHIFTING TERRITORIES
After a war between Poland and Bolshevik Russia, in March 1921 the **Peace of Riga** pushed the Polish border further east. Yugoslavia accepted Italian rule of disputed Fiume by the **Treaty of Rome** in 1924.

Peace conference delegates
Irish artist William Orpen was commissioned to paint this group portrait of the conference. Entitled *A Peace Conference at the Quai d'Orsay*, it shows Orlando, Wilson, Clemenceau and Lloyd George seated around the table.

FRENCH PRIME MINISTER Born **1841** Died 1929

Georges Clemenceau

"You ask what are **my war aims.** Gentlemen, **they are very simple: Victory.**"

GEORGES CLEMENCEAU, SPEECH, 20 NOVEMBER, 1917

In 1914, Georges Clemenceau was a 72-year-old maverick politician and journalist approaching the end of a long and chequered career. As a young man he had made his reputation as a radical critic of government, whose speeches in the Chamber of Deputies denounced colonialism, militarism, and the power of the Catholic Church.

When French life was torn apart in the 1890s by the Dreyfus affair – a scandal involving the mistaken condemnation of a Jewish army officer for treason – Clemenceau was among those who upheld Dreyfus's innocence. He became a hate figure for right-wing militarists, nationalists, anti-Semites, and Catholics. Around the same time, he was accused of taking bribes to cover up the bankruptcy of the Panama Canal Company.

In 1906, a time of political unrest in France, he accepted the post of minister of the interior. Socialists and anarchists were added to his list of enemies when he employed the army and police to suppress strikes and disturbances. In a subsequent three-year spell as prime minister, he earned respect for his tough handling of domestic issues and strengthened the Entente Cordiale (informal alliance) between France and Britain.

Outspoken critic

In the run-up to World War I Clemenceau founded a newspaper, *L'Homme libre* (The Free Man), to warn against the German threat to France and campaign for military preparedness. He described France as "neither defended nor governed" and fulminated against socialists who preached anti-militarism. When the war broke out in 1914, he turned down the offer of a government post as minister of justice. Instead, he stayed on the sidelines, using his newspaper to criticize the government and to demand a more competent execution of the war. After an issue of *L'Homme libre* was suppressed by military censors in September 1914, Clemenceau renamed it *L'Homme enchainé* (The Shackled Man).

Clemenceau was no champion of the freedom of others, however. He denounced

Ferocious reputation
French wartime prime minister Georges Clemenceau was known as "the Tiger" because of his fierce temperament. He was 77 years old at the time of the Paris Peace Conference in 1919.

M. le Docteur
Georges CLÉMENCEAU
dans l'exercice de son Ministère

The doctor of France
This cartoon alludes to Clemenceau's qualification as a doctor, depicting him as a crude surgeon who has operated on France's sick body. He was renowned for his ruthlessness towards his numerous enemies.

Interior Minister Louis-Jean Malvy as a defeatist and traitor for allowing the publication of the left-wing journal *Le Bonnet Rouge* and for failing to arrest left-wing "subversives and saboteurs".

As well as running his newspaper, Clemenceau was a member of the Senate, the upper house of the French parliament. As head of its army and foreign affairs committee from 1915, he met the military and political leaders of the Allied war effort and gained an insider's understanding of the conflict.

Becoming prime minister

By autumn 1917, the government was in disarray and public morale was low. Political unity had disintegrated. The fall of Paul Painlevé's government, defeated in parliament, left President Raymond Poincaré with two credible candidates for the job of prime minister: Joseph Caillaux, the leading advocate of a negotiated peace, and Clemenceau, the best known proponent of a fight to the death. He chose Clemenceau.

Clemenceau visits the troops
In 1918, the French prime minister made weekly visits to the front, both to talk with his generals and to meet ordinary soldiers in the trenches. His public appearances strengthened morale.

More like a dictator than a prime minister, Clemenceau filled his cabinet with nonentities and kept the key post of minister for war for himself. In an impassioned speech, he declared victory his sole aim and committed France to war "to the end". Alleged traitors and defeatists were arrested, including Caillaux and Malvy. Strikes in factories were resolved by addressing grievances while cracking down on anti-war activists.

Clemenceau's passionate commitment to the war tightened bonds with France's Allies during the fluctuating battles of 1918. He could claim a large part of the credit for installing Ferdinand Foch as Supreme Commander of the Allied Armies in spring 1918 and for the aggressive pursuit of the war on the Western Front from July 1918. His eloquent speeches raised French morale on the home front and in the army.

Tough stance

Celebrated at the Armistice as the architect of victory, he entered the Paris Peace Conference determined to ensure the security of France against a future resurgence of German militarism. Surviving an assassination

attempt by anarchist Emile Cottin – which left a bullet lodged in his chest for the rest of his life – Clemenceau argued tirelessly against what he saw as the naive idealism of US President Woodrow Wilson. Faced with the refusal of Britain and the USA to support his aims, however, he was forced to accept compromises. As a result, the Treaty of Versailles was denounced by French nationalists as too lenient on Germany. Exploiting Clemenceau's prestige, a "bloc national" of right-wing politicians campaigned under his banner at elections in November 1919 but then deserted him. Failing in a bid for the presidency, Clemenceau retired in 1920. He died nine years later at the age of 89.

Prime ministerial seal
Used by Georges Clemenceau during his tenure as prime minister of France, this seal was fashioned out of red gold and silver. It had a carved monogram – "GC".

> "With **snarls and growls,** the ferocious, aged, dauntless beast of prey **went into action.**"
>
> WINSTON CHURCHILL, DESCRIBING CLEMENCEAU AS WAR LEADER

TIMELINE

28 September 1841 Born the son of a doctor in the Vendée region of western France.

1858 Studies medicine in Paris and becomes involved in radical politics.

1865 Flees to the USA to escape arrest for opposing the regime of Napoleon III.

1869 Marries a US citizen, Mary Elizabeth Plummer.

1870 Returns to France and is present at the founding of the Third Republic. Appointed mayor of Montmartre in Paris.

1876 Elected to the Chamber of Deputies, becoming the leader of the radical left in the assembly.

CLEMENCEAU, PAINTED BY ÉDOUARD MANET

1880 Founds *La Justice*, the first of a series of radical newspapers he will edit.

1892 His reputation is severely damaged after he is accused of taking bribes in the Panama Canal scandal.

1893 Loses his seat in parliament and devotes himself to journalism.

1898 Becomes prominently involved in the Dreyfus affair, publishing articles attacking French anti-Semites, Catholics, and militarists.

1902 Elected to a seat in the French Senate.

1906 Appointed minister of the interior and then prime minister.

1907–08 Encourages the formation of the Entente Cordiale, an informal alliance between France and Britain.

1909 Forced to resign as prime minister by a vote of no confidence. Retires from politics.

1913 Founds the newspaper *L'Homme libre* (The Free Man) and campaigns for greater military preparedness.

1914 Refuses the offer of a government post on the outbreak of war. Renames his newspaper *L'Homme enchainé* (The Shackled Man) in protest at censorship.

1916 Denounces the Interior Minister Louis Malvy for "defeatism".

November 1917 Is invited, at the age of 76, to form a government by President Raymond Poincaré. Declares a policy of "total war".

January 1918 Has prominent pro-peace politician Joseph Caillaux arrested for treason.

March 1918 Presses for the unification of Allied military command under General Foch.

January–June 1919 Argues for imposing tough terms on Germany at the Paris Peace Conference.

19 February 1919 Survives an assassination attempt by anarchist Emile Cottin.

November 1919 His "bloc national" wins 437 out of 613 seats in French elections.

1920 Retires to private life.

24 November 1929 Dies at the age of 89.

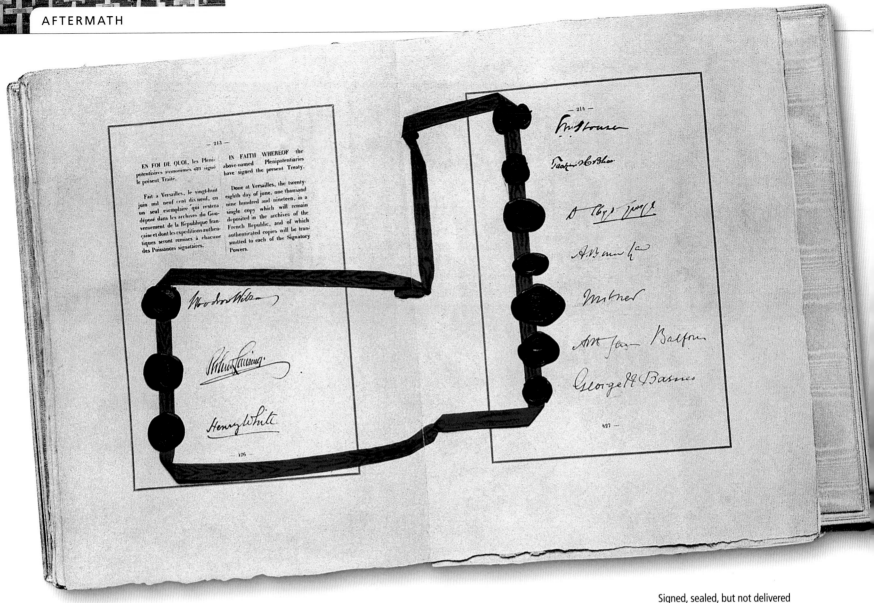

Signed, sealed, but not delivered
This page of the treaty was signed by all the main delegates at the conference. At the top is the signature of Woodrow Wilson, who later failed to get the treaty ratified by the US Congress.

The **Versailles Treaty**

The peace treaty signed by the Allies and Germany has remained controversial. The product of acrimonious debate between the leaders of the victorious powers, the terms it imposed on Germany were regarded by almost all Germans as excessively harsh and unjust.

BEFORE

The Armistice, signed on 11 November 1918, paved the way for a permanent peace settlement.

VICTORY AND DEFEAT
In Germany, a **revolution ‹‹ 320–321** overthrew the Kaiser and established a republic. The country was in political turmoil and its people suffered severe hardship, worsened by the continuation of the Allied blockade. In fulfilment of the Armistice terms, **German troops withdrew from foreign soil** and Allied forces occupied German territory west of the Rhine. Allied leaders assembled for the **Paris Peace Conference ‹‹ 334–35** in January 1919.

Discussion of the peace terms was primarily in the hands of three men: US President Woodrow Wilson, French Prime Minister Georges Clemenceau, and British Prime Minister David Lloyd George. Wilson and Clemenceau were very different characters. Wilson rejected the cynicism and self-interest of the European states; Clemenceau believed the American president was naive in his dealings with Germany.

Wilson believed in a settlement based on just principles. Future peace would be guaranteed through a League of Nations committed to oppose any act

of aggression. Clemenceau, steeped in European history, did not believe in a future ruled by principle rather than force. He told Wilson: "Do not believe the Germans will ever forgive us. They will seek only the chance of revenge." For Clemenceau, Germany had to be

Germany faces the guillotine
Commenting on the Paris Peace Conference, the German satirical magazine *Simplicissimus* shows a captive Germany facing execution at the hands of President Wilson, Lloyd George, and Clemenceau.

permanently incapacitated. Lloyd George, for his part, won an election in December 1918 with promises to "hang the Kaiser" and make Germany pay for the war. But Britain was satisfied with seizing the German fleet and German colonies. Lloyd George had no interest in backing French aims in Europe.

Key points
The easiest ground for Allied agreement was the founding of a League of Nations. Interpreted by Wilson as initiating a new era in international relations and by Clemenceau as a permanent military alliance against Germany, it was enshrined in Part I of the treaty.

There was also agreement on limiting Germany's armed forces. The German army was to be restricted to 100,000 men without tanks or aircraft, and the navy to a few small surface warships.

Territorial arrangements posed intractable problems. The Allies were committed in principle to "national self-determination", but they also

Anti-Versailles demonstration

Crowds on the streets of Berlin in 1919 protest against the terms of the Treaty of Versailles. Most Germans rejected responsibility for the war and did not accept that they must pay the price for defeat.

wanted to make newly founded Poland and Czechoslovakia viable states and had to address French security concerns. The result was a series of compromises. Clemenceau believed that French security could only be guaranteed if the French border was pushed forward to the Rhine. The Americans and British were happy for France to regain Alsace-Lorraine, lost to Germany in 1871, but would not accept French annexation of territory mainly populated by Germans. Instead, it was agreed that the Rhineland would be under Allied military occupation for 15 years. The Saarland, an area of

Area lost to Poland
Area lost to Denmark
Area lost to France
3,984
14,500
57,000 sq km

German loss of territory

After World War I, Germany lost 13 per cent of its territory. Most went to the new state of Poland, while France regained Alsace-Lorraine.

Germany rich in coal, was put under League of Nations' control, also for 15 years, during which time the French would exploit its mines. Some territorial changes were subject to referendums, including the transfer of part of the region of Schleswig to Denmark. Poland's borders with Germany were especially contentious. To provide the Poles with access to the sea, a corridor of territory linked the main body of Poland to the port of Danzig, separating East Prussia from the rest of Germany. Danzig itself, of

132 BILLION GOLD MARKS The sum set for German reparations payments by an Allied commission in 1921. In total, 20 billion marks was collected, mostly financed by loans from abroad that Germany never repaid.

predominantly German population, was declared an independent Free City. Poland and Czechoslovakia were left with large German minorities, while German Austria was refused permission to merge with Germany.

The issue that caused most dispute was reparations. It seemed to the Allies that Germany had been responsible for the war and should therefore pay for it. Germany itself had set the example by imposing heavy reparations on France in 1871 after the Franco-Prussian War. To justify demanding compensation in money and in kind, Article 231 of the treaty stated that "the aggression of Germany and her allies" had been the sole cause of the war.

German outrage

When the terms were presented to German envoys in May 1919, Germany erupted in shock. The Germans did not accept that they had been responsible for the war. Most of them did not even accept that they had been defeated. They believed they had been tricked into accepting an armistice on the basis of a promise of fair treatment, which was now being denied them. They bitterly resented the loss of territory and saw the military

limitations as humiliating. Above all, they rejected the "war guilt" clause as an insult to Germany's honour.

German Chancellor Philipp Scheidemann resigned rather than sign the treaty, but German President Friedrich Ebert was informed by the army that they were in no position to resume hostilities. Also, signing the treaty was the only way to end the Allied economic blockade. On 28 June, five years to the day after the assassination of Archduke Franz Ferdinand in Sarajevo, the treaty was signed in the Hall of Mirrors at the Palace of Versailles.

Some thought the Versailles Treaty too harsh on Germany while others thought it too lenient. Its terms left plenty of potential for future conflict.

SATISFYING NO ONE

The most **influential critic** of the treaty was British economist **J.M. Keynes**, whose book *The Economic Consequences of the Peace* denounced reparations payments. In the USA, **Congress refused to approve the treaty**, fearing membership of the League of Nations could draw the country into further foreign wars. In **France**, many **denounced the treaty** as too lenient. Marshal Ferdinand Foch declared prophetically: "This is not peace. It is an armistice for 20 years."

THE RISE OF HITLER

Germany **resisted reparations**, provoking a Franco-Belgian occupation of the Ruhr in 1923. In the end, Germany largely evaded payment. French troops withdrew from the Rhineland in 1930 and the Saarland was returned to Germany after a referendum in 1935. Leading Germany from 1933, **Adolf Hitler overturned the Versailles Treaty**. Polish refusal to give Germany control of **Danzig** was the pretext for the German invasion of Poland **in 1939**.

POSTAGE STAMP FROM DANZIG

Final act of defiance

A German warship lies half submerged in the British harbour at Scapa Flow off Scotland. Interned by the British after the Armistice, the German fleet was scuttled by its crews in protest at the peace treaty.

Signing the Versailles Treaty

The Treaty of Versailles was met by outrage and hostility when it was first presented to the Germans on 7 May 1919. They rejected blame for starting the war and refused to accept its terms. It was only when the Allies threatened to restart hostilities that the treaty was ratified. On 28 June, the German delegates signed the agreement in the Hall of Mirrors in the Palace of Versailles.

"The long hall was crowded with delegates, visitors, and newspaper representatives. The guests bobbed up and down in their chairs, trying to observe the great men of the conference. A score of Gardes Municipaux circulated among the crowd for a very good reason: they were instructed to keep a watch on the pens and inkwells in the hall, to prevent these articles being pilfered by souvenir hunters. The German delegation entered... and slipped almost unnoticed into its seats... It was led by Herr Müller, a tall man with a scrubby little moustache, wearing black.

At 3:15 o'clock, M. Clemenceau rose and announced briefly that the session was opened... M. Dustata then led the way for five Germans... and they passed to the table, where two of them signed their names. Müller came first, and then Bell, virtually unknown men, performing the final act of abasement and submission for the German people – an act to which they had been condemned by the arrogance and pride of Prussian Junkers, German militarists, imperialists, and industrial barons, not one of whom was present when this great scene was enacted.

At 3:50 o'clock, all signatures had been complete... Immediately afterward the great guns began to boom... The delegates rose and congratulated one another. The notables streamed out of the palace to join the crowd, which had begun shouting in wild enthusiasm... The Germans were the first to leave the Hall of Mirrors, passing out alone, and immediately took their automobiles for the hotel."

US PRESS JOURNALIST HARRY HANSEN ON THE VERSAILLES SIGNING CEREMONY, 28 JUNE 1919

Ratifying the treaty
Dignitaries gather in the Hall of Mirrors at the Palace of Versailles on 28 June 1919 to sign the Treaty of Versailles. The terms of the treaty helped destabilize Germany's new democratic government.

Postwar Conflicts

The armistice signed with Germany in November 1918 is generally taken to mark the end of World War I. In many parts of the globe, however, fighting continued or new wars flared up. A semblance of peacetime normality did not return until the mid-1920s.

Although victorious, Britain and France found their authority as imperial powers challenged in the aftermath of the war. In Ireland, the Republican Sinn Fein movement and its military arm, the Irish Republican Army (IRA), fought a war of independence against the British from 1919 to 1921. British World War I veterans played a significant part in the conflict, enrolling as paramilitaries (Black and Tans) to fight against the Republicans in Ireland. It ended in the establishment of the Irish Free State in 1922.

Meanwhile, in the Rif region of northern Morocco, Spain fought a colonial war against the local Berber forces of Abd el-Krim from 1921. The rebellion was only defeated with the help of France, after el-Krim invaded French Morocco in 1925. French troops were also in action in the Middle East, fighting a war in 1920 to overthrow the Arab Kingdom proclaimed by Prince Feisal in Damascus and establish French control of Syria. The British Empire also faced rebellions in its territories, with nationalist revolts in India, Egypt, and Iraq.

Events in Russia

The Russian Civil War, which had begun before World War I ended, continued through to late 1920. The Red Army of the Bolshevik government, organized by Leon Trotsky, faced White armies led by former tsarist military commanders – General Anton Denikin in southern Ukraine, Admiral Alexander Kolchak in Siberia, General Pyotr Wrangel in the Caucasus, and General Nikolai Yudenich in Estonia. The situation was further complicated by various nationalist movements and by the existence of a mass peasant army in Ukraine led by the anarchist Nestor Makhno.

The wartime Allies, desiring the overthrow of the Bolshevik regime, intervened tentatively in support of the White armies. In April 1919, a mutiny by French sailors sent to occupy the Black Sea port of Odessa highlighted the difficulty and unpopularity of military intervention, however, and most Allied troops were soon withdrawn. By the end of 1920, the Red Army had defeated the major

War in Ireland
British paramilitaries arrest an IRA gunman during the Irish War of Independence (1919–21). The war was on a small scale, costing around 2,000 lives, but fought with vicious determination on both sides.

« BEFORE

World War I destabilized much of Europe and Asia, causing the collapse of established states and raising expectations of change.

CIVIL WARS AND UPRISINGS
In Russia, the overthrow of the Tsar and the installation of a **Bolshevik government** **« 252–53** in 1917 were followed by a humiliating peace agreement with Germany at **Brest-Litovsk « 276–77** and the outbreak of **civil war** in 1918. The **disintegration of Austria-Hungary** destabilized Central Europe. In **Germany**, the shock of defeat and the overthrow of the Kaiser led to **political and economic dislocation**.

1.4 MILLION SQ. KM The area of land (550,000 sq. miles) that was to be ceded by Ottoman Turkey under the terms of the Treaty of Sèvres.

The defeat of the **Ottoman Turkish Empire « 316–17** ended Turkish rule in the Arab Middle East. The **Treaty of Sèvres** in 1920 imposed further harsh terms on Turkey. These were accepted by the Turkish government but rejected by nationalists. In Ireland, the **Easter Uprising « 164–65** against British rule in 1916 was followed by a surge of support for Irish republicans demanding independence.

White forces and could claim victory in the Civil War, but the Bolsheviks reigned over depopulated cities and a devastated countryside that was ravaged by famine.

Meanwhile, Bolshevik Russia was defeated in a crucial conflict with Poland. War broke out when the newly established Polish Republic, keen to advance its borders as far eastward as

15 MILLION The number of people estimated to have died in the Volga famine in Russia in 1921–22, a direct result of the Russian Civil War.

possible, sent troops into Belarus and Ukraine. A counter-offensive by the Red Army launched in June 1920 drove the Poles back and by August the advancing Bolsheviks were threatening Warsaw.

As Soviet forces pushed on towards Germany and Hungary, Polish leader Marshal Josef Pilsudski regained the initiative, executing a series of bold manoeuvres that inflicted a crushing defeat on the Red Army. Bolshevik leader Vladimir Ilyich Lenin was forced

to agree a peace that left the Poles in control of large areas of Belarus and Ukraine.

Greece versus Turkey

In 1919, Greece exploited the weakness of defeated Ottoman Turkey to launch a military occupation of parts of western Anatolia that had a substantial ethnic Greek population. Turkish nationalists led by General Mustafa Kemal defeated the Greek army in large-scale fighting through 1921 and 1922. Mustafa Kemal, later known as Ataturk, proclaimed Turkey a republic and deposed the Ottoman sultan.

Rejecting the option of reopening war with the Turks, the Allied powers accepted the need

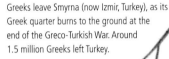

Fleeing the flames
Greeks leave Smyrna (now Izmir, Turkey), as its Greek quarter burns to the ground at the end of the Greco-Turkish War. Around 1.5 million Greeks left Turkey.

to renegotiate the peace treaty that had been imposed in 1920. The Treaty of Lausanne, signed in 1923, set Turkey's new borders, which it still holds today. The ethnic Greek population was expelled, leaving many towns and villages emptied of their inhabitants.

The rise of fascism

In Western Europe, the economic and social disruption caused by World War I led to chronic political instability. In Italy, nationalist extremist Benito Mussolini, who had served as a soldier in the war, led black-shirted Fascist paramilitaries in a violent campaign against socialists and trade unionists. In 1922, when Mussolini threatened to lead his followers in a "march on Rome", King Victor Emmanuel III allowed him to form a government, setting Italy on the road towards an eventual fascist dictatorship.

In Germany, postwar chaos peaked in 1923. In response to German failure to make reparations payments, France and Belgium sent troops to occupy the Ruhr region. The German government responded with a campaign of passive resistance. Hyperinflation led to the collapse of the German currency, wiping out savings.

When Nazi Party leader Adolf Hitler attempted a coup modelled on Mussolini's "march on Rome", however, his "Munich putsch" was suppressed by the army. The postwar world was still seeking stability.

Fascist propaganda postcard
A fanciful postcard celebrates the "march on Rome" by Italian fascist blackshirts in October 1922. A carefully stage-managed demonstration, the march led to Benito Mussolini becoming head of the Italian government.

AFTER

By the mid-1920s, some of the consequences of the chaotic aftermath of World War I were being addressed, although the return to normality proved shortlived.

RIGHTING WRONGS
In 1924, a US-brokered agreement, the **Dawes Plan**, created a basis for German payment of reparations and led to the **withdrawal of French and Belgian troops** from the Ruhr. In 1925, the **Locarno Treaty** settled outstanding issues with Germany, which was admitted to the **League of Nations** the following year. In the Middle East, Egyptian independence was granted in 1922 and Prince Feisal was made king of Iraq.

ECONOMIC CRASH
Normalization was ended by worldwide **economic depression** from 1929. Mass unemployment undermined democracy in Germany and brought Adolf Hitler's **Nazi Party** to power in 1933. Hitler tore up the Versailles Treaty and Germany rearmed.

The occupation of the Ruhr
An illustration from a French newspaper shows French soldiers confronting German workers in the Ruhr in 1923. The French and Belgians occupied the Ruhr in an effort to force Germany to make reparations payments.

> "I don't know if **war** is an **interlude in peace,** or **peace** an **interlude in war.**"
>
> FRENCH PRIME MINISTER GEORGES CLEMENCEAU

Never Again

« BEFORE

The experience of World War I cast a long shadow over the postwar period. Nations sought appropriate forms of public mourning and commemoration to grieve and honour the dead. There was an overwhelming desire that such a war should never be repeated.

During the war, Allied political leaders promised that a better, more peaceful world would result from victory over German militarism. These promises proved hard to keep.

THE WAR TO END ALL WARS
Declaring war on Germany in April 1917, US President Woodrow Wilson said his object was to **"bring peace and safety to all nations".** Celebrating the Armistice on 11 November 1918, British Prime Minister David Lloyd George said: "I hope we may all say that thus, this fateful morning, came to an end all wars."

The aspiration to a permanent peace was embodied in the founding of the **League of Nations** at the **Paris Peace Conference « 334–35** in 1919. Member-states of the League committed themselves to progressive disarmament and the peaceful resolution of disputes.

The emotional impact of World War I and its place in collective memory varied between countries. In Russia, for example, the war was almost forgotten, quickly eclipsed by the shattering upheaval of the Bolshevik Revolution.

In Britain and France, the war was commemorated intensively, with an annual Remembrance Day on 11 November established from 1919. By common accord they honoured the sacrifice of the dead rather than celebrated a victory. A two-minute silence was observed throughout Britain and its empire at 11am, a practice so rigorously followed in the early years that all traffic stopped,

factories turned off machinery, and pedestrians stood still in the street. Memorials to the war dead were erected in most towns and villages.

Unknown warriors

On Remembrance Day 1920, the British held a state funeral in Westminster Abbey for an Unknown Warrior, burying a soldier chosen at random from among the wartime dead. The French held a similar ceremony at the Arc de Triomphe in Paris, and the USA followed suit in 1921, burying an Unknown Warrior at Arlington National Cemetery in Virginia. The Unknown Warrior represented all those who had lost their lives, without

distinction of rank. This democratic spirit infused all commemoration of the war. Tens of thousands of plaques and monuments were erected in cities, towns, and villages, typically listing the fallen in alphabetical order, the officers intermingled with ordinary soldiers regardless of rank.

Britain decided against repatriating the dead. Instead, the Imperial (now Commonwealth) War Graves Commission created vast war cemeteries in France. Unidentifiable remains were marked: "A Soldier of the Great War Known unto God." The French placed the bones of their unidentified dead in ossuaries, such as the one at Douaumont near Verdun.

Flying the Nazi flag
The first version of the Nazi swastika flag is displayed outside Munich in 1920. Many who joined the Nazi movement had been too young to fight in World War I. The ex-servicemen who joined included Adolf Hitler.

University famously voted that "this House will in no circumstances fight for its King and Country".

Public promises

Governments were also inspired by the desire to fulfil the promise that World War I would prove "a war to end war". In the 1920s, there were international arms limitation agreements, while the League of Nations sought to substitute "collective security" and negotiation for armed confrontation. In 1928–29, all major countries signed the Kellogg-Briand Pact – named for US Secretary of State Frank Kellogg and French foreign minister Aristide Briand – publicly renouncing the use of war as an "instrument of national policy".

Nationalists and militarists in countries defeated in the war or disappointed by the peace drew a different lesson from the conflict. In the 1920s, the German Stahlhelm veterans' organization and the Italian Fascist movement harked back to the wartime experience of national unity. Fascist leader Benito Mussolini stated that war "put the stamp of nobility on those nations that had the courage to face it". Another ex-soldier who longed to reverse the defeat of 1914–18 was German Nazi Party leader Adolf Hitler. His accession to power in Germany in 1933 set the world on course for an even more destructive war.

World War I shows no signs of being forgotten a century after it was fought.

GONE BUT NOT FORGOTTEN
Despite the **deaths of the last surviving soldiers** from World War I, including Harry Patch in Britain in 2009 and Frank Buckles in the USA in 2011, the war continues to stir powerful emotions in the nations that were involved. Annual **commemorative ceremonies** – for example, Remembrance

36,000 **The number of communes in France that erected monuments to those who died in World War I.**

Day in Britain, Veterans Day in the USA, and Anzac Day in Australia and New Zealand – continue to be well attended, with the fallen in subsequent wars also remembered.

THREE OF THE WAR'S LAST VETERANS IN 2008

"Anything rather than war! Anything!… **No trial, no servitude** can be **compared to war.**"

FRENCH NOVELIST AND PACIFIST ROGER MARTIN DU GARD, PRIVATE LETTER, SEPTEMBER 1936

For Germany, remembrance was complicated by deeply divided attitudes towards the war. Local memorials were erected to the dead, but the Weimar Republic failed to agree on a national remembrance day, and commemorative events were often the occasion for political protests. Germany did not bury an Unknown Warrior until 1931.

Ireland was another place in which the memory of the war was politically contentious. For Irish Catholics, war service in the British Army became an embarrassment and commemorative ceremonies drew hostility from many republicans. For Protestants in Northern Ireland, war service was a badge of loyalty to the British Crown and Remembrance Day became a demonstration of Protestant superiority to the allegedly disloyal Catholics.

When the French erected a monument to mark the site of the signing of the armistice, they inscribed it with the words: "Here on the 11 November 1918 succumbed the criminal pride of the German Reich… vanquished by the free peoples which it tried to enslave." Such ringing endorsement of the purpose of the war was not often heard during the postwar decades. Disillusion was partly fuelled by the fate of ex-servicemen, who received far less attention from governments than the dead. Many

ended up unemployed, although veterans' organizations provided a source of support and companionship. The peace treaties were seen as unworthy of the soldiers' sacrifice.

A flood of memoirs and novels published during the late 1920s and 1930s – Erich Remarque's *All Quiet on the Western Front* the most prominent among them – fed the popular imagination with images of the horrors of the war. Americans in particular viewed the war as a mistake into which they had been lured by British propaganda.

US isolationism

Throughout the 1920s and 1930s, in reaction against the war, an isolationist mentality predominated in the USA. In Britain, pacifism grew into a mass movement, led by organizations such as the Peace Pledge Union. In 1933, students debating at the Oxford Union at Oxford

Pacifist protest
The youth section of the British Peace Movement at a demonstration in 1924. The movement was part of War Resisters International, founded in 1921.

In memory of the fallen
The Notre Dame de Lorette military cemetery near
Arras in northern France is the burial place of
40,000 French soldiers. Each grave is marked with
a simple white cross bearing the soldier's name.

In Memoriam

The first global conflict in history, World War I has never been forgotten. Memorials, monuments, and museums are found in all the combatant countries, the most moving of all being the vast war cemeteries built on or near the major battlefields.

AUSTRALIA

ANZAC Memorial
Set in Sydney's Hyde Park, this is New South Wales's principal war monument. Designed in an art deco style by Bruce Dellit, it is made of granite, with statuary and bas-reliefs created by the Australian architect Rayner Hoff. The buttresses are each topped by a mournful figure, while the bas-reliefs depict scenes from Australian campaigns at Gallipoli and the Western Front. Ceremonies are held at the memorial on Remembrance Sunday (11 November) and Anzac Day (25 April).
Hyde Park, Sydney
www.anzacmemorial.nsw.gov.au

Australian War Memorial
The national monument to Australia's war dead was built in the aftermath of World War I, though it serves to commemorate Australian service personnel killed in all conflicts. The main parts of the memorial are the Commemorative area (which includes the Hall of Memory), Anzac Parade, and the Sculpture Garden.
   The First World War Galleries occupy the west wing of the memorial's ground level galleries. A permanent display "Over the front, the Great War in the air" tells the story of aerial combat in World War I. It includes five original aircraft from the war and a sound and light show.
Remembrance Park, Canberra
www.awm.gov.au/visit

Shrine of Remembrance
Built to remember Victoria's war dead of 1914–18, this is one of Australia's great memorials. Inspired by the mausoleum to Mausolus, King of Caria, at Halicarnassus in Turkey, the shrine was inaugurated in November 1934. The sanctuary contains the Stone of Remembrance inscribed with the

Australian monument
The Anzac Memorial in Sydney, completed in 1934, has monumental figures sculpted by war veteran Rayner Hoff both outside and in an interior hall.

words "Greater Love Hath No Man", which has been designed so that a shaft of sunlight (or artificial light) falls on the word "Love" at a special ceremony held at 11am on 11 November each year.
St Kilda Road, Melbourne
www.shrine.org.au/Home

AUSTRIA

Museum of Military History
Located in Vienna's Arsenal, built from 1850–56 to house the city's garrison, this museum covers Austrian military history from the 16th century to 1945. Two halls are dedicated to World War I, including an exhibit housing the vehicle and blood-soaked jacket of Franz Ferdinand, preserved from the day of his assassination in Sarajevo.
Arsenal Objekt 1, Vienna
www.hgm.or.at

BELGIUM

Flanders Field American Cemetery and Memorial

The only American Battle Monuments Commission cemetery in Belgium, this commemorates the American contribution to the war on the Western Front. Smaller than most of the war cemeteries in Belgium, it consists of 368 burials, with the headstones arranged around a central chapel. Many of those interred here came from the US 91st Division, killed in October and November 1918. The chapel includes 43 names on the Walls of the Missing – rosettes mark the names of soldiers whose remains have been subsequently recovered and identified.
Southeast of Waregem, along the Lille-Gent autoroute E-17
www.abmc.gov/cemeteries-memorials

In Flanders Fields Museum

The Cloth Hall on the Market Square in the centre of Ieper (Ypres), site of three of the war's most significant battles, has been turned into a museum housing major collections of World War I artefacts and documents. The exhibitions and audio-visual displays cover the invasion of Belgium in 1914, the first few months of the war, and the four-year trench war in Westhoek. A documentation centre includes trench maps, a photographic library and postcard collection, and contemporary newspaper reports.

Visitors can climb up to the bell tower for views over the city and the sites of the surrounding battlefields. In the museum's research centre visitors can learn more about the global history of World War I, but also the history of the West Flanders region.
Lakenhallen Grote Markt 34, Ieper
www.inflandersfields.be/en

Langemark German War Cemetery

An official German War Graves Commission site, the Langemark Cemetery contains more than 40,000 burials of soldiers recovered between 1915 and the 1930s. The cemetery was designated German Military Cemetery 123 in 1930, and was inaugurated two years later. Of the soldiers buried in the cemetery, 24,917 lie in mass graves. The German Students' Memorial annex lists the names of 3,000 students killed in the Battle of Langemarck (part of the First Battle of Ypres) in 1914. Known in Germany as *Kindermord* (Massacre of the Children), First

Grieving soldiers
The German war cemetery at Langemark in West Flanders, Belgium, is guarded by figures of mourning soldiers created by artist Emil Krieger in 1956.

Ypres included many young German volunteers. In the cemetery stands a sculpture of mourning soldiers by German artist Emil Krieger. Also of note is a basalt cross on a small mound, marking one of the three original battlefield bunkers.
North of Langemark village, 6 km (4 miles) northeast of Ieper
www.volksbund.de

Menin Gate

One of the most visited sights on the Western Front, the Menin Gate Memorial in Ypres was designed by Reginald Blomfield and unveiled in 1927. It marks the point where most British soldiers marched out to the battlefields of the Ypres salient. The walls of the Hall of Memory are inscribed with the names of 54,896 British and Commonwealth soldiers killed at Ypres before 16 August 1917. Each night at 8pm, the traffic stops and the *Last Post* is played under the arches of the memorial.
Meensestraat, Ieper
www.cwgc.org

Messines Battlefield and Memorials

Around the village of Wystchaete, the St Eloi, Peckham Farm, St Yvon, Kruisstraat, and Spanbroekmolen craters bear testimony to the 19 enormous mines detonated beneath the German trenches at Messines. An information board in the village gives directions to the craters, and there are more than 1,000 burials in the Wytschaete Military Cemetery, a short walk from the main square. A smaller cemetery, the Lone Tree Cemetery, near Spanbroekmolen, contains 88 burials, mainly of soldiers from the Royal Irish Rifles.

Memorials of the battle include one to the London Scottish Regiment on the N365 between Wytschaete and Mesen (Messines), marking the spot

where they first went into action. In Mesen itself, which was completely destroyed in the battle, there are the New Zealand Memorial Park and the Messines Ridge Military Cemetery. It was in Mesen's church (rebuilt) that Adolf Hitler reputedly received treatment for combat injuries in 1914. To the south of Mesen is the modern Island of Ireland Peace Park, opened in 1998, to commemorate Irish soldiers killed during World War I.
Around Mesen (Messines)

Passchendaele Battlefield

Few battlefield areas evoke the tragedy of the Ypres salient more than Passchendaele, around the modern village of Passendale. The area is littered with memorials to individual battles and regiments, including the Canadian Memorial at Crest Farm, the 85th (Nova Scotia Highlanders) Battalion Memorial, and memorials to French soldiers and the British Seventh

Memorial to the missing
The Menin Gate arch at Ypres was designed as a memorial for British soldiers of whom no remains could be found for burial in a war cemetery.

Division, both at Broodseinde. Cemeteries in the area include the Passchendaele New British Cemetery, containing 2,101 British and Commonwealth burials, and the vast Tyne Cot Cemetery to the southwest of Passendale. In Zonnebeke, the Passchendaele Memorial 1917 Museum contains a large display of military artefacts.
Various locations in and around Zonnebeke and Passendale

Royal Museum of the Armed Forces and of Military History

This museum houses collections relating to the whole of Belgian military history, not just World War I, but it includes a large collection of World War I artefacts, documents, and memorabilia in a permanent 1914–18 exhibition. Exhibits include firearms, artillery pieces, uniforms, armoured vehicles, and even a Fokker triplane.
Jubelpark 3, 1000 Brussels
www.klm-mra.be

St Julien Memorial

This granite memorial, designed by the Anglo-Canadian architect Frederick Chapman Clemesha, stands 11 m (36 ft) tall. Known as the *Brooding Soldier*, it features at its summit the head and shoulders of a Canadian infantryman, his head bowed in mourning. The memorial remembers the Canadian troops killed around St Julien during the Second Battle of Ypres. Many of the dead were killed by the first use of

poison gas (chlorine) on the Western Front, as the memorial inscription attests: "This column marks the battlefield where 18,000 Canadians on the British left withstood the first German gas attacks on the 22–24 April 1915. 2,000 fell and here lie buried."
7 km (4.3 miles) northeast of Ieper, off the N313 towards Roulers

Sanctuary Wood Cemetery and Museum Hill 62

In 1914, Sanctuary Wood acted as a protective barrier between British and Commonwealth troops and the front line. During 1915–16, however, it was also swamped with heavy fighting, principally between Canadian and German forces.

Three Allied cemeteries were established in the area at the time. The remains of one of them formed the foundations for the present cemetery, designed by Sir Edwin Lutyens not long after the war. During the 1920s and 30s, the cemetery expanded with additions from the wider Western Front. Today, it contains 1,989 burials (spread over five plots), of which only 637 are identified.

Within a short walk of the cemetery is the Sanctuary Wood Museum Hill 62, a privately run establishment. An

Canadian remembrance
The National War Memorial in Ottawa, the focus of Canadian remembrance, has a bronze representation of 22 World War I soldiers and nurses, created by English sculptor Vernon March.

extensive series of preserved trench lines, all open to walk through, can be seen outside the museum. Another feature of the Sanctuary Wood area is the Canadian Memorial at Hill 62, remembering the thousands of Canadians killed in futile battles to retake Hill 62 in June 1916.
5km (3 miles) east of Ieper, off the N8

St George's Memorial Church

Field Marshal Lord Plumer, commander of the British Second Army in Flanders during the war, laid the foundation stone of St George's Church in Ieper in 1927. The building opened for services two years later and is still an active place of worship. The church serves the local community as well as the thousands of annual visitors from around the world. Though the church was built primarily to remember the British and Commonwealth servicemen who died at Ypres – its stained glass, wall plaques, banners, and kneelers reflect individual British regiments – it is now the memorial church for all those who died in battle in Flanders during both world wars.
Elverdingsestraat 1, 8900 Ieper
www.stgeorgesmemorialchurchypres.com

Tyne Cot Cemetery

The largest British war cemetery in the world, Tyne Cot contains a total of 11,953 burials, mostly of British and Commonwealth troops but also including four German soldiers. The majority of the men buried here were killed during the Third Battle of Ypres in 1917. The name Tyne Cot is thought to have British origins. According to a local story, the Northumberland Fusiliers thought a barn on the ridgeline here looked like their cottages on the River Tyne, back home in Britain. Landmarks of the cemetery include the Cross of Sacrifice Monument and the curved Memorial to the Missing, listing the names of 35,000 soldiers with no known grave.
Southwest of Passendale, signposted off the N332
www.cwgc.org

Vladslo German War Cemetery

This German cemetery is the burial place for 25,644 soldiers, most of whom were moved here from other locations in the 1950s (the site was used as a combat cemetery from 1914). Although some headstones date from the time of the war, most were inscribed afterwards. Each of the flat granite slabs bears 20 names, with name, rank, and date of death. *The Grieving Parents*, a pair of statues made by the German sculptor Käthe Kollwitz stand in the cemetery. Kollwitz's son died at First Ypres in October 1914.
3 km (1.8 miles) northeast of Vladslo, signposted from the N363 from Beerst
www.volksbund.de

Ypres Salient Battlefield

After the Somme, the area around the Ypres salient, centring on the modern town of Ieper, is the most frequented destination for battlefield visitors. Within the town itself are the Menin Gate and St George's Memorial Church, both moving memorials to those lost around Ypres, and the In Flanders Fields Museum.

Passchendaele war graves
The neat formality of the British Tyne Cot cemetery stands in stark contrast to the conditions in which most of the men buried there died in the Battle of Passchendaele.

There are many other sites in the area, including 140 military cemeteries and burial grounds. The cemeteries are tended by the British, Belgian, French, and Italian war graves commissions.

Among a number of interesting museums around Ieper are the Sanctuary Wood Museum Hill 62, the Hooge Crater Museum, the Memorial Museum Passchendaele (at Zonnebeke), and the Messines Historical Museum (Mesen). Poperinge, 13 km (8 miles) to the west of Ieper, was a centre for British troops heading to the front. The town's Talbot House Museum served as a club house for British Army troops. Opened by army Chaplain Philip Clayton as an alternative place of relaxation to the more debauched places in town, it was open to all ranks.
In and around Ieper

CANADA

Canadian War Museum
Although this museum covers the whole of Canada's military history, Gallery 2 focuses on the period 1885–1931. Reconstructed landscapes and trenches evoke famous battlefields of World War I, such as Passchendaele, while artefacts recall the personal experiences of those on the front line. References to World War I are also found in other parts of the building. Regeneration Hall displays a plaster model of Walter Allward's sculpture *Hope* (a figure from the Vimy Memorial), and the Memorial Hall contains the headstone of the Unknown Soldier.
1 Vimy Place, Ottawa
www.warmuseum.ca

National War Memorial (Ottawa)
Much like the Cenotaph in London, the National War Memorial in Ottawa was built for the dead of World War I but came to represent all of the country's war fatalities. Twenty-two bronze figures, representing Canada's armed forces, proceed through a granite arch, along with a cavalry horse and a piece of artillery. Two figures on top of the arch symbolize peace and freedom. In front of the memorial the Tomb of the Unknown Soldier contains the remains of a World War I soldier buried at the site in 2000.
Confederation Square, Ottawa

National War Memorial (Newfoundland)
Opened on 1 July 1924 by Field Marshal Douglas Haig, commander of the British Expeditionary Force (BEF) during the war, Newfoundland's National War Memorial features

five statues by English sculptors F.V. Blundstone and Gilbert Bayes. At the summit of the monument a figure of a woman holds a flaming torch and a sword, representing Newfoundland's loyalty to the British Empire. Flanking this central figure are statues of a soldier and a sailor, representing the Royal Newfoundland Regiment and the Royal Naval Reserve, and statues of a fisherman and a lumberman, recognizing the contribution made by the Merchant Marine and the Forestry Corps.
Between Water Street and Duckworth Street, St John's

FRANCE

Aisne-Marne American Cemetery and Memorial
This American Battle Monuments Commission site contains the graves of 2,289 American war dead, mostly killed in the fighting around the Marne valley in 1918. It is located at the foot of Belleau Wood, where the US Marine

Corps gained distinction. The cemetery is overlooked by the Memorial Chapel, the interior of which is inscribed with the names of 1,060 missing.
Follow signs from Chateau-Thierry
www.abmc.gov/cemeteries-memorials

Arras and Vimy Ridge Battlefield
Among the cemetery sites around Arras are the Zivy Crater Cemetery, the Lichfield Crater Cemetery, the La Targette French and British cemeteries, the Cabaret Rouge British Cemetery, and the large Neuville-St-Vaast German War Cemetery. The impressive Canadian National Vimy Memorial can be found on Vimy Ridge and memorials to the dead of specific battalions, regiments, and divisions dot the region, including those to the Ninth Scottish Division, the Seaforth Highlanders, and the Fourth and Seventh Royal Tank Regiments.
Around Arras, Pas-de-Calais

Cambrai Battlefields
The area around Cambrai was the scene of bitter fighting, particularly during the last two years of the war,

Memorial on Vimy Ridge
Designed by sculptor Walter Allward, the Canadian National Vimy Memorial stands on Vimy Ridge near Arras in northeastern France, the site of the Canadian Corps' most famous victory.

and the area has many military memorials. The major site for war burials in the area is the Louveral Military Cemetery, which also features the Memorial to the Missing, listing the names of more than 7,000 British soldiers with no known grave.

Other cemeteries within easy driving distance of Louveral include the Five Points Cemetery near Ytres, the Rocquigny-Equancourt Road British Cemetery, and the Ribecourt Road Cemetery near Trescault. On the side of the D15 road between Trescault and Havrincourt there is also a German bunker. A British Mark IV tank wreck, Deborah D51, can be seen in an open sided barn in the village of Flesquières. The tank, which served in the Battle of Cambrai, was excavated on the outskirts of the village in 1998.
Around Cambrai, northern France

Canadian National Vimy Memorial Park

The site of the Battle of Vimy Ridge, an epic struggle between Canadian and German troops in April 1917, this memorial park is dominated by the enormous Vimy Monument, with its 20 large stone figures (see p.351), and unveiled in 1936. In the grounds of the park, German and Allied

Ossuary at Verdun
Built on the site where the Battle of Verdun was fought, the imposing Douaumont Ossuary houses the bones of some 130,000 French and German soldiers killed there in 1916.

trenches have been preserved for public access; the contours of the land reflect the effects of shellfire. There are two Canadian cemeteries: Canadian Cemetery No. 2 and Givenchy Road Canadian Cemetery.
Near Vimy, between Lens and Arras, northern France

Douaumont Ossuary and Verdun Memorial
This is perhaps one of the most powerful memorials on the Western Front. Work on a provisional ossuary – a building where bones of the dead are kept – began in 1920 to provide a sanctuary for the hundreds of thousands of bones that were scattered throughout the Verdun battlefield site. Work on a permanent ossuary began in 1920, and bones were transferred here from 1927. The ossuary cloister contains the bones of 130,000

unidentified soldiers, arranged according to the area of the Verdun battlefield in which they were found. The tower houses a war museum.
Douaumont, near Verdun
www.verdun-douaumont.com

Étaples Military Cemetery
The many British military camps and hospitals around Étaples meant that the area required a large British and Commonwealth cemetery. In use from May 1915, this cemetery contains 10,733 burials from World War I, as well as burials from World War II.
Between Boulogne and Étaples
www.cwgc.org

Fricourt German War Cemetery
Although not the largest German war cemetery in the Somme area – Vermandovillers has 26,000 burials – Fricourt contains 17,027 German soldiers, about 10,000 of whom were killed during the Somme battles of 1916. Only 5,057 of the burials have individual graves; the other 11,970 are contained in four mass graves.
Near Fricourt, the Somme
www.volksbund.de

Meuse-Argonne American Cemetery and Memorial
This is the largest US military cemetery in Europe, with a total of 14,246 servicemen buried over 52 hectares (130 acres) of grounds. In the memorial chapel, panels are inscribed with the names of 954 soldiers missing in action (the bodies of those with rosettes against their names were eventually discovered and identified). Staff members at the visitor centre provide guidance on navigating the cemetery and locating particular graves.
Romagne-Sous Montfacuon
www.abmc.gov/cemeteries-memorials

Musée de l'Armée
One of the world's largest military museums, the Musée de l'Armée in Paris contains more than 500,000 artefacts from every period of French military history. The museum's World War I section contains large collections of uniforms and weaponry used during the conflict, displayed in the Joffre, Polius, and Foch rooms.
Les Invalides, Paris
www.musee-armee.fr

Ring of Remembrance

Designed by French architect Philippe Prost, the Ring of Remembrance memorial was created at the Notre Dame de Lorette war cemetery in 2014. It bears the names of 600,000 soldiers and civilians of all nationalities who died in the war.

Museum of Franco-American Cooperation

Housed in the 17th-century château of Blérancourt, the museum celebrates more than 200 years of Franco-American relations. During World War I, two Americans, Anne Morgan and Anne Murray Dike, turned the building into the headquarters of the American Committee for Devastated France. The historical artefacts now kept there illustrate the humanitarian aid given by Americans during the course of two world wars.

Château de Blérancourt, Aisne
www.museefrancoamericain.fr

Neuville-St-Vaast German War Cemetery

Established by the French in 1919 to hold German war dead, this German War Graves Commission cemetery, also known as La Maison Blanche, is the largest in France. The cemetery contains 44,533 burials, with four soldiers in each grave. There is also a mass grave containing the remains of more than 8,000 soldiers. A small chapel contains a list of the buried.

Neuville-Saint-Vaast, near Arras
www.volksbund.de

Notre Dame de Lorette

Religious buildings have occupied this ridge to the northwest of Arras since the 18th century, but the basilica and ossuary currently on the site were built in 1921 as memorials to the French soldiers who died in the Artois area during the battles of 1914, 1915, and 1917. The cemetery later became a national necropolis, and the ossuary contains the remains of some 23,000 unidentified soldiers from both world wars as well as French conflicts in Algeria and Indochina. The basilica, which was designed by French architect Louis-Marie Cordonnier, is decorated with colourful mosaics.

Surrounding the basilica and ossuary, the cemetery covers 13 hectares (32 acres) and contains 45,000 burials, the bulk of them from World War I. Behind the cemetery is a military museum, with dioramas, uniforms, artillery pieces, photographs, and a reconstructed trench and bunker system. Outside the museum, original World War I trenches have been redug.

Ablain-Saint-Nazaire, near Arras

Somme Battlefield

The site of one of the greatest and most costly battles in human history, the Somme region is one of the main centres of military tourism. To get the most out of a visit, it is advisable to buy a guidebook to the battlefield sites or join a tour run by one of the specialist companies operating in the area. The officially recommended

Americans fallen in France

The ranks of white crosses in the Meuse-Argonne American Cemetery are a stark reminder of the scale of US losses in France in World War I, twice the death toll of the Vietnam War.

"Tour of Remembrance" takes in the town of Albert (including the Somme 1916 Trench Museum and the CWGC-maintained Albert Communal Cemetery), Beaumont-Hamel, Thiepval, Ovillers-la-Boiselle (site of the Lochnagar crater), Longueval (including the New Zealand Memorial and Pipers Memorial), and Peronne. All these are packed with places of interest, including cemeteries, military relics, museums, and memorials. Munitions and artefacts are regularly dug up in the Somme countryside (remember not to touch any munitions you might find). The best way to get around the battlefield privately is by car; many of the sites are accessible from the A29 or A1 motorways.

The Somme
www.somme-battlefields.com

Thiepval Memorial to the Missing

This huge memorial in Thiepval was designed by Sir Edwin Lutyens and opened by Edward, Prince of Wales in 1932. It is inscribed with the names of 73,357 Allied soldiers who died in the Somme area between 1916 and 1918 but have no grave. A commemorative ceremony is held here on 1 July.

Thiepval, the Somme
www.cwgc.org

GERMANY

Bundeswehr Military History Museum-Berlin

While the Military History Museum in Dresden is concerned with the general history of warfare, the Berlin Museum focuses on aerial warfare. It has a collection of more than 600,000 items, including aircraft, major defence equipment – such as radar and missile systems – documents, art, uniforms, and training materials.

Am Flugplatz Gatow 33, Berlin
www.mhm-gatow.de/en

Bundeswehr Military History Museum-Dresden

Located in a former military arsenal in the Albertstadt neighbourhood of Dresden, this museum has a permanent World War I exhibit, which includes a range of uniforms, small arms, artillery, and aircraft.

Olbrichtplatz 2, Dresden

INDIA

India Gate

Built between 1921 and 1931, the India Gate in Delhi commemorates all Indian soldiers who died in World War I and the Third Afghan War of 1919.

Originally called the All India War Memorial, the arch is inscribed with the names of more than 70,000 men. Beneath the arch is the Amar Jawan Jyoti (The Flame of the Immortal Warrior) and also the Tomb of the Unknown Soldier. The cenotaph is surrounded by four flaming torches that are kept constantly lit.

Rajpath, Delhi

IRELAND

Irish National War Memorial Gardens

Built to remember the 49,400 Irish soldiers who died in World War I, these gardens were designed by Sir Edwin Lutyens in the 1930s. The park covers 8 hectares (20 acres) and includes a sunken rose garden and two book rooms, containing the Rolls of Honour listing the names of the dead.

The site also features the Ginchy Cross, built by soldiers of the Irish 16th Division and originally erected on the Somme battlefield. Inscribed on the floor of the temple on the bank of the River Liffey, is an extract of "War Sonnet II: Safety" by Rupert Brooke.

Islandbridge, Dublin

ISRAEL

Ramleh CWGC Cemetery

Established in December 1917 to serve the field hospitals set up in the area, the cemetery in Ramleh (now Ramla) was later augmented by graves moved here from other cemeteries in Palestine and Israel. Ramleh was occupied by the First Australian Light Horse Brigade from November 1917. The cemetery contains 3,300 Commonwealth burials from World War I, plus nearly 1,200 burials from World War II and a number of other

burials of non-Commonwealth and non-combat personnel. There is also a memorial, built in 1961, to Commonwealth, German, and Turkish servicemen buried elsewhere in Palestine and Israel, in cemeteries that are no longer maintained.

Near Ramla
www.cwgc.org

ITALY

Sacrario Militare di Redipuglia

Built under Mussolini and opened in 1938, after ten years of construction, the Sacrario Militare Di Redipuglia is a military shrine on the slopes of Monte Sei Busi, at the eastern end of the Isonzo front. It holds the remains of more than 100,000 Italian soldiers killed during World War I – the 22 steps to the top of the shrine alone contain the remains of 40,000 soldiers. The shrine also contains the tombs of five generals and the Duke of Aosta, the commander of the Third Army. The site includes a chapel and a museum containing a collection of artefacts from the Italian front and some original trench fortifications.

Monte Sei Busi

Buried in the east
Ramleh War Cemetery is the burial place of over 4,000 British and Commonwealth soldiers who died in Palestine in conflicts from World War I onward.

ITALY/SLOVENIA

Isonzo Front Battlefields

In terms of battlefield tourism, the Isonzo front is often overlooked in preference for battlefields in France and Belgium, but it is just as rich in places of interest. The challenges for touring the Isonzo front are the distances involved. A typical route might run from Kranjska Gora in northwest Slovenia down to Duino on the Adriatic coast in northeast Italy, although there are many other options. Highlights include the Soca Valley, containing numerous positions and gun emplacements in the rockface. At Kobarid (Caporetto during World War I) in Slovenia, it is possible to walk along former trench lines. The town also has an excellent museum devoted to the ferocious battles along the Isonzo front, with large-scale maps, artefacts, and photographs.

Along the Slovenian/Italian border

NEW ZEALAND

Auckland War Memorial Museum

Built in the 1850s, and more generally known as the Auckland Museum, this houses extensive general collections on the whole of New Zealand's history, not just military history. The modern annex, which opened in 1929, was built in memory of Auckland province's many war dead from World War I. The walls of the World War I Sanctuary are inscribed with the names of fallen soldiers with no known grave. Under the stained-glass skylight are the badges of their units and regiments.

Auckland
www.aucklandmuseum.com

ROMANIA

Mausoleum of Marasesti

The Mausoleum for the Heroes from the National Unity War, to give it its full title, is an imposing monument to Romanians killed in World War I. The Battle of Marasesti in 1917 was the last major battle on the Romanian front

Memorial "of the Hundred Thousands"
Sacrario di Redipuglia is Italy's largest memorial dedicated to soldiers who fell in World War I. Its three levels symbolise the army descending from the sky.

before the country was occupied. The mausoleum stands at around 30 m (100 ft) tall and the remains of 6,000 Romanian soldiers are contained within the crypts. The mausoleum also includes the sarcophagus of General Eremia Grigorescu, who died in 1919, and a rotunda containing the flags of the Romanian units who fought at Marasesti. The main edifice is topped by the "Dome of Glory". A great bas-relief on the dome depicts scenes from the battle at Marasesti.
Between Focsani and Adjud, Vrancea County

TURKEY

Gallipoli Battlefield

The Gallipoli Peninsula Historical National Park is one of the most rewarding sites for military history tourists and researchers. Covering around 33,000 hectares (81,500 acres), it includes 31 CWGC cemeteries, containing 22,000 graves, and numerous memorials.

There are three main areas of interest: Cape Helles (V-Beach Cemetery, Helles Memorial, and Redoubt Cemetery); Pine Ridge (the

Beach Cemetery, No. 2 Outpost Cemetery, Courtney's and Steel's Post Cemetery, Chunuk Bair Cemetery and Memorial, Fourth Battalion Parade Ground Cemetery, and Lone Pine Cemetery and Memorial); and Suvla (Green Hill Cemetery and Anzac Cemetery). The main sites can be covered in a day, but two to three days are recommended for a more thorough exploration. Also worth seeing on Cape Helles is the Canakale Martyrs Memorial, the principal memorial to the Turkish soldiers who died in the Gallipoli Campaign.

Memorials at Gallipoli

This stark monument commemorating New Zealand troops who died in the Gallipoli campaign stands on the summit of Chunuk Bair peak. Unveiled in 1925, the New Zealand memorial stands alongside a statue of the Turkish commander at Gallipoli, Mustafa Kemal, later known as Atatürk.

Special services are held at Gallipoli on Anzac Day on 25 April each year, commemorating the first day of the Gallipoli Campaign in 1915. Visits are best made via an organized tour.
Gallipoli peninsula

UNITED STATES

Arlington National Cemetery

Dating back to the American Civil War, Arlington has been a burial ground for the bodies of US military personnel for some 150 years. It covers 253 hectares (624 acres) and contains more than 300,000 burials, including those of many who were killed in World War I. One moving feature built in the aftermath of World War I is the Tomb of the Unknowns, containing the remains of an unknown US soldier, interred here in 1921. Similar tombs from subsequent wars are situated in the same area.

Numerous World War I memorials also grace the cemetery, including the Argonne Cross Memorial, in memory of US servicemen who died in the Meuse-Argonne offensive of 1918, the largest battle in US history; the Canadian Cross of Sacrifice, commemorating US citizens who served in Canadian regiments; and the World War One Memorial.
Arlington, Virginia
www.arlingtoncemetery.mil

Liberty Memorial

This towering monument in Kansas City is the National World War I memorial of the USA. Dedicated by US President Calvin Coolidge on 11 November 1926, it was designed in Egyptian Revival style by Harold Van Buren Magonigle, who won the commission in a competition set up by the American Institute of Architects.

The site's centrepiece is the 66 m (217 ft) Memorial Tower. Its four figures represent courage, honour, sacrifice, and patriotism. At night, a jet of steam illuminated by orange light emanates from the tower, giving the appearance of a burning pyre. The Great Frieze wall depicts the transition from war to peace, while another memorial wall features bronze busts of five Allied leaders present at the dedication of the memorial.

The memorial's accompanying museum, which opened in 2006, is one of the finest centres of World War I research in the USA. As well as extensive displays of documents and photographs, exhibits include a Renault FT-17 tank, replica trenches, Paul von Hindenburg's field jacket, and propaganda posters.
Kansas City, Missouri
www.theworldwar.org

UNITED KINGDOM

The Cenotaph

Designed by Sir Edwin Lutyens, the Cenotaph is a simple but imposing memorial in London's Whitehall. It was initially a temporary structure built from wood and plaster in the first year after the Armistice, but this was replaced by a permanent memorial of Portland stone in 1920.

Every year the Cenotaph is the focus for Britain's national Service of Remembrance on Remembrance Sunday (nearest Sunday to 11 November), which includes a minute's silence at 11am. Although the Cenotaph was built for the dead of World War I, it is dedicated to all of Britain's war dead.
Whitehall, London

Imperial War Museum London

Housing the UK's biggest collection of British military artefacts, London's Imperial War Museum principally focuses on 20th-century and modern conflicts. The World War I holdings are particularly impressive, and include

London landmark
In the middle of Whitehall, the Cenotaph is the site of Britain's annual Remembrance Day service. "Cenotaph" is a Greek-derived term for an empty tomb.

armaments and munitions, medals, uniforms, equipment, and ephemera from daily life at the front.

The museum's World War I art collection includes work by Percy Wyndham Lewis, Paul Nash, John Singer Sargent, and Sir William Orpen. The Department of Documents has holdings ranging from high-level strategic documents through to the personal writings of common soldiers such as diaries and letter.
Lambeth Road, London
www.iwm.org.uk

Scottish National War Memorial

Built to remember the 150,000 Scottish servicemen who died during World War I, this memorial occupies the North Barracks of Edinburgh Castle. Its architect, Robert Lorimer, faced much public opposition to his plans for redeveloping the castle, and the shrine was not finished until 1927.
Edinburgh Castle
www.snwm.org

Unknown Warrior, Westminster Abbey

Located at the west end of the abbey's nave, the Tomb of the Unknown Warrior holds the remains of an unidentified British soldier from World War I. The body was exhumed from the Western Front along with several others and chosen by Brigadier-General J.L. Wyatt as the individual to represent all those British soldiers who had no known place of death or who couldn't be identified. The body was buried, with full military ceremony, on 11 November 1920, including a stop at the unveiling of the Cenotaph in Whitehall by King George V. Soil from a French battlefield was included in the grave and it was covered with black marble from a quarry near Namur in Belgium.
Westminster Abbey, London
www.westminster-abbey.org

At the dedication of the National World War I Museum and Memorial (formerly known as the Liberty Memorial) in 1926, President Calvin Coolidge said it "had not been raised to commemorate war and victory, but rather the results of war and victory which are … peace and liberty."

NATIONAL WORLD WAR I MUSEUM

WWI   WWI

Remembering Passchendaele
At Tyne Cot war cemetery near Zonnebecke, Belgium, Irish Guards prepare for the ceremony commemorating Passchendaele, the Third Battle of Ypres, on 31 July 2017. The battle lasted more than three months and caused around 500,000 casualties.

Centenary events

The enduring impact of World War I on the collective memory of combatant countries was evident in the numerous centenary commemorations staged from 2014 onward. They fulfilled the promise made to soldiers by poet Laurence Binyon in 1914: "We will remember them".

4th August 2014
BRITAIN ENTERS THE WAR

As Britain prepared to enter World War I in August 1914, Foreign Secretary Sir Edward Grey commented forebodingly: "The lamps are going out all over Europe; we shall not see them lit again in our lifetime." This phrase was used as the theme for British commemoration of the centenary of the declaration of war. Individuals and institutions throughout Britain were urged to put out or dim their lights on the evening of the centenary in 2014. This Lights Out event was accompanied by a variety of light displays in the resulting darkness. In London these ranged from a single candle left lit by the front door of 10 Downing Street and on the Tomb of the Unknown Warrior in Westminster Abbey (see p.356) to the Spectra art installation in nearby Victoria Tower Gardens, a column of light directed into the sky to a height of 15 km (9 miles). Displays in other parts of Britain included a light and sound artwork devised by Welsh artist Bedwyr Williams at the North Wales Heroes Memorial Arch in Bangor and a large-scale video display on the façade of the Scottish National Gallery in Edinburgh. An installation of hundreds of thousands of ceramic poppies at the Tower of London was officially unveiled on 5 August (see pp.360–61).

Spectra installation
Commemorating the outbreak of war, Spectra consisted of 49 xenon lamps directed into the sky. Designed by Japanese artist Ryoji Ikeda, it was lit in London every night from 4 to 11 August 2014.

25th April 2015
GALLIPOLI LANDINGS

The tradition of commemorating the wartime service of Australian and New Zealand troops on 25 April, the date of the first landings by soldiers of the Anzac Corps at Gallipoli in 1915, dates back to World War I itself. The celebration of Anzac Day on the centenary of the Gallipoli landings in 2015 drew record numbers of people to dawn remembrance ceremonies at war memorials across Australia and New Zealand. More than 10,000 made the long trip to Gallipoli itself, where an all-night vigil preceded the dawn ceremonial. The scale of the commemorations reflects how important a role the memory of World War I plays in both countries' sense of national identity.

Far-flung commemoration
These Australian soldiers are observing the centenary Anzac Day service at the Australian War Memorial at Villers-Bretonneaux in France. The site commemorates Australians who died fighting on the Western Front.

Boots and poppies at Vimy
For the centenary of the taking of Vimy Ridge, 3,598 pairs of combat boots were displayed at the Vimy Memorial, one pair for each Canadian soldier who died in the battle.

1st July 2016
THE SOMME OFFENSIVE
see pages 362–63

9th April 2017
VIMY RIDGE

The assault on Vimy Ridge by Canadian troops in 1917 has a special place in Canada's sense of historical identity, seen by many Canadians as the moment when the country achieved true nationhood. More than 20,000 Canadians travelled to Europe for the centenary commemorations that took place at the Vimy Memorial (see p.352) on the site of the battle. Speaking at the event, Canadian Prime Minister Justin Trudeau said the Vimy monument was "symbolic of Canada's birth and our enduring commitment to peace". The commemoration was also attended by members of the British royal family and by French President François Hollande.

14th July 2017
AMERICA AIDS FRANCE

The annual Bastille Day military parade in Paris in 2017 also celebrated the entry of the United States into World War I in 1917, bringing vital support to France in its desperate struggle with Germany. Troops from the United States Army, Navy, and Air Force marched with French soldiers down the Champs Elysées, watched by French President Emmanuel Macron

Americans at Bastille Day
Wearing the uniform of the World War I "doughboys", American soldiers parade banners down the Champs-Elysées during Bastille Day celebrations in 2017. The United States entered the war in April 1917.

and his guest American President Donald Trump. In a speech at the event President Macron said: "I want to thank America for the choice made a hundred years ago". In the United States, World War I has sometimes been referred to as "the forgotten war". Pershing Park in Washington DC is the site for the National World War I Memorial.

30th July 2017
PASSCHENDAELE

The centenary of the start of the Third Battle of Ypres, more commonly known as Passchendaele, was commemorated by ceremonies at the Tyne Cot war cemetery and other sites in the Ypres salient. British and Commonwealth forces suffered a quarter of a million casualties in the battle. The ceremonies were attended by the Prince of Wales and Duke and Duchess of Cambridge for Britain, King Philippe and Queen Mathilde for Belgium, and German foreign minister Sigmar Gabriel. Thousands of descendants of men who fought in the battle were also present. Events included the opening of a Memorial Poppy Garden and of a restored dugout at Zonnebeke. Many people were struck by the contrast between the clean and neat current scene and the hideous rain and mud in which the battle had been fought 100 years before.

"We remember it… for the courage and the bravery of the men who fought here."

THE PRINCE OF WALES SPEAKING AT PASSCHENDAELE, 31 JULY 2017

29th May 2016
BATTLE OF VERDUN

Along with other European leaders, German Chancellor Angela Merkel and French President François Hollande joined in ceremonies to mark the centenary of the end of the battle of Verdun, which cost their two countries around 300,000 lives. The day began with a re-enactment of the start of the battle at dawn, staged by 300 men in period uniforms. Hollande and Merkel laid a wreath at the Consenvoye German War Cemetery and lit an eternal flame at the French Douaumont Ossuary (see p.352). The two leaders' speeches at the event stressed the importance of European unity as a way of avoiding future conflicts. President Hollande said: "We should love our country, but we should protect our common home, Europe." As part of the commemoration, several thousand young French and German people re-enacted battlefield scenes and ran through Douaumont Cemetery to fall as if shot at the feet of a figure of the Grim Reaper.

Eternal flame
Chancellor Merkel and President Hollande stand side by side after lighting an eternal flame in the Douaumont Ossuary at Verdun. The centenary commemorations stressed solidarity between France and Germany.

Ceramic poppy

Every single earthenware poppy in the display was made by hand at works in Derbyshire and Staffordshire.

Evolving display

A panoramic view of the Tower of London on 31 October 2014 shows the poppies spreading across the dry moat around the Tower walls and cascading from the "Weeping Window". Entitled "Blood Swept Lands and Seas of Red", the exhibit was constantly evolving as more poppies were "planted" over four months.

7th July–11th November 2014
TOWER OF LONDON RED POPPIES

The most visited commemoration of the centenary of World War I by far was a mass display of red poppies at the Tower of London in the summer and autumn of 2014. This installation was the brainchild of ceramic artist Paul Cummins, inspired by the discovery of an anonymous poem in the records office in Chesterfield, Derbyshire. Written on his will by an unidentified soldier who had volunteered at the start of the war, the poem began: "The blood swept lands and seas of red…". Cummins conceived of a work using ceramic poppies to recreate the soldier's impression of "seas of red" and succeeded in selling the concept to the authorities at the Tower of London.

Working with set designer Tom Piper, Cummins planned to fill the moat at the Tower with poppies. The moat was deemed especially suitable as a site because it already had associations with the war, being the place where volunteers from the City of London, known as the Stockbrokers' Battalion, had drilled in 1914. There would also be a flood of poppies streaming down from a bastion window, the Weeping Window, and a swirl of poppies around the Tower gateway, known as the Wave. Almost half a million kilos (1.1 million lbs) of Etruscan earthenware were used to manufacture 888,246 ceramic poppies, one for every British, Commonwealth, and Colonial, soldier who died in the war.

The first poppies were put in place on 7 July 2014. More than 17,000 volunteers worked on the project in the course of the following four months, steadily increasing the number of poppies and the scale of the display. The installation was officially declared open on 5 August, when it was viewed by the royal princes William and Harry, and the Duchess of Cambridge. The work immediately caught the public imagination. It attracted large numbers of visitors from the start and the crowds grew as the weeks passed. In a simple but moving ceremony initiated on 1 September, at sunset each day the names of 180 soldiers fallen in the conflict were read out and the Last Post was played.

The last poppy was put in place by a 13-year-old cadet, Harry Hayes, on 11 November, the anniversary of the

Armistice. After a 21-gun salute, the installation was declared over and dismantling began. It is calculated that by that time some 5 million people had visited the poppies installation. Cummins and Piper resisted pressure to extend the display beyond its term, arguing that the transience of the exhibit was part of its power. The poppies were sold, raising money for charity. However, a decision was taken to preserve the Weeping Window and the Wave. These were toured to sites around the United Kingdom, and destined for a permanent final home at the Imperial War Museum.

"The **blood swept seas** of red, Where angels dare to tread…"

POEM BY AN UNKNOWN SOLDIER OF THE GREAT WAR

Royal visit
Queen Elizabeth II and the Duke of Edinburgh walk among the sea of poppies during a royal visit to the Tower installation site on 16 October 2014.

Tower guard
One of the Yeoman Warders of the Tower of London, popularly known as "Beefeaters", holds a handful of poppies. The Warders were tasked with guarding the display.

All-night vigil at the Abbey
On the night of 30 June to 1 July 2016, British servicemen keep watch at the Tomb of the Unknown Warrior in Westminster Abbey. The vigil marked the centenary of the Somme Offensive.

Tribute of youth
Young people lay wreathes at war graves near the Thiepval Memorial to the Missing of the Somme during the service held there on the centenary. Some 10,000 people were present at the event.

1st July 2016
THE SOMME OFFENSIVE

The Somme Offensive is an event with a special significance in the collective memory of the British people. The battle involved many thousands of troops from Commonwealth countries, the French and, of course, the Germans. The first day of the Somme, 1 July 1916, produced almost 60,000 British casualties, the heaviest toll that the British Army has ever suffered in a day's fighting. The losses were rendered more poignant by the fact that so many of those killed or wounded were citizen soldiers, enthusiastic volunteers entering battle for the first time. The shock of the first day's casualties was followed by five months of grinding attrition for little or no gain.

On the eve of the centenary of the battle, vigils and services were held at Thiepval on the Somme battlefield, Westminster Abbey in London, and at other locations across the United Kingdom, including Edinburgh Castle, Manchester Cathedral, the Welsh National War Memorial in Cardiff, and the Somme Heritage Center in County Down. Queen Elizabeth attended a service at Westminster Abbey and made a gesture of homage at the Tomb of the Unknown Warrior. The Tomb was then guarded throughout the night by relays of four British service personnel and civilians who kept watch, heads bowed, at the corners of the memorial stone. At Thiepval, the Duke and Duchess of Cambridge led the vigil.

On 1 July, artillery rounds were fired both outside the Abbey and at Thiepval for 100 seconds, before the observation of a two minute silence began at 7.28 in the morning. The silence was broken at 7.30 by the blowing of a whistle, which had been the signal for the men to go "over the top" a hundred years before. Ironically, whereas the first day of the battle had been warm and sunny, the commemorations on the battlefield a century later took place in rain and under heavy skies. As well as royalty

Newfoundland remembrance
Prince Charles visits the Newfoundland Monument at Beaumont-Hamel on the Somme centenary. The Newfoundland Regiment suffered more than 90 per cent casualties on the first day of the Somme.

and political leaders, some 10,000 people were present, including descendants of soldiers who died on the Somme. After the main event, special ceremonies were held at specific sites, including the Ulster Tower in Thiepval, where representatives of Northern Ireland and the Irish Republic stood side by side, and the Newfoundland Memorial. Perhaps the most moving moment of the ceremonies was a reading of Siegfried Sassoon's poem *Aftermath*, with the lines: "Have you forgotten yet?… Look down, and swear by the slain of the war that you'll never forget."

Vintage horse-drawn artillery at the Somme
The King's Troop Royal Horse Artillery operate a World War I vintage field gun at Thiepval. Each team of gunners fired 26 rounds in 100 seconds as part of the centenary events.

Old soldier remembers
A Chelsea Pensioner wanders among the graves at Thiepval during the centenary vigil. The presence of the scarlet-coated Pensioners, all retired soldiers, was a prominent feature of the commemorations.

"We **lost the flower of a generation** … It was in many ways the saddest day in the story of our nation."

DUKE OF CAMBRIDGE, SPEAKING AT THE THIEPVAL VIGIL, 20 JUNE 2016

Index

Page numbers in **bold** indicate main entries.

A

Abbas Hilmi II, Khedive 75
Abd el-Krim 342
Abdul Hamid II 19, 74
Accrington Pals 181
Achi Baba 112
aerial photography 98, 145, 152, 227, 292
Africa
  campaigns **76–77**
  see also German East Africa; German South
    West Africa
African-American troops 131, 216, 287, 308
Afrikaners 76, 77
Agadir 18, 201
air combat **188–91**, 273, **294–97**
Arras 189, 227
  casualties 189, 295
  dogfights 189, 190–91
  Palestine 259
  pilot aces 189, 231, 298–99, 306
  St Mihiel 307
  Second Battle of the Marne 286, 294
  Verdun 131, 160
  Vittorio Veneto 319
aircraft 25
  anti-submarine patrols 257
  Belgian 192
  bombers 232, 233, 264, 295
  British 188, 192, 232
  Caproni 295
  fighter aircraft 160, 188–89, **192–93**, 232
  float aircraft 79
  Fokker Dr.1 299
  Fokker D.VII 192, 295, 299
  Fokker Eindecker 188
  French 188, 192
  German 64, 132, 188, 192, 232, 273, 294,
    295, 299
  Gotha 132, 232, 297
  Halberstadt 273
  Handley Page 295
  Ilya Mourometz 13
  Italian 232, 295
  Junkers 273
  LVG 294
  Nieuport 11 "Bébé" 188
  parachutes 189, 295
  reconnaissance 145, 152, 188, 227, 255,
    257, 294, 295
  Rumpler C.VII 295
  Russian 13, 24, 232
  Sopwith Camel 192, 232, 295
  Taube monoplane 64
  Vickers "Gunbus" 188
  Zeppelin-Staaken "Giant" 232, 233
aircraft industry 93, 294
airships 25, 79, 145
  blimps 132, 221, 257
  Clément-Bayard II airship 25
  Schütte-Lanz airships 132
  Zeppelins 14, 25, 131, **132–33**, 232, 255
Aisne river 55, 58, 59, 226, 279, 283, 285,
  305
Aisne-Marne American Cemetery and
  Memorial 351
Aitken, Max 261
Albania 141
Albert 305
Albert I, King of the Belgians 38, 42, 43, 59,
  312, 313
Alderson, General Edwin 230, 231
Alexandra, Tsarina 198, 199, 210
Alexeev, General Mikhail 174
Algeria 45
All Quiet on the Western Front (Erich
  Remarque) 303, 345
Allenby, General Edmund 73, 227, 258, 259,
  316
Allied Supreme War Council 247, 291
Allies, *see* Belgium; Britain; France; Greece;
  Italy; Japan; Portugal; Romania; Russia;
  Serbia
Alpenkorps 246–47

Alpini 106, 107
Alsace-Lorraine 22, **44–45**, 52, 159, 218, 339
ambulances 131, 187
  camel ambulances 258
American Civil War 187, 261
American Expeditionary Force (AEF) 213,
  217, 285, 286, 287, 305, 306–07,
  308–09, 310
American Field Service 131
American Relief Administration 333
Amiens 251, 283, 285, 287, 294, **304–05**,
  312
amputations 187
anaesthetics 187
anarchist movements 17
Anatolia 116, 117, 317, 343
Angel of Mons 47
Anglo-German Naval Agreement 221
animal messengers 145
anti-aircraft guns 132, 232
anti-Semitism 67, 135, 223, 321, 333,
  336
anti-submarine barriers 221, 292
anti-tank rifles 250
anti-war groups
  Austria-Hungary 198, 218
  Britain 33, 206, 218, 269
  conscientious objectors 177, 216, 218
  France 167, 199, 225
  Germany 33, 198, 199, 218
  novelists and poets 303
  Russia 33, 167, 234
  USA 131, 216–17
Antwerp 42, 43, 52, 58, 59
Anzac Cove 109, 112, 113
Anzac Memorial 348, 358
Anzac troops **108–09**, 227, 239, 358
  see also Australian troops; Gallipoli
    Campaign; New Zealand troops
Apollinaire, Guillaume 303
Aqaba 197
Arabic (White Star liner) 127
Arabs 122, 123, 317, 334
Arab Revolt 148, **196–97**
  nationalism 75, 196–97
Ardennes 44–45
Argonne Forest 308, 309
Arkhangelsk 300, 301
Arlington National Cemetery 356
armaments, *see* munitions production;
  weapons
Armenian massacre 75, **116–17**
Armenian nationalism 75, 116, 117
Armentières 283
Armistice 291, 301, 313, 322, **322–23**
  celebrations 264, 323, 324–25
  see also peace initiatives; peace treaties
armoured vehicles
  cars 25, 59
  tanks *see* tanks
arms limitation agreements 345
Army of the Orient 141
Arras, Battle of 59, 73, 189, 207, 224,
  226–27, 229, 231
Arras and Vimy Ridge Battlefield 351
artillery 24, **50–51**
  creeping barrages 181, 224, 225, 226, 239,
    241, 272, 287, 307, 309
  shells 24–25, 50, 105, 171, 226, 228–29
Artois-Loos Offensive 57, 98, **142–43**, 158
Asiago 107, 246, 319
Askaris 254, 255
Asquith, Herbert 199, 201
Atlantic, war in the 39, 83, 124, 126
atrocities
  Armenian 116
  German 38, 42, 77
  Turkish 116–17
Auckland War Memorial Museum 354
Aurora cruiser 252
Australia
  Australian and New Zealand Army Corps
    (Anzac) **108–09**, 227, 239, 358
  Australian Corps 109, 304, 358
  Australian Imperial Force 108, 109
  Australian War Memorial 348, 358
  centenary events 358
  navy 83

Australia (cont.)
  troops 73, 85, **108–11**, 184–85, 197, 227,
    239, 242, 259, 343, 358
  war memorial 348, 358
Austria-Hungary
  annexation of Bosnia-Herzegovina 15, 19
  anti-war groups 198, 218
  armistice 317
  Austro-Prussian War 66
  Balkan policy 18, 19
  civilian hardships 268, 319
  declares war on Serbia 12, 15, 29, 30
  disintegration of 257, 319
  Dual Alliance 14, 18
  early setbacks **68–69**, 70
  home front 268, 269
  invasion of Romania 195
  invasion of Serbia 68
  League of the Three Emperors 14, 18
  monarchy 17
  navy 78, 256, 257
  pre-World War I 14, 15, 16, 17
  relations with Italy 106
  and Sarajevo assassination 12, **28–29**
  social and political solidarity 32
  social unrest 269
  Treaty of St-Germain-en-Laye 319, 334
  Triple Alliance 14, 31
  war planning **23**
  see also specific campaigns and battles

B

backpacks 181
Baden, Prince Max von 320, 321
badges, German 64, 292
Baghdad 119, 122, 123, 316
Baker, Newton 310
Balfour, Arthur 197
Balfour Declaration 197
Balkan League 19
Balkan Wars 12, 17, 74, 188, 316
  First Balkan War 15, 17
  Second Balkan War 15, 19, 140, 194
Balkans 18–19
  see also Albania; Bulgaria; Greece;
    Romania; Serbia
Ball, Albert 189
bandages 187
barbed wire 25, 60, 61
Barbusse, Henri 199, 302, 303
Baruch, Bernard 217
Basra 75, 119, 122, 123
The Battle of the Somme (newsreel) 261
battlecruisers 124, 170, 171
Baucq, Philippe 167
Baupaume 305
Bavaria 321, 333
bayonet charges 25, 45
Beadle, James 259
Beatty, Vice-Admiral David 78, 124, 125,
  170, 171
Beaumont Hamel 184
Bedouin 197
Beer Hall Putsch 223, 333
Beersheba 258, 259
Belarus 277, 343
Belgium 153
  annexation 43
  Belgian army 42
  British advance into **46–47**
  centenary events 359
  civilian hardships 43
  colonies 77
  defence of Antwerp 59
  deportations 202
  German atrocities 42, 43
  German invasion of 38, **42–43**, 44, 45,
    46–47, 222–23, 302
  memorials, monuments, and museums
    349–51
  neutrality 22, 31, 42
  postwar 333
  resistance movement 43, 167
Belgrade 69, 140, 317

Bell, Alexander Graham 145
Belleau Wood, Battle of 283, **284–85**
Below, General Otto von 246
Benedict XV, Pope 218
Benes, Edvard 169
Berlin Conference 14
Berlin-Baghdad railway 14, 19
Bersaglieri 107
Beseler, General Hans von 203
Bethmann-Hollweg, Theobald von 21, 29,
  31, 152, 223
binoculars 286
Birdwood, General Sir William 108, 109
Bishop, Billy 189, 231
Bismarck, Otto von 12, 18, 20
Bismarck Archipelago 85
bite-and-hold tactics 242, 273
black African troops 76, 77, 118, 119, 254, 255
Black and Tans 342
Black Hand 29
black market
  Austria-Hungary 269
  Germany 198, 269
Black Tom Island explosion 213
Blériot, Louis 25
blimps 132, 221, 257
Blitzkrieg 273
blood transfusions 187
Blücher-Yorck Offensive 283
Blunden, Edmund 303
Boelcke, Oswald 160, 189, 298
Boer Wars 14, 21, 76, 77, 179, 187
Bohemia 319
Bolimov, Battle of 105
Bolo, Paul 167
Bolsheviks 174, 211, 234, 235, 236, 243,
  300, 301, 343
  and Brest-Litovsk Peace Treaty 276–77
  revolution 117, 128, 153, 197, 199, 218,
    252–53, 268
bombing campaigns **232–33**
  casualties 232
  London 132, 232
  night raids 232
  over Germany 295
  Paris 268, 295
  strategic bombing 232, 264, 294, 295
  Zeppelin raids **132–33**
Bonneau, General Louis 44
boots 304
Borden, Robert 230, 231
Boroevic, Field Marshal Svetozar 319
Bosnia-Herzegovina
  annexation of 15, 19, 28
  Sarajevo assassination 12, **28–29**
  Serbian invasion of 68, 69
Botha, Louis 77
Boué de Lapeyrère, Admiral Augustin 256
Boxer Rebellion 14, 21, 85
Brady, Mathew 261
Brest-Litovsk Peace Treaty 203, 211, 218,
  235, 253, **276–77**
Briand, Aristide 143, 224, 345
Britain
  aircraft industry 294
  Anglo-German Naval Agreement 221
  Anglo-German naval race 14, 18, 19, 78
  Anglo-Japanese alliance 14
  anti-war groups 33, 206, 218, 269
  British Empire 31, 77, 333
  centenary events 358, 360–61, 362
  civilian hardships 199
  coalition governments 93, 103, 199
  commemoration 344
  conscription 33, 128, 176, 177
  declares war on Germany 31
  declares war on Turkey 74
  domestic politics 93, 200, 201
  enters the war, centenary 358
  Entente Cordiale 14, 18, 23, 337
  home front 268, 269
  intervention in Russia 300, 301
  memorials, monuments, and museums 356
  mobilization 46
  monarchy 17
  munitions production 93
  pre-World War I 14, 15, 16, 17
  social and political solidarity 33, 199

Britain (cont.)
   social unrest 269
   Unknown Warrior 344, 356, 362
   war economy 93
   war planning 23
   see also British army; Royal Air Force;
      Royal Navy; Royal Flying Corps; and
      specific campaigns and battles
British Army
   British Expeditionary Force (BEF) 44, 45,
      46–47, 52, 55, 59, 60, 61, 177, 178
   colonial troops 60, 73, 76, 89, 99, 118,
      119, 122–23
   Fifth Army 242, 278, 279
   First Army 98, 103, 312
   Fourth Army 184, 304, 305
   Kitchener's New Army 142, 143, **176–77**,
      181
   medical examinations 176, 177
   Pals Battalions 177
   reforms 22
   Second Army 242, 283
   Special Reserve 176
   Tank Corps 248–49
   Territorial Force 22, 46, 143, 176, 177
   Third Army 248, 278, 279, 305, 312
   training 177
   volunteering 176, 177
British East Africa 254
British Legion 179
British Medical Corps 187
British Naval Intelligence Division 166, 167
Brittain, Vera 267, 303
Broodseinde Ridge 242
Brooke, John 260
Brooke, Rupert 303
Brooks, Ernest 260, 261
Bruchmüller, General Georg 278
Bruges 292
Brusilov, General Aleksei 70, 95, 174, 234,
   235, 237
Brusilov Offensive 107, 135, 149, 160, **174–
   75**, 194, 272
Brussels 42
Bryan, William Jennings 131
Bucharest 195
Buckles, Frank 345
bugles 123
Bukovina 194
Bulgaria 313, 317
   Balkan Wars 15, 19
   collapse of 264, 316, 317, 319
   enters the war 140
   invasion of Romania 194
   invasion of Serbia 140, 141
   Macedonian defeat 316
   territorial losses 316
   Treaty of Neuilly 317, 334
Bullard, Eugene 131
Bullard, General Robert 309, 310
Bülow, General Karl von 47, 53, 54, 55
Bundeswehr Military History Museum-Berlin
   354
Bundeswehr Military History Museum-
   Dresden 354
Byng, General Julian 231, 248, 279
Byng Boys 273

C

Cabrinovic, Nedjelko 29
Cadorna, General Luigi 107, 247
Caillaux, Henriette 32
Caillaux, Joseph 337
Cambrai, Battle of 73, 95, 243, **248–49**, 251
Cambrai battlefields 351
camel ambulances 258
camouflage outfits 273
Canada
   Canadian Corps 207, 231, 243, 304, 312
   Canadian Expeditionary Force (CEF) 230,
      231
   Canadian National Vimy Memorial Park
      351, 352, 359
   Canadian War Museum 351
   centenary events 359
   conscription 231
   Princess Patricia's Canadian Light Infantry
      230, 231
   troops 73, 102, 103, 226, 227, **230–31**,
      239, 242, 359
   war memorials 351, 359

Canal du Nord 312
Cantigny 285
Caporetto, Battle of 107, 243, **246–47**, 248, 319
Cappy-sur-Somme 131
Caproni triplane 295
Carden, Admiral Sackville 110
Carol I, King of Romania 194
Caroline Islands 85
Carpathian Mountains 70, 134
carrier pigeons 145, 167, 251, 309
Carson, Edward 33
Casement, Roger 164
Castelnau, General Noel de 155
casualties
   airmen 189, 295
   American 217
   Artois and Champagne offensives 143
   Australian 109, 332
   Battle of Arras 227
   Belgian 332
   bombing campaigns 232
   British 332
   Brusilov Offensive 175
   Canadian 231, 243, 332
   Caporetto 247
   civilian 332
   Gallipoli 113
   German 332
   Hundred Days Offensive 305
   Indian 119, 332
   influenza pandemic 269, 309
   Isonzo Campaign 246
   Jutland 171
   Lake Naroch offensive 174
   last fatality of the war 230, 323
   Mahiwa 255
   Marne (First Battle) 55
   Marne (Second Battle) 287
   medical treatment **186–87**
   Messines Ridge 239
   Mons 46
   Neuve Chapelle 99
   New Zealand 109, 242
   Romanian 194
   Russian 211
   St Mihiel salient 307
   Sarikamish 74
   Somme 181, 185
   Spring Offensives 279
   total 186, 332
   trench warfare 95
   U-boat attacks 220, 221
   US 285, 287, 307, 332
   Verdun 161, 224
   Ypres 241, 242, 243
   Zeebrugge Raid 293
casualty clearing stations 186
Cattaro 257
Caucasian campaigns 75, 110, 116, 117, 134,
   258, 259, 277
   see also Armenian massacre
cavalry 25, **72–73**, 145
   Anzac 109, 197, 259
   Arab 120
   Austrian 72
   British 46, 48–49, 73, 178, 179, 259
   Cossack 64, 69, 72
   Desert Mounted Corps 73, 316
   French 44, 72, 73
   German 72, 73
   Indian 118
   Kurdish 117
   Romanian 194
   uniforms 72
Cavell, Edith 167, 213
cemeteries 61, 185, 344, 346–47
   see also memorials, monuments, and
      museums
Cenotaph, London 356
centenary events 358–63
Central Powers, *see* Austria-Hungary;
   Bulgaria; Germany; Turkey
Champagne offensive 57, 59, **98**, 142–43,
   154, 158, 159
Chantilly Conference 174
Charles I, Emperor 153, 175, 218, 246, 319
Charteris, General John 91
Château de Beaurepaire 178
Château-Thierry 285, 287
chemical warfare 95, 102, 103, **104–05**, 131,
   160, 213, 279, **288–89**
   see also chlorine gas; diphosgene gas;
      mustard gas; phosgene; tear gas
Chemin des Dames 58, 159, 224, 283
children, evacuation of 268

China 84
   becomes a republic 15, 84
   Boxer Rebellion 14, 21, 85
   declares war on Germany 85
   foreign concessions 84
   Japanese aggression against **84–85**
   May Fourth Movement 85
Chinese labourers in Europe 85, 119
chlorine gas 88, 102, 103, 104, 105, 143, 230
cholera 71
Christmas Truce **62–63**, 95
Churchill, Winston 8, 20, 59, 82, 94, 171,
   300, 337
   First Lord of the Admiralty 110
   and Gallipoli 110, 112
   and tank warfare 250
Cigognes squadron 160, 189
civilians
   casualties 332
   hardships **198–99**
   morale 232, 268–69
   see also home fronts; women
Clemenceau, Georges 199, 225, 269, 323,
   333, 334, **336–37**, 343
   assassination attempt on 337
   biography 337
   character and qualities 336
   and Paris Peace Conference 201, 334, 337
   and Treaty of Versailles 338, 339
Clément-Bayard II airship 25
codes and codebreakers 124, 144, 145,
   166–67, 213
collaborators 323
Collins, Michael 165
Colmar von der Goltz, Baron 123
colonial troops **118–21**
   British 60, 73, 76, 89, 99, 118, 119,
      122–23
   French 45, 54, 77, 102, 118, 120
   German 254, 255
combat stress 187
commemorations, centenary 358–363
communications **144–45**, 166, 273
communism 85, 333
   see also Bolsheviks
concentration camps 14
Congress of Oppressed Nationalities 319
Connolly, James 164, 165
Conrad von Hötzendorf, Field Marshal Franz
   23, 29, 30, 68, 69, 70, 71, 140, 141, 175,
   319
conscientious objectors 177, 216, 218
conscription 22, 33, 128, 176
   Britain 33, 128, 176, 177
   Canada 231
   France 15, 19, 44
   New Zealand 108
   USA 216
Constantine, King of Greece 141, 256
Constantinople (Istanbul) 75, 110, 117, 153,
   316, 333
Constanza 195
convoy system 201, 220, 221, 257
Corfu 141, 257
Corfu Declaration 141
Coronel, Battle of 83, 124
Cossacks 64, 69, 72
Cottin, Emile 337
counter-intelligence 167
Courtrai Offensive 43
Cradock, Rear Admiral Sir Christopher 83
Creel, George 216
creeping barrages 181, 224, 225, 226, 239,
   241, 272, 287, 307, 309
Crimean War 145, 187, 261
Ctesiphon 123
Cummings, E.E. 303
Currie, General Arthur 231, 243, 304, 312
Cuxhaven 79
cycle corps 109
Cyprus, British protectorate 75
Czechoslovak Legions 169, 300–301
Czechoslovakia 169, 333, 334, 339

D

Damascus 73, 109, 197, 317
d'Annunzio, Gabriele 107, 319
Danzig 339
Dar es Salaam 255
Dardanelles 110, 257
   see also Gallipoli Campaign

Dawes Plan 343
de Valera, Éamon 165
Debs, Eugene 217
Defence of the Realm Act (DORA) 93
defence-in-depth tactic 226–27, 273
Degoutte, General Jean 286
Delville Wood, Battle of 184
demobilization 323, 332
Denikin, General Anton 342
Denmark 339
Dera 317
Derby, Lord 177
Desert Mounted Corps 73, 316
destroyers 79
Deventer, General Jacob van 255
Diaz, General Armando 247, 319
Dimitrijevic, Colonel Dragutin 29
Dinant massacre 42
diphosgene gas 105, 160
diplomacy
   pre-war 12, 14, 15, 16, 17, 23
   see also peace initiatives; peace treaties
      displaced populations *see* refugees
Dix, Otto 261
Dmowski, Roman 168
Dogger Bank, Battle of 79, 88, **124–25**
dogs, messenger 145
Dos Passos, John 303
Douala 76
Douaumont Ossuary and Verdun Memorial
   161, 352, 359
doughboys 306, 307
Douhet, General Giulio 295
Doyle, Arthur Conan 302
dreadnoughts 19, 74, 78–79, 80
Dreyfus affair 167, 336
Driant, Colonel Émile 155
Drocourt-Quéant Line 231
Dual Alliance 14, 18
Duisberg, Carl 104

E

East Asiatic Cruiser Squadron 82–83, 84, 85
East Prussia 70, 135, 223, 339
   Russian invasion of 64
Easter Rising 148, 164–65
Eastern Front
   Brest-Litovsk Peace Treaty 203, 218, 235,
      276–77
   campaigns (1914) 64–65, 68–71
   campaigns (1915) 134–35, 140–41
   campaigns (1916) 174–75, 194–95
   campaigns (1917) 234–37
Ebert, Friedrich 321, 339
École de Guerre 22
economies
   pre-war 16, 18
   see also war economies
Edward VII, King 14, 16
Egypt 122
   British protectorate 75, 196
   independence 343
   Turkish attack on 75
Eichhorn, Field Marshal Hermann 277
Eisner, Kurt 321
Elles, Brigadier-General Hugh 248
Emmich, General Otto von 42
Entente Cordiale 14, 18, 23, 337
Entente Powers, *see* Allies
Enver Pasha 19, 74, 75, 116, 117
Erzberger, Matthias 322, 323
Erzurum 73, 117
espionage **166–67**, 213
Espionage Act 213, 216–17
Estienne, Colonel Jean Baptiste 250, 251
Estonia 277, 342
Étaples Military Cemetery 352
Europe, war in, *see* Eastern Front; Italian
      campaigns; Mediterranean, war in the;
      North Sea, war in the; Western Front

F

Falkenhayn, General Erich von 30, 58, 71,
   95, 134–35, 143, 181, 223
   and Hindenburg 67, 134–35, 223
   and Ludendorff 67, 134–35, 223
   and Palestine 152

Falkenhayn, General Erich von (cont.)
  resignation 152, 161, 175
  and Romanian campaign 152, 194, 195
  and Serbian campaign 140, 141
  and Verdun 152, 154, 155, 160, 161
  and the Yildirim Force 152, 258–59
  and Ypres 60, 61, 102
Falklands, Battle of the 39, 83, 124, 126
Far East, war in the see China; Japan; Pacific, war in the
fascism, rise of 343, 345
Feisal, Emir 196, 197, 258, 317, 334, 342, 343
feminists, anti-war 218
Fenton, Roger 261
Ferdinand I, King of Bulgaria 316
Fez, Treaty of 15
field guns 50, 137, 249, 254
  see also artillery
field telephones 25, 144–45
Finland 276, 277
Fiume 107, 334
flamethrowers 160, 272
Flanders see Belgium; Lys Offensive; Messines, Battle of; Ypres
Flanders Field American Cemetery and Memorial 349
flare guns 249
flash-spotting 226, 272
Flers-Courcelette 185, 250
Flesquières 249
Foch, General Ferdinand 52, 59, 158, 179, **290–91**, 306, 311, 339
  and Amiens 304, 305
  biography 291
  character and qualities 290, 291
  criticisms of Armistice terms 291, 322–23, 339
  and First Battle of the Marne 54, 57, 291
  and Hindenburg Line Offensive 312
  Marshal of France 287
  and Meuse-Argonne Offensive 308
  offensive strategy 22, 290, 291
  and Second Battle of the Marne 286, 287, 291
  and Spring Offensives 279
  Supreme Commander of the Allied Armies 159, 279, 283, 291, 337
Fokker, Anthony 188
Fokker Dr.1 299
Fokker D.VII 192, 295, 299
Fokker Eindecker 188
Folkstone 232
food
  ersatz products 198, 269
  food riots 198
  production 93, 128, 152
  rationing 198, 221, 268
  shortages 198, 221, 268, 269, 271
  forced labour 64, 202
Fort Douaumont 119, 154, 155, 158, 160, 161, 162–63
Fort Vaux 145, 160, 161
France
  aircraft industry 294
  anti-war groups 167, 199, 225
  centenary events 359, 362–363
  civilian hardships 199, 271
  coalition government 143
  colonies 77
  commemoration 344, 345
  conscription 15, 19, 44
  declares war on Turkey 74
  Deuxième Bureau 166, 167
  domestic politics 32, 143
  Dreyfus affair 336
  Éntente Cordiale 14, 18, 23, 337
  Franco-Prussian War 14, 16, 24, 25, 66, 67, 187, 290, 339
  Franco-Russian alliance 14, 30
  home front 269
  intervention in Russia 301
  memorials, monuments, and museums 351–54
  mobilization 33, 44
  munitions production 93
  navy 78, 110, 256
  postwar 333
  pre-World War I 14, 15, 16, 17
  resistance movement 167
  social and political solidarity 32–33
  social unrest 269
  socialism 33, 225
  Unknown Warrior 344
  war economy 93, 119
  war planning **22**

France (cont.)
  see also French army; and specific campaigns and battles
Franchet d'Espèrey, General Louis 53, 54, 57, 316
Franco-American Cooperation, Museum of 353
François, General Hermann von 65
Frankfurt 295
Franz Ferdinand, Archduke 12, 15, 19, **28–29**
Franz Joseph, Emperor 12, 17, 28, 29, 175
Freikorps 333
French, Field Marshal Sir John 46, 52, 54, 57, 98, 103, 142, 143, 178
French army
  colonial troops 45, 54, 77, 102, 118, 120
  Fifth Army 45, 53, 54, 55, 57
  First Army 44
  Fourth Army 44, 52, 286
  French Foreign Legion 131, 169
  mutinies 159, 161, 199, 225
  Ninth Army 52, 54, 103, 291
  Second Army 44, 59, 159
  Sixth Army 52, 54, 55, 283
  Tenth Army 59, 143, 286, 305
  Third Army 44, 52
French Indochina 77
Fricourt German War Cemetery 352
Frontiers, Battle of the 44–45
frostbite 186
Fuller, Colonel John 248

G

Galicia 65, 68, 69, 70, 71, 73, 135, 169, 234, 235
Gallieni, General Joseph 38, 52, 53, 54, 57
Gallipoli Campaign 94, 95, 99, 108, 109, **110–15**, 119, 187
  centenary 358
Gallipoli Peninsula Historical National Park 355, 358
Gallwitz, General Max von 308
Gard, Roger Martin du 345
Garros, Roland 188
gas masks 103, 105, 274, 278
  for horses 73, 105
Gatling gun 25
Gaulle, Charles de 45, 159
Gaza 258, 259
Geddes, Walter 117
Geneva Protocol 105
Genocide Memorial, Yerevan 117
George V, King 15, 57, 210
Georges-Picot, François 197
German army
  colonial troops 254, 255
  Eighteenth Army 279, 281
  Eighth Army 64, 67, 223, 273
  Eleventh Army 135
  Fifth Army 44, 154, 160, 308
  First Army 42, 46, 52–53, 54, 55, 286
  Fourth Army 44, 59, 98, 239, 283
  Ninth Army 70, 152, 194, 195
  Second Army 42, 47, 52–53, 54, 55, 279
  Seventh Army 44, 286
  Sixth Army 44
  Tenth Army 134
  Third Army 55, 286
  German East Africa 38, 76–77, 119
  guerrilla campaign 254–55
  postwar division of 255
German navy 18, 19, 21, 78, 124–25, 293
  East Asiatic Cruiser Squadron 82–83, 84, 85
  High Seas Fleet 170–71, 293, 320–21, 339
  mutiny 320–21
  U-boats see submarine warfare
  see also naval conflicts
German New Guinea 39, 85
German Southwest Africa 73, 76, 77, 255
Germanization programme 203
Germany
  aircraft industry 294
  Anglo-German Naval Agreement 221
  Anglo-German naval race 14, 18, 19, 78
  anti-war groups 33, 198, 199, 218
  Armistice 317, 322–23, 339
  civilian hardships 148, 198, 268, 271, 333
  colonies 77
  commemoration 345

Germany (cont.)
  declares war 13, 31, 34
  domestic politics 32
  Dual Alliance 14, 18
  final bid for victory **282–83**
  German Social Democrats 32
  home front 268, 269, 271
  invasion of Belgium 38, **42–43**, 44, 45, 46–47, 222–23, 302
  League of the Three Emperors 14, 18
  Lebensraum 20
  liberalization of 320
  Mitteleuropa plan 202–03, 218, 223
  mobilization 30–31, 32
  monarchy 17
  munitions production 93, 202
  nationalism 20, 67, 202, 223, 332–33
  peace initiatives 313, 320
  postwar 332–33, 343
  pre-war I 16, 17, 18
  reparations 334, 339, 343
  revolutionary upheaval 320–21, 322, 332, 338
  social and political solidarity 32, 34
  social unrest 269
  socialism 32, 67, 199, 218, 320, 321
  Third Reich 203
  Treaty of Versailles 105, 132, 189, 291, 295, 321, 323, 334, 337, **338–41**
  Triple Alliance 14, 31
  under control of Third Supreme Command **202–03**
  unification 16
  Unknown Warrior 345
  war economy 93, 202
  war guilt, repudiation of 339
  war museums 354
  war planning **22**
  Weimar Republic 67, 223, 264, 321, 322
  Weltpolitik 20
  see also German army; German navy; and specific campaigns and battles
Ghent 323
Gibbons, Floyd 285
Glossop, Captain John 83
Godley, General Sir Alexander 108, 109, 113
Goering, Hermann 189
Gomes da Costa, General Manuel 283
Gorizia 107
Gorlice-Tarnow Offensive 102, 107, **134–35**
Goschen, Edward 31
Gotha aircraft 132, 232, 297
Gough, General Hubert 241, 242, 278
Gouraud, General Henri 286
governments-in-exile
  Belgian 43
  Serbian 141
Graves, Robert 303
Graves, General William 301
Great Depression 343
Great Retreat 47, **52–53**, 54, 57, 73, 135
Great Yarmouth 132, 170
Greco-Turkish War 343
Greece 141, 194, 343
  Balkan Wars 15, 19
  enters the war 256, 316
grenade launchers 249
grenades 26, 101, 110, 317
Grey, Sir Edward 19, 30, 358
Grignard, Victor 105
Grigorescu, General Eremia 355
Grimsby Chums 181
Groener, General Wilhelm 320, 321
Gronau, General Hans von 54
guerilla warfare 197, **254–55**
Gumbinnen, Battle of 64
guns, see weapons
Gurkhas 112, 118, 119
Gurney, Ivor 303
Guynemer, Captain Georges 189

H

Haber, Fritz 93, 104–05
Habsburg Empire 19, 28
  see also Austria-Hungary
Hague Convention 104, 105
Haig, Field Marshal Sir Douglas 46, 57, **178–79**, 224, 291
  and Amiens 304, 305
  and Armistice 322
  and Arras 226, 227

Haig, Field Marshal Sir Douglas (cont.)
  and Artois-Loos offensive 143
  attrition strategy 178
  biography 179
  and Cambrai 248, 249
  character and qualities 178, 179
  commander-in-chief 178
  and Lys Offensive 283
  and Neuve Chapelle 98, 99
  relations with Lloyd George 179, 201
  and Somme 155, 179, 180, 181, 185, 250
  and Ypres 103, 179, 231, 238, 239, 240, 241, 242, 243
Haig Fund 179
Haiti 130
Halberstadt aircraft 273
Haldane, Richard 22, 176, 178
Hall, Admiral Reginald 124, 166
Hamel 304
Hamilton, General Sir Ian 110, 111, 112, 113
hand-to-hand fighting 284, 285
Handley Page aircraft 295
Harbord, Brigadier James 285
Hardie, Kier 33, 218
Hartlepool 79
Hasek, Jaroslav 303
Hawker, Major Lanoe 299
Heidkamp, Wilhelm 125
Hejaz (Saudi Arabia) 75, 196–97
Heligoland Bight, Battle of 78, 124
helmets 43, 142, 152, 155, 168, 175, 243, 251, 285
Hemingway, Ernest 303
Hentsch, Lieutenant Colonel Richard 54–55
Herero massacre 77
Hildenbrand, Hans 260
Hindenburg, General Paul von 21, **66–67**, 70, 134, 135, 152, 153, 194, 223, 276, 320, 321
  and Falkenhayn 67, 134–35
  biography 67
  character and qualities 67
  and German economic and diplomatic policies 202
  and Ludendorff 66, 67
  and Tannenberg 64, 65, 67
Hindenburg Line 67, 95, 105, 185, 223, 226, 309
  Allied attack on **312–13**
Hipper, Rear Admiral Franz von 79, 124, 125, 170, 171
Hitler, Adolf 189, 203, 323, 333, 345
  appointed German chancellor 67
  failed putsch 223, 333
  Lloyd George's view of 201
  overturns Versailles Treaty 339, 343
  war service 60, 323, 333
HMAS Sydney 82, 83
HMHS Llandovery Castle 221
HMS Agamemnon 317
HMS Audacious 78–79
HMS Dreadnought 14, 18, 25
HMS Good Hope 83
HMS Indefatigable 171
HMS Indomitable 124
HMS Inflexible 83
HMS Invincible 83
HMS Lion 124, 125, 171
HMS Monmouth 83
HMS New Zealand 124
HMS Princess Royal 124
HMS Queen Elizabeth 80–81, 110
HMS Queen Mary 171
HMS Tiger 124
HMS Vindictive 293
Holt, Benjamin 251
Holtzendorff, Admiral Henning von 220
home fronts **268–71**
  civilian hardships **198–99**
  emergency measures 93
  food shortages 198, 221, 268, 269, 271
  social unrest 269
  see also under individual countries
Hooge 160
horses 136–37
horse-drawn transport 25, 52, 278
  see also cavalry
Horthy, Admiral Miklos 257, 333
Hottentot massacre 77
House, Colonel Edward 131, 214
howitzers 50, 51, 154
Hundred Days Offensive 109, 145, 179, 231, 249, 294, 305, 308
Hungary 319
  postwar 333
  Treaty of Trianon 319, 334

Hurley, Frank 260
Hussein bin Ali, Sherif 196, 197
Hussein Kamil 75
Hutier, General Oskar von 235, 273, 279
hydrophones 220–21

I

Ilya Mourometz 13
Immelmann, Max 160
Imperial War Museum London 356
In Flanders Fields Museum 349
In Flanders Fields (John McCrae) 102
incendiary bombs 132
Independent Labour Party 218
India Gate, Delhi 354
Indian Army 119
Indian troops 60, 73, 76, 89, 99, 118, 119,
    122–23
Industrial Workers of the World 217
infantry tactics, improved 272–73, 311
infiltration tactics 247, 249, 273, 274, 278
influenza pandemic 285, 309, 323, 332
Ingenohl, Admiral Friedrich von 78, 125
Inner Mongolia 85
intelligence **166–67**
    British 124, 131
    codebreaking 124, 144, 145, 166–67
    counter-intelligence 167
    espionage 166–67, 213
    signals intelligence 166
Inter-Allied Conferences 142, 143
International Congress of Women 218
Iraq 197
Ireland
    Black and Tans 342
    Easter Rising 148, 164–65, 342
    Home Rule 32, 33, 164
    Irish Free State 165, 342
    Irish National War Memorial Gardens 354
    Irish Republican Army (IRA) 165, 342
    Irish Republican Brotherhood (IRB) 164
    Irish Volunteers 33, 164
    nationalism 164–65
    troops 33, 164, 239, 345
    Ulster Volunteer Force (UVF) 33, 164, 239
    War of Independence 342
Irish Peace Tower 239
irregulars 197
Isonzo, battles of the 107, 246
Isonzo Front Battlefields 354
Italian campaigns
    Asiago 107, 246, 319
    Caporetto 107, 243, **246–47**, 248, 319
    Isonzo 107, 246
    Piave river 319
    Vittorio Veneto 247, 313, **318–19**
Italy
    civilian hardships 199
    colonies 77
    enters the war **106–07**
    fascism 343, 345
    invasion of Libya 17, 25
    Italo-Turkish War 15, 25, 74, 106
    nationalism 107
    neutrality 31
    postwar 333, 344
    territorial ambitions 106
    Triple Alliance 14, 31
Ivangorod 70
Izzet, General Ahmed 317

J

Jack, Richard 103
Jagdgeschwader (Flying Circus) 189
Jameson Raid 21
Japan
    Anglo-Japanese alliance 14
    convoy escort duties 257
    declares war 31, 84
    intervention in Russia 300, 301
    postwar 334
    pre-war 16
    Russo-Japanese War 14, 25, 60, 145, 187
    territorial ambitions 84, 85, 300
    Tsingtao expedition 84–85
Jassin 254
Jaurès, Jean 32
Jean Bart French battleship 256

Jeddah 196
Jellicoe, Admiral John 78, 79, 170, 171, 220,
    221
Jerusalem 109, 258, 259, 316
jingoism 17, 32
Joffre, General Joseph 15, 22, 41, 44, 45, 46,
    56–57, 58, 145, 158, 159, 290, 291
    and Artois-Loos Offensive 98, 142, 143
    and Battle of the Marne 54, 55, 56, 57
    biography 57
    and Champagne Offensive 57, 98, 142–43,
        154
    character and qualities 56, 57
    and the Great Retreat 52, 53, 57
    Marshal of France 57, 287
    Plan XVII 44, 45, 56, 57
    relations with British allies 57
    replaced by Nivelle 57
    and Verdun 57, 154, 155, 160
    and Ypres 60, 61
Jonas, Lucien 284
July Days 235, 252
Jünger, Ernst 303
Junkers J4 273
Jutland, Battle of 125, 145, 166, **170–73**

K

Kaiser Wilhelmsland 39, 85
Kaiserjäger 68
Kamerun 76, 77, 255
Kaulbach, Friedrich August von 31
Kellogg-Briand Pact 345
Kemal, Mustafa (Ataturk) 112, 259, 317, 343
Kent, Thomas 164
Kerensky, Alexander 234, 235, 252
Kerensky Offensive 169, 195, 211, **234–37**, 248
Keyes, Vice-Admiral Roger 292, 293
Keynes, J.M. 339
Khalil Pasha, General 123
Kiel 321
Kindermord 61
Kingdom of Serbs, Croats and Slovenes 169, 334
Kingdom of Transjordan (Jordan) 197
King's African Rifles 38, 76, 77, 255
Kipling, John 143
Kipling, Rudyard 143, 302
Kitchener, Lord 33, 46, 52, 110, 113, 119,
    142, 176, 177
Kluck, General Alexander von 46, 53, 54, 55
Kolchak, Admiral Alexander 300, 301, 342
Kollwitz, Käthe 61, 350
Komarow, Battle of 73
Königgrätz, Battle of 66
Kornilov, General Lavr 235, 252
Kosovo 141
Kostiuchnowka, Battle of 168
Kriemhilde Stellung 309, 312
Kruger, Paul 21
Krupp 202
Kuhl, General Hermann von 241
Kun, Bela 333
Kurds 116, 117
Kut al-Amara 119, 122, 123, 258

L

La Bassée, Battle of 59, 60, 119
La Voie Sacrée 155, 160
labour unrest 269
    see also strikes
Lafayette Escadrille 131
Laffert, General Maximilian von 239
Lake Doiran 316
Lake Naroch offensive 174
Landships Committee 250, 251
Langemarck 60, 241
Langemark German War Cemetery 349
Lanrezac, General Charles 44, 45, 46, 47, 57
Lansing, Robert 131
Latvia 277
Lausanne, Treaty of 334, 343
Lawrence, T.E. (Lawrence of Arabia) 196,
    197, 258, 317, 334
Le Bonnet Rouge 167
Le Cateau, Battle of 47
League of Nations 85, 215, 255, 334, 338,
    339, 343, 344
League of the Three Emperors 14, 18, 197

Lebanon 197
Lee-Enfield rifle 24, 231
Leman, General Gérard 42
Lemberg 69
Lenin, Vladimir Ilyich 33, 167, 211, 218,
    235, 243, 252, 253, 276–77, 343
Léon Gambetta cruiser 256
Leopold of Bavaria, Prince 276
Lettow-Vorbeck, Lieutenant Colonel Paul
    von 76, 77, 254, 255
Lewis, Percy Wyndham 261
liberty bonds 216, 217
Liberty Memorial, Kansas City 356–57
Libya 15, 25
    Italian invasion of 17, 188
Liebknecht, Karl 33, 218, 320
Liège 42, 167, 223
Liggett, General Hunter 308, 309
Lille 59, 313
Liman von Sanders, General Otto 19, 74
Limonova 71
Lithuania 135, 277
Lloyd George, David 199, **200–201**, 224, 230,
    240, 258, 323, 344
    becomes prime minister 201
    biography 201
    domestic politics 200, 201
    munitions minister 93, 103, 201
    and Paris Peace Conference 201, 334, 335
    relations with generals 179, 201
    and Treaty of Versailles 338
    war, support for 210
Locarno Treaty 343
Lochnagar crater 181
Lody, Carl 167
Lodz, Battle of 70–71
London, bombing of 132, 232
London, Treaty of 15, 31, 42, 107
Lone Pine, Battle of 109, 112, **114–15**
Loos, Battle of 103, 105, 119, 177, 178, 179
"Lost Battalion" 309
"Lost Generation" 303
Louvain 43
Lowestoft 170
Ludendorff, General Erich 4, 21, 66, 67, 70,
    71, 134, 135, 153, 209, **222–23**, 276,
    320, 321
    and Amiens 305
    biography 223
    character and qualities 67, 222
    and Falkenhayn 23, 67, 134–35
    and German economic and diplomatic
        policies 202, 203, 223
    and Hindenburg 66, 67
    and invasion of Belgium 42, 222–23
    and Lys Offensive 282, 283
    and Michael Offensive 278, 279
    and Second Battle of the Marne 285, 286,
        287
    and Tannenberg 64, 65, 67
Ludendorff Donation Fund 222
Lüderitz 76
Luftwaffe 189, 295
Lusitania, sinking of the 79, 89, **126–27**, 131,
    213, 214, 220
Lutsk 175
Luxemburg, Rosa 33, 218, 320
Luxembourg 42
LVG reconnaissance aircraft 294
Lvov, Prince Giorgi 211
Lys Offensive 279, **282–83**

M

McCrae, John 102
Macedonia 316
machine-guns 15, 24, 25, **138–39**, 227, 241,
    252
Mackensen, General August von 70, 71, 135,
    140, 194, 195
MacMahon, Sir Henry 196
MacNeill, Eoin 164
Madras 83
Maginot Line 159
Mahiwa, Battle of 255
Makhno, Nestor 342
malnutrition 195, 198, 268, 269, 271, 332, 333
Malta 256
Malvy, Louis-Jean 167, 337
Mametz Wood 181
Manchuria 85
Mangin, General Charles 118, 119, 160, 161,
    286, 305

Mann, Thomas 302, 303
Mannheim 295
maps
    world in 1914 38–39
    world in 1915 88–89
    world in 1916 148–49
    world in 1917 206–07
    world in 1918 264
    world in 1919–1923 328–29
Marasesti, Battle of 355
Marconi, Guglielmo 145
Mariana Islands 82, 85
Maritz, Solomon 77
Maritz Rebellion 77
Marne
    First Battle of the 23, 53, **54–55**, 56, 57,
        145, 291
    Second Battle of the 279, 283, 285,
        286–87, 291, 312
Marshall, Colonel George 307, 311
Marshall Islands 85
Martini-Henry rifle 196–97
Marwitz, General Georg von der 279
Masaryk, Tomas 169
Masurian Lakes, battles of the 65, 134, 223
Mata Hari 167
Matz, Battle of 283, 285
Maubeuge 52, 58
Maude, General Sir Stanley 123
Maunoury, General Michel-Joseph 54
Mauser rifle 164
Maxim, Sir Hiram 25
Maxim guns 14, 24, 25
Maxwell, General Sir John 165
Mears, F.J. 238
Mecca 196
medals
    British 112, 170
    French 31
    German 44, 298
    Italian 19
    Japanese 85
medical treatment **186–87**
Medina 196
Mediterranean, war in the 78, **256–57**
Megiddo, Battle of 316
Mehmed V, Sultan 15, 74–75, 119, 196
memorials, monuments, and museums 117,
    161, 239, 255, 348–57
    see also cemeteries
Menin Gate 349
Menin Road 60, 242
merchant shipping 82–83, 126, 127, 213,
    220–21, 256–57
    convoy system 201, 220, 221, 257
Mercier, Cardinal 202, 203
Mesopotamia 75, 119, **122–23**, 197, 317, 334
Messines, Battle of 109, 227, **238–39**, 248
Messines Battlefield and Memorials 349
Metz 306
Meuse-Argonne American Cemetery and
    Memorial 352
Meuse-Argonne Offensive 285, 305, 306,
    307, **308–09**, 311, 312
Mexico 166–67, 213
Meyer-Waldeck, Alfred 85
Mézières 323
Michael Offensive 277, **278–81**, 282
    see also Spring Offensives
Middle East, war in the *see* Arab Revolt;
    Caucasian campaigns; Gallipoli
    Campaign; Mesopotamia; Palestine
Military History Museum, Austria 348
Military Service Act 177
military technology **24–25**, **272–73**
    see also aircraft; airships; artillery;
        dreadnoughts; tanks; weapons
mines 25, 78, 79, 238, 239, 292
minesweepers 110
Mitchell, General Billy 295, 307
mobilization 22, 33
Moldavia 195
Moltke, General Helmuth von 21, 22, 30, 31,
    42, 45, 53, 54–55, 57, 58, 95, 223
Monash, General Sir John 108, 109, 242,
    304, 313
Monastir 194
Monchy-le-Preux 73
Monro, General Sir Charles 113
Mons, Battle of **46–49**
Montagu, Edwin 119
Montenegro 15, 19
Montfaucon d'Argonne 309
Moravia 319

Morgenthau, Henry 117
Morocco
    First Moroccan Crisis 14, 17, 18, 21, 201
    Rif Rebellion 159, 342
    Second Moroccan Crisis 12, 15, 17
    troops 45, 54
Morse Code 144, 145
mortars 50, 51
Moscow 253, 300
Mosul 123, 317
Mulhouse 44
Müller, Captain Karl von 82–83
munitions production
    Britain 92, 93
    France 93, 119
    Germany 93, 202
    USA 13, 130
Murmansk 300, 301
Murray, General Archibald 258
Musée de l'Armée, Paris 352
Muslims 122, 196
    troops 119
    see also Turkey
Mussolini, Benito 343, 345
mustard gas 105, 243
mutinies
    Canadian 332
    French 159, 161, 199, 225
    German 293, 320–21
    Indian troops 89, 119

N

Namibia 255
    see also German South West Africa
Namur 42
Nancy 52, 132
Napoleonic Wars 24
Nash, Paul 244, 260
National Defense Act 131, 216
national self-determination 334, 338
National War Memorial (Newfoundland)
    351
National War Memorial (Ottawa) 351
nationalism
    Arab 75, 196–97
    Armenian 75, 116, 117
    Czech 169
    German 20, 67, 202, 223, 332–33
    Irish 164–65
    Italian 107
    Polish 168–69
    Russian 342
    Slav 18–19, 28, 29, 153, 168–69
    Turkish 19, 117, 343
Naumann, Friedrich 202
Naumann, Captain Heinrich 255
Nauru 85
    naval conflicts 78–79
    Coronel 83
    Dogger Bank 79, 88, 124–25
    Falklands 39, 83, 124, 126
    Heligoland Bight 78, 124
    Jutland 125, 145, 166, 170–73
    see also submarine warfare
Nazi Party 203, 223, 343, 345
Nek 109, 113
Netherlands 167, 333
neutrality 22
Neuilly, Treaty of 317, 334
neutrality 22, 31, 167
Neuve Chapelle, Battle of 98–99, 103, 119,
    179
Neuville-St-Vaast German War Cemetery
    353
New Zealand 85
    centenary events 358
    conscription 108
New Zealand Expeditionary Force 108, 109
    troops 108–09, 110–15, 242, 259, 358
Newfoundland Regiment 230, 231, 362
newsreels 261
Nicaragua 130
Nicholas II, Tsar 15, 31, 33, 135, 153, 174,
    198, 300
    abdication 210, 300
    execution 211, 300
Nieuport 11 "Bébé" 188
Nikolai Nikolaievich, Grand Duke 70
Nivelle, General Robert 57, 159, 226
    biography 225
    dismissed 225

Nivelle Offensive 153, 159, 224–25, 227
    and Verdun 160, 161, 224
Nixon, General Sir John 122
No Man's Land 94, 95, 119
North Sea, war in the 78–79, 88, 124–25,
    126, 145, 166, 170–73
Norway 333
Notre Dame de Lorette 353
novelists and poets 302–03
Nungesser, Charles 189
Nur ud-Din Pasha 123
nurses 186, 187

O

observation balloons 145
Odessa 74, 301, 342
oil fields 75
Old Contemptibles 61
    see also British army, British Expeditionary
    Force (BEF)
Omdurman 179
Operation Georgette see Lys Offensive
Orlando, Vittorio 247, 334, 335
Orpen, William 261, 335
Ostende 293
Otranto barrage 257
Ottoman Empire
    decline of 17, 19, 74
    dismembered 317
    see also Turkey
Owen, Wilfred 303, 323

P

Pacific, war in the 39, 84–85
pacifism 345
    see also anti-war groups
Painlevé, Paul 337
Palestine 73, 109, 119, 152, 197, 258–59,
    313, 316–17, 334
    division of 197
    occupation of Jerusalem 259, 316
Pals' Battalions 177, 181
Pankhurst, Emmeline 33
Papen, Franz von 131
parachutes 189, 295
Paris
    aerial bombing 268, 295
    defence of 38, 52
    long-range bombardment of 279
Paris Peace Conference 85, 197, 201, 215,
    291, 311, 323, 328, 334–35, 337
Passchendaele, see Ypres, Third Battle of
Passchendaele Battlefield memorials 349
Patch, Harry 345
patriotism 17, 33, 67, 302
Patton, Colonel George 307
peace initiatives 152–53, 218–19, 313
Peace of Riga 334
Peace Pledge Union 345
peace treaties 334
    see also Armistice
Pearse, Patrick 164, 165
Péguy, Charles 303
Penang 83
penicillin 187
Pershing, General Jack 149, 213, 217, 285,
    291, 310–11, 320
    and Armistice 322
    biography 311
    character and qualities 310, 311
    distrust of Europe 310–11
    and Meuse-Argonne Offensive 308, 309, 311
    pre-war combat experience 310
    and St Mihiel Salient 306
Persia 75, 122
Pétain, General Philippe 103, 158–59, 285,
    286, 287
    and Artois Offensive 158
    biography 159
    character and qualities 158
    commander-in-chief 225
    and Spring Offensives 279
    and Verdun 155, 158–59
Peter I, King of Serbia 140, 141
Petrograd 199, 210, 211, 234, 235, 252, 253,
    300
Philip, Prince of Eulenberg 21

Philippines 130
phosgene 105, 279
photography 260–61
photo-reconnaissance 98, 145, 152, 227, 292
Piave River, Battle of the 319
Pilsudski, Jozef 70, 168, 169, 319, 343
pistols 101, 143, 203
plastic surgery 187
Pless Convention 140
Ploesti 195
Plumer, General Herbert 103, 238, 239, 242,
    283
Pohl, Admiral Hugo von 125
poilus 155
Poincaré, Raymond 30, 32, 33, 57, 337
poison gas see chemical warfare
Pola 257
Poland 69, 70–71, 152, 319, 333, 339, 343
    18th-century partition of 168
    deportations 202
    Germanization programme 203
    independence 169, 334
    nationalism 168–69
Polish Legions 70, 168, 169
Russian Poland 70, 168, 169
    Russian retreat from 135, 169
    Russo-Polish War 73, 343
Polar Bear Expedition 301
poppies, Tower of London 358, 360–61
Portugal 152, 282–83
    colonies 77
Portuguese Expeditionary Force 283
posters 79, 93, 128–29, 131, 159, 176, 177, 203,
    216, 231, 234, 265, 285, 295, 306, 320
postwar conflicts 342–43
Potiorek, Oskar 68
Potorièes 109, 184–85
POWs see prisoners of war
Preparedness Movement 130, 131, 216
Price, Private George 231, 323
Princess Patricia's Canadian Light Infantry
    230, 231
Princip, Gavrilo 28, 29
prisoners of war
    Austro-Hungarian 319
    British 281
    German 242, 305, 333
    Portuguese 283
    release 332
    Russian 202
Prittwitz, General Maximilian 64
profiteering 93, 199, 269, 323
propaganda
    art and photography as tools of 260, 261
    Bolshevik 300
    British 47
    French 44
    German 12, 67
    posters see posters
    writers 302
Prussia
    Austro-Prussian War 66
    Franco-Prussian War 14, 16, 24, 25, 66,
    67, 187, 290, 339
    Prussian War Academy 22
    see also East Prussia
Przemysl 69, 71, 134, 135
psychiatric medicine 187
Putnik, Field Marshal Radomir 68, 141

Q

Q-ships 127
Qurna 122

R

Race to the Sea 58–59, 60, 73
radio communication 25, 144, 232
railway networks 22, 24, 25, 238
Ramleh CWGC Cemetery 354
Rasputin, Grigori 149, 198, 199, 210
Rathenau, Walther 93
rationing
    Austria-Hungary 268
    Britain 221, 268
    Germany 198

Rawlinson, General Sir Henry 180–81, 184,
    250, 304
Raynal, Major Sylvain-Eugène 160
reconnaissance aircraft 145, 152, 188, 227,
    255, 257, 294, 295
    observers 188, 294
    photo-reconnaissance 98, 145, 152, 227,
    292
Red Army 276, 301, 342–43
Red Baron, see Richthofen, Manfred von
Red Cross 187
Red Guard 252
Redel, Colonel Alfred 167
Redmond, John 33, 164
refugees
    Armenian 88, 116, 117
    Belgian 42, 53
    East Prussian 64
    French 53
    Serbian 141
Reims 52, 58, 286, 287
Remarque, Erich 303
Remembrance Day 344, 345
remembrance poppies 179
Rennenkampf, General Paul von 64, 65
reparations 334, 339, 343
reserved occupations
    Britain 93, 177
    USA 216
reservists 22, 60
resistance movements 167
    Belgium 43, 167
    France 167
    see also governments-in-exile
revolutionary upheaval
    Arab Revolt 148, 196–97
    Germany 320–21, 322, 332, 338
    Irish War of Independence 342
    Russia 117, 128, 153, 197, 199, 218,
    252–53, 268
revolvers 175, 312
Rhineland 291, 332, 339
Richthofen, Manfred von (Red Baron) 189,
    227, 297, 298–99
Rickenbacker, Eddie 189, 297, 306
Rider-Rider, William 260
rifles 14, 24, 25, 26–27, 72, 113, 138, 139,
    164, 196–97, 225, 250
Riga, Battle of 95, 235, 252, 273
Rizzo, Luigi 256
RMS Leinster 221, 320
Robeck, Admiral John de 110
Robertson, General Sir William 201, 240, 257
Robinson, Lieutenant William Leefe 132
rockets 145
Rohr, Captain Willy 273
Romania 203, 218, 234
    Balkan Wars 15, 19
    civilian hardships 195
    enters the war 175, 194
    invasion of 152, 194–95, 234
    territorial ambitions 194
Rome, Treaty of 334
Rommel, Lieutenant Erwin 246, 247
Roosevelt, Theodore 131
Rosenberg, Isaac 303
Royal Air Force 189, 232, 295
Royal Australian Navy 83
Royal Flying Corps 227, 231, 259
    see also air combat
Royal Marines 292–93
Royal Museum of the Armed Forces and of
    Military History 349
Royal Navy 18, 23, 30, 78–79, 80, 127
    and the Arab Revolt 196, 197
    British Naval Intelligence Division 166,
    167
    East African operations 77, 82
    Gallipoli 110–11
    naval blockades 38, 79, 82, 93, 124, 126,
    131, 198, 322, 333
Royal Naval Air Service 79
    South Atlantic Squadron 83
    Zeebrugge Raid 221, 292–93
    see also naval conflicts; submarine warfare
Ruhr, Franco-Belgian occupation of 339, 343
Rumpler C.VII 295
runners (messengers) 145
Rupprecht, Crown Prince of Bavaria 44, 99,
    104, 241, 242
Russell, Bertrand 218
Russia
    Allied intervention in 300–301
    anti-war groups 33, 167, 234
    armed forces, mobilization 15, 23, 30, 33, 64

Russia (cont.)
Balkan policy 18–19, 30
Bolshevik Revolution 117, 128, 153, 197, 199, 218, **252–53**, 268
Bolsheviks *see* Bolsheviks
Brest-Litovsk Peace Treaty 203, 218, 235, **276–77**
civilian hardships 198–99, 211
declares war on Turkey 38, 74
exit from the war 153, 276–77, 278
Franco-Russian alliance 14, 30
invasion of East Prussia 64
League of the Three Emperors 14, 18
monarchy 17
nationalism 342
overthrow of tsarist regime **210–11**, 213, 218
postwar 342–43
pre-World War I 14, 15, 16, 17
Provisional Government 207, 211, 234, 235, 252
Russian Civil War 73, 169, 174, 253, 265, 277, 342–43
Russo-Japanese War 14, 25, 60, 145, 187
Russo-Polish War 73, 343
social and political solidarity 33
war economy 93
war planning **22–23**
see also Russian army; and specific campaigns and battles
Russian army
Fifth Army 71
First Army 65
Red Army 276, 301, 342–43
Second Army 64, 65
Tenth Army 134
Third Army 135

S

Saarland 339
sabotage 131, 195, 213
Sacrario Militare di Redipuglia 354
St George's Memorial Church 350
St Julien Memorial 349–50
St Mihiel Salient 251, 265, 285, 295, 305, **306–07**
St Quentin Canal 249, 312–13
Salandra, Antonio 106–07
Salonika 141, 256
Sambre, Battle of the 45
Samoa 85
Samsonov, General Alexander 64, 65
Sanctuary Wood Cemetery and Museum Hill 62 350
Sarajevo assassinations **28–29**
Sargent, John Singer 261, 288
Sarikamish, Battle of 74, 75, 116
Sarrail, General Maurice 141, 194
Sassoon, Siegfried 218, 303
Sazonov, Sergei 30
Scapa Flow 339
Scarborough 79
Scheer, Admiral Reinhard 170, 171
Scheidemann, Philipp 321, 339
Schleswig 339
Schlieffen, Alfred von 14, 22, 44
Schlieffen Plan 14, 22, 31, 42, 44, 52, 55, 64, 222
Schütte-Lanz airships 132
Schutztruppe 76, 77, 254, 255
Schwieger, Captain Walther 126
"scientific warfare" 291
Scimitar Hill, Battle of 113
scorched-earth tactics 135, 169, 224, 255
Scottish National War Memorial 356
Scramble for Africa 76
seaplanes 79
Sebastopol 74
Sedan 307, 309
Seeger, Alan 131
Selle, Battle of 313
semaphore 145
Serbia
Austria-Hungary, pre-war relations with 19
Austro-Hungarian invasion of 68
Balkan Wars 15, 17
Bulgarian invasion of 98
defeat of 107, 135, **140–41**, 152
invasion of Bosnia 68, 69
liberation 141
and the Sarajevo assassination **28–29**, 30

Sèvres, Treaty of 117, 317, 334, 342
shells 24–25, 50, 105, 171, 226, 228–29
shell shock 187
shortages 93, 103, 104
shrapnel 50
Shrine of Remembrance, Australia 348
Siberia 342
Sidi Bair 112, 113
Siegfriedstellung 248, 312
Sikorski, Igor 24
Silesia 69, 70
Singapore Mutiny 119
Sinn Fein 165, 342
Slav nationalism 18–19, 28, 29, 153, **168–69**
slave labour see forced labour
Smith-Dorrien, General Sir Horace 47, 103
smoke helmets 105
SMS *Blücher* 124, 125
SMS *Breslau* 74, 75, 124, 256, 257
SMS *Derfflinger* 124, 125, 172–73
SMS *Dresden* 83
SMS *Emden* 82–83
SMS *Gneisenau* 82, 83
SMS *Goeben* 74, 75, 124, 256, 257
SMS *Karlsruhe* 82
SMS *Königsberg* 76, 77, 82, 254, 255
SMS *Moltke* 124, 125
SMS *Novara* 257
SMS *Panther* 18
SMS *Pommern* 171
SMS *Scharnhorst* 82, 83
SMS *Seydlitz* 124, 125
SMS *Szent István* 256, 257
SMS *Wien* 257
Smuts, General Jan 77, 232, 254–55
social and political solidarity 32–33, 198, 199
socialism 17, 269
France 32, 33, 225
Germany 32, 67, 199, 218, 320, 321
USA 217
Solomon Islands 85
Somme Battlefield 353–54
Somme Offensive 73, 95, 109, 148, 155, 177, 179, **180–85**, 230, 231, 272
centenary 362–63
The Battle of the Somme (newsreel) 261
Sonnino, Giorgio 107
Sopwith Camel 192, 232, 295
Souchon, Rear Admiral Wilhelm 74, 75
South Africa 76, 77
South African troops 73, 77, 184, 254, 255
South Atlantic Squadron 83
South Tyrol 319
Spanish influenza 186, 269
Spartacus League 33, 218, 320
Spectra installation 358
Spee, Admiral Maximilian Graf von 82, 83
Spring Offensives 67, 95, 159, 201, 223, 277, **278–79, 282–83**, 286
SS *Glitra* 126
SS *Kronprinz Wilhelm* 83
SS *Sussex* 215, 220
St-Germain-en-Laye, Treaty of 319, 334
Stalin, Joseph 211
Stefanik, Milan 169
Stevenson, Frances 200
Stinktruppe 104
Stopford, General Frederick 112
stormtroopers 249, 272, 273, 274–75, 279, 281, 283, 287
Strasser, Captain Peter 132
stretcher-bearers 177, 186
strikes 199, 218, 268, 269, 337
Sturdee, Vice Admiral Frederick 83
submarine warfare
Austro-Hungarian submarines 257
ending of 320
long-range U-boats 221
Lusitania, sinking of the 79, 89, **126–27**, 131, 213, 214, 220
merchant ships, sinking of 82–83, 126, 127, 206, 213, **220–21**, 256, 257
prize rules 126, 127
U-boat guns 221
U-boat losses 221
unrestricted 21, 79, 124, 126–27, 131, 153, 171, 213, 215, **220–21**, 223, 256–57
submarines 14, 25, 30, 127
submarine pens 292–93
Suez Canal 75, 122
suffragettes 15, 17, 32, 33
Suvla Bay 112, 113

Swakopmund 76
Swinton, Colonel Ernest 250
Switzerland 167
swords, ceremonial 255
Sykes, Sir Mark 197
Sykes-Picot Agreement 197
Syria 73, 75, 109, 197, 334, 342

T

Talaat Pasha 74, 117
Tamines 42
Tanga, Battle of 76, 119, 254
tanks 179, **250–51**
Amiens 251, 304–05
anti-tank rifles 250
British 184, 185, 248–49, 250, 304
Cambrai 248–49, 251
French 225, 250, 286, 307
German 250, 251
Nivelle Offensive 225, 251
St Mihiel 251, 307
Second Battle of the Marne 286, 287
Somme 185, 250
tank crews 250–51
Ypres 242, 251
Tannenberg, Battle of 38, **64–65**, 67, 145, 223
Taube monoplane 64
"taxis of the Marne" 54
tear gas 104, 279
tetanus 187
Thiepval 185
Thiepval Memorial to the Missing 354, 362
Three Year Law 19
timelines
1870–1914 14–15
1914 40–41
1915 90–91
1916 150–51
1917 208–09
1918 266–67
Tirailleurs Annamites 119, 207
Tirailleurs Sénégalais 118, 119
Tirpitz, Admiral Alfred von 18, 21
Tisza, Count István 29
TNT 25
Togoland 76, 255
torpedoes 25, 79, 130, 171
total war concept 8, 337
Tower of London red poppies 358, 360–61
Townshend, General Sir Charles 122–23
Trabzon 117
trade blockades 152, 198, 339
trade unions 33, 201, 202, 268, 269
Trans-Siberian Railway 300, 301
Transylvania 194, 195
Trebizond 73
trench warfare 55, 59, 60, 61, **94–97**, 98, 152
casualties 95
saps (short trenches) 94, 226
trench construction 94
trench fever 186
trench foot 95
weaponry **100–101**
Trenchard, General Hugh 227, 232, 295
Trentino 106, 107, 246, 247, 319
Trevelyan, G.M. 319
Trianon, Treaty of 319, 334
Trieste 257, 319
Triple Alliance 14, 31
Trotsky, Leon 235, 252, 253, 276, 342
Trouée de Charmes 291
Tsingtao 39, 84, 85, 334
Tudor, General Hugh 248
Tunisia 45
tunnelling 238
Turkey (Ottoman Empire)
and the Arab Revolt **196–97**
Armenian massacre **116–17**
armistice 259, 317
Balkan Wars 15
defeat in Palestine 313, 316–17
enters the war 31, 38, **74–75**
Gallipoli 94, 95, 99, 108, 109, **110–15**, 119, 187
Gallipoli Campaign centenary 358
Greco-Turkish War 343
Italo-Turkish War 15, 25, 74, 106
jihad (holy war) 75, 119, 196
Mesopotamian campaign 122–23

Turkey (Ottoman Empire) (cont.)
nationalism 19, 117, 343
navy 74, 256, 257
Palestinian operations 258–59, 313, 316–17
postwar 333, 343
Treaty of Lausanne 334, 343
Treaty of Sèvres 117, 317, 334, 342
Turkish Republic 112, 317, 343
Young Turks 15, 19, 74, 75, 317
Turnip Winter 198, 268
Tyne Cot Cemetery 350, 358, 359
typhus 71, 187, 333

U

U-boats see submarine warfare; submarines
Uganda railway 254
Ukraine 276, 277, 342, 343
Ulster Volunteer Force (UVF) 33, 164, 239
Umberto I, King of Italy 17
uniforms
Australian 82, 108–09
Austrian 72
British 46–47, 72, 188–89
Canadian 230
cavalry 72
French 44–45, 72
German 21, 43, 70, 72, 77, 293
Italian 107, 247
naval 82, 217, 293
pilots 188–89
Russian 135
servicewomen 217
stormtroopers 274, 275
Turkish 113
US 217, 306
Unknown Warrior 344, 345, 351, 362
US army
African-American troops 131, 216, 287, 308
Air Service 307
American Expeditionary Force (AEF) 213, 217, 285, 286, 287, 305, 306–07, 308–09, 310
First Army 306, 308, 309, 311, 312
Second Army 309, 311
standing army 130, 131
Tank Corps 128
USA **130–31**
aircraft industry 294
anti-war groups 131, 216–17
Associate Power status 213
casualties 285, 287, 307
conscription 216
declares war on Austria-Hungary 247
enters the war 127, 153, 207, **212–13**, 215
first military actions 285, 287
industrial capacity 130, 131
intervention in Russia 301
isolationism 345
mobilization 282
munitions production 13, 130
National Defense Act 131, 216
navy 130
neutrality 31, 39, 130, 131, 213, 214
Preparedness Movement 130, 131, 216
"Red Scare" 333
and the sinking of the *Lusitania* **126–27**, 131
socialism 217
Unknown Warrior 344, 356
volunteer principle 216
war economy 216, 217
war effort **216–17**
war memorials 356
see also US army

V

Van 116–17
Venice 319
Venizelos, Eleftherios 141, 257
Verdun, Battle of 57, 105, 119, 143, 145, 148, 152, **154–57**, 158–59, 160–61, 224
centenary 359
Verona 319
Versailles, Treaty of 105, 132, 189, 291, 295, 321, 323, 334, 337, **338–41**
conditions 338–39

veterans' organizations 345
Vichy regime 159
Vickers gun 25
Vickers "Gunbus" 188
Victor Emmanuel III, King of Italy 107, 343
Victoria, Queen 14, 20
Victoria Crosses 112, 170
Vienna 319
Villa, Pancho 149, 310, 311
Villers-Bretonneux 251, 279
Vilnius 135, 174
Vimy Ridge 207, 226, 231
  centenary 359
Vistula Offensive 70, 135
Vittorio Veneto Offensive 247, 313, **318–19**
Vladivostok 300, 301
Vladslo German War Cemetery 350
Volga famine 343
Voluntary Aid Detachment (VAD) 187

W

war art and artists 31, 48, 99, 102–03, 103, 131, 133, 170, 180–81, 190, 223, 238, 244–45, 258–59, 260, **261**, 284, 288–89, 307
  see also posters
war bonds 93, 128
  Germany 202, 203
  USA 216, 217
war correspondents 285
war economies 93, 269
  Britain 93
  France 93, 119
  Germany 93, 202
  Russia 93
  USA 217
War Resisters International 345
war weariness 201, 211, 218, 234, 268, 301
Warsaw 70, 343
wash kit 259
water bottles 123
Watter, General Oskar von 249
weapons
  anti-aircraft guns 132, 232
  anti-tank rifles 250
  artillery 24, **50–51**

weapons (cont.)
  bayonets 25, 45
  field guns 50, 137, 249, 254, 363
  flamethrowers 160
  grenades 26, 101, 110, 317
  howitzers 50, 51, 154
  incendiary bombs 132
  machine-guns 15, 24, 25, **138–39**, 227, 241, 252
  Maxim guns 14, 24, 25
  mines 25, 78, 79, 238, 239
  mortars 50, 51
  naval guns 79, 80
  pistols 69, 101, 143
  revolvers 175, 312
  rifles 14, 24, 25, **26–27**, 72, 113, 138, 139, 164, 196–97, 225, 250
  shells 24–25, 50, 171, 226, 228–29
  torpedoes 25, 79, 130, 171
  trench warfare weaponry **100–101**
  U-boat guns 221
Weimar Republic 67
Wejh 197
Wells, H.G. 302
Wemyss, Admiral Rosslyn 323
Western Front
  campaigns (1914) 42–49, 52–55, 58–61
  campaigns (1915) 98–99, 102–03, 142–43
  campaigns (1916) 154–57, 158–59, 160–61, 180–85
  campaigns (1917) 224–27, 232–33, 238–45, 248–49
  campaigns (1918) 277–87, 304–09
  Spring Offensives (1918) 277, **278–79**, **282–83**
Western Thrace 317
Wet, Christiaan de 77
Wharton, Edith 302
Whitby 79
White, Victor 131
White Feather movement 177
White Lady resistance network 167
White Russians 300, 301, 342
Whitehead, Robert 25
Wilhelm II, Kaiser 13, 14, 18, **20–21**, 29, 30, 31, 33, 34, 60, 67, 84, 125, 132, 202, 206, 223, 320, 321
  abdication 21, 321
  aggressive militarism 18, 20, 21
  approves unrestricted submarine warfare 21

Wilhelm II, Kaiser (cont.)
  attitude towards Britain 20–21
  biography 21
  character and qualities 20, 21
  and the First Moroccan Crisis 18, 21, 201
Wilhelm, Crown Prince 34, 44, 154, 160
Williams, Christopher 181
Wilson, Woodrow 13, 15, 127, 130, 153, **214–15**, 216, 269, 301, 307, 310, 344
  biography 215
  character and qualities 214
  Fourteen Points 215, 218, 320
  and Paris Peace Conference 201, 215, 334, 335
  Peace Note 153, 213, 214
  takes America into the war **212–13**, 215
  and Treaty of Versailles 338
Windhoek 77
Wintgens, Captain Max 255
wireless telegraphy 25, 144, 145
women
  military service 217, 234, 253
  munitions work 92, 93
  nurses 186, 187
  voting rights 15, 17, 32, 33, 269
war work 92, 93, 128, 199, 201, 268
Women's Social and Political Union (WSPU) 33
Wood, General Leonard 131
Woodville, Richard Caton 48
World War I
  background to **18–19**, **28–29**
  commemoration **344–45**
  deadlock **152–53**
  outbreak of war **30–31**, **34–35**
  peace treaties 334, **338–39**
  postwar conflicts **342–43**
  pre-war period **14**–17
  war planning **22–23**
  war weariness 201, 211, 218, 234, 268, 301
World War II 159, 273, 295, 339
Wrangel, General Pyotr 342
Wright, Wilbur and Orville 14, 25
Württemberg, Albrecht, Duke of 44
Wyllie, William 190

X

xylyl bromide 105

Y

Yenbo 197
Yilderim Force 152, 258–59
York, Alvin C. 308
Young Turks 15, 19, 74, 75, 317
Ypres
  First Battle of 59, **60–61**, 73, 89, 102, 240
  Second Battle of 99, **102–03**, 105, 119, 230–31, 240
  Third Battle of (Passchendaele) 105, 109, 179, 206, 221, 225, 227, 231, 239, **240–45**, 248
  Third Battle of (Passchendaele) centenary 359
Ypres Salient Battlefield 350–51
Yser, Battle of the 59
Yser, flooding of the 59
Yudenich, General Nikolai 73, 117, 342
Yugoslavia 141, 169, 317, 334

Z

Zborov, Battle of 169
Zeebrugge 59
Zeebrugge Raid 221, **292–93**
Zemstvo Union 198
Zeppelin, Count Ferdinand von 25, 132
Zeppelin raids 14, 25, 131, **132–33**, 232, 255
Zeppelin-Staaken "Giant" 232, 233
Zimmermann, Arthur 166, 213
Zimmerman Telegram 131, 166–67, 213
Zionism 197
Zouaves 102, 142

Acknowledgments

The publisher would like to thank the following for their kind permission to reproduce their photographs:

(Key: a-above; b-below/bottom; c-centre; f-far; l-left; r-right; t-top)

1 Dorling Kindersley: Gary Ombler (c). 2-3 Corbis: Hulton-Deutsch Collection. 4 Corbis: Alinari Archives (br); Hulton-Deutsch Collection (l); Bettmann (tc); Manuel Litran (ca). 5 Alamy Images: Interfoto (bl). Corbis: Hulton-Deutsch Collection (c). Photo Scala, Florence: The Print Collector (br). 8-9 TopFoto.co.uk: The Granger Collection. 10-11 Dorling Kindersley: Gary Ombler / Collection of Jean-Pierre Verney. 12 akg-images: (crb). Getty Images: Imagno (tl, clb); Topical Press Agency (cb). Mary Evans Picture Library: Interfoto (tr).13 Corbis: Bettmann (cra). Getty Images: Boyer / Roger Viollet (cb); Hulton Archive (tc). 14 akg-images: (br). Alamy Images: Interfoto (c). Dorling Kindersley: Gary Ombler / Collection of Jean-Pierre Verney (cl); Gary Ombler / Courtesy of the Royal Artillery Historical Trust (bl). Getty Images: Roger Viollet Collection (cra). 15 akg-images: Interfoto (clb). Corbis: Heritage Images (cb); (c); Hulton-Deutsch Collection (br). Getty Images: Paul Thompson / FPG / Hulton Archive (cra). Mary Evans Picture Library:

Grenville Collins Postcard Collection (cla). 16-17 Getty Images: Roger Viollet Collection (t). 16 Dorling Kindersley: Gary Ombler / Collection of Jean-Pierre Verney (cl). Mary Evans Picture Library: Grenville Collins Postcard Collection (bl). 17 Getty Images: Imagno (tc). 18 akg-images: (tr). Getty Images: Imagno (bl). 18-19 Corbis: (b). 19 Getty Images: Topical Press Agency (t). 20 akg-images. Corbis: (bl). 21 akg-images: Interfoto (c). Corbis: (tl). Getty Images: General Photographic Agency (br). 22 Mary Evans Picture Library: Onslow Auctions Limited (tl). 23 Lebrecht Music and Arts: Sueddeutsche Zeitung Photo (t). 24 Dorling Kindersley: Gary Ombler / Collection of Jean-Pierre Verney (cla). Getty Images: Hulton Archive (b). 25 Corbis: Alinari Archives (tl); National Aviation Museum (cb). Dorling Kindersley: Gary Ombler / Courtesy of the Royal Artillery Historical Trust (tr). 26 Dorling Kindersley: Gary Ombler (c, clb); Gary Ombler / Collection of Jean-Pierre Verney (cra); Gary Ombler / © The Board of Trustees of the Armouries (br, cla, cl, ca, bl/a). 26-27 Dorling Kindersley: Gary Ombler / © The Board of Trustees of the Armouries (t). 27 Dorling Kindersley: Gary Ombler / © The Board of Trustees of the Armouries (cb, c); Gary Ombler / Collection of Jean-Pierre Verney (fbl); Tim Ridley / Courtesy of the Ministry of Defence Pattern Room, Nottingham (ca).

Toucan Books Ltd: Imperial War Museum / Norman Brand (br). 28 Corbis: Bettmann (b); Hulton-Deutsch Collection (cla). 29 Corbis: Bettmann (bl). Getty Images: Dieter Nagl / AFP (tl); Imagno (cra). 30 Getty Images: Paul Thompson / FPG / Hulton Archive (tr); Topical Press Agency (b). 31 Dorling Kindersley: Gary Ombler / Collection of Jean-Pierre Verney (cr). Mary Evans Picture Library: Interfoto (l). 32 Corbis: Heritage Images (bl); Hulton-Deutsch Collection (br). 33 Corbis: Hulton-Deutsch Collection (tl); Reuters / Tobias Schwarz (br). Getty Images: Topical Press Agency (br). 34-35 Corbis: Hulton-Deutsch Collection. 36-37 Lebrecht Music and Arts: Interfoto. 38 akg-images: IAM (clb). The Art Archive: Imperial War Museum (tl). Getty Images: Images of Empire / Universal Images Group (crb); Popperfoto (tr). Lebrecht Music and Arts: RA (cb). 38-39 Corbis: Hulton-Deutsch Collection (t). 39 Alamy Images: The Print Collector (c). Australian War Memorial: Order 6173929 (clb). Lebrecht Music and Arts: Pictures from History / CPAMedia (t). 40 akg-images: Interfoto (c). Alamy Images: Photos 12 (tr). The Bridgeman Art Library: National Army Museum, London (bl). Corbis: Daniel Deme / epa (cr). Dorling Kindersley: Gary Ombler / Collection of Jean-Pierre Verney (cla). Getty Images: Popperfoto (br). 41 akg-images: Interfoto (c); Interfoto / Hermann

Historica (cr). The Art Archive: Imperial War Museum (crb). Australian War Memorial: Order 6167241 (bc). The Bridgeman Art Library: Musee de l'Armee, Paris, France (cl). 42 Getty Images: Central Press / Hulton Archive (ca). Lebrecht Music and Arts: RA (bl). 43 Dorling Kindersley: Gary Ombler / Collection of Jean-Pierre Verney (r). Getty Images: Hulton Archive (clb). 44 akg-images: (tl); Interfoto / Hermann Historica (bc). Alamy Images: Interfoto (bl). 44-45 Dorling Kindersley: Gary Ombler / Collection of Jean-Pierre Verney. 45 Getty Images: ND / Roger Viollet (br). 46 Getty Images: Hulton Archive (cla). The Stapleton Collection: (bl). 46-47 Dorling Kindersley: Gary Ombler / Courtesy of the Royal Artillery Historical Trust. 47 The Stapleton Collection: (ca, br). 48-49 The Bridgeman Art Library: National Army Museum, London. 50 Dorling Kindersley: Gary Ombler (fcl, tr); Gary Ombler / Courtesy of the Royal Artillery Historical Trust (cra); Gary Ombler / Courtesy of the Royal Museum of the Armed Forces and Military History, Brussels, Belgium (bl, c); Gary Ombler / By kind permission of The Trustees of the Imperial War Museum, London (cl). 50-51 Dorling Kindersley: Gary Ombler / Courtesy of the Royal Museum of the Armed Forces and of Military History, Brussels, Belgium (b). 51 Dorling Kindersley: Gary Ombler / Courtesy of the Royal Artillery Historical Trust (tl, cl); Gary Ombler / Courtesy of the Royal Museum of the Armed Forces and of Military History, Brussels, Belgium (tr, cr, br). **52 akg-images:** IAM (c). **Getty Images:** Popperfoto (b). **53 Corbis:** Bettmann (bc). **54 akg-images:** ullstein bild (t). **Lebrecht Music and Arts:** RA (bc). **55 Dorling Kindersley:** Imperial War Museum, London (tr). **56 Mary Evans Picture Library:** Rue des Archives / Tallandier (l). **57 Getty Images:** Popperfoto (tc). **Lebrecht Music and Arts:** leemage (br). **RMN:** Paris - Musée de l'Armée, Dist. RMN-GP / Emilie Cambier (bc). **58 Getty Images:** Hulton Archive (b); Topical Press Agency (tr). **59 The Bridgeman Art Library:** Musée de l'Armée, Paris, France (br). **60 akg-images:** Interfoto (bc). **Lebrecht Music and Arts:** Interfoto (cl). **60-61 Australian War Memorial:** Order 6167241 (c). **61 Alamy Images:** Arterra Picture Library (br). **Getty Images:** Hulton Archive (tr). **62-63 The Art Archive:** Imperial War Museum. **64 akg-images:** Interfoto (tr). **Getty Images:** Hulton Archive (br). **66 The Bridgeman ArtLibrary:**Heeresgeschichtliche s Museum, Vienna, Austria (bl). **66-67 akg-images:** Interfoto / Hermann Historica. **67 Alamy Images:** Pictorial Press Ltd (br). **Corbis:** Hulton-Deutsch Collection (tc). **68 akg-images:** Imagno (bc). **68-69 Nationaal Archief / Spaarnestad Photo:** Het Leven / Fotograaf onbekend (t). **69 Corbis:** (bl). **Dorling Kindersley:** Gary Ombler / Collection of Jean-Pierre Verney (cr). **70 akg-images:** Interfoto (b). **Alamy Images:** The Print Collector (c). **Getty Images:** Hulton Archive (tl). **71 Dorling Kindersley:** Gary Ombler / Collection of Jean-Pierre Verney (cr). **Mary Evans Picture Library:** AISA Media (b). **72-73 akg-images:** Interfoto (t). **Corbis:** Hulton-Deutsch Collection (b). **73 akg-images:** Interfoto (tr). **Australian War Memorial:** Order 6167241 (bc). **74 The Bridgeman Art Library:** Private Collection (ca). **75 akg-images:** ullstein bild (tr). **74-75 Lebrecht Music and Arts:** RA (b). **76 Dorling Kindersley:** Gary Ombler / Collection of Jean-Pierre Verney (cla). **Getty Images:** Images of Empire / Universal Images Group (b). **77 Alamy Images:** Interfoto (tl). **Getty Images:** Hulton Archive (tr). **78 Corbis:** Bettmann (b). **79 Corbis:** Swim Ink 2, LLC (cr). **Dorling Kindersley:** Gary Ombler / By kind permission of The Trustees of the Imperial War Museum, London (b). **Getty Images:** SSPL (tl). **80 Australian War Memorial:** Order 6183492 (r). **80-81 The Art Archive:** Imperial War Museum. **82 Australian War Memorial:** Order 6180421 (cl). **83 Alamy Images:** The Print Collector (bl). **Dorling Kindersley:** Harry Taylor / Trustees of the National Museums Of Scotland (br). **Lebrecht Music and Arts:** Sueddeutsche Zeitung Photo (tr). **84-85 Lebrecht Music and Arts:** Pictures from History / CPAMedia. **85 Australian War Memorial:** Order 6173929 (tc). **Dorling Kindersley:** Imperial War Museum, London (cr). **86-87 Dorling Kindersley:** Gary Ombler / Courtesy of the Royal Museum of the Armed Forces and Military History, Brussels, Belgium. **88 Alamy Images:** Photos 12 (bc). **The Art Archive:** Imperial War Museum (tc); Marc Charmet (bl). **Getty Images:** Hulton Archive (tl). **Mary Evans Picture Library:** Interfoto / Pulfer (tr). **89 Corbis:** Bettmann (tr). **Corbis:** Lebrecht Authors / Lebrecht Music & Arts (tl). **Lebrecht Music and Arts:** Pictures from History / CPAMedia (bc). **90 Corbis:** Derek Bayes Aspect / Lebrecht Music & Arts (tr); Hulton-Deutsch Collection (cl). **Dorling Kindersley:** Gary Ombler / By kind permission of The Trustees of the Imperial War Museum, London (cr). **Getty Images:** Leemage (br). **Museum Victoria, Melbourne:** Order 18373 (ca). **91 akg-images:** (clb); Interfoto (tr). **The Art Archive:** Imperial War Museum (c). **Dorling Kindersley:** Gary Ombler / Collection of Jean-Pierre Verney (cl); Gary Ombler / By kind permission of The Trustees of the Imperial War Museum, London (br). **TopFoto.co.uk:** Roger Viollet (bl). **92 The Art Archive:** Imperial War Museum. **93 The Art Archive:** Musée des 2 Guerres Mondiales Paris / Gianni Dagli Orti (tr). **Lebrecht Music and Arts:** Sueddeutsche Zeitung Photo (bl). **94 Alamy Images:** Trinity Mirror / Mirrorpix (bl). **Australian War Memorial:** Order 6173929 (c). **94-95 akg-images. 95 Toucan Books Ltd:** Imperial War Museum / Norman Brand (c). **96-97 Corbis. 98 Getty Images:** Popperfoto (cla). **99 The Art Archive:** Imperial War Museum / Eileen Tweedy (t). **Dorling Kindersley:** Imperial War Museum, London (bl). **100 Dorling Kindersley:** Gary Ombler / John Pearce (cl); Imperial War Museum, London (br). **100-101 Dorling Kindersley:** Gary Ombler / Collection of Jean-Pierre Verney. **101 Dorling Kindersley:** Gary Ombler (r, bc); Imperial War Museum, London (tc); Gary Ombler / © The Board of Trustees of the Armouries (cr). **102 Corbis:** Lebrecht Authors / Lebrecht Music & Arts (clb). **102-103 Canadian War Museum (CWM):** Detail of The Second Battle of Ypres, 22 April to 25 May CWM 19710261-0161 Beaverbrook Collection of War Art / www.warmuseum.ca (t). **103 akg-images:** (bl). **Lebrecht Music and Arts:** RA (tr). **104 Dorling Kindersley:** Gary Ombler / By kind permission of The Trustees of the Imperial War Museum, London (tr). **Getty Images:** Hulton Archive (b). **105 Australian War Memorial:** Order 6180421 (c). **Corbis:** Hulton-Deutsch Collection (cra); (tc). **106 Getty Images:** Leemage (tr). **106-107 Corbis:** Hulton-Deutsch Collection (b). **107 akg-images:** Electa (br). **Dorling Kindersley:** Gary Ombler / Collection of Jean-Pierre Verney (tc). **108 Corbis:** Bettmann (bl). **108-109 Australian War Memorial:** Order 6173929 (c). **109 Alamy Images:** Global Travel Writers (r). **Australian War Memorial:** Order 6173929 (cb). **Museum Victoria, Melbourne:** Order 18373 (tc). **110 Corbis:** Bettmann (cra, clb). **Dorling Kindersley:** Gary Ombler / By kind permission of The Trustees of the Imperial War Museum, London (cb). **111 Getty Images:** Philip Schuller / The AGE / Fairfax Media (tr). **112 Getty Images:** Keystone-France / Gamma-Keystone (tc). **112-113 The Art Archive:** Imperial War Museum (b). **Dorling Kindersley:** Gary Ombler / Courtesy of the Royal Artillery Historical Trust (t). **113 Dorling Kindersley:** Gary Ombler / Collection of Jean-Pierre Verney (br). **Getty Images:** Keystone (tr). **114-115 Corbis. 116 Alamy Images:** Photos 12 (b). **117 akg-images:** ullstein bild (tr). **Corbis:** Atlantide Phototravel (br). **Dorling Kindersley:** Gary Ombler / Collection of Jean-Pierre Verney (bl). **118 akg-images:** (tr). **Alamy Images:** Photos 12 (b). **119 Dorling Kindersley:** Gary Ombler / © The Board of Trustees of the Armouries (cr). **Lebrecht Music and Arts:** Pictures from History / CPAMedia (bc). **Mary Evans Picture Library:** Imperial War Museum / Robert Hunt Library (tc). **120-121 Mary Evans Picture Library:** Rue des Archives / Tallandier. **122 Lebrecht Music and Arts:** Sueddeutsche Zeitung Photo (t). **Mary Evans Picture Library:** Imperial War Museum / Robert Hunt Library (tr). **123 Dorling Kindersley:** Gary Ombler / Courtesy of the Royal Artillery Historical Trust (c). **Toucan Books Ltd:** Imperial War Museum / Norman Brand (crb). **124 Mary Evans Picture Library:** Robert Hunt Library (c). **124-125 The Art Archive:** Imperial War Museum (b). **125 Mary Evans Picture Library:** Imperial War Museum / Robert Hunt Library (tl). **Toucan Books Ltd:** Imperial War Museum / Norman Brand (cra). **126 Corbis:** Bettmann (b). **Dorling Kindersley:** Gary Ombler (cl). **127 Corbis:** Hulton-Deutsch Collection (cr). **Dorling Kindersley:** Gary Ombler / By kind permission of The Trustees of the Imperial War Museum, London (tl). **National Maritime Museum, Greenwich, London:** (br). **128 The Art Archive:** Eileen Tweedy (tr); Imperial War Museum / Eileen Tweedy (clb). **Getty Images:** Buyenlarge (bl); DEA / G. Dagli Orti (tc); Universal History Archive (br). **Mary Evans Picture Library:** Interfoto / Pulfer (cr, bc). **129 akg-images:** (tr). **Corbis:** (cl); Heritage Images (bl); K.J. Historical (fbl). **Getty Images:** Archive Photos (br); DEA / G. Dagli Orti (tl); The Bridgeman Art Library (tc). **Smithsonian Institution, Washington, DC, USA:** Armed Forces Division, National Museum of American History, Kenneth E. Behring Center (bc). **130 Getty Images:** Boyer / Roger Viollet (br). **Library Of Congress, Washington, D.C.:** Harris & Ewing Collection (t). **131 Alamy Images:** The Protected Art Archive (cr). **TopFoto.co.uk:** Roger Viollet (tc). **U.S. Air Force:** (bc). **132 Dorling Kindersley:** Imperial War Museum, London (tl). **Getty Images:** Hulton Archive (cra, bl). **133 Corbis:** Derek Bayes Aspect / Lebrecht Music & Arts. **135 akg-images:** (bl). **Alamy Images:** The Print Collector (br). **Dorling Kindersley:** Gary Ombler / Collection of Jean-Pierre Verney (tc). **136-137 Corbis:** Underwood & Underwood. **138 Dorling Kindersley:** Matthew Ward (c); Gary Ombler / © The Board of Trustees of the Armouries (cr). **138-139 Canadian War Museum (CWM):** CWM 19390002-268 (t). **139 Australian War Memorial:** Order 6175160 (tl). **Dorling Kindersley:** Gary Ombler / © The Board of Trustees of the Armouries (br, cr, cl, tr); Gary Ombler / Collection of Jean-Pierre Verney (cla, bl). **140 The Art Archive:** Marc Charmet (b). **Getty Images:** Universal History Archive (tr). **141 Getty Images:** Hulton Archive (br). **Toucan Books Ltd:** Imperial War Museum / Norman Brand (c). **142 Alamy Images:** Military Images (ca). **142-143 Photo Scala, Florence. 143 The Stapleton Collection:** (cra). **144 akg-images:** ullstein bild (b). **145 Alamy Images:** Interfoto (bl). **Dorling Kindersley:** Clive Streeter / Science Museum, London (tl). **Getty Images:** SSPL (cra). **Lebrecht Music and Arts:** Sueddeutsche Zeitung Photo (tc). **146-147 Dorling Kindersley:** Gary Ombler. **148 The Art Archive:** Imperial War Museum (bl). **Corbis:** dpa (bc). **148-149 The Bridgeman Art Library:** Private Collection (t). **Dorling Kindersley:** Anthony Haughey (tl). **Lebrecht Music and Arts:** Sueddeutsche Zeitung Photo (tc). **TopFoto.co.uk:** (br). **149 Getty Images:** MPI (bc). **Lebrecht Music and Arts:** Imagno (tl). **150 Corbis:** (c). **Dorling Kindersley:** Andy Crawford / By kind permission of The Trustees of the Imperial War Museum, London (br); Gary Ombler / Courtesy of the Royal Museum of the Armed Forces and Military History, Brussels, Belgium (cr); Gary Ombler / Collection of Jean-Pierre Verney (cl/a, tr). **Getty Images:** Universal History Archive (bl). **151 Alamy Images:** Pictorial Press Ltd (tl). **The Bridgeman Art Library:** Dublin City Gallery, The Hugh Lane, Ireland (br). **Dorling Kindersley:** Gary Ombler (cr). **Getty Images:** Galerie Bilderwelt (bc); Mansell / Time & Life Pictures (cl). **152 Australian War Memorial:** Order 6185010 (cl). **Dorling Kindersley:** Gary Ombler / Collection of Jean-Pierre Verney (tr). **Getty Images:** Hulton Archive (bl). **152-153 Alamy Images:** Trinity Mirror / Mirrorpix (b). **153 Getty Images:** Hulton Archive (tc). **154 Alamy Images:** Interfoto (t). **Lebrecht Music and Arts:** Sueddeutsche Zeitung Photo (bc). **155 Alamy Images:** Interfoto (cl). **Lebrecht Music and Arts:** RA (tr). **156-157 Lebrecht Music and Arts:** RA. **158 Getty Images:** Universal History Archive (l). **159 akg-images:** (c). **Getty Images:** Apic (bl); Galerie Bilderwelt (crb). **160 Corbis:** adoc-photos (c). **Dorling Kindersley:** Gary Ombler / Courtesy of the Royal Museum of the Armed Forces and Military History, Brussels, Belgium (bl). **161 Alamy Images:** Hemis (bl). **Getty Images:** Galerie Bilderwelt (tl). **162-163 Mary Evans Picture Library:** westernfrontphotography.com. **164 The Bridgeman Art Library:** Private Collection (cl). **Dorling Kindersley:** Anthony Haughey (cla, t). **165 Alamy Images:** Trinity Mirror / Mirrorpix (t). **166 Getty Images:** Hulton Archive (b). **167 Getty Images:** Leemage (cra). **Lebrecht Music and Arts:** RA (bc). **168 Alamy Images:** Interfoto (bc). **169 akg-images:** Rainer Hackenberg (tr). **Getty Images:** Hulton Archive (br). **170 Alamy Images:** Interfoto (br). **The Bridgeman Art Library:** Private Collection (b). **171 Alamy Images:** Mary Evans Picture Library (tr). **Dorling Kindersley:** Andy Crawford / By kind permission of The Trustees of the Imperial War Museum, London (bc); Gary Ombler (t). **172-173 akg-images:** Erich Lessing. **174 akg-images:** RIA Novosti (cl). **Lebrecht Music and Arts:** Imagno (tr). **175 Alamy Images:** Interfoto (c). **Dorling Kindersley:** Gary Ombler / Collection of Jean-Pierre Verney (tr). **176 Corbis:** Daniel Deme / epa (cl). **Getty Images:** Central Press (b). **177 The Art Archive:** Imperial War Museum (br); Musée des 2 Guerres Mondiales Paris / Gianni Dagli Orti (cl). **Getty Images:** Hulton Archive (tr). **178 Getty Images:** Topical Press Agency (r). **hemis.fr:** Francis Cormon (l). **179 Alamy Images:** David Osborn (crb). **Bonhams Auctioneers, London:** (t). **Getty Images:** Topical Press Agency (bc). **180 The Bridgeman Art Library:** National Museum Wales (b). **181 The Art Archive:** Imperial War Museum (cr). **Corbis:** Michael St. Maur Sheil (tr). **Dorling Kindersley:** Gary Ombler / Courtesy of Birmingham Pals (bc). **182-183 Alamy Images:** Pictorial Press Ltd. **184 Cody Images:** (bl). **184-185 Lebrecht Music and Arts:** Sueddeutsche Zeitung Photo (b). **185 Getty Images:** Scott Barbour (cr). **186 Corbis:** (b). **187 Corbis:** (c). **Dorling Kindersley:** Jerry Young (b); Gary Ombler / Collection of Jean-Pierre Verney (crb). **Toucan Books Ltd:** Imperial War Museum / Norman Brand (t). **188 Getty Images:** Fotosearch (bl). **189 Alamy Images:** Classic Image (tr). **Lebrecht Music and Arts:** Sueddeutsche Zeitung Photo (br). **190-191 Ministry of Defence Picture Library:** UK MoD / Crown Copyright 2012. **192 Dorling Kindersley:** Gary Ombler / Courtesy of the Royal Museum of the Armed Forces and of Courtesy of the Royal Museum of the Armed Forces and of Military History, Brussels, Belgium (crb, cl). **192-193 Dorling Kindersley:** Martin Cameron / Courtesy of the Shuttleworth Collection, Bedfordshire (b). **193 Dorling Kindersley:** Gary Ombler (crb, cr); Gary Ombler / Courtesy of the Royal Museum of the Armed Forces and Military History, Brussels, Belgium (cl). **194 Mary Evans Picture Library:** Illustrated London News Ltd (r); Sueddeutsche Zeitung Photo (bl). **195 Lebrecht Music and Arts:** Sueddeutsche Zeitung Photo (bc). **Roland Smithies:** Luped. com (crb). **196 The Art Archive:** Liddell Hart Centre (tr). **Dorling Kindersley:** Gary Ombler / © The Board of Trustees of the Armouries (c). **TopFoto.co.uk:** (b). **197 Alamy Images:** Interfoto (tc). **The Bridgeman Art Library:** The Illustrated London News Picture Library, London, UK (br). **198 Corbis:** dpa (tr); Hulton-Deutsch Collection (bl). **Dorling Kindersley:** Gary Ombler / Collection of Jean-Pierre Verney (tl). **199 The Art Archive:** (b). **200 Getty Images:** Mansell / Time & Life Pictures (l). **201 Corbis:** Hulton-Deutsch Collection (br); Underwood & Underwood (tl). **Mary Evans Picture Library:** (bl). **202 Corbis:** Bettman (tr). **Dorling Kindersley:** Karl Shone (bl). **Getty Images:** Mansell / Time & Life Pictures (br); Popperfoto (cl). **203 akg-images:** (l). **Dorling Kindersley:** Gary Ombler / © The Board of Trustees of the Armouries (cra). **204-205 Dorling Kindersley:** Andy Crawford / By kind permission of The Trustees of the Imperial War Museum, London. **206 akg-images:** (br, c). **The Art Archive:** Imperial War Museum (bl). **Corbis:** (tr). **Getty Images:** Bentley Archive / Popperfoto (tl). **207 Corbis:** (tr); Bettmann (tc). **Getty Images:** DEA / G. Dagli Orti (tl). **Mary Evans Picture Library:** Imperial War Museum / Robert Hunt Library (cb). **208 akg-images:** Interfoto (tl); ullstein bild (b). **Alamy Images:** akg-images (clb). **Dorling Kindersley:** Gary Ombler / Collection of Jean-Pierre Verney (tr, crb). **TopFoto.co.uk:** RIA Novosti (c). **209 Corbis:** (bl). **Getty Images:** Universal History Archive (crb). **Lebrecht Music and Arts:** RA (ca). **Smithsonian Institution, Washington, D.C., USA:** Armed Forces Division, National Museum of American History, Kenneth E. Behring Center (cr). **TopFoto.co.uk:** Imagno (cl). **210 Dorling Kindersley:** Sergio (cl). **210-211 Getty Images:** Popperfoto (b). **211 Dorling Kindersley:** H. Keith Melton, spymuseum.org (br). **Getty Images:**

Popperfoto (tl). **TopFoto.co.uk:** RIA Novosti (tr). **212 Corbis**. **213 Corbis:** Bettmann (cl). **Dorling Kindersley:** Gary Ombler / Collection of Jean-Pierre Verney (br). **214 Corbis:** Bettmann (clb, r). **215 Corbis:** Smithsonian Institution (br). **Getty Images:** Fotosearch (bl); SuperStock (tl). **216 akg-images:** (cra). **217 Corbis:** (t). **Smithsonian Institution, Washington, D.C., USA:** Armed Forces Division, National Museum of American History, Kenneth E. Behring Center (bl). **218 Corbis:** Bettmann (tr). **Getty Images:** Bentley Archive / Popperfoto (bl). **219 Alamy Images:** akg-images. **220 Getty Images:** Time Life Pictures / Mansell / Time Life Pictures (cl). **220-221 Getty Images:** MPI (b). **221 akg-images:** (cla). **Dorling Kindersley:** Gary Ombler / By kind permission of The Trustees of the Imperial War Museum, London (tr). **222 Alamy Images:** akg-images (bl). **Getty Images:** Imagno (r). **223 akg-images:** (tc). **Corbis:** Hulton-Deutsch Collection (bl). **Mary Evans Picture Library:** SZ Photo / Scher (crb). **224 akg-images:** ullstein bild (b). **225 Alamy Images:** World History Archive (tl). **Dorling Kindersley:** Gary Ombler / Collection of Jean-Pierre Verney. **226 Dorling Kindersley:** Gary Ombler / Collection of Jean-Pierre Verney (cr). **226-227 akg-images:** ullstein bild (t). **227 Dorling Kindersley:** Gary Ombler / Collection of Jean-Pierre Verney (cr). **Lebrecht Music and Arts:** RA (bc); Sueddeutsche Zeitung Photo (bl). **228-229 Corbis**. **230 Corbis:** Bettmann (b). **Dorling Kindersley:** Gary Ombler / Collection of Jean-Pierre Verney (tr). **231 The Art Archive:** Culver Pictures (bc). **Corbis:** Reuters / Chris Wattie (br). **Getty Images:** Buyenlarge (tl). **232 akg-images:** ullstein bild (tr). **Dorling Kindersley:** Gary Ombler / Courtesy of Royal Airforce Museum, Hendon (cl); Gary Ombler / Courtesy of the Royal Museum of the Armed Forces and Military History, Brussels, Belgium (b). **233 akg-images:** ullstein bild. **234 Alamy Images:** RIA Novosti (bl). **The Art Archive:** Musée des 2 Guerres Mondiales Paris / Gianni Dagli Orti (r). **234-235 Corbis:** Bettman (b). **235 Corbis:** Hulton-Deutsch Collection (tc). **Dorling Kindersley:** Imperial War Museum, London (r). **236-237 Alamy Images:** The Print Collector. **238 Alamy Images:** The Print Collector (tr). **The Bridgeman Art Library:** Moore-Gwyn Fine Art (bl). **239 Dorling Kindersley:** Gary Ombler / Collection of Jean-Pierre Verney. **Getty Images:** Travel Ink (tr). **240 Dorling Kindersley:** Karl Shone (cla). **241 The Art Archive:** Imperial War Museum (t). **Dorling Kindersley:** Gary Ombler / Collection of Jean-Pierre Verney (b). **242 Canadian War Museum (CWM):** 19390001-759 (r). **242-243 The Art Archive:** (b). **243 Australian War Memorial:** Order 6189723 (tl). **Dorling Kindersley:** Gary Ombler / Collection of Jean-Pierre Verney (cr). **244-245 The Bridgeman Art Library:** The Fine Art Society, London. **246 Corbis:** Hulton-Deutsch Collection (r). **247 Dorling Kindersley:** Gary Ombler / Collection of Jean-Pierre Verney (c). **Getty Images:** Universal History Archive (bl). **248 Mary Evans Picture Library:** Robert Hunt Collection (r). **248-249 Dorling Kindersley:** Gary Ombler / By kind permission of The Trustees of the Imperial War Museum, London (tr). **249 The Art Archive:** (tr). **Dorling Kindersley:** Imperial War Museum, London (br). **250 Alamy Images:** Martin Bennett (tc). **Dorling Kindersley:** Gary Ombler / Courtesy of the Royal Artillery Historical Trust (bl). **250-251 Corbis:** Underwood & Underwood (b). **251 Bovington Tank Museum:** (cra). **Dorling Kindersley:** Andy Crawford / By kind permission of The Trustees of the Imperial War Museum, London (r); Kim Sayer (br). **252 Alamy Images:** ITAR-TASS Photo Agency (bl). **The Art Archive:** Private Collection / CCI (ca). **252-253 Dorling Kindersley:** Imperial War Museum, London (b). **253 akg-images:** Erich Lessing (cr). **The Art Archive:** (tc). **254 akg-images:** Interfoto (bl). **Lebrecht Music and Arts:** Sueddeutsche Zeitung Photo (t). **255 akg-**

images: (tr); ullstein bild (crb). **Alamy Images:** Interfoto (bl). **256 Alamy Images:** Interfoto (cla). **Mary Evans Picture Library:** Robert Hunt Library (c). **256-257 Getty Images:** Hulton Archive (b). **257 Dorling Kindersley:** Karl Shone (cra). **Mary Evans Picture Library:** Robert Hunt Library (tl). **258 akg-images:** (cla). **Alamy Images:** Prisma Bildagentur AG (cra); Yagil Henkin (b). **259 Corbis:** (br). **Dorling Kindersley:** Gary Ombler (tc). **260-261 Dorling Kindersley:** (b). **261 The Art Archive:** Imperial War Museum (cb). **Dorling Kindersley:** Gary Ombler / Collection of Jean-Pierre Verney (cr). **Toucan Books Ltd:** Imperial War Museum / Norman Brand (tl). **262-263 Dorling Kindersley:** Gary Ombler. **264 Corbis:** Bettmann (b). **Getty Images:** Galerie Bilderwelt (tc); ullstein bild (bl). **265 Corbis:** (tr); K.J. Historical (b). **TopFoto.co.uk:** Fine Art Images / Heritage-Images (cr). **266 akg-images:** ullstein bild (cr). **Australian War Memorial:** Order 6191798 (c). **Mary Evans Picture Library:** (cla, cra); **TopFoto.co.uk:** (br); ullstein bild (bc). **267 akg-images:** Interfoto / Hermann Historica (bc). **Corbis:** Reuters / Chris Wattie (br). **Dorling Kindersley:** Gary Ombler / Courtesy of the Royal Museum of the Armed Forces and Military History, Brussels, Belgium (clb). **Lebrecht Music and Arts:** Interfoto (cl). **Library Of Congress, Washington, D.C.:** (tc). **Canadian War Museum (CWM):** The Signing of the Armistice / CMW 19830483-001 Beaverbrook Collection of War Art © Canadian War Museum / www.warmuseum.ca (cr). **268 Getty Images:** A. R. Coster / Topical Press Agency (b); Popperfoto (cla). **269 Corbis:** Bettmann (br). **Dorling Kindersley:** Gary Ombler / By kind permission of The Trustees of the Imperial War Museum, London (bl). **Lebrecht Music and Arts:** Interfoto (tr). **270-271 The Bridgeman Art Library:** SZ Photo / Scherl. **272 The Art Archive:** Imperial War Museum (b). **Australian War Memorial:** Order 6191798 (tr). **273 The Art Archive:** John Meek (cr). **Australian War Memorial:** Order 6203877 (tl). **Dorling Kindersley:** Imperial War Museum, London (bc). **274 Dorling Kindersley:** Gary Ombler (clb, br, tr, b); Gary Ombler / The Board of Trustees of the Armouries (c). **275 akg-images:** Interfoto / Hermann Historica (tl). **Dorling Kindersley:** John Pearce (cra); Gary Ombler / Collection of Jean-Pierre Verney (tc); Gary Ombler / John Pearce (r, c, bc); Gary Ombler / Courtesy of the 5te. Kompagnie Infanterie Regiment nr.28 'Von Goeben' (cl). **276 Corbis:** Hulton-Deutsch Collection (bl). **276-277 akg-images:** ullstein bild (b). **Mary Evans Picture Library:** (cla). **277 akg-images:** ullstein bild (tl). **278 akg-images:** Interfoto (tl). **Australian War Memorial:** Order 6191798 (br). **Dorling Kindersley:** Geoff Dann / Courtesy of David Edge (bl). **279 akg-images:** ullstein bild (bl). **Lebrecht Music and Arts:** Sueddeutsche Zeitung Photo (cra). **280-281 Corbis:** Bettmann. **282 Dorling Kindersley:** Andy Crawford / By kind permission of The Trustees of the Imperial War Museum, London (clb); Gary Ombler / Collection of Jean-Pierre Verney (tr). **283 Mary Evans Picture Library:** (tc); Sueddeutsche Zeitung Photo (br). **284 TopFoto.co.uk**. **285 Getty Images:** Buyenlarge (cl); Pictorial Parade (bc). **286 Dorling Kindersley:** Gary Ombler (bl). **Getty Images:** Universal History Archive (cl). **286-287 Dorling Kindersley:** Gary Ombler / Courtesy of the Royal Museum of the Armed Forces and Military History, Brussels, Belgium. **287 The Art Archive:** Culver Pictures (bc). **Corbis:** Bettman (tr). **288-289 The Art Archive:** Imperial War Museum. **290 Getty Images:** Leemage (cl); Universal History Archive (r). **291 age fotostock:** Dennis Gilbert (br). **Getty Images:** Hulton Archive (tl); Three Lions (bc). **292 akg-images:** Interfoto (bl). **TopFoto.co.uk:** (tr). **293 Australian War Memorial:** Order 6206941 (tc). **Getty Images:** A. R. Coster / Topical Press Agency (br); FPG / Archive Photos (cl). **294 Dorling Kindersley:** Gary Ombler (tl). **294-295 Dorling Kindersley:** Martin

Cameron / Courtesy of the Shuttleworth Collection, Bedfordshire (b). **295 Dorling Kindersley:** Imperial War Museum, London (crb). **TopFoto.co.uk:** ullstein bild. **296-297 akg-images:** ullstein bild. **298 Dorling Kindersley:** Imperial War Museum, London (clb). **TopFoto.co.uk:** ullstein bild (r). **299 akg-images:** (bc). **Alamy Images:** National Geographic Image Collection (br). **Corbis:** Bettmann (tc). **300 Alamy Images:** Interfoto (br). **The Art Archive:** Musée des 2 Guerres Mondiales Paris / Gianni Dagli Orti (c). **Corbis:** Underwood & Underwood (clb). **301 TopFoto.co.uk:** Fine Art Images / Heritage-Images (tc, b). **302 Getty Images:** Universal History Archive (b). **303 Corbis:** (tl). **The Kobal Collection:** Universal (crb). **Lebrecht Music and Arts:** Ben Uri Art Gallery / Collection (c). **TopFoto.co.uk:** (bc). **304 Australian War Memorial:** Order 6206941 (tr). **305 Corbis:** Bettmann (tl). **TopFoto.co.uk:** (bc). **306 Dorling Kindersley:** Gary Ombler / Collection of Jean-Pierre Verney (bc, bl). **TopFoto.co.uk:** The Granger Collection (tr). **307 Corbis:** (b). **TopFoto.co.uk:** The Granger Collection (tc). **308 Dorling Kindersley:** Gary Ombler / Collection of Jean-Pierre Verney (tl). **Lebrecht Music and Arts:** RA (cr). **TopFoto.co.uk:** The Granger Collection (bc). **309 Smithsonian Institution, Washington, D.C., USA:** Armed Forces Division, National Museum of American History, Kenneth E. Behring Center (tl, b). **310 Library Of Congress, Washington, D.C.:** (l). **311 Corbis:** David Pollack (c). **Getty Images:** Hulton Archive (bl); MPI (tl); Paul J. Richards / AFP (br). **312 Dorling Kindersley:** Gary Ombler / © The Board of Trustees of the Armouries (cl). **TopFoto.co.uk:** (bl). **313 TopFoto.co.uk:** (tc) Fine Art Images / Heritage-Images (b). **.314-315 Getty Images:** Three Lions. **316 TopFoto.co.uk:** (bc, cr). **Toucan Books Ltd:** Imperial War Museum / Norman Brand (cl). **317 Corbis:** Bettmann (b). **Dorling Kindersley:** Gary Ombler / Collection of Jean-Pierre Verney (tl). **Mary Evans Picture Library:** Grenville Collins Postcard Collection (tr). **318 TopFoto.co.uk:** (b). **319 Alamy Images:** Interfoto (c). **Dorling Kindersley:** Andrzej Chec / National Museum, Cracow (bl). **TopFoto.co.uk:** Imagno (tr). **320 Dorling Kindersley:** Gary Ombler / Collection of Jean-Pierre Verney (cl). **Getty Images:** Galerie Bilderwelt (tr). **TopFoto.co.uk:** ullstein bild (tr). **321 TopFoto.co.uk:** ullstein bild (t, bc). **322 Canadian War Museum (CWM):** The Signing of the Armistice / CMW 19830483-001 Beaverbrook Collection of War Art © Canadian War Museum / www. warmuseum.ca (t). **323 Dorling Kindersley:** Gary Ombler / Collection of Jean-Pierre Verney (cl). **Mary Evans Picture Library:** Hulton Archive (cr). **TopFoto.co. uk:** (br). **324-325 TopFoto.co.uk:** The Granger Collection. **326-327 Alamy Images:** Glen Harper. **328 akg-images:** Rainer Hackenberg (bc). **Alamy Images:** Global Travel Writers (tr). **Corbis:** Bettmann (tc, br); Hulton-Deutsch Collection (tl). **Getty Images:** Time Life Pictures (bl). **329 Corbis:** Bettmann (tc). **Mary Evans Picture Library:** (cb). **330 Alamy Images:** DBI Studio (br). **The Bridgeman Art Library:** Imperial War Museum, London (tl). **Corbis:** DaZo Vintage Stock Photos / Images.com (bl); Hulton-Deutsch Collection (b). **Lebrecht Music and Arts:** Interfoto (cla). **Toucan Books Ltd:** Imperial War Museum / Norman Brand (bc). **331 age fotostock:** Jose Antonio Moreno c (bl). **akg-images:** Andrea Jemolo (tc); ullstein bild (br). **Alamy Images:** The Print Collector (tr). **Corbis:** Hulton-Deutsch Collection (c). **332 Corbis:** DaZo Vintage Stock Photos / Images. com (c). **Lebrecht Music and Arts:** RA (tl). **332-333 Getty Images:** Hulton Archive (r). **333 akg-images:** ullstein bild (br). **Corbis:** Bettmann (tc). **334 Corbis:** Bettmann (bc). **Lebrecht Music and Arts:** Interfoto (c); RA (clb). **335 The Bridgeman Art Library:** Imperial War Museum, London. **336 Mary Evans Picture Library:** (bl). **336-337 Alamy Images:** Photos 12. **337 The Art Archive:** (tr). **Lebrecht Music and Arts:** Interfoto (bc). **TopFoto.co.uk:** Roger Viollet

(tc). **338 The Bridgeman Art Library:** Roger Viollet (t). **Mary EvansPicture Library:** (bc). **339 Alamy Images:** DBI Studio (cr). **Getty Images:** Hulton Archive; Popperfoto (br). **340-341 Getty Images:** Time Life Pictures. **342 Corbis:** Hulton-Deutsch Collection (tl). **342-343 Corbis:** Hulton-Deutsch Collection (b). **343 akg-images:** Andrea Jemolo (tc). **Alamy Images:** The Print Collector (crb). **344 Corbis:** Hulton-Deutsch Collection (tl). **345 Corbis:** (tl); Hulton-Deutsch Collection (b). **Getty Images:** Peter Macdiarmid (cr). **346-347 age fotostock:** Jose Antonio Moreno. **348 Alamy Stock Photo:** CulturalEyes-DH (br). **Getty Images:** Joseph Gruber / EyeEm (t). **349 Alamy Stock Photo:** DC Premiumstock (tr). **Getty Images:** Arterra / UIG (b). **350 Alamy Stock Photo:** Francis Vachon (tr). **Getty Images:** Philippe Lissac / Corbis (bl). **351 Getty Images:** Sylvain Lefèvre. **352 Getty Images:** Francois Nascimbeni / AFP (tl). **352-353 iStockphoto.com:** Sjo (b). **353 Getty Images:** Robert Grahn / AFP (t). **354 Alamy Stock Photo:** Ian Nellist (tc). **Dreamstime. com:** dragoncello (b). **355 Getty Images:** Steve Heap. **356 Alamy Stock Photo:** Peter Phipp / Travelshots.com (t). **Dorling Kindersley:** Stephen Oliver (b). **357 Getty Images:** Eddie Brady / Lonely Planet Images. **358 Getty Images:** Thierry Chesnot (br); Leon Neal (r); Joseph Okpako (bl). **359 Getty Images:** Thierry Chesnot (tr); Sean Gallup (b); Pierre Suu (tl). **360-361 Getty Images:** Ian Collins. **360 Getty Images:** Chris Jackson / WPA Pool (b). **361 Getty Images:** Andrew Cowie / AFP (cra); Chris Jackson / WPA Pool (tr). **362 Getty Images:** Niall Carson / Pool (cra); Jack Taylor (tl); Chris Radburn / Pool (br); Gareth Fuller / Pool (bl). **363 Getty Images:** Phil Noble / Pool.

Endpaper images: Front & Back: **Alamy Stock Photo:** Chronicle (L: 6th row, 1st from left), (R: 2nd row, 1st from left); **Getty Images:** adoc-photos / Corbis Historical (L: 4th row, 3rd from left), Corbis Historical (L: 1st row, 4th from left), FPG / Hulton Archive (R: 1st row, 4th from left), Imperial War Museums (R: 6th row, 2nd from left), (L: 3rd row, 4th from left), (L: 5th row, 2nd from left), (R: 2nd row, 6th from left), Past Pix / SSPL (L: 5th row, 1st from left), (R: 3rd row, 1st from left), Popperfoto (R: 2nd row, 3rd from left), (L: 1st row, 3rd from left), (R: 4th row, 1st from left), (L: 2nd row, 3rd from left), Topical Press Agency / Hulton Archive (L: 3rd row, 2nd from left), (R: 1st row, 3rd from right), (R: 4th row, 3rd from left), (R: 6th row, 1st from left), War Department / Buyenlarge (L: 6th row, 4th from left); **iStockphoto.com:** duncan189 (R: 5th row, 1st from left).

All other images © Dorling Kindersley

For further information see:
www.dkimages.com